Antonia White

Antonia White
A Life

Jane Dunn

JONATHAN CAPE
LONDON

Published by Jonathan Cape 1998

2 4 6 8 10 9 7 5 3 1

Copyright © Jane Dunn 1998

Jane Dunn has asserted her right under the
Copyright, Designs and Patents Act 1988 to be identified
as the author of this work

First published in Great Britain in 1998 by Jonathan Cape
Random House, 20 Vauxhall Bridge Road, London SWIV 2SA

Random House Australia (Pty) Limited
20 Alfred Street, Milsons Point, Sydney,
New South Wales 2061, Australia

Random House New Zealand Limited
18 Poland Road, Glenfield,
Auckland 10, New Zealand

Random House South Africa (Pty) Limited
Endulini, 5A Jubilee Road, Parktown 2193, South Africa

Random House UK Limited Reg. No. 954009

A CIP catalogue record for this book is available from the British Library

ISBN 0-224-03619-X

Papers used by Random House UK Limited are natural,
recyclable products made from wood grown in sustainable forests.
The manufacturing processes conform to the environmental
regulations of the country of origin.

Typeset by Deltatype Ltd, Birkenhead

Printed and bound in Great Britain by
Biddles Ltd, Guildford, Surrey

'Thou art a soul in bliss; but I am bound
Upon a wheel of fire, that mine own tears
Do scald like molten lead.'

King Lear Act 4 Scene 7

Eric said, 'You're bound to the fiery wheel.'
And Djuna: 'Are you a writer or a weeping woman?'
Both I fear. Oh I DID want to be happy as a woman. . . .
But I'm a monster and must accept being one. Not *all* writers are
monsters.
But my kind is.

Diaries I 2 January 1953

For Nick
mo mhuirnín rua

Contents

Illustrations

All photographs are courtesy of Susan Chitty, unless otherwise stated.

Acknowledgements

The biographer is authorised to snoop; there is a thrill in the directness of communication in opening a dusty handwritten journal, in the uninvited intimacy of a letter meant for another's eyes alone. But a biographer also has to be true to the material. This biography would not have been possible without access to a wealth of unpublished material. Thanks to Susan Chitty for permission to quote from Antonia White's diaries, letters and other unpublished writings; to Lyndall Hopkinson Passerini for permission to read and quote from her own letters to her mother; to Carmen Callil for permission to quote from the material in her possession, including her own correspondence and details of Antonia White's publishing renaissance with Virago; to Amanda Hopkinson for permission to quote from her father Tom Hopkinson's diaries and letters. Thanks too for their hospitality, generosity and various candid and illuminating conversations about Antonia, life and the rest.

I am grateful to Joseph Geraci for permission to quote from Emily Coleman's letters and diaries, and The Author's League Fund for permission to use Djuna Barnes material. Thanks to Skoob Books Ltd for permission to quote from Kathleen Raine's *Autobiographies* and David Gascoyne's *Collected Journals*.

Thanks for the kindness, and in many cases hospitality too, of those who knew Antonia and her circle and shared their memories and insights: Janet Adam Smith; Neville Braybrooke; the late Joan Cochemé (Souter-Robertson); Kay Dick; David Gascoyne; Judy Gascoyne; Kathleen Hale; Ian Henderson; Michael Holroyd; the late Lady Hopkinson; Lyn Isbell; Harry Isbell; Elaine Lingham; Professor Frederick Marnau; Cynthia Moody; Mary Palmer; Maggie Pringle; Isabel Quigly; Isabel Waley; Susan Watson; Mary Siepmann (Wesley). I am particularly grateful to Kathleen Raine for taking the trouble to explain Antonia's search for spiritual integrity.

Thanks too to the University of Delaware Library for access to the Emily Holmes Coleman papers, including all of Antonia White's letters to Emily. I have fond memories of the associate librarian, Rebecca Johnson Melvin, and library analyst, Anita Wellner, who put up with me for so long. Thanks to Carl

Spadoni, archivist at McMaster University in charge of the Bertrand Russell archive there; to Mrs Inglis at Sussex University Library, home of the Leonard Woolf papers. I am particularly grateful to Patricia Allderidge, curator and archivist at Bethlem Royal Hospital Archives and Museum and to Eric Byers, chief executive of the Bethlem and Maudsley NHS Trust, for permission to quote from Antonia White's medical records. The London Library provides the backbone of any biographical research and I am always grateful to their cheerful, helpful staff.

I have been asked to make it clear that only in the exceptional circumstances of Antonia White having breached her own confidentiality, by writing and discussing her time in Bethlem asylum, was the Maudsley and Bethlem NHS Trust willing, in her case, to lift the hundred-year closure order on all medical records.

I would like to thank the following individuals and organisations for information and explanation: Howard Bailes, archivist at St Paul's Girls' School; Gordon Bowker; Monsignor Ralph Brown, Vicar General Westminster Cathedral; Sister Mary Coke, archivist at Society of the Sacred Heart; Michael Cudlipp, History of Advertising Trust; P.F.A. Denman; Reverend Ian Dickey, archivist at Westminster Diocese; Louise Frith of The Book Trust; Penny Hatfield, archivist at Eton College; Eleanore Hofstetter, Towson State University, for a most useful bibliography; Clare Hope, librarian at RADA; Michael Lattey; Susan Lattey; Jerry Lee, Cabinet Office; Jeremy Lewis; Sheila Murphy; Tim Padfield, Public Records Office; David Rustidge, Housemanager Oldham Coliseum; Bonnie Kime Scott; Mrs Sehgal, St Paul's Girls' School; Dr Peter Shephard; Jane Simpson.

Many thanks to my agent, Deborah Rogers, who combines a gimlet eye for a contract with maternal patience and encouragement. On the publishing side, affectionate thanks to Candida Lacey for the idea and her confidence and support of it through the years, and to David Godwin, my publisher at the time. I am very grateful to his successor Dan Franklin and his enthusiastic team at Jonathan Cape for all they have done for the book: thanks especially to my editor, Charlotte Mendelson, who asked all sorts of awkward questions, and with style and good humour subdued this unruly manuscript.

During the last long haul, inevitably I have ignored and neglected friends and family – for which some may be thankful. My children, Ben and Lily are the unimpressed antidote to this obsession; Nick has provided a necessary stark insensibility of Johnsonian proportions, and I am as grateful to the rest of my family and friends for being the dependable elastic of life – keeping things up, and on, and breaking every fall.

One could not live with the spirit of Antonia for all these years and not become changed somehow oneself. Her life has made me understand the force of religious experience, and the despair at its loss. Antonia has also shown me at first hand the terrors of mental illness, and the everyday courage needed to survive; bound to her fiery wheel.

Foreword

Where do I believe *she* is now?
I go on praying for her as if I believed what I *should* as a Catholic believe.
  IF that belief is true, she has, I am sure, found peace and happiness.
But how much instinctively stronger in me is the sense of *natural* mystery
  of life, death, change – of the mysterious natural, wonderful, terrible,
  inexhaustible, incomprehensible universe in which we find ourselves.

Antonia White on the death of a friend: 8 October 1966, Diaries II

16 April 1980 was a sunny spring day. Antonia White's two daughters, Susan and Lyndall, arrived at the West Grinstead Roman Catholic Church after lunch. They went into the vestry to arrange the flowers for the service; Father Mulvey was checking the last details in the church, anxious about having to conduct the Mass in Latin. Antonia's coffin arrived bearing her daughters' large wreath of spring flowers, and an unexpected small wreath of purple chrysanthemums from the surrealist poet David Gascoyne. The service had just begun when a handsome black cat walked through the open doors.

Antonia's friends and family watched, transfixed. Tail erect, it made a deliberate promenade up the aisle, circled under the coffin and then strolled into the neighbouring pews. Everyone there knew of Antonia's passion for cats, her extraordinary ability to empathise with them and the transforming nature of the love they inspired. Tom Hopkinson, her third husband, was deeply shaken: he was certain it was Antonia, he whispered to his wife sitting beside him. Antonia's devout friend Fred Marnau, who was due to read one of the lessons, thought the cat had been sent by her as a sign of approval. Even Father Mulvey recognised a significance in this feline presence. When the cat had had enough of the service it slipped out through a side door and waited in the churchyard.

After the last hymn was sung and everyone was gathered in a circle around the grave, the great invocations De Profundis and Miserere were said over the coffin. As Antonia's remains were committed to the earth, the singular cat once more appeared, walked round the grave, 'gazed down into the void and withdrew with dignity'.[1] For most present, this was too much to be pure coincidence. Antonia had approached death wracked with spiritual doubt and full of fear: for those who cared for her during this last struggle some consolation was needed. Here, perhaps, in the role of emissary, the cat had come to tell them that all was well.

At the memorial High Mass at St Ethelreda's, Ely Place, London, the following month, a larger congregation was blessed at the reception afterwards by the presence of another black cat, with as much a sense of its own right to be there. It had greeted the guests on arrival and mingled with them as they drank wine and talked of the past – and of the cat, and the first cat. The poet Kathleen Raine felt that Antonia was somehow part of these ceremonies of farewell: 'I hope she saw us all at that funeral, which was so very much in her own style, both the truth of her faith, and the human comedy. And the cat! And the *second* cat! . . . that is just too much to doubt – she sent us those cats, surely with love and perhaps laughter as well. To tell us all was well with her.'[2] The American writer Emily Coleman had once pointed out that Antonia always stayed too long at parties because she was unsure that she was ever wanted there at all. Perhaps, even after death, there was a need for reassurance that all these people had cared for her after all.

Now finally laid to rest, Antonia's legacy was not a simple one, either artistically or emotionally. She had left behind four novels, a book of short stories, a few poems, two novellas about her cats, an epistolary exposition of her struggle with her Catholic faith, a fragment of autobiography, an aborted fifth novel, a few miscellaneous short works, thirty-five full-length translations from the French – and her master-work, over a million words of her diaries, movingly honest, painful, self-obsessed, revelatory, and ultimately heroic. This lifework was an extraordinary testament to the human and spiritual quest for integration and meaning in a life that was never free of mental illness and the threat of madness.

The story of Antonia White's life is also a family drama where injuries abound. Unhappy families may be more interesting than happy ones, but they are much more destructive to the lives they touch. And Antonia's is a drama on a grand scale encompassing large questions of faith, the needs of the soul, the struggle to become both a writer and a woman; the impossibility of being a wife and mother when fighting for your sanity. Antonia herself was defenceless and clear-sighted about her weaknesses and shortcomings; particularly when young she plunged into life heedless, blinkered, with little regard for the consequences to herself or others. In the process she was to learn much about her own nature and the havoc of her disease: in the end she was full of remorse for the suffering which she caused. In all her letters and journals, highly critical as she was, she was hardest always on herself.

She had a quick and devastating temper. Too often she was submerged in the terrors of mental illness but never sought to anaesthetise herself with excessive alcohol, and had little recourse to psychiatric drugs. This made her essentially shell-less, exiled and self-obsessed and she struggled all her life to breach this isolation, seeking always to connect. Antonia had a real gift for friendship, a tolerance and understanding of fear and weakness in others. She continued to extend her hand even when her fingers got bitten or backs were turned against her, persevering with her friendships to the end.

But her story is also one of unremitting struggle: struggle in a material sense to find enough money to pay the rent and bills; struggle to maintain a mental equilibrium in order to live and work; struggle to remain true to her art, her honesty and her faith. But despite the seriousness of her quest she had a deep vein of frivolity and amusement at the condition of herself and others. Her conversation was erudite and witty, her laughter quicker than her tears. Particularly in her later years, when she had given up on men, Antonia entered a calmer more expansive period when her friends and daughters brought her increasing joy.

As Antonia White's biographer, I have set out to discern the springs of her life and the motivations of her art. I have tried to trace the source of her power and the reasons for her sense of powerlessness: the intellectual nature so dislocated from feeling. She was frightened of contentment and mediocrity and, uncertain of her own identity, she courted drama and risked disaster, just to prove that she was real.

I have hoped that the wealth of original material, the letters and diaries and autobiographical fiction, would allow Antonia to speak, to be the main commentator on the progress of her life and the impetus of her work. In her detailed fragment of autobiography, she could not take the account of her life much beyond the age of four. In her autobiographical fiction, she left her *alter ego*, Clara, standing on the shore of adult life, aged barely twenty-five, her future blank before her. A writer's block of monumental proportions prevented her from telling the story of that girl's rollercoaster progress through further marriages, motherhood, literary endeavour, faith lost and refound, breakdown, betrayal, madness.

But even while her creative work dried up in the desert of more than twenty years' unproductive labour, her life continued to be lived generously, foolhardily, courageously. And most of it she examined closely in the steady stream of letters and the diaries: remarkable, in their entirety, for intellectual curiosity, comfortless insights and the obsessiveness of their gaze. These records are in part a continuation of the story which Antonia, for complex psychological reasons, failed to progress as fiction, although her efforts to do so were exhausting and self-destroying.

Antonia's life, nevertheless, had been so marked by upheaval, so strained by extremes of experience, that it was bound to produce aftershocks in the lives of those closest to her. As literary executors she had appointed her daughters – Susan, Lady Chitty, and Lyndall, Countess Passerini, who lived in Italy – and Carmen Callil. Carmen, as founder and publisher of Virago, had resurrected Antonia's novels and her literary reputation in the last years of her life, and had become a close friend. Susan was herself a biographer. They were a powerful triumvirate who were bitterly to fall out; Susan on the one side, and Lyndall and Carmen on the other. As a result Susan took legal action and, being a trustee of Antonia's will as well as the sole beneficiary, was awarded the executorship of her mother's works.

In a complicated relationship, the fundamental cause of friction became the daughters' differing viewpoints on Antonia's character and motives. Their two published memoirs of their mother and the relationship with her detailed their unhappy childhoods and the effects on their lives. Susan Chitty's *Now to My Mother: A Very Personal Memoir*, published in 1985, was a headlong ride, highly personal, at times expressive rather than exact, and driven with hurt and anger: Lyndall Hopkinson's *Nothing to Forgive*, published three years later, was a more thoughtful journey from fear and hurt to a certain reconciliation, even love. As a result the question of who should edit the diaries became fraught, and Susan's insistence on being the editor was the cause of the final breach.

The kind of biography I am attempting here, with Antonia's character and voice at the centre, could not have been written without full access to her papers. I have been treated with utmost friendliness and co-operation by everyone involved: Susan Chitty, who holds the bulk of the papers, and her husband Thomas; Lyndall Passerini Hopkinson with her invaluable archive of letters from her mother and father; Carmen Callil with her own letters from Antonia, Silas Glossop's letters and the details of her publishing renaissance; Amanda Hopkinson with her father's diaries.

I have also been given permission to read the letters and journals relevant to Antonia and her friends in public archives. In the University of Delaware library there is a vast archive of Emily Coleman papers, where Antonia's letters to her offer essential insights to her story. I am particularly grateful to the Bethlem and Maudsley NHS Trust for lifting a hundred-year closure order on Antonia's case-notes, allowing me to read and quote from her doctors' clinical observations while she was in the asylum in 1922–3.

Her friends, and even an enemy or two, have generously talked to me, sometimes fed me, and in the process revealed something of her vivid nature and what she was like to know. Despite the passions Antonia aroused in her lifetime, and after her death, I have not been impeded in my research or had any influence exerted on my interpretations of character or events. This freedom has been helped, no doubt, by the fact that all her husbands, and nearly all the friends and lovers most intimately connected with her life, are now no longer alive. Antonia, wary herself of encroaching on the privacy of the men she had loved by portraying them in her fiction, would have known Virgil's view of the matter: *Hi motus animorum atque haec certamina tanta/Pulveris exigui iactu compressa quiescent* – Such fiery passions and such fierce assaults/A little sprinkled dust controls and quells.[3] The dust has settled, the passions have been quelled, and the story can be told.

I was at first attracted to this task through an admiration for Antonia's novels, particularly *Frost in May* and *Beyond the Glass*. The cool precise language she used to describe momentous things conveyed both a sense of absolute truth about what is, and a kind of absolution. The disintegration of a mind, the killing of a soul, the fundamental isolation of one being from another, the seduction of suffering and its intense affirmation of self; these large experiences she charted through small moments of being, in prose completely free of self-pity. The complete diaries were also a gift to any biographer who was interested in the interior journey of a profound, unsentimental and flawed woman whose quest was power, integration and truth. She was practised socially, with a variety of masks with which she attempted to contain her disintegrating self; to become more acceptable and, she felt, more deserving of love. Only in her diaries did she reveal that self without disguise.

I had begun work admiring Antonia for her honesty and the sharing of herself, yet not quite liking that self: grateful to have been neither her daughter nor a lover. A woman of extremes, in the grip of her own mental anguish, Antonia was capable of terrible blindness to the feelings of others and of impetuous acts of harm. I have ended years of living with her literary presence, however, profoundly moved by her courage, her saneness, her intellectual energy and generosity of spirit. If I had had the good fortune to have been her friend, I think I would have found her fascinating company, always stimulating, even lovable, frights and all. Any biography of Antonia White has to explore these contradictory aspects of her nature. She would not have wished to have her life or character made tame, so critical was she anyway of herself; exercised always by the unravelling of the truth.

But ultimately this can only be my interpretation of the life, using her words and the words of those who knew her in an attempt to reveal the layering of character and will, the growing humanity, the gaining of self. I am aware that the truth of any life can never be contained in one medium or labelled by one mind. All one can hope for is a glimpse of something real and reminders of a shared humanity and experience.

Antonia had known that: '. . . somewhere in everyone there must be a love which gave one independent life, not father, mother, lover or friend, but oneself . . . one's own spark that persists in spite of every loss of beauty, money, good opinion, human affection. I have known mine go right out in madness, lost all sense of personal identity . . . and yet it is there. Call it life, call it nature, call it God. . . .'[4] Perhaps the black cat in the church had come to signify this spark: her family, friends and faith united, drawn by her persisting presence at the centre, the continuity of life.

I

Born in Captivity

Honestly I do not think anyone could have had an odder pair of parents
than I had.

11 November 1970, *Diaries II*

When caged lions are suddenly set free they cower, frightened of
the sky. Two poets who were friends of Antonia at different
times in her life wrote of her as an untamed animal who resisted the
cage, yet was fearful of freedom. Kathleen Raine thought Antonia had
cultivated an intricate social mask behind which she pursued her own
subtle journey of the soul: 'she was, though a highly trained creature,
not a tame one.'[1] And Dylan Thomas, who met Antonia when she was
in her late thirties, wrote of her escaping her suburban zoo into
dreamed-of liberty. But with this came madness. She too was frightened
of the sky, 'and crawled back to the zoo, through a million strange and
frightening places full of human wild animals. . . . She wants to be tame
again, but she's been let loose once.'[2] He thought that this had done for
her.

Antonia too saw herself as partially compliant in her own imprisonment: 'There is, of course, still the big chain to break – the *habit* of being
a prisoner and the belief that life out of prison is not ever worse than life
inside. . . . It means freedom, insecurity and the possibility of being
completely neglected.'[3]

Antonia had many analogies for her life and state but a recurring one
is similarly primal. She referred to her madness as 'the beast' but this
term meant something much more, an untamed, natural, even ruthless,
energy out of which her best creative efforts came. But, inevitably, this
was at odds with the demands of her exterior life: 'I am much more
afraid of the beast than of death. If I could come to terms with the beast,
real terms, I would be an artist instead of a Clever Little Thing' she

wrote to a friend.[4] She felt at times that only religion could contain her rampant egotism and will for power: she was attracted to this untamed self and saw it as the greatest source of creative energy and yet she was repelled by its consequences in the kind of life she felt she ought to lead, the life where she hoped to be 'happy as a woman'. She wrote to Cyril Connolly in partial (and only partially joking) justification of her philosophy of life, 'though superficially civilised, I am a barbarian and a lunatic.'[5]

Antonia and her women friends and writers, Djuna Barnes and Emily Coleman particularly, were very much exercised by the real conflict they saw between being both an artist and a woman – the one intrinsically untamed and the other domesticated, defused, made safe. For Antonia there was also the conflict between the untrammelled flight of creative energy and the necessary trammels of her religion. She claimed the falcon as her patron bird; 'As an artist I would like to balance and hover for a long time and then fall dead on the prey.' And the taming of the falcon she saw as a metaphor for God's breaking-in of the soul – the bird is starved and kept in darkness until it will feed only from its master. She longed to be willing 'to accept the hood and jesses and only flying and striking at the Master's word.'[6] But under this harsh training, a falcon might sulk and sicken and have to be allowed back to the wild, to be lured again into semi-captivity. The nature of her own untamedness, her longing for yet abhorrence of constraint, fascinated Antonia all her life.

The taming of Antonia began young, and at first she could resist it. As a child she had longed to be a soldier and would sleep with an old sword by her side.[7] Even as an adult, she claimed that had she been a man she would have gone into the army and at eighteen was still manoeuvring a vast army of lead soldiers, collected from early childhood, which she retained through all the vicissitudes of her life. It was the soldier's sense of honour and willingness for a clean fight which attracted her so. 'It wasn't the soldiers who betrayed Christ . . . it was the priests and the lawyers.'[8] Uninterested in dolls, she cared only for animals, real or toy, and 'military accoutrements'.[9]

In a formal photograph taken when she was seven, she stands beside her mother who is dressed in full Edwardian style with beribboned dress, fur stole and a picture hat. Rather than appear in her best dress, Antonia has insisted on wearing her plain school uniform and, to her mother's greater frustration, her favourite hussar's cap. This was the cap which she slept with on her pillow. For her, dressing-up fulfilled fantasies of leadership and valour rather than romance and submission; a favourite accessory was a pair of sequined wings of her mother's which, fastened to a brown paper helmet, allowed Antonia to become a Viking chief, or, when they were stuck to the back of her shoes, helped her imagine she was Hermes, messenger of the gods.[10]

The classics and their pagan gods were Antonia's earliest religion. The first deity she learnt to identify as a child was Athene, goddess of war and wisdom. Sprung from Zeus's head, fully-armed, she was born of her father and essentially motherless. For a small soldierly girl who wanted only her father as parent, this might have been a happier classical connection than that of her given name, Eirene, meaning 'peace'. '"Peace" seemed a very inappropriate name for me,' she wrote much later in a letter to a friend.[11]

Courage, honesty and combativeness were qualities she exhibited from the start. It was partially these characteristics which made her mother comment often on how like her father 'Tony' was. Christine Botting called her daughter by this boyish nickname, refusing to use Eirene, which had been unilaterally chosen by her husband, the classics scholar and teacher, Cecil Botting. Spelt in the Greek manner this rarefied first name allied to the earthy 'Botting' caused the schoolgirl Antonia embarrassment and shame. Those two rogue letters – the redundant E which, when she had to spell out her first name, made her sound affected, and then that rude B which left her open to all sorts of undignified misnomers. Eirene Botting was a name which did not reflect her idea of herself, 'with such a name could I ever be anything?'[12]

Eventually she added her mother's maiden name to 'Tony' and became Antonia White. But in constructing this new name for herself she felt she had come up with something worse, a nothing sort of name, bland and meaningless. Even more painful was the implicit denial of a fundamental part of herself and the loss of her identity: 'It is a source of great unhappiness to me that I have no name,' she reflected years later.[13] How strange, she thought, to have rejected her father's name, the name of the man whom, as a child, she loved and admired more than anyone, and to have taken instead her mother's names, despite a passionate antipathy to her at the time.

There were deep strains and confusions in the family: her parents were as unalike as two people could be, with very little understanding of each other. There remained a residual attraction between them and socially they were a charming and lively pair, but in effect Antonia White was born into a covert domestic war where a conventional exterior masked running skirmishes and long term attrition. Her mother had no explicit authority and used charm and subterfuge to manipulate her husband into accommodating some of her wishes; she was an attractive and vain woman who kept her expenditure on herself hidden by raiding the housekeeping and her own child's clothes allowance. (Antonia remembered wearing shoes which were too tight for her because the money for new ones had been spent on some adornment for her mother.)

Cecil Botting worked long and hard at his teaching in a job which did not provide him with the status and intellectual satisfaction he considered his due: he brought his disappointment home and exercised his authority over his wife and child with an unimaginative and heavy hand. Rigidity and self-righteous conviction made him blind to the points of view of others. Both parents were engaged in this power-struggle and, as an only child, Antonia received the concentrated fall-out. A natural fighter, she did not cast herself as the go-between or conciliator but quickly allied herself to the apparently more powerful side. But this, as Machiavelli would have warned her, was a risky business – if you ally yourself with someone more powerful than yourself, victory will see you emerge as his prisoner.

Cecil Botting looms as the most imposing, demanding and threaten-ing male figure in Antonia's life. No other man ever deposed him in the hierarchy of influence. He was born into a family of yeoman farmers who, in his parents' time, had slipped a little down the social scale. His father ran the village shop. Cecil never glossed over the fact that his father was a small shopkeeper, but his daughter realised how much distress this caused him at times.

His own parents were deeply rooted West Sussex people of not much education. His father, George Frederick 'Fred' Botting, was a tall good-looking man with striking blue eyes who was virtually stone deaf, having been viciously boxed on the ears by a schoolmaster when he was a child. He was lazy, good-natured and unbusinesslike. His only perceived talent was for exquisite copperplate handwriting; he could write the Lord's Prayer on a threepenny bit and his granddaughter remembered a foxed and yellowing piece of paper framed on the wall in his bedroom on which every petition of the prayer had been written by him in a different fancy script. He named his son 'Cecil' after the horse which had won him some money in the St Leger that year. His son described his father as the passion of his life.

And Cecil was the passion of his mother's life. He had the misfortune to be born on 25 September 1870, the day his elder sister of eighteen months died of the croup. This new baby, born in the midst of grief, was destined to be a solitary child watched over and cossetted almost to extinction. He lived in the heart of Sussex in Storrington near Chanctonbury Ring, and yet had little of a country childhood. Young Cecil was not allowed out without coat, hat, gloves and muffled to the eyes. He learnt nothing of the names of plants or animals nor of the ways of rural life. Discouraged from climbing trees or playing outside with other children, he missed the robust physical confidence that comes from being a young animal at home in the natural world. Instead he played croquet by himself and read voraciously indoors. One of the highlights of his childhood, during a rare sombre visit to relations, was being offered a particularly delicious sherry trifle.

The source of this close-focused passion was Adeline 'Ada' Botting (née Jeffery), a small dumpling of a woman with no pretensions to beauty. Good-hearted and practical, she fussed over her son and solidly supported her husband. Her own inheritance of one hundred pounds a year helped. Her family were also long-established Sussex folk, mostly carpenters who had acquired small packets of good farming land over the years. Ada's possessiveness of her son continued until she died, spreading its invasive roots under the foundations of his marriage (she considered her daughter-in-law selfish, lazy and neglectful) and plucking at her only grandchild, Antonia. 'Every inch *Daddy's* girl!' she would point out with evident pleasure, reinforcing the Botting alliance against Antonia's mother.[14]

An unexpected inclination for learning combined with reclusivity as a child made Cecil a natural scholar. When he was only seven he bought Latin and Greek primers from a stall in Storrington market and taught himself the rudiments of both languages. His parents' modest ambitions for him were suddenly expanded. They employed a tutor for their precocious son and eventually he won a scholarship to Dulwich College. There is no mention of the personal cost to his parents involved in transplanting themselves from their centuries-old tenure in deepest Sussex to a shop in a back street of Dulwich, so that Cecil could be a day boy. He too suffered. His country accent was marked, his clothes were clumsy and odd, having been handmade for him by his mother. After school he had to help out as the errand boy in the local corner shop and post office, now run by the family. Amongst the clientele whom he served were his teachers, fellow pupils and their parents.[15] A deep sense of social inferiority became entrenched in him with the obvious disparity between his own family's financial and social position and that of the majority of his fellow pupils.

He learnt early that nothing comes free and worked hard and uncomplainingly in what was to become the pattern of his life. Already by the age of sixteen he was taking private pupils to help supplement his parents' income. A photograph of him at this age showed 'a singularly weak-chinned boy with a high forehead & plump hands'.[16] This picture puzzled his daughter because she always remembered him with a strongly defined chin and a heavy almost underhung jaw. In 1889 he won a scholarship to read Classics at Emmanuel College, Cambridge and a photograph taken there showed he had developed this characteristically determined jawline sometime during the hard graft of his early adulthood. His undergraduate days were the only interlude of carefree extravagance in his fifty-nine years.

It was while he was at Cambridge that he made the most passionate friendship of his life. Nevinson de Courcy was a charming Irishman who was a distant cousin of Lord Kinsale: in his looks, his social ease and aristocratic connections he embodied to Cecil Botting the romantic ideal of manhood. For the first time, this rather priggish, conscientious young man had a true friend with whom he could share his taste in literature (they were both keen admirers of George Meredith), his past frustrations and his hopes for the future. De Courcy, who was always called Toby by Cecil, guided his friend through the pitfalls of social etiquette and introduced him to some of the more sophisticated ways of the world. The importance of this social patronage cannot be over-emphasised. Oxford and Cambridge in late Victorian England were largely élite clubs for the young men of upper-class families who knew each other, came from the same great public schools, had been imbued from birth with the manners and voice, the dress code, and the natural expectations of their class. It was very easy for a clever lower-class boy to feel inferior in every way; he was essentially in exile in a foreign land.

Even after they had both completed their degrees and gone down from Cambridge, such was their closeness and loyalty to each other that Cecil Botting found it very hard to admit to his friend that he was about to marry. This seemed to be an emotional betrayal. The tone of his letter breaking the news was contorted with anxious justification and reassurances of his unchallenged love for his friend. He resorted to a not entirely accurate quote from Shelley 'True love in this differs from common clay/When you divide you do not take away.'[17]

De Courcy was to become Antonia's Church of England godfather and although she met him only on his rare visits from Egypt, where he had gone to work, she remembered him vividly, reminded of his attractiveness by the fading photograph in her father's study. But most of all, in her girlhood, his fascination lay in the romance of his name. How much better, she would fantasise, if she were to discover that her parents were only her adoptive parents and that really she was Toby's daughter and her name was not Botting but Eirene de Courcy! She would go on living quite happily with her adoptive parents; it was only the glory of his name and lineage which she coveted. This desire to disclaim her own family connections was a mirror of her father's embarrassment over his;

in his letters to de Courcy if he mentions his doting parents at all it is in passing as 'my people', the whole family written off as barely literate.

When she was in her late sixties and reading her father's letters to de Courcy Antonia was gripped by a different fascination. Here was the exposure of her father's lineaments of love. She noted with excitement, 'Daddy really did love him – he often writes "My own Toby".'[18] There is a sense in which Antonia's unspoken question is whether in fact this intense love between her father and godfather was not in part sexual. Certainly Toby was not expected to marry and did so only very late, dying tragically of asthma on his honeymoon. Her own father was a man of sensual nature and aesthetic tastes, drawn to Oscar Wilde and Aubrey Beardsley. She was much amused by Compton Mackenzie's fond memories of being tutored by him, before he had married, and waiting to see which of his eight or more magnificent greatcoats he would appear wearing. For a man of limited means the number and quality of these coats, one trimmed with astrakhan collar and cuffs, was a statement of his concern for the outward appearance of things, as well as his sensuous appreciation of luxury.

The letters to de Courcy were not only a revelation to her of her father's emotional nature but also of the qualities of his mind. She noted the many similarities between herself and him, 'So many things like me – depression – torment of conflicting opinions – feeling of being all bits and pieces and having no personality.' It made her long to have a real talk with him, adult to adult, but of course by then he had been dead for nearly forty years.

It was in one of these letters, read with such close attention by his daughter, that Cecil Botting admitted rather shamefacedly to his best friend that he was secretly engaged to be married to 'a charming girl just back from Germany who talked "Pessimism"'.[19] This young woman was Christine White, Antonia's mother, who embodied the other, more shadowy, side of Antonia's inheritance.

The Pessimism Christine White espoused, which proved to be so attractive to Cecil Botting, was a fashionable philosophical stance during the 1890s, when she was working as a governess in Hamburg. Closely allied to German romanticism, the overwhelming sense of anguish at the human condition resonated with the mood of increasing *fin de siècle* disillusionment and decadence. Schopenhauer and von Hartmann were propogandists of the Pessimism movement, an ultimate expression of romantic *Weltschmerz* where pain outweighs pleasure and evil triumphs over good. Men and women, it was argued, in bondage to the will-to-live, can only alternate between desire and ennui in a world that was irredeemably bad.

Christine's life to this point had not given her much reason for optimism. Born 24 April 1871, she was the youngest of five children (a sixth having died in infancy), and was only two and a half months old when her mother died at the age of thirty-four. She could not recall any mother-like woman in her early life; through her childhood memories strode the figure of her elderly father alone. Her grandfather had been born in the reign of George II, in 1732, and was already ninety years old when Christine's father, Antonia's grandfather, was born. This child spent most of his own childhood in a Masonic orphanage and was unwilling to extend much charity to his own children. He had his daughters schooled in the skills necessary to gain them positions as governesses: there was never any suggestion that he might support them until they married. At eighteen each was delivered by her father to a family of strangers in a foreign land. The eldest sister was sent off to a job in Vienna: apart from one visit nearly twenty years later she never returned to her own country. The second sister, Beatrice, was dispatched at eighteen in 1883 to an aristocratic family also in Vienna, where she would inhabit, as did her sister, that shadowy place in the family hierarchy of neither lady nor servant, socially invisible. She would earn probably less even than the cook.

When Antonia visited her aunt forty-five years later, when she was still in Vienna, her story of her father's pragmatic insensitivity was still vivid. Before handing his daughter over to her new Austrian employer, 'Papa' White gave Beatrice a five pound note with the valedictory words: 'This, my dear Beatrice, is the last money you will ever receive from me. But do not think I have made no provision for your future, should you ever be in need.' He then took her to a gloomy house where 'several old ladies were sitting knitting or playing patience'. Then he said, 'For the rest of my life except in the unlikely event of your marrying [Antonia here interjected that Beatrice was the plainest of the sisters and her mother recalled that their father never tired of telling her so] I shall subscribe a guinea a year to this excellent institution which provides a home for governesses when they are too old for employment. So you will have the satisfaction of knowing that, whatever happens you will always have a roof over your head.'[20] As Aunt Bee confided to Antonia, at eighteen that was no comfort to her at all.

The next sister, who was the cleverest, pre-empted her father's chilling dispatch by going off and becoming a teacher in a girls' school. But Christine had not the force of character to withstand the paternal will. Although her brother interceded on her behalf for permission for her to take the examinations necessary to become a clerk at the Post Office, she failed by one mark to get a place. This seemed such an unfair thwarting of hope and desire that it rankled for the rest of her life. Yet Antonia herself felt that the governess solution was probably a happier one for her mother, as it turned out, than the drudgery of the Post Office, which she had been so close to achieving.

Escorted by 'Papa' to Hamburg, Christine had the good fortune to be employed by a family who liked and respected her. She was paid £25 a year. She also discovered a talent for languages and learnt German with ease. Always hungry for admiration, this young woman found that there were young men there, willing to reflect her best qualities back at her, enhanced by their own romantic need. She was in the country of Goethe and *Sehnsucht*, a yearning for something necessarily unattainable which made for a peculiarly Germanic kind of romanticism, encapsulated in Goethe's poetry of continuing desire. And so, it was quite natural for her to read Schopenhauer, begin to 'talk Pessimism', and consider herself consumptive.

Christine White worked in Germany for nearly four years, and in that time had not only gained confidence from the respect and admiration which she attracted, but also discovered an independence in herself and a natural feminism. Watching the behaviour of the young women around her, to whom marriage to an officer in the Prussian army was the height of ambition, she was shocked by their submissiveness to these mostly rude and arrogant men. Being pushed prematurely, and rather brutally it seemed at the time, out of the nest, Christine at least had learnt some valuable lessons in how to survive, if not exactly how to fly.

She had been born into an upper-middle-class family who had fallen on hard times. Although no longer well-off, the fact that her branch of the White family could be traced back to the fifteenth century and a Robert White, Keeper of the Parks of Farnham, whose own grandson, John White, rose to be a Bishop of Winchester and preach the funeral sermon for Queen Mary, gave Christine the gratifying sense all her life, that despite her current modest circumstances she was in fact almost aristocratic and therefore superior to everyone in her acquaintance – especially, as it turned out, her husband's family.

She came back to England at the end of the summer of 1893 and joined a Dulwich tennis club. Cecil Botting was still living with his parents in Dulwich, having graduated from Cambridge and taken up his first job as junior master at Colet Court, a preparatory school for boys. Lonely and miserable, by chance he had himself joined this tennis club. He was not a good player, but his keenness for the game increased dramatically after his first introduction to the faintly exotic Miss White. He told Antonia that the first thing that impressed him about her mother was the little continental bow she gave him when they first met.

Quite quickly things progressed. The 'pessimistic' talk perhaps found resonance in the temperaments and experiences of them both. This lonely young school teacher and this young woman, whom only marriage could rescue from the social limbo of a lifetime spent as a governess, found their futures seemed more promising together than apart.

Acutely aware of his modest financial situation and his inability as yet to support a wife, Cecil Botting nevertheless was impatient to declare himself formally. Within about five months of meeting he rushed over to Christine White's house early one morning and proposed. Although she was unprepared for visitors, she did not hesitate to accept, rather pleased, as she confirmed many times to her daughter, that though she was caught unawares and not looking her best, he was not deterred from his quest: 'Daddy must really have been truly in love to propose to me at that moment for I had a bad cold and was looking my worst. And as I wasn't expecting visitors at that time of day I was wearing a hideous old pink blouse I'd made myself and hadn't even done my hair properly.'[21]

They did not marry for four and a half years. Christine had to continue to work as a governess, but this time in England for a horsey family who lived in Berkshire. Cecil worked even harder than usual, taking in private pupils after work in the pattern he was to follow all his life. In this way he could increase his basic salary of £130 per annum to more than £200. Then in 1896 his skills and hard work were rewarded: so many of his pupils had won scholarships to St Paul's School that he was invited to join that prestigious but confining school, as junior Classics master, where he was to remain for the rest of his working life. For thirty years he taught boys Greek and Latin, both in school, latterly as Senior Greek Master, and in home tutorials. His name was to become well-known to further generations with his co-authorship of the well-used textbooks, by Hillard and Botting.

By the spring of 1898, their long engagement was over. Christine White and Cecil Botting were married on 18 April at St Andrew's Church in Fulham. Her father, predictable to the last, had refused to finance her wedding dress so her dreams of a romantic and suitably stylish wedding celebration had to be foregone. She married instead in her going away suit. This was the first disappointment of married life. Within three months Christine Botting was pregnant and Cecil's longed for son was born after a difficult and traumatic labour on 31 March 1899. Only the baby was not a boy, but a little girl.

2

Consciousness

At the moment I represent the womb as a brick wall, a prison.
Mental claustrophobia describes my present state.

24 February 1966, unpublished diaries

Consciousness begins in the womb. There is plenty of proof that the foetus in the later stages of pregnancy can hear sounds and respond to pain and pleasure. The mother's steady heartbeat is reassuring. The physiological changes in her caused by anxiety, fear, depression and anger are not. Antonia's relationship with her mother, and to a lesser extent with her father, might be speculatively traced from the beginnings of her consciousness: at least two of her doctors believed some of her psychological troubles evolved out of prenatal experience. And Antonia in her maturity, still struggling to understand the mainsprings of her life, found this explanation illuminating and useful.

Being treated by Dr Philip Ployé, a psychotherapist at the Cassel Hospital in Richmond, when she had declined into a serious depressive state in her mid-sixties, Antonia wrote in her diary about the revulsion she had felt at the idea of being inside her mother when she was first told the facts of life. 'I am sure [Ployé] is right when he said my mother hated being pregnant. He seems to think something may have affected me in the womb, perhaps during intercourse between my parents.'[1]

Her mother hinted often at this distressing something which happened between herself and her husband while she was pregnant. The story which fuelled so much feeling involved Cecil Botting coming home drunk one night and apparently forcing his sexual attentions on his wife. So disturbed had Christine been that she attempted to kill herself with an overdose of sleeping pills or aspirin. Antonia thought this crisis might have been during the latter months of her own gestation for her mother mentioned that this unforgiven event happened at Christmas time and she was born on 31 March. It was an episode which was recalled by her mother in old age on virtually every visit Antonia made to her; so impressed was it upon Antonia that she returned to it herself time and again in her own attempts at unravelling the origins of her neurosis.

Christine White had many possible reasons for hating being pregnant. She was a vain woman and Antonia had noted in her own 'Autobiography' how proud her mother had been of her extremely slim figure; how she managed to retain it while working in Austria for a family and in a culture where everyone tucked into mountains of rich food – and looked as well-filled as their plates. There may have been a strong element of control in her eating habits; powerless and fearful of that powerlessness, she may have exerted her will over the one thing in her power – herself and her body. And pregnancy threatened physical anarchy. Deprived of her own childhood, there was every reason also for her to be unwilling to grow up and assume her womanly destiny. Being a child was safer and, in her family, womanhood was not a happy lot.

The attraction to Christine of the 'Pessimistic' school of philosophy may have corresponded also with her own apprehension that the world was a basically unredeemable place, where the advent of a new life was an occasion of foreboding rather than joy. She was a particularly childlike woman who would have been ill-prepared and possibly resentful of this forced change of status. 'She wanted to be the romantic mistress not the wife.'[2] Whatever the reasons, whatever the trauma that her momentarily uncontrolled father had inflicted on her mother, it seems that maternal depression, fear and disgust were probable companions for Antonia in the womb. But then escape was to be just as difficult.

The terrors of childbirth was another woe rehearsed too often by mother to child; Christine had told her daughter 'you go down to the gates of Hell'.[3] She had described how her waters had broken and so the birth had been 'dry' and therefore particularly agonising: she had bronchitis at the time and her doctor had refused her even the crude anaesthetic of chloroform. The whole nightmare story had left Antonia horrified and guilty at being the cause of so much suffering: 'My mother had a very bad time at my birth. . .'.[4] All her life Antonia was to recoil at the idea of the pain of childbirth, so much so that she was moved to write of it as the worst kind of torture where death itself would be preferable, 'some really fearful, rending horror like unaesthetised childbirth which is so awful that I would rather let the child die inside me and die of bloodpoisoning than face it.'[5]

Christine's horror of childbirth had to be revisited three more times but with the terrible and tragic result of three still-born daughters. Her granddaughter Lyndall argues persuasively in her book, *Nothing to Forgive*, that Christine probably belonged to the rhesus negative blood group while her husband was rhesus positive. This would have accounted for Antonia, their first baby, being healthy but all the subsequent ones dying as a result of the antibodies increasing: the only chance of salvation being an immediate transfusion. In her husband's desire for a son, Christine had continued to get pregnant but each time facing the death of a baby after an agonising labour. She can only have approached each new pregnancy haunted by a feeling of grief, dread, even morbidity at the potential for suffering and death growing inside her.

Antonia was not breastfed as a baby. Years later, she noted that she nevertheless 'sucks at things and people' and could not give up smoking. Yet with all this need for oral stimulation she was relieved she was never breastfed, feeling as she did 'a spasm of nausea at the thought of physical contact with my mother'.[6] Her reactions were extreme; 'terror, pain and *repulsion*' are the words she used to describe the whole process of pregnancy, childbirth, nurture.[7]

The last year of the century still had a very old and remote Queen Victoria on the throne and the Boer War in South Africa was just about to break into bitter confrontation. Culturally and philosophically, there were some glimmerings of a new age; Elgar's *Enigma Variations* was first performed to rapturous applause and Freud was preparing his magnum opus, *The Interpretation of Dreams*, for the press, eventually publishing the following year, the beginning of the twentieth century. Colette too, with whose writing Antonia was to be so closely connected through translating most of her work, was about to publish her first 'Claudine' novel. That modern cure-all, aspirin, was also invented in 1899.

22 Perham Road, the house where Antonia grew up, was in a terrace of Victorian houses in West Kensington, a genteel and modest suburb of London. Antonia remembered every fine detail of this house and described it vividly in her 'Autobiography', and also in each of her four novels where Perham became Valetta Road. Overlooked and lacking in light, with dark paint and wallpaper and mahogany furniture, this was an enclosed world and a rather dull one where the most had to be made of whatever diversion came a young child's way.

Her earliest years were spent largely with the servants. Christine Botting had lost her own mother when she was a baby and was geographically distant from her sisters and had no advice or support in looking after a young baby. She did have a good-hearted but interfering mother-in-law, who had always thought her feckless and vain and in no way good enough as a wife, or now a mother. Christine, quite understandably, did not wish to ask for help and advice from that quarter, and in any case considered her mother-in-law not nearly good enough in terms of breeding and social standing. Christine was in fact temperamentally unsuited to the task of mothering a small baby, being extremely childlike herself, self-obsessed, escaping often into a fantasy life and detached from the needs of someone more vulnerable and needy than she was. The everyday care of the baby fell to the already busy housemaid or cook, as the family could not afford a nanny.

In retrospect Antonia considered her mother not so much neglectful, as Granny Botting so clearly did, just unaware. Between four and seven years old, her relationship with her mother was at its happiest; they could play imaginary games together, riding their imaginary horses to the shops, or playing with her clothes and jewel box. They would indulge in 'orgies of wishful thinking' together, discussing what they would buy if they were rich.[8] But already Antonia was aware of the servants' ridicule of her mother below stairs, which she herself uneasily was party to, living as she did a life intimately with them in the kitchen, while belonging upstairs, acting grown-up with her parents at approved times of the day. This propensity in her mother to evade responsibility for her adult life; her inability to offer a secure bond of attention and care to the real child; her impulse to identify or compete with rather than support: all these were characteristics Antonia was to recognise in herself. 'If only one could bring oneself to accept each loss as it occurs, one would gain something. Refusing to turn into a fruit does *not* mean one remains a flower.'[9] Christine Botting intended to remain a flower all her life and rather valiantly kept the illusion going, spending more than she had, dressing theatrically and continuing to charm most of the people she came across. For she was affectionate and without malice, frivolous, imaginative and, as she got older, an increasingly blithe and uncomplaining spirit.

But as a child, Antonia had been frightened of her and had grown to distrust her for her 'terribly irritable and capricious temper . . . I never knew what would bring the storm on'.[10] Antonia noted that only after the menopause, and after her husband had died, when Christine was taking lovers and retreating into a euphoric fantasy world, did she become 'practically irritation-proof'.[11] It is quite possible that Antonia's mother suffered from a less severe form of the same bi-polar mood swings which were to make her daughter's life, and the lives of those who lived with her, so painful. Antonia wrote that up to her fifties, her mother 'suffered from intense depression and melancholy but was very resilient. I have never known anyone gayer than she could be.'[12]

Christine's later life was characterised by a consistently inflated view of herself and her surroundings; even as an old woman: 'she really did think she was one of the most beautiful women in the world.'[13] Antonia had so disregarded her mother for most of her childhood and youth that it never occurred to her that Christine was much closer in nature to her than she could ever admit. Tragically, it was the same unpredictable temper with which Antonia frightened her own young daughters, in a terrible repeat pattern of unawareness of her effect on others and erratic loss of control. In retrospect, Antonia did come to see how, in times of crisis, her mother had been a stalwart support to her, courageous and independent-minded; 'if I was in serious trouble I always found her much more understanding and reasonable than my father.'[14]

Antonia's father also suffered from excesses of feeling, but mostly kept them under rigid control. He never indulged in imaginative play with his daughter, or anyone else. He did not approve of nicknames or baby talk. He worked so hard that the only time Antonia saw him during the week was when he came home from St Paul's School for a quick lunch. Otherwise, at the end of the teaching day he would arrive back in his study to find one of his private pupils already there, and so he would continue with his tutoring until long after Antonia was in bed. He was a clear and patient teacher, but had a quick and frightening temper which his daughter from her earliest years could provoke.

Cecil Botting was also a man of iron routine. Neighbours could set their watches by the sight of his stocky figure hurrying past their window on his way to school. At home his inflexibility was extended to mealtimes; 'it would have been unthinkable that we should have dined at 7 or 8 instead of 7.30, that we should ever have gone into the kitchen and cooked ourselves eggs on a Sunday night instead of sitting down to the same inflexible meal of cold meat and undressed salad.'[15] There is something significant about the fact that he was a Classics master who became famous for his published textbooks. A grammarian is less interested in the power of language to express the great myths than in structure and form.

His meticulousness about form extended into all areas of his life; he always wore exactly the correct clothes for the occasion, right down to his gloves and walking stick. Antonia's memory was etched for ever with his uncompromising ritual of rolling an umbrella: 'Each fold had to be shaken out, smoothed of creases, then lapped one over the other as neatly as fish scales before, taking a firm grip with his strong white hands, he worked them slowly upwards in a spiral movement, squeezing the folds together as ruthlessly as if he were wringing the umbrella's neck. Then, keeping a tight hold on the victim with one hand, he deftly slipped the elastic noose round it with the other and finally throttled it.'[16] The admiring young daughter, mesmerised by this rigorous procedure, could have been left in no doubt as to how Cecil Botting would be inclined to deal with the irregular creases in her own character. His tastes in music extended to favourite hymns and Gilbert and Sullivan – he liked familiarity in all things. But his daughter commented in one of her recollections of her father that he had an odd passion for Wagner, or rather for *Tannhauser* in particular, a sentimental opera he would see on every possible occasion, an outlet for the sensual romantic nature beneath the tightly controlled façade. The one defining accessory, without which Cecil Botting was incomplete, was his pipe. One of Antonia's earliest memories was of the sound of his pipe being knocked out on the study mantelpiece. The smell of his specially powerful tobacco imbued his room and person. It was sold as 'Botting's Mixture' in their local tobacconist and was a fierce mix of his own devising, rich in Latakia, a Turkish tobacco, which he had to give up smoking in later life because the effects were too much for his heart.

Her father's presence loomed large in Antonia's life from the start. He did not have much to do with her as a small baby; what little contact he might have had was curtailed by the fact that his bristly moustache made her cry anytime he tried to kiss her. But once she was old enough to play in her nursery she became highly sensitised to the man in the room next to hers.

Cecil Botting's study and Antonia's nursery shared the ground floor, with a lavatory in between. Both looked out on a brick wall in a backyard which never saw the sun. The nursery had none of the brightness and colour of a modern nursery. There was not a decoration in sight; the room was painted a tired chocolate brown with equally light-defying wallpaper, and was furnished with cast-off bits and pieces. The nursery had no fire and so was particularly chilly and cheerless in winter. Antonia spent a good deal of time in this room alone, her only resources being Mr Dash, her passionately loved black toy poodle, a few toys and dolls, and books, paper and pencils. Her imagination therefore became her greatest ally. Stories were concocted, plays enacted starring her motley collection of toys, but always with Mr Dash the central part of any fiction.

When imaginative games no longer distracted her solitariness, Antonia would slip downstairs into the warm kitchen and listen to the colourful conversations of the cook and the housemaid. Her parents had no idea how much time she spent with the servants, and how much she learnt from their talk and company: murders, ghost stories, superstitions, and a general disrespect for their mistress upstairs. Although Antonia found herself in the uncomfortable territory of occasionally defending her mother from their scathing comments, it was a warm, jolly and appreciative world which offered the young and curious girl something of the human companionship she was missing. She was particularly fascinated by stories of violence and cruelty: 'A cabman had his head bashed in by a lamp-post in Hammersmith' found its way into an occasional newssheet which she wrote as a very young child, the *West Kensington News*.[17] Years later Antonia mused on her liking for violence and extreme experience, enjoying film of storms, explosions, fires and fiercely running rivers. She thought Mickey Mouse an expression of pure genius: 'all wit and violence . . . a real release of the most violent impulses in pure fantasy.'[18] She wondered too at how her first creative writing, when she was only four, was an imaginary letter from her much loved companion toy poodle, Mr Dash, facing an imminent and desperate end. 'The waves are drifting High alas. Our ship is sinking Alas now we must die.'[19]

Antonia's liking for hard experience, for conflict and opportunities for valour which made her long to be a soldier, was clear from her earliest days. She recounts two episodes of her reckless defiance of her father's authority when she was very young and very vulnerable. On the first occasion, Lizzie, the maid with responsibility for Antonia, was requested to take her away after lunch, as was the custom, so that her parents could enjoy their coffee in peace. Apparently Antonia said something rude to Lizzie and her father lost his temper and bellowed at her to apologise. She refused. Further enraged, her father picked her up and carted her to the top of the house where he locked her in his dressing-room, informing her that she would not be let out until she apologised. This she still refused to do. Her parents then tried to resume their coffee drinking, but Lizzie was distraught and Christine was remonstrating with her husband that their daughter was far too young to be punished in this way.

When they all eventually trooped upstairs to release what they thought would be a traumatised and sobbing child they heard behind the locked door an indomitable little person stamping around the room, unrepentantly shouting, 'Shan't apologise, shan't, shan't, *shan't*.'[20] This had a peculiar resonance with Cecil Botting's own behaviour when thwarted. Antonia remembered years later 'fearful scenes when I was very small: my father almost foaming at the mouth, stamping and shouting "I will and I *shall*".'[21] Antonia admitted she could only feel admiration and awe for the irrepressible spirit of her earliest youth. She recognised: 'the *enormity* of my terror of my father's disapproval' and yet was amazed that 'it *never prevented* me from doing things he disapproved of.'[22]

The second episode also happened when she was only four years old and has the more sinister aspect of a power struggle where one protagonist is unreasonably more physically powerful than the other. Scribbling on the walls of her nursery was strictly forbidden, Antonia knew; therefore, deciding to fill in a few idle moments in the dining room by scrawling a huge noughts and crosses diagram on the florid wallpaper by the door, and then proceeding to fill it in, was an act of gross wrong-doing. Her father was outraged, her mother bewildered: everyone knew that Antonia was guilty but her father insisted on asking if she was the culprit. She insisted on denying it, although she knew full well that in her father's eyes, disobedience was bad enough but barefaced lying was worse. She recalled wilfully defying him, but was unprepared for the force he could exert against her. He grabbed her arm in a fury and despite the protestations of her mother, dragged her into his study and closed the door.

Antonia recalled, in her extraordinarily lucid memoir, that her father trapped her in between the spare desk and a bookcase and picked up a ruler. His face was flushed and he had a peculiar lop-sided smile, as if, she wrote, he was in some way pleased as well as angry. She did not speculate as to whether his pleasure was in recognising the spirited courage of his young daughter or in contemplation of the power he had over her and the punishment he was about to mete out. He had controlled himself enough to speak quietly, but that made his words seem even more menacing. Antonia continued the story:

'You see this ruler?'

I nodded. It was a stout yellow wooden one, with spots of red ink on it.

'Turn round and bend over that desk. I'm going to take down your knickers and beat you with it.'

I was too horror-struck to obey. What horrified me was not the idea of being beaten . . . but those dreadful words, 'I'm going to take down your knickers.' No one except the maid who acted as my nurse, ever saw me naked. I would have been shy of being seen with nothing on even by my mother. Certain parts of my body I knew were 'rude' and must be always covered up, except in the bath, by my knickers. The thought of these most secret and shameful areas being exposed bare to the person I most revered, and not even accidentally, by his own hand, was so shocking that I felt I should never survive such shame.[23]

Antonia wrote that she could not remember what happened next. Her mind was a blank. All she knew, she writes, was that her father did not carry out this terrible threat. Amateur psychologists would have a field day with this episode. However, there are other episodes later in her life where Antonia herself questions the nature of her powerful and not entirely healthy obsession with her father, and his with her. At this stage in the story, it was Antonia's own vivid recollection of the horror and shame which was important; she wrote about it seventy-odd years later with the emotion still trembling in her words. It is interesting that this young child, at four just aware of her own possibilities, already an independent thinking being, should deliberately provoke her father's wrath. Was it to dominate proceedings and demand attention, even of a painful kind, from a child who never was offered enough attention and admiration voluntarily by her parents? Was it because she liked to test her evident strength of character and will in conflict with the most powerful being in her universe? Antonia's imagination was caught by the stories of the battles of the gods on Olympus. She wrote of her father as a Zeus in their world at Perham Road; had she already assumed Athene's desirable persona, the warrior goddess born armed and with the power to resist her father should she choose? Certainly, she recalled never being particularly frightened by her father's temper and scoldings until he imposed Catholicism on her and she was no longer Athene to his Zeus but a sinner in the shadow of a forbidding and implacable God. 'I don't think I was ever carefree again ... God the Father was a very terrifying figure.'[24]

It should be pointed out in partial mitigation, perhaps, of Cecil Botting's behaviour, which looks to the modern eye as an unforgivable bullying of a small defenceless child: Antonia's father had been a school master all his life, institutionalised from when he had gone off to Dulwich College himself as a boy. Beating for even casual misdemeanours was commonplace in such places at the time; the beating of them on their bottoms whether clothed or bare caused little concern and very little reflection on the effect on the beater or the boy. Cecil Botting was a literal and unimaginative man. He possibly had no idea of the profound effects such punishment could have when taken out of the impersonal and routine context of institutional life and introduced into the intimacy of the home, disturbing the complex balance of the father/daughter relationship. Certainly he and his wife, together with the majority of Edwardian parents at the time, had little idea of the emotional needs of their children and the responsive movements of the human psyche.

When her father was at home he was invariably working in the study next to her nursery. Antonia was aware of every noise that came through the wall, and knew the rituals they represented. The rhythmic knocking out of the pipe on the mantelpiece was a leitmotiv of her father's life. There was also the clunk of his wooden desk chair being pushed back into the big bookcase filled with Delphic Classics, a sound which heralded the arrival or departure of each of his students. As teaching the Classics had by necessity become his life, he could not wait to introduce these to his intelligent little daughter. To his mind, it would have been better had she been a son, but her enjoyment of his attention and her eagerness to learn made her a rewarding pupil.

One Sunday, when Antonia was only three, her father decided the time had come at last to try and teach his daughter some Greek. He taught her to recite parrot fashion the first line of the *Iliad*, first in Greek and then in translation, 'Sing, oh Goddess, the wrath of Achilles, the son of Peleus'. Both were equally incomprehensible to the small girl. This began a regular Sunday tutorial in Greek mythology. This precocious knowledge was to reward her with her first earnings – but more significantly led to an incident which gave her a concomitant sense of cataclysmic deprivation and disappointment which remained with Antonia for life. She had happened upon one of her father's students waiting in the study for Mr Botting's return. The young man had been charming and urbane and shown a real interest in this self-possessed child who not only recited the first line of the *Iliad* but could converse intelligently on the gods and goddesses of the Greek pantheon.

Antonia recalled that for a child who was hungry for attention this young man's admiration was sweet indeed. And there was the heady sense of power, she had discovered, to keep him attending and amused. When he called her an infant prodigy who deserved a reward, and pulled a glinting half-sovereign from his pocket, she was too overwhelmed to speak. But just as she was contemplating this unimagined wealth – and what she could buy with real money, not just the imaginary riches of her fantasies with her mother – her father came into the room. Disapproval and deprivation ensued. Of course she couldn't accept money from a stranger, however well-earned the work, however kind the stranger. She was too young to have control of such money: she was his daughter and had to comply with his will. Hopes crushed, joy blighted, Antonia returned to her nursery and overheard her father tell the young man that she wouldn't be disappointed, that she would soon forget. . . .

'He was wrong. After seventy-two years I have not forgotten the breathless moment of possession and the bitter sense of injustice when the treasure was snatched away. I wonder if that pupil whose name I never knew and whose face I do not remember, ever realised that, unintentionally, he had sown the seed not only of as pretty a complex about money as any psychologist could be called on to resolve but of a conviction that the more passionately I wanted something, the more unlikely I was to be allowed to have it.'[25]

In retrospect too, Antonia felt the burden of having her intellect forced at the expense of her carefree, childish spirits; 'my brain was forced on & my emotions, natural joy in life crushed down by that too early forcing.'[26] Her intellect became her enemy, denying spontaneity and distrusting instinct. To try and apprehend everything through the intellect, as she did throughout her life, Antonia believed made her shallow and disconnected from herself and others: 'woman was the first scientist who tried to see for herself *what happened* instead of taking it for granted!' she wrote to her friend Emily Coleman when she was in her late thirties, 'It's just a pity she ate the wrong fruit!'[27]

But there were times of sublime happiness too in her childhood. Antonia remembered the unalloyed pleasure of going off with her father alone on an expedition to the British Museum to see the classical statues and the Elgin Marbles (possibly, she surmised, to make up for the disappointment over the half-sovereign). It was having him to herself that Antonia remembered as the main delight that day. While walking about, looking at the statues and identifying the god each represented, Antonia made another useful discovery. She had long puzzled over how parents knew they had a boy baby or a girl baby: there seemed to be no obvious differences when you looked at them in their prams, whereas with grown-ups it was easier to tell because women had long hair and wore dresses. Peering up at these larger-than-life statues without any clothes concealing them, she was fascinated to see that what seemed at first to be elaborately carved bosses stuck on the front of the male gods actually appeared to be part of them, growing out of their bodies, whereas the goddesses were smooth like her.

Suddenly she realised that here was the defining difference between men and women, and her mind immediately turned to her father who, as a man, must possess one of these carved bosses too: 'a large ornate one, like Apollo and Poseidon.'[28] Up to that point she had thought that her parents must have decided arbitrarily that she was a girl and therefore condemned her wilfully to grow up into a lady, rather than the soldier she longed to be. The perfect outing was capped by tea with her father in Appenrodts, a tea room near the Museum, where they ate rich and delicious Viennese pastries in a conspiracy together, for her father asked her not to tell her mother that he had been indulging in such fattening food. 'That was my crowning bliss, the thought that he and I were sharing something highly pleasurable from which my mother was excluded.'[29] She was in sole possession of the prize of her father's attention and love.

Throughout her childhood, Antonia was aware that they did not behave like a united family, doing things together, the parents arm in arm with their child between them. Rather it was 'a conspiracy of twos; my father and mother, myself and my father or myself and my mother. We were not a family.'[30] In considering her father's character after his death, she recognised that the family was unbalanced in one crucial way which threw everything else out of kilter, 'He [her father] treated his wife like a child, his daughter like a wife.'[31]

Only at Binesfield Cottage, her grandmother's old home in Sussex where her two unmarried sisters still lived, did Antonia get a semblance of family life. Her Botting grandparents and her great aunts, Agnes and Clara Jeffery, offered an unconditional love which provided a constant warm light in her childhood memories. The house and the life in it and the countryside around exerted the greatest pull on Antonia's heart and imagination throughout her life.

Again, it was at the magic age of four that Antonia was first introduced by her grandparents to this idyll. She had long heard the stories of her grandmother's girlhood with Agnes and Clara in this fascinating never-never land of ducks and geese and cows grazing in meadows where wild flowers grew. She could not wait to see if it was really true. She was pleased to be leaving her parents behind, escorted by her grandparents with just Mr Dash for company. They arrived at night and the first time that the great aunts saw their little niece became in its frequent retelling a part of Antonia's family legend. She had been lifted down from the horse-drawn trap by the driver Mr Tidey who was preparing to carry this small child across the wet grass to the front door. The first the aunts heard was a high little voice saying with authority, '"Please put me down, Mr Tidey ... I'm not a baby" ... You were only a little mite, but so independent.'[32]

The house was once an Elizabethan farmhouse, furnished and decorated by the aunts in an ingenious mixture of mend and make-do. Nothing was ever wasted; if it could not be composted, cut up and re-made into a blouse or a patchwork quilt, or improvised to mend a three-legged table, then some new use was found for it, like bottle corks which, fitted out in bright crochet jackets, became decorative wasp-crushers. There was so much to enchant a young child both inside and outside in the garden, Antonia found herself delightedly inhabiting a quite different world from the world of her parents in Perham Road.

She was to write sensuously of every small detail of the place; throughout her life, Binesfield was lovingly revisited in reality and memory. As a teenage schoolgirl Antonia wrote to a friend who was staying nearby, full of nostalgia even then for the magical place of her childhood: 'Your description of the place where you are is so typical of Sussex. Our own little cottage is bedecked by my maiden-great-aunts with texts and memorial cards – don't I know those thin paper doors with the latch & the piece of string. It brings back me infancy as Miss Gray & Ishbell Costello would say.'[33] While she was there, Antonia had no desire to invent imaginary surroundings or impersonate imaginary characters. Her daydreams and reveries could not begin to compete with the interest and fascination of her daily life.

She was surrounded also by grown-ups who were interested in what she thought and did and were never too engrossed in their own affairs, as her parents were, to talk with Antonia about hers. They were also skilled in practical ways, which included a young child; gathering and cooking fruit for the baked fruit pies, sewing and wood carving, and gardening. '[My grandfather] was a wonderful companion. He taught me the names of birds and butterflies and wild flowers, to recognise the different crops and distinguish between barley and bearded wheat, to know mushrooms from toadstools and tell the time by "dandelion clocks". . . . He made me a miniature wheelbarrow which was the joy of my life. Sometimes I gave Mr Dash rides in it but more often I used to "help" Aunt Clara or Mr Stepney with the gardening.'[34]

In this atmosphere of affection and encouragement, Antonia first learnt about God. Both her great-aunts were religious in an uncomplicated way. They said grace at mealtimes and taught Antonia how to kneel by her bed and pray, for goodness and safety for those she loved. Aunt Agnes also used to give her Scripture lessons on Sunday afternoon. The God Antonia learnt about in the house of her great-aunts was a benign figure who held no great terrors in a place where goodness seemed to be endemic.

The return to London was depressing. Antonia felt more than ever the lack of stimulation of real animals to feed, real activities to engage in, people to talk to about the things which really mattered. The experience of Binesfield had separated her even more from her parents; it was something they had not shared and grew tired of hearing her endlessly relive. More than ever she longed for another child as a companion. It was hard to be an only child 'being the only thing of its kind in the household'.[35]

From as early as she could remember Antonia had longed for a brother; in her adulthood she wrote, 'I *hated* being an only child. I think all my life I've been searching for a lost brother.'[36] It was soon afterwards that an extraordinarily intense friendship began with a boy whom she met at the Round Pond in Kensington Gardens. Gérard Sinclair-Hill was half French and to Antonia's admiring eye terribly grown-up at seven. He sailed his boat with natural authority and flair and stood out from the pink-and-white-skinned English boys with his tawny skin and his blue eyes, intensified by dark brows and lashes. But most singular of all was the fact that on being introduced to Antonia by his aunt – a friend of Antonia's mother – he gave her a solemn kiss.

He became a regular visitor to Perham Road. There was the usual shared childish games of riding the rocking horse and playing soldiers, and dramatising all sorts of reckless adventures and terrible tortures from which each had to rescue the other. Religion also came into their discussions, now that Antonia had been alerted by her great-aunts to the existence of God. Gérard preferred God to Jesus because he seemed to be less soppy and more of a man; 'I bet God wouldn't have let anyone crucify *him*.'[37]

There was, however, a far more passionate strand to the relationship which seemed to fulfil a part of Antonia's need for physical affection and intense emotional engagement. The two children had an on-going fantasy which brought satisfaction to them both: they were a married couple, Mr and Mrs John Barker, the rich owners of the grandest shop in Kensington. This 'marriage' involved a great deal of kissing and cuddling and lying together under the nursery table covered by a shawl to make the imaginary bedroom as dark and intimate as possible. There, in the semi-dark in the arms of another child, with the thrill and fear of her father's presence next door and the knowledge that for some as yet inexplicable reason he would be angrier than she had ever seen him if he was to happen upon them under the table, Antonia experienced her first sexual *frisson*.

At night in her own bed, with Mr Dash beside her, she could revisit this thrilling feeling by imagining Gérard lying there too, his arms around her, his body pressed close. 'One night I discovered that by touching that most secret part of my body which I knew it was "rude" to touch I could produce it all on my own. I began to invent new ways of producing it, sometimes not even thinking of Gérard. I imagined doing extraordinary things which it would have shocked me beyond words to do in real life, such as running out into the street without any clothes on and letting strangers see me naked.'[38]

This fantasy made her feverish with excitement at the idea of shocking people, the thought of all those eyes upon her, fascinated and intent. Rebellious and hungry for attention she certainly was. But there was this love of violence, conflict and heroic action too. Her most exciting fantasy as she lay close to sleep was of the always indomitable Gérard reduced to tears and abjection by a series of grotesque tortures from which she, the shining heroine, would release him. But she would let him suffer a bit longer than was absolutely necessary, the more to impress him with her power and heroism when salvation eventually came.

Gérard's family, his half-sister Yvonne, his French mother, and his stepfather, Osman Edwards, were very important to Antonia throughout her childhood and youth. She remained in love with the dashing Gérard from the age of three until about thirteen 'when he jilted me for a more sophisticated girl'.³⁹ But his stepfather was also a fascinating figure for her. Though tamed and domesticated by an unappreciative wife and domestic duties, he had once been a decadent from 'the wicked world of art & literature', Antonia's first exposure to such a person from such a world. His passion for France and for Japan enlarged her imaginative universe: his genuine love for literature opened her mind to the pleasures of an aesthetic life.

For a while, Osman Edwards had been romantically in love with Christine, Antonia's mother, and had written her charming poems which had made her husband intensely jealous. He wrote poems to his daughter Yvonne on her birth and his unconditional love for her helped make her into one of the most assured, competent and uncomplicatedly attractive young women Antonia ever knew. The warmth and charm of his personality was experienced by everyone; when he read a poem of Antonia's in the school magazine he took the trouble to write her an appreciative letter, a gesture she never forgot.

Osman Edwards extended to Antonia the kind of benign encouragement she seldom received from her parents. He offered too an inspiring interest in the world of the artist, an awareness of the foreign, the other – beyond the narrow confines of suburban London and the modest material ambitions of her own family. He was responsible also for introducing into Antonia's young life the only interesting people she met, the Noh actors from Japan, the Belgian connoisseur and avant-garde critic Emile Verhaeren and, through his own ardent suffragist sympathies, Christabel Pankhurst. He gave Antonia a sense that there was an exciting world of feeling, ideas and sensation waiting for her: she in return felt she alone appreciated his intellectual and artistic qualities; 'I think I would rather have liked this shocking, easy-going, art-loving man as a father though of course I thought Daddy more admirable in every way.'[40] Her own father disapproved of and patronised Osman, who was a failure in the conventional sense, but Antonia believed that there was a secret identification with him too, for his unexpressed side shared an interest in decadence in his liking for Wilde and Beardsley.

Antonia recalled her earliest life in the most distinct, almost eidetic detail, in the autobiography embarked on in the summer of 1965 at the suggestion of Malcolm Muggeridge, enthusiastically endorsed by family and friends, as a final attempt at breaking the writing block from which she had suffered most of her adult life. Initially the project of the autobiography seemed to release her writing energy, but then Antonia hit the wall again. Writing about her life somehow defined her and made her real, but there were great stumbling blocks in that life which she could neither climb over nor go round. At those points in her fiction or her autobiography she shuddered to a halt and stayed miserably pawing the ground and pacing, unable to move on.

She worked on and off at her autobiography during the last fifteen years of her life and produced more than seventy thousand words of close packed prose, yet she did not cover much more than the first four years of her life. Antonia commented herself on the wealth of events she remembered, yet was unable to progress much beyond the age of four. A possible reason she gave for this was that by then she could read and write and so memories became focused by language. But she could give no reason why she seemed to be transfixed at that age, unable to remember much of what came next.

There is some evidence that Antonia was naturally left-handed but forced, from a very early age when she was first drawing and beginning to write, to be right-handed. Left-handedness was considered a characteristic which needed to be cured and was actively, sometimes cruelly, discouraged. When Antonia was a child, left-handedness was allied in the popular and quasi-scientific mind to mental retardation, lack of civilisation and even sinister practices. There was no way that Cecil Botting could have countenanced his precious daughter showing any such dangerous aberration, let alone writing and doing her classical studies with that awkward backhand motion.

There are clues which make this worth considering. Antonia smoked with her ring hand, her left hand. There is a photograph of her in this book doing precisely this. Her handwriting was also amazingly controlled, regular and unexpressive, with the simplicity and rounded-ness of a child's. In extreme emotional distress it broke down into letters which leant in all directions. On at least two occasions when on the verge of madness, and when she was clawing her way back to sanity in the asylum, she wrote in a reversed form of mirror writing, forming the letters from right to left, the natural way for a left-handed person to write and one of the abilities left-handed writers, who have been turned into right-handers, retain.

On another occasion when she was nearly forty and in analysis with her Freudian Dr Carroll, she began writing in her diary a diatribe against her father, her letters breaking up in the process: 'Yes I will write backhand in spite of my father I will WILL WILL. Couldn't even write – filthy dirty beastly old man – the way I WANTED TO – Well I will. You'll see. . . .'[41]

One of the most mortifying memories from Antonia's early days at her convent school was making the sign of the cross across her body using her left hand, instead of the right. This terribly shaming and disrespectful action would have been almost impossible for a right-handed person to make by mistake. To a left-handed child, it would have been the most natural thing to do.

Also, one of her practical friends, with whom she stayed during the beginning of the war, was amazed by the difficulty Antonia had manipulating everyday domestic objects; 'even the laying of a table completely foxed her', which is an odd thing in a well-brought-up and socially sophisticated woman of forty.[42] Unless she was a left-handed person having to masquerade as right-handed, perhaps not even conscious of her natural orientation, but remembering the ghost of it when engaged in physical activities: confused by which was her dominant hand. She was also remarkably bad at games as a child, and felt incompetent even when crossing the road.

If it was the case that Antonia had been forced, in her writing at least, to become right-handed, it might be a significant factor in explaining something of the sense she had of being disconnected from her imaginative, creative self. The right hemisphere of the brain is connected to the left hand: there are many theories about the right hemisphere being involved in perception, imagination, creativity and dreams. The left hemisphere of the brain, connected to the right hand, controls the more logical and linear kinds of thought involved in language, mathematics and science.

In fact there is much more interrelation between both sides of the brain than this crude formulation allows but, in Antonia's case, if she was performing her main creative activity, her writing, with the wrong hand for the particular connections in her own brain, then it is reasonable to think that she may have been inhibited by a certain blockage or disconnection between the thought and the hand. Might this have contributed to the pathological writing block which tormented her for much of her adult life?

A left-handed person forced to write with his or her right hand is made to feel powerless and incompetent until she learns a new way of writing. And this hesitancy in the natural flow might continue throughout her life. Antonia was haunted always by a fear of powerlessness, it was one of the defining emotions of her life. Again there were strong psychological reasons for this, but the elemental sense of her own basic impotence might have started when she first began to write as a small and precocious child: her natural competence frustrated at the source.

The first four years of Antonia's life were intensely lived and vividly recalled. There was a powerful sense of her character and individuality already formed. Her intelligence and curiosity, her combativeness and courage, her need for attention and for extreme emotion, her toughness and self-centredness: all were part of her heroic persona. In her autobiography she portrays herself as a child poised on the edge of life with her gifts, her strength of character and her confidence primed for her disposal. But something happened to change everything.

3

The Garden of Good and Evil

'Your will had to be broken and re-set in God's own way.'

Nun to Antonia, quoted in 'A Child of the Five Wounds', *As Once in May*

If learning to read at the age of four was one of the seminal experiences of Antonia's intellectual life, then the defining moment of her spiritual life occurred at the age of seven. Her father converted to Catholicism and she and her mother followed him into the Church. This was a profound step for Cecil Botting. It had a significant secular impact too, for it cramped his career prospects and made it impossible for him ever to be considered for the post of Headmaster at St Paul's. It barely ruffled the surface of his wife's life, although many years after Cecil's death it did become important to her. But for his young daughter it had a convulsive effect on her heart, her mind and soul: she was to learn about sin and to assume an attitude of irreducible guilt. 'I never did feel free again.'[1] Her intellect too was absorbed by her faith's conundrums and her soldierly energies exhausted in a lifelong combat with her adopted religion. Or rather, a religion which she felt had been imposed on her; at the age of only seven, she protested, how could she ever be said to have made a free choice? In a letter to Cyril Connolly in 1942 Antonia explained the ambivalence of being neither born to Catholicism nor drawn to it by intellectual, emotional or spiritual conviction. This was at the heart of her personal struggles with her faith: 'I am, I think, incurably religious by temperament. I wanted to be *pratiquant*; what I found exceedingly difficult was to be *croyant*.'[2]

Cecil Botting had been baptised into the Church of England and at Cambridge had become an atheist, but one who had wanted to believe. In a sentimental way he had liked the rituals and traditions of the Catholic Church, having been introduced to them by his beloved 'Toby' de Courcy. The sensuous, hedonistic side of him, so long suppressed beneath his ferocious capacity for hard work and filial responsibility, was also attracted to the forbiddenness of what appeared an exotic religion with its foreign bells and smells and theatrical rituals. For a man so burdened by his lower-class background, the Catholic Church, then in triumphalist mood, gave him the sense that he was joining a spiritual aristocracy when the temporal one he longed to be part of was closed to him. Cecil Botting explained something of what brought him finally to become a believer in a series of letters to Dorothy Seaton (who later became Lady MacAlister), an erstwhile pupil of his who had given him some simplistic Catholic Truth Society pamphlets in response to his professed inability to believe. Her youth and beauty may have added an extra intensity to his deliberations.

> May 7 1906 . . . You made me realise more than anyone that a belief in Catholic Christianity was not incompatible with a sane view of life . . . it is rather humiliating for an almost middle-aged person like myself to make all these admissions to you. . . . But I shall never understand why it is that for some months I have felt a sort of inward compelling force drawing me on to investigate the claims of the Catholic Faith. . .
>
> May 21 1906: You will be glad to hear that I am receiving instruction from Father Sidney Smith – my wife is also – & I am a happier man than I have been for over fifteen years. During all those last years I have been trying to open a lock & at last I have found the key.[3]

He told his daughter that he had experienced something like a personal calling. He had been kneeling in a Catholic church and had suddenly felt a definite presence at the altar. The words 'I am the way and the truth and the life' were so clear in his mind it was as if someone had spoken to him. He became a Catholic at the age of thirty-five and practised devoutly for the rest of his life, only once revealing any sort of doubt to Antonia. In Antonia's fictional depiction of this epiphany in *The Lost Traveller*, she used exactly the same words to describe her father's calling, but made it follow spiritual despair over the uncontrollable lustfulness of his imagination and a sudden apprehension of evil: 'He was conscious of something corrupt in the depths of his nature; something at once frigid, impure and violent.'[4] Certainly there were times when Antonia believed that someone with a nature as extreme as her own needed the cage of a hardline Catholicism to keep her in check. She may have sensed that her father too, alarmed by the excesses of his own nature, sought to strengthen his defences with the proscriptions of his faith.

As an autocratic Victorian father with little imagination about the needs of others, Cecil Botting would not have recognised that just as he could only make this grave decision after years of searching for belief, and then with a sense of conviction, so his daughter might need to find her own way to certainty. He could not provide her with the acceptance and security of being a cradle Catholic, yet had robbed her of the conviction he had felt in finding his own truth at last. She was condemned to be always in an ambivalent position towards her faith: to be always the outsider.

When she was told that she was to become a Catholic, Antonia remembered being 'very shocked inside but of course told no one.'[5] She had a devoutly Anglican grandmother and great-aunt, and had been taught by them that 'the very worst thing was Catholicism, the scarlet woman and all that'.[6] This visceral sense of shock was soon overborne by the proffered pleasures of feeling special – and superior. She embraced instruction with all the natural enthusiasm of a clever and curious girl. Emotionally, she was following and pleasing the father she looked up to and adored: intellectually it was an adventure on which she was well equipped to embark. She too took instruction from the same priest who had instructed her parents, Father Sidney Smith, an old and kindly Jesuit. She came to him knowing all the Greek gods and goddesses but never having heard of Our Lady. Antonia thoroughly enjoyed the intellectual rigour of her preparation; it all seemed to her perfectly logical and interesting. She read every appropriate religious book she could lay her hands on and learnt her catechism with ease.

Part of the attraction for her too was that she was treated in an adult way, given difficult abstract ideas to understand and commanded the undivided attention of a venerable adult to whom she could display her intellectual talents and diligence. She later recalled that Catholic teaching encouraged a sense of being right when everyone who was non-Catholic was wrong – an attractive conviction at any age. As a child she also associated intelligence with Catholicism; her father had become a Catholic because he was so *clever*. It was another bond of identification and distinction. But it also made her lonely. 'Becoming a Catholic cut me off from others: it was eccentric, like becoming a foreigner.'[7]

Antonia was baptised into the Faith at Farm Street Catholic Church on 8 December 1906: then followed two happy years at the breezily secular Froebel school; 'the hooks [of Catholicism] didn't go right in till I went to Roehampton.'[8] At this co-educational school she was encouraged, was popular and did well. Then, aged nine, she was sent as a boarder to the Convent of the Sacred Heart at Roehampton in the September term of 1908. This was an English school, but the Society was founded by a French saint and there was an international group of pupils, many drawn from the great European Catholic families. Amongst the girls, some of whom could barely speak English when they arrived, Antonia was the only true outsider. Catholicism and class was their uniting nationality, and Antonia, as a very raw convert and a middle-class girl from West London, stood out awkwardly from the rest. 'I had none of the Catholic manners and graces. I wore neither scapulars nor miraculous medals under my serge uniform; I could not boast of having been dedicated to Our Lady and dressed exclusively in blue and white for my first seven years; I had not even a patron saint.'[9]

For years afterwards she would grow cold with shame when she remembered some of the mistakes she made; making the Sign of the Cross with the shameful left hand, and finishing the Lord's Prayer with the Protestant clarion, 'for Thine is the Kingdom, the power and the glory, for ever and ever' instead of stopping at the rather more downbeat, 'deliver us from evil'. Each mistake trumpeted her alienness. Her first few weeks at the Convent were miserable, as she had expected them to be. To begin with, desperate to belong, Antonia was fervent in her faith and diligent at work. But mental pride and physical vanity were considered two of the worst temptations and, even while trying so hard to be good, her natural pleasure in her talents was made to seem sinister, and was quickly deflated.

The school was an even more hermetic place than most boarding schools. It had a unique and complicated set of rules and obligations, treats and punishments, decorated with the remnants of an 18th century French etiquette, and overlaid by a respect for grand lineage and established wealth. Antonia was disadvantaged in all the categories which mattered in this world. Neither was she good at sports, another badge of success. All she had was her intelligence and her talent and these were the very qualities in which she was taught not to take undue pride: the reckless display of these very gifts was to become the direct cause of her devastating fall from grace.

In her first novel, *Frost in May*, she revisited her schoolgirl life at the Convent. It began with the child in tightly-laced gaiters, her cold hands in a muff, travelling to the Convent in a horse-drawn bus, her father by her side. There is a thick yellow fog outside and inside, an intrusive and rather repellent old Catholic Irishwoman falls into conversation with them. There is a strong sense that the uncomfortable, trussed child is being offered as a sacrifice for her father's social and religious aspirations. The Irishwoman says to the father 'And wouldn't it be a beautiful thing

now if she was to offer her life to God as a thanksgiving for the great
blessing of your own conversion, sir?'[10] The child knows enough of her
Catholic teaching to see how appropriate such a sacrifice would be and
shrinks from the thought. She sees a different destiny for herself.

Many times Antonia asserted that this novel was an accurate account
of her life at the time, and that almost every incident she wrote about
was true. Antonia recreated the powerful atmosphere of the place and
the effects on a child who was naturally religious and technically a
Catholic, still trying to familiarise herself with the ideology of her
religion while having to learn how to live it too. She knew she had
none of the easy grace of her dashingly attractive friend Charlotte
d'Erlanger (Léonie de Wesseldorf in the book), who had been born into
a well-connected Catholic family. She was a granddaughter of the
eminent historian Charlotte Blennerhassett, born Countess Leyden, who
had passed on to her daughter, Lady Galway, and to her granddaughter,
Charlotte, the wider perspective of an intellectual and artistic European
culture. This gave the young Charlotte a confidence and style which
Antonia could not attain; she had a natural acceptance of her faith and a
light-hearted but affectionate irreverence too, as one might for an old
friend, rather than a slavish devotion or anxious straining to be good.

During her years at the Convent of the Sacred Heart Antonia
exhibited both of these convert's traits: a habit of inferiority which left
her with a legacy of rigidity and a fear of letting go. 'Why is it I can't be
"natural".... The silly thing is I'm always even now trying to be
"good".... It is true I was systematically educated to mistrust and check
every natural impulse. Yet the nuns were by no means bad judges of
character....'[11]

They used their good judgement of character, honed on generations
of schoolgirls, to go straight to the weaknesses in a child, to break down
the integrity of the self to make it conform more easily it to the proper
demeanour of a young Catholic girl. The convent girls were watched at
all times for the smallest signs of independence of mind or subversive
activity. They could not walk in pairs, only in threes, as a way of
discouraging discussion and solidarity in dissent. They were not allowed
to touch each other or hold hands. Their letters were opened and
censored, their gifts suspected, pockets and workboxes could be
swooped on without warning. Every book was inspected and even the
Bible given to Antonia as a parting gift by her father was banished to her
trunk, with the explanation that there were many passages in the Old
Testament which were quite unsuitable for any girl under eighteen.
Fine psychologists, the nuns could recognise an incipient rebel by the lift
of an eyebrow or the glint in an eye and confided these suspicions in

secret weekly reports to their superiors. Many years later Antonia realised that a fundamental part of her fatal insecurity was due to having had her individuality constantly under attack; 'it took me a long time to realise I existed!! As a child I was immensely more aware of other people than of myself.'[12] This became embedded in her view of God; 'It is *so* difficult not to think of God as waiting to catch me out. The convent training seemed to me *always* waiting to catch one out, to nip any self-confidence in the bud.'[13]

All kinds of sins, most of them previously unheard of and incomprehensible to someone not brought up strictly in the Faith, lurked ready to insinuate into one's thoughts and deeds, some with the direst effects on the soul. The young Antonia, who had had the reckless courage to provoke her father's considerable wrath in an effort to assert her own independence and test her mettle, knew the thrill of soldierly fear when she dared to confront her father's anger. This was a tangible fear of pitting one's will against a greater force and having the chance, however slight, of victory. The punishment risked was also finite. But here she learnt about fear of a different order. 'God the Father was a very terrifying figure', and his cruel punishments could not be evaded and might be eternal. 'I did realise [at seven] that there was no appeal.'[14]

In the Convent she learned to fear an enemy which was invisible, apparently immanent, and liable to ensnare you without your knowledge. Antonia had the kind of combative energy which could have dealt with a concrete assailant. But the silent enemy and the enemy within were much more mysterious and frightening things. One of the nuns, Mother Radcliffe (Mother Bradshaw, the Mistress of Discipline in *Frost in May*) had some kind of clairvoyant powers which she would exhibit in a game with the pupils who would pass an object, usually a key, secretly between them and then one would conceal it. Charlotte d'Erlanger confirmed to her son that this story, related in the novel, was true. Invariably Mother Radcliffe detected in whose safekeeping the object was to be found. In the exercising of these powers the nun would grow white with exhaustion, which added to the tension and melodrama. This uncanny skill was used as a way of subduing her charges with the threat of her omniscience. In the novel's version, Léonie (Charlotte), of course, was unimpressed by what she called spiritual showing off, but the point went deeper with Antonia. This sense of being watched, stalked, intruded upon in the most private recesses of one's mind was never to leave her; 'after I became a Catholic . . . I have never been free of fear for more than the briefest intervals.'[15]

Antonia was also undermined by the sheer mundanity, the unheroic nature of sin in the pupils' daily lives, while their imaginations were engorged with the grisly details of horror-shop martyrdoms and the tortures of a Hell hungry for the unrepentant sinner. In *Frost in May* we hear Antonia's own voice, in the person of Nanda, named after the Nanda in Henry James's *The Awkward Age*, a young girl of beauty, precocity and lack of irony with whom Antonia identified at the time. She answered a question about the number of venial sins: ' "Hundreds," said Nanda gloomily. "Almost everything's a venial sin, in fact. If I don't eat my cabbage, or if I have an extra helping of pudding when I'm not really hungry, or if I think my hair looks rather nice when it's just been washed . . . they're all venial sins. And then, as if one's own sins weren't enough, there are nine ways in which you can share in another person's" . . . Nanda shut her eyes and gabbled. "By counsel, by command, by consent, by provocation, by praise or flattery, by being a partner in the sin, by silence, by defending the ill-done." '[16]

Antonia dated her years of insecurity from this education in sin. All her adult life she was afraid of falling and recognised she feared to fall in a different sense: 'Fear in childhood that I might have committed a mental sin. Rigid hairsplitting "examinations of conscience" we had to make every night increased the fear. . . . Then each confession added yet another sin to the list. Fear of "sins of omission". Difficulty of judging the exact gravity of sins of thought and word, especially of thought. Terror of dying unprepared, in mortal sin, & being condemned to hell for ever. . . .'[17] A scrupulous, literal-minded and sensitive child could get herself into a frenzy of anxiety, trying to understand logically a labyrinthine scheme of rules which seemed to shift their intricacies as she moved. It left her envying criminals under sentence of death because they knew when they were to die and had time to prepare.

The changes in her adolescent body were also a focus for inexpressible fears. She was not told the facts of life until she was eighteen, and remembers being shocked and incredulous that people should be expected to do these bizarre things. She felt there was so much prurience and veiled threats in the whole area of Catholic sex education that she dreaded going to confession when she was about twelve because she had been kissed by a schoolboy at a party and had actually enjoyed it. Two years later when she began to grow bodily hair, she lived through months of fear that she was turning into an animal as punishment for some terrible sin which she had inadvertently commit-ted. The girls at the convent bathed in calico tents which came down to their ankles ('the reason being that we mustn't shock our guardian angels') and were never meant to see themselves naked.[18] They were certainly not likely to see anyone else naked. For too long Antonia

thought she was suffering uniquely this humiliation of pubic hair, that
she alone was expressing the bestial side of herself in this horribly
concrete way.

Fear and power were two of the strongest strands in the densely
ravelled skein of Antonia's psyche: 'I do know there is only one thing
for me and that is to be drawn by love and not driven by fear. Too
much stress was laid on fear in my childhood and my own nature was
too responsive to fear, anyway.'[19] And of human love there was very
little. Natural affection between the girls was blighted before it stood a
chance of even the tenderest growth. In *Frost in May*, Nanda was
threatened with loss of privileges when a letter she had written to her
parents mentioned in passing the unusual colour of a friend's eyes. She is
told by the nun who chastises her that an interest in another girl's
appearance is inappropriate and that special friendships are against
charity, but even worse, can lead to 'dangerous and unhealthy
indulgence of feeling'. Told to cultivate two other girls who are deemed
more suitable companions, Nanda was left with the chilling rhetorical
question: 'And do you know that no character is any good in this world
unless that will has been broken completely? Broken and re-set in God's
own way. I don't think your will has been quite broken, my dear child,
do you?'[20]

Yet despite this psychological warfare, the Convent years for Antonia
were also years of intensity and significance. What she learnt there
imbued her for life with a passion for literature, an ability with
languages, her capacity to write. The nuns might not approve of what
she wrote, but without their education, Antonia believed she would
never have picked up her pen to write in the first place. The Convent
certainly gave her the most powerful subject for her first and most
perfectly realised book. Antonia claimed that she had never forgotten
anything she had learnt at the Convent of the Sacred Heart, but neither
was she able to throw off her dependency. Although she was unable to
conform fully, even as a girl (she was bored or disgusted by so many of
the saints she was meant to revere, and the robust ones like St Augustine
and St Theresa she liked for all the wrong reasons), she accepted the
Catholic Church wholeheartedly. As her convent schooling began to
get more of a grip in her teenage years, the Church had become an
integral part of her nature and to break away, it seemed, would have
required a mutilation of her self. For a child with a strong sense of
herself as an outsider, becoming part of a powerful institution gave her a
welcome sense of familiarity and belonging.

Antonia had come to love the whole atmosphere of the Convent,
'the rather exotic atmosphere, hearing people talking Spanish and

French' and the place itself was very beautiful. 'I liked all this ritualised life – you knew exactly what you were to do at every moment of the day.'[21] And so when her father, hoping to save some money and also have his daughter prepared for university entrance to Cambridge, suggested that she leave at the age of fourteen and go to St Paul's School for Girls, the academic (and secular) sister school to where he taught, Antonia was overwhelmed with horror. Everything she did and thought was related to her life as a Catholic; she was alternatively thrilled by contemplating it, and frustrated and rebellious at its petty restraints. She could not imagine life without it. 'Wherever she looked, it loomed in the background, like Fuji Yama in a Japanese print, massive, terrifying, beautiful and unescapable.'[22] She burst into tears at having to contemplate leaving it and her father withdrew his suggestion, for the time being.

As Antonia became more disenchanted with the morbidity or pathetic meekness of so many saints, she was increasingly drawn to poetry and literature, stepping dangerously close to being independent-minded in the matter. Francis Thompson, the Catholic poet, provided something of the ecstasy she was missing in the practice of her religion. She may not have understood more than half of his sensuous rush of words but they excited and inspired her, as did little else at the time. 'As a child I had such a passion [for Francis Thompson] that I would have given a finger to have seen him once [she would have been eight when he died]. I knew all the long Odes by heart when I was 11 and believe I still do,' she wrote in her early forties.[23]

But she resisted strongly the idea that her talents, anyone's talents, were only to be used for the glorification of God. The official line was memorably expressed in a letter sent to Nanda by her class mistress, in which she upbraided her for not paying enough attention to the qualities of obedience and self-denial, when she insisted that it was a hundred times better to knit a pair of socks humbly for the glory of God than to write the finest poem or symphony for mere self-glorification. Antonia could never bring herself to agree; it worried her that Catholic opinion at the time could seriously claim that a bad poem by Father Faber, for instance, was considered 'better' than a sublime poem by Coleridge – because it was more edifying. She wanted works of art, above all, to be free of the weight of religious interpretation – unless that message was so intended. They should be complete in themselves, as things of beauty.

The admonishing letter written to Nanda in *Frost in May* was provoked by an earlier incident when Léonie had been prevented from continuing with playing the part of Beatrice in the school play, *The*

Vision of Dante. Although everyone agreed she was the star of the production, the play and her part in it was sacrificed, because she had taken a 'wilful and sensuous pleasure in the performance'. To Nanda's incomprehending outrage at the injustice of this, Léonie languidly explained, 'Have you forgotten that we are not here to acquire vain accomplishment but to form our characters? And don't you realise that there's nothing worse for the Catholic character than to do something it really enjoys?'[24]

This was a lesson which Antonia learnt too well, a lesson which was to haunt her in various guises all her life. If she wanted something badly enough, she knew it would be denied her: if she enjoyed something too much, undoubtedly it was wrong. For a while, she applied herself diligently to her schoolwork and enjoyed the pleasure of learning and doing well. She received prizes for everything; English, French, German, Christian Doctrine, Latin and Literature. She loved writing and was pleased to be asked to read pieces out in class. The plays and tableaux too fired her with a love of theatre. The nuns were wonderful at making costumes and one production, Tennyson's *Morte d'Arthur*, had them all dressed in superb armour, thus serving well Antonia's long obsession with soldiers. However, this embodiment of masculinity was only allowed from the waist up; they still had to hide their legs under long skirts.[25] In another production Antonia was an angel in a Fra Angelico tableau, and she remembered into old age the beauty of her wings. But there was a kernel of rebellion growing, which the ever vigilant nuns knew about and monitored before Antonia herself realised what was happening.

In 1910, when she had been at the Convent nearly two years, a particularly exquisite punishment was exacted which spoiled for her the most important day in any young Catholic's life, her First Communion. Her friends at school were the essential human heartbeat at the centre of life in the Convent; they made the privations more bearable and the pleasures a delight. The nuns had attempted to break up her friendships with particular girls, suggesting she was aspiring too much in her choices and should be concentrating on girls closer to her in age and status. Perhaps Antonia had not shown the required obedience and humility because, as her First Communion approached, set for the important feast day of Corpus Christi on 26 May, she was prevented from participating along with her friends. Instead she had to take her First Communion alone, except for one other girl, not surrounded by friends, and at the wintry end of the year on the much less important feast day, the Presentation of The Blessed Virgin, on 21 November.

The reason given for this harsh deprivation was that she had talked too much in the corridors. Fifty-one years later she still recalled her disappointment with bitterness: 'I would have kept silence all day rather than have it postponed! . . . Six whole months and all the joy of the great feast & making it with the others denied me . . . it made me feel disgraced, set apart, not like the others when I so desperately wanted to be like them.'[26] It is not surprising that, devout as she was, and desperate to experience a profound spiritual recognition of something transcendent, at the moment of partaking of the greatest sacrament of her faith, she was flat and disappointed. She was confirmed two months later on 26 January 1911, but left no written memoir of that ceremony.

Years later she remembered: 'On my First Communion day, November 21st 1914 [1910], I felt nothing at the actual receiving of the sacrament but in reading Francis Thompson's poems that day (my mother had bought them for me not knowing what she was giving me) I found something terrible, sweet and transforming which really did make me draw breath and pant after it. . . .'[27] She called it her first revelation. In an interview when she was sixty she explained the nature of this revelatory. Having been brought up by a classical scholar with a love for that ancient world, its gods and myths, she had felt that after her conversion any imaginative return to this love would be a sin and branded as heresy. 'Suddenly Francis Thompson restored me all my "old gods" in a new light, symbols, pre-figurations of the ancient mystery. I realized, for the first time, that Catholicism wasn't narrow and exclusive but wide and inclusive. I can't tell you the sense of release.'[28]

It is significant that it was her mother, at this time despised by Antonia for her perceived frivolity and lack of intellect, and marginalised by her daughter's obsession with her father, who had shown in this gift just how good her instincts could be and how sympathetic she was to her daughter's passionate character. Significantly, in *Frost in May*, so truthful to her experiences in virtually all respects, Antonia made this revelatory book of poems a gift from her father.

The effect on Antonia of this delayed First Communion was to make her feel once more that she was an outsider, that she could never be good enough to be included in the golden circle of the chosen ones. She went home for the Christmas holidays and immersed herself deeper in Francis Thompson and wrote passionate essays. Most significantly she read Wilde's novel *The Picture of Dorian Gray*, which inspired her with the determination to write her own novel.

In *Frost in May* Antonia described with warmth the girls' welcome of any illness which would land them up in the sick bay where there was an inevitable relaxation, where one need no longer obey the bells and regulations which harried and marshalled them throughout the day, from dormitory to classroom, to playground, refectory and chapel and back again. She wrote of an epidemic of measles which the friends did their best to catch from each other so that they all ended up in quarantine together. The female camaraderie of those days of free speech and relaxed living are lyrically evoked in the book. We know that Antonia was ill during the spring term of 1914, and although we do not know how many of her friends joined her in convalescence, we do know that it was there that she began her great project – a novel which would demonstrate to everyone not only her talent but her piety too. She was specifically writing this work for her father's approval.

The plot was hazy but she wanted the ending to be a highly moral one, with the heroine finally becoming a Carmelite nun and the hero a Jesuit. With a true novelist's appreciation of storyline she knew that such a suitably Catholic conclusion would make the most impact if her characters were presented as sinners reformed by faith. And so she set out to paint them as decadent and rakish as she could. The trouble was that her lack of experience of this kind of reprobate life rather failed her: she had to content herself with descriptions of the hero's yellow silk dressing gown and the geranium red of her heroine's lips. The heroine's wanton behaviour did not extend much beyond kissing a stranger on a balcony 'to the wild throbbing strains of a Hungarian band'. However, Antonia was rather pleased with her first three chapters. But one of those new sins she had been taught to recognise was lurking in the convent corridors, and it caught her out. 'Vanity was my downfall. I could not resist showing the three chapters to my best friend.'[29]

The sword of Damocles, which had been suspended increasingly precariously over her, this time proved too heavy for its fraying thread. The next day there was one of the secret random checks on their desks. The manuscript disappeared. And the exquisite torment began. Antonia could see the sword slicing its way towards her in slow motion. It took a week to fall. Even more painfully, she had to endure this wait in Holy Week, with all its attendant ceremonies and re-enactment of the suffering of Christ. It was on her fifteenth birthday that Antonia was eventually summoned to face not Mother Superior but her father, with her mother in unhappy attendance. The interview was so deeply shocking to her that she could barely bring herself to contemplate it even twenty years later, in a memoir of her schooldays. She was confronted with the errant manuscript and accused of perversity, corruption and indecency. She was given no chance of defending herself, of explaining her story and about the beautiful conversions to come. It was her father's harshness which shocked her more profoundly than anything the nuns could have said or done to her. She had written these chapters with excitement and joy, she would have something that would impress her father with her intelligence and piety. And he was using it in the most terrible way as a weapon against her, impugning her very soul. 'My superb gift to my father was absolutely my undoing.'[30] The interview between Nanda and her father in *Frost in May* is the searing climax of the novel. It was also in reality the annihilation of her belief in her writing talent, her joy in imagination. It destroyed too her hopes of love and acceptance, her trust in God, in her father and in herself. Antonia herself called it a catastrophe, 'the most traumatic experience of my life.'[31] The father's words she recorded in the novel are her own father's words which she would never be able to forget: 'if a young girl's mind is such a sink of filth and impurity, I wish to God that I had never had a daughter.'[32] With that he abandoned her to her personal hell.

So great was her disgrace, he said, she would have to leave the Convent the following day. The late frost had come stealthily and with deadly effect. In one pitiless half hour, her tender new growth was blackened and shrivelled on the bough. All the nourishing roots of faith and friendship and learning were also brutally severed: she was torn out of the ground and transplanted into a different soil. She physically survived, but her flowering was to be late, and then only a poor reminder of what it might have been.

There is mention in her later diaries of a second part-novel, read to her father and now lost. His reaction was mild but unenthusiastic. We cannot know what sort of story it told, but with her adult writing Antonia was never able to sustain a purely imaginative work of fiction again. She mentioned derisively the slick commercial work she managed to knock off occasionally, but anything more ambitious and profound, requiring invention rather than fictionalised fact eluded her. Antonia allied writing creatively with the conceiving and bringing forth of a child. She saw, in this painful metaphor, the idea for that first book, 'began in the year following the beginning of menstruation. My father, as it were, killed the child. He thought of it as *having been conceived in sin.*'[33]

Antonia was unable to write a creative work for public scrutiny with anything like the ease and joy with which she wrote this first attempt at a novel. From that moment, she became fearful of what evils her writing might unloose. As a writer she was sentenced to 'hug the shore' as she described it, staying within her depth, revisiting every crisis in her life and every twist and turn of her soul. After half a lifetime of struggle to advance in her fiction beyond the emotional reef of her first sexual encounter, her father's complicity and her first abortion, Antonia wrote in her diary of the staleness and 'squalidity' of this autobiographical approach. 'I long for something fresh, something unconnected with my wretched self. Yet I seem quite incapable of invention. I am something of a freak as a writer and know it.'[34] Fear of pleasure, fear of the imagination, distrust of the unauthorised mind, these were the shackles on her art.

4

Outside the Railings

The heavy door shut behind me and I was back again in the suburban
lane, in the world to which I, an outsider from first to last, really
belonged.

'A Child of the Five Wounds', *As Once in May*

Although Antonia did not know it at the time, she was not expelled
from the Convent. In the Roehampton School Register was
written 'Left for a time in order to help her to get through a difficult
phase and to work for her degree.'[1] The Mother Superior had offered to
let her go to another house in the Order, one in Newcastle, but her
father had refused. He insisted that she was removed the following day
and sent to St Paul's Girls'. The shock of his anger and vilification of her
self, the injustice of the punishment, her voicelessness and impotence,
the brutal rooting up of her life: these finally achieved what the nuns
had failed to do. A fundamental part of herself was lost. 'I often feel as if
I had never been a "whole" person since that day [the day of her
interview with her father]', she wrote, 'from that moment, my religion
became *comparatively* superficial though still potent through fear.'[2]

Antonia gave up believing in her potential for goodness and beauty:
she feared she had lost the capacity to love. Contemplating her life years
later she saw it clearly. 'I don't think I was intended by nature to be
either "beautiful" or "good". . . . Acquired virtues seem to me very
much like rouge on a corpse.'[3] But neither did she have the confidence
to focus her considerable energies on the worldly success which she had
also wanted all her life. Not tamed enough, yet not free to be truly wild,
Antonia was paralysed between conflicting energies and desires,
between the cage and the open plain.

There was nowhere now for this cast out child to feel she belonged.
Antonia blamed neither the nuns nor the Catholic Church for this

expulsion; in fact, her faith became for a while even more fervent. Her father refused implacably to discuss the matter further. She could not explain herself or get a more reasonable account from him of his motives and feelings. Once when she was thirty years old she summoned up the courage to broach the subject and his face hardened and he said, 'I prefer not to discuss it'.[4] She was never able to tell him how she felt or to explain the purpose of the novel she had been writing for his approval. Her mother's attempted interventions on her behalf at that fateful interview had been brushed aside and she remained in Antonia's mind as ineffectual and irrelevant to the main drama of her life as she had always been. It was her father's terrible disapproval and emotional abandonment of her which did such violence to her spirit. As a child she had defined love 'as giving someone the power to hurt me'.[5] Certainly the person she loved most had done her the gravest damage, yet would not acknowledge it nor mitigate it. This confusion of anger and misunderstanding became a barrier between them which lasted until his death, 'a cloud . . . which was never entirely dissolved'.[6]

One of the most painful aspects of that cloud was the sense Antonia had of having fatally destroyed her father's approval and good opinion of her. This was the man she loved to the exclusion of anyone else, whose estimation and recognition of her were of defining importance. She felt almost annihilated by his thundering denouncement of her character and denial of her precious filial connection to him. She had been Cordelia to his blind and blundering King Lear, cruelly rejected and fatally misunderstood. Then a chance encounter with Mother Bradshaw, thirty-six years after the fatal incident, threw a new and surprising light on Antonia's years of shame.

The incident which Antonia had described often as the greatest shock in her life was put into a different perspective by Mother Bradshaw's admission that she had quite forgotten the exposure of Antonia and her sinful manuscript. But the real revelation came with the old nun's memory of her conversation with Mr Botting. She was adamant that it was Antonia's father who wanted Antonia to leave, and quoted his reaction, which sounded absolutely plausible to his daughter, 'If this is how she is spending her time, the sooner she comes home and works with me the better.'[7] This left Antonia with the extraordinary new slant on her father's behaviour. He had used the situation for his own ends. She remembered that he had wanted her to leave the Convent the previous year: the discovery of the manuscript had probably given him his chance to manipulate her into accepting his decision that she should go to St Paul's. But of course, in his heavy-handed way, he completely overplayed this delicate card and could not appreciate the malign effects of his action; 'it was so upsetting for my relations with my father and I was never able to write anything of my own, as I call it, until after his death.'[8] With amazement she realised that in his anger he had lied to her; the father who she had always thought could not lie. At fifty-one years old, with her father long dead, Antonia accepted, for the first time, that he was human and fallible.

Slowly Antonia realised that for all those intervening years, she had felt too insecure herself to be able to allow that her father could be wrong. She had needed him to be this idolised god-like figure, and it seemed less painful for her to blame herself, her own 'irreparable badness', with all the destructive effects on her own sense of worth, than to give up the crutch of her father being 'a representative of God on earth'.[9] In the same diary entry she wrote that she had known for some time that if her father, during her childhood, had said he no longer believed in Catholicism she would have left the Church at once, even if she had been at her most devout at the time. His authority was absolute: her guilt apocalyptic. She could not question her father's or her Church's rightness and truth, only ever her own. Always one to embrace the extreme of human experience, Antonia had made herself no less than 'responsible for the Fall of Man.'[10]

So as Antonia started at St Paul's at the age of fifteen, she had no concept of her father's fallibility. She was under the cloud. She was already familiar with the sense of her own intrinsic badness. Antonia entered her new school with a hardened heart. As her attempts to be the model pupil, the devout disciple, had reaped such sour rewards, she was not even going to try. Here her behaviour was the opposite of that of her convent days. The liberal regime meant nothing to her, the good teaching left hardly a mark. She became lazy and could barely be bothered to do her best work, gaining prizes only for English and French essays. Clothes and make-up instead became her new enthusiasms. Uniform was not compulsory at her stage in the school and she responded by never wearing the sober gymslip, except on the few occasions when she had to, and sporting wild, colourful and entirely unsuitable clothes the rest of the time. In her own words she behaved outrageously, a rebellious schoolgirl refusing to do games, fancying herself much more mature than her contemporaries and making great theatrical play of her religion. 'I became more Catholic than the Pope; carved my desk with pious mottoes and festooned myself with scapulars. My history essays had a Catholic bias which would have shocked even Mr Belloc; I invariably wrote Protestant with a small "p" and always spoke of "Good Queen Mary" and "Bloody Bess".'[11] She was treated with kind tolerance and on the whole had a good time as one of the

eccentric characters of the Sixth form. It became in retrospect the
happiest time of Antonia's life, 'when I was least afraid of public
opinion.'[12] 'During my two years at St Paul's I really did *not* care what
people thought of me, flouted all the most sacred school conventions
and was known as 'the cat that walks by itself".'[13] People liked her, she
was popular, and Antonia discovered for the first time that she had
power over others and enjoyed using it. But the moment she cared
again for someone and wanted to be loved, she became once more
'agonisingly sensitive' to the opinions of others. This wild time at St
Paul's was the only time in her life, since her early childhood, when she
felt careless enough, free enough, to just be.

A contemporary of hers at the school, Rhoda Dawson, whose father
was a well-known Arts and Crafts engraver working in Hammersmith,
remembered Antonia as 'a pretty, almost fluffy girl with an air of
sophistication new to us'. She was the first girl at school to use a powder
compact, and to keep it on top of her desk, but she tempered this
frivolity with a penetrating intellect and could win the annual essay
competition with a stunning effort on the set subject, 'Poetry Redeems
from Decay the Visitations of Divinity in Man.'[14]

Antonia explored most of the feelings and events of her life between
the ages of fifteen to eighteen in *The Lost Traveller*, a novel which
followed Nanda's life after *Frost in May* and the leaving of the Convent.
However, in this and subsequent novels, Nanda became Clara, named
after Clara Middleton, the heroine in Meredith's *The Egoist* – her
father's favourite book. In *The Lost Traveller* Antonia described with
astuteness how the exhilarating freedom which St Paul's offered her
became burdensome and problematic. 'The change from the convent
discipline had been too violent . . . In the enclosed world of [the
Convent of the Sacred Heart], every moment of her time was arranged
for her' but at St Paul's the girls organised their own time and imposed a
measure of self-discipline which was beyond Antonia. 'She felt
compelled to fritter away her time simply because it was her own to
squander . . . She was so used to obeying other people that it was almost
impossible to obey herself.'[15] This led to a sense of dissipation and
dissatisfaction. Her lingering to gossip in the corridors with friends was a
reaction against the Convent's rule against going around in twos: her
sudden obsession with clothes and how she looked a response to six
years of wearing an unflattering uniform and being forbidden to use a
looking-glass.

She became particularly conscious of her looks at this time. Her
father's insistence that she should be equipped to earn a living because
she might not marry made Antonia believe that she was not pretty

enough for any man to want her. The nuns had convinced her that she
was 'very plain', having the habit of calling attention to the girls' defects
not their attributes. 'I was so conscious (made so by them) of my ugly
teeth that I was afraid to smile. They never told me I had nice hair or
skin.'[16] Her longing to be attractive, and the fear that even when people
complimented her they were really jeering, lasted all her life. It might be
appropriate, therefore, to quote Antonia's description of her fictional
alter ego, Clara, the spitting image of herself:

> Though Clara was still thin, she was squarely-built, like her father,
> with broad shoulders and hips. The slender arms and legs were
> oddly matched with the heavier bones of the torso. . . . There
> were the same elements of lightness and heaviness in her face. . . .
> Her hair, brushed severely back, showed a high masculine forehead
> and small feminine ears. The modelling round the eyes was delicate
> but the dented obstinate chin and blunt tip of the otherwise well-
> drawn nose seemed to have been added by a coarser hand.

She then added a peculiar characteristic which many of her friends were
to comment on. 'According to her mood, her face could look vivid,
almost beautiful, or dull. The transformation was sometimes so sudden
that in a moment not only the contours, but the size and colour of the
eyes and even the texture of the skin would appear entirely different.'[17]
In writing about this variability to a friend, Antonia recalled being told
by someone who knew her very well that in the course of a day she
could veer from being 'a daughter of the morning to a debauched
Roman Emperor and back again.'[18] Her best features perhaps were her
pink and white skin, and the soft fair hair which rose in waves from her
high forehead. In her lively conversations with vivacious schoolfriends
like Marian Abrahams (Patsy Cohen in *The Lost Traveller*) their
speculations ranged over how to improve their looks, the possibilities of
finding husbands, future ambitions, art and literature and the universe.

Nothing she experienced during her years of easy camaraderie at St
Paul's impressed her with anything like the power and substance of her
years at the Convent of the Sacred Heart. Antonia was drawn back
periodically to visit the nuns, and would watch new girls walking about
under the plane trees eating their bread and jam as she had, listening to
the same old stories about the saints' lives and the venerable foundress of
the school. Nothing there appeared to have changed and its certainty
and timelessness attracted her still. It was Antonia who had changed.
After a while these visits felt strained and uncomfortable and she would

leave with relief, returning to the world outside where she felt she now belonged more, yet still was not quite at home.

Antonia's father's ominous insistence that she would have to earn her own living may have been just practical; the plight of unskilled, unmarried women was not a happy one. While she was at the Convent Antonia had found galling the contrast between her family's circumstances and those of most of her friends. They had none of her constraints and privations; they travelled abroad, they lived in elegant houses, had ponies, holidays, any clothes they needed. Training for a job and earning a living were not part of their world, and Antonia wished it did not belong in hers. She knew that her father wanted her to become a schoolmistress and resisted this with all her power. To her mind becoming a 'schoolmarm' was equivalent to admitting to being 'a grotesque, unloved spinster'.[19] Yet years later she was to write that she actually loved teaching, thoroughly enjoyed explaining ideas and 'laying down the law on any subject I know': she wrote that she was in fact a gifted teacher.

But rather than express her intelligence and her naturally competitive and ambitious nature through her work at school and university ('I have always wanted to be first and best in everything') Antonia decided to disappoint her father, and inevitably spite herself, by failing.[20] She was discouraged by her father from doing English as her subject for the scholarship exam for Cambridge. Later she felt that he was jealous of her writing talent (he wrote well himself but never escaped from his schoolmaster's yoke) and that this was the only explanation for his denying her the chance of a scholarship. Like many classically trained minds, he also did not consider English suitably intellectually rigorous, and perhaps thought that his clever daughter might have gained a scholarship with something a bit more challenging, like Classics or modern languages.

When Antonia turned seventeen she began to put her hair up and walked out occasionally with ex-pupils of her father, who were impressed by her owning 'a real beauty' of a canoe which she paddled on the river. She had been left £25 in Nevinson de Courcy's will and, although her father had urged her to buy something solid like a gold watch, Antonia, to the surprise of everyone, had insisted on buying a canoe. She became quite proficient at handling it, 'which was just as well as I couldn't swim.'[21] This confidence with paddling a canoe on the busy and dangerous River Thames, without being able to swim, showed the carefree, independent – even reckless – side of Antonia, which the intellectually free and secular St Paul's Girls' School seemed to have encouraged.

One of her earliest extant letters was to her schoolfriend Rhoda, who was spending part of the summer holiday in Sussex. This letter revealed the liveliness of Antonia's personality and style at the time, her affectionate intimacy with her favourite poet, and her deep and romantic love for the Sussex landscape of her forebears:

> Please give my love to the downs; and sacrifice to every god on them for me. There are a great many gods there, you know. There's a god who has a private and particular dew-pond by the Chanctonbury Ring; there's a very terrible god, who sometimes takes the form of a snake, by the Lancing Clump (you feel a horror come over you, as of Pan, as you go by there) there is a god in every copse between Amberley & Storrington. I wonder Francis never met any when he was at Storrington all that time . . . perhaps he did, but he never says anything about it, only 'the wind that sings to himself as he makes his stride/Lonely & terrible . . . on the height.'[22]

Unfortunately, Antonia did not persevere with Cambridge entrance, as her father had hoped. She was to regret this later, and even in her last year at school, if we can read the truth between her lines of fiction. In *The Lost Traveller* Clara speculates with one of her intellectual friends about the excitement of Cambridge and the sense they have of a life beginning: 'All over England there must be people just like themselves, waiting to meet and set each other on fire . . . [they] invented a place which was a combination of Mediaeval Paris, Plato's Academy and an eighteenth century coffee-house. The dons in this dream city talked like Coleridge and Wilde and the undergraduates were all brilliant and fantastic.'[23] If she had gone to Cambridge she might have found her home, for a while at least. She chose instead to leave school at seventeen, against her father's wishes, because she was attracted by the idea of earning money.

Money, or rather the lack of it and resentment at her real or comparative poverty, was to be one of the major motivations in her life. It affected significantly the work she did, her state of mind, even the men she chose to marry. As we have seen, the seeds for this obsession were laid in the early years of her life. Money was power, allied closely in her mind with her father. He controlled the money; she and her mother had none and were dependent on his goodwill for everything. He was not ungenerous, but she recalled her frustration that he would only give what he wanted to give, never considering the desires or needs of the recipient. Money was also love; withheld, as love was withheld, if she did not attain the expectations put upon her. Antonia learned early the painful lesson that there was no point in her even voicing her wishes and asking for anything. She grew up feeling deprived of power, of love, of money: the easiest to try and remedy was her need of money, but for too long it masked the deeper needs in her to feel significant and worthy of love.

The Convent increased her sense of material deprivation and inferiority: in a personality which cannot bear to be less than first and best, this lack of evident power and distinction rankled. So as a restless schoolgirl with a financial chip on her shoulder, the chance of having her own money at last was seductive indeed. 'It was the magic words "£10 a term" that made me leave school and my friends and go and live with strangers. It has made me do jobs that bored me, give up what I knew to be valuable, made me fear to take risks . . . Money comes into all my relations with men. I have never made a single sacrifice for "Art" and I have grovelled for money.'[24]

The money may have focused her mind, but Antonia at seventeen was already impatient with school life. It was 1916 and the full horror of the First World War was becoming clear to those back home. Poison gas had been used by the Germans at Ypres the previous year: there was public shock with the realisation that this was a war like no other that had been before, with casualties so great in the terrible offensives on land and sea that every family was to be touched by the death of at least one young man close to them. Half a million allies perished in 1916 in the Battle of the Somme alone. Conscription had been hastily pushed through in the first part of the year. And young women were going off to war as ambulance drivers, nurses and auxiliaries on the Western Front.

As a child Antonia had longed to be a boy so that she could be a soldier when she grew up; now she felt she had been cheated a second time by being born just a couple of years too late. All around her was adventure and extremities of human courage and suffering. Young men whom she had seen as schoolboys visiting her father's study were now suddenly important in uniform. Those few who returned to visit came marked with a world of experience which had turned them from children into men, a world from which she was excluded. To make her sense of exclusion even more complete, those few soldiers she saw on leave were reluctant to talk about the war, more intent on forgetting for the few days' respite they had left to them. She saw her father's accumulating grief over the succession of deaths amongst his old pupils. For a while she was no longer his central concern.

Antonia's faith too, while not exactly diminishing, was inevitably less integrated in her daily life than it had been at the Convent. It was hard for her to see how to anchor her newly emerging personality in her Catholicism without the external structure and reinforcement of daily rituals and community consciousness. Increasingly her face was turned outwards to the world, and her intense moments of inner revelation were more often than not the result of reading a poem, or the sight or sound of something beautiful in nature, which seemed to have no moral imperative attached to it at all. For a while she seemed freed from the burden of doctrinal debate, able to share her mother's relaxed, intuitive attitude to her faith.

Having money of her own was an increasing preoccupation, and so when the seductive £10 a term was offered by a Catholic family, the Cumming Latteys, who wanted a good Catholic as governess, she had little compunction in leaving friends, family and her education behind to become something very close to the 'schoolmarm' she had so feared as her destiny. In *The Lost Traveller*, Antonia wrote with great effectiveness about the love Clara felt for the precocious boy she was sent to teach. His was an ideal family with a kind, devout and distinguished mother who lived in a wonderful country house; 'when I was little I used to dream about such places and pretend I lived in one', and an intelligent, rumbustious boy who represented the longed-for younger brother with whom she could play war games and by whom she was adored.[25] As was her custom, Antonia kept her fiction very close to reality.

The house was a Jacobean manor house just as she described it, Priors Court in Callow End in Worcester, and the beloved only son of the book existed too. He was Henry James Cumming Lattey, and was nine at the time Antonia went to stay. He did go on to the Catholic public school Downside, as he was due to in the story, and all the wild games of soldiers he and Antonia used to play together bore fruit; he eventually went to Sandhurst to become a career soldier. In the book everything ended tragically with the accidental death of the boy, for which Clara blamed herself and wished herself dead. She made expiation of this guilt the reason for her unlikely engagement to Archie Hughes-Follett (in real life Reggie Green-Wilkinson, who was to become her first husband). More happily, her young pupil in reality distinguished himself in the Second World War, emerging a Lieutenant-Colonel, and went on to become a High Sheriff of Worcester, dying at the more timely age of seventy-four.

Within six months Antonia was home again. Two terms of teaching at a boys' school followed. She replaced a young teacher who had gone to war and recalled with amusement that the boys, aged from twelve to fifteen, hardly much younger, and many much taller than herself, were asked to continue to call their teacher 'Sir'. She recalled wearing a lace and tulle hat, her hair frizzed out at the sides and her face laden with make-up. Her dress was a tube dress, bought by the yard, and on her feet were 'high yellow top button boots'.[26] She taught Latin, French and Greek, but the classes were a riot and she had to negotiate the boys' good behaviour by agreeing to tell them ghost stories at half time, as long as they had done their work first. She also took them for football and shared her love of military headgear with them, showing them a German helmet she had acquired: 'Oo, look, Sir's got a German helmet'.[27] Later, writing to a friend, Antonia recalled that she found presiding over the boring bits, ' "lines", walks & "cloakroom" much the worst part.'[28] Antonia's liking of the masculine and her longing for a brother made her a collaborative and entertaining teacher for the twenty boys in her control. But she was asked to leave after two terms. The head of school had visited the classroom during the second half of the lesson, when a ghost story was in full swing.

Between the ages of eighteen and nineteen Antonia went through a stage of thinking she should become a nun, 'mainly because it was the most awful thing I could think of.' She had spent much of her time at the Convent terrified that she might have a vocation. There were all sorts of chilling stories of young women fainting with fear if they heard the call, but becoming nuns regardless. 'You get these absurd ideas that if you enjoy anything it must be wrong so that what God wants of you is the worst thing you can think of.'[29] She distressed her family with the idea and made herself utterly miserable: the feeling soon went away.

Already, while in her last months at St Paul's Girls' School, Antonia had happened by chance upon advertising as a possible area of employment. Along with her friends, she had pored over beauty advertisements and had thought that one, by Dearborn's for a product called Mercolised Wax, could be improved upon. She wrote to the company with her suggestions and was asked for more. This developed into a freelance copywriting contract which paid her the enormous sum of £250 a year (800% more than she was paid as a governess) at the age of nineteen. It would last until 1921, when her mental health started seriously to decline. The money she earned from her teaching and subsequently from a temporary job as a clerk in the Ministry of Pensions (now the Department of Social Security) could hardly compare with these freelance riches.

Antonia was also writing occasional stories for the *Westminster Review*. But it was Dearborn's money which meant she could afford to leave her job as a clerk, which she had endured for a year, and pay for herself to go to study at the Academy of Dramatic Art (now RADA) in Gower

Street. This may have been a further sign of her growing independence from her father's opinion, for she had loved acting both at the Convent and at St Paul's despite his disapproval. More negatively, it may have been evidence of how much she was still in thrall to him, making the flouting of his deepest wishes and aspirations for her the more important motivation. Acting was an activity for which her father had nothing but contempt: 'What he absolutely *abhorred* my doing was not writing but *acting* and acting to me was of course the greatest *pleasure* of all.'[30] To any father, born a Victorian and devoutly Catholic, acting would seem a precarious and morally dubious occupation for an intellectual daughter. Certainly, in the post-war frivolity of the 1920s, it was a raffish and rather rackety life.

But none of these considerations crossed Antonia's mind. Although she was twenty she was still surprisingly ignorant of the ways of the world, the emotional and sexual dealings between men and women; even the bare facts of life. When she was eighteen, a young medical student, whom she had been considering marrying, so desperate was she not to remain a spinster, took her to a ball and afterwards told her the facts of life. Perhaps she still believed that a woman could get pregnant by kissing in a certain way, for she must have displayed some surprising gap in her knowledge for him to launch into a full explanation. The news he gave her, as she admitted to her elder daughter years later, was enough for her to break off the relationship instantly. It had already been somewhat strained by the fierce theological arguments in which he and Antonia would embroil themselves. He was one of the McVicker brothers, either Robin or Wilfred, and his parents were devout Ulster Protestants; Antonia at that time was in her fervent Catholic period.

Her father could still thwart her longings and cramp her joy. As a child Antonia had longed to have a pony but 'always knew it was *inconceivable* I should ever have one.'[31] Her father had said he would give her riding lessons but then insisted he could not afford to. When an aunt came into a legacy, when Antonia was about eighteen, and wanted to buy her a riding habit and pay for some lessons, her father refused, saying it was too great a present. Antonia's disappointment and bitterness was an echo of the time her father had taken the half-sovereign she had won for her precocious talent at Greek.

She was at the age when she had ambitions to be something in the world, to make her mark and claim her share of all the things she had felt were lacking in her life so far. By her own admission she was not a good actress, being too 'feeble of voice and constrained of gesture' but she was driven by the romantic desire just to *be* an actress, legitimately centre stage, holding everyone's attention, with the power to affect the minds and hearts of others, to win people's notice, perhaps even their love.[32] She joined the Academy of Dramatic Art initially for a four term course, starting in the autumn of 1919, living at home and paying her twelve guinea fee per term herself. She still called herself the hated name she had been lumbered with by birth and her father's classical pretensions and was yet to manufacture for herself the more anaemic 'Antonia White'.

Notwithstanding the fact that she was still Miss Botting, London in 1919 was a good place to find oneself, particularly if you were twenty with your life before you and a dream of what you could be. Women, who had played such a crucial part in the war effort in factories and hospitals, were not going to return to the narrowness of their pre-war roles. Nancy Astor was elected that year as the first woman to represent a constituency in Parliament. Young men were flooding back from the Front, many of them febrile in their need to celebrate life after years of physical deprivation and proximity to death. One of these young men was a fellow student at the Academy, Philip Reeves. Antonia fell 'madly in love'[33] with him, but he was already married. He had come back from the war and was much older – and a much more talented actor, moving quickly through the Academy classes and then getting a part in *Charley's Aunt*.

Years later Antonia was to write of what she most desired: it was to be a list which had changed little during her lifetime. Significantly perhaps, this version – written at the age of almost forty – had more the feel of an adolescent's hopes than the plans of a woman who has reached the halfway point in her life with three marriages, two children and one acclaimed novel behind her. 'What then is it I most want to have? A great, indisputable, demonstrable creative talent. I also want money, a few nice enviable possessions, to be popular, desired and powerful.'[34] She did not mention love or marriage, but then this very lack suggested too a woman who had failed to find much value or comfort in lovers or children.

For a while, the Academy of Dramatic Art seemed to be one route for Antonia to find that creative talent, and to assert herself against her father in the process. Housed in adjoining Georgian buildings in Gower Street, it was a lively and uninhibited place where people swore and drank and made love to each other without being married. Founded in 1904 by Sir Herbert Beerbohm Tree, it was blessed with some illustrious patrons; George Bernard Shaw and Gerald du Maurier sat on the Council in the year when Antonia entered, and Mrs Patrick Campbell, Gladys Cooper, Ellen Terry, Somerset Maugham and Jerome K. Jerome were among its Associates. The Academy's aim was to be the equivalent of the Paris Conservatoire, and to provide a thorough general training for the stage.

There were more female students than male and more male parts than female, which meant that the female parts had to be shared. This was confusing and unsatisfactory for everyone, not least the young woman thespian who wished to think herself deeply into her role, rather than be part of a randomly interchangeable group. It seemed very unfair to Antonia that some male student could swagger about on stage throughout the whole performance, being Hamlet, for instance, from beginning to deathly end, while she and the other women were having to slip in and out of the character of Ophelia, or Gertrude.

Part of the attraction of auditioning for a touring company who wanted a minor *ingénue* was the chance of having her part, however meagre, entirely to herself. When Philip Reeves left to take his part in *Charley's Aunt*, Antonia was very keen to try and get a part in the same company, but she was only taken on by 'this rough touring [company].'[35] Her audition consisted in having her teeth inspected and her legs checked to see she was not bow-legged or knock-kneed. She was offered the part because it seemed as if the clothes of the actress she was to replace might fit. She was offered £3 a week and accepted, even though it meant leaving the Academy before her last, fourth, term. The play was *The Private Secretary* and the tour was due to start in York. Antonia was duly dispatched with the rest of the company on the night train, and thus rudely introduced to the discomforts and forced camaraderie of the touring player. Fortunately she was taken under the wing of another young actress in the company, Trixie, with whom invariably she had to share their succession of dingy lodging rooms. She was a much more capable and worldly young woman than Antonia, and had an entirely different temperament: optimistic, opportunistic and pragmatic, she bowled through life without much thought or self-doubt, devoutly Catholic yet unconcernedly sexual. Antonia's third novel, *The Sugar House*, began with this tour and evoked so well a world of seedy lodgings, petty feuds and easy friendships; 'all the part about the tour: I think that is absolutely as it was.'[36] The vivid Trixie became in fiction a memorably realised character called Maidie.

Antonia also wrote of this experience in a memoir, 'The First Time I Went on Tour', and recognised the debt she owed this high-spirited and contradictory young woman: 'I could neither rise to her heights of old-maidish refinement nor follow her in her moods of rollicking relaxation. We shocked each other profoundly, we quarrelled bitterly, we went for days without speaking . . . yet we continued to share bed and board . . . I have never met anyone like Trixie, and I probably never shall again.'[37]

Quite soon the tour began to run down; a week's booking in good cities like York declined to three days in smaller towns, and Antonia was relieved to be dismissed along with the rest of the company after six months. Despite emotional farewells and promises to keep in touch, Antonia was never to see Trixie, nor any other members of that temporarily close-knit company, again.

Someone she did see again was a young man who had been demobbed and become a stage-door Johnnie, hanging round the Academy in Gower Street in his desire to be something in the theatre. Reggie Green-Wilkinson was the same age as Antonia, gawky and painfully lacking in the qualities which were then expected of a young man of his background. He had had an undistinguished time at Eton, where he showed neither intellectual nor sporting prowess and left without a trace at fifteen, having been there for only a year. He was not a natural leader. Loathed by his overbearing father but adored by his mother, he had almost enjoyed the war, despite its horrors, because it took his mind off his unhappiness and for a while provided a dramatic theatre for his aimless existence. It was remarkable he should survive when so many did not, and it was quite possible that he suffered something of the guilt survivors feel who have come through some terrible catastrophe that kills most of their contemporaries. He was soon an alcoholic.

Reggie had no real aptitude for a profession but there was the promise of a good deal of money in the background. He was kept by his family on a tight allowance, most of which went on drink. Antonia remembered him as 'good and simple'.[38] Not a Catholic, although made one in her novel, he came from a well-connected family; his uncle was Tom Sopwith, already a legendary aviator and aeroplane designer whose firm produced, during the First World War, the Sopwith Pup, Camel and Triplane. At the same time Antonia met another man who was going to become even more important in her life: Eric Earnshaw Smith, also a war survivor, older than Antonia and Reggie but just as ill-equipped for the hard knocks of life.

In Antonia's diaries she discussed all the men in her life, sometimes obsessively and at length. Yet there is barely anything about Reggie Green-Wilkinson, apart from a few dreams of marrying him a second time when the security of his money and his unquestioning devotion to her seemed so attractive. He did feature, however, as a central character in *The Sugar House*, where Antonia wrote of the love he and the heroine bear for each other in an embryonic and asexual marriage. She never quite knew why she married him; perhaps it was just the recognition of their mutual despair which united them in a hostile world. 'His face, as he looked up at her with a toy locomotive in each hand, had been blind with misery. It was then, simply to wipe away that hopeless look that matched her own sense of numb despair, she had, for the first time, said that she would marry him.'[39]

She wrote touchingly of this doomed connection between them. But they were like two lost children: Hansel and Gretel, their sibling fates entwined, both outsiders, unhappy and incompetent, clinging together in a hostile and encroaching world. The escape for each was a dislocation of the self – alcoholism for Archie (Reggie), and for Clara (Antonia) the beginnings of a terrible descent into madness.

Antonia and Reginald Green-Wilkinson became engaged some time during her six-month tour, when she was about to turn twenty-one. It all happened rapidly and with heightened emotion. Reggie Green-Wilkinson had to endure yet another familial attempt at reform and was packed off by his father to work for an uncle in South America, that graveyard of adventurers, bounders and black sheep. Antonia went with him to the station to see him off. Desperately unhappy to be banished, 'he sort of poked his head out of the window just as the train was leaving and said "will you marry me?" '[40] She found herself yelling back above the noise, the simple word that would seal her fate – yes.

Although it seemed such an odd union, there were all kinds of stresses in Antonia at this time which may have contributed to her decision. She had been terrified of marriage; she was still vague about the sexual side of it, and what little she did know filled her with dismay. But Antonia was also terrified of being unmarriageable, of being alone and unloved. She wanted to prove to her father that she could find herself a husband, and one of whom he would approve. Antonia's father was always liable to hero worship men of a higher social status than his own, and he was delighted by his only daughter's engagement and subsequent marriage to this young man.

Her mother, who recognised that status and money had very little to do with marital happiness, was surprisingly firm in her opposition. This was an occasion when her intuitive understanding of the situation was entirely correct, and her unconventionality allowed her to express her misgivings, largely to do with Reggie's character and suspected homosexuality. However, it was always her father's opinion which mattered to Antonia; his conviction that she was doing the right thing and his affection for this weak but well-bred young man, whom he could accept as a son, meant that some of the cloud of disapproval and resentment which had hung over her relationship with her father since the terrible interview at the Convent of the Sacred Heart had now dispersed.

In *The Sugar House* she expressed this complex family dynamic. 'This marriage had restored her to her father; henceforth the three of them were bound in a new tie from which her mother was excluded. She thought how passionately [her father] had wanted a son; how passionately she herself had wanted a brother.'[41] In fact the one great bond between Antonia and Reggie was a fraternal love for each other and a shared enthusiasm for the theatre and for playing toy soldiers. A whole room was set aside in their tiny first home for their armies, set up in permanent warfare.

On a more trivial level, she was mortified by the idea of having to be seen naked of make-up. 'I thought I should look so repulsive in the early morning that a lover would be disgusted.' The fear of her unadorned self, without the safety of her mask, had grown so great that she felt her need for face powder and cream had become almost pathological, 'almost like a lust or kleptomania'.[42] Being loved innocently and unconditionally as Reggie appeared to do, removed some of Antonia's fear of censure, of not being attractive or lovable or good enough, merely as herself, without disguise.

But most significant of all in the influences which drew Antonia to marry Reggie was the fact that she was beginning to disintegrate mentally. She 'began to crack up – the year before I married Reggie' and started at that time to keep a diary, in a black notebook like her father's, little knowing that this was to be the beginning of the most remarkable document of her life.[43] This was a time when she was finding it impossible to do any work at all; even her advertising copy failed to flow fluently from her pen. She felt that her only expression of any kind went underground into her diary. 'It is as if I keep my identity in these books' and she used them during the worst times of breakdown and disintegration as a photograph of herself to which she could refer.[44]

Sadly she was to destroy this and the subsequent volume. But all the volumes which were to follow were a lifelong conversation with herself; sometimes harsh, often obsessional, always unfailingly honest. In unflinching detail they illuminated the life of a working woman, a mother and sometime lover, struggling with a manic-depressive illness, with the threat always of madness upon her: they charted too the progress of a soul in search of meaning and truth. In the world she assumed a variety of masks in an attempt to contain her disintegrating self, make it more acceptable and herself more deserving of love: only in the diaries does she lift the veil.

Slipping on the downward track of her own unhappiness, Antonia perhaps also accepted Reggie's proposal of marriage in an attempt to bring some point into her chaotic life. Her mother, frivolous as Antonia always liked to consider her, cared more for the happiness of her daughter than she knew. Marriage to a potentially rich young man did not blind her to her uneasiness about her daughter's motives and Reggie's basic unsuitability to be a husband in any conventional meaning of the word.

Cecil Botting was always careful to be seen to do the right thing and he insisted, against the wishes of both the bride and the groom, on a big wedding ceremony at the Brompton Oratory. Reggie's father was adamantly against the union and refused to meet Antonia's family or attend the ceremony, increasing her sense of unworthiness and of being a social outcast. Antonia and Reggie were married on 28 April 1921, just after her twenty-second birthday. She wrote in *The Sugar House* of the bride almost sleep-walking down the aisle, barely recognising herself, let alone the young man who waited for her at the altar. Their wedding photograph shows a touchingly ill-matched pair, one so short and round, the other elongated, asthenic and thin, his bony wrists and ankles making him seem even more vulnerable and overgrown. They seem innocent and shy and ill-equipped for the world.

For their honeymoon, Reggie's aunt, Mrs Tom Sopwith, lent them her monstrous gothic mansion Horsley Towers, between Leatherhead and Guildford in Surrey. While Antonia was changing into her going-away clothes, her mother entered the room to give her daughter her valedictory best wishes. Antonia told her younger daughter years later that her own mother had attempted to enlighten her about her wedding night, but could only say that something 'so appalling was going to happen . . . she could only pray to God and make sure there was a glass of milk and biscuits by her bed to console herself with when it was all over'.[45]

The building itself was oppressive, with its cloisters and towers and vast, sunless, stone-flagged rooms. Built by the Earl of Lovelace, who married Byron's daughter, it was a 'Nightmare Abbey' of warring styles and unhappy associations: for many years it was to haunt Antonia's dreams. On her honeymoon night Antonia was overawed and depressed by the rambling, gloomy building. Like two children lost in a grim fairytale, she and Archie were alone in this alien, ghost-ridden place, surrounded by knowing and rather sinister-seeming servants. Antonia went to bed exhausted and full of foreboding, but soon fell asleep. Archie added a hefty nightcap to the quantities of champagne already drunk and eventually stumbled up to join her. Antonia related the rest of the story to her daughter: Archie had woken her with his clumsy entrance and, barely glancing her way, had noticed the biscuits and milk.

' "Biscuits. Oh good!" he mumbled and ate the lot.' He then collapsed fully dressed on to the bed and went to sleep.

The embracer of extreme experience, Antonia felt a mixture of relief and disappointment; she had been half hoping, as her heroine Nanda had, that 'that unknown, violent contact with another person would break down some barrier in herself'; instead she had been denied the experiment which may have made her feel more a part of the human race.[46] As she explained to her daughter 'although I was petrified, I was also curious to know what happened. I had only the haziest ideas of the facts of life, although I had read Thomas Hardy and other authors which had given me some intimation of what went on between men and women. But I had no idea what had to go where for children to be conceived, and had some vague idea that it was connected with some particular way of kissing. And of course I'd never seen a naked man, except in statues, and I knew nothing about – er – *phallus erectus*.'[47] It was to be many more years before Antonia even began to understand the real nature of what went on between men and women.

By the age of twenty-two this highly intelligent but unworldly ex-convent girl had written two abortive part-novels, finished school, was earning £250 a year on a freelance copywriting contract, and had been a governess, a teacher in a boys' school, a civil service clerk and a professional actress. She had fallen in love for the first time, married another man whom she barely knew, and had already met her second husband-to-be. She did not know who she was, where she was going or where she wanted to be. Somehow separated from her true self, she felt immune from experience. As her fictional self explained, 'I used to want to grow up as fast as possible . . . Especially since the war. I felt as if I'd miss everything otherwise. But, since I've come up here, I don't care. What is there to grow up *for*?'[48]

5

The Land of Lost Content

I said there was an image that had always haunted me . . . .. the traveller
who must not lie down in the snow and sleep or he will die.
[Dr Ployé] said 'Now I know what you're up against: you really *want*
to go to sleep and die.'
I said *eagerly* – '*Yes* – beautiful oblivion.'

18 January 1968, *Diaries I*

A ntonia and Reggie escaped from the gothic towers of their
honeymoon retreat and set off for Cornwall on Reggie's motor-
bike. They wandered around Mevagissey and Polperro, amazed at how
timeless and unspoilt were these two North Cornish fishing villages.
They returned to set up home in rented furnished accommodation in 38
Glebe Place, in Chelsea. This was a pretty Georgian cottage of doll's
house proportions in a smart part of London, and it was well beyond
their means. But Antonia had been so keen to move away from the
dreary Victorian terraces of her home in West Kensington, and this
could not have been more different. With its quietness, the prettiness of
the buildings and their lack of uniformity, and the prevalence of trees
and gardens, Chelsea still felt like a village. More important to Antonia,
however, was the fact that the 'villagers' were predominantly artistic,
bohemian types, whose garrets were not too cold or dingy: the kind of
people with whom Antonia would always feel a kind of kinship.

This move, ruinous as it turned out to be for their finances, was
meant to be for Antonia the beginning of her life as an artist. This was
how she had seen herself all her life. She did not see herself ever as a
wife, or a mother, or an actress, an advertising executive or a journalist –
or even a 'learned person' as another learned person, her second
husband Eric Earnshaw Smith, once called her – to her horror. She only
ever wanted to be an artist, and that meant for her being a writer. On

her marriage certificate she had given her profession as Authoress, declaring before God and State that this is where she would make her mark. In a heartfelt entry in her diary years later she sounded less confident, resisting her natural talent for academic pursuits: 'I don't *want* to be . . . a schoolmistress. Yet perhaps it is all I am fitted for, if only I could be humble & accept it. . . . But oh, I want to be *in* it – not an outsider – however small an artist, yet a true one.'[1]

Her father, of course, could not appreciate her vision. And if he had, it would have frightened him. Writing was good enough as a hobby, but as a profession he considered it disreputable and risky; 'I think this ties up with Wilde and his homosexual side.'[2] To him, this ridiculously furnished shoe box of a house was pure folly. He had saved hard for four and a half years before marrying her mother and then prudently had moved into his parents' home, and been grateful for their furniture. Chelsea and the writer's life held too many uncontrollable elements and temptations for a repressed hedonist, such as he was, to accept it as an appropriate place for his headstrong daughter.

But it was not just imprudence which brought Antonia down. Reality for her and Reggie had never stood much chance of measuring up to the dream. The deterioration in Antonia's mental state had begun before her marriage. It is possible she was already eating in the desperate and uncontrolled manner she described in *The Sugar House*, 'stuffing herself with anything she could find; sponge cakes, chocolates, old heels of bread and cheese, like a ravenous child.'[3] The photograph on her wedding day showed her much plumper than she appeared in any other photograph, even those of her soon after having given birth to her children.

Neither Reggie nor she was working consistently: he had the odd menial job driving vans for Lyons bakery, and the occasional position in the theatre or small part in a play, but nothing lasted for long. Antonia, increasingly sunk under a weight of torpor and guilt, was incapable of writing. She lost the will to care for herself, growing increasingly dishevelled in a physical expression of the depth of her depression. Their house, the Sugar House of the title, lost its superficial brightness and became an increasingly sinister prison for unsuspecting Hansel and Gretel. Reggie was absent for long periods, drinking recklessly and spending money like a fool. Within only a few months, chaos, debt and despair had overwhelmed their inchoate yearnings for the artist's life. Antonia recognised in retrospect that 1921, the year leading up to her terrible first breakdown, was: 'one of the worst years of my life when I first felt this awful inertia, depression & impotence.'[4]

Because of her destruction of her diaries for this time, there is very little factual evidence of what passage her life took in this downward slide. But all her novels follow closely the events and emotions she experienced during the time that they encompass and Antonia, when she was in the middle of the painful struggle to write *The Sugar House*, stated that she had to face and interpret in this book 'all that queer, horrid Chelsea time leading up to the asylum.'[5] On rereading the novel, years later, she surprised herself with how closely she had managed to trace the pattern of her despair. 'I read through Sugar House and thought it rather good. How painfully well it describes this state of mind which I first knew in 1921.'[6]

She wrote from the intense experience of the fear and disorientation which oppressed her: 'The more she was alone, the more she became conscious of her own emptiness. Sometimes she even doubted whether she existed at all. Once this sense of non-existence was so acute that she ran up from the basement to the sitting-room full of mirrors almost expecting to find nothing reflected in them.'[7] Years later she explained to her friend the American writer, Emily Coleman, that there was a time at this house when she had felt so invisible she was startled to see letters addressed to her. Antonia charted the encroaching paralysis of depression; 'Each anxiety was like an actual weight on her diaphragm pinning her down on the rumpled bed: the bills, Archie's drinking, her own impotence to write, the impossibility of going either backwards or forwards in any direction. But more crushing than any of these was an overall sense of guilt, not localised, as if all these were a punishment for some mysterious sin she did not remember having committed.'[8]

Before her diaries of 1921 were destroyed Antonia allowed Emily to read them in the mid-thirties: Emily recorded her reaction to them in her own diaries: 'She is a strange, frantic little doll, as mad as a March hare.'[9] One entry in particular struck her, which she quoted: ' "And yet as I dress tonight, putting on my pink frock, I shall catch my own face sidelong in the mirror and dimple at it and think, 'Tony you fascinating thing.' Ugh! I'm a reptile that should be trodden under foot".'[10] This extreme reaction to her own looks might have been an echo of her Catholic training against the sins of vanity. However, most significant is the fact that the voice of encroaching madness and self-disgust in *The Sugar House* was as authentic as this surviving fragment.

Nothing seemed to halt Antonia's spiralling descent. Neither Reggie nor she could extend the hand that would help the other out of the vortex. The house which had so delighted her became her cell, its small rooms appearing to shrink, its bright furniture seen as the gimcrack stuff it really was. The redbrick Catholic church opposite, already out of scale with the tiny houses, loomed even larger and more forbidding. It was like the witch guarding Hansel and Gretel's escape-route, a reminder of the full weight of Catholic expectation, of the indissolubility of marriage and the duty of procreation.

Outside the house, they could pretend for a while that everything would work out; that they were like any other young, bohemian couple in their rumpled clothes, strolling aimlessly down the King's Road to a café for a coffee or a cheap meal. They went to Antonia's parents for Sunday lunch, and would manage somehow to tidy themselves up and act the parts of the happy newly-weds. Antonia had commented once that she might not have been much good as an actress but in extremis she could be 'a tolerably good actress off the stage.'[11] Although her father thought it ridiculous that they had rented such an expensive and fashionable place and refused to visit them there, he was still delighted with his son-in-law. This, momentarily, lifted Antonia's spirits with the false hope that her marriage would turn out to be right. But it was not to be. She was the first to grow tired of the endless childish games which, together with mutual fear and pity, seemed to be their substitute for the usual bonds of marriage, love and sexual desire.

In fact the catalyst for change came not from themselves but from an outsider, one of the Chelsea artistic community to which Antonia longed to belong. The painter Eliot Seabrooke, who in the previous year had just become a member of the London Group of painters, had a studio nearby. Thirteen years her senior and a good deal more experienced than she, his career seemed to be in the ascendant at the time when Antonia met him. His first one man show was held that year in 1921: he had all the credentials to appeal to her romantic imagination. He had been an official war artist and had shared dangers and privations with the soldiers. A large, impressive and handsome man, he had a head like Napoleon's. Antonia appeared to amuse him, and his healthy libido for a time was directed casually her way.

Seabrooke introduced her to some of the artists and their exhibitions during her Chelsea period. In his expansive company she fleetingly entered the rarefied air of Bloomsbury when he took her to a party in Vanessa Bell's studio in Gordon Square. Virginia Woolf was the hero-writer of Antonia's youth. She seemed understandably overawed in a description she wrote of the sisters: '[Vanessa Bell] is a tall slim quiet woman with blue eyes and a very spiritual expression. Her sister, Virginia Woolf, is also tall and quiet, vague and yet perfectly contained and poised.' They were two decades older, and their grandeur, beauty and literary and artistic successes made them commanding presences in London's cultural life. Antonia was struck by 'their deep quiet charm . . . as if there were a door always open in their minds through which you too might catch a breath of the wind beyond the world.'[12] Years later she was to deplore the morals of their set in a later letter to a Catholic friend, as 'childish and disgusting', but as they did not differ markedly from the morals of her own Chelsea set, this outrage may have been slightly synthetic to appease the more judgemental man to whom she wrote.[13]

But Eliot Seabrooke's importance in Antonia's life extended beyond his sociable opening of studio doors. She wrote in a later diary, while working on *The Sugar House*, 'The Seabrooke thing must be given something of its true importance. It is a pity, I suppose to have left myself so little space for its development.'[14] This suggests that the conclusive role the artist Marcus Gundry in *The Sugar House* played in helping the heroine to confront her impossible situation, and to show her the way out, reflects Seabrooke's pivotal role in Antonia's own life at the time. Because of this importance, it is interesting perhaps to see her fictional version of the unlayering of the moment of truth.

Clara, attracted to Gundry, visited his studio in the middle of her desperate state of lethargy and non-being. Half-excited, half-repelled by his attempts at seduction, she was overcome suddenly with hysterical crying. Gundry backed off, bemused at such an extreme level of response. Barely able to answer his part-formed questions, Clara intimated that although married she was still a virgin. Gundry, genuinely shocked and concerned for her, subjected her to the first straight talking about any sexual matter she had ever heard:

'Well, what are you going to do about it?'
'Do, what can I do?'
'You're not seriously proposing to go on with this farce of a marriage?'
She stared at him.
'But I have to go on. We're both Catholics. We have to go on whatever happens. Even if I were ever to leave Archie there's no question of divorce for either of us.'
He then explained that as long as she remained a virgin it became a matter of routine to have the marriage annulled by her Church.
'You really mean you hadn't the least idea?'
'No . . . Not the remotest . . . I never even dared imagine. . . .'

She began to faint with the emotion and shock of this revelation and as Gundry revived her and saw her to the door he said, 'Well, young woman, I hope you're grateful to me.'

'Oh I am. . . . I am. . . . You'll never know how much.'

But the interview had given her more than just the truth. After weeks of isolation and disorientation, leaden with the sense that there was something bad and corrupting within her, haunted by the other self in the mirror, Antonia found in the presence of this large and centred personality a raft of sanity on which she could rest for a while – 'It's been like coming to life after being dead for months. . . .'[15]

Seabrooke had not only given her the chance of a future emotional and sexual life, he had opened the door on what it meant to be an artist. She was attracted to the general scepticism and devotion to art amongst the writers and painters whom she met at this time. Their enthusiasms and attitudes infected her and she found herself questioning the fundamental truths of her religion for the first time since she was converted to Catholicism. She was amongst people who worshipped art and thought orthodox religion rather a quaint or irrelevant activity; 'to be a practising Catholic was considered, at the worst, mentally dishonest and at the best an amiable eccentricity.'[16] Although Antonia did not consider relinquishing her belief in God or the teachings of Christ, she became less sure of the Catholic Church's claims to be the one infallible repository of truth. 'Gradually the artists came to replace the saints (I had always found the saints a little repellent) in my private pantheon.'[17]

Twenty years on, Antonia remembered that only after meeting Seabrooke did she begin to doubt her faith. She also credited him for first pointing out that sex and creativity were interconnected: 'that sex was essential to the artist,' although she had come to believe that for her the opposite was truer – sex destroyed art, but out of madness came art.[18] The missing link, which she failed to make, was that the sexual relationship allied with love was so difficult and problematic for her that she either evaded it or risked madness, at times even death.

As far as one can tell from *The Sugar House*, it was Reggie who insisted that she proceed with the annulment for her own sake more than his, and he and Antonia parted with all the bittersweet affection and fear for the future which had brought them together in the first place. Both felt torn apart and full of regrets. Antonia went home to her parents in Perham Road and despite alternating periodically between numb passivity and extreme irritability, she appeared to them to be less distraught. She herself felt she would never feel anything passionately again. It was even possible, it seemed to her in this state of deadly inertia, that she would remain in her parents' house for ever. Her old fear had gripped her; there was something in her which repelled others and condemned her to permanent exile from life, love and creativity. Like

Clara in *Beyond the Glass*, her last novel and the one which dealt specifically with her irruption into mania, and just as violent a recovery, Antonia felt unwholesome and disconnected: 'She had an instantaneous vision of herself as someone forever outside, forever looking in through glass at the bright human world which had no place for her and where the mere sight of her produced terror.'[19]

The ecclesiastic process was begun. It took more than two years for the Catholic Church to annul her marriage on the grounds of non-consummation, '*propter impotentiam mariti*', as always retreating into Latin for the important, hieratic or embarrassing bits. Antonia had to endure an interview and a physical examination before the Holy See could declare her an Official Virgin. The civil plea for non-consummation was a separate and not quite so lengthy procedure, but that also involved a physical examination and intrusive questions. There was one ridiculous and distressing time when Antonia had to identify Reggie through a glass door in which her own distraught image was reflected, their mutual isolation and despair caught in the superimposed reflection. Of the two processes, the religious one was by far the most unpleasant. Antonia described the way the Church conducted the annulment as 'an obscenity'.[20] When asked to elaborate, she explained, 'The State was searching, but impersonal. I don't think I'm exaggerating, but there seemed to be a definite element of *gloating* in the other.'[21]

Antonia made occasional forays into the world outside her parents' house in an attempt to break out of the deadness of her feelings, to connect again with life. She saw Eric Earnshaw Smith, whom she had first met before her marriage to Reggie, and who always lifted her heart with his peculiar cat-like personality and his intellectual originality and open-mindedness. He was a companionable yet unintrusive presence who always seemed to know more than he expressed. Neurotic, solitary, mysteriously appearing and discreetly disappearing, he flitted inscrutably through the margins of other people's lives while working at the Foreign Office in a job of mind-soothing routine and urbanity. Music was one of his passions and Antonia, on looking back on her long relationship with him which lasted until he died, recalled that they would manage at least one concert a year together, regardless of the other demands of their lives.

Now in the early days of their friendship, Eric came to her rescue momentarily with his cerebral and imperturbable acceptance of her neuroses, with his fascinating, allusive conversation. In October 1922, little more than two months after her separation from Reggie and return to the parental home, Eric showed her a photograph of a handsome young man in uniform, perhaps because he found him attractive himself, and Antonia recognised that she had 'an extraordinary feeling about him'.[22] Eric had an invitation to a party given by this young man's sister and took Antonia with him to an artist's studio, where a young pianist was giving a recital of a Beethoven sonata.

After months of deathly torpor and depression, that evening Antonia was jolted violently into the opposite extreme; wild elation, extravagance and eventual mania. This was the pattern of the manic-depressive illness she was to suffer with all her life. Deadening depression was suddenly transformed into a heightened sense of limitless power and inexhaustible life. The catalyst was a chance encounter with the young man in the photograph who roused her passions: her over-stimulated senses appeared to make her able to communicate telepathically with him, as he could with her. His name was Robert Legg, an Officer in the King's Own Scottish Borderers. He was handsome and dark, with distinctive eyebrows framing striking grey eyes. On leave from his duties in Ireland, he arrived at the party, given by his sister Dorothy in her studio. There he made his psychic connection with Antonia by somehow interlacing his own thoughts with hers. They were soon dancing and, magically it seemed, simultaneously and spontaneously in love. For Antonia the extraordinary metamorphosis had begun.

In that moment of human connection she felt something fundamental in herself change; the weight of her past was sloughed off like a confining shell and she was released into her essential self – her senses supernaturally enhanced. She felt she could see in the dark; she could make out each layer of scent in the room; mundane objects were alive with fanatical detail. Antonia and Robert Legg spent three weeks in each other's company. Love, marriage, children, all the aspects of a domestic life which she had felt she would not want and could not have, seemed now perfectly natural and free from fear. In retrospect she realised this was the only time in her life when sexual desire was uncomplicated for her: 'wanting a man, wanting children by the man.'[23] He had said he wanted to live on a desert island with her and build everything himself; he could divine water. 'He was someone who *was* functioning properly. Every other love affair I have ever had was with someone who *wasn't*.'[24] But he also evoked that old passion of hers for the soldier and the soldier's honourable and active life. In listing what some of the men she had known had meant to her she wrote, 'Robert the soldier: simple: active: intuitive: *good*. The Public School type: the Brushwood Boy. *Actually the type my father most admired.*'[25]

He was also perhaps the only man who could break Antonia free from her father's emotional domination: he even managed to demystify that most holy of places and centre of power – her father's study – by imposing his sexuality there, and awakening a quiver of sexual response in her. In a highly symbolic act they engaged in an erotic game of wrestling, amongst the books, tobacco and pipes and old leather chairs, the talismans of her father's power. The intense attraction Antonia experienced for Robert Legg was a fairly straightforward sexual response, but the access of extreme elation and heightened perception which followed came from the same place as the deepest depression which had dogged her previous year: her feelings for Robert were merely the switch. Antonia began her dizzying upwards spiral. It struck her that she had never before realised what it was like to be truly alive. Life seemed to have flowed into her in such abundance and with such force that she could pour her benison on everyone, her family and friends, even passing strangers in the street. She felt she could embrace the world. Everything seemed possible. She would make her fortune, of that she was sure; she would write a magnificent book; she was full of brilliant schemes and plans: energy radiated off her like heat and light from a sun. 'She is going mad without knowing it,' Antonia explained this fictionalised episode to Emily, 'and this false ecstasy is the sign. And *yet* her feeling is real as a feeling, though everyone else begins to suspect there is something odd & hallucinated about it.'[26] In *Beyond the Glass* she wrote vividly of the rapture of this mania, which she first experienced in its full intensity during these weeks with Robert.

> It was difficult sometimes not to burst out singing or laughing from sheer ecstatic joy. Sometimes it seemed to her that she could savour the ecstasy even more fully when she was alone than when she was with Richard [the Robert Legg character] . . . Sleep was a sheer waste of time if one were really alive. Night after night she would lie awake, neither restless nor impatient for the next day; content simply to feel this high pulse of life throbbing through her. . . . She also began to discover that it was hardly necessary to eat. Her appetite had almost vanished yet everyone was saying how amazingly well she looked. She wondered if she ought to tell someone about these remarkable discoveries. Supposing she had hit on the secret of life?[27]

They seemed to have supernatural powers, and would play a game whereby they would not communicate verbally where they were to meet but would just turn up simultaneously, knowing without telling where and when to arrive. This extraordinary phenomenon, which Antonia wrote of in *Beyond the Glass*, she assured Emily had actually

happened between herself and Robert; 'that odd second-sight business. . . . All that is true . . . but it *was* odd.'[28] Second sight was reputed
to run in her family, but for her it was only a temporary phenomenon,
connected to the mania. During these three weeks anything seemed
possible; even her anxiety at introducing Robert to her father was
dissolved in the general elation of mood which cushioned her from
apprehension of anything outside her own thoughts. Her parents were
bemused at the sudden change in their daughter, but grateful to see her
apparently so happy. Her behaviour, however, seemed troublingly
strange. She had lost all her old impatience and irritability, was no longer
prickly, and showed a spontaneous affection for her mother. Her energy
seemed prodigious.

Robert too, initially swept up in the peculiar romance of recognition
and identification, grew uneasy at the inflated heights to which Antonia
seemed to have flown. In the novel his character confides his fear that
Clara is hardly real at times, barely human: 'It's as if you were on fire
inside. I look at you sometimes and it's as if you were melting away.'[29]

Antonia was flying too close to the sun, and her crash to earth was
inevitable. It was to prove almost fatal. '3 weeks of utter happiness, of
feeling *completely* alive, with no anxiety – but I was "manic" at the time!
I suppose I'll always be haunted by that . . . by having missed love.'[30]
Suddenly the tenuous grip she had on reality gave way. She struck out at
Robert for no reason, hitting him hard in the face. Antonia's fictional
description of her breakdown and subsequent incarceration in Bethlem
Royal Hospital, the famous public asylum for the insane, was
extraordinarily close to the facts in the fascinating document in the
hospital archives of her committal.

In *Beyond the Glass* Clara is with Richard, his sister and a friend in a
studio in Chelsea by the river. It is November, and there is a dense,
impenetrable fog. Aware of an exquisite happiness, the Antonia
character is in thrall to a voice in her head which tells her, 'This is the
perfect moment. Go *now*.'[31] She leaves the studio quietly and with utter
deliberation walks down the slippery alley that leads to the river, and
then on into the icy water. She is rescued by Richard and taken back to
his sister's rooms. Here she tells his sister that she can see that Richard
will die in a car or plane crash. In real life, Robert's sister was so struck
by the clarity of this premonition that she wrote it down and years later,
meeting Antonia by chance, she tells her that 'it happened as I "foresaw"
long ago'.[32]

In the next two days Antonia's mind was assailed by extremes of
exhaustion, elation, hallucination and violent impulses. The family
doctor was called. Her mania had moved into a psychotic stage: assailed

by delusions and hallucinations, her flight of ideas was so extreme that she became incomprehensible and inaccessible to ordinary communications. Her father appeared to her in the brown habit of a monk. She was repelled; he was an evil spirit disguised as her father: she felt that she was possessed by the devil. So violent and intractable was Antonia's behaviour that she seemed beyond understanding, help or reason: her father was shocked and terrified by what might become of her. Her mother was much more sanguine, inclined to try and nurse their daughter at home. But Cecil was persuaded that Antonia's case was so serious that she should be committed to Bethlem. Possibly Antonia's breakdown frightened him more because he was himself fearful of losing control, aware of his own blanketing depressions and how close he came at times to a sense of personal dissolution. Their doctor argued for Bethlem, a public institution rather than a private asylum, because it had a reputation for employing experienced psychiatric doctors. It had no commercial interest in its patients, and its waiting list meant that the administrators would not be tempted to hold a patient incarcerated for any longer than was medically necessary.

The Bethlem duty doctor's history of the five days preceding Antonia's admission to the hospital was laconic but expressive of her distressing state:

> On Sunday 12th [1922] November patient became very emotional. She stated that she was weeping because she was so happy. Patient attempted to throw herself into the river. Patient was prevented. Patient stated that she was in the possession of an evil spirit. Patient became excited. She stated that she believed that her father was dead. She kept saying that she was fighting against evil powers. Her excitement became toned with a religious phase. She decided to see a priest but without doing her any good. Patient has always had eccentric tastes as regards literature; herself interested in the supernatural with a keen interest in the stage.[33]

There was a letter from her father appended, written ten days later, and pathetic in its concern that Antonia's case should not be made to look too hopeless. He wanted to make clear that his suggesting Antonia had 'a rather morbid taste' in literature was an exaggeration.[34] He pointed out that she had a very high standard of literary taste and by 'morbid' he had merely meant she was interested in modern psychological novels. Her ramblings too, he had listened to carefully. Mad though they seemed, he vouched that much of what she ranged over could be located in her past experience.

Many years later, and after many hours of introspection and analysis, Antonia had realised that it was the possibility of normal sexual relations with a sexually uncomplicated man which made her retreat in panic into madness; although they had not yet consummated their affair, 'at the mere approach of the real husband–wife situation (Robert) I go out of my mind.'[35] This chance to become a fully sexual woman had come too soon; she was not yet able to release her father's central hold on her and give herself up to the experience. 'I have never yet learnt the language of the body' she wrote when she was thirty-eight, 'and I think that is why I feel so false and shallow and incomplete. I felt the same thing without quite understanding it with Robert . . . but I was not ready for it and the shock drove me out of my mind.'[36]

6

Breaking the Glass

She was changed into a salmon. The salmon was suffocating in a dry,
  stone-floored cell behind iron bars.
Just beyond the bars was the life-giving waterfall.
It lay wriggling and gasping, scraping its scales on the stone floor,
  maddened by the noise of the water it could not reach.

Beyond the Glass

On 17 November 1922 Antonia was helped in through the impressive
doors of the great Wren building which housed the Bethlem Royal
Hospital. Her father was with her. She was twenty-three years old and
raving. She seemed to be oblivious both of herself and of the outside
world; Antonia was sealed in her own pandemonium. Without
inhibitions, violent, frightened and fearsome, she was deemed a risk to
herself and to others. For nine months she lived with her demons, and
they gave her a sense of overweening power and a unique intensity of
experience.

Bethlem asylum had two categories of patients – 'Voluntary Boarders'
and 'Certified'. Mrs Eirene Green-Wilkinson was not there voluntarily.
The two doctors' reports certifying her insane show how violent were
Antonia's impulses at the time of her entry into hospital: 'maniacal
excitement . . . suicidal tendencies, is dangerous to others.'[1] She had
already hit her family doctor on the head and said 'There's one for the
Holy Ghost.'[2] The second doctor noted her incoherence and hyperac-
tivity, her wishing to play a game of letters centred on her name
(reminding him that this name was Eirene, spelt in the Greek way) but
then she had wanted to kill him. Her 'Rank, Profession or Occupation'
was given as Authoress, a poignant detail probably supplied by her
father.

But even this last remnant of her worldly identity was to be lost while she gave herself up to madness. 'Once I was right in the power of the beast and it was terrible and wonderful.'[3] She came to value this extreme and frightening experience as adding a deeper dimension to her life, something that could make her a writer instead of a 'Clever Little Thing'.[4] Certainly her writing of her experiences in the asylum, in Part Four of *Beyond the Glass* and in the short story 'The House of Clouds', is amongst her most powerful and moving achievements. In them she captured a remarkable poetic truth. 'In a way I was more in my right element during the asylum's intense waking dreams than in much of my "normal" life. The "right element" being a peculiar heightening of life, intensity, awareness.'[5]

However, with the evidence of her Bethlem medical records, it is possible to appreciate just how brilliantly she maintained, within her fiction, an extraordinary connection to the literal truth. It was as if she was both in the belly of the beast and also detached, observing the processes of her madness and the treatment meted out to her from a distant perspective. To entwine both strands of experience, the external – the doctor's reports – with the internal – her own voice – shows the extent of the suffering she endured, and the flight of her mind as it transcended the material world.

Almost the first thing that was done on her entry to the hospital was the issuing of 'A Warning', stating the patient was 'suicidal and must not be lost sight of'. She had already attempted suicide in the hospital by 'swallowing her handkerchief'. The warning was signed by the Resident Physician and sixteen attendants.

[17/11/22] This patient is [in] an excited, restless and confused state. Patient passes her time singing snatches of hymns and popular songs as 'Sing a Song of Sixpence'.

Sometimes she was in sharp pain; sometimes she was happy. She could hear herself singing over and over again, like an incantation:
> *O Deus, ego amo te*
> *Nec amo te ut salves me*
> *Nec quia non amantes te*
> *Aeterno punis igne.*

. . . [the doctor] tried to give her an injection, but she fought him wildly. She had promised someone (was it Robert?) that she would not let them give her drugs. Drugs would spoil the sharpness of this amazing experience that was just going to break into flower.[6]

[18/11/22] Patient is unwilling to take her food. Patient has a gastric odour. Patient's stomach was washed out. . . . The vomit consisted of offensive undigested food.

[13/12/22] Patient is tube fed. She is still confused, excited and restless. Patient talks incessantly, her utterances consisting of incoherent details rich in associations.

Then she was Richard, endlessly climbing up the steps of a dark tower by the sea, knowing that she herself was imprisoned at the top. She came out of this dream suddenly to find herself being tortured in her own person. She was lying on her back with two nurses holding her down. A young man with a signet ring on his finger was bending over her, holding a funnel with a long tube attached. He forced the tube down her nose and began to pour some liquid into the funnel. There was a searing pain at the back of her nose, she choked and struggled, but they held her down ruthlessly.[7]

'The Christmas Eve Fancy Dress and Entertainment was a greater success than ever,' according to the 1922 hospital Year Book. There was a Christmas tree, with little presents donated by charitable members of the local community; some even came to celebrate with the patients. '[13/1/23] Patient is still tube fed. Patient is suffering from a seborrhoeic rash most pronounced over buttocks.'

On the Prescription Sheet, amongst the sedative drugs Chloral and Veronal, was a request for carbolic soap and calamine lotion, presumably to treat her rash. 'Continuous baths and other forms of hydro-therapy' were favoured for the treatment of acute excitement and insomnia.

Then two nurses dragged her, one on each side, to an enormous room filled with baths. They dipped her into bath after bath of boiling water. Each bath was smaller than the last with gold taps that came off in her hands when she tried to clutch them. . . . They took her out and dried her and rubbed something on her eyes and nostrils that stung like fire. She had human limbs, but she was not human; she was a horse or stag being prepared for the hunt. On the wall was a looking-glass, dim with steam.[8]

[16/1/23] Rash has practically disappeared. Patient is still tube fed. Patient is still restless, excited and deluded.

The rubber room was a compartment in a sinking ship, near the boiler room which would burst at any minute and scald her to death. Somehow she must get out. She flung herself against the rubber walls as if she could beat her way out by sheer force. The air was getting hotter. The rubber walls were already warm to touch. In a second her lungs would burst. At last the door opened. They were coming to rescue her. But it was the torturers who entered: the young man and the two nurses with the basin and funnel.[9]

[20/2/23] Patient is now taking her food a little better. She is spoon-fed. Her mouth is in a very bad state – marked pyorrhoea. She talks continually to herself, a confused jumble. Is looking very ill.

They stripped her, forced her struggling limbs back into the heavy canvas garment and fastened her down under the sailcloth again. Exhausted, she fell asleep. When she woke up again, a nurse was sitting beside her, holding a plate with some porridge in it and a spoon. The nurse kept spooning up bits of it and trying to make her eat. She did not want to eat, because she knew the porridge was poisoned, but the nurse forced a little between her teeth and she had to swallow it. The nurse smiled.[10]

[20/3/23] Patient is much more demented. She has regressed considerably. She has to be tube fed entirely now. She secretes enormous quantities of saliva. Does not speak at all now. Occasionally smiles in a dull sort of way. Stuporous condition. Mouth has much improved.

She lost herself again; this time completely. For months she was not even a human being; she was a horse. Ridden almost to death, beaten until she fell, she lay at last on the straw in her stable and waited for death. They buried her as she lay on her side, with outstretched head and legs. A child came and sowed turquoises round the outline of her body in the ground, and she rose up again as a horse of magic with a golden mane, and galloped across the sky.[11]

This was a serious set-back which the doctors had not been expecting. The excess saliva, the 'stuporous condition' may have been an extreme reaction to the drugs. However, her condition did not bode well. Cecil Botting had been visiting his daughter every Sunday; usually he was able to see her, not that she recognised him. Just once she had shown a glimmer of her old self, and mentioned the scarf he was wearing, and he had clung to this as an omen that she was going to recover. On his visit towards the end of March he was told, however, that this latest deterioration in his daughter's condition made it unlikely that she would fully recover before her late forties, or even early fifties. Perhaps in the doctors' minds was the thought that a woman's hormones were implicated in her madness, so their decline at menopause might signal a return to greater sanity.

This news was a shattering blow to Antonia's parents; with this prognosis, they might not live to see her restored to health. In his own despair, Cecil Botting thought it only fair to tell Robert Legg that she was unlikely to recover in the near future. He had continued to visit Antonia's parents while she was in the asylum. In years to come, Antonia believed that her father carried a secret guilt about being too hasty, 'that he ought to have waited and not told R that she might not return till she was 50.'[12] This news made Robert give up his hopes of marrying Antonia: he returned to his patient former fiancée, and was lost to Antonia for ever.

Within a month the crisis had passed.

> [20/4/23] Patient now takes her food herself. She sometimes eats meat, cabbage etc with her fingers. Does not speak sense at all yet. Talks continually again.

> *Another thing that recurred was finding herself sitting up in the manger bed with a plate of food balanced on her knees. The food looked strangely unreal, like the painted cardboard food in dolls' tea-sets. The knives were blunt, too, like dolls' knives. She usually ate the unreal, completely tasteless food because she wanted to see the pattern on the plates. She could see all the printed letters round the rim now. They read NAZARETH ROYAL HOSPITAL . . . What and where could this hospital be? And why was she in it?*[13]

Years later, Antonia recalled her old cell at Bethlem: 'when I was there it had dirty distemper on the walls and something like a large manger to sleep in with thick cotton sheets.'[14]

> [20/5/23] Is now up in the ward. Very talkative. Confused. Will not answer sensibly at all. Sings a lot. Rather exalted. Eating & sleeping well but no mental improvement.

> *She was born and re-born with incredible swiftness as a woman, as an imp, as a dog, and finally as a flower. She was some nameless, tiny bell, growing in a stream, with a stalk as fine as hair and a human voice. The water flowing through her flower throat made her sing all day a little monotonous song, 'Kulalla, kulalla, kulalla, ripitalla, kulalla, kulalla, kulalla, kulla.'*[15]

[3/8/23] Rapid improvement the last few days. Two days ago on being questioned she described her life up to the age of twenty-one & then said there was a gap of two years for which she could not account. Very emotional. Today she remembers what has happened the last two days. She is anxious for something to do or read. Is beginning to take a keen interest in her surroundings.

In the garden women and nurses were walking; they did not look like real people but oddly thin and bright, like figures cut out of coloured paper. And she could see birds flying across the sky, not real birds, but bird-shaped kites, lined with strips of white metal, that flew on wires. Only the clouds had thickness and depth and looked as clouds had looked in the other world. The clouds spoke to her sometimes. They wrote messages in white smoke on the blue.[16]

[5/8/23] The improvement of the past few days has been maintained. Dr Beaton interviewed the patient's father to-day. He was imperative in his desire to take his daughter away. This attitude was much aided and abetted by the patient herself. The net result is that the patient has gone on 14 days leave.

In Looking-Glass Land one must use looking-glass writing. She began again at the right hand side and wrote backwards, reversing the letters. Her hand moved quickly and easily. . . . Then it occurred to her that her father was on the other side of the looking-glass. It would be more sensible to write the way they did there. . . . With a great effort she made her hand begin at the left. It was extraordinarily difficult. . . . 'Dearest Daddy, I do not know where I am but I think it is Nazareth Royal Hospital. That is what it says on the plates. Please try and find me. I want so much to see you again. Please try hard. Perhaps you thought I was dead. I am alive but in a very strange place. Doctor Bennett(?) has promised to post this. Your loving daughter, Clara.'[17]

[22/8/23] Patient was today discharged by Committee 'Recovered'.

They ran down the step hand in hand, like children escaping from school, and did not pause for breath till they reached an iron gate at the end of an avenue. Beyond it, buses and trams were racing past. Clara was nearly deafened with the noise. Her father waved his free arm shouting frantically 'Taxi! Taxi'.[18]

It was, she thought, like Orpheus bringing Eurydice back from the underworld.

Antonia had written of her father's inevitable guilt at allowing her to be certified insane and incarcerated in such a notorious asylum. Even his Aunt Edith had protested at his action in allowing her to be sent there. But by the 1920s, Bethlem Royal Hospital was an enlightened place, given the current limitations in understanding and treatment of mental illness. The doctors there were open to the use of psycho-analysis, although quite reasonably they pointed out in the 'Physician Superintendent's Report' that for many of their more serious patients there was not much opportunity to practise the talking cure. One of their recent senior appointees was Dr Thomas Beaton O.B.E., who had come highly recommended from the Maudsley Hospital and had been in the Navy during the First World War; he had considerable experience of battle-traumatised men. Rather remarkably, the annual recovery rate at Bethlem was just under fifty per cent.

The descriptions of Antonia's extreme and unreachable condition during the onset of her breakdown made it clear that she needed some kind of secure and specialist care. In the psychotic stage of her mania, she could have easily harmed herself or others. There was no real treatment for these kinds of severe manic-depressive illnesses. The great textbook on this bipolar affective disorder states: 'Until the middle of this century, manic-depressive illness had remained intractable, frustrating the best efforts of clinical practitioners and their forebears. This long history ended abruptly with the discovery of lithium's therapeutic benefits.'[19] Hitherto people suffering from manic-depression led lives painfully interrupted by illness and often prematurely ended by suicide. Suicide remains a serious risk: about one in five people with this illness succeed in killing themselves.

It is a debatable point whether the drugs used to treat Antonia, with the intention of calming her down and subduing her – and possibly with the hope that through sleep and a tranquillised brain she might more easily recover her sanity – actually contributed to the intensity and prolongation of her illness. Chloral, which recurred throughout her prescription list during the early part of her treatment, is a hypnotic which could present some unfortunate side-efects, like nightmares, incoherence and paranoid behaviour. Its possible effects on the skin were also well-known, causing allergic rashes and eczematoid dermatitis.[20]

However, the fact that Antonia seems to have had all drugs withdrawn by the middle of May 1923, when she had been deemed well enough to join the women's ward, but was still reported to be exalted and showing no mental improvement, does suggest the hospital's relatively enlightened policy towards sedative drug use. Her rapid improvement over the following two months was doubtless due to a number of factors, some of them mysterious and a function of her own will, but her freedom from major sedative drugs may have been an important factor in this stage of the restorative process.

Antonia herself described in barely disguised fiction this crucial moment in her recovery, when acceptance and passivity were exchanged for the pain and effort of returning to the world on the other side of the glass. It was a measure of her strength and courage, and her will to rise to the struggle, that she was able to win this battle. She had not chosen to remain in her own isolated fastness. 'Beyond the glass, however agonising the nightmare experiences, they had had a peculiar intensity. If some had been terrifying, others had been exquisite. When these experiences had ceased, she had been as passive as a child until the tremendous, absorbing effort of willing herself back to consciousness.'[21]

Antonia wrote in her diary that she had resented her father committing her to a public asylum; one whose notorious reputation dated from medieval times, with a name, contracted to 'Bedlam', which had become a generic term for madhouse, and general behavioural chaos. But the soldierly part of her was proud of the fact that she had been somewhere so extreme and come through such a profound and shocking experience. This was not a genteel sanatorium for the well-behaved ill: it was a place for people who had slipped over the edge and were travelling without a map. Antonia had not had just a minor mental breakdown but had been starkly, staring, mad; she had been incarcerated in a padded cell; she had been constrained in straitjackets; she had been force-fed. And she had survived and willed her way back to sanity. 'It was the real thing,' she told a journalist when she was old, 'strait-jackets, being plunged in and out of cold baths. The interesting thing about madness is that your sense of time goes. I could watch the leaves unfolding on the trees like those nature films. Madness is never boring; it may be unpleasant but never boring.'[22]

She had been through an initiation as testing as any and Antonia wore the fact, when she chose, as a badge of honour and courage. Her soldierly nature had helped her survive; she recognised there was a steely core to her nature, 'something . . . tough, harsh and, to many people, repellent.'[23] She had been into the darkest recesses of her psyche and returned changed by her experiences; 'though superficially civilised, I am a barbarian and a lunatic.'[24]

Antonia returned to the embrace of her family on a wave of euphoria. She still expected to see Robert Legg and her father, afraid that an emotional shock would return her to the asylum, chose not to tell her the truth and let her continue instead with the hope that he would come for her still. It was summer and she was taken down to the great-aunts' cottage at Binesfield for the family holiday. Her future seemed empty and featureless and the recent past in the asylum so vivid; it was all she wanted to talk about, yet it was the last thing her family wanted to hear. The associations were too painful for them and they feared for her fragile newfound sanity. The careful concern which enfolded her in a protective blanket very soon became claustrophobic.

So great had been her father's shock at losing her to madness, so ecstatic was his response to her miraculous return, that Antonia sensed he hoped she would not remarry, but would remain with him for ever. He too had an extreme and tempestuous character like his daughter's and, although usually so tightly controlled, he may well have come close to breakdown himself. Cecil tried to make up for what Antonia had been through by buying her presents, among them the riding habit and riding lessons which, when she was a teenager and longing to ride, he had prevented her accepting as a gift. Captain Green-Wilkinson, Reggie's father, had given Antonia £500 as a sort of compensation for the annulment of her marriage to his son. Cecil had taken half of this as expenses, he explained. 'So you might say it was I who paid for [the presents] in the end' wrote Antonia.[25]

Only many years later did Antonia experience any understanding or sympathy for her parents' suffering during the time she was in the asylum. It was not until her father was dead that she came to appreciate Christine's absolute loyalty and non-judgemental acceptance of her daughter's character and life. Antonia felt the shock of her incarceration in Bethlem would not have shattered her mother in the same way as it did her father. 'Possibly because she was not in the least self-questioning or guilty. She was an entirely spontaneous person ... even in her affectations. She never *brooded* although she was subject to fits of depression.'[26]

Once Antonia had been decertified on her last visit to the hospital, she had stronger ground for pleading to be able to leave the country for London. People were still trying to protect her from the truth about Robert, and only after 'months of agony trying to find out where he was & what had happened' did she learn, possibly from Legg's sister, that he had been told she had little chance of recovery and had married his former sweetheart.[27] She accepted this fact with little apparent grief. She had learnt early that something she really wanted with all her heart would inevitably be taken from her, and through the agency of her father. Perhaps Antonia already knew something that she told Emily many years later – that the ecstatic love she had felt for Robert was 'abnormal', a function of her madness, and bore no real relation to the object of this passion. 'I couln't "know" [Robert] as I "know" say Eric or my father . . . I could only describe him as seen by a crazy girl during 3 weeks. I suppose he was just a nice, straightforward young soldier, with only a physical poetry *plus* that odd second-sight business.'[28]

That Christmas Robert sent her a present of a rosary, from the Holy Land, made of stones from Mount Olivet; 'The one thing Robert . . . gave me . . . I thought it a strange present at the time because he was not a Catholic.'[29] She may have suspected the extremity of her feelings for Robert at the time but her memory of her love for him never faded: every other man was only ever 'second best . . . It was the one chance of absolutely natural human happiness I ever had and the madness cut it right off'.[30] She never saw him again and only received this one letter and present, and a letter twelve years later, when she was miserable about an affair in which her then husband Tom Hopkinson was involved. In this he enclosed a photograph and intimated that he was not happy.

Prevented from working, Antonia approached the end of 1923 not knowing what the next year would bring or what she hoped for. She re-established the easy occasional companionship she had enjoyed with Eric Earnshaw Smith. Possibly by this time Antonia had met Eric's friend of Oxford days, Alan Walker, who was also in the Civil Service. She was taking Spanish lessons at London University, and felt full of life and vigour. Her euphoria continued; when contemplating the sequel novel to *Beyond the Glass*, she reminded herself of her mood in the months after the asylum: 'extremely gay. . . . She is almost a "good-time-girl" for the first time in her life.'[31]

Antonia was still waiting for the Papal annulment of her marriage. But at twenty-four, despite having been married, engaged at least twice and ecstatically in love, Antonia was still a virgin and remarkably unaware of the nature of sexual love, let alone the mechanics of sex. For a highly intelligent young woman with a curious mind and active feelings, this sexual blankness was significant, not merely accidental. However, Antonia was to endure something that on the surface appeared more threatening to her sanity and sexual innocence than Robert, and yet, emotionally disengaged, she was to remain surprisingly unmoved throughout the event and its shocking aftermath. Some time in the early part of 1924, Antonia met Jim Dougal, a rather shady character whose stories of his life and circumstances hardly tallied with the truth. He had a pronounced limp as the result of polio when he was a child, but he pretended that he had been injured during the war.

Dougal's apparent injury in the call of duty to his country roused her imagination and pity. Also the mutilated body held a peculiar fascination for her. Her fantasies of saving her childhood friend Gerard from cruel torture and suffering always involved him in some physical wounding. She considered herself to be a mutilated man, and therefore somehow an incomplete and 'despicable being', and thought that the sight of someone else's mutilation somehow reassured her about her own.[32]

Dougal was amusing to talk to; he admitted to being a kind of journalist, which also attracted Antonia. He had been married, was a lapsed Catholic and currently, he claimed, divorced. Antonia remembered being particularly affronted by his saying that all art was just unsatisfied sex, but then thought him rather more charming and chivalrous to his wife when he admitted, 'We're both bad pickers'.[33] She was flattered by his interest and affected by her father's enthusiasm for him. Dougal made up to Cecil with his easy charm and heroic stories: Antonia's father was as gullible as he was insecure; he admired this apparently swashbuckling side of Dougal and, according to his daughter, would have liked them to marry. This was odd given that just a few months previously Antonia had felt that he never wanted to let her go. Perhaps the reality of having a young, grown-up and wilful daughter under his roof again, kicking her heels and needing distraction, had made the idea of living with her for the rest of his life less attractive. To an old-fashioned and conventional man, it was preferable to have his daughter marry, despite his own possessiveness and passion for her, and have some other younger and, he hoped, richer man take on the responsibility.

But Antonia was not thinking about marriage. Dougal entertained her, she enjoyed talking to someone who worked in an area allied to the ambition she had taken for her own, long before her illness, to be a writer. She had been beginning to think that she feared sanity as much as insanity; sanity was too easily confused in her mind with mediocrity and 'total lack of fire and imagination.'[34] He was there when she first went riding in her new riding clothes, the disputed gift from her father. It was in fact the first time in her life that Antonia had ever sat on a horse and Dougal's presence gave her the confidence to ride with him for twelve miles, straight off. She remembered she was rather nervous, but 'tremendously excited'.[35] However, her equestrian activities did not proceed much further than that, largely because she came to realise that Dougal was someone she could never trust again.

The Dougal episode was the one event in Antonia's life which was truly puzzling, both to herself and to others. It was also something she barely talked to anyone about, apart from her grown-up daughters. She

found it both 'trivial' and 'shaming'.³⁶ The shaming part of it was her
peculiar complicity. She even spoke of having 'provoked' it. Her post-
manic euphoria may have had something to do with it, enhancing her
optimism and recklessness, keeping her still suspended slightly above the
ground. One night, about six months after Antonia had been discharged
from Bethlem Royal Hospital, Dougal had stayed late talking to her
father. Antonia had said goodnight and gone to bed early, still subject to
her doctors' ten o'clock curfew. She had no idea that Dougal had been
invited by her father to stay, perhaps due to the lateness of the hour.
When she was awoken by her door opening and a man entered her
room wearing one of her father's old dressing gowns, Antonia thought
she was dreaming.

It soon became clear that this man was not a figment of her sleepy
imagination but Dougal, intent on having sexual intercourse with her.
Antonia neither protested nor resisted. Her apparent unconcern at the
time of the seduction turned to mild distaste the following day when she
noticed him for the first time as a person with his own individual
characteristics, some of which she did not like. Subsequently she
discovered that he had lied about his divorce; 'his wife was very much
about' and was actually in hospital having their baby.³⁷ The friendship
was over and Antonia never saw Dougal again. He had left her,
nevertheless, an unforeseen and shocking legacy. The first sexual coition
of her life, and a shabby, stolen one at that, had resulted in pregnancy;
'Dougall [sic]. The Liar: the man who got me on false pretences.'³⁸

Antonia's Catholic faith was still strong, but just as she was detached
from powerful feeling at this time so she seemed to be much cooler in
the practice of her religion. Her father, however, had become
increasingly devout. Antonia's fear, when she had her pregnancy
confirmed, was not for herself and the consequences this turn of events
would have on her life but rather at what her father's reaction would be.
His rages were awesome and could be terrifying. She also felt some
concern for the effect another such catastrophe would have on both her
parents. She broke down and told her mother first, and Christine took
the responsibility of telling her husband. Cecil was angrier than she had
ever seen him, her mother reported, but the anger and blame were not
directed at Antonia, as it had been so often in the past. It was Dougal
whom Cecil wanted to kill. His first reaction was that Antonia should
go abroad to have the baby, possibly to Spain. This she interpreted as a
way of punishing her.

As a true Catholic, Antonia believed he should have said, 'Have it
here and we will see you through' and she felt, in retrospect, that had
that been his attitude then there was a chance that she might not have

opted for an abortion.[39] As it was, she could not contemplate exile and giving birth to an unwanted child alone, without emotional support from home. Antonia therefore persuaded her father, with unexpected ease, to lend her the money for the abortion. She went for advice to her worldly painter friend, Eliot Seabrooke, who put her in touch with a woman who could help. That woman was Wyn Henderson, who was to feature, along with her family, in Antonia's life in many guises and for many years to come. Wyn gave her the name of an abortionist. The injections cost ten shillings each, and Antonia got her own back on her father for his meanness to her by cheating him, telling him they cost twice as much and pocketing the difference.

The fact that Cecil was participating in a mortal sin against his God and his Church did not seem to cause his conscience too much trouble: neither did the religious impact of what she was doing shake Antonia's own conviction at the time that this was what she had to do. In fact, her father did not absent himself from a distressing and sinful act, but was very kind when Antonia was in pain as a result of the injections she was given. When the pain worsened and she entered a nursing home, with the possibility that she had blood poisoning, she described her father's concern for her with a peculiar choice of phrase, 'If he had been my husband he could not have been kinder'.[40] Antonia was told by the nursing staff that the baby she had aborted was a son.

At this point Antonia's unnatural euphoria was pierced by a stab of emotion; 'I did not seem to feel *guilt* about having had an abortion but just human sorrow because I had killed my little boy'.[41] At the time both her father and herself seemed to deal with this traumatic episode with little apparent disturbance of conscience. 'My father realised he shouldn't consent to it but he did because it solved the problem'.[42] Neither was much thought given to the danger and illegality of this action. Cecil Botting salved his own fear of mortal sin by shifting all the blame firmly on to his daughter's shoulders, and her shoulders seemed, at the time, to be strong enough. In fact, Antonia remembered continuing to practise her religion after the abortion, feeling 'perfectly serene and unguilty'.[43] This period was remarkable in her memory for the sanity and clarity of her mind; 'Remember with great pleasure weeks recovering from abortion in 1924 and for once holding my life in suspension, not wanting anything, never even concerned with the future, but perfectly happy reading Proust.'[44]

In her early fifties, however, struggling to write *The Sugar House*, she was struck by how much the abortion of her first child was worrying her and although she accepted that the guilt was hers, she felt that her father made it easier for her to have the abortion than to go ahead with the pregnancy. She still found this one of the inexplicable parts of her father's behaviour and thought perhaps there was something which her father wanted to destroy in her; 'I wonder if it was the writing?'[45]

The extraordinary events of these couple of months in the beginning of 1924, were to prove the final and greatest obstacle for Antonia's published writing in the years to come. Writing every one of her novels was a terrific struggle, with the partial exception of *Frost in May*, although even that was delayed by more than fifteen years and then only wrung out of her with weekly deadlines. Antonia finally ground to a miserable halt with Clara's emergence from the asylum at the end of her last novel *Beyond the Glass*. She tried year after painful year to deal with the Dougal episode which would begin the next book in the sequence, but was unable to proceed. She told herself that she was sick of Clara and all her doings; that Clara would lose her readers' sympathy with the strangely inexplicable events around Dougal and the abortion; that in keeping the book faithful to the facts, as had been the case with the previous four, she would expose her father's moral weakness (even though he was by then long dead). But she feared also that this novel should have been a particularly important one for her, marking her emergence from the nursery, asserting a more complete and 'more masculine side as a writer' and that she was unable to rise to the challenge to grow into independence and maturity.[46] It was meant to be 'the story of a girl really getting away from her father' and by failing to write it she was somehow foiling that necessary escape.

Antonia's life was full of such extremities of experience that although she recorded them truthfully in her novels and short stories as 'almost photographic reports of experience', sometimes they struck her critics as being too far-fetched to be believable.[47] Life, for Antonia, was much more Grand Guignol than the average fiction. Consequently she was angered by reviews which suggested she was faking: 'Whatever my faults, I don't fake about things which I have experienced first hand. . . . No one could try harder to record an experience truthfully.'[48]

But this was the one experience which finally dammed up the sequence of novels and prevented Antonia from dealing with any of the other experiences of her life in fictional form, except for a few short stories and poems. She was to revisit all aspects of her life many times in her diaries and letters, but her creative weaving of autobiographical experience into novels for publication came to an end when Clara, her fictional self, was only twenty-four years old: poised, rather belatedly, on the brink of adult life.

It was the experience, however, which catapulted Antonia into her next eccentric marriage.

7

The Rational Construct

'But what really enraged me was the calm, almost casual way she announced it: "I hope you won't mind too much Daddy if I don't come to Mass with you.
You see I'm no longer a Catholic."'

'Clara IV', *As Once in May*

Antonia had known Eric Earnshaw Smith ever since she had been a student at the Academy of Dramatic Art in Gower Street in 1919. From the start she had been drawn to his enigmatic, watchful, cerebral character. He had been on the periphery of Antonia's life for nearly five years and had given her always the feeling that he accepted her without question; for the first time in her life she neither had to apologise nor explain. He had taken her to the fateful party where she had met Robert Legg and had then disappeared discreetly into the night, and left Antonia to her ecstatic three weeks; he had been kept informed of her progress in the asylum; he was there still living in Chelsea when she emerged. He and his friend from pre-war days, Alan Walker, were part of a small number of acquaintances whom Antonia saw in the months of rehabilitation after Bethlem.

Eight months after her release, and in the wake of her abortion, Antonia's father took her to Paris. It was April. The Olympic Games were staged there that summer (the year Harold Abrahams and Eric Liddell were to win gold medals running for Britain) and springtime in Paris had even more of an air of expectation and excitement than usual. This was another occasion, like the time he had taken her as a treat to *Tannhauser*, when their relationship became rather too intimate; Antonia remembering it as being like a honeymoon. On the conscious level, at least, she was a willing participant in this emotional trespass which bound her and her father in a conspiracy which excluded her mother.

Within a couple of months she was off abroad again, this time with Eric and Alan to Italy. Mussolini's fascist party had just swept to victory, and lone voices were raised in protest at the corruption and fear that had been endemic in their electioneering. Political assassinations were common. Eric worked for the Foreign Office, Alan in the Home Office and later the Diplomatic Corps and they all must have been aware that a sea change was in process. Antonia had a sea change of her own; encouraged by Eric, she became engaged to Alan. However, it was obvious she had not really given her heart or any kind of real commitment to Alan; a minor incident occurred on this holiday which showed him up as a rather fussy man with a 'peculiar character', and Antonia immediately decided to cancel the engagement.[1] By the autumn she was engaged to Eric instead.

This was the one relationship of her life which she never had cause to regret. Cool, impartial, tolerant, Eric was the antithesis of her father, yet he became the only other man to have as much authority in Antonia's life. 'I submitted to him absolutely and unquestioningly *exactly* as I did to my father. And through him I did in actual life escape from my father's domination, but only on the surface.'[2] Although he had played rugby football in his youth, Eric was not a physically or emotionally robust man. He had been invalided out of the trenches in the First World War, having lost a kidney. He was excessively thin and very tall, with a small head and sparse but silky ginger hair; a friend recalled 'his movements, though elegant, were angular, and his long bamboo fingers stuck out in all directions when he smoked his cigarettes in their long holder, like stick insects.'[3]

Eric was also a practising homosexual, although Antonia did not know it consciously at the time. However, she knew that she was embarking on a marriage that was not going to encompass a sexual relationship. Her only real experience of sexual passion had been truncated by her retreat into madness. The Dougal episode had not been sexual love but carnal theft, and had resulted in the suppressed horror of pregnancy and the abortion. Everything in her recent past Antonia came to see as the 'only logical lead-up' to the marriage with Eric.[4] With him she would feel safe, anchored and free from the dangers of passion.

Antonia's capacity for sexual love remained focused on her father. As long as she was obsessed with him, and allowed herself to be dominated by him, she was incapable of fully loving another man. She realised that Eric and her father were rivals, both in a real and symbolic sense. Eric was the first person to make Antonia question her father's infallibility and the purity of his motives. 'The two most abidingly important people in my life,' she wrote more than thirty-five years later; 'it is Eric who makes the revolutionary statement . . . "your father is a bad man . . ." i.e. of course meaning "bad for you".[5] The fates of these two men were also bound together in their relationships with Antonia. While Eric began the process of freeing Antonia from her father, he was sowing the seeds also for his own loss of her to the world of heterosexual men, where she would try to make an adult and complete relationship, with children.

She was choosing to marry for the second time a man who was unable to offer her sexual love. The union she sought was of a different nature. With Eric she sought a marriage of escape and safety, a union of intellectual companionship. Many years later, in considering the novel which she hoped would be an exploration of this marriage, she wondered if *The Invisible Ring* might not make an appropriate title. 'There is a marriage that is not a physical marriage; the escape from the father that is no escape, even when he dies.'[6] In fact, Eric referred to himself in relation to her as 'your old Daddy' and 'your Old Master'. She valued the intellectual friendship he offered; 'My relationship with him was unique: it wasn't exactly "love" but a kind of mental blood-tie. . . . There was nothing we would not say to each other though we were so unalike. . . . I suppose it was the perfect, inexplicable friendship. I really married him in order *to be able to see enough of him!*'[7]

The dissolution of her marriage to Reggie *'per dispensationen summo Pontificis Decretum'* came through at last, dated 20 January 1925. On 15 April Antonia married Eric at the Church of the Holy Trinity in Brook Green, a neighbourhood in West London she knew well from her time at St Paul's Girls' School. She had just turned twenty-six; Eric was thirty-one and marrying for the first time. Their honeymoon in Paris and Provence Antonia remembered as one of the best holidays of her life.

Antonia had been living with her parents in Perham Road since her discharge from Bethlem. Finally she was leaving the family home for good when she moved into Eric's Chelsea maisonette, in Paultons Square. This alone must have been quite a difficult transition for someone as confirmed in his bachelorhood as Eric. He was preternaturally tidy, while Antonia never got the better of the material world and tended to live in some chaos. He was a man of unwavering routine with which he hoped to keep his small neuroses in check. The only anarchic component of his otherwise highly controlled life was his big black cat, Mr Pusta, who could sleep where he liked, do what he pleased, with both Eric and his new wife securely under his paw. He was born in the Foreign Office and never forgot it. Coal black with yellow eyes, he was 'a Civil Servant to the last, he would sit on no paper but *The Times*.'[8]

Antonia was quickly installed in the domestic hierarchy as Eric's other pussycat, and treated with the same amused indulgence. 'I hope you'll have a really good time on your voyagings' he wrote when she was away on a short holiday without him, 'and come back to Master with a lovely glossy fur and renovated whiskers.'[9] His new pussycat seemed happy to accept his intrinsic authority over her. She had grown used to ceding power to the most important people in her life.

At the beginning of their marriage Antonia was in the early and successful stages of a career in advertising. The previous summer she had taken on a job at Crawford's, one of the biggest and most important agencies in the inter-war years. She was employed to write copy as a junior, and quite quickly was promoted to the post of senior copywriter. On a salary of £600 a year, 'considered good money in those days!', she was responsible primarily for the beauty and fashion accounts.[10] Her greatest achievement during her years with this firm was to create a more classic and sophisticated image for Jaeger's clothes. Until she began work on it, the company was 'known chiefly for "long vegetarian underpants" of a type favoured by George Bernard Shaw'.[11] William Crawford prided himself on promoting women right up through the company hierarchy. Florence Sangster was the Managing Director, her sister Margaret Havinden was the account executive and the space-buyer was also a woman. But like everything Crawford did, there was hard commercial sense in employing a significant number of influential women. He once wrote, 'It is not merely easy, but it is the most practical common sense in life to fall back on the phrase "I must ask my wife". Women are better buyers than men. They are shoppers – professionally.'[12]

Antonia was highly skilled at the work; she could produce excellent copy which pleased the clients and promoted their product, and on her good days she could be charming and effective at getting her own way. But her heart was never in it. On the whole she was contemptuous of the work she did, and felt alienated from many of her colleagues. She found it an interesting if unwelcome idea that in providing the tools of seductive advertising copy she became a kind of legitimised fraudster. 'I have not the guts to rob a single individual but I can indirectly rob thousands of people through advertising and feel no guilt about it until people not in the advertising world think of me as "an advertising woman"'.[13]

It was the term 'advertising woman' when applied to herself which triggered the self-disgust. So fragile was her own sense of identity that the labels by which she was known in society mattered greatly to her. Just as the term 'schoolmistress' suggested to her someone untalented and unloved, so too the term 'advertising woman' repelled and alarmed her. To be successful as that person, Antonia believed, she would have to lose all interest in art, to become 'reserved and autocratic' and, with that fear again of being unlovable, 'I shall lose any feminine charm; become harsh, dried up, ugly.'[14]

These were extreme reactions. In the same diary entry she used intemperate words to describe her ambivalent attitude to her work in advertising; 'On the whole I loathe it and find it disgusting', but she also admitted that she sometimes found it quite interesting, and could treat it as just a job to earn money. This last attribute cannot be underestimated in Antonia's case, for money was a practical commodity of which she never had enough, but it also symbolised power. The fear and loathing seemed to enter her mind only when she felt that she somehow became identified with this work in the eyes of the world; she was a writer, the only identity she ever wanted. Virginia Woolf became her icon; she cut a picture of her out of *Vogue* and stuck it above her desk. 'It used to comfort me while I wrote advertisements for corsets and disinfectants and baking powder,' she explained when she finally wrote to her heroine.[15] But as an 'advertising woman', Antonia played the part well. She was smartly dressed and carefully made-up. She found herself taking her own advice and becoming more fashion-conscious and fastidious in her dress and grooming. The fact that she did not respect the profession perhaps explained her lack of fawning respect for the directors of the agency, whom she would charm when she was in a good mood but with whom, just as readily, she would flare up and lose her considerable temper. In this way Antonia, consciously or unconsciously, wrong-footed her superiors into a defensive position where they had to abandon the original criticisms or demands which had enraged her and work instead to restore her to equilibrium and productivity.

She and Eric lived a well-regulated life, with enough money from their joint incomes to be able to afford holidays, expeditions to theatres and concerts and to eat out every evening they were at home together. Their life was orderly and ritualised and provided a framework within which Antonia could safely contain her extreme nature without risk of spinning out of control or disintegrating into fragmented parts. In a section of an unpublished novel, one of the exhausting attempts at a sequel to *Beyond the Glass*, with the working title 'Julian Tye', Antonia drew directly from life to give a vivid impression of the singularity of their relationship. 'There were moments when life with Clive [Eric] seemed to be as prescribed and ceremonial as it had been at her convent school. She had adapted herself surprisingly well to Clive's peculiarities and considered this discipline a small price to pay for the extraordinary pleasure of living with Clive. From the moment she had met him, when she was only nineteen she had regarded him as the rarest of human beings.'[16]

One of the most valuable things Eric did for Antonia was to remain unruffled by her violent temper. This was something over which she had little control, an alarming expression of her mental disease. She herself feared she was a destructive, even evil, influence on everything good in her life: she was shamed and bemused by the pattern her serious love affairs seemed to run. 'They're always attracted because I seem so gay & then I proceed to make their life and mine a perfect hell of torment.'[17] But the only person who had never threatened her security and triggered this overwrought behaviour was Eric. Once, in the early days of her marriage to him, Antonia had entered into a familiar frenzy of over-sensitivity and fear which would have ended with bitter accusations and self-contempt. But as she began to wind herself up he 'merely watched and listened with such an air of respectful interest that she had to laugh and the scene collapsed.'[18] And that was the last time she came close to losing her temper with him. His calmness reassured her that she was after all not quite the monster she feared she was, that she might even be a little bit lovable. Uninterested in power, he did not inflame her own fear of powerlessness: by failing to be intimidated, he removed from her the burden of her own oppressive nature.

Antonia's enthusiasm for Eric was not shared by everyone. Two women friends of hers who knew him well saw him with a less worshipful eye. Emily Coleman, who stormed into Antonia's life in the early thirties, thought him 'nervous, neurotic to a point of lunacy, empty, pathetic; yet he has this abnormal intensity, which he puts into reading; and into Tony [Antonia's nickname].'[19] Joan Souter-Robertson, a painter and one of Antonia's longest standing friends, found him spider-like and 'rather creepy'. They became sufficiently friendly for him to propose to her at a later date; 'but he really wanted a housekeeper'.[20] She recognised, however, that he was a kind of soulmate to Antonia. These women were responding to Eric as a man, while Antonia only saw him as a mind, ' "a thoroughfare for all thoughts" as Keats said.'[21] It was only as they grew older and more distant that Antonia began to see that Eric had flaws as crippling as her own.

However, the pleasure of his intellect never palled for her. Hardly a husband, he was more an education – the university education Antonia had never had, with Humanities, life, art, music and religion elegantly combined. His freedom of thought, and his denial of the imperative 'ought', on which her life had been based, helped to release her from some of the fear and insecurity on which her own mind and relationships so readily foundered. She had not known before that someone could love her and yet not want to change her, possess or dominate her. The workings of a brain which she considered to be so superior to her own and so different from any other she had ever known, brought her a new and airy philosophy to contrast with 'the old terrors of religion, the fear of hell, the agonised preoccupation with conduct, the heavy yoke of Catholic exclusivity and rigidity'.[22]

Eric also set out to teach Antonia to think for herself. She had been so schooled by her father's dominant personality and by her reverence for his opinion that she could only either do or defy his will, barely aware of her own will in the matter. Her convent education had zealously continued the regulation of every movement of her body and mind throughout her time there and extended its tentacles of expectation and guilt into the remainder of her life. Eric was deeply steeped in the works of the Spanish-American philosopher, George Santayana. Santayana had grown up in Boston and spent his working life at Harvard. He was defiantly proud of his Latinity and his Catholicism, although he was no longer a believer. Philosophically his truest affinities were with the Greeks, a connection which resonated with Antonia's earliest suscepti- bilities. She was to bring Eric into her pantheon of heroes when she described him as 'a Greek born out of his time'.[23] Santayana as seen through the prism of Eric's mind held a great fascination for Antonia. She was predisposed to respect his philosophy by his foundation in Catholicism. In his writings she found her own instincts about art and life and religion given elegant and erudite voice. Santayana argued convincingly for the freedom of art from moral judgement; a work of art was a more or less abstract symbolisation of the natural world and the experience of human beings within it. There can be no absolute principles for criticising works of art, only our own aesthetic preferences modified in the wake of experience. The ultimate justification of art, Santayana believed, was simply that it added greatly to human enjoyment and therefore to human happiness. Beauty he defined as 'pleasure objectified'. This realisation lifted from Antonia part of the burden of anger and frustration she had felt when told by the nuns that for a work of art to be good it had to be created for the glory of God alone. Santayana brought the same naturalistic philosophy to bear on religion. He saw religion as myth: it could not therefore be judged by the standards of literal truth, but rather by the imaginative richness of its expression of our moral experience. To see religion as *poetic* truth was like a draught of fresh air for Antonia. It 'disinfected religion of every superstitious, repulsive and sentimental aspect', she claimed.[24]

Although an atheist, Eric was forbearing about Antonia practising her religion; in fact he showed the utmost interest in Catholicism and in her experiences of it. Antonia characterised her relationship with him much as Alice's with the Caterpillar in Wonderland:

> 'Who are *you*?' said the Caterpillar.
> This was not an encouraging opening for a conversation. Alice replied, rather shyly, 'I hardly know, sir, just at present – at least I know who I *was* when I got up this morning, but I think I must have changed several times since then.'
> 'What do you mean by that?' said the Caterpillar sternly. 'Explain yourself!'
> 'I can't explain *myself*, I'm afraid, sir,' said Alice, 'because I'm not myself, you see.'
> . . . 'Come back!' the Caterpillar called after her. 'I've something important to say!'
> This sounded promising, certainly: Alice turned and came back again.
> 'Keep your temper,' said the Caterpillar.
> 'Is that all?' said Alice, swallowing down her anger as well as she could.

The Caterpillar then outlined to Alice ways in which she might grow back to her normal size. Like the Caterpillar, Eric never said 'do this', or 'don't do that' but rather steered her towards previously unconsidered avenues of discovery, encouraging her to take the risks always with the attitude of 'try it and see'. There was possibly a level at which Eric lived vicariously on the results of Antonia's more reckless and extreme nature. However, the unconditional support he offered her in her work and her personal life was something she valued until she died. When she was nearly seventy she wrote: 'Eric had more influence on my mind than anyone in my life, even my father. And he never aroused any guilt in me, as my father so painfully did – and still does. And, of course, my father had all the weight of religion behind him – and has left that insoluble problem with me.'[25]

For a while she was confident that she could see at last, with help from the clear light of Eric's rational mind. After a progressive loosening of the ties that bound her to Catholicism, Antonia finally lapsed in 1926. As her father had been her god, now Eric was elevated to that demanding role. 'My relation with E. is really "fantastic". . . . It is a phenomenon, there's no other word for it' was how she tried to explain to a friend his importance to her.[26] Thus Antonia attempted to liberate herself from the fears, to disconnect from the prescriptions and prohibitions of Catholicism, feeling perhaps she was free for a while to be Santayanan and enjoy her adopted religion more as a poetic expression of ethical experience, a 'rich and complex essence, a wonderful work of art of the human spirit'.[27]

However, she was to discover that freedom was a state of mind, and hers was as much in chains as ever; she was 'quite as hag-ridden' as when she was still within the Church.[28] She was to remain in this spiritual battleground, outside the Church, for fifteen years. Unhappy within it, lost without it, lacerating herself with doubts, Antonia was able to find little nourishment in the Christian teachings yet was incapable of purging them altogether from her system.

Antonia's apostasy was the deepest cut she could have inflicted on her father. Cecil had become more devout as he grew older. His health was declining, the strain of such unremitting work, teaching by day and tutoring by night, had caught up with him, raising his blood pressure and exacerbating diabetes. Within two years he was to take early retirement at only fifty-six and would be dead before he was sixty. Such a fundamental rejection of her father was only possible because she had partially transferred her filial allegiance to Eric, and he had given her the confidence to develop a philosophy of her own. In 'Clara IV', Antonia's attempt at a sequel to her last novel, *Beyond the Glass*, in which she explored this time in her life, Antonia described the intellectual fresh air and space which Eric offered her in a marriage unburdened of passion:

> they were unconventional without being messy, their home was equally free from quarrels and from boring domesticity and, though it was definitely understood that either could be invited alone without giving offence to the other, people usually preferred to ask them together because they shone in each other's company . . . Their life together was a kind of art: it involved suppressions and exclusions but it had its reward for Julian [the Antonia character] in an extraordinary delight that she knew she would never find with any other human being.[29]

The suppressions and exclusions referred to the sexually open nature of their arrangement. Both Eric and Antonia were free to pursue their sexual lives elsewhere, with neither jealousy nor resentment from the other. Antonia at this time was giving a most convincing performance of being a well-organised and sophisticated career woman, always turned out immaculately in her business suits and high heels. Eric too was a natty dresser, in his characteristic 'mauve suit, cream shirt and black

Borsolino'.[30] He frequented homosexual bars and clubs, but with the utmost discretion, as was his way.

It took Antonia two years before she embarked on a tentative and fleeting affair with Yvon, a young man considerably younger than herself, whom she met on holiday in the South of France. She did not appear to be driven by her own sexual needs, although perhaps her curiosity, and encouragement from Eric, played its part. Eric's sexual adventures, which were becoming more evident to her, may well have made Antonia feel she needed some similar experience to balance against his in the equipoise of their relationship. She described in a tender and lyrical short story, 'Mon Pays c'est la Martinique', something of her own psychology and the character of the boy who managed to breach her deep-seated recoil from erotic contact. The following meditation on her heroine's previously preferred celibacy was revealing: 'If she hadn't a lover herself yet it was just because she didn't want one. She liked the idea in the abstract. But whenever a young man presented himself. . . . She would like him well enough until he came too close, and then, as if her eyes were distorting mirrors, he would appear ridiculous and even horrible.'[31] The boy himself had an epicene quality: 'His body was slender and small boned, like the body of a very young girl.'[32] This, together with his youth, made him somehow more familiar to her and not a threatening, masculinely sexual, 'other'. This was the first of a few passing love affairs Antonia had while married to Eric. In a diary entry in middle-age she denied the impression that some of her friends had that she had lived an erotically adventurous life. In fact the opposite was more true; she was uneasy and disengaged in most of her sexual relations, never able to abandon herself or to find much pleasure. Her most passionate sexual feelings she experienced in fantasy or dreams when she was released from fear, guilt and the powerful need to maintain control. Years later she wrote of this; 'terrified of getting carried away . . . I am *afraid to let go* (the old fear which stopped me always from so many physical activities – skating, cycling, swimming etc)', and sex.[33]

Antonia listed in her diary the 'sporadic "affairs" while I was married to Eric. Yvon, the Austrian boy [Edo], I[an] B[lack], B.H.[unknown].'[34] She contrasted these with her 'genuine affairs' – the next two men who played a serious emotional part in her life, and who fathered her children. There is little information about these 'sporadic' men; Ian Black was another man with a 'cat-like nature', an expert on economics, who befriended her and later, during the early part of the war, rented her two rooms in his flat.[35] B.H. appears as 'Brian' in another list and possibly could be Brian Hill, a poet friend of largely homosexual inclination, like most of the men to whom she was attracted. Antonia also had a brief relationship, probably about this time, with an 'exuberant "golden giant",' Géry Forsythe, who had wanted to be a writer but never became one because it was too much like hard work, he told her. He came back into Antonia's life nearly forty years later, when he was dying of cancer. Antonia could welcome him then with greater understanding and affection; 'somehow underneath the same ebullient, restless, dissatisfied, eternally young and self-centred and frustrated Géry, [he is] desperately needing, as I see now I am old, to be loved and not, perhaps, capable of loving.'[36]

Having overcome an initial pang of possessiveness, Eric was the model of disinterest when it came to Antonia's extramarital affairs. She explained in 'Julian Tye' his peculiar – and to her precious – detachment: 'One of the many endearing things about Clive [Eric] and one which made him so unlike any other man she had ever known was his impersonal interest in a situation. At any moment he could detach himself from his own feelings (he was fond of assuring Julian [Antonia] that he had none though she knew this to be untrue) and examine any circumstance, a friend's deception, a lapse of Julian's, some piece of neurotic behaviour of his own with exactly the same quality of attention he gave to a book or a picture.'[37]

Although it was not consummated, during this time of experimentation Antonia conducted an episodic teasing flirtation with Bertrand Russell. She had attended one of his series of lectures in January 1926 and had invited him back to Paultons Square, possibly to a small Sunday afternoon gathering of friends. Unable to make that date, he invited himself the following Thursday evening for a drink. Ever keen to make the most of any attractive young female's admiration he wrote, 'I have been wishing to make your acquaintance almost since the beginning of the lectures. (This is not a polite fiction.)'[38]

Antonia wrote more letters to him than she received; he was extremely busy pouring out articles, lectures and books but still found time to counsel her provocatively, 'What I fear for you is not just Sin, but Repentance. See Spinoza on the ethics of the latter.'[39] Antonia was working on a 'convent memoir' at the time, which Russell asked to see. In July 1926, Antonia went to Paris, either in the company of an unknown admirer or meeting someone there whose interest in her she used to titillate Russell's already inflamed desire. He replied to her brilliantly crafted letter: 'You do write the most charming letters, & you are yourself *most* delectable. . . . I am amazed at your strength of mind in resisting the Frenchman. I should have wanted to see what were the bad things he could do, & whether I couldn't do worse. Goodbye my darling Tony – I *do* want to see you again.'[40]

One letter he wrote to Antonia in early 1928 which, as she explained, fifty years later, to Mr Blackwell, the Russell archivist at McMaster University in Canada, gave a misleading impression about the level of intimacy of their relationship. 'My darling' Betrand Russell began, 'I was quite intoxicated by your kindness to me yesterday ... I keep wondering whether it was just a mood, or whether you feel the same way still ... Will you dine with me? And will you join me again after my lecture? And stay with me till next morning? Or is that asking too much? And if it is, what is the most you will concede? I feel so much that I can hardly write the words. You know how long I have wanted you, & now hope makes me dumb & shy. Your devoted B.'[41] Antonia had told her daughter Lyndall that she did not sleep with Russell, although she had considered it before the dinner referred to in this letter. However, his rather ludicrous passion in the taxi afterwards when he had slipped to his knees and pleaded with her, 'bleating like a sheep "Please, p-l-e-a-s-e" made it seem preposterous.'[42]

In her letter to Mr Blackwell she made her point clear, '[Russell] misunderstood something I had said & thought I *had* at last agreed to go to bed with him – something of course he wanted to do with any young woman he liked. But though I admired him tremendously, was enchanted with his wit and much flattered by his friendship, I didn't want a physical relationship with him.'[43] She did however ask him to be an honorary godfather to her first child Susan, born the following year, and added his name, Russell, to her list of Christian names on her birth certificate, thereby trying to maintain this precious connection with him, if only because she felt some of his intellectual lustre and world celebrity was thereby reflected a little on to her.

The only affair which seems to have had some unhappy consequences for Antonia was with the 'Austrian boy' whose name was Edo. He also appeared in the list dated 1928, with the single word 'demoralisation' after his name. Those are the only facts she left but her fiction, usually so accurate about the events of her life and state of her mind, suggested a rather dramatic débâcle, where her *alter ego* too has been reduced to a similarly 'demoralised state'.[44] In 'Clara IV', Antonia has Clara having turned twenty-nine, the age she herself was at the time of the affair. We know that Antonia had been on holiday to Vienna, quite probably to visit her Aunt Beatrice who was a governess there. In the fragment of this abortive novel, Clara is returning home from a holiday in Austria, in a state of quite severe mental distress. She has gone without her husband, as was Antonia's custom, but this time is desperate to get back to him to restore some equilibrium to her life – or as she characterised it, to be delicately remoulded into the familiar form and identity she had feared she had lost for ever.

Over everything hung the memory of Antonia's past insanity, and her fear that she was collapsing into that black hole again. Something had happened in the last week of her holiday which had shaken her to the core and actually made her fear that she was in danger of going mad; 'she had lost contact with her rational self to such an extent that she could not remember it well enough to reconstruct it'.[45] Antonia did not elaborate in diary or fiction form on what had destroyed the fragile integrity of her mind, but in the fiction she hinted darkly at things her heroine had done which she would be ashamed to tell her husband, even though he condoned everything; she felt almost that she was 'under an evil spell' where she had lost all vestiges of what she liked to consider her civilised self and was now 'less than human'.[46]

8

Striking Out from the Shore

The whole of the rest of my life has been conditioned by what happened in 1928 and 1929, by my relation with Eric, the birth of Sue, and my father's death.

31 December 1961, *Diaries I*

As Antonia's bonds with her Church and her father were weakened, Eric's authority over her was no longer needed to replace them, and so was diminished. He had set out to help her become independent of the autocratic masculine influences in her life. With such independence came greater self-knowledge and the confidence to meet others on equal terms; the courage too to write something serious and revealing of herself; perhaps even the chance to make a real marriage at last. But any loosening of the regulations in her daily life was inherently dangerous. Antonia acknowledged throughout her life how important strict external structures were to her in order to keep her restive character in check and functioning. This always had been one of the practical benefits of her religion. 'Naturally good and unselfish people seem to do very well outside the Church but the best place for aggressive and egotistical ones like me is in it . . . *well* in!'[1]

In moving further away from the directives of others, she was breasting new and emotionally uncharted waters. She decided to extract herself a little from the claims of her advertising work and arranged to work at Crawford's part-time, an unprecedented privilege which showed how highly her work was valued. Although, since her marriage to Eric, Antonia had moved on the edges of literary and artistic life in London, the publication in the April 1928 issue of the *New Statesman* of her first short story, 'Strangers', was a welcome breakthrough. There is no record of her own or others' reactions to this, but the story of mistaken identity and the impossibility of really knowing another person has all the hallmarks of her later work, with its bleak and chilly view of human relations. Desmond MacCarthy offered her a job as his assistant on his new review *Life and Letters*, and Antonia was pleased to accept. Desmond was of the inner circle of Bloomsbury, civilised, charming, highly Europeanised: Virginia Woolf had insisted he had the nicest nature of them all. He had started the journal in June with money from a patron, and turned it into an esteemed literary review, although young show-offs like Cyril Connolly enjoyed criticising its catholic, dinner-party level of taste; '[it was] as august and readable as any late Victorian arse wiper, and as daring and original as a new kind of barley water.'[2] The first issue of *Life and Letters* had a scintillating piece by Santayana (written two decades earlier) on *Hamlet*, a choice which might well have been a reflection of Antonia's influence. The journal's coverage of French and Russian literature was amongst its stronger characteristics, interests which Antonia would have been well-qualified to encourage. By the time Antonia was working with Desmond MacCarthy he was middle-aged, much loved and respected in grand social and literary circles, sought out for his brilliant gifts of conversation and sympathetic understanding. Quentin Bell recalled his early promise, 'he had so charmed and domesticated that intractable creature the English Language that it would do anything for him, give him a force, a range of subtlety that would take him anywhere.'[3] This promise never material-ised in any great creative work of his own, but he was a generous critic and facilitator of others. In his benign company Antonia was at the heart of the kind of literary life to which she aspired. She too was a gifted conversationalist and when on form could be as brilliant in her richly allusive talk.

1928 was the year when the equilibrium in her life with Eric began to shift. She had returned from whatever adventure she had had in Austria in distress, threatened with the possibility of further mental disintegra-tion. She felt that only Eric's dependable control could restore her to herself. But the separation from her 'Old Daddy', her 'Old Master', eventually had to come. 'The inevitable happened. I fell in love in the ordinary way.'[4] As she separated further from Eric's mastery, she could see more clearly the anomaly of their relationship; loved by him and loving him but not in the way that she now wanted her relationship with a man to be. 'He is right – it was a kind of sin in him to ask me to marry him and heaven knows he has expiated it by trying to give me back to my own nature.'[5] She saw this nature as having been 'born natural' but somehow to have been sidetracked into 'dreamy platonic friendships'. Above all she most feared becoming 'a freak, something against nature, however intelligent or rare.'[6]

Feeling she was ready at last for the adventure of sexual love, in September of 1928 she fell in love with an innocent romantic, Silas Glossop. She was to write that she had never loved anyone 'so naturally' as she loved him – apart from Robert of course. But the relationship, however spontaneously it may have started, was never going to be easy.

Silas, named by his parents Rudolph Glossop, had preferred to keep his nickname, given to him at school by friends who likened him to Professor Silas Q. Porter in Burroughs's novel *Tarzan of the Apes*: the stereotypical absent-minded intellectual who preferred study to action. He was a handsome young man of twenty-six, a qualified mining engineer, who had recently returned from three years prospecting in Northern Quebec. He had been offered a temporary post at Birmingham University, lecturing in mining engineering, and travelled down to London to renew his acquaintances from University days there, hoping also to catch up on some of the culture he had been missing during his long Canadian exile.

For Silas had talents and interests which straddled both the arts and the sciences. He wrote poetry and was a voracious reader, full of the poetry of Keats and Swinburne and much struck by H.G. Wells's Utopianism, a construct of social harmony and scientific advance which offered more in the way of aesthetic satisfaction and romantic escapism than any hard sociological solutions. Silas's attachment to such a philosophy showed, however, how in tune he was with the mood of the times. Later he acknowledged that he owed Antonia a debt of gratitude for her role in his subsequent questioning of the validity of Wells's vision. It was a young man's enthusiasm, and the perfectibility of human nature and society offered an imaginative antidote to Silas's natural pessimism. A.J.P. Taylor has called the period of the late twenties 'The Years of Gold', marked by a general uplift of hope and expectation that human potentialities, not yet fully realised in societies which distort and suppress, could attain increasing levels of enlightenment and happiness. Science was in the forefront of dramatic changes which affected everyone; television, the possibility of flying round the world in a good deal less than eighty days, the discovery of penicillin. It even seemed that the mainsprings of human nature and the established dynamics of society could be transformed. It certainly *appeared* transformed; dresses had lost their padding and strict seaming, corsets were thrown to the winds, skirts shot up as far as the knees, men wore flamboyant Oxford bags like folded sails. The Charleston and other modern dances, and the concomitant abandoned behaviour, provoked dire warnings of immorality from churchmen and doom-laden prognoses from various medical experts, fearing that young women would jeopardise their chances of healthy childbearing by such energetic and unmaidenly carryings-on.

Silas had been staying with his painter friend Frank Freeman in his borrowed studio in Cheyne Walk in Chelsea. One afternoon, Frank decided to introduce Silas to a friend who lived in the neighbourhood. The door was opened by a pretty blonde woman with a charming and feminine manner which gave no hint of her impressive intellect or her volatile emotions. She was already entertaining two young men to tea and was happy to welcome these further two. The talk ranged over topics which seemed, to a young mining engineer long isolated from European culture, to embody everything which he had hoped to find on his return to London. William Gerhardie was a colourful object of literary speculation at the time; his third novel *Jazz and Jasper* had been received with terrific excitement, but it was his first novel, *Futility*, a Chekhovian tale of the Bursanov family, veering between tragedy and comedy, which Antonia discussed so memorably with her guests that afternoon. She wrote some years later that she thought Gerhardie 'a feeble, peevish, exhibitionistic kind of baby satirist'; if she had expressed something like that at this tea party the debate would have been lively.[7] The talk ranged from current Chelsea scandals to the latest play running at the Arts Theatre Club, and may have touched on the furore over Lawrence's *Lady Chatterley's Lover*, which dominated literary gossip at the time, or the more subtle subversions of Virginia Woolf's ambisexual *Orlando*. Each subject was deftly introduced and interwoven with significance by their hostess.

Antonia had an irreverent sense of humour and she had a great success at at least one of the 'boasting parties' which were popular amongst her friends at the time; she produced the peerless boast that she had been married twice and had a certificate from the Pope vouching for her virginity. Antonia's bizarre claim beat Eddy Gathorne-Hardy's, that he had contracted ringworm from the Archbishop of Canterbury, into second place. She also wrote, for a birthday party celebration, a memorable play called Young Sodley. This was probably a spoof of the play *Young Woodley*, by a young Anglo-American, van Druten, in which he explored the sexual initiation of an adolescent. It was made a *succès de scandale* by the Lord Chamberlain's subsequent ban. Somehow the police got hold of Antonia's version, and so the birthday production turned into a mock trial of Antonia instead.

Antonia was delightful company at these kinds of relaxed gatherings on the periphery of smarter social circles. Her conversation could fascinate and flatter, weaving connections between people and ideas, with references subtly introduced from the classical authors, mythology or any number of the multitude of books that she had read. And all of it done with the lightest of touches, spiced with a sharp wit. Silas likened this conversational skill to a musical accompanist's, in whom resided the control of tempo and inflexion, imposed so discreetly that anyone else engaged in the performance felt the brilliance was theirs. Years later he was to tell her, 'You are the only person who understands me and in whose presence I become articulate.'[8] Certainly that first afternoon Antonia's charm and intelligence drew him in, and he was eager to return for more. For Antonia, Silas was an unthreatening and attractive young man whose alien experiences in the wastelands of Northern Canada made him a refreshing change from the bohemian artists and tea-party politics of Chelsea. Perhaps she recognised that under their conventional exteriors both had been cast beyond the pale of polite society by the extremity of their experiences of solitariness and exile. When Antonia asked him years later if he remembered ever being really happy Silas had replied, 'Yes – driving a dog team alone in Canada.'[9] And she, cherishing her revealed self in Bedlam, feared monotony, safety, sanity, as much as she feared madness.

When they met, Silas was in the middle of sitting for his portrait by his friend Frank Freeman. Nine years later the American writer, Djuna Barnes also decided to paint his portrait as 'the young Bull-heifer . . . When his hair is rumpled, full across his forehead, & he's a little heated, he's *exactly* a baby bull. . .'.[10] This description of Silas pointed up his androgynous good looks. He himself said he had caught sight in a shop window of what he thought was a remarkably attractive woman: then he realised that he was gazing at a reflection of himself. Although not homosexual, Silas fitted into the broad type of man who attracted Antonia, gentle and unassertive, the opposite to her father. She recognised this quite early on, and explained 'he is not in the least overbearing, is tolerant, comes out strong in moments of crisis. He is incapable of conscious exploitation. His greatest difficulty is to make decisions.'[11] He also suffered from anxiety and depression, expecting the worst and suspicious of happiness.

The courtship proceeded rapidly. Antonia seemed to be part of a lively, artistic, gossipy set of friends centred on Chelsea, a raffish and less serious pole to Bloomsbury, but with members like Desmond MacCarthy, Logan Pearsall Smith and various artists who navigated between both. Antonia's liveliness and vitality promised Silas release from his own melancholy. Her attraction was enhanced further by the intimated presence of other admirers, most impressive to Silas at the time being Bertrand Russell, with whom Antonia was still conducting the flirtation which had begun in the early part of 1926. She certainly used it to amusing and provocative effect in her conversation with her new admirer; competition from other males being an unfailing aphrodisiac. Older than him by three years, twice married, sophisticated, cultured and urbane, she appeared to this naïve male to be experienced in the unknown land of social and sexual relations. Within a week of meeting, Silas was writing from his parents' house in Bakewell in Derbyshire, begging a reply to reassure him that it had not been just a dream. 'Of course in my heart I know that it is all true, for even in dreams I could never have created your loveliness.'[12] He was soon back in his grim little flat in Edgbaston which, as the weather grew colder, he christened 'esquimaux villa'. But hope had now come to keep him warm; how unexpected, he thought, and sudden, had been his transformation from unhappiness to joy. He was back in London before the end of the month and took his new love dancing.

Antonia was still married to Eric and living in civilised amity in his house in Paultons Square. On the surface, this affair was merely part of their agreement in the 'companionate marriage' they shared, to use Bertrand Russell's term for a sexually open arrangement. Antonia's love for Silas, 'a natural, happy ecstasy', seemed to be the real thing at last.[13] But this was prior to its sexual consummation. In retrospect, Antonia felt that this certainty of feeling, this freedom from anxiety and doubt, had only lasted for about a week. The sexual side of their relationship was not a success. Many years later, Silas explained that he had come to her completely inexperienced but filled with romantic notions gleaned from exalted literature such as the love poetry of Keats, while Antonia, despite the appearance of sophistication in such matters, he came to consider as sexually maladjusted and unable to find any pleasure in the sexual act. Never one to avoid harsh truths, Antonia called herself 'frigid' throughout most of her active sexual life. 'Actual sex became a kind of ordeal mixed up with all sorts of terrors and feelings of extreme guilt.'[14] Fear on her side and disappointment and disillusionment on his quickly entered the heart of their love affair.

Antonia was beginning to wonder if she would ever manage a complete relationship with a man. She enjoyed Silas's company, loved going dancing with him, shared some happy and close moments, even thought of him as 'my true love'.[15] But at heart she was uneasy; he was a romantic and therefore bound for disappointment and she was haunted by the old fear that she was a freak of a woman, able to make neither herself nor others happy. Despite his natural melancholia, Silas was young and eager and more committed and hopeful, perhaps, than Antonia. In a letter written in the latter part of 1928, he thanked her for showing him how beautiful and innocent love could be. He was keen that Antonia come to Edgbaston to spend the weekend with him. He cleaned up his bachelor rooms and wrote her a letter asking for her preferences in beverages, bed-warming, and breakfast. Soon he was walking the streets of Birmingham in search of the weekend's necessities: Oxford marmalade, Ryvita biscuits, Lapsang Souchong tea and a hot water bottle. Antonia was introduced to his landlady as Mrs Smith, his cousin.

On either the second or third visit – it could not have been any earlier than the beginning of December – Antonia arrived in his flat, sat down and said without preamble that she was pregnant. The news stunned Silas; he had assumed that this twice-married woman of the world would somehow know how to prevent this natural outcome of their love-making. His shock obviously showed. With some reluctance Antonia said she could have an abortion, but this Silas did not want to countenance. He suggested that as her marriage to Eric was only a matter of form, which in fact was not emotionally the case, she should divorce Eric and marry him.

Again, a kind of hope rose in Antonia that with Silas, so obviously decent and kind, she could learn how to be a natural woman, with sexual desire for her man and maternal feelings for her children. Antonia had, by now, superficially cast off the weight of her religion and had distanced herself from the force of her father's opinions. Eric had consoled her, when she had told him of her fear of the mediocrity of living a sane life, by pointing out that sanity is only being what one was intended to be by nature. But Antonia was always to wonder, what exactly *was* her natural self? She was more sure of her vices than her virtues: 'I know my vices: fear & greed . . . I must have some [virtues] since all human beings have. Some moral courage, I *think*; at least the *desire* to be honest. I think a certain capacity for understanding, perhaps understanding more truly strong than feeling; my emotions are v. intense but very irrational & unstable. . . .'[16]

Both Antonia and Silas were anxious about the idea of the coming child. Silas was still finding it hard to come to terms with the fact that at so early a stage in the relationship they were facing parenthood and the reversal of all their individual hopes and plans. He asked if Antonia was sure that the baby was his and not Bertrand Russell's: Antonia assured him that it could not have been Russell's since their flirtation had never developed into an affair. Silas wrote to her, possibly after this fateful weekend, apologising for any clumsiness in his responses and the wrong impression he may have given her. He was just worried in the short term, he said, about money and how to support a family. He reiterated that he loved her and although the situation was difficult and complicated (they were particularly fearful of the reactions of Antonia's father and Silas's mother) together they would find a solution. Already, by the end of 1928, when Antonia can only have been about four weeks' pregnant, he had a name for the unborn baby – Francis, for both hoped it would be a boy.

Antonia experienced all her familiar ambivalence at any change in the *status quo*. The desire for a child with a man she loved had nothing much to do with wanting an individual child, she said, but rather needing the security and love which the idea embodied, and the pleasure of producing something masculine from her own body. But set against this in her mind was the real fear of childbirth, vividly inculcated in her by her mother's gruesome experiences. Her wish to prove herself as a woman was at odds with her disgust at the physicality of pregnancy, its 'acute discomfort and distortion', and the sense that among her smart friends there was something unbecoming and socially inferior about the pregnant woman.[17] The twenties was a time when women began to see themselves as beings separate from their ability to procreate. Fashions minimised the breasts and hips, women began dieting in an attempt to make their bodies thinner and more boyish, hair was straightened and cropped. The elaborate hair, pronounced curves and full bosom of the Edwardian feminine ideal had disappeared with the practical exigencies of war work and the feminist advances, particularly female suffrage, of the postwar period.

Antonia was also a working woman and would consider herself to be such throughout her life. She was harried by her father's emphasis on finding work in case she remained unmarried, and her anxieties at how best to earn her living became at times obsessive. The working mother is not an easy conjunction even now; then it was much rarer and much more difficult – for many jobs such a double role was not even countenanced and motherhood meant the end of a career. In fashionable circles, children were considered tiresome and overt maternal love vulgar. '*Children* weren't smart in the 20s' she wrote to her daughter Susan, many years later. 'Girl friends commiserated with anyone who was breeding! . . . MAHVellous was the key word. Favourite silly games "Beaver" (spotting men with beards), treasure hunts & stunt parties . . . everyone dressed as babies or murderers. . . .'[18] It was an adolescent society where emotional responsibility was evaded for as long as possible. It was against these attitudes and fears that Antonia was considering becoming a mother, initially without the protection and security of marriage to the baby's father. And unmarried pregnancies and illegitimate children still carried a powerful stigma of shame in society at large. Never having been encouraged when a child to believe she had a choice, or even could ask for what she wanted, Antonia was paralysed always by the need to make decisions. Eric suggested they remain married and the child be brought up under his protection. But Antonia wanted to try and live a 'natural' life with a man she could love in the usual way, with a child as the seal on this normality. To achieve this, however, she had to risk everything in the hope of love with Silas.

Marriage to Silas would also mean bringing another annulment suit, this time against Eric, whom she loved and respected and for whom privacy and discretion was a precious thing. Antonia had confused feelings about this as well. Giving up Eric was not easy; he represented a rare safety and so much of what she loved and valued. The idea of having to go through the ordeal of annulment for a second time made her faint-hearted. Eric too had feelings which had to be considered. Antonia recognised how much he cared for her and wrote some years later, 'He gave me up (& I know what that meant) for what he thought was my happiness.'[19] Silas had his own anxieties. His future was uncertain. He was having to look for work where he could find it in order to earn enough money for his new and unexpected responsibilities. Quite soon he realised these responsibilities were more onerous than he had at first thought, for Antonia was already in debt and appeared to have a cavalier attitude to her creditors. His father had been very ill for a year, and in December suffered another stroke which had left him half-paralysed and without speech. Silas and his sister Elspeth were summoned back to Derbyshire to find him unable to recognise them. He died on 21 December and Silas immediately succumbed to flu.

He and Antonia spent Christmas apart. She was already tired and not sleeping very well. He was assiduous with his letters, trying to reassure her that he loved her, that things would turn out all right in the end. Silas was also anxious and over-protective of his sister Elspeth, who collapsed while staying with him in Edgbaston that January, with something akin to a bad dose of mumps. This meant that Antonia's visit had to be put off because Silas thought it unwise for her to risk any infection herself now that she was pregnant. This was a blow, for Antonia was lonely on her own in a room in the King's Road. She had had to move out of the civilised home she had made with Eric in order to bring the divorce suit against him. She also had not been well herself. Antonia seemed to be losing everything that mattered; the structure and routine that helped her to function, the security she needed, her health, her figure, her independence. She loved Silas and he professed to love her, but they were so much apart (they had only managed to see each other for one day during the first three weeks of January) and it was in her nature to expect the worst. She had an uneasy feeling too that she was at her least attractive when ill or unhappy; some years later she recalled, 'When I am gay, Silas is strongly drawn to me. When I am unhappy he flies me like the plague'.[20] She came to think he was haunted by what she called an 'escape-motif', never realising that the one thing he wanted to escape was really himself.

They went dancing when they saw each other in London, and planned a short holiday in France together in the spring of 1929. Interestingly, Antonia had begun to experiment with writing again, something which Silas called 'the Convent book'.[21] Bertrand Russell had also mentioned her 'convent memoir'. Her short story 'The Saint' was published in *Life and Letters* in November 1931, but elsewhere she claimed it was not closely rooted in personal experience, so the 'convent book' must have been the beginnings of what was to become *Frost in May*. This Antonia had begun writing soon after leaving the Convent of the Sacred Heart. She was to return to it spasmodically and was probably working on it again at this time as Silas suggested she bring the manuscript with her on her next trip to see him.

Antonia was suffering badly from headaches. These were extreme and sometimes lasted up to three days at a time: for more than twenty years they were an intermittent part of her life. They were not, however, migraines, for Antonia did not suffer the concomitant visual disturbances which characterised that particular affliction. Silas, on the other hand, did. Antonia continued to work at Crawford's and Silas was teaching his last term at Birmingham University, and wondering where on earth he was to go next. Increasingly, it seemed sensible for him to go abroad as technological revolution promised great expansion in all manufacturing industries, with an increased demand for more raw materials. The influence of Wells's scientific utopianism remained strong. He was offered a job in Canada as a mining engineer with the possibility of working for his doctorate at Harvard. He discussed it with Antonia; perhaps she could come out at the end of the year, once the baby was born, and live in Toronto or Boston? She was upset: he apologised in a letter at the time for making her cry, perhaps over the idea of losing him. Antonia, in the end, agreed it was best that he go and earn the required money to keep her and their baby secure. But for two fragile, depressive temperaments, separation and distance were a danger. They were both insecure, self-centred and uncertain of their identities, and the eighteen months they were apart involved each in extreme experiences which were emotionally inaccessible to the other.

Silas left on 3 May 1929 from Liverpool docks and sent a flurry of excited, euphoric notes to Antonia. How happy they were going to be;

he promised her his true and faithful love; he said he longed to be married. These were the last of his uncloudedly optimistic letters. Money, or rather the lack of it, began to loom larger in their correspondence. Silas sent everything he had, which was not much and came by circuitous and unreliable routes. Antonia was alone and fearful, her pathological anxieties over money having been reactivated; not having enough money meant not only practical inconvenience but the more frightening sense of her own impotence and lack of love. Even though she knew rationally that Silas was away from her for the very sake of earning some money to support his new family, she felt emotionally abandoned by him; she feared he did not really love her and was not ready to marry her.

Silas was also suffering physical hardship, illness, loneliness and his familiar old depression. He started off on $300 a month as an assistant manager in a mine in Timmins, in Ontario, a place 'extravagantly noxious' where he found it hard to imagine Antonia fitting in.[22] 'Imagine a collection of 15,000 mid European wage slaves, 500 predatory Canadian storekeepers, & a sprinkling of incredibly po-faced engineers with their beastly wives, all despising one another. The whole set in a desolate burnt out wilderness of sand plains & cyanide slimes', he wrote enticingly to her.[23] In June Silas had moved to a job doing geological surveying for the Keeley Silver Mines, 200 miles to the south. He seemed happier with the work, but still anxious about the unhappy letters arriving from Antonia, and the endless requests for money which he seemed unable to fulfil to the level that was needed.

She had told her parents of her pregnancy; she knew that her father had long hoped for a grandchild but, through fear of his shock and displeasure, had allowed them to think that the baby was Eric's. However, at the beginning of July, with just six weeks to go before her baby was due, Antonia on an impulse, told her mother the truth. She was worried about her father's reaction, and also that the expected explosion of anger would be bad for his heart, but Christine encouraged her to risk telling him. She was amazed at his generous and tolerant response and related the good news to Silas; 'he said that he had had suspicions all along, but did not want me to tell him unless I wanted to. I can't tell you how extraordinary it seems, & what a relief it is . . . he has been sweet about you, which is best of all.'[24] This, however, did not seem to give Silas the impetus to broach the coming marriage and baby to his formidable mother. Antonia was particularly pleased that the new revelation had not spoiled her father's pleasure in his first grandchild, but he too '*very* much wants it to be a boy'.[25] However, her relief and gratitude were short-lived; her anxieties about money must have been acute because she asked her father to lend her £30 for the costs of having her baby and his reluctance made her lose her temper. She fumed that he had been keener to lend her the £50 necessary for her abortion.

Antonia had suffered a bout of measles and was also having to endure in July the humiliation of the divorce from Eric without Silas's support – or even a sympathetic letter, for which neglect he apologised. She was pleased to be able to report that she had told Bertrand Russell that she was pregnant and he had agreed to be an 'atheistical godparent' to the new baby.

Antonia had worked for Crawford's up to the last month of her confinement, sometimes while staying with her parents, who had retired to Sussex, to Binesfield. Her two great-aunts were still alive and her father had begun his longed-for improvements of the ancient and ramshackle cottage and gardens. But they were improvements of which she could not approve, for they destroyed the essential makeshift and make-do quality of the place which had so reflected the genius of her beloved great-aunts. Antonia's lack of enthusiasm hurt her father's feelings; he had created his lifelong dream of a croquet green on the lawn by the house, but Antonia felt a sense of loss and outrage which she realised years later was because the cottage represented herself, '"Forcibly converted" by my father & not altogether suiting my nature.'[26]

In the middle of August she returned to London to have her baby in the Royal Northern Hospital. Labour started on Friday afternoon, 16 August, and after a long and difficult birth a daughter was born on Sunday 18 August. This new and central relationship was wrong-footed from the start.

By having a daughter rather than a son Antonia felt she had disappointed everyone; (years later her psychoanalyst was to tell her she had a 'compulsion to *disappoint* people', with which she agreed.)[27] Her mother had had a tragic succession of miscarriages and stillborn girls in her attempt to give her husband a son. Antonia had not only failed to be that son but now had been incapable of giving him a grandson: he had told her subsequently that he would have found it easier to overlook the circumstances of this baby's birth [her illegitimacy] if she had been a boy. Antonia's own desire for a son involved her need to restore what she saw as the mutilated part of herself. 'I can understand the extraordinary satisfaction of producing a son. A woman has not a penis but she can produce a being with a real penis.'[28] The penis was also symbolically connected to her writing, as something powerful and creative, with the ability to fertilise ideas in others.

On hearing the news two days later of his daughter's birth, Silas wrote with frankness but some insensitivity. 'I am so glad that everything's all right; I had been so worried about you, particularly as I was so hopelessly out of touch [he had been on a long trip into the outback and had almost collided with a bear] . . . So it's Anne-Elspeth after all . . . I am quite stunned at having a daughter, I could have faced a son, but the responsibility of Anne E. is almost too much, I hope that you feel equal to the occasion.'[29] It was as if, unable to identify with a daughter, he was emotionally retreating, shifting the responsibility back to Antonia, who was by now even less equipped to shoulder it. Even Eric, who was still Antonia's husband and the nominal father to this baby, gave her the impression he would have preferred it if she had produced a boy. On the second night of Antonia's labour he had sat in his club until one in the morning drinking, thinking of her and waiting for news. When word finally came the following day, he wrote with sympathy for her long labour and then, masking disappointment with irony, he made a discouraging joke: 'I wish you had not added yet another woman to the army of sinners.'[30]

Antonia took her new baby back with her to her parents in Sussex. She was having great difficulty in breast-feeding; part of the problem, perhaps, was her own physical recoil from the idea of such physicality and intimacy. 'And fear of suckling the child: vanity is only a conscious element & could easily be overcome: no just terror and pain and *repulsion*.'[31] Antonia was also troubled by her lack of maternal feeling for her baby and wrote to Bertrand Russell about it. He, naturally so experienced in such things, gave her a partial but hopefully reassuring answer: 'I shouldn't worry, if I were you, over not feeling the correct emotions as per copy book – very few women do, especially with a first child. They lie about it as a form of boasting. You will find that affection will grow; it is a result, not a cause, of the care one takes of the child. At least that is usually the case with civilised people.'[32] Antonia was left alone to try and reconcile the reality of this defenceless baby daughter in her arms, so needy, pathetically vulnerable, yet separate, with the intellectual ideal she had carried in her mind of the boy child, the extension of her other self and symbol of her power and womanliness. Antonia was herself too much that needy infant, unequal, she felt, to the responsibility of another more vulnerable being, and terrified of the practical and emotional demands of raising a baby ('it is *babies*, not *children* that alarm me').[33] It was in this way that Antonia came to see her children too often as her competitors for love, power and all her precious resources, 'as enemies out to take away everything I have.'[34]

She was overcome at times by 'a morbid terror of their annihilating me.'[35]

Full of fear of emotion and distrust of herself, Antonia recognised that in loving Silas she had achieved 'my first complete love-affair because it went to full lengths and resulted in a child'. However, she also expected, from the patterns she had already traced in her life, that pain and loss would follow close behind. 'To fall in love means for me giving someone the power to hurt me. And frequently my falling in love with someone is the signal for their falling out of love with me.'[36] She had created a bleak narrative for herself; it was as if she held her breath waiting for the disappointments to come. Many years later Antonia made the connection of the birth of her first child with her having lost the ability to cry. '[The analyst] asked me if something inside me was "crying"', and she could only recognise with shock and grief that this was true.[37]

9

We Have Shot the Lovely Albatross

I said, 'If I am so wicked, what is my worst vice and wickedness?' She
said 'Giving poison to the wrong man.'

Conversation between AW and Djuna Barnes 27 September 1937, *Diaries I*

As Antonia struggled with new motherhood, back in Sussex with her
parents and longing for London, Silas was still working long hours
at the Keeley Silver Mines and going off on trips prospecting, feeling all
the more cut off from his former life. Mention of his baby being ill gave
him a sudden pang, arousing his parental affections. A photograph of her
and Antonia touched his heart. He was growing used to the idea that he
had a daughter and enjoyed speculating about her character and
planning her education (at Bedales). Silas professed an even greater love
for Antonia, which had grown with the realisation that he had created a
family with her. But he was also often low spirited and anxious,
prostrate with exhaustion or mired in his familiar despondency,
bordering on despair. Silas, at least, was planning for Antonia and the
baby to move out to be with him by Christmas 1929. He was still calling
their daughter 'Anne' well into September, although Antonia had
registered her names, Susan Elspeth Russell Glossop on 27 August;
'Elspeth' reflected Silas's love for his sister. However, on Susan's birth
certificate Antonia did not name the father, and so her baby took her
name: Earnshaw Smith.

Silas was not sure where work might take him. He had had to turn
down the place he had been offered at the Massachusetts Institute of
Technology, the prestigious institution which led the field in the
engineering and technological contribution to the vastly expanding US
economy. Affiliated to Harvard University, MIT was situated in
Cambridge, on the outskirts of Boston: Silas particularly had hoped to
do his doctorate there but decided the $150 a month he was offered

would not be enough to keep his new wife and baby. Instead he mentioned the mine at Timmins as their most likely destination, but this time he expressed a not entirely plausible enthusiasm for the place. Unfortunately, Antonia could remember his memorable first descriptions of it as 'extravagantly noxious' and was far from keen. To add to his woes, the Wall Street crash of 24 September that year seemed to arrive without warning, at a point when everyone was thinking the boom would go on for ever. It wiped billions off the value of companies across America; all sectors collapsed, but mining shares were particularly badly hit. Personal savings, businesses and jobs were razed overnight. There were eleven related suicides in New York alone. Silas was given a month's notice, with nothing definite to look forward to as an alternative. Reassuring Antonia of his lasting and true love for her, he asked if it were possible for her to support herself and 'Su' (for Anne had become Susan) for two months while he came back to London on the cheapest ticket available, and then looked for work abroad again, perhaps in South Africa.

Although all these attempts to set himself up with a good paying job were well-meaning and admirable, although he continued to send Antonia letters expressing his affection and his longing to be married to her, Silas's continued absence and the confusion of his plans filled Antonia with insecurity and foreboding. She felt certain he had stopped loving her, just as she had come to expect her love affairs would end. She explained it when she was much older and could look back with some equanimity: 'That 18 months, beginning when I most needed him there – when the child was born – shook my confidence in him. And he must know in his heart of hearts that he was not wholeheartedly set on marrying me till he came home and found he had a rival.'[1] But she was not afraid of taking responsibility for the damage she caused in not marrying him, when he finally did return. In rereading his letters, more than forty years later, Antonia was touched by the love and concern Silas revealed in them, a love she had been unable to appreciate at the time. The telegram he had sent after their baby's birth, which had gone astray (possibly destroyed by her father, Antonia came to suspect) struck a splinter of bitterness into her heart. 'If I had had that telegram, things *might* have turned out differently.'[2] With the clarity of hindsight, she noticed how they had let each other down by their inability to enter into the experiences and feelings of the other. How different their emotional responses were: 'It's such a sad, ironic story, Si's & mine. For I was so awfully in love with him & so hurt by his apparent coldness . . . which as he tells me over & over again is 90% his inability to feel things at the time and to *express* what he feels most strongly . . . It was those *masks* in Si . . . that tormented me so for I'm impatient & always *conscious* of what I'm feeling and . . . always madly needing re-assurance. I always supposed everyone else was *completely* confident!'[3] The geographical distance between them became an emotional gulf.

Silas's best friend Frank Freeman, who had just married Antonia's painter friend Joan Souter-Robertson, wrote to her on Silas's behalf. He reminded her of Silas's moodiness, and his fundamental goodness: 'I am afraid you will always find him somewhat undependable at fixed times – but he is always all right in the end.'[4] But Antonia had no such confidence in her future with Silas. She knew she could not continue living with her parents and her two great-aunts in the cottage, however extended and converted it now was. There no longer seemed to be the money, or indeed the wish, for her and baby Susan to travel out to Canada to live with Silas in a mining town – if in fact Antonia had ever seriously considered such an upheaval. After all, living in such a transitory community could only offer a precarious and uncomfortable life in a social desert, thousands of miles from any kind of familiar place or accessible culture.

Antonia's main concern was to get back to work to earn some money and so she returned to a part-time position at Crawford's Agency in November. Baby Susan, who was only three months old, was left with a nurse in the overall care of her grandparents in Sussex. Antonia considered where best to live herself now that she was back in London. The attraction of life with Eric had never faded: the annulment of their marriage was through by the autumn and so she could go back to live with him again in Paultons Square, almost as if none of the momentous experiences which had separated them for over a year had ever happened.

Another momentous and unexpected event was soon to follow. Cecil Botting died unexpectedly on 17 November 1929 of a brain haemorrhage. Antonia was surprised at how little she felt. The person who had been the focus of all her passion and the source of so much fear was dead: she experienced at first only relief. Standing beside his body in the bedroom at Binesfield, she was overcome by a 'strange temptation . . . to which mercifully I did not yield'. She longed to strip him naked, to divest him of his mystery and authority, 'to see for myself that my father was a man like other men'; as frail, as human, as insignificant. The opposite effect, however, was to occur.[5]

She wrote to Silas with the news of her father's death. He was still in Canada, desperate for work and hoping to hear that he had a job at the Narcozari Copper Company in Mexico, recommended to him by Professor Gratton at Harvard. On receiving the letter, more than four weeks after the event, Silas replied at once full of loving concern, and promises that a job would turn up soon, although he assured her he wished he could be home with her. This vague ambivalence merely underlined Antonia's insecurity about his true feelings – if he really cared would he not have come home already? All these professions of love meant very little when he was so far away and making little effort, it seemed to her, to come back to see her and his baby. She fired off one of her accusatory letters, which left him puzzled and contrite like an old dog who has been kicked unjustly but wants to make amends. Silas's reply showed him apparently more confused than ever – should he give up on Mexico and the hope of some worthwhile earnings or should he come home? There may have been something tacitly obdurate in him, however, which passively resisted her requests that he should return. For in the same letter he threw in the bogey of the chance of his disappearance to a job in North Africa, where there was no opportunity for her to join him. Compared to that threat, the mining job in Mexico seemed more palatable to his impatient fiancée back home. By the end of December 1929, Antonia had not seen Silas for nearly eight months, their daughter had been born, her father had died, and she was officially single again.

Silas slipped out of focus in Antonia's mind, preoccupied as she was with the everyday demands of work and the aftermath of her father's death. She was beginning to wonder whether he might ever make it home again. Susan also seemed to slip out of her immediate field of concern. With her husband's death, Antonia's mother seemed less happy about having her granddaughter and her nurse living with her. Rather than install her baby, together with the nurse, in Eric's immaculate household, or try and set up a home herself for her child, Antonia sent her to a private residential nursery in Roehampton, interestingly not very far from the nuns at the Convent of the Sacred Heart. It was expensive and well-run, but this was the era when childcare expert Truby King's theories of child training were all the vogue. He advocated a particularly strict series of routines. Babies were treated rather like clockwork toys – they were to be fed every four hours, put on the pot every two hours, only played with and spoken to at stated times. There was little appreciation of the emotional needs of the growing infant, and great emphasis on training the child, from infancy, to submit its desires to some arbitrary external authority.

Antonia, whose own babyhood was isolated and chilly, and by modern standards missing in close parental involvement, was not likely to see in this smart nursery provision that the lack of a reliable mother-figure for Susan was crucially damaging. She had never really attached herself emotionally to her daughter; Antonia visited Susan and relayed her progress in her letters to Silas, but the baby was not in the forefront of her thoughts. Years later she tried to understand what were the forces which led her virtually to abandon her child during the first year and a half of her life. 'Si ran away at such a critical moment. Again if my mother had looked after her it would have been better. But I am by far the most to blame. It all seemed so impossible at the time to have her with me. I suppose I was really too selfish and too cowardly.'[6] Although so blind at the time to Susan's plight, Antonia over the years gained a greater awareness and understanding of the suffering of others and came to regret bitterly the damage she had done her child. 'How terribly wrong it was of me to let Sue be with strangers, however kind, the first 18 months of her life. How can I wonder that she hates me now.'[7] The most painful realisation was that however hard Antonia might try and make it up to Susan once she was grown up, it was by then too late. She had betrayed the most primitive maternal compact, to put the welfare of one's baby first, and nothing she could do subsequently could restore that bond of trust and dependable love.

It was Antonia's greatest misfortune that she saw all relationships in terms of a power struggle. It was a measure of her own painful insecurity and fear of powerlessness, but it had a particularly tragic outcome when she applied it to her children. So often she interpreted familial relationships as a battle between herself and them, she alternated between resentment and fear, combativeness and submission, much as she had with her father. The bully and the victim had become one in dangerous and unhappy combination. The death of Antonia's father was not the end of his influence over her; instead, it was the beginning of an ascendancy of a different kind. He left her an intolerable legacy: 'I loved him dearly and he died feeling that I had failed him in every important way,'[8] she wrote years later to a friend. Her longing for his approval and yet her need to defy him and disappoint him resulted in another of her unconsidered decisions which went against natural good sense. On her return from his funeral, feeling 'rather shaken', a young man who worked as a copywriter at Crawford's was particularly sympathetic and kind to her.[9] This conjunction of loss and loneliness with the possibility of rescue was to prove fatally irresistible.

Antonia had first noticed Tom Hopkinson when she returned to part-time work at the agency after Susan's birth. She had acquired her own office, partly because she was highly valued for her work and had negotiated for it, and partly so that her unique part-time status and irregular hours would not be too evident to the other staff, who might then expect similar concessions. It was a space she had made her with personal bits and pieces, and where she also kept some of her private work in the drawers of her desk. She was understandably irritated to find that this young, and rather smug, man had been using it in her absence. Being Antonia, her natural irritation quickly escalated into unreasonable anger. In 'Julian Tye' she described this confrontation with the Tom figure, and in the process illuminated the pattern of her temper, which frightened even herself. 'Anger at her own anger made her more furious than ever. She was going to make a fool of herself and this intolerable young man would be responsible . . . "At least," she said roughly, "you might have the decency to answer when I speak to you." The note in her voice appalled her. Was it her father working up to one of those scenes that used to paralyse her into idiocy or her mother screaming at a housemaid?'[10]

Antonia had been predisposed to dislike Tom Hopkinson. Her first impressions were not favourable – she thought him 'shamefaced' and conceited. Certainly he was charming, good looking, and six years her junior, all qualities which usually attracted her; he was also intelligent, with a strong poetic streak. But he had appealed so much to the young women in the firm, who gossiped admiringly about his long lashes and blue eyes, that Antonia had decided she was not going to join the adoring throng. There was, however, a smaller faction who found him condescending: ' "Thinks himself much too good to be here." '[11] Tom also had a sentimentality and lack of solid integrity which made her uneasy. So against her will, her better judgement, even her understanding, she bolted into a relationship with him within the month; '[he] suddenly assumed this violent, almost compulsive importance soon after my father's death. Why? It had never occurred to me that *anyone* could be a rival for Silas for me.'[12]

There was an element of defying her father again, even though this time he was beyond her in death. He had accepted her proposed marriage to Silas; he had liked Silas, and regularising their relationship made Susan's birth more acceptable to his own conscience, and to the public opinion which mattered so much to him. But there were other reasons for beginning this affair. It was Christmas, a time when she was vulnerable to feeling especially alone and unloved. Silas was still so far away, with little prospect, it seemed, of either returning home or making a home out there for a new wife and baby; Susan was in the children's home, emotionally detached from her and cared for by others; her father, for so long the centre of her own experience of family, was dead. Tom, with his ready sympathy, his witty conversation, his warm talk of brothers and sisters (he was one of five), seemed suddenly attractive to this solitary only child: 'Tom in some way stood for me that

Christmas as security, respectability, a *family*. I remember how I wished I could have gone up with him to spend Christmas with his family'.[13] Ever since she was very small she had longed for a sibling; a sister would have done (she was haunted by her mother's grief over the three lost sisters, all stillborn) but it was a brother whom she wanted most. 'I *hated* being an only child. I think all my life I've been searching for a lost brother.'[14] And it was Tom, she felt, who appeared to fulfil that brotherly role. He was her masculine counterpoint; 'The sort of young man I should like to have been myself?'[15] Antonia was a woman with a strong male side, unsure of her femininity and Tom was a man with a strong female side who was himself insecure in his maleness: '[he] had a deep desire both to be a woman and to prove himself a man' was how Antonia categorised this ambivalence in Tom, but she could have been talking just as acutely about herself.[16]

Tom Hopkinson was born in 1905 into a well-established intellectual family. His father had a sweet but ambivalent nature and in his mid-thirties gave up a promising academic career to become a priest in the Church of England. It was as dramatic and unworldly a decision as Cecil Botting's conversion to Catholicism. Both men had limited their careers in the pursuit of a spiritual life. He eventually ended up as Archdeacon of Westmorland, but it was a difficult and impoverished life on the way for his wife and five children. Tom's mother was austere and self-denying, which meant she also denied her own children open affection, encouragement, a sense of joy. It set Tom up, the clever, sensitive second son, to be desperate for affection and approval for the rest of his life. It also made him as an adult emotionally vulnerable to dominating women.

He won a scholarship to read Greats at Oxford and managed to maximise his chances of approval by being both good at rugger and an academic, in with the aesthetes. But each clique felt slightly suspicious of him for his allegiance to the other. This desire to please everyone all the time was to be another of the emotional burdens he carried into his adult relationships. Wanting to be a writer but short of money and influential connections, Tom found himself in the spring of 1928 working as a junior copywriter in Crawford's. He became aware of Antonia long before she noticed him. Tom was waiting for a lift on one of the upper floors when the sound of high heeled shoes clacking down the corridor at quite a pace first caught his attention. He looked down to the floor below and saw a young woman in a green knitted suit, not very tall, slightly plump and walking quickly with small steps: 'From her chin thrust forward, and the way she set each foot down as though wanting to knock a hole in the tiles with her heel, the impression I took in was of smouldering indignation. The sharpness of that instant impression remains, as though in it I had seen an essential aspect of her personality.'[17]

When Tom met Antonia face to face he was struck by an apprehension that here was 'a woman born to be unhappy'. By that he explained, he meant that her fine sensibility and limitless feeling left her ill-protected against the outside world. However, when he knew her better her realised the limits of her fragility and the underlying power of her strength; ' "You are so strong. You needn't be afraid" [he said to her during one of their fights] "You're made of iron". That too was true.'[18] After their first territorial confrontation over the use of Antonia's desk, the relationship between them was combative and flirtatious, not remotely serious – in Antonia's mind at least. Then at the Christmas party something happened which showed Antonia her feelings were not as disengaged as she had thought. Some drunken men had apparently tried to push Tom out of a window and Antonia sprang to his defence with such ferocity that she knew in some way she identified with him; 'My instinct of protecting someone? A writer? My male side?'[19]

Tom, at nearly twenty-five, was still a virgin, as had been Silas when first he met Antonia. She appeared to both young men to be an experienced older woman. To Tom she seemed particularly sexually exotic, given that she was living with, although divorced from, her second husband, who was openly homosexual, and had a fiancé who sounded like a 'Nietzschean "wild man" ', working in the outback of Canada and possibly moving on to the Wild West of Mexico.[20] She already had had a baby by him and perhaps had told Tom, in her witty conversational way, of her escape from Bedlam, and her other escapades with admirers, seducers and rogues. Still uncertain about what exactly it was which propelled her, Antonia fell into Tom's willing arms.

Right from the start there was an imbalance in their relationship. She was more romantically in love with Tom than he was with her, but he was much more sexually attracted. For Antonia, this remained the aspect of any love affair where her lack of confidence, fear and incomprehension made pleasure impossible. Sex, on the other hand, was for Tom 'almost mystically important', and the sharing of intimacy and pleasure with a woman was essential to his enjoyment and sense of identity.[21] 'I was very cold sexually in our first years which was very distressing to both of us'; Antonia also recalled how, with the perversity of human nature, she only really desired him at all when he took a mistress and no longer felt attracted to her.[22] Only once, after they had separated, did their desire for each other coincide, but this was too much for Antonia. She suddenly ruptured their harmony by destroying his fragile sexual confidence with a single word: 'I said he was an "unconvincing" lover and he never forgave me for that.'[23] Her brutal honesty could shrivel more sensitive souls. Her unawareness of the effect she had on others was part of her self-centredness, the fall-out of her mental disease, but also a symptom perhaps of her fearful sense of her own insubstantiality. Antonia tried to justify to herself such a casually devastating comment by writing in her diary that other lovers of Tom's had said the same to her, but what she did not appreciate was that none of them seem to have said it to *him*.

Initially, Tom knew that he was just an interim lover while Antonia waited to be reunited with Silas. One of his early letters to her in the spring of 1930 referred to his acceptance that there were more permanent rival claims on her affections; 'I try to remember always those Americas that will, it seems, slide in between us, & I try while remembering them, not to have them so very much in mind – it *is* wrong, Tony, just to steal you for as long as possible & not to mind about everybody else. . . . It is wrong & I shall do it.'[24] It was expressive letters like this, his literary flourishes, his gushing affections, which compared so favourably with Silas's more prosaic communications. Only with hindsight would Antonia see that what appeared to be so wooden in comparison was also seaworthy, straight and true. 'I can see now how marvellously attractive Tom's quick responses & his *articulateness* & his vivid, living letters (Si's are so touchingly flat & bald, like a schoolboy's) & the feeling of firmness and security he gave me (for even when he was letting me down flat, as he did at times, he was so full of remorse and consideration and interesting reasons!) must have been.'[25]

Determined to try and impress them with her writing ability she sat down and wrote, almost in one sitting, a recreation of her time in Bethlem asylum. She called it 'The House of Clouds': it had all the intensity and authority of felt experience. In an interview when she was an old lady she confirmed that she had remembered the whole of her experience of madness 'absolutely vividly'.[26] It had been difficult for her when she first came out of Bethlem because her memories were so powerful, her experiences so extreme, that all she wanted to do was talk about them and try and make sense of the whole. It had been the most frightening and the most ecstatic time of her life and, like a veteran of some terrible war, she returned with a profoundly altered consciousness to a world that had not changed and people who could not know, and did not want to know, the nature of the cataclysm which had befallen her. So the memories remained inside, charged with energy and significance, until they suddenly gushed up and on to the page. Bringing them to light 'took the "haunting" away.'[27]

'The House of Clouds', and its expanded re-appearance in *Beyond the Glass*, is one of the finest pieces she wrote, something she was very proud of having created. Antonia's need to explain herself to herself informed all her writing, from the voluminous journals to her painfully wrought fiction. Her writing provided a structure which contained her experiences and gave them form and reality. Antonia's sense of her own identity was so fugitive that she seemed only to exist when she could capture herself in words on paper. Explaining the effect of writing 'The House of Clouds', she wrote to a friend: 'I can only deal with a difficult or painful situation in two ways – by facing or being made to face the full horror of it and then getting it into its right relation or by expressing it in what one loosely calls "a work of art". The second is really an extension of the first.'[28] This extra burden that her writing carried of proving her existence meant that her barren, unproductive periods were doubly frightening, as she felt her identity slip away. To Emily Coleman she wrote of this crucial connection: 'as I always have had great difficulty in believing I could write at all I often feel like a kind of ghost.'[29]

'The House of Clouds' was a significant point for Antonia in the development of her 'real work', as she liked to call it: her mission to be a writer. In writing something mirroring her own experience she found that others were violently affected; they were touched, sometimes shocked, and generally admiring of her writing talent, and the personal courage which she revealed. With this kind of intimate writing she had discovered the value, indeed the necessity for her, of reworking her own past in the conventions of fiction. She sought some identity with, a validation from her great heroine-writer, Virginia Woolf. She had read *Mrs Dalloway*, with its searing depiction of madness, and felt excitement, recognition, acceptance; 'This is it . . . the real, right thing'.[30] She wrote to tell Virginia Woolf that in this book she had shown her there was a reason and a pattern in madness. Antonia passionately identified with Virginia Woolf as a fellow survivor. There was no record of a reply.

In the summer of 1930, Antonia and Tom decided to take a holiday in the South of France. Antonia was not entirely happy; she was anxious about her personal life, with Silas on the distant Mexican horizon and Tom attentive to her closer to home. She was also under pressure from work. Florence Sangster the financial partner, had had enough of Antonia's obvious contempt for the profession and lack of wholehearted commitment to the company. Antonia returned to London to face the sack, Crawford's had thought that, good as she was, they could do without the trouble that came with her. Antonia now had to try to earn her living as a freelance writer. Tom came to understand what a perilous step this was for her. 'Her father said when she was 15 that she must work or be destitute & starve "because I can't leave anything". This was to her not just a casual remark but a combined command & prophetic utterance'.[31]

After they had returned from holiday, Antonia took Tom to see Susan in the nursery in Roehampton for the first time. She had described her to him after a visit in early summer when she was about ten months old. Antonia appeared to be surprised by her own pride in this little stranger; 'she is really very sweet and gay and pretty and dazzlingly healthy – her new trick is to pull my hair which she does with ferocious competence'.[32] Tom had a strongly caring nature, a 'maternal' streak as he called it, and he was shocked to see this little creature, wrapped in a blanket, but with her feet sticking out and blue with cold. This symbolised poignantly her neglect, the lack of someone in her life who cared especially for her. Lyndall believes that it was after this visit that Tom pointed out to Antonia that a one-to-one relationship with a foster mother would be a much better way of looking after Susan's physical and emotional welfare. In this way Tom inadvertently had laid claim to Silas's daughter; he had seen the baby before her own father had, and had been instrumental in a decision about her health and happiness. This was another reason for Antonia to feel, on some subliminal level, that Tom would make a most reliable and sympathetic parent too.

Silas, meanwhile, was unaware that there was a distinct shift in hope and expectation back home. He was completely taken up with the insecurity of his own career. By February 1930 he had accepted the job with the Narcozari Copper Company at their Los Pilares mine 3,000 feet up in the mountains of Sonora in north-western Mexico. But the Depression that followed the Wall Street crash was to continue to thwart his ambitions. Hoping to be involved with further exploration he was met with the news that any expansion had been abandoned for the time being as the price of copper had fallen so drastically. The only job available was as '*jefe de las muestras*', head of the mine sampling department, which was responsible for the calculation of the reserves of copper in the rock already being worked. This was a dead-end job, as far as Silas was concerned, but he felt he had to take it in order to continue to earn enough money to send back for Susan's costs in the nursery and for partial support of Antonia. He also was trying to save a lump sum to buy his passage home and begin a new life with his wife and their baby. As he surveyed the magnificent mountain landscape of the Sierra Madre, which made access from vertiginous mine to precarious settlement alarming and strenuous, Silas realised it was increasingly unlikely that Antonia would settle happily there. Listening to the sounds of gunshot at night from the Mexican village in the valley across from the mine (in the eight months that Silas was living in the compound twelve men were killed in gunfights) it became clear that a metropolitan woman, however much she liked the idea of soldierly honour and war, was not going to appreciate this lawless, frontier brawling: neither would someone so lacking in competence in either physical or practical ways feel a natural affinity for this hard, uncultured, rudimentary life. Some of the murderous activity was the result of the settling of old scores after a violent rebel uprising, against the revolutionary-turned-repressive dictator, Plutarco Elias Calles, was ruthlessly crushed. Rebels had been summarily hung from the telegraph poles beside the railway and their corpses left to rot in the wind as a terrible warning. There was a campaign too against the Roman Catholic Church; the stand taken against this by individual priests, and their subsequent persecution, is the subject of Graham Greene's masterpiece *The Power and the Glory*.

It is interesting that Antonia's attraction to the idea of being a soldier did not come from a longing for a physical and adventurous life. She was drawn much more to the institution of the Army, its orderliness, discipline, hierarchy and structures, bound by what she saw romantically as the pure masculine principles of simple valour and incorruptible integrity. The idea of joining Silas in some pioneering, backwoods community never seriously crossed her mind.

If Silas had been happier about his personal circumstances he would have enjoyed his time in Mexico more; as it was he felt defeated by fate. He began to rise at 4.30 in the morning to study mathematics before work, so determined did he become to get an academic job that he might live a more civilised life. His letters to Antonia became less frequent, as hers were to him. He had been keen that she go and visit his mother in Derbyshire, which she did after the New Year, possibly taking Susan with her. But Antonia had thought that as she and Silas were engaged, Silas had writtten to his mother to tell her the news, and was rather disconcerted to find that Mrs Glossop never once referred to this fact during the whole visit. Silas assured her that this was only a symptom of a family trait: 'as soon as we really want to express our feelings we intravert at once.'[33] Silas's sister Elspeth wrote to him that she had been to an enjoyable party at Antonia and Eric's house in Paultons Square where charades were riotously acted out; and his best friend, Frank Freeman, wrote how 'ravishing' Antonia was looking, which made Silas quite jealous he told her in a letter. Reading this letter years later Antonia was seized with guilt at the unhappiness she had caused: '. . . of course, all that meant . . . Tom!'[34]

Silas, feeling even more isolated from that gay Chelsea life of which he had fleetingly been a part, wrote rather wanly, 'Would you mind a normal husband so much, I sometimes feel that work in London, and a flat in Fulham with Tony, is all that I ask of fate'.[35] And in a letter written five days later he admitted he was thinking a lot about his daughter. He felt 'that she should be supported with something resembling normal parents; as near as you & I can get to it anyway'.[36] From Silas's half of the correspondence it was clear that Antonia alternated between sending him occasionally inspiring letters full of interest and affection and unhappy, even accusatory, ones where she felt utterly abandoned and unconvinced that he ever meant to return. Both types of communication were liable to include a request for money, which Silas appeared to do his best to fulfil, although he kept on asking her to be as frugal as possible as he had to save for his passage home. His life consisted solely of work and study, with neither the time nor spare money for play; there was little drink, no cigarettes or entertainment (the brothel being the centre of all leisure activities) to enliven his life. But, as Silas had stayed away for a total of nineteen months, perhaps Antonia had good reason to fear that he was not as keen to return and get married as he professed to be.

Still living with Eric, Antonia's affair with Tom continued through the summer of 1930. Tom was engaged in some prison visiting, and also bought a small and rickety car he called their 'horse', for trips to the country. Not only was he seeing Antonia daily, he was also full of the kind of sympathy and admiration which flowed so easily from him. He also offered her the greatest gift of all – interest and encouragement to continue with her writing. He was a fellow aspiring writer whom she could work alongside at last, someone with whom to share similar frustrations and hopes, reading each other's work and offering praise and constructive criticism. Tom was working on a novel at the time and was reading one of Antonia's stories, still in progress. Set in the South of France, it was most likely to be 'Mon Pays c'est la Martinique', a story particularly noticeable for the tenderness of its feeling and tone. Perhaps, the romantic, yet protectively fraternal, affection that she felt for Tom at the time informed something of this story's sweetness. Having read her story he wrote to her: 'It is intolerably beautiful. You are an artist – much more an artist than I am. You are the perfect pancake – I the Irish Stew'.[37]

Although Silas was still writing in early summer that he would need at least until the end of the year to have saved enough money to be able to afford his fare back, the dramatic decline in the price of copper at the beginning of September 1930 meant the mine immediately made him redundant. This external event propelled him home a few months early.

He caught the boat train to London via Southampton and arrived late at night, some time around 12 September. Antonia met him at the station. Silas recalled that he took one look at her and by the extraordinary change in her looks he knew immediately that trouble was coming. Emotional confusion and having to make a choice always paralysed Antonia with fear. Everyone who knew her intimately and had seen her through one of her distraught and destroying moods knew the frightening physical metamorphosis which came over her. She knew it too, and feared and hated it; 'Why can't I be like other people? . . . I never know when I look in the glass what I shall see'.[38] Tom gave the most complete description of this distressing phenomenon:

> Nothing is more startling than the rapidity of her physical changes . . . I've known her undergo changes which could, I am certain be verified with tape-measure and scales. I have seen her put on six pounds in an hour under the influence of misery. I have seen her unable to wear clothes today, & to-morrow, when she is well, have to haul them in round her. I have seen her hair radiant & glossy in the morning, fall to rank snakes' tails in the afternoon. I have seen [her] old one day & next morning for next to no reason become a girl, really a girl. I have seen her face a perfect, most delicate & ethereal oval: her features exquisite: her skin as fresh & new as a child's: her whole face *sweet*, contented witty. I have seen it in a few hours collapse & put on twenty years, her features stiffen & set, her skin crinkle & age, the flesh of her face sag into a heavy Neronian scowl. She could be a daughter of the morning or an 18th century debauched marquis all in the same day.[39]

It was not the daughter of the morning who greeted Silas on his return home after nineteen months away. The uneasy couple took a taxi to the lodgings Antonia had arranged for him. In an attempt to defuse the situation, Silas began to talk about his plans for their life together. But Antonia could not contain her anxiety and fear, and suddenly the anger this engendered in her fizzed up: 'Can't you see that I have been living with this man all the time?' she blurted out harshly.[40] This came as a shattering surprise, but Silas was not one to react emotionally immediately. He asked who this man was and for the first time was told about the existence of Tom Hopkinson.

This was the beginning of ten weeks of emotional turmoil for all three of them. Antonia's confusion and inability to choose between the two men in her life, and the resultant stress, propelled her into a pathological state. 'Uncertainty, suspense . . . they have always been a

torture to me producing an absolutely paralysing effect.'[41] She veered
from one to the other. Each of the men found his desire to marry
Antonia intensified by the existence of a rival and the heightened
emotion of the situation. For Antonia, their contrasting claims on her
affection seemed impossible to resolve. Silas was someone she had
considered as her 'true love'; he was the father of her child; their
forthcoming marriage was approved by her own father before he died;
he was a decent and good man who would do his best by her and Susan.
But Tom was the brother she had never had; the literary collaborator;
the ready sympathiser and emotional support. There was Eric too to
consider, with whom Antonia was still living. He had reluctantly agreed
to have their marriage annulled, but would happily continue just as
before, as a loving companion with both of them free to pursue their
erotic lives elsewhere.

After the inauspicious reunion, Antonia decided at first that it was
Silas whom she should marry after all, and wrote to explain this decision
to Tom. His letter in reply, was eminently civilised, generous and fond:
'We have shot the lovely albatross, my dear & you must make
something out of what we have done . . . & in the end you will make it
right & you will make all three of you happy.' He was also very clever,
for he mentioned the things, precious to Antonia, which he had offered,
and which they could no longer share; the criticism of each other's
writing, the tender concern for her welfare, and most telling of all, his
promise of money. 'You must do this for me, Tony. You must
remember I have money. I have lots in hoard. Soon I shall be making
more than I use. For my sake, if you need some ask me, let me.'[42]

This was to prove one of the deciding factors for Antonia. A few
years later she was to recognise the significant connection: 'Money
comes into all my relations with men . . . I believe I wouldn't marry Si
because he had no money. I believe I married Tom because he had a
regular job and a hundred pounds or two. Reggie the same . . . It's
something very important I have never faced before.'[43] The pendulum
swung back in Tom's favour. But once Tom had broken the news of his
and Antonia's engagement to his parents, and they had heard the bare
facts of their prospective daughter-in-law's former life, everyone was
plunged into another emotional imbroglio. On the face of it, their
anxieties were only to be expected; Antonia was six years older than
their twenty-five-year-old, boyish-looking son. It was his first serious
relationship: she had been twice married before, the marriages each
annulled for non-consummation. There was a period of incarceration in
the notorious Bethlem Asylum and, somehow along the way, she had
had an illegitimate child by a man other than her two previous husbands.

It was a mercy that Antonia's future parents-in-law were spared the details of the certificate of virginity signed by the Pope, the other affairs and the abortion. Tom's father was so concerned as it was that he travelled down to London from Carlisle and offered in anguish to help Tom disentangle himself. Tom was adamant that he intended to marry Antonia, but realised that his usually supine and inexpressive parent must have been driven into a state of some despair to risk such an emotional scene. However, he and Antonia, and Silas, were exhausted by the fraught emotional see-sawing of the situation. Every nerve was raw. Great poetry was enlisted in the debate. Antonia gave a copy of Shakespeare's sonnets to Silas, with numbers 107, 109 and 122 marked for his particular attention. Sonnet 109 carried a particular message of hope:

> O, never say that I was false of heart,
> Though absence seem'd my flame to qualify!
> As easy might I from myself depart,
> As from my soul, where in thy breast doth lie:
> That is my home of love: if I have rang'd,
> Like him that travels, I return again;
> Just to the time, not with the time exchanged,
> So that myself bring water for my stain.

Meanwhile both Tom and Antonia were disturbed, for different reasons, by his parents' uncompromising opposition to their marriage. They had gone on 21 October to see Noël Coward in the first night of his new play *Private Lives* at the Phoenix Theatre. In the interval, stirred up by Coward's desolate view of love, and undermined by the rejection of Tom's family, Antonia provoked a row with Tom. Hurt by her inability to elicit from him the usual reassurances, she rushed out of the theatre and hailed a taxi, on 'a headlong flight to Silas after Tom's rejection of me'.[44] She fell into Silas's arms and enjoyed a sexual intimacy that night which she claimed was more profound than anything she had known before. 'I felt true & positive' she wrote, believing that it was here, after all, that she belonged, with the father of her child, the man she loved and had promised to marry.[45] Silas told his daughter Susan of his own relief and pleasure. 'In all the years that I knew her it was the one occasion on which her company brought me unalloyed happiness. She was kind, she was sympathetic, she was gay, she was fond: but all too soon she said she must go'.[46] He had thought then that after the weeks of hope and despair, the nightmare at last was over. But in retrospect he felt that Antonia had already finally made up her mind to marry Tom.

In fact she was as racked with uncertainty as ever. Tom came round to Paultons Square the next day to apologise and explain, and once more Antonia was bound to the fiery wheel, unable to stop her tortured spinning. She dragged everyone else into the flames. This was one of the manifestations of the manic swing in her disease. Her mind was racing, her senses overstimulated, her actions impulsive and bizarre. Antonia had a compulsive need to take violent action to escape fear and pain: she was prone to flail wildly rather than contemplate the situation, or withdraw. At this point, recognising that she had become so over-wrought she was incapable of any rational decision, Eric made his point of view known. He thought she could be happy with Tom: to make the transition from living with him to living with Tom easier, he was willing to swop Paultons Square with Tom's flat in Great Smith Street. Antonia would thereby continue to live in the same place, but with a different man. This sounded the death knell for Silas's hopes. This may have been an unwarranted and self-interested intervention on Eric's part. His opinion carried enormous authority with Antonia. Perhaps he preferred the idea of Tom as Antonia's next husband, rather than the less-known Silas, who may have threatened Eric's supremacy in Antonia's life. In retrospect, Antonia recognised with remorse that this ultimate rejection damaged Silas profoundly. Djuna Barnes, who was to know Silas even better than Antonia did, later accused her of giving poison to the wrong man. Silas recalled that those ten weeks of emotional turmoil, renewed intimacy and hopes destroyed were 'the most unpleasant period of my life'. Antonia thought in retrospect, however, that although she would never know if she had made the wrong decision, she feared that 'to have married him in the state I was in could have brought him no happiness'.[47] And that was the saddest fact of all, for when Antonia was in the grip of her 'beast', there was no happiness for anyone, least of all herself.

Having made the fateful decision, Tom's father's final anxiety had to be addressed. He had told his son that he was frightened that Antonia's history of madness might make it inadvisable to have children. The thirties were a time when the new science of eugenics was being employed even by otherwise liberal governments, like Sweden, with the intention of cleansing the nation of physical and mental defectives of various kinds. Gross mental illness, such as Antonia had suffered, was one of the human propensities whose eradication, through sterilisation and isolation, was least disputed by adherents to this movement. As an idea that had entered the collective unconscious of the time, Antonia must have found the legacy from her childhood of self-loathing and the sense of unworthiness was etched even deeper by this quasi-scientific judgement on people who suffered like her. Sensitivity to this movement might explain some of the extremes to which Antonia and Tom went in order to put Canon Hopkinson's mind at rest – and perhaps Tom's own. He managed to track down one of the doctors who treated Antonia in Bethlem and took her to see him again on 20 November. They went armed with an affidavit as to her mental fitness from a doctor friend of Antonia's, Douglas McClean, who was himself married to Kathleen Hale, the artist who was to become famous as the creator of 'Orlando the Marmalade Cat'. The doctor from Bethlem, Percy Smith, wrote the required letter declaring that her acute collapse in 1921–22 was due to prolonged mental stress, and was unlikely to be any kind of inherited disorder which could threaten any future children with mental disease.

By the time that this assurance arrived in the last week of November, Antonia was already pregnant, and may well have just become aware of the fact. The dates of the conception and birth of Lyndall, her second daughter, are significant. Given the emotional turmoil and confusion in the lives of Antonia and her two suitors at the time, no one could be certain who was the father. Lyndall was born at midnight between 22 and 23 July 1931. Antonia mentioned that she was late. If she was a week late, then that put her conception date at around the third week in October the previous year, just when Antonia was at her most distraught, fleeing from Tom to seek reassurance with Silas, only to be wooed back again by Tom.

By the time she can have known that she was most probably pregnant, Antonia had already thrown her lot in with Tom. It suited her now, whatever her doubts about who this baby's father might be, to make it a child which she and Tom had created. She had married Tom for security and a sense of family and it was essential that no doubts about the paternity of this baby should be allowed to surface in his mind, or even hers. It suited her also to allow Susan to believe that Tom was her father too, although that deception was to end when she was eight. Years later Joan Souter-Robertson, who knew and was fond of all the members of this extended family – and brought her portraitist's eye to bear on their likenesses – pointed out something very obvious. Lyndall not only looked like her elder sister Susan, Silas Glossop's acknowledged daughter, but as she grew older she looked increasingly like Silas himself. Neither of the girls, in height and build particularly, looked much like Antonia. At bad moments in Antonia's life, when her daughters were unfurling their beauty as they reached their teens, this disparity in looks between her and them was a source for her of irritation and jealousy.

Joan was a very good friend to Silas and his family until she died, and she mentioned to him one day her suspicions that not only Susan but Lyndall too was his daughter. He told her it was certainly possible, and left it at that. By then, the family connections had become so complicated and painful that perhaps it seemed better to leave that stone at least unturned. Joan had also mentioned this to Lyndall, to whom of course it did matter. Obscuring the truth of a child's origins can deprive her of a natural sense of identity and belonging. Antonia did not set out to deceive, for she could not have been certain whose baby she was carrying at the time she got married. However, it was convenient for her to assume this baby was Tom's and to continue in that assumption, long after Tom had relinquished his emotional care for Lyndall. Never at ease in triangular relationships, Antonia was fearful of too close a conspiracy between her two daughters, for she always saw it as an alliance against herself. Even though she may have wondered at the likeness between them, it probably suited her to keep these girls fundamentally separated in one crucial area, their paternity. That way she remained the only one in the complex family dynamics of Silas, Tom, Susan and Lyndall, to be the central cog, intimately connected to them all. In pursuing a course of action which seemed to make life easier for the adults involved, Antonia inevitably ignored a much more important factor for her child's own emotional integrity. Again, as had been the case with her first baby Susan, Antonia was incapable of empathising with this child as an individual with her own needs, and the right to knowledge and the truth. With Susan, the deception that she was Tom's daughter was only ended on the urgings of an analyst. For these two girls, the confusion and resultant rivalries over their fathers was a hurtful opposition manufactured by this negligence of the truth. Certainly Antonia knew that her third choice of husband was as 'against nature' as her first two, for different reasons, had been. 'Silas came back from Mexico, loving me like a man and I rejected him. I knew Tom to be at that time cowardly, undecided, unstable, yet I accepted him, believed in him, married him though with a cold exhausted heart'.[48]

Within a week of Dr Smith's letter being written, Tom and Antonia were married in Carlisle Cathedral with Tom's father, as Canon in Residence, officiating. It was early in the morning of 29 November 1930. The great austere cathedral was still bitterly cold, and Antonia was emotionally half-dead and physically drained. There were no friends to support them: not even her mother was there. The hostility of Tom's parents to this marriage was palpable, and yet only on their insistence were she and Tom enduring this dispiriting ceremony against their own convictions, Tom's atheism and her own lapsed Catholicism. On their marriage certificate Antonia was married with the full panoply of her baptised names: Eirene Adeline Prisca Mary Magdalene, and the hated surname, Botting – of which two previous marriages had failed to relieve her. She chose not to give her age and both gave their profession as 'writer'. Perhaps it was a measure of the disintegrated state of her mind that she could have overlooked something so fundamental to her Faith; only years later did Antonia realise that this Anglican marriage resulted in her excommunication from her own Church.

At the small reception afterwards Antonia was overcome with exhaustion and emotion, and collapsed. Already six weeks pregnant, she was probably suffering from the tiredness and vulnerability of early pregnancy, but, more obviously, it was the culmination of a desperate ten weeks of near madness for them all. It was the end of the hopes Antonia had had for herself and Silas. She never felt any sense of rightness and inevitability about her union with Tom, but she thought she had made a pragmatic choice which would protect her and her children and bring them all some security and happiness. 'I *always* thought there was a "curse" on our marriage: my father's curse presumably & this was heavily re-inforced by his [Tom's] parents' extreme disapproval of me and the marriage.'[49] As Tom had said, they had shot the lovely albatross and now had to make what they could of it. Antonia expressed it with a bleak matter-of-factness, eight years later:

> I killed Silas's natural, if late-born, affection for his child by my refusal to marry him when he wanted it so much. I salved my conscience by thinking that Tom would never in any circumstances desert Susan & Lyndall and I was wrong.[50]

10

The Writer . . .

Tom's the only man who has ever *stimulated* me to write. Though mixed
with jealousy and various things, I did get that from him, especially at
first.

26 May 1948, unpublished dream diaries

After such an inauspicious wedding day, the honeymoon was hardly
much warmer or more expansive. As chilled November turned into
frozen December, the newly-weds borrowed Canon Hopkinson's little
car and set off for Scotland, where they snatched a few days walking in
the hills round the Solway Firth; it was all the leave Tom had been able
to negotiate from Crawford's. They returned to London to a new flat
off the Fulham Road, a less fashionable and attractive neighbourhood
than Chelsea, where Antonia had always felt most at home. 18 Cecil
Court was a large flat with spacious, light-filled rooms in the front, and a
warren of smaller less-favoured rooms at the back. These were to
become the children's quarters. It was more than Tom felt they could
afford; already there was a conflict in his and Antonia's attitudes to
money. Tom hated to be in debt and tried to manage his affairs by
staying within the bounds of his resources. Antonia, it seemed, could
only manage to live on credit and if ever, by fluke or good fortune, she
should slip from the red into the black, she would rapidly release the
brakes on her spending and restore her debt to its previous level.
Redecorating her apartments, buying furniture and beautifying herself
with new clothes, hair styling, and especially hats, were the areas where
she was most drawn to extravagance. At times her compulsion to spend
money she did not have on things she did not need reached pathological
proportions, an expression of the manic stage of her mental illness. It
was the cause of terrible guilt and grief.

However, Tom and Antonia's first joint purchase augured well. They
asked a local carpenter to make them an identical pair of plywood desks.
These cost £5 each and were installed side by side in their main living

room. This was a statement about the priorities in their marriage, and an intention to fulfil their marital promise that they were writers, as witnessed before State and God. Writing was at first the most important area of harmony and collaboration between them. They read each other's work, and encouraged and criticised. Each felt from the start, however, that this was in the end all their relationship should have been and that the marriage was somehow deeply bogus. Tom, assessing his life years later, admitted that he had 'made use of Tony' in order to lose his virginity and gain 'the knowledge I needed' to love other women. But he felt that his betrayal of her was as a result of feeling he was himself cheated and used. 'I felt that, by our marriage, she had used me to get herself out of a situation: & I was taking my revenge.'[1]

Antonia had always said that she was puzzled by why she suddenly attached herself so strongly to Tom. She did not love him – she barely liked him in the beginning – but he was somehow connected powerfully in her mind with her father. Cecil Botting would certainly have disapproved most strongly of her taking yet another lover, and would have deplored her dishonourable treatment of Silas, but there was a compulsive attraction in the fact that Tom was the sort of man her father would have liked to be, charming and attractive, cerebral and poetic, yet with evident sporting prowess and an ability to get on in the world. Perhaps most tellingly, she thought he was the sort of man she might have been herself, if she had been the son for whom her father had longed. Yet her guilt in marrying him, and her sense of her father's disapproval, increased markedly after the wedding. Her relationships remained complicated and distorted by her father's clutch, even from beyond the grave.

Antonia's own analyses of her third marriage were complex and extensive, and the 'soulmate' motif, the lost brother, the male side of herself, appeared in different guises. 'Funnily enough, on my side it has always been rather like [Platonic love]. I've always felt that whatever it is that Tom & I have doesn't naturally express itself in sex . . . our real thing has been something different . . . a sudden marvellous harmony of spirit.'[2] Antonia also gave Tom all the credit for her completion of her first novel, sixteen years after she had first begun.

But before Antonia was able to pick up her pen again for her own neglected writing, she had to go back to work. She took a job in Harrods's advertising department, but still managing to retain her freelance status. She hated working there; she was treated like a hack with none of the appreciation for her work she had commanded at Crawford's. But also she was growing more tired and alienated from her increasingly pregnant body. The few letters between Antonia and Tom which exist from that time are full of affection and gratitude for each other's kindness, but there is an underlying strain of anxiety and problems to which both allude. These two letters give an idea of their expectations and responses to each other, hers showing her battle with her approaching depression.

> Tom, my darling dear, [Antonia wrote in the spring of 1931 when six months pregnant] . . . Oh, sweetheart, you *are* good and patient with me. I wish we could get away by ourselves just for a little bit and forget all about families . . . I've got everything any reasonable person could want to make them happy. I think I'm just tired of always having to carry another person about with me & never be either by myself or alone with you. Darling, I am a selfish pig, but it's partly because I love you & we've had so little time together without worry of some sort or another . . . Please stop me from getting altogether dead: I think you can . . . we're all right really – if we don't go to sleep in the snow. Or rather, if I don't. You're too much alive to be in real danger.[3]

> Dearest and only Tony, [was Tom's reply] Your letters . . . are so full of you it almost makes me cry to read . . . Oh Tony you're not silly to wish to have time to see things & one another, and I wish to God we had. And oh you must be tired of always having someone else sitting on your chest. It is such a load for you that it is quite hard to remember this monster may even be an actual positive source of happiness to us . . . Remember too Tony that your sadness is for want of your own self again, & I do guess how you must long to have it. I do too. And when you have that you will find far more pleasure in our lovely house & in going about & meeting people on fair & equal terms & in building up your book – which will be a real building made of proper bricks.[4]

Antonia was at her best and happiest when she was in a social situation, preferably playing the host to friends in her own home. She was not a relaxed or natural cook, and she and Tom were not well off enough to fund drinks parties, so instead she invited friends to tea on Sunday afternoons where talk was the main attraction. Geoffrey Grigson, who was just beginning to make his way as a littérateur, remembered these gatherings with gratitude. 'I learned much (if in a timid way) from Sundays *chez* Antonia White, in which I experienced a sub-Parisian *chic*, I suppose I might call it, a Chelsea *chic*.'[5] He dismissed her literary skills but warmly recalled her physical charms: 'exquisitely pretty, and pink, and plump (and mentally insecure).'[6] Tom, like Silas, described the particular fascination of Antonia's conversation and her gaiety and quick sense of humour. Unlike Silas, however, Tom found the disparity between her social facility and his shy moroseness in such situations was something which he resented. He was proud and competitive and did not enjoy activities where he could not excel. Antonia had many more friends, and they were a varied and interesting bunch: Tom always felt he would rather be off in the country or playing sport, where at least his own sense of inadequacy would be stilled.

This group of friends included at the time: Geoffrey Grigson and his attractive American wife Frances; the artist Kathleen Hale, who had been secretary to Augustus John; Alick Schepeler, a tall, thin, dissatisfied beauty who worked for *Vogue* and had also been singled out by John to become his model and mistress; Eliot Seabrooke, Antonia's old friend from the pre-asylum *Sugar House* days, an attractive Post-impressionist painter and prominent member of the London Group of artists; the architectural writer John Summerson; and Frank Freeman and Joan Souter-Robertson. Sunday tea time at Antonia's was an established event, frequented by an even wider range of friends once she became famous after the publication of *Frost in May*.

But first of all Antonia had to deal with certain domestic matters, not least her coming baby. The pregnancy went on for at least a week longer than expected. Antonia naturally suffered from extreme impatience in all situations; hating being heavily pregnant as much as she did, those extra days must have been very difficult for her to bear. Her mother, who had so terrorised her with stories of the torment of unanaesthetised childbirth when she was younger, came up to stay at Cecil Court to be close to her. Tom too was sympathetic for he surmised that his new wife felt physical pain much more acutely than the average person. He had noticed with some amazement how literally thin-skinned Antonia was: how even a silk dress which chafed would cause a weal, how easily she bruised, how taking her arm to draw her attention to something hurt her. He realised she was mortified by even the thought of pain. At home, with his mother-in-law, Tom wrote a fond note to his wife on the verge of entering once more, what was to Antonia, the personal hell of labour: 'Oh my darling cat I do want you back. There is a nice swept hearth & warm coals & a boiling kettle, and blue & white chintz curtains, and everything except the one essential puss. Shall I ever cease to bear a grudge against my own descendant for taking up so much of you & of your time.'[7]

At last the baby was born at midnight between 22 and 23 July, another girl, although Antonia was not as disappointed that she had failed to produce a son as she had been at Susan's birth. The birth was easier than her first, but the post-partum was much more difficult and Antonia had to stay on at the nursing home, unwell and recuperating, possibly from the effects of having a retained placenta which had had to be extracted. She and Tom named the baby Lyndall, after the main character in *The Story of an African Farm*, Olive Schreiner's classic novel which they had both been reading and much discussed.

For Antonia, childbirth combined in her mind extremes of humiliation and suffering with the threat of permanent loss of something intrinsic and precious to herself. 'Funny how I literally *retained* my second child and was ill for long after and still bear physical traces [six years later]. I recovered completely from Susan. I think I *accepted* the experience of having Susan in a way that I was unable to accept the experience of having Lyndall. I think I regard both children as having robbed me of something vital.'[8] Part of Antonia's lack of acceptance of the experience of having this baby was to do with her continued ambivalence about Tom. She never really managed to overcome her reservations about him, or her sense that she may well have made the worst decision of her life in choosing him over Silas. The sense of being robbed expressed something she felt for many years about her children, that she forcibly had had to relinquish to them her own claim on the care of others. Motherhood robbed her of physical youthfulness; her freedom from responsibility; her independence and her identity. Children were also an added financial burden in a life blighted by anxiety about and mismanagement of money. Antonia tended to see their existence in these negative terms until she began to appreciate her daughters as interesting individuals who could offer her pleasure, affection, and the chance to learn. But by then she had damaged profoundly their natural filial love and trust in her, and had nurtured instead competitiveness, jealousy and a struggle for power; her rights and needs against theirs. Her love and appreciation of them came too late to overcome those baleful early lessons of fear and rejection.

While Antonia was at the nursing home, a young woman came to see her, recommended by Tom's boss's nanny as a good person to look after babies and children. Mary Hitchcock's experience had been gained working in a Dr Barnardo's home. She was hired by Antonia and Tom to live in and take full responsibility, not only for the baby Lyndall but for Susan, who was now nearly two years old. Mary Hitchcock, who was to become known as 'Nurse' by her two charges, took the baby back to Cecil Court, leaving Antonia behind in the nursing home to regain her strength. She had not even attempted to breastfeed Lyndall after the difficulties and physical revulsion she had experienced when attempting to feed Susan. According to Mary Hitchcock, a few days after her arrival at Cecil Court, a woman came to the flat with Susan and handed the little girl over to Mary's care. Susan called this woman 'Mummy'. She was probably a foster mother who had been arranged to care for Susan as a result of Tom's outrage when he first saw Antonia's little daughter at her residential nursery, a year previously. This move made Susan suffer a double emotional wrench. The woman she had grown to think of as her mother had disappeared, never to be seen again, and the woman who now looked after her had another more demanding little person to care for, whom she appeared to favour. In her memoir, Susan recalled being unimpressed with her 'cry-baby' sister whom 'Nurse had to fuss over continually.'[9]

Antonia eventually returned to the flat and Nurse's routine and the 'maternal' affection Tom showed both these infants soon established a continuum of family life which was secure and happy enough. When undistracted by personal woe or his own romantic entanglements, Tom loved these children with a tenderness which showed in his diary entries, charting their progress and the charming and interesting comments they made to him and each other. His affection for Antonia deepened: the creation of this small family unit gave him a purpose and status and made him feel more secure. While Antonia was still recuperating, they decided to take a quick break in the South of France again. Cassis was their destination, a dazzlingly picturesque fishing village where the Bloomsbury painters Vanessa Bell and Duncan Grant had made their Mediterranean base and attracted the other 'Bloomsberries' on various occasions over the years. It had already gained great cachet with a select band of well-connected writers and artists, and, although she never became a part of this society, walking through the streets of Cassis gave Antonia a sense of being part of a milieu where she felt she belonged, with people and a way of life to which she aspired. Cast over all was the magic of the Mediterranean evening light, 'when the whole air used to thicken and grow coloured.'[10] Tom believed that Antonia's return to health dated from that holiday. He remembered particularly one evening when they scrambled home along the base of the cliff, caught out by a sudden storm, and he noticed a change for the better in Antonia's strength and stamina.

Soon after their return, however, Tom had to go to hospital to have his appendix removed. It was November, the hospital was the Hampstead General in Haverstock Hill, Antonia was serving her unhappy sentence at Harrods in Knightsbridge: almost every night after work she would set off on the cold and difficult journey up the hill carrying some special foodstuffs or books to keep him amused. As a result of her own suffering, Antonia was capable of great kindness and insight when she was able to apprehend the suffering in others. Too often she was blinded to the unhappiness of those around her by the demands of her own obsessive nature, but when someone was reduced to helplessness and required her aid, she forgot her own neurotic battles and was generous and selfless in her care. Antonia had written about how great was her pleasure as a young child, when fantasising about saving Gerard, the boy she loved, from some terrible torture and threat and then consoling him and restoring him to fitness. She began to understand better her children and more readily sympathise with them on the few occasions she was called upon to nurse them through illness. It was one of the expressions of the grand leitmotiv of her life; her need for power and her fear of the power of others – under which lay her sense of her own powerlessness.

During this time of dependency, Tom was never more in her thrall, his letters to her from the hospital were full of love and a peculiar abjectness. 'I love you Tony. I love your beautiful, soft, bright body. I love your bright eyes & your lovely skin & your little hands & small neat feet & I love your fine golden hair & little teeth. I love them & I love you & I long to be back where I ought to be, by your side, at your table, at my desk, by your fireside, in your bed.'[11] All his letters read as an attempt to make Antonia seem domestic and tame, something small and cosy and pet-like. She expressed this aspect most clearly while Tom was disabled in hospital, but he knew and she knew, all too well, that this was only a small part of the truth about her. Antonia was anything but tame, and could be a very frightening animal indeed.

One of her less tame parts was her writing, not the advertising copy nor the slick magazine articles, but the work wrought from her own experiences and shaped by the hard-edged part of herself. That November 'The Saint' was published by Desmond MacCarthy in *Life and Letters*. It was a story she had written to have something to read to Tom. Drawing on the knowledge she had gained from her time at the Convent, and the distinctive atmosphere of a religious establishment, it was nevertheless not directly based on experience. Nevertheless, it was a precursor to *Frost in May* and had as one of its main characters a spirited girl called Charlotte, the friend Charlotte d'Erlanger who became Léonie de Wesseldorf in her novel. This story dealt with the unexpected nature of sainthood and the perception of miracles, and Logan Pearsall Smith, an elderly American aesthete and habitué of Chelsea and Bloomsbury, wrote her an enthusiastic and encouraging letter. He said she and her story were discussed at a lunch party where Arnold Bennett had declared it a 'perfect story, & that he has read it three times.'[12] He went on to tell her she had a real talent and should make the most of it. The contents of this letter had been relayed to Tom in his hospital bed, along, perhaps, with a sense of disappointment that she had wasted so much time already and was thirty-two years old with nothing significant to show for her gift. Tom then gave her the confidence and permission to excel in her writing – something her father she felt had destroyed in her – with a work that was bigger and more demanding; the novel which she was just beginning to resurrect. 'You have all the best years for writing ahead, & need have no fear to set your ambition out of sight above the snow line.'[13] It was interesting that he used this snow metaphor when one of the folk tales which obsessed Antonia was about the dangers of lying down to sleep in snow because there you would die, overcome by the cold or a new fall of snow. He was encouraging her not only to be ambitious with her writing, but also to break out of the stasis of the snowbound, and live.

He was himself planning to write a novel, autobiographical and unpublishable as it turned out, about a young man who went into advertising but really wanted to be a writer. Antonia had come across a few half-formed chapters of a novel about her convent experiences which she had first sketched out at St Paul's when she was about sixteen. She was laughing as she read them to herself and Tom asked her what was so amusing. She began to read aloud to him and he was immediately impressed. However, she was distracted from progressing with it by anxiety and negativity about what she had already done. Tom urged her to concentrate instead on getting the book finished, and only start the analysis then.

By the beginning of 1932, Antonia had returned to a full-time job again at Crawford's, forced back by her unhappiness at Harrods and the household's general lack of money. By the spring, Tom had left Crawford's for the publicity department at Odhams Press, where he was largely employed in thinking up ideas and writing copy for the gifts used to lure people into signing up subscriptions for the Odhams group of newspapers, the *Daily Herald*, the *People* and *Sporting Life*. Their writing consoled them for the uncreativity of their jobs and bound them together in mutual support and endeavour.

More importantly for Antonia, Tom's belief in her and encourage-ment of her writing self released her from the curse of her father's words: '. . . sink of filth and impurity . . . never had a daughter'.[14] This thundering denouncement had made Antonia fearful of the depravity her real writing might reveal; Tom offered a benign reflection of herself as a writer. Her fractured sense of her own identity was pieced back together, for a time at least, by his belief in her talent and his reassurance of her lovableness. 'Tom destroyed my guilt about writing' she wrote in her diary, and was never to lose her gratitude to him for this.[15] It was an extraordinary liberation for her after nearly twenty years of stops and starts and 'one or two decent short stories'.[16] However, it gave Tom a power over her which made her uneasy. What he could give he could also take away.

They instituted a routine of sitting side by side in the evenings after work, or sometimes at the weekends, and working on their respective novels. Tom set Antonia a deadline of one chapter a week, to be read to him every Saturday night. This teacher-pupil relationship was familiar to her from her Greek lessons with her father, and then her time at the Convent with the nuns. She had found strict discipline helped her most; she responded to constraints and had been eager to please. Tom provided her again with a structure within which she could perform, but proved to be a benign and encouraging teacher. Suddenly the words which had been dammed up inside her for so long began to flow. *Frost in May* grew into a perfect work of art, a small masterpiece, 'the only book I have written with no trouble.'[17] Strongly autobiographical, it told the story of Nanda Grey, a young convert who entered the exotic and hermetic society of the Convent of the Five Wounds at seven, and then after a shocking débâcle was forced to leave at the age of fourteen, before her time there had run its natural course. She was an outsider to this highly ritualised, hierarchical and seductive world where there was an unstable, at times hysterical level of emotion in both the pupils and the nuns.

But Antonia recorded everything through the intelligent, curious, spirited persona of Nanda. She used a detached, precise style which conveyed brilliantly the outraged spirit of a naturally fair-minded child, as well as the passion she felt for the place, the religion which animated it and the friends she found there. This and a cool ironic humour justified Elizabeth Bowen's claim, in an introduction written in 1948, that Antonia's style as a storyteller shared much with Jane Austen. Her characters were real and memorable too; the dashing figure of Léonie de Wesseldorf had a life all her own, much more subtly drawn than the usual schoolgirl heroine but sharing some of the swash and buckle of the best of them. Mother Bradshaw too, with the psychological finesse of the Grand Inquisitor, loomed as a sinister figure, yet also tragic and vulnerable. Years later Antonia realised that she had not given any thought to the nuns' stories, their own fears and feelings, yet it was the very narrowness of the viewpoint in following Nanda's experience alone which made the book so intense and distilled.

Perfectly poised, *Frost in May* leads the reader on pitilessly to the climax which, although it shows Nanda overwrought and prostrate with grief, keeps to its characteristically pared down style. And there was something right and true about Antonia's courage in leaving Nanda at the end, neither redeemed nor reconciled, but broken and alone. In fact the intimation of what had actually happened to Nanda is even more shocking; the nuns had warned their new charge that their job was to break her will and then re-set it in God's own way. There is a sense that with the final denouncement by her father, reinforced insidiously by Mother Bradshaw, the Mistress of Discipline, Nanda's will has finally been broken. But, before the second part of the conventual contract can be completed, she is prematurely and violently uprooted and trans-planted out into the world. With her natural strengths and talents thus dismantled, Nanda is left to fend for herself, her will reduced to wilfulness, her soul corrupted with fear and self-loathing, her psycholog-ical integrity in pieces.

By November 1932, Antonia had finished to her liking her first novel: her eye caught by the headline of an article on roses in a gardening magazine, she called it *Frost in May*. She had crowned her work of art with the perfect, understated but ominous title, for what can be more devastating to blossom, fruit, growth, life even, than the unexpected frost at night when the tender new buds are just unfurling? And in acknowledgement of his help and involvement, she dedicated it to Tom. She first tried the publishers Cobden-Sanderson who, having been impressed by her short stories in *Life and Letters*, had written to her and asked to have first refusal on any novel which subsequently she might write. They were a refined literary outfit who advertised themselves to new authors as 'publishers of books suited to fastidious production . . . mostly of a slightly elegant flavour'.[18] Cobden-Sanderson sent the manuscript back to Antonia as being too slight to be of interest to anyone. She then tried Heinemann, who kept it for nearly two months before turning it down. Duckworth too rejected it. While her manuscript was at Heinemann, Antonia and Tom went with the children, Susan aged three and Lyndall at sixteen months, to Cocker-mouth in Northumberland where Tom's father was now Archdeacon. Although the Hopkinsons cared little for Antonia, they had some affection for her children. Susan remembered her step-grandparents' house well and described it in her memoir as a kind of Cold Comfort Vicarage, damply situated by the river, overhung with laurels and run by a half-mad servant and the Archdeacon's alcoholic secretary. Antonia's diary entries mentioned none of this (but then neither did she mention her children) but she did list the amenities, the chill bedrooms, the grim brown walls, the religious books and the cheerless meals. She was interesting on the reason for the general air of strain she felt every time she was in her family-in-law's company. 'It is Tom's father who is the key to the strain . . . I wish he would come out with open hostility instead of this gentle, insulting Christian tolerance.'[19]

Tom's own love and admiration for his father had soured somewhat with the old man's continued disapproval of Antonia and his inability to accept that Tom had chosen freely, and felt increasingly committed to his wife. They both escaped into long walks round the Lakes, breathing 'the odd, cold, liquid quality of the air'.[20] Then they returned with relief to London, where Antonia had to continue her search for a publisher, but was also worrying about what writing project she should be concentrating on next. Comparing Thomas Carlyle and D.H. Lawrence interested her, for an intellectual article perhaps, but she was also wanting to sort out what way she wanted to go with the next novel.

Wyn Henderson, a friend now of Antonia's, was a woman of phenomenal energy and appetites whose sphere of influence was as wide and surprising as anyone else's she knew. She was a typographer by training, but could turn her hand to most things, having extraordinary social talents and zest for life. Antonia had told her of her difficulty in finding a publisher and the redoutable Wyn took it in hand. She was having an affair with Desmond Harmsworth, who had won some money on the Irish sweepstake and wanted to start a publishing company, and she gave the manuscript to him, suggesting he start with that. Antonia was offered an advance of £50, which she accepted. Wyn, who had been the key to procuring her abortion ten years previously, was now to turn midwife at the birth of her first novel. Another friend, Joan Souter-Robertson, was godmother to the book and had painted a jacket for it of a wreath of virginal white flowers against a sky of icy blue. *Frost in May* was dedicated to Tom and published in the summer of 1933. It cost seven shillings and sixpence and was immediately greeted by the critics with shock and admiration. The *Times Literary Supplement* felt that 'The story . . . is only saved from being too painful by the simplicity and sincerity of the telling'.[21] William Plomer in the *Spectator* was much exercised by how it displayed 'how dreadfully people behave when they are "acting for the best"', the conversations of the girls reminded him of the satires of Ronald Firbank and the painful dénouement recalled for him *Mädchen in Uniform*, although he allowed that Nanda's undoing was not a homosexual passion, as it was in the film.[22] Most of the papers reviewed it, all agreeing to its affective power, and Wyn Henderson said there was little doubt that they would sell out of the initial print run of 2,000 copies, declaring that the book 'could not have had a greater *succès d'estime* if you had sold 100,000 copies'.[23]

Tom informed her that in the literary roundup at the end of that year her book was mentioned in all lists of best novels of the year. However, Desmond Harmsworth, the fledgling publishers, had barely any distribution organised and could not manage to service even a modest success. Luckily Francis Meynell, son of the poet Alice Meynell, came to the book's aid. He took on the rest of the stock and under his imprint of the Nonesuch Press he published the subsequent editions of *Frost in May*.

But the unexpected success of Antonia's first novel and the acclaim that came her way upset the personal equilibrium between herself and Tom. The cosy and valued teacher-pupil relationship was tilted off balance. Tom's hopes for his own writing career were becalmed and already his sense of growing inferiority was evident in his valediction at the end of a letter written in December that year: 'don't forget your foolish, incompetent, ill-writing, conceited, detestable, unintelligent & worn-out husband, Tom.'[24]

Even Eric, who was not professionally competitive with her, realised that this success altered something in the balance of their relationship. 'My dear daughter' he began, 'How do, or will, you like being a success? For the Book is indubitably that. Perhaps you will now be able to believe in yourself? I need not tell you how profoundly gratified and fond your poor old Master is'.[25] Not as masterful as usual, but obviously pleased for her, he passed on Logan Pearsall Smith's comment that with *Frost in May* Antonia had achieved 'a real solid work of art'. It was the effect her success had on Tom, however, which knocked away the fragile supports to her creative and personal life. The impetus for this reversal was just a trivial discourtesy. Wyn Henderson had organised a post-publication party for Antonia in the autumn of 1933, where she was inevitably 'mildly lionised'. And there Wyn introduced Tom to someone as the husband of Antonia White: this, Antonia believed in retrospect, set a series of interconnected events in train. '[Tom] suddenly fell in love with this girl whom we had both known for years and in whom he had never shown any special interest.'[26] Tom confirmed this implicitly in a conversation with Lyndall many years later when he related how, at a party of Wyn's, he had thought that this young woman, whom he had known for almost three years, suddenly looked very interesting. This woman was Frances, already married to Geoffrey Grigson. When she insisted she had to leave, Tom went with her to call a taxi and suddenly they found themselves inexorably drawn into a passionate embrace, the intensity of which he was to remember with emotion all his life. In the progress of their love affair and Frances's subsequent mortal illness, trauma and heartbreak touched everyone involved.

In his autobiography, Tom confirmed Antonia's recognition that her success, in the face of his own lack of progress, gave him reason to pause and change course, although he did not mention Frances as the direction in which he was to leap; 'Though I had encouraged Tony to write her book and been happy with her over its success, I was not happy to be introduced at parties as "the husband of Tony White who's just written that marvellous book".'[27] The encouraging mirror he had held up to Antonia, which reflected her back at herself as both a writer and a woman, was suddenly cracked and clouded.

She had analysed many times that first unforgettable occasion in the Convent when her pride in her first embryonic novel had destroyed everything that mattered to her, and had 'upset relations with my father'.[28] Now it would seem that this book, recreating that very time, had blighted her hopes for the future as brutally. '[*Frost in May*] wrecked our marriage . . . so I thought psychologically whenever I wrote anything I destroyed love.' Here again her gift of herself through writing brought punishment and rejection: from another man who had assumed the all-important teacher/lover role, the role which had vested such authority all those years ago in her father and the Church. Tom's 'betrayal' of her was to bring back the guilt and the writer's block with a vengeance. 'I see now that only two men have *seriously* damaged me: my father and Tom.'[29] Once she discovered his rejection of her, the fear of writing for publication, the terrible doubts about her identity and worth, the sense of her own corruption, all forcefully returned. But this time, madness was riding pillion.

. . . and the Wild and
Weeping Woman

'Why look at me as if I were the enemy?'
'Not an enemy. A stranger,' she said wearily.

'The Moment of Truth', *Strangers*

At first Antonia said it was just tiredness, 'nerves and general strain'. She had thought that after writing out her experiences in the asylum in 'The House of Clouds' in 1930, she might be free of 'the beast' for ever.[1] This was not a ruminant beast, nor a gorilla in the mists, but a beast of prey, the kind that stalks, moves stealthily and springs when you least expect it. Its aim was to kill. From the publication of *Frost in May* to her desperate submission to a full Freudian analysis two years later, Antonia was subjected to every stage of this predatory cycle.

The stalking wracked her nerves. Antonia was now deeply into the depressive stage of her illness and incapable of much sense of achievement or pleasure in her success. She was to convince herself that the very unanimity of the critics' praise was suspect; 'I doubt if a book which went deeper would get such unthinking approval.'[2] It is remarkable that in her diaries for July 1933, the month of the publication of her masterpiece, there should be no mention at all of anything to do with her book. All her life she longed for literary acclaim, fame, the possibility of money in return for good creative work, the recognition of her peers; when it came she made not even an oblique comment about any aspect of this momentous experience. In fact in June, on the eve of her book's publication, she went down to see her mother at the cottage at Binesfield and meditated with some despair on her failure at love.

> When I am in love I think of the person all the time. I am not happy unless I am in 'a state of grace' with them. But each time I

meet them, the deeper I get, the worse I handle them. I take offence at the smallest thing, I stay too long, I become a bore and then suddenly a black curtain of melancholy descends and I feel shut in, cut off – I cannot go away though I know I should have gone an hour ago because I cannot live through tomorrow.[3]

This was the state she was reaching with Tom. Soon after the publication, Tom and Antonia were on holiday in Porthcurnow in Cornwall. Tom was feeling humiliated by the recent shift in his status. He played sports with some young friends of his on the beach and could no longer hold his own against them. More importantly, his marriage was increasing his sense of inferiority. He wrote in retrospect that he had never really accepted Antonia as his wife, but then she had never shown much interest in their relationship being an equal partnership either. '[Antonia] maintained towards me a curious, friendly, critical aloofness – the underlying assumption of which always was that she was the senior partner.' The success of her book had meant that even in the sphere of their writing, where it had been important to him that he had assumed the superior role, it was made painfully clear, now, that 'she was the senior partner in writing, too'.[4]

This was to be one of the lasting preoccupations of her life; how to be both a woman *and* a writer. By being a woman, she meant being loved, attracting others, being receptive, approved of, intuitive, soft-hearted. But her desire to be this kind of culturally authorised woman was made problematic for her by her deep-seated contempt for the female side of human nature. 'A woman *is* more corruptible, I believe, than a man because of the slower rhythm of her life, as still water breeds scum. And haven't you often noticed, in men, that it is their female side that betrays and corrupts them?'[5] Part of Antonia's recoil from her womanly self came from her strong identification with her father, but her Church too had impressed her from young girlhood with its harsh misogyny, its dismissal of woman as a 'bag of tripe' which ruined and degraded. Alienated from her own feminine nature, Antonia considered that the most precious part of her self was hard-edged and uncompromising: 'something in my nature which is tough, harsh and, to many people, repellent'.[6] This was the very attribute she called masculine, her soldier side, from which she believed her best work would come. But she could not integrate the undervalued 'feminine' with this fiercer beast: 'I can't "act" gentle when I feel fierce and hard – There is a lion & a lamb inside me – and they *won't* lie down side by side.'[7]

Antonia was already growing increasingly depressed by the idea of writing her second book. She was thinking about basing it on her relationship with her father, having always wanted to memorialise him in some way. Tom told Lyndall years later that Antonia had thought once her father was dead she would be free to write again. But with the publication of *Frost in May*, she felt terrible guilt at exposing his cruelty to her, and she found he returned to haunt her. Rereading *Anna Karenina* she longed to be able to tackle something on a similarly grand scale. She had also been pursuing her interest in Carlyle and his wife Jane, with whom she readily identified; 'passionate, melancholy, impatient, fame-loving – fame-hungry almost – and nervous.'[8] At some point she was commissioned to write a biography of Jane Carlyle. Logan Pearsall Smith had told her not to do it quickly, but to give it the full scholarly treatment, but she was never to settle happily into it. Tom went back to London and started the book which was his riposte to his wife's literary fame. He wrote in six weeks *A Strong Hand at the Helm*, an exposure of the government's incompetence and inconsistency using a series of quotations and photographs.

Meanwhile Antonia went to spend a week with a new set of friends in a rented house on the edge of Dartmoor in Devon. Here she was in the company of a group of women who, with their abandoned behaviour and intellectual aspirations, provided Antonia with larger horizons and more dangerous possibilities. She had always looked to men as the powerful sex, the interesting and worthwhile half of humankind: she had considered the 'masculine' qualities of tough-mindedness, uncompromising honesty and an unemotional perspective the most valuable qualities she possessed. Therefore, to find in a group of women, highly unorthodox as they were, intellectual stimulation and a freedom from convention and restraint, demanded a disturbing re-evaluation of her own philosophy. It also required a partial release of her strictly disciplined social self. These women were not interested in cultural chit-chat at polite Chelsea tea parties. Their style on these summer retreats was pagan and rustic; Bacchantes drunk on wine and unsafe talk, tearing limb from limb, not the wild animals on the moor but each other and the few naïve men who wandered their way. This was to be an exhilarating, alarming and exhausting initiation for Antonia into the power of women.

Antonia had first met Emily Holms Coleman in the spring of 1933 at a party given by Wyn Henderson. Emily had been struck by how similar to herself was the description of Antonia given in *Life & Letters*; Emily wrote that Antonia was 'like me with the life left out.'[9] This was a characteristic statement of Emily's. She was an irresistible force with an irrepressible belief in her own genius. In later life she acknowledged that she was a manic depressive, who lived most of her life at full tilt with the accelerator slammed flat to the floor. Throughout her seventy-five years she poured forth letters, poems, diaries, and eventually paintings, with an extravagance of energy which was breathtaking. She fought with and for her friends; was passionate about everything and rational about nothing. She was committed to her vision, and at times certifiable. She had one published novel to her name, *The Shutter of Snow*, the story of her experience in an asylum during a breakdown after the birth of her only child in 1924, told with poetic intensity, and humour too. While she was in the asylum, Emily thought she was God, and a sense of her own divinity never really left her. When she converted to Catholicism she brought her prodigious energies and self-belief to her religion, and added 'saint' to the appellation 'genius'.

Emily Coleman was working for the international anarchist Emma Goldman who had been deported from the United States and was then living in St Tropez. She was helping this other great egotist to ravel her memoirs into book form, when she met Peggy Guggenheim, the richest egotist of them all. It was 1928; Emily was twenty-nine with a four year old son. Peggy was a year or two older, with a son the same age and a daughter who was still a baby. She was monstrously rich, energetic and emotionally crass to a dumbfounding degree. She befriended Emily whom she described as: 'a mad American girl [who], unlike most people who are mad, did not hide it. On the whole it was a pleasant quality because it manifested itself in terrific enthusiasms and beliefs. . . . She shared with Blake the persuasion that all things are possible if you have faith.'[10] Peggy led a purposeless, itinerant life in pursuit of sensation, picking up and discarding her own and other people's husbands, until she found her place in history as a flamboyant patron of twentieth-century art. Her memoir, *Out of this Century*, was madcap and unintentionally hilarious, a monument to her prodigious ego and chilling in its total absence of insight and feeling. Her family were so horrified by its publication that they attempted to buy up every copy in existence.

Peggy Guggenheim had already met the American writer Djuna Barnes, who was working as a highly regarded journalist in Europe and was part of the raffish and the literary Parisian scene. Djuna was yet to write the 'stream of unconsciousness' novel, *Nightwood*, which Emily was instrumental in getting published by T.S. Eliot at Faber & Faber in London. She was living in Paris with her lover Thelma Wood, a sculptor and silverpoint artist, and was celebrated already as an erudite and witty woman who could characterise a person or a situation in a couple of devastating phrases. Djuna described Antonia as all brain, disconcertingly disguised; 'Her mind ticking away behind that great blonde head, like a veiled Big Ben.'[11] Emily's character invited aphorism more than most; Djuna described her as a 'rivet in a cream puff'. When Peggy complained that on a particular occasion Emily had gone too far, Djuna's whiplash response was 'That's one of her destinations'.[12]

In the middle of July, Antonia at Emily's instigation joined the party at Hayford Hall near Buckfastleigh, where Peggy Guggenheim had based herself for the summer. There was a rotating group of visitors, of whom the core were Peggy's children Sinbad and Pegeen, along with Djuna Barnes, Emily and her son John, and John Holms, a sphinx-like (or plain inarticulate) Englishman who roused terrific passions and loyalty in most of the men and women who knew him. He appeared to be a man more generously gifted than anyone, and yet by the point of his untimely death at the age of thirty-seven had left nothing to remind people of his nascent genius but their own memories and the fond anecdotes which circulated amongst his friends. Some thought his manner mere posturing and his philosophical reputation pure humbug. Edwin Muir considered him 'one of the most remarkable men of his time, or indeed of any time . . . Sometimes he seemed to breathe a goodness so natural and original that one felt the Fall had not happened yet.'[13] Everyone agreed on his magnificent physique and athletic prowess, combined with a surprising asthenia which stopped him in his tracks. Peggy thought he talked like Socrates and Djuna simply (and ironically) called him 'God'. Emily had met John Holms and his, at that time, common-law wife Dorothy, an astrologer, in St Tropez and had him as a lover. She introduced him to Peggy who took up where Emily had left off. She decided, however, that John should agree to marry Dorothy, who had long requested this to satisfy her family's sense of propriety, so that he could then go off with Peggy – with Peggy contracted to pay Dorothy alimony. Emily meanwhile had become obsessed with Samuel Hoare, whom they all called Peter, a clever senior civil servant in the Home Office. Hoare was fascinated by Emily and her milieu, but far too confirmed a bachelor and too buttoned-up an Englishman to risk marrying her. For many years she continued to try and batter him into submission, but all in vain.

Antonia was plunged into this disconcerting world of uninhibited expression and volatile passions where the women called the shots, and many of them went astray. The house was a bizarre combination of Victorian baronial and modern kitsch, creeper-hung and decorated with ancestral portraits and various extremities of dead animals. But the gardens and the situation, on the edge of the Moor, were magical and mysterious; 'a dream place, a lovely poetic garden, a Paradise, far from nowhere, deep in the trees beneath the moor.'[14] There was tennis and riding, made more exciting by the treacherous moorland bogs and the wildness and loneliness of the scenery, strewn with enormous boulders and animal bones and inhabited only by tough little Dartmoor ponies. Antonia loved the soft countryside of Sussex, although she could never be described as an outdoor or country woman in predilection or temperament: the unsafe grandeur of this landscape that encroached on the garden boundaries increased her sense of disorientation and danger.

Tom was there also for a few days, and liked Peggy but was less sure of Djuna, whose cleverness and lack of sentimentality could be daunting. According to Emily, Tom became besotted with her and 'would have done anything I said'.[15] She, who considered herself the laureate of suffering, inveighed against his innocence of this defining process. She made him cross, he recalled, because this was partially true, but also because she failed to see that suffering, for some people, was not a nourishing and creative experience but 'destructive and paralysing'.[16] Antonia noticed how ill-equipped Tom was to contribute to the glittering, quick-fire talk that characterised this kind of gathering where Djuna, in particular, shot from the hip. '[Tom] does not generate that peculiar electric atmosphere in which people really become transparent to each other and talk becomes music. . . . He is the onlooker, contributing occasionally but not *in* it. I used to feel this very much at Hayford Hall; he was for no apparent reason a constraint and a drag on the rest of us.'[17] He was much happier outside, playing sports with Peggy's and Emily's children and encouraging them to ride.

Antonia played tennis rather badly but her conversation was brilliant. 'She talks as well as any woman I have ever met', declared Emily.[18] The quality of Antonia's conversation was renowned. She was light and witty yet erudite, full of insight and illumination. She drew others out and made them feel more articulate and interesting themselves. It was an expression of the thrill for her of the pursuit of ideas and the sharing of discoveries. Emily attempted to capture the elusive essence, in her description of a subsequent late night discussion between Antonia and Peter Hoare back in London:

> Then they got into Baudelaire, and thence to Balzac, and they discussed his novels for some time, delighting in his idiosyncracies. The conversation flew. I sat silent, delighted. Tony's face was all lit up, she was quite lost, speaking in a high, well-modulated voice, rippling, perfectly in tune, Peter gay and very lively, jumping . . . I wish I could remember every word of what was said for about three hours last evening, because it was rare, and good, a taste of the kind of human exchange that all too seldom occurs.[19]

Her brilliant social talk, however, was often a smokescreen to hide the real despair and sense of her own fugitive identity. For a moment, on stage, she saw herself reflected back from the faces of her audience and knew that she existed in their response to her. In the evenings, everyone would drink too much, play games, insult each other and grow more outrageous as the night wore on. Emily's favourite game was a lethal 'Devil's biography' called Truth.[20] With wit and vitriol, lubricated by alcohol, everyone collected in the drawing room after dinner and wrote a phrase, or paragraph on a particular aspect of one of the people present. The subject might be sex appeal, trustworthiness or that person's chances in hell, and the anonymous contributions were read out by a nominated reader. Djuna's were the most distinctive and memorable, Emily's the most unconstrained. She was also the most obsessed with who had written what and was found one night, after everyone had gone off to bed, crouched over the wastepaper basket trying to decipher the handwriting of the contributions to which she had taken most exception.

They were dangerously stressful games for Antonia, already in a depressed and rawly sensitive state: *Frost in May* was discussed; Djuna tried to like it but failed. Antonia, on the other hand, was amazed at the prolific outpouring of words from Djuna, who gave her *Ladies Almanack* to read, her satiric and mythic insider's view of the lesbian circle of which she had been a part in Paris. She was in the middle of writing *Nightwood*, sitting up in bed in the mornings at Hayford Hall, immersed in what would become her most celebrated novel. (Djuna was afraid to leave the house because Emily had threatened to burn this manuscript if something she had told her, in private, was incorporated in her story.) She had also published *Ryder*, her carnivalesque version of a family saga, and presented a copy to Antonia on her departure: Antonia was inevitably depressed by the comparison with her own meagre oeuvre.

The two writers sat together much of the week, Antonia perceptive and admiring, Djuna accepting and encouraged: 'They munched away together,' Emily wrote in her diary, 'a proper feast for Tony, and a further satisfied appetite for Djuna, who doesn't get this here.'[21] Emily considered that flattery was much more essential for Djuna than for Antonia, who only liked it as a means of making her feel she was accepted and belonged. 'Djuna would die without flattery, but Tony would go rattling right along.' Antonia turned to Peggy and asked her how she would take news of Antonia's own death. 'Very absentmindedly', Peggy replied.[22] John Holms told Antonia she looked like 'a something Queen Elizabeth' which she rather liked, but then he would not tell her the defining adjective.[23] Holms later told Emily the 'something' was 'Surbiton', the eponymous London suburb. A Surbiton Queen Elizabeth did not sound quite so flattering.

The week was soon over and Antonia returned to London dazzled and exhausted. They all talked about her after she had gone and continued to challenge each other about the relative merits of their geniuses, their work and the men they professed to love. Emily expostulated in her diary that she feared she was nothing but a middle-class college girl: 'I told P[eggy Guggenheim] she could not know what I was like inside, an elephant trying to sit down on a dime – That is just what I am like. If I *were* nothing but a middle-class college girl I would have it settled; unfortunately I've got poetic genius.'[24] She had turned to Djuna and told her that she felt sure that just one word from her would put her on the right tracks once and for all. Emily then asked the others what might this one thing be which was the answer to everything for her. A strait-jacket was Peggy's immediate reply, and Djuna chipped in, 'Lydia Pinkham's Vegetable Compound.'

Tom welcomed Antonia back to Cecil Court. He was working away hard on his *Strong Hand at the Helm*. Antonia's admiration and awe for Djuna Barnes had made her feel the urgency of progressing with her own writing, beginning with this second book about her father which seemed to resist all her attempts at exegesis. But the intensity of the experience at Hayford Hall, where she was put on her intellectual mettle and was up until late every night fencing with ideas and personalities as prickly as her own, took its toll. Exhaustion accelerated the creeping paralysis of depression; malaise gained more of a grip on her mind and her headaches returned. She was still managing to keep her inner torment from her colleagues at Crawford's; she remained a far better actress in life than on the stage. But all this pretence and suppression had a price. As Antonia descended further she manufactured great obstacles to progress: the lack of green typing paper; anxiety about her autumn wardrobe; confusion about her real attitude to her religion: 'The worst thing about being mad in my particular way is that all these things seem of equal importance', she confided despairingly in her diary that autumn.[25]

During this period of mental disintegration, Antonia mentioned her children for the first time in this diary, caught as she was by their interest in death. 'Yesterday Lyndall found a dead fly. S[usan] said "Lyndall likes making things killed" and this morning they were both pretending to be dead. Susan lying quite still and Lyndall waving her arms and shouting "I'm dead too".'[26] They were four and two years old respectively.

So austere and unchildlike was her own experience of childhood in Perham Road, that Antonia found little understanding and no pleasure in the intellectual and emotional progress of her two young daughters. Perhaps she recorded their conversation about death because for the first time she had found them interested in something which preoccupied her and belonged in her world, so incapable was she of entering imaginatively into theirs. It was Tom who wrote about them affectionately in his diary. His visits to the nursery were the highlight of their day. But it was Nurse who was responsible for all their daily care, and Antonia remained frightened of them, emotionally and physically absent and terrifyingly prone to unpredictable and transforming rages.

From early on, Susan had attempted to deflect her fear and loneliness by pretending she was a horse and steeling herself not to cry. Lyndall, as a very young child, cried often and attached herself to her elder sister for solidarity and comfort. When she was only four and a half, Susan said something to Antonia which had an eerie echo of her own early and powerful identification with her father and denial of her mother. 'I suppose you had Lyndall and Tom had me.'[27] It bleakly expressed her lack of a mother from her earliest days and her alienation from Antonia even once she was physically united with her under the same roof. There was also some recognition of the difference in the sisters' experiences of babyhood, and jealousy perhaps of Lyndall's closer bond with Nurse; the sense that she had been mothered, however meagrely, by someone. Perhaps too, it was an expression of Susan's response to and possessiveness of Tom's own maternal qualities, for he was in some ways much better endowed with the 'female' qualities of empathy and care than Antonia.

The children's lives continued very separately from Antonia's and Tom's, both of whom changed jobs that autumn. Antonia gave up Crawford's for good and decided to go freelance again, driving herself into a frenzy of activity trying to make, and renew, contacts with other advertising agencies and newspapers. She secured two freelance contracts that year, writing the fashion page on the *Daily Mirror* under another pseudonym, Ann Jeffrey, and securing for herself the post of theatre critic for the literary journal *Time and Tide*. She never considered her journalism to be worth anything, yet she was very skilled at knowing what was needed and, except when she was really ill, producing what was required in elegant and spare prose. She wrote three short stories for inclusion in anthologies, the flurry of requests being the result of her fame after *Frost in May*. 'A Child of the Five Wounds' was a brisk description of her time in the Convent, written for Graham Greene's collection *The Old School*; an essay about Brighton for a collection of pieces celebrating English seaside towns, *Beside the Seaside*; and 'The First Time I went on Tour' was for an anthology edited by Theodora Benson called *The First Time I. . .* , where her story rubbed shoulders with pieces by William Gerhardie, P.G. Wodehouse and Rose Macaulay.

Tom's *A Strong Hand at the Helm* was published in November to an interested public, and on the strength of that he was offered a job with an already struggling newspaper, the *Clarion*, starting in the new year. They were very short of money and Tom managed to sell back to his uncle the share he had been given in his company. He was offered £500, half its face value, but it was a financial lifeline for them at the time. After paying off their debts and putting some by for emergencies, Tom decided they each had £50 to spend. He bought a small boat, *Scud*, which he moored on the Thames, and Antonia went shopping for clothes.

Around this time too, Antonia was spasmodically pursued by Alexander Keiller, another of Wyn Henderson's connections. Heir to the Keiller fortunes, Antonia called him 'the Marmalade King', although so varied were his interests and so great his energy and ego that he would have claimed for himself a variety of other titles. His most noble achievement, perhaps, was as the man whose vision and money excavated and restored the prehistoric stone avenues and circles at Avebury in Wiltshire. His least noble might have been his roughshod treatment of other people's feelings, which earned him a reputation for sadism. Antonia told Lyndall that she ended her flirtation with him when he begged, and then offered to bribe, her to submit to one of his sexual peccadilloes; he wanted her to climb into a laundry basket dressed only in a mackintosh while he poked her through the wicker with a rolled umbrella.

Antonia's mental state was such that she was finding living with Tom at Cecil Court increasingly distressing. She was not yet consciously aware that Tom's passionate feelings were deflected towards Frances Grigson, but she sensed his distraction and was feeling alienated and bereft. She escaped for the middle part of June to the Old Mill Guest House at Aldermarston so as to be able to see Bob Gathorne-Hardy, a close friend of Logan Pearsall Smith. Bob and his brother Eddie were well-known literary figures in London at the time. Both brothers sported monocles and shared a passion for botany and archaeology and were great experts and collectors of seventeenth- and eighteenth-century English books. Bob was 'a natural highbrow' and worked for a time as Logan's literary assistant.[28]

Staying in the old mill, which still smelled of flour and old sacks seven years after it had ceased its working life, Antonia relaxed a little. Logan had suggested that she use her diary as a portable memory. It helped her to look outwards a little and she began to record some of her observations of the natural world rather than her own obsessional thought processes, and the struggle to understand. Antonia's mental state, however, was now dominating everything. She was unable to concentrate, full of fears and lassitude, with occasional bursts of vivacity when she found herself in a new and demanding social situation. Since March 1934, she had been seeing a psychologist, James Robb, who was a member of the Arcane Society and whom Antonia came to distrust because of his complicity, she believed, in occult matters. She dated her 'terrible black depressions' from her first visits to Robb and his probing of her dreams and unconscious.[29] Antonia was suffering from oppressive nightmares again from which she would awake sobbing, or calling out in a thin keening voice: only Tom's presence and reassuring words it seemed could give her the route back to waking consciousness.

She was ambivalent about the merits of analysis and remained in the grip of profound misery and black despair. She decided she had to make Tom love her again, and in this brittle frame of mind set off on 12 July for the annual Guggenheim Bacchanale.

That summer, Peggy had rented a spacious eighteenth-century farmhouse, with the remains of a twelfth-century castle, with a tower and a moat, in the middle of its gardens. It was called Warblington Castle, near Havant, close to the Hampshire coast, and was periodically open to the public who occasionally stumbled upon the bizarre inmates engaged in riotous discussion or shambolic sporting contests. "'Anybody can ask anybody they want," said Peggy, "if they'll sleep with them.'"[30] The main guests were Peggy and the new man in her life, Douglas Garman, a multilingual young Englishman who worked as a publisher and had seven remarkable sisters, whom Peggy found rather more unorthodox and interesting than their decent and straightforward brother. He had taken the place of the now heroised John Holms, who had died the previous January from the effects of anaesthetic administered during an operation to correct a badly-mended fracture of his arm, which he had broken in a fall from a horse at Hayford Hall the previous summer. Emotion in the household was still high over his unexpected and wasteful death and Emily Coleman and Peggy were to be found occasionally weeping together, or wishing that they too were dead.

Emily was a guest again, along with Phyllis Jones, Emily's friend, who was a lean and handsome woman with a zestful attitude to life and men, and a saintly generosity with her time and care to friends in need. She had been invited by Peggy who thought she would be good with the children. Her own two were there, as was Emily's son John, and also Garman's little daughter and his niece. Phyllis became a stalwart friend to Antonia too and remained so all her life, a godsend to her as companion, nurse and typist during some of the worst periods in her life. She was a sometime Agony Aunt on the *Mirror* newspaper, and certainly lived the kind of life herself which meant she could draw from personal experience – heavily censored – for most of her advice.

Antonia felt that at least in this company she was accepted for what she was and not disapproved of for being selfish, neurotic or mad. But she arrived very near breakdown and Emily and Peggy were so concerned about her that they insisted she ring Eric Earnshaw Smith and try to get him to come down to be with her. When he could not manage it, they suggested Frank Freeman, but he could not afford the train fare. Antonia somehow pulled her social self together and that first evening entertained them with the story of how Wyn Henderson had penetrated the Bloomsbury inner circle at last. Emily repeated part of the conversation in her diary; 'Julian Bell [Vanessa and Clive Bell's elder son] took her to a club. They all went in a char-a-banc. Tony said, "They all changed tarts for supper." At the end she said, "They formed a lobster quadrille".'[31]

Tennis was the main daytime activity. Antonia organised a tournament for the end of her week and there was lots of frenzied practising in the days leading up to it. Emily mentioned how fat Antonia looked in her shorts: she added, however, what an intelligent and highly trained social creature she was, but also someone who made rather a lot of gaffes (from Emily this was a bit rich). Peggy had wanted to keep it quiet that she was having an affair with Garman, afraid it appeared unfeeling so soon after John Holms's death. But then one evening after a 'peacherino' of a row was had by everyone, except Phyllis, Antonia 'with a bitter smile wafted her cigarette and spoke feelingly. She admitted she wanted to sleep with Garman [Peggy had earlier said that sleeping with Garman would be like sleeping with fly tox – he would come to life again to annoy you!] . . . Tony, very ugly, sat on the sofa smiling. She says she loves me [Emily]. Her face gets fatter, her mouth more trained, she rolls her eyes in dejection. She never believes one decent word anyone says (about her).'[32] Emily was sensitive to Antonia's longing for romance and felt it was 'indecent' to deceive her about Garman's relationship with Peggy.

In fact, Peggy had taken the tower bedroom for herself and Garman, hoping that it was separate enough from the main party not to arouse comment. But when Antonia came into her bedroom to talk and spotted a large pair of Garman's flannel trousers on the bed, Peggy came down the next day wearing them, even though they were many times too big, in an attempt to deflect any suspicions. Not surprisingly Peggy felt that nothing she said to Antonia was right; just when Peggy thought she was getting on well with her and had determined to buy her a croquet set, the mood collapsed when she implied she could not remember whether Antonia had been a guest only once or twice last summer. Immediately Antonia had felt the sudden deflation of the unimportant and forgotten. Emily, meanwhile, thought Antonia did not like her. Phyllis, who was the only person there who was not filtering every utterance and event through her own ego, realised that Antonia was in such a fragile state that she could not take quite so much exuberance and forcefulness of character: '*Adorable* as you are,' she said to Emily, 'Tony's had enough of you.'[33] However, Antonia told Emily and Phyllis all her trouble with Tom, and they were sympathetic and worried for her sanity. She had a peculiar way of talking about the most terrible things in a calm conversational way, which both women found strange and disconcerting.

Antonia wrote to Tom the day after the row described by Emily as a 'peacherino' but which Antonia plausibly laid at Emily's door. Emily had flung a full wine glass at Garman, screamed at him and slammed out of the room. 'I am a perfect Minnie Mouse compared to E. in a rage.'[34] Mad as the whole atmosphere was, it made Antonia feel that she was not the only crazy, impossible woman, that actually there were even more extreme versions of herself in the world. Also, as she explained to Tom, it took her mind off herself for a precious while.

Antonia was capable also of rising magnificently to a social occasion, and at one of their evening dinners had entertained them all with a story about one of Silas's girlfriends, Mabel Lethbridge, a young woman with 'sheer brute vitality' and a wooden leg.[35] 'She was blown up in a munitions explosion, during the war, and has been plated since, and is very successful with men. I asked Tony where she was plated, Tony said she had seen a map once but couldn't remember. Said her leg had a spring inside which she got wound up every year at the hospital, then it went so fast that she couldn't keep up with it. Garman said it must be strange for a man to have to climb over barbed wire entanglements . . . Tony said she got run over once; everyone said how brave she was but it was her wooden leg. Garman said "she did not flinch".'[36] The talk then became cruder and Emily did not bother to report the rest of the night's conversation, but she commented to her diary that the talk all the week was so rich and witty that she wished she had 'a dictaphone in the living room'.[37]

On 18 July Antonia left Warblington: Emily's verdict was 'Tony very much impressed with everything, though we drive her crazy'.[38] Despite the unbearable strain of keeping her beast from breaking out, she enjoyed being with women who could dominate proceedings, and be so interesting in themselves. The men at these Guggenheim summer parties were always adjuncts – had not Peggy's directive been, you can invite any of them as long as he is your possession, the one you sleep with, for whom you are responsible? They were kept firmly in their places, as sexual objects of amusement and desire, and as butts to the women's superior wit and repartee. But this unbuttoning of Antonia's strictly controlled social persona was a dangerous thing. No longer able to contain the chaos, she entered a kind of accelerated mental process: the mania before the depressive collapse.

Tom had arranged a holiday in Brittany for both of them in a desperate attempt at restoring some equilibrium to Antonia's mind: they left for France soon after her return from Devon. They had planned to be away for longer but the trip was cut short after they had endured a most terrible and frightening couple of weeks, with Antonia back in the hallucinating madness of her first catastrophic breakdown. Out of this torment she wrote a remarkable and disturbing short story 'A Moment of Truth', which was published in *Horizon* in June 1941.

The wife in the story is struggling to hang on to her sanity, while assailed by dreams, hallucinations, and an oversensitivity to the harsh and primitive environment which mirrors her own degeneration. 'Something inside her seemed to have died and to be filling her mind, even her body, with corruption.'[39] The husband is vigorously sane, kind and reasonable: 'It wears one down being married to a man who always gives such excellent reasons for everything he does'.[40] When she discovers he is having an affair with another woman, suddenly all her festering self-hatred is exposed; '"It's not safe for anyone to come near me. You don't understand. I am poisoned, poisoned right through." He did not dare to deny or to interrupt. The terrible words multiplied and multiplied, till he seemed to be watching the multiplication, cell by cell, of a cancer.'[41] The moment of truth is the husband's and wife's realisation that they both wanted her dead.

Like all her serious work this story was very closely based on actual events and experiences; a letter Antonia wrote to Emily Coleman gave the same minatory detail of landscape and experience. The inn they had decided to stay in at St Germain de la Mer was remotely situated on the very edge of the sea. At high tide the water crashed against the outer walls, so close to the bedroom that Antonia noticed you could dive into it from the window. Peculiarly repellent to her was what was revealed at low tide; 'two miles . . . [of] a stinking expanse of greyish sand and soft black bubbling mud, littered with copulating crabs, sardine tins and festering marine matter of various kinds.' She found the landlady of the establishment particularly sinister with her intrusive presence and sombre psychic warnings and the few locals they came across on 'desperate walks through slime & gorse' seemed, to her terrified eye, to be as primordial as the creatures of low tide. Her language, usually so unemotional and precise, had a Shakespearian richness in her description of the baseness and corruption of these people. 'Being fed on nettles, unripe apples, sour mead & clammy barnacles [they] are suspicious, surly and filled with hate for each other and contempt for everyone else.'[42] And in her crazed imaginings their contempt was for her, someone even more degenerate than they were, one of the creatures of the slime.

In the middle of one of her self-lacerating diatribes, Antonia suddenly attempted to launch herself out of their bedroom window onto the half-exposed rocks below. She was only saved by Tom's desperate intervention when he hauled her back into the room. A year or so later Tom explained just how manipulated he felt, what an impossible situation she put him into in her pleading for him to kill her or attempting to kill herself which equally forced him into involvement on her terms. 'The exasperation I felt towards you in Brittany . . . was a typical masculine resentment at what seemed an "unfair trick" . . . we were as it were in a battle, we were at that moment arguing, suddenly you spring out of bed & run towards the window – "Damn the woman" I think, "that's not an argument. She knows I feel for her. She knows I don't want a hair on her head hurt. She wants her way & she'll even go & kill herself to get it."'[43]

When the story was published in *Strangers* in 1954 and Emily complained that she had made the woman so unsympathetic, Antonia explained: 'I wanted to get out of my cocoon of misery & try & see what it must be like to live with & be loved by a woman in that state.'[44] Antonia's unsentimental, unsympathetic portrayal of this woman revealed the terrible self-knowledge of how madness destroys love, personality, reason. She showed the bleak impossibility of happiness. She and Tom cut short their holiday and returned a week early at the beginning of August.

Soon after her return to London, Antonia telephoned Emily and made a date for lunch. Despite the complete degradation of her mental state she managed to maintain her social self. 'She sat in her jolly way and told me tragic things. She tried to commit suicide with Tom,' Emily noted with amazement in her diary. 'She sits talking, as Phyllis said, in a social way, to such a point that you cant believe the things she says are real. But they are real. Tony is not a tragic woman, and this life doesn't

suit her – but there she is – shes violent, and could go out of her head –
and die.'[45]

Tom had written to Antonia, 'pain to your pride, & there must have
been much of it, is being avenged. But I know very well that is not all
that has been hurt between us.'[46] He resented having been used by her
to escape an impossible situation; he then betrayed Antonia to get his
revenge: this was his reasoning to himself. He had longed all his life to
be passionately loved by a woman, and he felt Frances Grigson was that
woman. Antonia, sensing she had lost him, now desperately wanted to
make him see that she could give him what he needed. But the
equivocation of her madness caught her longing for something which
she had convinced herself could never be: 'If the *whole* of Tom & of
myself could have come together it would have been ... the ideal
marriage. Well we didn't & couldn't because neither of us *were* whole.
Hence dislocation, collision, disaster, flight. . . .'[47]

12

Dicing With Death
and Life-in-Death

I have been an object of exaggerated love, exaggerated envy, exaggerated
contempt all my life.
I have always been afraid no one would love me for what I *was* &
invented various disguises in which I had seen other people loved.

22 March 1936, letter to Tom Hopkinson

During the summer of 1934, the children had left London with
Nurse to stay with their Hopkinson grandparents up in Cumberland. There they celebrated their fifth and third birthdays and for a time,
mercifully, were out of the gyre of fighting and despair in which their
parents spun. At this stage in Antonia's daughters' lives they barely
featured in her thoughts, particularly when she was struggling to
maintain even a minimum of mental equilibrium against the onslaught
of her disease.

In fact, Antonia's feeling for her cats, and to a lesser extent for all
animals, was much closer to the kind of maternal unselfishness and
passion which she seemed unable to express for her own children,
particularly when they were very young. Fascination with their
individual characters; a willingness to put herself out for their needs;
delight in their company; the ability to intuit their wants and assuage
their suffering: all this she could feel spontaneously for her animals, but
her own children made her frenzied with anxiety. The two books she
wrote about a Siamese and a ginger tabby who shared her home for
many years, *Minka & Curdy* and *Living with Minka & Curdy*, bear witness
to her deep affection and the insight she had into the feelings and mind
of creatures dependent on her for care and love. In her letter to Tom
from Warblington Castle, teetering on the edge of the abyss of madness,
she nevertheless asked him to give her love to 'the pussies'. The
recipients of this love were not Sue and Lyndall, who were far away

from her both emotionally and physically, but Fury and Vanya, a ginger-and-white spitfire and an imperious Russian Blue. With her cats love was easy; simple affection, acceptance, companionship flowed both ways with none of the sense of 'them against me', the checks of expectation, criticism and risk of failure which accompanied human relationships. 'However much they teased [her], they had never snubbed or criticised her', was how Antonia had described Fury and Vanya's charms in the beginning of *Minka & Curdy*.[1] Whereas to someone like Antonia, with her fragile sense of self, the crying baby was too easily interpreted as rejection of her love; a badge of her own failure as a mother and a human being. Later, the expressive child with her raw emotions was too painfully close to Antonia's own childlike self, with her skinless irritability and accesses of feeling over which she had little control. It was frightening to have to deal with the legitimate lack of control in a child when she herself was so close to the edge of rationality herself.

And running throughout her life, and magnified in her intimate relationships, was the strain of her mental illness. She explained in a stricken letter to Tom a year later something of what it felt like to be her, in the grip of the beast:

> This perpetual internal torture is a disease & productive of no good to myself & no one else. But no act of will can destroy it – only faith & patience of which I have so little . . .. This meaningless suffering is like a cancer, making one repulsive to oneself and everyone else. I am not one that feeds & flourishes on misery. I love happiness & gaiety but my cancer drives them from me. You would have to be a saint to love me as I am now.[2]

Apart from her own, discounted, mother, the human being who came closest to expressing that unconditional love for Antonia was Eric Earnshaw Smith. On her return from Brittany, it was to Eric that she longed to run for some comfort and solace. He was on holiday in Devon at Shaldon, near Teignmouth, in a bungalow called Ye Olde Cottage: Antonia went to spend the second week of August with him. She was worried by her lack of faith and yet her longing to believe. Eric told her to make to measure a morality to suit herself, not try to cut herself to fit something ready-made. She was overwhelmed again by the 'blank depression' which had almost destroyed her in Brittany.[3] Everything had lost its point and purpose; she did not think she had any 'creative' genius, only the ability to interpret things truthfully. If only she were a painter like Vuillard, she wrote in her diary; 'Why *can't* one do the same thing in writing?' She returned to London having decided that she should take a room in Eric's town house, where she would go daily to work.

While Antonia was struggling with total disintegration, Tom's emotional life had capsized again. Frances and Geoffrey Grigson had returned from Spain and Frances came to the flat in Cecil Court to see Tom and renew their intimacy. She also told him that she had conceived a child by her husband, while they had been together in Spain. With the news of Frances's pregnancy, she and Tom were parted again, leaving Tom to struggle with his bitter sense of lost love. It made him decide to try and make something of his marriage to Antonia, although she was in such a frightening state of mind and almost impossible for anyone, including herself, to live with.

During the day of 17 August Antonia was writing in her diary of the terrible way jealousy distorted the relationship between two people, how having been hurt she wished to hurt herself further, 'to degrade oneself to less than human.'[4] Part of this degradation had to do with the distortion of her sexual self. Antonia told Emily that from not having desired Tom at all, she now suddenly wanted 'sex' with him. Emily thought this pathetic and comic too, because she did not believe that Antonia was sexual at all; '. . .. she thinks she *ought* to want it . . .. Desire like that is only roused by jealousy.'[5] Yet in the midst of all this suffering, Antonia could pull herself together enough to go to dinner that night with Emily and Samuel Hoare and become the entertainer that was expected of her:

> Tony extremely amusing last night talking about her mother [Emily wrote]. She told how she went to Monseigneur's, 'took up all the table decorations and put them behind her ear.' Returned from the lavatory with her dress awry, 'showing art silk knickers behind.' At which she danced. Aged 64 and has a priest of 20, who kisses her hand . . . She said: 'He took a bee out of my hair, so nicely, not at all flirtatiously'.[6]

But none of this fleeting forgetfulness of self made much difference to Antonia's underlying misery. Tom was miserable too, but aware of her suffering and filled with remorse for not being the kind of support she needed in her extremity. He was self-critical too, apologetic for seeming to her stupid and dull. Tom's sense of inferiority in Antonia's company was bolstered by her intellectual mind made hypercritical with her illness, her articulacy, the *succès d'estime* of her book: '. . . you are far too clever . . . I can't imagine anything duller, more depressing, more maddening, more boring, more irritating than for you to be with me at present. If I could suddenly blink & sit up wide awake I would . . . If you ever loved me – help. Blink a little yourself for a few weeks. Don't be too all-seeing. Even be a little stupid, if you can.'[7]

Towards the end of September Antonia had three weeks of unexpected respite, when clarity returned to her and people, including Tom, felt drawn to her once more. She was detached and cool and felt that if she could maintain an attitude of indifference allied to some pretence of sexual passion then she could hold him for ever. But she had to 'possess' herself too, to love and not just be loved. As suddenly as the relief came it disappeared again. Antonia was plunged back into nightmares, hallucinations, disintegration, and impulses towards suicide. Tom told of how suddenly she would fling back the bedclothes and make a run for the window to launch herself out, much as she had done at the inn in Brittany. He could only counter this by clinging on round her waist until she had tired herself out and the impulse had passed. At other times he had had to pursue her in the middle of the night as she ran for the Embankment and the river, half-dressed and intent on drowning herself, as she had tried to do when she had first gone out of her mind in 1922. Tom was more than willing to shoulder his share of blame for the situation: 'though physically present, emotionally I was somewhere else – a fact which Tony would have perceived even if I had been much better at concealment than I was.'[8]

Naturally an antagonist, Antonia became more edgy and aggressive when in the grip of this disease, picking fights with Tom in an attempt to get a reaction from this preternaturally reasonable and passive man, who had become even more detached and submerged in his own world. The bitter arguments took two forms, the first kind when Antonia, full of self-hatred, would accuse herself of ruining his life and with a sudden poignant and tender remorse tell him they would both be better off if she were dead. ' "Oh Tom, darling I am so awful. Do please kill me, Tom. I wouldn't mind a bit, honestly I wouldn't. Just kill me quietly, Tom . . . It would be much the best thing for you to do" and she would be soft & convincing as a pleading child "really Tom, it would be much the best thing you could do." '[9] It was a chilling and incongruous juxtaposition of sweetness with nightmare; an aggressive passivity of a most terrifying kind. And yet in the blackest depression, death often seems the most logical and compassionate solution. The implication of Tom in this desire, suggested that Antonia was asking him to love her enough to release her. In retrospect, Antonia recognised for herself the connection between sexual desire and death. In a letter to Tom she recalled the night in Brittany when she had tried to throw herself out of the window and for a moment Tom too had wanted her to die. 'That is why I sometimes say I want to die at your hands', she explained to him, 'since in a sense it is what we both unconsciously want and, in a world of madness, could give us the supreme satisfaction we have never known in sex.'[10]

In these terrible arguments, Antonia could switch from self-destruction of this extreme kind to being the destroyer of others; accusing Tom of every weakness and sin. Most destructively, she undermined his sense of masculinity, or denied that he was as creatively talented as he hoped. He accepted it philosophically, at times masochistically: 'I am always telling you you destroy me. So sometimes you do. You also *make* me. . . . You gave me the whole idea of trying to see what I was like & of turning myself into someone. No-one else ever saw or took the trouble. Man to man I owe you a great deal.'[11] That last sentence suggested that Tom accepted what Antonia had always believed, that she was more of a man than he.

Towards the end of the year, Antonia's state was beyond her will to control and Tom's ability to endure. She was leaving him notes in mirror writing, the same kind of reversed handwriting which she used during her time in the asylum. Antonia had decided she could not live at Cecil Court any more because it was tainted by Tom's betrayal of her there with Frances. In the middle of November Tom went to Eric for advice and was told by him: 'Tony needs something desperate doing. Do something mad for her sake.'[12] This was alarming advice for someone who naturally did not court hardship and uncertainty: he was also writing very well at the time and feared disrupting the rhythm of his life. But Tom knew Eric was right; at this time this sphinx-like man was a kind of sage father-figure for both himself and Antonia. Tom put the flat in the hands of agents to find new tenants, sent Susan and Lyndall once more back to Cumberland with Nurse and rented 16 Godfrey Street on a three-month lease.

This was a move which was to run him into debt, but Godfrey Street was a place Tom looked back on with a warm nostalgia, so for a while they must have been happier. They called it 'the little house', fondly so in his memory. But that winter Antonia's experiences were so bad that Tom considered having to send her away to some sort of psychiatric institution. He wrote on 4 December from his office, 'You have been so good & you are having such a dreadful time. If what you really need – as perhaps it is – is to go away, you must be a good girl & go. I will find somewhere human for you. I will come continually to see you.'[13]

The idea of incarceration was abandoned but in the next few days Tom was so worried about Antonia that he took her to see Dr William

Brown, whose work with shell-shock victims after the First World War had sprung him to eminence. Antonia's experience, however, suggested he was then past his best. He had had some success with hypnosis and tried this on her. She found him 'So bloody pleased with himself.'[14] It also disconcerted her that when she was in a semi-hypnotised state he would pop his head over the screen to see how she was getting on, and then, mumbling the reassurance 'better in yourself, stronger, calmer, more capable,' she would see him fiddling with things on his desk, paring his fingernails or stumbling over the fire-irons.[15]

Ineffectual as he may have seemed to her, Dr Brown was instrumental in getting Antonia treatment which finally helped her understand something of her nature and the reasons for her suffering. He suggested a young Freudian psychoanalyst, Dr Dennis Carroll, whom she attended four times a week for nearly four years, from the middle of February 1935 until mid-September 1938. At the end of this time, she wrote that the best she could hope for was that Dr Carroll would literally 'make an honest woman of me'.[16] She described to a sceptical friend the practical results of this long, slow and painful process she had been through: '[it] is as if, before, you had been swimming with your feet tied together and now you are swimming with them free. But swimming is still difficult and where you swim is your own affair.'[17]

Dr Carroll's verdict on her was uncompromising and Antonia recorded it in her diary without protest or any attempt at palliation: 'He tells me I have the nature of a torturer, that my ruling passion is money, that my voice is powerful and aggressive, frequently rising to a scream and that I tend literally to talk people to death. Whereas I would *like* to write them to life!'[18] This was Antonia's distillation of a much more complicated and subtle analysis of her character, but it was interesting that she should have picked on these particular aspects and accepted their harsh evaluation, shouldering it as her cross to bear.

Antonia was a rare person who could look herself coldly in the eye and accept the most unbearable truths about herself. But she was also someone who, so schooled in the evils of pride and hypocrisy, could not accept the slightest praise nor the smallest allocation of good to her nature. She was continually failing to live up to the unattainable ideal set her as a child that no outsider's favourable view of her could ever colour the inveterate belief that she was a shameful disappointment in the eyes of her God and her father.

There are two descriptions in Antonia's version of Dr Carroll's summing-up which most demand explanation. 'The nature of a torturer' sounds chilling but in fact is some way removed from actually being a torturer. It suggests a fear of powerlessness in a person with an overwhelming need for power and control. To have this nature is to feel powerless and afraid, and only able momentarily to gain a sense of potency and freedom from fear by oppressing someone weaker and more afraid than you are. In the act of torture there is an inevitable dehumanisation of both the tortured and the torturer. It involves an isolation from one's universal connection with others, and a personal detachment from feeling. All these qualities Antonia exhibited at some time in her life, but most devastatingly when her mental state was disintegrating. The other prong to Dr Carroll's diagnosis also implied quite a threat: 'I tend literally to talk people to death.' Literally to death?

This referred not to Antonia's conversational skill but to her over-analytical approach to herself and the world. Every movement of her heart and soul was discussed, either with herself in her voluminous diaries, or in her unhesitantly fluent letters, or face to face with the protagonists in her life. She analysed and ravelled and unravelled a problem to a standstill, and then started all over again. In fact, after the three fascinating hours of talk once admiringly recorded by Emily, Antonia then turned to a discussion about Tom, and for the next hour obsessively worried over every nuance of their latest drama. Hoare complained to Emily the next day that Antonia may be the most intelligent woman and a wonderful talker but, 'it was sickening to hear us go portentously on, pulling Tom's liver solemnly to bits when all that was needed was a little irony.'[19] This continual reworking and fanatical analysis of conditions and situations was just another manifestation of the list-making, the compulsive need to impose order on a frightening, incomprehensible and chaotic world.

The harrowing effect of this obsessive debate on her intimates was particularly obvious in her relationship with Tom, who was kept up half the night in highly articulate but circular arguments over the irresolvable problems of their relationship. She was like a cat with a bird which she would not kill but could neither let alone nor allow to flutter free; each one as much a prisoner of this obsessive ritual as the other. Victim and torturer were caught in a deadly symbiosis where fear, pain and power were in continuous flux between them. Some years later Antonia was to recognise that she gained 'exquisite pleasure' from comforting someone she had hurt, but did not care much for comforting those hurt by others: 'Yes. I *have* a torturer's nature. And yet the person I torture most of all is myself.'[20] Here, it seemed clear to her that it was power, more than pain, which motivated her; the power to hurt and the power to take away hurt eased for a while her own fear of powerlessness and non-being.

Tom was a willing, or perhaps mesmerised, partner in this dance. His letters often exhibited a cloying abjectness which he himself traced back to his childhood at the mercy of a domineering nanny supported by a strict and inexpressive mother. When Antonia eventually left him, after more than four years of extreme stress and strain in the relationship, he wrote, 'You have done me the rarest service in the world. You have seen quite through me. You have shown me how quite imaginary, false & beclouded a world I had built up round myself. You have shown me how much needed breaking down.'[21] And he was to take as his third wife Dorothy Kingsmill, another powerful woman, who professed to be an analyst herself, who would carry on the breaking down and remaking of his uncertain, protean self.

Despite her obliterating depressions and private despair, Antonia was still managing to maintain the act of being 'frightfully jolly & sociable' amongst her friends and acquaintances.[22] She was establishing an epistolatory friendship with Emily Coleman, who had returned to America at the beginning of 1935, writing, when she had the energy, intimate letters about her own life and attempting to answer the torrent of directives, questions and exhortations which poured from Emily's incontinent pen. She also had met a handsome Jamaican sculptor called Ronald Moody, who was working as a dentist to earn his living while devoting every spare moment on developing his sculptures in wood and plaster. He began sculpting Antonia's head. One of the symptoms of her illness was an exaggerated sense of her own physical ugliness: she felt repellent and gross, particularly in comparison to the willowy, cool blondeness of her rival Frances Grigson. Ronald Moody's artistic appreciation of her: 'I love the way your hair leaves your forehead – it does it so *virulently*', and eventually his sexual appreciation and general acceptance of her in all her moods, made her feel a little less repulsive, a little more lovable, more human and whole.[23]

Still very ill, Antonia managed to go down to Sussex with Tom for the funeral of her ancient Aunt Agnes, who had been bed-ridden for the last few years and was the last of her much-loved old great-aunts to die. She was racked with guilt that she had neglected her in these last years. By the second week in February, however, Phyllis Jones was called on to prove what a stalwart friend she could be. Having returned from an exhilarating holiday in America, paid for by Peggy Guggenheim, who considered 'she badly needed a change of thought', Phyllis was back in London looking handsome and healthy and admitting to feeling more confident and happier than she had ever been.[24] Tom asked her to come and stay with them, as Antonia had become afraid of being on her own during the day and would dissolve into tears if left for too long. Phyllis was a kind and willing companion, but found Tom's attitude to his wife very trying. 'Tom brings such a sick bed atmosphere with him. . . . He hangs over Toni – rolls his eyes after her all the time – pets her & kisses her. I find it sickening, but I think she likes it from him. . . . He seems to reproach me silently every time I chatter & laugh.' Yet when they all went out dancing he danced inappropriately intimately with Phyllis; '– of course – was too loving. . . .'[25] This was the last thing she wanted to happen; she had come to be a comfort to Antonia, she protested to Emily, not a serpent in the bosom! Phyllis was blessed with good sense and a big heart and grew increasingly fond of Antonia during this stay. She had much less time for Tom, whom she saw as a narcissistic and sentimental idiot, living out a variety of self-conceived roles.

The great Freudian analysis began in the middle of February, Antonia felt resistant, suspicious and superior towards Dr Carroll, whom she thought 'undersized, rather stupid: cockney accent'.[26] However, quite quickly she grew more confident in him and his ability to help remove 'an unbearable obstruction' in her life.[27] Dr Carroll thought it would be fruitful to concentrate at first on her relationship with her father. A good deal about faeces came up in the first few weeks. In fact Antonia had an alternative name for analysis – 'anal lusis'; lusis being the Greek word for letting go.[28] Then suddenly it seemed significant to recall the layout of her father's study and her own nursery, with the lavatory between which both shared almost exclusively. She also realised that a particular clicking sound, connected in her mind with her father's presence, seemed to be the precursor for her of weighty disapproval. In a later session she linked this frightening clicking sound with the sound of her father's latchkey; 'Convulsive horror aroused by C[arroll]'s shaking his bunch of keys.'[29] It was as if she was a child again for, soon after this revelation, she was in bed one night with Tom and felt almost embryonic next to him; 'Wished there was another "big" person curled at the back of me to keep me warm.'[30]

Antonia became fearful that Dr Carroll seemed to interpret much of what she related in dreams and associations as a sexual desire she harboured for him. Yet she was rather amused by the overtly sexual imagery of a dream she described to him; '. . . someone gave me a gigantic tube of lanolin-like stuff to rub on my scorched leg. . . . A great deal came out of the tube, rubbed it on burn. Hands covered with it. Rather disgusted & didn't know how to get rid of it so ate it (I think).'[31] Within three months she was writing to Emily that in some extraordinary way the obstruction was shifting. The 'disintegration which was the result of years of strain, pressure & irrational fear' was in the process of being shored up; painfully, mysteriously, inexplicably, analysis seemed to be working.[32] Even to be able to cross a road without fear was a new and precious achievement for her, she told her friend.

In the process, even during these first three months, Antonia gained a certain new courage and focus. She was managing still to do some freelance work, although continuing to agonise over it, putting it off and then, in one great outpouring of energy, finishing it in a rush. She was writing advertisements for Innoxa beauty products and still keeping up with some of her *Daily Mirror* fashion articles, researching shops and their new stock. She had also gained enough confidence to think about leaving Tom, even though he had given up his affair with Frances Grigson and was making love to his wife again with a simulacrum, at least, of passion. Antonia's intention was hardened by her unauthorised reading of his notebook. She had let Tom read her diaries and he had been deeply touched by the 'extraordinary pathos' which appeared to hang around Antonia's head. She was a shell-less, vulnerable creature, ill-equipped to deal with the outside world. But then he recognised too that she was also far stronger than he, at times it seemed 'made of iron' and certain to survive.[33]

His notebook was less reassuring to her. She was shocked how full it was of Frances and his discovery of sexual ecstasy with her. It was terrible too to be confronted with herself through Tom's eyes as someone who aroused pity. She would have rather aroused fear than pity, would rather be monstrous than mediocre, and yet perversely she wanted to be protected and adored. Above all she wanted to count for something. Reading Tom's diary, she said, made her feel that her life was over; no man would ever love her again. She would become 'cranky and vinegarish' because she had wasted whatever chances of love she had been offered through fear and horror of the sexual relationship.[34]

Jealousy too was a difficult emotion to integrate into one's life; to destroy one's rival was not possible in a civilised world, and so that force was turned inwards. 'We have lost love and so want to make ourselves too foul to have love again. That terrible destroying impulse has always been very strong in me. . . . I seem to have experienced everything in the world except positive, continuous, productive happiness.'[35] And yet that very kind of happiness, Antonia realised, frightened her for it would possibly mean renouncing everything she valued. The news of the birth of Frances Grigson's baby at the beginning of March also reinforced this feeling of her rejection by love and life. When she told Tom the news she was seized by a fit of cold shudders and chattering teeth, just as she had been after a particularly bad nightmare.

However, it seems that analysis too was freeing Antonia a little from the torture of self-hatred and obsession, for she began to consider the children's feelings a little more in the scheme of her life. Her separation from Tom was the last thing that Susan and Lyndall needed in their young lives. 'They love him and he is so good to them. Emotional disturbances are so bad for them,' she wrote in her diary, considering for a time at least that Bertrand Russell's brand of 'companionate' marriage might be the only answer, 'with all its risks, frustrations, painted-over miseries.'[36] Eight days later, however, these concerns were brushed aside; Antonia had steeled herself to leave. Having lived a life so shaped by fear, with hope as a delusion, Antonia felt now that for the first time she had to try and live without the impetus of either hope or fear.

She intended to move into Shelley House at 105 Oakley Street, Chelsea, and to take a room next door to Phyllis. The children, she thought, would be less traumatised if they stayed in the flat with Nurse and Tom. They were growing increasingly interesting and individual, although it remained Tom rather than their mother who seemed to notice and delight most in them. Susan was nearly six and 'introverted, self-absorbed, imaginative and poetic. Almost from the first she attempted to speak in sentences ... and would go white with concentration in trying to find the exact expression she wanted.' One stormy day when the river was running wild and high, Tom took her down to the Embankment to watch the racing tide. She gazed down into the water for a long time and then said 'I'm the sort of person that likes coldness and wetness and loneliness and lostness.'[37] Lyndall was nearly four and naturally warm and gregarious. As a little girl she was more aesthetically sensitive than verbal, being drawn most to colour and form and the specific appearance of things. She also made friends easily and seemed more relaxed than her older sister in her relationships with others. Having made the decision, Antonia was afraid but determined to carry it out: 'I feel a sinking in my stomach as if I were standing on the edge of an aeroplane and had to make a parachute jump. I will not try and force myself not to love him. If I love him, I must accept that too as a fact.'[38] She went to lunch with Tom to discuss their separation. He recalled their conversation:

> 'If anyone wants to know where you are, Tony' I said, 'I shall tell them you're taking a holiday from me.' ... Tony looked at me with a little smile. 'Still afraid of the truth?' she asked. 'Why,' I said 'surely that's true?'
>
> She looked at me. 'Darling' she said very gently, 'I'm leaving you.'[39]

13

Living With the Stranger

Alone, alone, all, all alone,
Alone on a wide wide sea!
And never a saint took pity on
My soul in agony.

'The Rime of the Ancient Mariner', Samuel Taylor Coleridge

Just before her thirty-sixth birthday, Antonia moved out of the family home. She was never to share her life intimately with a man again. All her life she had made her decisions from a position of weakness, driven by fear: it was fear too which then had prevented her from turning the major decisions she had made into something adequate and good. Fear of powerlessness, fear of letting go, fear of disapproval and failure, shame over her body, and a profound fear of sexual love, all imprisoned her in an emotional straitjacket as effective as anything in which they encased her at the asylum.

It was March 1935; spring was beginning to lengthen the evenings and put a haze of green on the trees. There was some relief for Antonia in being isolated in her little room, high up, looking out on Oakley Street. There were no extra demands on her there. And yet the lethargy and sudden convulsions of fear which Tom's presence had been able to calm now alarmed her, for there was no one to restrain her from a sudden impulse to throw herself from this high window. She placed three small dahlia plants in their pots on the sill, 'to remind me to keep my head.'[1] Antonia also was overcome with an irresistible desire to physically attack Tom when they met, and this she did, only to feel overwhelming depression and suicidal thoughts afterwards. The feeling of isolation and the sense of her own grotesqueness overwhelmed her. A young man at the window in the opposite house, engrossed in his reading and writing, became a focus of this despair; 'He is aware of me, I am pretty sure, but resents the intrusion of that monster the "writing woman". Yet here am I a creature in distress, only half in my mind, at any moment to be assailed by an impulse to fling myself out of *my* window as he may, for all I know, want yet fear to do out of *his*.'[2]

So concerned was Eric Earnshaw Smith about Antonia's state of mind that he went to see Dr Carroll, three months into her analysis. He related to Antonia that the doctor had told him she was really ill; although he felt he could give her some years of self-possession the madness might return in the end, sometime between fifty and sixty, but possibly even sooner than that. Antonia surprised herself with how well she took this serious prognosis. Her initial reaction was one of relief, 'that there *is* a beast in the jungle.'[3] So good was she at putting on her acceptable social face that there were people who found it hard to believe in the extremity of her suffering; others thought she was merely subject to fits of hysteria. She had an argument with Emily who said that women, particularly, could choose madness as an escape from the daily pain of living. She had herself. On the contrary, Antonia had said, it was something that was thrust upon you, that lurked and stalked and then pounced. After the initial relief had worn off, however, the shock of this sentence took its toll. She wrote in her diary that she had often felt on the verge, even over the edge, of madness, but to be told that truly she was in the grip of it, and that the abyss was real, was terrifying. A few months later she wondered if it was the will of God that she should go mad again and again, and in the end irretrievably. Was this her place in the scheme of things? And yet, if this was her fate, one which she had to endure without help and with no attempt at deflection, she could not contemplate going on living. She would only ever be 'a horror to myself and destruction to others.'[4] It was a fearful thought. Antonia was wounded by Tom's reaction, which appeared academic and indifferent to her terror. Her mother, however, wrote with a heart-wrenched sympathy from Binesfield, the note undated and her handwriting disintegrating:

> Darling Tony, I wonder if you realise how I agonise over you, & the tragedy of your life pierces my heart like a sharp sword. Every day I pray for you, make a communion when I can for you, you are never out of my thoughts. If I could die alone for you I would, if by dying I could give you happiness – I would, and that is true. Your loving Mother *Christine*. [She then added a line:] I never have told you all this, not wishing to depress you my dearest child.[5]

Nightmares began to crowd Antonia's sleep again. That May the streets of London were full of bunting and celebrations marking the Silver Jubilee of King George V's reign. In Antonia's mind, however, she was back in Bethlem asylum, her tortures refined to incorporate the features of her recent life. In one she was an old woman who knew she was mad, 'trying to plead with the nurses, explaining to them that things which looked normal and harmless to them were terrifying to me.' Listening, apparently with sympathy and understanding, they nevertheless pushed her towards 'the machine with the clippers which frightened me so.'[6] But this time there was no Tom beside her in bed who would bring her a cup of warm milk and talk her down from her terrors. By day she would sit frightened in her room, writing letters or her diary, longing for the company of someone else, even just sitting silently beside her, 'reading or knitting, but *tethering* me.'[7] Antonia inevitably turned to Phyllis in her lonely despair, but Phyllis found this increasingly difficult to deal with especially as she was having a rumbustious affair with a passionate Hungarian, Stefan Lorant, a gifted photographer, cameraman and journalist. Phyllis was very aware that while she was in the arms of her lover, Antonia was next door struggling alone with a terrifying desire to kill herself. She felt that Antonia was so full of envy of her during this terrible time that on more than one occasion she did not pass on phone messages from Lorant. However, such a flouting of this trust may have been as much to do with the broken state of Antonia's mind and memory at the time.

There were lighter moments too. Phyllis described in a letter to Emily how comic Antonia looked doing exercises to her gramophone, but had improved her figure greatly in the process. Then, trying to fix something, she had burst out with 'If it isn't right this time I'll eat my Dutch cap.'[8] One of the places where Antonia sought solace at this time was Ronald Moody's studio, which he had converted from a little greenhouse on the side of his small flat in Chelsea. She would sit and read in the adjoining room, listening to the tapping of Ronald's chisel as he worked away at his latest sculpture. Here Antonia felt uncritically cared for and accepted. On the first Sunday in June, afraid of what she called 'Sunday neurosis', Antonia went round to the studio. Some time during that day Antonia overcame her self-confessed colour-prejudice, and Ronald his fear that he would awaken all her old demons, and they made love. Almost immediately Antonia recognised this as an event with some great symbolic import for her. 'It was as if that day I came of age, took a new name, was initiated into a rite, given, as in fairytales, the sealed packet with the instructions for my journey.'[9] The sexual act had not given her pleasure: Antonia was cold with terror and in pain; all her old anxieties and sense of sin assailed her. It was the first time she had been unfaithful to Tom since their marriage, and she felt that this act had cut her off somehow from him for ever. Emotional instability loomed: she wept. But Ronald was calm and sure-footed in his treatment of her. He put on a record of 'Deh Vieni', Susanna's famous aria from *The Marriage of Figaro* and lay beside her breathing steadily. She became calm; the music and Ronald's solid presence helped release her from the obsessive workings of her own mind. When she found she had been bleeding 'like a virgin' she felt all the negative accretions of the years slip away and in the mirror her face seemed transformed from a swollen-eyed, distorted mask, to the face of a young, contented woman with bright eyes and radiant skin.[10] For a time she had been connected in her humanness with another, with none of the anxieties and fear and self-absorption which kept her isolated and always alone. Briefly, she thought she had been shown her adult self. Out of Ronald's company the old insecurities returned. But Antonia realised that for the first time she was being dealt with honestly by a man; it was hard for her, but positive. In reply to her clamour for reassurance he said, 'No, you may not be young and beautiful, but if you were young you would not be what you are and to me your face is beautiful.'[11]

This moment of connection and acceptance of another human being was not as dramatic an epiphany as Antonia had at first thought. The affair with Ronald ended after about a month, although she continued to like and admire him all her life. She still longed to be able to respond naturally and wholeheartedly to a man who loved her; 'It would be most "rational" for me to love R[onald] who is so much ahead of me; most desirable for me to love Tom.'[12] To her shame she could do neither. Without meaning to, she did tell Tom, however, about her revelation with Ronald and was a little disappointed that the news barely ruffled him. But he was distracted himself by a new affair, with a married woman called Vesti, and his emotional energies had a different focus. Nevertheless, for about four weeks that June Antonia was suddenly able to get through a remarkable amount of her hack work. She still was not attempting her major writing, and had been barely able to read anything serious for months. But she managed to write her *Daily Mirror* fashion pieces regularly and with relative ease, she delivered articles for another magazine, *Everyman*, finished the copy for two shoe catalogues and then wrote, in two intensely productive days, about 12,000 words of copy for Theodora Benson. This ease passed, and the work and emotional troubles returned, but underneath she noticed there was something more secure and solid; 'a sort of hope or rather resignation & sense of life one day to flower.'[13] Then later that summer, she bought a pen just like Dr Carroll's; this similarity was unconscious, she said. The recognition that her writing block was connected with impotence released her from taboo for a week: suddenly filled with creative energy, she wrote 15,000 words of a new book about Tom and Frances. But the block returned as quickly as it had passed.

She had attracted the attentions of two other men. The architectural writer John Summerson was a friend, but Antonia felt ambivalent about him. He was a closer friend of the Grigsons, and seemed to get some pleasure from giving Antonia hurtful information about Frances; he had in fact been the one to break the news of her baby's birth to her, before even Tom knew. The writer and journalist Eric Siepmann was more of a challenge, and much more interesting to her as a focus of friendship and for a while, she hoped, of passion too. Antonia considered him to be fiendishly clever and was to grow obsessed with him. She described him in terms of his polarised qualities, the very qualities she might have used to describe herself at the time: 'demon and angel so mixed in his face . . . needs affection & drives it away . . . cruel with the extreme cruelty of the sensitive . . . so much alive and so completely dead at the same time.'[14] That summer, however, she was too emotionally fragile to pursue him.

By August, when Dr Carroll gave her a holiday from analysis, Antonia was much more able to deal with the demands of everyday life, even to the extent of sharing a communal life for a couple of weeks with the experimental Group Theatre, which was holding its summer school at A.S. Neill's progressive school, Summerhill, in Suffolk. Two acquaintances of Antonia's, Rupert Doone, who had trained in classical ballet and had worked with Diaghilev, and the painter Robert Medley, were among the founder members of the Group Theatre three years earlier in 1932. Auden too was of their number and 'Uncle Wiz', as he was called, was most influential in forming the ideas of the Group. They considered that new forms of drama were needed to reflect the changes in modern life. The Group Theatre had both aesthetic ideas and a philosophy based on Communism, and Doone thought the plays they produced should have a form analagous to modern musical comedy or the pre-medieval folk play. To effect this he proposed there should be a permanent company of actors fertilised with a changing group of guest artists, poets and musicians. It was as a guest writer that Antonia was invited down to Suffolk in August, and it was on impulse that she accepted: 'What on earth am I doing here?' Although it was self-consciously progressive, full of idealistic young people insisting on the benefits of hearty outdoor living, physical exercise and fresh-faced ideology, all usually anathema to her, Antonia really rather enjoyed herself. As a writer she was exhorted by Doone to become socially conscious and work for the collective good, eschewing 'old bourgeois pride and prejudice and individualism.'[15] Antonia found herself feeling guilty at how politically supine she was and worrying about what was really meant by 'the bourgeoisie'. She realised that the Catholic Church was definitely The Enemy – fascist, capitalist and bourgeois – and she was amused to find herself defending it so eloquently and silencing some of its detractors; 'I have the advantage of having read the Communist Manifesto while they haven't read the Catechism.'[16]

Antonia needed action, challenge and drama in her life, and the Summer School provided a bizarre combination of all three. In a letter to Phyllis Jones begging to be sent a bath towel and a couple of new brassières (bought by Nurse with Tom's money) she described her days there.

> Such a pandemonium as you never dreamed, but it's rather fun. I sleep with another woman, there are no locks on the bathroom door, bath itself filthy & inches deep in matted hair, hot water boiler burst etc. etc. yet I really am rather enjoying it. We do the most convulsive exercises for hours in blazing sun, sing rounds, read plays, all in the most arty way imaginable. . . . Believe me or not I dragged my mattress into an open field last night & slept under god's stars & crawled over by god's earwigs & awakened by god's larks, cocks, dogs, willow-wrens etc. etc. This place is *so* like an asylum that I feel quite at home. . . . Rupert Doone invites you to roll on your belly on the tennis court 'feeling the hardness, the soul, the personality of the ground,' the problem children prowl round with knives in their belts but I feel remarkably well on it.[17]

This was the first time that Antonia managed to overcome her embarrassment when undressing in front of anyone. Usually the fear of her body instilled in her by the Convent, together with her fear of self-exposure, made it an unbearable task.

Along with the institutionalised communing, the Group Theatre were rehearsing Auden's play *The Dog Beneath the Skin*, which became rather a fashionable hit. As a drama critic, Geoffrey Grigson voiced a common criticism of Group Theatre productions; 'We should like less prancing and bad dancing, less complacence, less guidance, and more stiff thinking combined with spontaneity.'[18] When Tom went in the New Year with Antonia to see this particular play he had found it 'very scrappy & disconnected, but disturbing', and had lain in bed that night unable to get to sleep.[19] However, the play was almost saved from its over-stylisation, its masks and fragments of ballet, by the rolling magnificence of the poet's choruses, even though they may have smacked a little of what Cyril Connolly branded 'homo-communism'.[20]

> Now the ragged vagrants creep
> Into crooked holes to sleep:
> Just and unjust, worst and best,
> Change their places as they rest:
> Awkward lovers lie in fields
> Where disdainful beauty yields:
> While the splendid and the proud
> Naked stand before the crowd
> And the losing gambler gains
> And the beggar entertains.[21]

Auden's line about awkward lovers lying in fields was particularly apt for Antonia that August. She was flattered by the attentions of a young Quaker, John Greenwood, 'half prig and half poet', who was writing a history entitled *Protestant Dissenting Deputies*, and managed to be both a pacifist and a revolutionary in his politics.[22] Admiring his integrity and fleetingly attracted to him sexually, they had attempted some kind of sexual relationship, but once again impotence thwarted desire. She continued to see him when she returned to Oakley Street, grateful for his affection and care but ambivalent about 'his commonness, narrowness, cockiness. . . .'[23] Antonia's search for faith was one of their topics of conversation, and Greenwood persuaded her to come to a meeting of Friends, convinced that she would find her God among the Quakers. She did not doubt their sincerity but was disappointed in the apparent joylessness and complacency of the gathering; the silences tense, she felt, rather than contemplative. But their strange friendship would continue for more than a year.

The volatility of Antonia's feelings, particularly when she felt she had been rejected in some way, were demonstrated by a sudden intemperate outburst in her diary against Greenwood, a month after they had first met: 'How horrible, how horrible human beings can be. Even when one knows how many actions are prompted by unconscious fears, it is impossible not to be disgusted by them. Even though I know there is something true, warm, incorruptible in J[ohn] G[reenwood] how he stinks of corruption. I feel as if I had been covered with slime by contact with such a creature.'[24] There is reason to believe from a later diary entry that the incident which turned her so violently – and temporarily – against Greenwood had to do with his strong feelings for her and his desire to somehow overcome his impotence in his relationship with her.

Her outburst shows how deeply distressed, even disgusted, Antonia could be by sexual behaviour and the concomitant sense of failure and rejection. She consoled herself by considering some good had come out of this incident – she had introduced him to a therapist of some kind and therefore 'put him in the way of being cured.'

Antonia saw Peggy Guggenheim and Emily again that summer of 1935. Peggy had rented an ancient cottage at the foot of the Sussex downs, called Yew Tree Cottage, named after the five hundred-year-old yew which grew at the front and towered over its roof. They had to pump their water from a lake and use an old unreliable generator for electricity. Peggy lived there for much of the time with her lover Garman, who embarked on landscaping the large romantic gardens and restyling and decorating the house. They were not as social as they had been at Hayford Hall or Warblington Castle, but Antonia was invited for a visit at the end of summer. Emily had grown to love Antonia and she appreciated that, while Antonia seemed incapable of writing her own novels, she was a most gifted literary critic and editor on other people's behalf. Her intelligence and perceptiveness, and generosity with time and energy, made her comments always valuable and often inspired.

The last weekend in July, Antonia went to stay at the Cottage. Emily had insisted Antonia work on her own book for her entire time there. This vast, rambling, impossible work was to be called 'The Tygon', on a suggestion by Djuna, who considered it the best novel yet written on jealousy from a woman's point of view. It was hardly light reading for Antonia, struggling to emerge from the morass of her own feelings of abandonment and loss. But Emily, in the grip of her obsession, was utterly irresistible. Antonia returned to London almost erased with fatigue and Tom came to her aid. He was cross that her two friends seemed to be oblivious to the fact that Antonia had a very small resource of energy: it could be catastrophic for her when she ran it dry. He took her to their local restaurant and then put her to bed. His heart was touched by the things she said in a sad matter-of-fact way: 'I am like a person who's been left behind on an island. Everything goes on without me. I have no place. It isn't that I haven't had chances. I've had lots of them, but now I'm too old to start afresh . . . If you have chances and don't take them life goes on giving you them for a time, then it decides regretfully that it's no use giving you them any more. . . .' Tom had been talking earlier about what he ought to do with his career and Antonia added in her quiet sad voice, 'You made me feel like the corpse in the coffin; hearing all the people saying what they'll be doing on Thursday week and knowing that by then he'll be under the ground.'[25]

Part of her sense of isolation and inconsequentiality was a result of her having left the family home. She realised that Tom and the children carried on, with Nurse's continuity of care, much as they had before. She felt shut off from what seemed to be a happy self-contained little family; 'I've just dropped out of it like a book gone from a shelf. Nobody notices even that I'm not there.'[26] But Tom was also rather miserable himself, not knowing what he should be doing, becalmed in his work and his emotional life. Susan and Lyndall were one of his few unalloyed pleasures, increasingly interesting themselves, but also uncomplicated in their emotional demands on him. In May he had travelled to his parents' house to bring them home and had been met with resistance. His father, particularly, had had all his worst fears fulfilled by the latest news of Antonia's mental state and absence from the family home. The Hopkinson grandparents had grown fond of their two little granddaughters, who seemed to their distant and conventional eye to be in a most unsuitable environment. They thought it unwise that Mary Hitchcock, the children's nurse, and Tom should be under the same roof without a third adult there for the sake of propriety. Tom had to stand up to them, something he always found very difficult to do, and bring the children and Nurse home to Cecil Court.

Antonia's fears that she was extraneous to this little family unit were founded on intuition and fact. The children were growing increasingly fond of Tom and he of them. He enjoyed their company, listened to their stories, was sensitive to their troubles and the difficult emotions with which they had to deal. He recognised how jealous Susan was of Lyndall at times, sometimes pretending to be a baby in the hopes that she would receive more of that precious attention and concern. He noted that she was beginning to steal, small trivial things like the toy money from school, which she hid in the elasticated leg of her knickers. But Tom knew that this was a signal that she was feeling insecure, in need of love, and wanted more attention. Susan was also afraid of parental disapproval and Tom thought her stealing was a way of getting what she wanted without having to risk admonishment. Lyndall, on the other hand, at four was a more confident little person who quite readily stood up to be counted, and 'was prepared for a fight in the last resort.'[27]

For Antonia, the return to analysis that autumn unsettled her equilibrium and by the end of the year she had declined into a desperate state once more. She suffered from an excessive nervousness; she was afraid to leave her room but afraid also to stay. There was no pleasure for her in anything. Even though Tom's affair with Frances was long over, she was wracked by an overwhelming desire for revenge against both of them. Every time she saw Tom she would say to him, 'Vengeance really *is* the Lord's' in an attempt to subdue the impulse in herself.[28] (She did not quite manage to do so and wrote a 12-page letter to Frances.) During one of her visits to Dr Carroll, Antonia was asked by him to demonstrate something she was saying and suddenly, without warning, a very deep voice burst out of her; 'It didn't sound like my voice at all' she told Tom. 'It abused Carroll like anything for about twenty minutes.'[29]

Antonia also abused Tom, in her own voice, but to just as shocking an effect. One day, for an entire lunch and then for three hours that evening, she attacked him continually for past injuries in such a fluent and irrefutable stream that Tom was reduced to speechlessness, as he often was with her. His only possible response that night was to put her into a taxi and take her back to her home bodily, barely saying a word. 'When she is at her most vindictive I am suddenly filled with passion – not of hatred which is slow-smouldering & often present but never flooding me suddenly like a revelation – with a passion of pity. It has come over me sometimes so that I could cry. When she said "*Please* kill me, Tom. Really I could bear it quite well from you. It would be much the kindest thing that you could do."'[30]

Antonia recorded in her diary a conversation with a mild man she had met in a café. He confessed to having tortured animals when he was a boy, in the company of a gang of other boys. They competed to see who was the chief torturer, or 'executioner' as they called him. He then became the leader of the gang, the one with all the power. On at least one occasion Dr Carroll associated her outbursts of rage 'with impotence, with fury at not being able to work miracles.'[31]

Antonia's sense of powerlessness provoked terrible outbursts of rage against those she felt had some advantage over her. Tom was an obvious focus for her hurt, and Joan Freeman, her own painter friend, who was engaged fleetingly in an affair with him. Tom's susceptibility to women and his need of their love was the main prop of his life: 'I do need, if I am to be strong & happy, a person whom I can love, with all the breath in my body & all the fibres of my mind.'[32] This need in him meant that almost any woman, including most of Antonia's friends – Emily, Joan, Phyllis, Kathleen McClean, Dorothy Kingsmill – was a focus at some time for his narcissistic desire.

At the beginning of the bad times that autumn, Antonia was reading Djuna Barnes's novel *Nightwood*, and identified closely with the description Djuna had written of a character. '"She was avid and disorderly in her heart. She defiled the very meaning of personality in her passion to be a person. . . . She was nervous about the future and that made her indelicate. She wanted to be the reason of everything and so was the cause of nothing."' She thought of Djuna's deadly eye, her saying to Antonia, 'For God's sake go out of your mind if you want it that way. At least that would be something definite.'[33] By the end of November Antonia was so reduced she had not the will even to do that; 'Utter exhaustion and a despair which has nothing in the least grand about it – just a weeping whining infant unable to cope with life. I do not know, literally do not know how to go on living.'[34]

In the midst of this mental collapse that November, Antonia lost her job with the *Daily Mirror* and her eight guinea weekly salary. This meant her income dropped to virtually nothing. Remarkably, despite her despairing mental state, Antonia decided to approach Michel Saint-Denis for work. He was an avant-garde French theatre director whose theatrical experiments with his company of acrobatic actors, the 'Compagnie des Quinze', had attracted her when she was drama critic the previous year for *Time and Tide*. He had recently established his acting school, the London Theatre Studio, which followed the Stanislavski method and offered a two-year course, including classes in breathing and voice, calisthenics and readings from texts and improvisations, as well as lectures in the history of theatre. He needed someone to lecture on Greek drama. Antonia had decided that it was work which would save her, not rest. She needed a congenial climate in which she could expand, and had 'something to fight for.'[35] She had pinned all her hopes on being able to have some association with this company; Saint-Denis was so full of life she felt that contact with him would revive her from her half-life; she had also been reminded how much she loved the theatre. However, he was concerned about her mental state, and initially would only offer her a part-time, unpaid post, starting at the beginning of 1936, as his literary adviser. By early spring Antonia had convinced him of her capability, and she was delivering a series of lectures on Greek drama at the Theatre Studio in Islington in North London. These lectures were deemed to be 'brilliant': reluctantly Antonia had to admit that not only was she good at teaching, but she rather enjoyed it.[36]

She had also managed to write a couple of plays for the students to perform, *Alcibiades*, and another about Nausicaa, the daughter of Alcinous in the *Odyssey*, who comes across Odysseus after his shipwreck, and clothes, feeds him and sends him on his way, while wishing he could stay. Tom saw the play performed in April and found it very moving; 'very simple & fresh & well constructed. . . . Tears kept on welling up.'[37] Antonia's dramatic vein continued with a sketch which she wrote for a comic revue that the Group Theatre were due to put on, probably for Christmas. She was not proud of it and did not own up to its authorship. Although the Theatre Studio only lasted about three years, it had at least two eminent students; Peter Ustinov and a young

Canadian woman, the poet Elizabeth Smart, who was to fall irrevocably and memorably in love with George Barker, memorialising her doomed passion in *By Grand Central Station I Sat Down and Wept.*

Antonia's extreme suffering lasted right up to Christmas; an expedition with Tom and the children to spend time with her mother at Binesfield filled her with unspecified but 'fearful anxiety.'[38] But Antonia recovered suddenly on realising that the book she wanted to write was not the Tom and Frances one, on which she had inevitably become stuck, but an earlier idea, begun just over a year earlier, about her father. Christmas was saved and both Tom and Antonia felt it was a successful and happy time; the first night Antonia played the piano and then the children started singing sweetly and competently a medley of songs, both known ones and others made up by them. Granny Botting had made them cakes specially for tea and was, as Tom said, 'less loopy than usual.' Susan and Lyndall danced and delighted everyone with their welcome to any visitors and their beautiful manners. Tom was also struck that Christmas by how gentle they were with each other: '"You take it, sweetheart" said Susan to Lyndall.' To which Lyndall replied, ' "Susan, you can have my dolly to play with sometimes if you like."'[39] On Christmas night, as Tom and Antonia were getting ready for bed, there was a commotion of shouting and crying coming from the children's bedroom. Antonia went to investigate and then called for Tom's adjudiction. Susan and Lyndall were sharing a bed with Romeo, a huge tabby-and-white cat who had just come home from hunting, thoroughly wet, and had snuggled down between the two girls and lain his head on the pillow with theirs:

> Lyndall was crying. 'I don't *want* a wet cat in my bed – besides he's pushed me all up & there isn't enough room.'
> Susan was very contemptuous. 'Poor Romeo' she said. 'Let him stay, he only wants to be warm like you do Lyndall.' Then, looking at Lyndall with contempt 'I can't have a crying child in my bed.'[40]

Tom ruled that no one should be forced to share a bed with a large wet cat and Romeo was banished for the night. Tom was very touched by this Christmas holiday, believing that they somehow had become the sort of family that he had always wanted, where there was a sense of pulling together, being part of a team. Celebrating Christmas with her children was always to be symbolically important for Antonia but, sadly, playing happy families like this was a rare conjugation of mood and circumstance. It was to grow much less likely through the rest of the children's childhoods as Tom extricated himself from their lives, and Susan and Lyndall's fear of their mother's unpredictable moods cast an increasing shadow over their relationship with her.

Antonia was still in a fragile mental state when a sudden tragedy affected her deeply. In the middle of February, Elspeth Glossop, Silas's much-loved younger sister, had had an illegal abortion which had gone horribly wrong. She was rushed to hospital and subjected to several blood transfusions, but was not expected to live through the night. Mrs Glossop was summoned to London from Derbyshire and arrived at six o'clock the next morning. She knew no one and rang the Cecil Court flat, hoping to find Antonia. Instead Tom came to her aid and took her to the hospital and waited for her while Elspeth died. Antonia saw Elspeth's body in the mortuary and was shocked and yet strangely elated by the sight. When she related the events to Emily the next day, Emily was very disapproving; '[She] becomes as cheap as an old woman. She seems to get a great excitement out of it. She talked as I imagine her mother talks.'[41] Antonia had to attend the inquest, and Emily and Phyllis were both very protective of the doctor they believed to have been responsible. He was a well-known illegal abortionist 'who saves women's lives' according to Emily and did not charge when a woman could not afford to pay. Emily warned Antonia not to say anything which might make things worse.

This tragic and untimely death affected Antonia much more deeply than Emily understood. 'This is the first death I have completely realised: even my father's death was not so real to me. I was glad at last to be able to weep for someone.' The sight of Elspeth's body and the obliteration in one wilful act of her intense aliveness and beauty shocked Antonia; 'I wanted to write a poem about her. I wanted to put on her grave that she was young and beautiful so that people should not remember her as she looked dead with her face swollen and yellow, cotton wool carelessly stuffed in her nostrils, her hair that used to be sleek as spaniel's ears, dead and dull.'[42] In her illness, Antonia saw everything in relation to herself. She felt that in that mortuary she could have been looking at her own corpse, still young, her body poisoned, her face distorted in death; so close had she come many times to an equally violent destruction of self.

Antonia did in fact write her poem, titled 'Epitaph', suddenly that October. At that time she was struggling with what appeared to be a perfectly rational decision to end her life. There seemed no alternative, given her conviction then that she was incurable and did not know how to go on living any more. The *New Statesman* rejected the poem as 'too violent and emotional.'[43] It was published in April 1938 by Henry Miller and Alfred Perlès in Paris, in their newly reincarnated literary magazine *Delta*. Antonia was proud of the poem: it said something true about the horror and seduction of untimely death. She admitted to Emily: 'I have a conviction, perhaps illogical, that this [life] must be lived through and accepted, however dull & painful. Believing as I do that fear is the root of all evil . . . fear would distort the face of the one who died *stealing* death instead of *earning* it.'[44] She may have been remembering her own abortion, which had also threatened her with blood poisoning, and the son she had never had. She later told a friend, 'You can also take it as being an epitaph on myself too, had I killed myself at a certain time of my life.'[45]

> . . . Bury me deep
> Lest my love look on me asleep
> And see the time-stained face with which I died.
> This hasty, swollen mask of yellow wax
> Which fear, the clumsy workman botched me up
> Blasphemes death's patient marble.
> Calmer my living brow,
> Purer my cheek that flushes now
> With dark decay like rouge.
> I wear the face of one who could not stay
> For heaven's slow marriage day
> That stamps me as death's whore and not his bride. . . .[46]

14

Young Poets' Society

It is so absurd that I can hardly bring myself to set it down on paper: a
woman of 37 – a woman who has had three husbands and two
children, has been in an asylum, is being psycho-analysed and,
having been living alone for about a year, is starving not so much
for sex as for simple affection, or rather an object of affection – has
fallen in love with *me*.
We sat up talking about it until six o'clock in the morning.
She wants to explore, not so much my body, as my soul! (And she has
only met me once before.)

David Gascoyne, *Collected Journals*

The beginning of 1936 was marked by the death of King George V
and the accession to the throne of the dashing Prince of Wales, who
was for just twelve months the uneasy and uncrowned king, Edward
VIII. In December, after months of personal and national agonising, he
abdicated and left his kingdom for an ignominious exile with the
woman he loved. It was to be an ominous year. German troops entered
the Rhineland, the Spanish Civil War erupted bloodily and Oswald
Mosley's Blackshirts appeared at anti-Jewish demonstrations in London's
East End. However, none of these events or upheavals found their way
into Antonia's voluminous diaries of the time. Only when she was
actively engaged with war work and suffering the privations and dangers
of the blitz in London, did her journals, and particularly her letters,
become more concerned with ordinary people, with everyday detail and
the world outside. It is a well-known phenomenon that war and other
kinds of national crisis have a remarkably steadying effect on most
neurotic states of mind. Antonia's was no exception. But in the slow,
menacing approach to world war, Antonia's own war against personal
annihilation continued, punctuated with a sporadically febrile social life
and extreme enthusiasms for various young men. She was touched by

their frankness and freedom from preconceptions about morality and art and for a time they energised her own intellectual life, and made her feel she was part of a new spirit of experiment and enquiry. In their company Antonia could believe that she still had something valuable herself to give.

But first Antonia's obsessive gaze returned to Eric Siepmann, who had assumed a 'violent importance' to her at the end of January.[1] She was often attracted to men whom she could cast in apocalyptic roles, her dramatic instinct was expressed in the melodrama of her relationships. She told Tom what a dangerous and destructive man she considered Siepmann to be; 'The most dangerous of all because he hates what makes him happy. . . . He's a real homicidal maniac.'[2] Yet Siepmann's few surviving letters to her show a kindly man, an intellectual, interested in religion and politics and admittedly, at the time, drawn to drink, whorehouses and excitement, but honest and generous in his impulses towards her. He had his share of mental instability and fascinated Antonia, in part because she recognised so much of herself in her version of his character. 'He is terribly split and divided against himself. Much more naif and childish than I had supposed, but with a much keener drive of mind and imagination too . . . a real Judas betraying himself.'[3] She was meant to go to stay with him in Cornwall that January but he panicked, dispatching a telegram telling her not to come. An undated letter from him explained his reasons for holding himself more aloof: 'I suspected you, after our last meetings, of approaching me via some ready-made idea that somebody or something would be good for you at this point, and choosing me as it!' Tom was greatly relieved; he had rung Emily, his voice trembling 'in a clergyman's way', to ask her if Siepmann knew that Antonia could go out of her mind.[4] Emily said he certainly did and was terrified by the thought. Tom was also still strongly attached to Antonia emotionally, as she was to him, despite the serial affairs in which he was engaged.

On receiving the telegram and a following letter, Antonia immediately went round to Emily's flat where they spent the day, as Emily described it, talking like harpies. The subjects were as usual – their assertive demands for love, their own characters, the failings in the characters of their men, and sometimes the problems of their writing projects: different speculations, analyses and glosses were endlessly discussed in the light of the latest turns of the screw. Emily had cheered Antonia up, making her rock with laughter over the story of her only lesbian affair. Antonia had always thought Emily reckless and headlong in her behaviour; now a certain raciness was added to her aura.

Some of the most intellectually lively discussions within this group of friends occurred when Peter Hoare and Antonia were together and on top form. They brought out the best in each other in the literary arena, although he was frightened of her madness and she was afraid of his disdain. One Sunday in April to entertain the literary friends, Hoare read out loud an autobiographical fragment by Antonia's mother. Emily wrote that 'It was screamingly funny, just like Ouida.'[5] Emily's diaries contained pages and pages on the theme of unrequited love for Peter, although it seemed to be more about her need to possess, his recoil from possession. She had been trying to bludgeon him into greater declarations of passion for three years and he had resisted every ploy: Djuna Barnes called him Emily's little indomitable Scotch rubber plant. That spring she wondered whether she could use the poet George Barker's growing interest in her to ginger up Hoare's desire. Hoare's sexuality, however, was too complicated and subtle a matter for Emily's gale-force personality. He confided to her that he had gone to a prostitute because he thought there was something wrong with him, but had never got over the sense of violation. He still thought sex was frightful and preferred instead to imagine what it felt like to be a woman, fancying himself as 'a black frump, quaking with desire'.[6]

But neither was Barker a straightforward sexual conquest for Emily. He was very young, at twenty-three fourteen years younger than she or Antonia. He was one of the new generation of poets: non-establish-ment, state-school educated, and already published and recognised. T.S. Eliot was his mentor, in his role as poetry publisher at Faber & Faber. He was a man with a mission; he had known he was a poet when he was barely sixteen and his life was lived in the light of that grand plan: he was to befriend both Antonia and Emily. In her diary Emily related convoluted conversations about how much Barker was attracted to her, although never before had he been attracted to a woman, or so he said (despite being married). Yet, he told her, when he finally made love to her he did not like it a bit. Emily did not take this personally: nothing ever seemed to ruffle her immutable sense of her own rightness. As always she had her own analysis of the situation; it was the peculiar combination in her of the masculine and feminine which attracted him, she decided, 'the hermaphrodite he longed for in his dream.'[7]

These conversations were related to Antonia, who could offer a richer perspective from the Greek myths, psychoanalysis and her own fractured emotional experiences: 'I do not really believe Emily *wants* to be loved. . . . She chooses instinctively the most difficult people and demands from them what is most impossible for them to give: from H[oare] sexual love without guilt and reaction, from B[arker] romantic devotion'.[8] However, Emily also had what her exhausted husband had called 'Joan of Arc energies'; she desired to save people as well as dominate them. She recognised the penury in which Barker lived and pledged a pound a week to support him, forcefully persuading Peggy Guggenheim into adding another two pounds to his stipend.

Meanwhile, Eric Siepmann was planning his trip to Spain. The political situation was fevered, elections were due at the end of February and Siepmann set off to be there during these historic times; he was to cover the crisis for the *News Chronicle* and anywhere else he could sell his stories. Civil War was to erupt in July in terrible acts of atrocity on both sides. The shaky Republican government was challenged by Nationalist rebels, centred on the army. General Franco was one of the rebel leaders, corralling his forces from his headquarters in Morocco, ready to set off north across the Straits of Gibraltar. Young idealistic men and women streamed to the Republicans' cause, although they represented an extraordinarily varied coalition of hopes and ideals: some fighting to defend the constitution, others seeing the struggle as the beginning of extensive social revolution. As the war progressed these factions began to break apart in their own internecine struggles. Siepmann wrote to Antonia for the first time from Spain on 1 March, having received a letter from her with unhappy news, the effects of which he considered to be 'an outrageous misfortune' for her. He invited her to Torremolinos for escape, to recover. But he warned her 'it would be an impersonal visit – not at all what we had planned – for, as you say, we have become remote.'[9] The news which called forth such a sympathetic reaction was most probably Elspeth's death and the fact that the investigation of the police and inquest rebounded on Antonia. By the second week of April, Antonia was on her way to Spain. This was a much longed for holiday, away from the strains of her life in London: Antonia surely hoped there might be also some chance of love. Tom made a point of seeing her off. Things went badly from the start. A terrible storm-tossed crossing left her weak with sea-sickness. Bad became worse when the boat ran aground as it approached Torremolinos in a gale. Antonia finally made it to Siepmann's whitewashed house with its garden a jumble of roses, hibiscus and herbs. But before she could begin to recuperate, her host declared that he was off to Gibraltar, ordered there by the *News Chronicle* to cover a story for the paper. She went with him, tired from the trip out and in a still perilous frame of mind. Siepmann was worried, perhaps already regretting his generous invitation. On the second night of her visit he burst into Antonia's room, roaring drunk, and abused her for two hours or so. It frightened her, not least because she felt trapped – an immediate passage home was not easily come by at the time. Also this was a man about whom she had spent many hours speculating as to the exact extent of his dangerous nature and divided self. On their return to Torremolinos she succumbed to a nasty bout of food poisoning: Siepmann could not have been kinder. Meanwhile, back in London, news of her plight was filtering through to Eric, Tom and Emily. While the two men were fussing about what to do, Emily confided to her diary her lack of respect for them both, and thought Siepmann would be 'about as much help as a tarantula.'[10] Antonia's mental state deteriorated. In fact Siepmann was very sympathetic but had been warned of Antonia's imminent madness and was not keen to be responsible for her in any collapsed state. Years later he related to his wife Mary, who became the well-known novelist Mary Wesley, that he too had seen how Antonia's physical self went through a peculiar metamorphosis when very disturbed; before one's eyes, her face and body appeared to become heavier and coarser and rather menacing. It had terrified Siepmann.

Tom borrowed £70 for the fare and flew out to bring Antonia home. She arrived back in London after almost three weeks of increasing ill-health and renewed fears. Emily found her pale and enervated and, despite her good intentions, practically talked her to death with the latest machinations of the Hoare/Barker axis she had set up in her emotional life. When she could summon the energy and get a word in edgeways, Antonia wanted to discuss her own analysis of the situation with Siepmann: 'It is Siepmann who is most in my thoughts just now, though he is always straying into my desires from which I must exclude him . . .'[11] she confided to her diary. However, she did send him long letters about his character, her failings and their writing. Unsurprisingly, he was not as responsive as she would have hoped, thanking her rather stiltedly for a letter of hers on self-hate which he said would be very useful to him in his work. She admitted to feeling resentful, for these long letters to him were the only sign she had of her writing block easing a little: his silence dammed up even this little trickle of expression in her.

That June Antonia faced a minor operation on an infected cervix, something which she dreaded. But Tom was sympathetic and supportive, taking her into hospital, waiting for her to come round from the anaesthetic afterwards and returning to visit her when she was recuperating. Emily also postponed her trip to Yorkshire so she could visit and reassure her if anything went wrong. In fact Antonia had thrown a fit when she first went in, she told Emily, because the place reminded her of the asylum. But the following day she felt more lighthearted; she told Emily how her surgeon had come into the room as lugubrious as an undertaker and said to her in sonorous tones that Dr

Beaver would give her what she wanted, anything she wanted. The two women giggled and Antonia said to Emily that she hoped Dr Beaver, whoever he was, did not realise exactly what she did want. Antonia was reading Henry Handel Richardson's novel *Maurice Guest,* and was immensely impressed that any woman could write so brilliantly about a man; she recommended it enthusiastically to her friend. Peggy brought her two dozen yellow roses and Dr Carroll also visited. Kindly attention always cheered Antonia up; the feeling that she mattered to people reconfirmed her existence. One of the night nurses had made a sexual advance to her and she told Emily with amusement that Matron had said 'If these girls can't pick up a man, they turn themselves inside out.'[12] Obviously Matron was used to odd complaints; another woman, who was put in a double room, protested that the patient in the next bed was so deaf that she could not hear herself fart, and therefore never apologised. This Antonia related with much merriment to Emily. With small distractions, human company and some care and attention, she could be briefly taken out of herself.

Ill-health and loneliness, however, exacerbated her depression and once out of hospital she was plagued again with 'impotence and indecision, guilty about everything.'[13] Emily wrote from Yorkshire, full of concern, telling Antonia how fond she was of her and how much she valued her piercing intelligence and sensibility. She had already pointed out what other friends had said, that this analysis seemed to be making such a difference to her: how far she had travelled on the road to recovery. But Antonia could only appreciate the blank misery she was suffering and dread the distance she still had to go. She went down to stay with Peggy Guggenheim and Garman at Yew Tree Cottage for a few days' recuperation, but left feeling despair at how destructive most people's lives were of their own and other people's happiness.

Djuna was in England again and staying at Emily's flat in Oakley Street in Chelsea. She had come to see T.S. Eliot at Faber & Faber and get a contract for her novel *Nightwood.* There were flashes of the old abandon of Hayford Hall days. Emily and Hoare, Djuna and Antonia set off in early June for an excursion to the country, Antonia very keen that they should visit Horsley Towers, the gothic mansion where she and Reggie had had their disastrous honeymoon, and to which she so often returned in her dreams. On the journey the conversation flowed as headlong and acerbic as it ever had been at Hayford. When Tom's name came up, Djuna said 'Do you remember how he used to fling his torso into the brook, thinking he was giving the brook a moment?' which had Antonia overcome with laughter. Djuna then said that she could not imagine an English husband 'indulging in connubial bliss . . . "I can't see them bending"'. Antonia had replied, 'Well they sway a little' and the car erupted with female cackling.[14] Antonia was always rather intimidated by Djuna's brilliance and wit and did not flower in her company. Nevertheless she was swept along in the exhilaration of the conversation and laughter.

Emily had an exuberant way with other people's masterpieces. She would correct and rewrite bits of Wordsworth, *Wuthering Heights*, even Shakespeare. Anything which caught her imagination and she felt could be improved upon, she had no compunction in deleting, rearranging, altering, imposing her vision upon. She did this even to Antonia's letters to her. Antonia explained: 'She does not read; she flings herself upon and passionately possesses a work.'[15] Djuna was horrified to find that Emily, who had acted as a tireless and inspired agent for her novel *Nightwood*, promoting it to Eliot, badgering him, believing in it utterly, also had seriously tampered with the manuscript, without mention or permission, while Djuna was absent in the States. She forgave her however when they read together Emily's last letter to Eliot, which he had not answered – and never would, so Djuna declared, full of admiration and amusement at how Emily had the nerve to patronise Eliot so. But Djuna noticed something which her friend was too self-involved to see, that underneath the bright social exterior, Antonia was utterly miserable and insecure. George Barker's faith in her ability to write poetry had been the one flare of light for Antonia in the depression of that summer. He had told Emily how he had suggested to Antonia that her mental illness could be the temporary illness suffered by a poet in the process of writing a poem. He himself had suffered seizures when he had become obsessed by a poem, 'when reality becomes extraordinary and distorted because of an internal metamorphosis.'[16] He suggested the cure for her madness was to write, or at least try to write, poetry. 'I think that the intensity of her thinking is lyrical.'[17]

Spurred on by his enthusiasm, Antonia managed to work on a poem 'with happiness & difficulty' for two hours and produced seven lines. The light, however, went out and she could do no more, but in the process she had learnt something important about poets and poetry: 'You can muffle the lie in the soul in prose but not in a poem. . . . A poem *must* aim at perfection. The eternal image stays still for you to contemplate. But a novel unrolls in time. Its values are human, not eternal. It can only deal with a certain section of truth as revealed in time & mixed with the natural imperfections of any human life while being lived.'[18]

Antonia's work for Saint-Denis oppressed her greatly – it was not even work which she wanted to do, not central to her creative effort.

Her mind was 'overdriven' and yet she drove herself on even harder, so guilty did she feel at holding up the whole school programme by her failure to write two plays for them. She was also expected to mark forty examination papers at the end of the summer term, which was drawing to a close. Under extreme strain, and close to suicide, Antonia wrote a long, terrible, faltering letter in pencil to Emily:

> . . . you do not know how hard it is for me to trust anyone . . . I *must* talk to someone. I *have* to hold back with Eric [Earnshaw Smith] because he is such a sensitive antenna that he suffers everything *with* me & I cannot unload any more misery on to him and this illness of mine is like an acid bath which has developed everything neurotic in him. I feel like a leper – I have to hold my breath for fear of infecting the people who come near me. . . . With Tom I have to use double control because one thing I am resolved to do – not to use my illness as a weapon. Things are terribly difficult for him and underneath all his worldliness and cowardice and double dealing there is a sensitive creature turning towards the light. . . . The pull towards madness, annihilation of reason is fearfully strong. One part of me is a screaming child, terrified to face life at all. The other part adult & fairly clear sighted. These two *have* to be reconciled. . . . I am full of shame – I feel I am gifted in some ways above the ordinary run of people, yet as a human being I know I am far below the humblest person who accepts the facts of their life, deals with them, lives through them uncomplaining. We pride ourselves on our extreme sensitiveness, our capacity for feeling pain. Yet what feels such fearful extremes of fear, love, despair, desire for total possession of someone's love as the infant. Add that to an adult's power of memory, thought, rationalisation, communication – and you have a terrible thing.[19]

In the midst of this fearfulness, Antonia had returned on a visit to the grand Wren building which had once housed Bethlem Hospital and had recently become a new home for the Imperial War Museum. She found her old cell, and described what she felt to Emily: 'all beautifully painted now & heated to keep a case of shells warm – the old high grated window replaced by a smart new one. The agonies that place has seen. I thought of all those lives of horror lived in those cells – those people lost & despised, laughed at for centuries – no one even trying to understand. I am one of the lucky ones. . . . But how can I believe in a kind god who lets such things happen? . . . Did God create us, or are we, through infinite ages, in pain & darkness, creating God?'[20] Much later she was to recreate this experience in her short story 'Surprise Visit'.

It was very hard for her to get Emily to understand just how serious was her plight; Emily herself was always quick to threaten madness, murder or suicide. Antonia also had made a practice of making light of her suffering, turning it into an entertainment rather than a plaint. Desperate to make Emily hear her cry, she wrote: 'As regards the mental illness, I know you think I exaggerate & think it is a joke. Everyone does except Tom & Eric. It is not a joke though I make jokes about it when I can. Your life is tormented I know. But you are not at this moment fighting for your reason. . . .'[21] This heart-rending letter was enormously important: in it Antonia tried to explain her madness, to rationalise and make sense of the fundamental springs in her which seemed to be broken. She told of how she had tried to make light of it, suppress it or, finding rational causes for it, make it go away. But it persisted, living on within her, at war with her.

Undermining this courageous struggle just to carry on living was the intractable self-loathing Antonia had dragged with her since childhood: 'I feel for all my apparently sincere attempts at goodness, at bottom I am vile & disgusting. Sometimes I wallow in my own nastiness. If I were pure & clean perhaps I wd. wish immediately to dirty myself again.'[22] The intemperance of her language belonged more to hell-fire preachers on sin than to the analyst's couch, but Antonia's sense of being irredeemable in her depravity came from somewhere that pre-dated either Christ or Freud; it had more in common with the Gorgons of the Greek myths.

Eric Earnshaw Smith was Antonia's most rational friend and it was with him that she decided that summer of 1936 to discuss her desire to kill herself, 'Not in hysterical despair this time but quietly as the only possible solution.'[23] It seemed to be the kindest thing to do for everyone concerned: she was certain then that she was incurable; her insanity might ebb and flow but she would never be free of it and all the destruction it wreaked in her own and others' lives. 'Better kill myself than destroy other people', she wrote in a despairing letter to Emily.[24] Eric begged her to give herself six months and if she still felt the same then she would know that it was a fair decision. He took her away with him to a hotel in Lyme Regis for a short holiday.

In the first episode of a pyschic synchrony which seemed at times to exist strongly between Susan and her mother, Antonia's mental collapse was mirrored by a crisis in seven-year-old Susan. Tom had been worried for some time about bouts of jealousy which would flare out of her, possessiveness of Tom and jealousy of Antonia on one occasion, reminiscent of the dynamic between Antonia's young self and her parents. Only in this case Tom was not a forbidding father and Antonia not an indulgent and uncritical mother. Tom had been concerned also about Susan's unhappiness which had resulted in her stealing and secretiveness. There had been some talk between him and Antonia of his adopting Susan, who had never been given any reason to doubt she was his daughter: her surname had been changed by deed-poll to Hopkinson after she came to live with them. But nothing came of the suggestion. However, Tom must have been disturbed enough for him to go to see Dr Carroll and ask his advice. Carroll suggested Susan should go and see her own analyst, four times a week. If he could not get her into a clinic then she would have to go privately at half a guinea a time, for a year. This would have cost exactly what Antonia had been paid by the *Daily Mirror* for her weekly fashion piece.

Meanwhile, Antonia and Tom had already discussed the plan that she should move back into the family flat at Cecil Court and take overall responsibility for the children. This seemed rather rash, given Antonia's terrible state of mind at the time. Tom would move out, but came every morning to take Susan and Lyndall to school, and see them at the weekend: he would be almost as involved in their lives as before. Perhaps this was one of the suggestions that Carroll had made as a way of helping both Antonia and Susan to feel more secure.

Through her analysis, Antonia had become, on the surface, more able to cope with everyday life; she herself recognised a change in her perception of things, a greater detachment and clarity. This did not stop the underground stream of her own violence and fear, but it helped to channel and divert it. In her solitary bedsitting room in Oakley Street, Antonia had been much more inclined to feel distanced and cut off from people and the social life she used to know which stimulated and sustained her. Her return to the flat meant she could start inviting friends round again, as she used to for Sunday tea and conversation. But it meant too that Tom had to tell Susan and Lyndall, still only seven and five years old respectively, that life at home was going to change. They were at the stage of their lives when they passionately loved Tom, at times possessively loved him. He had been a sensitive, fair and loving father to them both: their mother was a much more shadowy figure, already a more unpredictable presence – an inevitably less attractive proposition as resident parent, at the time, than the one they knew and loved so well. Their faithful nurse, Mary Hitchcock, was still with them, but emotionally grown more distant, as she had fallen in love with Gordon Palmer, a corporal in the RAF: her emotional attention and energy were focused less now on the two girls, to whom she had been an important maternal substitute. Lyndall, particularly, remembered feeling the loss once she was no longer central to Nurse's life.

Tom took the children and Nurse up to his parents in Winster Vicarage at Windermere in Westmorland for the August holidays, and there they had a happy time of boats and picnics and excursions in Grandfather's rackety old car, on one occasion going to Morecambe Bay for a day of sand, donkey rides and sandwiches. Tom chose the last day of his holidays to explain to the girls the shift in the family dynamic – that their mother was moving back home and he would be moving out. Many years later Tom told Lyndall that their reaction was not the overjoyed one he had related in a letter to Antonia but an altogether more subdued affair; 'you never took your eyes off me, and said after every explanation, "I see Tom," "Yes Tom," "All right Tom," "I understand Tom," until I had to turn away because I couldn't bear to see your sad little face any more.' Lyndall wrote in her memoir: 'I had joined my father and mother and sister in knowing what unhappiness meant. I was just five years old.'[25]

Tom's unhappiness was compounded by the news he had heard recently from Frances Grigson. The woman for whom he had felt such passion the previous year was now suffering from TB. She loved him, she said, but Tom had been unsure for quite a while about his true feelings for her. The poignancy of her situation and the possibility of her death intensified everyone's emotions. Despite her own suffering, Antonia managed to be sympathetic and encouraging of Tom's feelings for Frances. None of Antonia's emotions were writ in stone: great generosity one day could turn to ranting irritation the next; affection and desire could transmute into antipathy and recoil.

On the last day in August Antonia had moved back into the family flat, spruced up and partly repainted by Tom and Norah the cook and housekeeper, in an attempt to make her reinstatement as easy and welcoming as possible. After a week's camping out in the room in Oakley Street, Tom moved into a bedsitting room at 15 Gunter Grove in Fulham, within walking distance of the old flat. Although continuing to live apart, they were still lethally connected. Tom made love to her unexpectedly, which encouraged Antonia to think that the spark could be fanned into a flame again: then two days later he asked if she minded about his affair with Joan Freeman. This prompted an understandable bitterness; Antonia admitted to herself that although he made a good friend he was a treacherous lover, who smiled as he stabbed you. Blood, vengeance, betrayal; she was gripped by primitive passions. She often wrote of how much she needed a physical expression of the violence within her, as a relief, if only temporary, of the intolerable pressure and stasis: 'I want nothing but a fight at the moment – a real physical battle. And that would mean losing everything I have worked patiently for, disciplined myself to for months.'[26]

Yet Antonia realised also that she had to make some effort to re-establish relationships with her daughters. During one of her worst periods of disintegration, just before they went to their grandparents for the summer holidays, Antonia had let her control slip to frightening effect. She admitted to Emily: 'I was in such blind misery I did one thing I swore not to do & have kept for 18 months – showed bitterness in front of the children. They are so sweet. I begin really to love them. And they kept asking me to come back. I lost all control.'[27] She was fearful of their reactions to losing Tom, only to gain her in his place. Indelibly, in her own experience as a daughter, a father was everything and a mother of negligible value. On Antonia's return to Cecil Court, Emily wrote to encourage her, fearing 'a perpetual chorus of "We want Papa!". I hope you have been spared that chorus & that you aren't finding old associations depressing.'[28] She then went on to say how close she had come to suicide herself, or if not that then doing Hoare some dreadful violence. This prompted Antonia to reply: 'You & I are very much alike in temperament. At one time I would not admit my violence even to myself, grew a protective social shell and became mentally apathetic & shallow. You acted yours out in your life but brought great unhappiness to yourself and frightened people you loved. I have been doing the same for 18 months. But in the end we have both got to find a third way ... writing & the imagination.'[29] If only the treatment could be as easy as the diagnosis.

However, that autumn writing and the imagination suddenly seemed possible again. Now that Antonia was installed again in a spacious flat, her social circle began to widen. Through Barker she met Humphrey Jennings, who was another of the revolutionary poets but was to become a film director, and the surrealist poet David Gascoyne who, at only nineteen, was the youngest of them all. At the end of the year she also met Dylan Thomas.

These four young poets were a refreshing addition to her social and imaginative life. They brought an active political intelligence to their discussions. No one so matched her intellectually as did David Gascoyne. His cultural world was European rather than narrowly British, and he opened for Antonia a wider, deeper landscape: it was to him that she was immediately and violently drawn. Theirs was to be an eccentric but significant relationship, which was to benefit them both, leaving them with a lasting gratitude and affection. David had published his first book of poetry three years earlier, and his first novel when he was seventeen. His *A Short Survey of Surrealism* had been published the year before he and Antonia met. That summer of 1936, he had been one of the organisers of the International Surrealist Exhibition held in the New Burlington Galleries. Salvador Dali appeared in a diver's suit, complete with weighty diver's helmet. He proceeded to give a lecture, which was largely inaudible, and then almost suffocated when the helmet became jammed and refused to budge. David himself contributed a surrealist event; rumour had it that he escorted in Trafalgar Square a girl whose head was entirely encased in roses.

David Gascoyne was an elusive prodigy, with an innocence and otherworldliness about him which inspired love and protectiveness in those who knew him. His sweetness of character led him to expect the same generosity and lack of guile in others. Kathleen Raine, herself a poet and a lifelong admirer of David as man and poet, described him as being: 'like a wild animal who has never yet had cause to fear man, open and expectant of receiving the same goodness and out-flowing love that was in him.'[30] He met Antonia at Emily's flat towards the end of September; Hoare was there, as was Humphrey Jennings. Antonia noted 'the feeling I like best – of flow and communication between people the other night, sitting up till 4.30 a.m.'[31] It seemed to David then that out of that group of people Emily was the most likely to become his confidante. But Antonia had other ideas. At their next meeting a few days later, she and he stayed up talking until six in the morning: she told him the strange, grotesque story of her life and then confessed that she was in love with him. This shocked him with its unexpectedness and absurdity. He recoiled, confused and afraid: he had liked her lively intelligence, but she was so old, it seemed to him at nineteen, and he felt no physical attraction for her at all. Antonia sought to reassure him by implying that she hoped for a spiritual intimacy rather more than a sexual relationship, but even this he felt was beyond him: 'But why, O why, has all this come upon me? the egoist asks. Why should my precious inner solitude be disturbed into a deliberate consciousness of itself? . . . Why should the poor thing have chosen me?'[32] David had none of the sophistication and self-protective instincts of Eric Siepmann. He was also more generous. Rather than turn away from the voracious grasp of Antonia's unhappy self, he decided that the best he could offer her was a sympathetic companionship, walking arm in arm through life as Babes in the Wood, orphaned, bewildered, pathetic. There was a similarity between them which was not just the poignancy of the outsider; both shared too a suppressed violence, and a desire for violence as a sign of life, an antidote to mediocrity and boredom, the equilibrium both dreaded. His fantasies often returned to the images of explosion, icebergs and the underground river, and the Marquis de Sade was one of his heroes.

At the beginning of October, David took Emily on the enormous anti-Fascist demonstration in the East End, when one hundred thousand people turned up to barricade the streets against Mosley's Blackshirts, and he was dumbfounded by her naïve and inappropriate remarks. She had been warned that as an American she risked immediate deportation if she should be arrested. They returned intact to her flat where Phyllis Jones, who had also been there, and Antonia, who had not, joined them later. Antonia was terribly nervous and unwilling to meet David's gaze. He was struck at how unhappy all Emily's women friends seemed, 'You are all eating your hearts out', he told her and she replied, 'yes, a queer nest you've fallen into.'[33] Antonia was keen to go once Humphrey Jennings had arrived and started talking about film stars, and she offered David a place to stay for the night rather than his having to struggle back to Teddington in Middlesex, where he still lived with his parents. He was reluctant, but did not want to hurt her feelings, and so found himself in an awkward embrace at four in the morning after an analytic and harrowing conversation, 'Entrails, entrails. . . .', in front of the gas fire.[34] Tom found him still there when he came to the flat in the morning to take the children to school, and gave him a sheepish grin when he popped his head round the door.

By the end of October David had asked for some money on account from his publishers and received £20 which meant he could join his friends, Roland and Valentine Penrose, who were heading for Barcelona. The Civil War was growing in violence and the Republicans seemed to be losing ground to Francisco Franco's Nationalist forces. Antonia begged David to spend his last night in England with her. He was exhausted, and had an all-night journey ahead of him, but reluctantly he agreed. She told him the extraordinary news that Emily, who had been having an affair with Barker, was now madly in love with Humphrey Jennings, and he with her. Like Barker, Humphrey too was married, and as with Barker, this passion for Emily would not last long. She was strong medicine whom mortal men could only take in homoeopathic doses. On parting the next morning, Antonia slipped a ten shilling note she could ill afford into David's coat pocket as she ran for a bus. He was reluctant to accept it but she insisted – after all he had just had his twentieth birthday and could buy some books with it in Paris on his way to Spain. David thought it revealed 'the disillusioning truth' about his relationship with Antonia that when he came to look for the note he discovered it had slipped through his pocket without his noticing – only to be picked up by an old man.[35] This he thought was a perfect example of Freud's 'objective chance'.

Antonia, meanwhile, was fearful for David's safety; he looked like the type who would get killed, she wrote in her diary – but felt alarmed even at giving shape to the thought. She had no regular work, only the continuing series of lectures and her occasional literary consultancy for the chaotic Michel Saint-Denis. She pondered on just what the company of these young poets meant to her these last few months. It pleased her that her poem about Elspeth's death was admired by the new revolutionaries while the old guard, in the form of the *New Statesman*, thought it too violent and excessively emotional. Humphrey Jennings managed to get Robert Roughton to publish it in *Contemporary Poetry and Prose*. She was energised by their own work and enthusiasms; although expressly suspicious of surrealist dogma, Antonia was surprised at how much she liked Andre Breton's *Nadja*. It evoked her adolescent love of the magical and made her wonder if she could somehow manage to throw off her autobiographical approach to fiction and begin to write more freely, using a different part of her mind where fantasy, play and invention slumbered. Dr Carroll had suggested that a good sign of her being cured would be her ability to write from her imagination, instead of tying her creative fiction so closely to the actual events of her life. Antonia increasingly understood how guilt had blocked her inventiveness; she could use her dreams as material but only because she did not feel responsible for them and was therefore free of guilt.

While David Gascoyne was in Spain, and Emily was pursuing Jennings, Antonia spent a good deal of time with Barker and got to know him better and even grew to love him a little. He was born on 26 February, the anniversary of Keats's death and Antonia's lifelong love for that great poet added to her affection for this young one. She found him inspiring in the realm of her own work and, on his urgings, embarked on a private piece of writing for him on her experiences in the asylum. But it was to David Gascoyne that Antonia looked for liberation from herself. Restlessly waiting for David to telephone on his return from Spain, she recalled Djuna's words 'are you a writer or a weeping woman?' and determined she would never be a weeping woman again.[36]

The news from Spain was of daily atrocities, and she was puzzled by her recoil from others' acting out of hidden thoughts she believed were shared by all. 'We are all wild beasts at heart and have raped, tortured and murdered in our imaginations.'[37] No doubt having discussed David's experiences and the exhilaration on the Republicans' side, Antonia thought that she too would like to go to Spain that December, but then dismissed it as having 'too much of "love in dreams" about it – "action rapidly performed in the sight of all".'[38]

Antonia was seeing a good deal of David at the end of 1936. His sudden departure to Spain in the autumn, on his own admission, had confused matters for both of them, but on his return their friendship moved into a deeper layer of affection, interest and support. In a long analytical diary entry, Antonia wrote about her feelings for him and her assessment of his powerfully contradictory character: 'The general tone of his work melancholy – the feeling of someone imprisoned & impotent. But tenderness and real feeling too. . . . He is not only sensitive, warm-hearted & imaginative at his best, but also calm, honest, deep and wise.'[39]

Having for some time believed that he was bisexual, David was anxious to be able to express his affection for Antonia sexually. One evening, either at the end of December or the beginning of the next year, encouraged by a particularly satisfactory encounter with a French doctor with whom he was sexually involved at the time, who was himself enthusiastically bisexual in his behaviour, David went round to see Antonia. He was 'convinced that my libido was sufficiently strong and versatile to enable me successfully to accomplish what I had not until then had the confidence to attempt'. He was only twenty at the time and, as Antonia recognised, still rather frightened of her. 'I do not believe I have often indulged in wilful self-delusion, but so genuine was my desire physically to satisfy this distraught and vulnerable woman in the manner customarily appropriate in such a situation that I persuaded myself that I was up to the challenge. . . . I deliberately put myself in a situation that was bound to leave me faced with the admission that heterosexually I am virtually impotent.'[40] This did not sour the relationship for either of them and in fact, as a result of her continuing analysis, Antonia was considerably calmer and better able to deal with such a setback. In her assessment of the past year she wrote that the fears which had so crippled her were quietened, and in that quietness she had learnt how to be receptive to others, and to life, in a completely new way. 'This enrichment is so wonderful so magical and so frequently accessible (I could only touch it in the briefest flashes before) that I can never tell anyone what a miraculous thing it is. Its immediate instrument is my relationship with David.'[41] She described this relationship as delicate and difficult 'but perhaps the most beautiful thing that has ever happened to me'; the most touching thing for her about it was the sense of intimate communion with another person, something which in her previously isolated, self-obsessed state had seemed an impossibility.

Dr Carroll had told Antonia 'something very sweet and womanly is beginning to appear in you'.[42] Tom too had noticed a distinct change in his wife. She was much more tender and gentle towards him, guilty and saddened as he was over Frances's inexorable decline in health. Talking to him in the new year when Frances's death seemed inevitable, she said, 'though your loss will be terrible you will not really lose Frances. You, Frances & Tom, cannot be destroyed like that. You will find the value of Frances & of what she means to you somewhere in your own life.'[43] He was strengthened and consoled. That Christmas of 1936, Antonia went with her children and Tom to Binesfield to stay once again with her mother. She and Tom shared a bed, as they always did on these visits, and Tom was again impressed that although Antonia had another terrible nightmare she was not terrified and distraught, as was so often the case in the past, but calm and interested in finding some meaning in it. She was also unusually sensitive to his feelings.

By the end of the year two of the females closest to her, due to her influence, had trod the path to her analyst's door. Emily had been so concerned about her deteriorating state of mind once Humphrey Jennings had cast her off that she went to see Dr Carroll, deciding she liked him on the spot. She cannot have been completely in the grip of her mania because she demurred from telling him something she had believed all her life; 'I am not adapted to this world – because I have genius.'[44] Susan, who was seven that autumn, began seeing her own analyst, on the suggestion of Dr Carroll. Miss Searle lived in Notting Hill and four afternoons a week Sue, accompanied by Lyndall and Nurse, travelled to her house, where Lyndall and Nurse sat in the waiting room for the requisite forty minutes. In her own memoir, Susan described the sessions as a battle between the testing will of the young analysand and the inexpressive endurance of the put-upon analyst. Lyndall recalled the excruciating boredom of the wait, alleviated once by the extraordinary sight of her heroic elder sister on the back of the poor elderly analyst who, on all fours, was being ridden up the stairs as if she were a horse.

Susan gave her little sister to understand that analysis was a grown-up activity which she shared with their mother, and would not talk about to a non-initiate like Lyndall. But it was obviously a disturbing process for her. Tom recorded in his diary at the end of the year that on a particular occasion Antonia had spent an hour talking to Susan alone and had relayed her daughter's anxieties: 'I do hate having the private parts of my mind poked about in.'[45] Antonia, looking back on this time, recognised how much Susan's need for privacy was breached, 'what she absolutely could not stand about her analyst as a child was when the woman spoke to her affectionately. Though obviously one part of her wants love another regards it as an impertinent intrusion on her private life.'[46] Sue had also told her mother that she much preferred living in her mind than in the outside world, then had said with a sigh, in what struck Tom as an exact echo of her mother's words and manner, 'Oh, when shall I be able to get on with my own work?'[47] The conversation continued with Antonia reassuring her that it was perfectly normal for a young girl to prefer her father to her mother. Susan had looked relieved and then added – as if to balance the fact that she loved Tom more – that she really did like talking to Antonia. This was to be increasingly the leitmotiv of Antonia's life; the love she demanded was offered elsewhere but the fascination of her conversation and the wisdom of her mind, when she was in a state of relative equilibrium, was ever valued and sought out.

1936 ended well for Antonia; she was in a better state mentally than she had been for years. She was able to make a deeper, more human connection with others: she was beginning to know how to listen and respond rather than demand; offering solace rather than battery with accusation and bitterness. The last of the young poets too hoved into view. Emily met Dylan Thomas through a mutual friend and then joined him on a pub crawl round Chelsea. At twenty-two he had published two collections of poetry and that winter had just received a dream review from Edith Sitwell in the *Sunday Times* which claimed his work was 'nothing short of magnificent.'[48] His second book, *Twenty-five Poems*, was into its second printing although he was still as impoverished as Barker and Gascoyne. Emily was immediately taken with Thomas, 'a round-eyed animal with a chuckling guttural laugh, and a rosy personality.'[49] When she saw him again, a few days later, she was delighted that he was raving about Antonia's writing – *Frost in May*, 'The House of Clouds' and her poem 'Epitaph', which had just come out in *Contemporary Poetry and Prose*. Emily rang Antonia, who was gratified to have his reaction relayed but, of course, found it difficult to believe. Effervescent in the company of Thomas, Emily was beginning to forget her unhappiness over Jennings, but it was a wild, drink-induced euphoria. She was hoping her father would finance her psychoanalysis, as she was very short of ready money now that she was helping support Barker. Although Thomas was already involved with Caitlin Macnamara, who was to become his wife the following year, he and Emily started an affair which was conducted 'in pubs and clubs and cinemas and beds.'[50]

Thomas was intrigued by Antonia. He thought of her as a wild animal tamed in a suburban zoo, dreaming of freedom; '. . . and then, one waking day, obsessed by those dreams, she escaped into liberty, a liberty that for her – necessarily because of her long, tame imprisonment – was far more terrifying than the safety behind the suburban-zoo bars.' But this taste of freedom, frightening as it was, meant that she could not return happily to tameness, which was sanity. It was this, he believed, which made her search for intimate companionship so difficult: she was bored by the tame ones but terrified by those who were uncompromisingly wild (Dylan rated himself among the beasts). She could only really relate to friends like David Gascoyne (and Emily herself) who, like her, had been born into captivity but were barely able to contain their feral natures, to keep their madness in check: 'she is done for, done for ever perhaps. She wants to be tame again, but she's been let loose once. . . .'[51]

15

The Lithopaedion

The Lithopaedion is a child which fails to be born and is petrified into a limestone fossil in the womb where it may remain for half a lifetime. I think that is what has happened to my creative talent, if I have one.

15 March 1936, *Diaries I*

On 27 January 1937, Antonia became a chief copywriter for J. Walter Thompson, the prestigious American advertising agency, at a salary of £1,000 per annum. This was the largest amount of money she would ever earn (the equivalent salary today would be £90,000) and it bribed Antonia to return to the profession she had sworn she had left for good. It was full-time work in a highly professional agency, and Antonia felt bleakly that she was renouncing the only life she thought worth living, the life of an artist. However, the positive side of this decision was the thought that within three months she would have paid off her debts. Dr Carroll also considered that this kind of discipline, and the ensuing freedom from money concerns, might release her from her writer's block and allow her to begin to make some real headway with the next novel.

Antonia had been struggling for four years to produce something significant and had got nowhere. Despite her commission to write a biography of Jane Carlyle and her initial enthusiasm for the woman and the work, she had quickly tired of both, finding Jane arch and trivial, and accusing her of 'sham highbrowism'.[1] For her next work of fiction she had tried repeatedly to write about the relationship between a daughter and her father, dealing with the 'hopeless impossibility of an adjustment between two people so different when one person will not allow for differences'.[2] The crystallisation of their differences would be expressed in their Catholicism. Analysis had helped her to look at her father with neither bias nor fear and it was his character that she had wanted to explore centrally in this book: 'I will *not* be afraid of him any more. It is a pure accident that we were father and child. I have a *right* to look at him, yes, sexually too.'[3] It took more than thirteen years for her to write this book; published at last in 1950, it was called *The Lost Traveller*. After this, Antonia wrote in relatively quick succession the other two novels in her quartet about a young girl's coming of age. *The Sugar House* and *Beyond the Glass*, brought Clara through an unconsummated marriage, love and madness. They left her standing on the edge of adulthood, with the doors of the asylum barely closed behind her. And then another terrible writing block descended on Antonia. But this time it was chronic and her inability to move Clara forward, into a life like her own, embracing literary success, marriages, lovers, friendships, children, drove her to despair and mental collapse; the obsessional and sterile struggle to write intertwined with madness in a vicious circle of cause and effect.

Antonia gave many reasons for her monumental writer's block but most paths ultimately led back to Rome – to the preternaturally inflated figure of her father, reinforced by his Catholicism. His reaction to her first imaginative work had forced her to rely on the safer facts of her own life, but she was then faced by the shame of revealing her own unworthiness, and also by her fear of exposing others, particularly her father. The final obliterating block Antonia suffered almost continually from 1954 until her death revolved around her inability, she believed, to write from anything other than the actual events of her life. The obstacle she could not quite bring herself to overcome was exposure of her father's complicity in the Jim Dougal episode, and her own feelings of hurt and betrayal. Her father had put his fear of society's disapproval, she felt, before the physical and spiritual welfare of his daughter.

So important is this father in Antonia's life, so destructive his effect, his presence so mixed up in her mind with God, sex and her own unworthiness, that it is necessary to examine, as far as we can, the extent of his influence on her. Had it encompassed sexual abuse, in all the subtle variations of meaning and effect in that crass and over-used phrase? Was this the source of the fear and longing that she expressed for him? Antonia was extremely candid in her diaries and in her conversations with her women friends, related in their diaries and letters. Djuna Barnes was unembarrassed about admitting to Emily and Antonia the gross and criminal sexual behaviour that her own father exhibited towards her. Yet there was never any answering admission, or even implicit hint of impropriety that Antonia offered in their discussions. She had no taboo on relating in matter-of-fact language her sexual problems, her masturbatory habits, her fantasies of whipping and inflicting pain, her lurid dreams. She was an honest woman with an unflinching, analytical mind which could turn a problem over and look at it from all sides, interpreting it through a variety of guises. There were disturbing events between herself and her father which she described; admitting that they were unhealthily close. But never once did she give any reason to believe that she thought there was ever the smallest chance that her father had sexually abused her, in the usual physically intrusive meaning of the word.

When she was in the early stages of her analysis with Dr Carroll, the layout of the nursery in relation to her father's study and the lavatory they shared had seemed significant to her. But the significance seemed to centre on Antonia's fear of his disapproval. Her recollection in the early days of her analysis of the sound of her father's latchkey, his 'warning of disapproval', had precipitated her into a terrible state of depression. Her lethargy and drowsiness had lasted for days; even her handwriting was affected, becoming painfully slow and tiny.[4]

Antonia's father was certainly emotionally oppressive and invasive of her integrity. He had been insistent that she conform to his idea of how his daughter should conduct herself, as an extension of his will and a fulfilment of his frustrated dreams. The fact that Antonia was clever and quick to learn and also particularly keen to please the father she had cast as a god, fuelled his expectations. She was left with a lifelong sense of never being good enough, or loved for herself alone. In a pathetic letter to Tom, during one of her crises, she explained: 'Having never been loved when I *was* myself as a child, gay & independent, I feel I never *can* be loved that way . . . & longing passionately for tenderness I never had, unconsciously try to get it the wrong way, feeling pity is the most I can ever hope for.'[5] Cecil Botting's overbearing attitude towards his young daughter was common enough given that, at the time, it was generally accepted that children were the property of their parents and were not expected to have a voice. However, his intrusion into the individual integrity of her self was made more powerful and far reaching by being reinforced so relentlessly, and seductively, by the zealous nuns of the Convent of the Sacred Heart.

This destruction of a child's spirit and natural belief in the goodness of the world, and the rightness of her self within it, was the real abuse which crippled Antonia's life. Many times she described herself despairingly in terms of being like a broken spring, with only her negative attributes left to her; 'at the convent, they deliberately set out to break my will, which was a tough one . . . I've never had a proper will since, only compulsive rushings-to and rushings-away-from. The old tough will has relapsed into blind obstinacy, which works almost

entirely (though mercifully not quite) negatively.' Her longing to be
constructive in her life, she wrote, was always undermined by her fear of
her own power; 'it all gets frittered away in rebellion, uncertainty &
remorseless bullying of myself . . . [AW's ellipses] and sometimes others
. . . combined weight of my father, the church & my own inner fears
was just too much.'[6]

Although there is no evidence that it extended to any kind of physical
interference, there was a strong suppressed erotic element in her father's
possessiveness of her, domination over her and intrusion into her life. As
she said herself in a later interview '[the relationship was] much too
close, really.'[7] This was made all the more psychically damaging for her
by the fact that her legitimate – if extreme – romantic love for him was
inflated by his own inappropriate complicity in her fantasy. She wrote
about this in fictional terms in *The Lost Traveller*, where the heroine
Clara is recalled from her convent school because her mother has been
very ill after a miscarriage. While she is home her father invites her to a
production of his favourite Wagner opera, the sentimental *Tannhauser*.
This is a most precious and rare treat for his daughter, who luxuriates in
being the focus of his attention while he is at his most charming and
benign. Afterwards, he takes her to his favourite restaurant and in the
middle of what appears to the young girl to be an almost magical meal,
they have this conversation:

> He looked at her intently for a moment and then sighed: 'Ah,
> Clara.'
> 'What is it, Daddy?'
> 'Nothing. I was just toying with a wild notion I sometimes have.'
> 'Tell me.'
> 'Well, now and then, I try and fancy how it would be if you and I
> were not father and daughter.'
> She took it up eagerly.
> 'Oh, I've often thought that too.'
> His eyes grew bright.
> '*Have* you? That's remarkably interesting.'
> 'Of course I don't mean I want anyone else for a father. But just
> that now and then. . . .'
> 'We could forget,' he nodded. 'Exactly. Sometimes the idea is so
> vivid to me that it is almost like a memory. We meet, you and I, in
> a lonely tower . . . we talk without any self-consciousness.'

After the meal they go home together and, although the amatory mood
in him is gradually being replaced by his old admonishing parental

mode, 'he kissed her goodnight, more lingeringly than he had done for many months, stroking her hair while she tried to tell him what a wonderful evening it had been. The dining-room clock struck half-past one with a fretful ping. The afterglow vanished from his face.'[8]

Cecil Botting's repressed sexuality was expressed in a self-indulgent romaticism. Inappropriately focused on his young daughter, his fantasies inflamed Antonia's natural daughterly desire for her father into a complex of Electra-esque proportions. In the unhealthy grip of this complicity, she ruthlessly diminished her mother and carried the burden of her father's longing for her: consequently her sexual relationships with other men were blighted from the start. Despite a number of sexual partners, three marriages (two of them chosen deliberately as non-sexual unions) and the birth of two children, Antonia remained in a profound sense sexually untouched, truly the Virgin Queen of Surbiton. Towards the end of her life Antonia admitted that 'in some curious way she [Clara and herself] feels guilty at being in bed with a man', and that this guilt was something to do with her feelings for her father.[9] As she described it, 'my illness, which I did not understand, made me unable to create any happiness for myself or other people as long as any sex relation came into it. Eric I could make happy because sex & its guilt never came into it. . . . But I am not homosexual; I have all a woman's natural inclinations to a man . . . but it is in the *expression* of them that I am overwhelmed with fear, guilt, coldness or nausea.'[10]

There were two other events in her life which showed the uneasy configuration of filial love with sexual desire. The first was the recurring focus of her writing block; the pregnancy which resulted when Jim Dougal, a friend of her father's, unexpectedly entered Antonia's room one night when she was asleep, *wearing her father's dressing gown*. She was a virgin, she did not care for him nor even know him very well, but she not only allowed him to engage in sexual intercourse with her, she admitted that she 'certainly "provoked" this intercourse'.[11] In her relation of this bizarre event her father's dressing gown seemed to be a significant factor. To a drowsy mind, the sight of this familiar garment was reassuring initially, perhaps. Yet one would think that what the imposter proceeded to do to her was not what the usual wearer of the dressing gown would be expected to do. Was this a psychologically safe way for her to fulfil her dream of incestuous love for her father? It is perhaps more that for Antonia, at that stage of her life, in the euphoric postmania of her illness, her virginity was an anachronism which she was happy to relinquish, with as little significance and fuss as possible. She was not driven by erotic impulses but by intellectual curiosity, and perhaps the opportunity had arrived fortuitously for her to find out what the whole mystery of sex was about.

Antonia always found sinister Cecil Botting's surprising agreement to her abortion of the baby which resulted from this union, despite his devout Catholicism and his implication in what was a mortal sin. However, Antonia had only recently left Bethlem asylum; her nine months there had been the most terrible ordeal of Cecil's life. When he had been allowed to see her she would have been a pitiful sight, seldom able to recognise him, sometimes physically ill, sometimes raving. He had been told that she would probably not recover until she was beyond middle-age, when he might well be dead himself. Her return to sanity and to him was like a miracle: if he could help it, she would never be allowed to get into such a desperate mental state again. He had seen his own wife's suffering over Antonia's prolonged and difficult birth and then the cruel series of agonising labours and stillbirths which had followed. Birth itself, in his experience, was more an occasion of unbearable pain, fear and grief than of happiness and fulfilment: Antonia realised in retrospect that he feared for his daughter's health and sanity if she had proceeded to have the baby, either to care for it herself or give it up for adoption.

This consideration, together with his fearful social insecurity and concern with propriety, helps to explain his defiance of his Church's most central teachings, his willingness to risk damnation, to support his daughter's abortion by lending her money. Antonia herself analysed it as: 'horror equally of the disgrace, of poss. consequences to her reason: of the sin if she has the abortion. But the disgrace must, I fear, be uppermost.'[12] However, Antonia continued to use sexual symbolism involving her father when talking about her longing to write creatively: 'it seems clear from several indications I want my father's penis or a child by him e.g. a work engendered with his loving approval. What am I fussing about? I can't have his loving approval because he is DEAD/I couldn't have had intercourse with him anyway because presumably apart from morals (a) he didn't want it (b) I couldn't have endured it without mutilation'.[13] This was an extraordinary diary entry, for Antonia wrote as if intercourse with her father was something which she would welcome not only symbolically, as a creative act, but in reality too – only his lack of compliance and her fear of mutilation stood in her way, or so she implied. The entry becomes even more bizarre; it quickly disintegrates into a frenzied rant against him, and even her handwriting degenerates into stabbing fragments and disorder. He is a 'filthy dirty beastly old man', for preventing her from writing 'backhand' when she was a child. 'I spit on your corpse ... I hope you've been punished.

You punished me enough. I've forced myself to be sorry for you and admire you. You've ruined my life. . . . You never loved me for a second . . . I was hurt and wanted your approval. . . . You only gave me what *you* wanted, never what I wanted.'[14]

Antonia was still in the depths of her Freudian analysis with Dr Carroll when this was written, and the sexual symbolism may have been in part a reflection of that. However, ten years later she described a dream in extraordinary precise detail, in which she was ritually raped by her father. Antonia was unflinching about the sexual content, sensual but matter-of-fact in her description of the pressure of his penis and the mixture of terror and desire in her. Too long to quote, it was nevertheless a magnificent dream, dense with archetypal imagery. It would be a mistake to interpret such a dream literally and superficially, in all its shocking incestuous detail, for its more profound meaning was recognised by Antonia. She saw the significance of the act as an important symbolic union which was both creative and conciliatory, and awoke cold and shuddering, 'not in terror, but in a kind of awe and thankfulness'.[15] In Antonia's own mind, there was a sexual component to the fear of her father's disapproval, just as sexual pleasure was conflated with her relief at his approval and the joy of reconciliation. In a later dream in which Antonia meets her long dead father and they greet each other with intense happiness and relief (for now they will not be lonely again) Antonia awakes to 'a very faint sexual tremor.'[16] She realised it was a dream of forgiveness and reconciliation also; the idea of being reunited with her father in joy and acceptance, the nearest she could get to bliss.

And so, although there is little reason to believe that there was any kind of genital contact between them, there was an erotic element in his love and interest in her, combined with a heavy-handed expression of power invested with the weight of paternal disapproval and reinforced by the threat of supernatural retribution. There is enough straightforward explanation from her own pen of the obsession that existed between them and the oppressiveness of his expectations. The extremes of passionate longing and violent resentment which Antonia felt for him all her life dominated her emotional landscape and blighted her creative and sexual life.

Her identification too from her earliest years with the father, the masculine in life, and her rejection of her mother and the feminine, made for an exaggerated emphasis on the intellect at the expense of the feeling and intuitive side of her nature; 'I have tried to apprehend everything through the intellect and that is why I am shallow & disconnected' she explained to Emily, adding how much she was attracted to people who had this strong spring of spontaneous instinctive knowledge.[17] Her Church reinforced contempt for the feminine and only when she was old herself did Antonia realise, with some anger, what her mother had always known; 'The Church really *does* hate women – you can't get away from *that*! We are still "bags of tripe" to them as we were to the Early Fathers.'[18] But as the years brought a greater understanding of herself and of the fears and insecurities of others, Antonia came to make her peace with both her parents. Her reconversion to Catholicism during the war brought her an inevitable reconciliation with the figure of her father, who was always so closely identified with her God: 'I begin at last to understand & love my own father with whom I found it an agonising strain to be alone . . . I feared him more than I loved him. . . . I *know* he is in Heaven now but I had a strange idea that he was for some time in purgatory & that in some way my coming back to the Church & his release were connected.'[19] This had echoes of the beginning of *Frost in May* where the child Nanda on her way to the Convent is being sacrificed for her father's religious aspirations.

And so in the first part of 1937, Antonia found herself in that unproductive desert of masculine intellect, cut off from her creative self. She was wrestling with the 'bleak boredom' of office life at J. Walter Thompson and resentful of how little energy or time she had left for the real work, her writing.[20] After three months she had not even managed to pay off her debts. Her social life with the young poets continued to sustain her a little, although no longer could they inspire her to poetry, or even prose. The interconnections too between them all were growing more complicated by the month. Antonia still shared an intellectual bond with David Gascoyne, who admitted she was one of the rare people who could speak his language, but the emotional intimacy of their early relationship had been diluted by David's own recoil from her immoderate criticism of herself and others, her pathological fear of just letting things be: 'It's all very well to be frightened of complacency;' he wrote in his journal, 'but A. seems to suffer from a ceaseless compulsion to smash all the chairs in the house with a hatchet – every day.'[21]

Antonia had drawn closer emotionally to George Barker, who had once been Emily's lover and to whom David now was increasingly attracted. Emily, meanwhile, had been conducting an affair with Dylan Thomas which she was to bring to an end finally in June, for he had decided to marry Caitlin and did so within the month. That Easter Antonia went to Paris and on to Germany for a short holiday with Norman Cameron, a Scottish poet and friend of Geoffrey Grigson's, who made a good living on the side writing advertising copy for J. Walter Thompson. He was rather proper: 'Norman the Nagger' Dylan Thomas called him; Antonia thought him marinated still in public-school values, with rather too much of the head prefect about him. Laura Riding, the American poet and muse to Robert Graves, christened him 'Zero the companionable', which summed up perfectly his relationship with Antonia.[22] She had entertained for a while painful romantic longings for him but they came to nothing, and Cameron turned into an entertaining, if lightweight, companion. While in Paris she called on Djuna Barnes, although it had taken an effort of will for she was shy and insecure in the presence of her bitter brilliance. For once Antonia could be sympathetically helpful to Djuna, who had been attacked by a section of the Parisian lesbian community for allegedly ruining Thelma Wood's life with her depiction of her in her book *Nightwood*.

For Antonia, depression was very close to the surface, and it suddenly broke through again in April; she was once more afflicted by what David sympathetically recognised as 'that load of gloom and restless lifelessness'.[23] In her search for relief from this miserable inertia, Antonia sought the opposite extreme; she had the chairs and began to look for the hatchet. By the beginning of the next month, she had formed a violent attraction to another man, the opposite kind from her young poets, a man whom she had known for two years and had always thought 'cynical, cold-hearted and devoid of any interest in human beings except to use their own weaknesses for his own ends.'[24] Basil Nicholson was a famous Fleet Street journalist, who worked on the *Daily Mirror* and was considered by his proprietor to be a brilliant man, full of initiative and energy. Antonia saw him more as a boy prematurely stricken with old age, intelligent but emotionally desiccated and essentially solitary. His most touching characteristic seemed to be his love and knowledge of birds, once camping on an island for three months just watching the birds until he identified with each colony to such an extent that he could predict their behaviour as certainly as he knew his own.

The connection between Antonia and Basil was a tenuous one, and on his side based largely on lust and a misapprehension. She and Tom had known him for many years and she had always disliked him and never understood his attraction to women, suspicious of his 'habit of pursuing women violently'.[25] However, Antonia was feeling so diminished by Tom's lack of desire for her that when Basil suddenly and passionately declared his interest, implying that he thought she was 'a man-eater', Antonia was grateful. They did not meet often, and then only on his terms. His sexual ferocity frightened Antonia, her recoil inflamed him; 'It seemed to me that my frigidity & shyness appealed to a touch of sadism, more than a touch, in his character.'[26] Avid for sensation and drama, however, Antonia became rather fascinated by what she saw as the degradation of her self into a focus solely for another's sexual desire. It gave her a sense of her own power, passive though it may have been, yet the skeletal relationship itself rendered her utterly powerless, dependent and without rights or expectations. She analysed it in her diaries at length, on one occasion veiling the matter by expressing herself in French, and spoke obsessively to Phyllis Jones, who had herself had an affair with Basil Nicholson. Phyllis, however, was a much more spontaneously erotic woman and quite bemused by the fuss Antonia was making; 'makes me wonder what Tony's other men have done to her in bed, if anything', she wrote wryly to Emily, adding that unless Basil had changed radically there was nothing much in her memory of him worth making such a song and dance about.[27]

Antonia, bored at work, frightened of stagnation and 'longing for action', transformed in her mind this temporary mismatch of desire into a love affair.[28] She even imagined herself married to Basil and fired up by this crazy idea started divorce proceedings against Tom. He was already living with Gerti Deutsch, a Viennese photographer who had come to see him at *Weekly Illustrated* in search of work, and was in no hurry to change anything. But Basil was already on the run; 'what had originally attracted him had been my ruthlessness & of course what he aroused in me was all my softness!'[29] This grab for a chance of sexual happiness came partly from Antonia's sense of time fleeing from her, and the urgent desire to join the mainstream of human life before it was too late. There was still a yearning in her to be like other people. She looked at those closest to her, singularly unlike other people, and wrote in her diary a brilliant sketch characterising how each approached the crucial examination of life in which, not only did one have to come up with some sort of answer, but to do so in a time limit: 'Silas has so far done little more than write his name on the examination paper. Djuna has given brilliant answers to questions that were never set in this life. I have just finished, when time is getting short, reading the questions. Tom has read all the books thoroughly and found that they haven't set the paper he expected. Emily has altered most of the questions, is writing a wonderful answer to one headed "to be attempted only when obligatory ones have been answered"; . . . Eric will get a second on an aegrotat on the quality of his work during term; unfortunately when the time came he could not put pen to paper but dazzled everyone in the Viva. Basil, having failed to bribe the examiners openly, is using *his*

paper to write them blackmailing letters.'[30] Antonia knew they were all
astray and the prize of conventional success and happiness would be
awarded elsewhere.

At the end of June, in the midst still of her obsession, Antonia had left
Saturday free, as she always did, in the hopes that Basil would ring – as
he never did. Having frittered away the afternoon in the cinema she
returned to the flat, restless and needing some action. She began ringing
up anyone she could think of, even those whose company she did not
care for, in her desperate desire to see someone, to do anything. Then
something so unusual and surprising happened to her, she felt it merited
a special entry in her diary, 'because it will be reassuring another time'.
Unable to find any outside distraction and on the verge of her familiar
hysteria, 'Out of a pure sense of duty I went to say good-night to Susan.
I stayed half an hour. Then to Lyndall. They were both so fresh and
sweet and alive. Susan hugged me which she very seldom does. We
laughed and made plans to celebrate the end of analysis. And somehow
that lifted all the dead weight and relieved the tension.'[31] But this
revelation of the pleasure of her young daughters' company did not last.
In her paper in the great Examination of Life, Antonia had not yet
reached the question to which this was the answer: she was still too
afraid of human intimacy, fearful of facing the undistracted self.

At the very end of August 1937 Antonia set out a second time with
Norman Cameron to Germany, more peaceful in herself about his lack
of romantic interest in her, and resigned too to the end of her sexual
relationship with Basil Nicholson. Instead she became fascinated by the
phenomenon of Laura Riding, with whom Norman Cameron seemed
besotted. Antonia recognised qualities in this wild and extreme woman
which seemed to be mirrored in herself; her undoubted power over
others, her vanity, her lack of confidence despite her assertions of
uniqueness and superiority. But all was deployed with a consistency and
ruthlessness which Antonia felt she lacked. 'I wonder why all women
writers who are any good have been and are sexually very odd', she
mused to herself, wishing she had acquitted herself better as either a
writer or a woman.[32]

During this trip, Antonia's diary had a few rare entries about the
external world, she commented on the red swastika banners everywhere, the overflying of massed aircraft, the *Hitler Jugend* in their black
corduroy shorts. But then the sense of brooding guilt and anxiety which
she wrote about also was not a comment on the state of a nation on the
edge of the abyss but of her own internal struggles with depression and
mental collapse. However, on her return to London she had a terrifying
dream, full of fear and the threat of unimaginable tortures, the torturers

conducting themselves with an awful jocularity, a dream which conflated Hitler and the bullying nurses of the asylum.

Antonia's sense of aloneness that summer was exacerbated by having relinquished her fantasy of reconciliation with two of the important men in her past, Tom and Silas. When she was daydreaming about marrying Basil, Antonia had suggested seriously the idea of a divorce to Tom. Those wheels were in motion and she knew she would now be alone again. Frances Grigson by then was dying of tuberculosis and had slipped from Tom's focus. Antonia noted indulgently that Tom could not exist without a woman. But when he had a woman he seemed both abject and duplicitous. Having discussed their divorce he wrote to Antonia, 'I continually wonder that you should have married me, & I am constantly grateful for the immense and loving trouble you have taken over me. . . . You have put me in the way of being a writer, & you have perhaps even made me capable of marriage.' Given Antonia's nature, which he knew so well, and her struggle with both intimacy and her writing, Tom ended his letter with the most glib of blessings, 'I wish you everything in the world, first, a strong, alive & loving husband, second, a rich flowering of your lovely talent'.[33]

Although the Basil episode had been quickly truncated by his escape, Antonia, who was keen always to salvage something from her accesses of feeling, claimed, 'he did set me free from a prison in which I have been for so long and gave me the power to love, however incompletely, an image that was not my own.'[34] Even now, without her possible husband number four, Antonia felt that the divorce from Tom should proceed anyway. She was very concerned about the children's unconditional love for him, which inevitably cast her in the role of villain; she was anxious too at her own lack of love for them and her fear of the extra responsibility. However, this forced reponsibility brought a real if belated sense of maternal feeling for Susan and Lyndall, which struck her occasionally. She told Phyllis that she was beginning to love them, now that she had to, being responsible for them. Although by now her preference for Susan was beginning to be marked: 'I would find it very hard to part permanently with Susan . . . having her was one of the few genuine things in my life. I loved Si and wanted Susan, in spite of all the difficulties.'[35]

In fact Silas was also lost to her in a real sense that summer for he and Djuna met at dinner at her flat and fell deeply in love. Djuna thought him 'a perfect angel, & *why* some idiot Englishwoman hasn't grabbed him long since is really beyond me.'[36] These female friends' relationships with each other's men made for some convoluted emotions and easy indiscretions. (Their men's relationships with each other's men had their problems too.) Silas's version of his engagement to Antonia, and subsequent abandonment by her, gave Djuna a new slant on Antonia's character. Djuna's love for Silas and her sense of his woundedness as a person brought out her protective side. Ruthless hunger for power – the Borgia connection as she defined it – even a predisposition towards evil, became the currency of Djuna and Emily's analysis of Antonia's nature that autumn, and it excited and disturbed Antonia to have such an uncompromising interpretation draped around her shoulders. Both Emily and Antonia recorded in their diaries the main conversation where her character was discussed in these terms. Emily and Djuna had gone round to Antonia's flat for dinner some time in the third week of September. Emily had attacked Antonia for wasting her gifts on writing an article on Horsley Towers, the honeymoon house, for which she was paid five pounds (and had published in *Night and Day* that November). One of the things that irritated Antonia about Emily was the fact that she had a private income from her father and, generous as she was, had never understood the real pressures of having to earn a living at a precarious profession. This blind criticism from her friend pushed Antonia too far, and she began one of her frightening apoplectic fits. Djuna had never before seen Antonia out of control and was really alarmed; she started talking rapidly while Emily, who recognised the signs, and knew them well from her own history, continued phlegmatically to eat her meal. The women then adjourned to the sitting room and began to talk about *The Egoist* and Meredith's qualities as a novelist. This was her father's favourite author and Antonia was fascinating in her analysis; 'Tony illuminating at any point on literature' Emily conceded in her diary. But then Emily wanted to move the conversation on to 'truth telling', her favourite dangerous, party game.

It is interesting to see the tenor of their conversation. As Emily recorded, Djuna began addressing Antonia:

> 'You're a bad, bad woman. . . . Why don't you see it through, instead of trying to be a good woman?'
> 'I daren't,' said Tony. She was alive and interested, replied in that calm lively tone, possessing everything. . . .
> I said. 'Yes Tony, you've had everything. Youve had Tom, Eric and Silas eating out of your hand, giving you everything, you've given nothing, just got benefits. Yet you think youre the little abandoned woman.'
> 'I am,' she said.
> 'Youve got even the cats,' Djuna said. 'Youre a bad little spider.'

'The flies have always managed to bite me hard, before they got away,' said Tony.[37]

Antonia's own diary then recorded some more of the conversation:

> [Djuna] said 'You crash right into other people's lives and wreck them – look at Silas – you've done for *him* all right – look at Tom. . . . I saw him on his boat the other day and that engine just kept right on stuttering "Tony . . . Tony . . . Tony . . . Tony . . . Tony."'[38]

Then Emily's diary took up the commentary:

> 'Am I really so bad?' said T[ony] to Djuna.
> 'Not bad enough,' said Dj. 'You ought to be the real poisoner.' [Djuna had accused Antonia in this exchange of giving poison to the wrong man, i.e. Silas]
> 'Yes, I haven't courage enough,' says T. 'I'm afraid no one will love me.'. . .
> She doesnt realise her power. I told her she has literary genius, as a poet, a mystic and a novelist, and why the hell didn't she stop being so greedy for money and power and follow her talent.

But Emily concluded that it was not the power of the creative artist which Antonia wanted but power over men; she was a Borgia and had to follow through her fate before she could write to her full glory. In Antonia's diary entry dealing with this evening, she agreed she loved power, but more in the role of the Old Testament God. 'I want the whole universe dependent on me & to be able to wipe it out and create a new one with a word'.[39] This grand megalomania belonged in the nursery, at a pre-socialised stage of infancy. But it was interesting, perhaps, that this sweeping destruction and recreation should be effected by one *word* – not one blow, one gesture, an order or whim. Emily was right; this kind of creative power should have been Antonia's through the medium of her writing. Instead, she felt, her friend was destroying herself in pursuit of material goals and dictatorial power.

Antonia recorded also her friends' delineation of her evil, which exhilarated her but made her uneasy; having assumed a religious and civil outlook on human responsibility, she wrote, she had struggled to be more aware herself of the existence and rights of others, but was this now shown up as mere hypocrisy? She consoled herself, however, with Emily and Djuna's insistence that she could write, and recorded Djuna's backhanded compliment: 'there is nothing you couldn't do. You could write something quite extraordinary. . . . You're all brain & you've got a heart of leather and with that face & those little feminine ways, there's not a thing you can't get. You trample on them – & they'll love you for it.'[40] What had amazed Emily, during this extensive and hard-hitting dissection of Antonia's qualities, was that she accepted it without flinching, with neither anger nor self-defence, 'as if she was accustomed to hear every night the most dreadful truths about ones soul that anyone could ever utter.'[41] But Emily did not know that no one could say anything more damning of Antonia's soul than what she had already heard from her own heart, hammered into it in her fall from grace in the Convent twenty-three years before. No one could be crueller to Antonia than she was to herself.

16

Sexual Swansong

[Dr Carroll] says the same characteristics appear in every man to whom I am attracted – the strong homosexual element, the fear of castration manifesting itself either in impotence or in over violent sexuality, the trait of disappointing women.

30 November 1937, 'Basil Nicholson diary'

At the end of the summer of 1937, Antonia was coming to accept reluctantly that what she had experienced with Basil Nicholson was not a real emotional connection but merely a sexual collision, and now even that was over. With this on her mind, she visited her mother in the family cottage, Binesfield, in Sussex. In a brilliant diary entry she described the luxuriance of the country in late summer, naming the wild flowers, and noting the birds with a real knowledge and lyrical appreciation. Her elegiac eye rested too on her mother as she portrayed, with exasperation and some fondness, the tatty remnants of her valiant if deluded life. These visits were always unsettling, partly because it was distressing to find an elderly woman taking refuge still in girlish romantic fantasies while her self and her physical world declined into shabbiness and squalor; 'the terrible sense of sweet decay.' But Antonia was more disconcerted by the recognition that there was something very similar in their emotional make-up: 'When she sits up in her shabby bed in a soiled flowered night-dress, with a velvet coat and a moth-eaten fur collar, she thinks she is the Pompadour.' She was disturbed too by her sexual incontinence: 'She talks of nothing but sex. With a giggle she tells me, in veiled language, that she masturbates.'[1]

Masturbation was a subject of some concern for Antonia. She did not gain much, if any pleasure, from sexual intercourse and during the periods when she wrote in her diary of episodes of masturbatory activity invariably she was left feeling guilty and increasingly isolated from human connection. 'The private thrill, followed by shame & disgust & guilt.'[2] It never seemed to concern her overmuch that in her Church's teaching it was also a sin. Antonia's fear of sin was selective and cerebral, focusing on heresy, hypocrisy and lack of grace. Although she was straightforward and candid in her diaries about all matters of the soul and body, and would describe without embarrassment the violent fantasies which sometimes accompanied masturbation, Antonia implied that she considered such behaviour a failure of control, a sign of her continuing immaturity. Even when she was engaged in the last sexual relationship of her life, when belatedly she began to find occasional enjoyment in the act, she still felt her inadequacy; 'Even now know that I am only half awake sexually. Outward stimulation still more exciting than penetration. Not wanting anything to *come too close*.'[3]

In all Antonia did not treat masturbation as a sensual exploration of her body's responses, but rather as an impulse from which she was intellectually detached, something which, in a business-like way, she dispatched to rid herself of an unwelcome discomposure. In her waking life she was her father's daughter, an intellectual and sensation-seeker, cut off from her feeling, intuitive side. Only in her dreams did the erotic, imaginative, and inspired part of her nature stand a chance of surfacing. In her dreams she was connected more truly with her mother. Only then was she disconnected from the control of her mind, whose fear of letting go, of confronting her real self, kept her clinging to the mask that kept her sane. And there were times in her life when her dreams and the hallucinations of her madness seemed a much more real and fertile place for her to be. This alienation from her creative, intuitive self made her greedy for connection with the posse of young poets, David Gascoyne, George Barker, Norman Cameron, and then the two young sons of Wyn Henderson – who were to be her last sexual partners. This hunger sprang not from a sensual or sexual need so much as from fear of the vacuum of lack of life, of lack of love. And that vacuum was as much in her as in her interaction with others.

Within a couple of months from the end of her relationship with Basil Nicholson, Antonia had taken Nigel Henderson as a new lover. He was the younger son of her friend Wyn, who was herself larger than life in physical bulk and carnal appetite. Wyn also had a daughter, Susan, who remembered with gratitude how Antonia, who seemed so sophisticated, treated her as an adult and an equal. Nigel was only twenty, Antonia was thirty-eight and had known him since he was a child. This history and the discrepancy in age and experience did not seem to trouble her: 'I accept, partly . . . from desire to have some human warmth in my life again, a boy of 20 for my lover'.[4] The very youth of young men like these allowed the balance of power to remain in Antonia's favour. Uncertain and ambivalent at the time, Nigel and his elder brother Ian were to attract the attention of two of Antonia's other loves, Eric Earnshaw Smith and David Gascoyne. And so the incestuous interrelations continued. Ian attracted Antonia's attention too and within about six weeks she was engaged in affairs with both brothers, initially without either knowing of the other. This was a hurtful and damaging thing to do to Nigel, a young man who was himself recognised by Antonia as tentatively approaching adulthood, someone she thought of as intelligent, impressionable, highly sensitive and with an artistic, hysterical temperament; a young man who suffered also his fair share of complex passions and rivalries with this elder brother. Antonia had no personal experience of the passions between siblings and the destructiveness of setting one against the other. Nigel's reaction was bitter; 'he thinks I have knifed him in the back'.[5] This was either another example of Antonia's blindness to the feelings of others when she was in the grip of obsession with her self, or a conscious act of revenge on Nigel for his inability to love her. This latter and ruthless possibility was suggested by Dr Carroll, and Antonia, as ever willing to believe the worst of herself, merely wrote in her diary: 'This is a terrible truth to face, if it is so.'[6]

Nevertheless this highly charged *ménage à trois* continued fitfully for four months, from December 1937 until April 1938 when Nigel, perhaps in revenge for the hurt she had done him, or so Antonia thought, slept with her friend Kathleen McClean. This turn of events possibly occurred on the occasion Kathleen recalled when Antonia and Nigel were staying with her in her house in Hertfordshire and in the middle of the night Nigel had fled from Antonia's bed and sought refuge in her own. Nigel continued to hover in the wings of his brother's and Antonia's relationship, in the confused hope of re-establishing some sort of sexual connection, until the end of the year when Antonia finally committed herself to Ian. Antonia was obsessed with analysing the young men, their relationship with her and with each other. She found Nigel more satisfactory intellectually and emotionally, but Ian was a steadying influence and seemed to be sexually more rewarding: he remembered, however, being surprised that such an apparently mature and experienced woman should be so naïve about the male body and its sexual functions, exhibiting a detached curiosity which was more prepubescent than lover-like. Antonia felt she was learning at last about the intimate relationships between men and women, 'The best thing about my relationship with Ian is that I can sometimes allow myself to be dull and happy with him.'[7]

Through analysis, she had grown more aware of the aspects of her behaviour which made her such a restless and difficult companion; she had always been terrified of the boredom that descended on her when nothing special was happening, and would create scenes, look for trouble, demand attention. She would even wake up Ian to ask for reassurance. So uncertain was Antonia of the fact of her own existence that she needed always to be reflected in the concern, love or even distaste of another's gaze. Above all she realised that unless she was working on her real writing she was a liability; otherwise 'there is NO happiness possible for me or for people closely connected with me'.[8]

The people most closely connected to her were Susan and Lyndall – not that Antonia was thinking of them when she made that comment. She had not yet reached the point where she appreciated the baleful effects her moods and behaviour could have on her children. They were not yet nine and seven years old respectively, but were already aware of the ways that their mother was often emotionally absent to them, and even more alarmingly present when in the grip of her own anxieties and obsessions. In the autumn of 1937, with the divorce from Tom finally becoming reality, and Silas's liaison with Djuna proving to have some durability, Antonia became sentimental in conversation with Djuna about her 'dear fatherless creatures . . . whom nobody seems to want'.[9] Djuna gave this short shrift, as she considered Antonia to be the chief offender; however, this plaint was as much about Antonia's own sense of abandonment and lovelessness. It was she whom nobody seemed to want. She had told Phyllis Jones, who was now running the agony column on the *Daily Mirror*, that with Basil Nicholson no longer a marriage prospect she would like to break up Tom's relationship with Gerti and get him back for herself; 'She thinks it is the BEST THING for all of them. BALLS!' was Phyllis's well reasoned, professional response.[10]

In the same conversation with Djuna, Antonia also mentioned that she had told Susan that Silas, not Tom, was her father and that the little girl had liked the idea. Silas now had to take Susan to tea once a week, and rather liked that idea himself. The truth of the matter, of course, was much more complicated and distressing for both children, but particularly so for Susan. Her analyst, Miss Searle, had decided that the time had come for Susan to be told who was her real father. Perhaps Antonia's impending divorce from Tom and his possible remarriage made such a clarification all the more desirable in her mind, but she was to admit to Susan years later that this piece of advice was the worst mistake she had made in her professional life, which can only suggest that the psychological repercussions were serious and destructive.

Susan described in *Now to my Mother* being called into the drawing-
room by Antonia. Her mother sat with her back to the window, neatly
upright and smoking a cigarette. She said in a matter-of-fact voice,
'Now, darling, if I were to tell you that Tom is *not* your father, who
would you guess *was*?'[11] Susan remembered her mind running through
the list of men friends of her mother's, none of whom seemed to fit the
fatherly bill, and then suddenly she recalled Silas Glossop, who mostly
lived abroad and turned up occasionally bearing a big present for her and
a smaller one for Lyndall. 'Is it Silas?' she asked and was told it was. It
seemed that Antonia had been unable to bring any sympathetic
imagination to bear on the situation. Her own father had been the most
important person in the world to her, and she would have been
devastated to have been told that in fact he did not belong to her after
all. Because her daughter did not react adversely Antonia, isolated herself
from the deepest feelings of others, thought that this was a satisfactory
exchange: Susan seemed pleased and that was that.

In fact, Susan's immediate feelings were painfully mixed. She was
proud to have a father all to herself, one who was a romantic and
attractive figure, who had given her a toy dog called Dingo and carried
some of the exoticism of his foreign travels with him. But she barely
knew him, and it was to be many years before she could look to him as a
father, to his family as her family. The overwhelming emotional impact,
however, came from the realisation that Tom, the father she had
known, and loved, and been nurtured by since she was an infant of
eighteen months, was no longer hers. In her own words she had to
'surrender' this father to Lyndall, and face the fact of her own
illegitimacy. It was painful that she could no longer think of herself as a
true member of the Hopkinson clan, the grandparents, the aunt and
uncles who had been an important part of her emotional landscape and
had supplied a sense of familial security and normality in an unpredictable and chilly childhood. This new distinction which separated her
from Tom and Lyndall and the rest of his family increased her feelings of
loneliness and difference. To compensate for this fundamental loss,
Susan assumed a fragile superiority. There was no defensive action,
however, on her part which could heal the increased feeling of self-
loathing which had dogged her short life.

The realisation that she had lost a real father to gain only a shadowy
promise of one also drove a wedge between her and Lyndall. They were
no longer totally united in sisterhood. Susan had already suffered the
jealousy of realising that Nurse gave more attention to Lyndall as a new
baby than to her. Now she had had to withdraw, and leave Lyndall in
possession of the prize father and his extended family. At that moment it

seemed she had nothing much to fill this newly-created void. When Susan came out of the fateful meeting with her mother, Lyndall had been waiting anxiously for her. Lyndall remembered her appearing at last, holding her head high. Then before Lyndall could say a word, Susan burst out 'Tom's only your father. Mine's Silas Glossop.'[12] Lyndall was astounded, but admired Susan for what appeared to be her equanimity.

With the clarification of Silas's paternity, Tom requested a renegotiation of maintenance payments, suggesting Silas should take on the financial commitment for Susan. Silas was still paying for Susan's analysis and found this extra burden hard to bear; in February, he and Antonia had a bitter argument where old wounds were aired, but peace was re-established with a meeting with Tom to discuss finances and commitment.

The only evidence we have about Susan's subsequent reaction to this new father comes from a letter of Djuna's to Emily in the following summer. Djuna and Silas had come to dine with Antonia and had gone with her to say goodnight to Susan and Lyndall: 'Funny, seeing Tony and Silas standing by the bed of their girl, and she looking cunning and sweet and wicked like her mother, and shy of Silas because he has not taken her into his life. Remember me? he said and she answered Yes, sly little yes with sting and hurt in it.'[13] Of all these women friends, Djuna showed herself to be the most sensitive and feeling towards others. In the same letter, Djuna described Antonia's unawareness of her child's needs that night, and the brilliance of her conversation, her preening in the light of Silas and Djuna's admiration for her talk.

For both girls, the regular parental appearances of Tom in their lives was less consoling, as he struggled with his own emotional maelstrom. Frances Grigson finally died of tuberculosis in October 1937, by which time Tom had already replaced his subsequent lovers with Gerti Deutsch, whom he was to marry once his divorce from Antonia was through. Another family was to follow and although Tom would continue to treat Antonia's daughters with concern, interest and affection, they would inevitably feel displaced by his new connections and responsibilities. Nurse too, who had been Susan and Lyndall's ever-present carer, left in October to marry. Lyndall had always been more attached to her than was Susan, but her departure was a loss for both girls after all those years of predictable and affectionate presence.

With Nurse replaced by less permanent help, and as Tom slipped increasingly out of their lives, Antonia's state of mind affected the girls more directly. She was almost as demanding and critical of others as she was of herself, and quickly roused to anger. Susan and Lyndall were at full-time school, King Arthur's in Bolton Gardens. Each learnt that it was less painful to keep out of Antonia's way for much of the rest of the time. As Antonia recognised herself, when she was not writing she was dangerous; when she was involved with a lover she was distracted and obsessed and when she was without either work or love she was panic-stricken and in despair. The beast of her mental illness spread its claws into all areas of her life.

None of these conditions allowed her much emotional energy left for love and empathy with her young daughters, whom she alternately feared and resented with occasional flashes of interest, pride and love. It was a lonely, anxious and unpredictable home life for these young girls, when each other's company and support was the only secure marker. Lyndall called it the '"Babes in the Wood" phase of our childhood . . . our only remaining security was each other.'[14] Pretty much unsupervised, they roamed the streets on their way home from school, playing horses and hanging around the real horses at the United Dairies stables. The sisters once set off trotting behind an Express Dairies milk cart on its way to the depot; they wanted to find out where the ponies of the rival dairy were stabled. Lyndall soon dropped back, unable to keep up, but Susan cantered on and finally reached the stables at Hammersmith. She was eight years old and had been away from home for at least two hours. No adult seemed to know or care.

Work also was a problem for Antonia that autumn. J. Walter Thompson were not as indulgent as their English counterparts of staff, however creative, who did not offer one hundred per cent of themselves. After nine months of half-hearted commitment from Antonia they sacked her, giving her notice to leave at the end of November. Antonia was not so much upset at losing the job, which was boring her into rebellion, as disconcerted by the thought that she had been sacked from every job – ten in all, she thought. She was very good at getting jobs, men and money, she realised, but useless at keeping any of them. Driven by her continual need to earn a living, Antonia applied to eight or nine advertising agencies, two newspapers and answered six advertisements.

She was still ambivalent about taking advertising work, professing to loathe it and the people in it, but it offered a regular and more than adequate income. She felt she was most successful when she was teaching the public about the product, once more employing the didactic skills she had always loathed. All her advertising work, even the best, was always derivative of someone else's work whereas her writing, like her poetry, she felt was truly original and peculiar to herself. The decision, however, was made for her. No advertising job was forthcoming and Antonia was reconciled to the idea of returning to the perilous but less constricting world of the freelancer.

Just after Christmas, in January of 1938, she threw financial caution to the winds and set off for a week in Paris, to see David Gascoyne who was languishing there in a subdued state. He had shown her short story 'The House of Clouds' to Henry Miller and Alfred Perlès who were Fashion/Literary Editor and Managing Editor respectively of the *Booster*, and both were impressed. Miller wrote to Antonia to tell her how much he admired the piece and how he would like to publish it. The *Booster* was an avant-garde literary magazine, ostensibly the house magazine of the American Country Club of France, whose financial backing and advertising patronage were quickly exhausted by its editors' policy of uncompromised (and subversive) editorial freedom. The last straw came with the publication of an obscene story about an eskimo which resulted in a public denunciation by the Club President. Advertising was immediately withdrawn and the magazine limped on before being turned into *Delta*, which ran for three more issues. In the April 1938 issue of the *Booster*, Miller and Perlès published three of Antonia's poems, 'The Crest', inspired by Nigel Henderson, 'The Double Man' about Ian Henderson, and 'Epitaph', on Elspeth Glossop's untimely death. 'The House of Clouds' appeared in the summer edition of *Delta*, called the 'Special Peace and Dismemberment Number with Jitterbug-Shag Requiem', contemporaneous as it was with the Munich Crisis that September. She shared the contents page with Miller, Perlès, Lawrence Durrell, Dylan Thomas and Anaïs Nin.

But despite the literary welcome given her by the wild man of American letters, Antonia suddenly was suffering again from deadening depression and an impulse to kill herself. To Miller, and to a lesser extent Perlès, insanity was a mysterious conundrum to be embraced as intellectually inspiring, an ennobling risk one ran in the creation of great art. But this was not much consolation for those who had to endure the anguish of such a condition. When Miller heard that his friend Richard Osborn had gone mad he wrote 'Hurrah. Let's go and see him. Let's have a drink first, and put ourselves in the right mood. This is rare, superb, it doesn't happen every day. I hope he is really insane and not faking.'[15] Perlès, seeing Antonia in this parlous state, however, was moved to write a poem about her. Due to her influence, he told Miller, his conversion to a new seriousness happened on New Year's Eve. He told his friend it would change the course of his life: perhaps this new seriousness was part of his dramatic decision to transfer his allegiance to Britain and join the British Pioneer Corps in 1940, when he was forty years old, in which capacity he worked heroically under fire saving civilians in the East End during the war. As a Czech Jew living in Paris, this decision may have saved his life. Despite the important effect she apparently had on Perlès, there was no mention of anything in Antonia's diary or letters beyond the cold beauty of Paris under frost, her own despair, and David's enervated state.

David had been lonely and looking forward to her visit and some good profound talk, but her depression and her unrelenting critical eye had deflated his fragile mood. His emotional nature was vulnerable and absorbent. She left him as she was, inert yet restless and distracted; as he described it, he felt '*le monde désert*, a terrible fundamental boredom, a terrible sense of being alone among people who are all alone with themselves and inarticulate, a terrible dry interior sobbing.'[16]

Antonia returned to the Henderson brothers and the necessity of finding enough work to earn her living. Tom was due to decrease his allowance to her in September by £300, and that added to her anxieties. She also had to find somewhere else to live. When she was facing unemployment at the end of the previous year, Antonia had suggested tentatively to Cecil King, the proprietor of the *Daily Mirror* and *Sunday Pictorial*, that he might finance a new magazine for children. She thought the children aspect would interest King, although it would seem hardly of burning interest to Antonia herself. With Eric she discussed the idea of a paper for women, which she would edit. Cecil King did not respond positively to either proposal, but perhaps it was at that point that he realised that this rather intellectual writer, Antonia White, was the same competent fashion journalist, Anne Jeffrey, who had written for the *Daily Mirror*. As a result of this he offered her a well-paid job as fashion editor of the *Sunday Pictorial*, for which she wrote under the name of Jane Marshall. This was the beginning of a rare period of freedom from pressing financial concerns, which lasted until the outbreak of war.

Cecil and Margot King were to be significant friends to Antonia until the war intervened, and she remained into old age good friends with Margot. That summer of 1938 saw the fascist tide advance through more of Europe, with Franco unassailable in Spain and Hitler welcomed ecstatically by the Austrians in Vienna. With the growing menace from outside, Antonia's internal threat of madness seemed to be in retreat. She was learning how to be less at the mercy of her fears and obsessions and more attuned to the needs and natures of others.

In the middle of June, Antonia was invited to stay with the Kings in some grandeur at their country house, Culham Court in Oxfordshire. She was drawing to the end of her intensive four-times-a-week analysis with Dr Carroll, and Antonia was becoming more aware of the world around her. She vividly described in her diary the orderly routine of self-sufficient country life, recognising too the wilful nature and hidden power of a conventionally submissive wife like Margot. Musing on the boredom of the wealthy, she felt again the contrast of her own material poverty, which she resented and feared, and the richness of her own extreme experiences. 'The most striking thing about madness, painful and terrifying as it was was the sense of continued intensity of experience. I was often agonised, miserable and terrified, but I was never bored.'[17] Nevertheless she felt that the self-centredness of her nature had led to a strangely impoverished life, despite the apparent freedom she had enjoyed, and the breadth and nature of her experiences. Dr Carroll had suggested to Antonia that her real desires were 'towards power, achievement, dominance & success' but she felt that this was militated against by the strength of her inner life: 'the most important thing I have.'[18]

As she faced the loosening of her dependence on analysis, so her mystical side once more began its ascendancy. She had been told by a mutual acquaintance that Robert Legg, the ecstatic love of her youth, had died three years before in a flying accident. In her mania before Bedlam, Antonia had had a premonition he would die that way: now there was a confusion of feeling about having her foreboding confirmed, 'I do not quite know what I felt – triumph, dismay, blankness', but she and Robert had been so psychically connected during that euphoric three weeks that she expected too that he would send her a sign.[19] She concentrated, asking for a message – even finding a jay's feather would have been enough – but no sign came and she felt cheated. She had come to realise that the extreme emotion she had felt for him had been pathological, part of the mania which preceded the fall into a suicide attempt and raving madness. Nevertheless, that elation had become for her a standard of human happiness against which she always compared her subsequent life, and always found it wanting. That night as she was falling asleep, Antonia had a vivid sense of a man bending over her; he had a mocking, even hostile, presence, just as Robert had when he appeared to her in dreams.

Increasingly her thoughts were returning to religion. She wrote in her diary how she needed a plan into which her struggles and sufferings could be fitted and dignified with meaning. She was fearing the loss of Dr Carroll and the lack of any other legitimate human figure of support; 'It may be an illusion to rely on God, yet it makes it more possible not to lean on human beings. . . . Yet can I ever again accept the restrictions and superstitions of an organised religion?'[20] If she was drawn back to organised religion, it was always Catholicism which seemed the only possible one for her. With the withdrawal of Dr Carroll from her life, her identification of him with her father was weakened. Some months after analysis was over she had met Carroll again and had been surprised to find him clean-shaven; she was even more surprised to realise that he had always been so, 'though all through my $3\frac{1}{2}$ years of sessions I had always seen him with a little moustache, like my father.'[21] As Carroll prepared to abandon her at the end of September, her resentment and fear of her real father suddenly flared up in that extraordinary outburst against him in her diary where she had assessed his impact on her creativity: 'I hope you've been punished. You punished me enough. I've forced myself to feel sorry for you and admire you. You've ruined my life. . . . I'd like to fight and kill you both, trample on you, take your money away. . . . You never loved me for a second and I'm damned if I'm going to go on loving you. . . .'[22] There was much more in the same angry, hurt, defensive vein.

That July Antonia had two short holidays with Ian at his mother's cottage, Summer's Heath near Henley-on-Thames. Both were unsatisfactory. On the first visit Wyn Henderson was also there, and too much in possession of the place for Antonia to feel relaxed and at ease. Ian was supposed to be revising for his Civil Service exams, and was seeking success yet courting failure. Antonia was in an ambivalent state over him, attacking him when he ignored her and made her feel insecure, then suffering guilt at how quick-tempered and frightening she could be to her intimates. She resented his financial dependence on her own limited funds, and yet liked him to be reliant on her: she was relieved to be able to enjoy a sexual relationship at last, but burdened by his sexual demands. Although Antonia admitted the relationship seemed incomprehensible to everyone else, without Ian she feared she would become cold and inhuman, '& grow claws & fangs'. The best thing he did for her, she told Emily, was to treat her like a woman '& not like a dangerous or dazzling or embarrassing *phenomenon*.'[23]

Overwhelmed by her longing for a husband – she told Dr Carroll anyone would do, but preferably someone like him – Antonia was consumed with envy of Gerti Deutsch, not because she had married Tom particularly, but becasue she had a husband at all. To try and assuage her feelings of deprivation, Antonia decided to play house with Ian during their second visit to Summer's Heath at the end of July. They were alone this time and assumed cosy married personae. Antonia put on a pinafore and started to cook macaroni cheese and roast joints, as she related to an amazed Emily, who was back in Connecticut again. Antonia had told Emily that they were both handicapped by a lack of female wit; they had to work out on paper what other women knew instinctively. 'Work out on paper' was an interesting turn of phrase and perhaps explained part of Antonia's compulsion to describe, analyse and dissect in her diaries, letters and conversations her relation with herself and the world. A fundamental human relatedness, which others approached intuitively, was inaccessible to her and women like her, who could only try and work it out through the intellect. Emily could only agree. She added that she and Antonia were also alike in the way they needed men; 'My weaknesses regarding men . . . are a combination of vanity, which must be served by adulation . . . a childish and surely insane adolescent longing for romantic love (without sex); and a genuine terror of life.'[24]

Djuna Barnes was back in London and in reckless despair over her love for Silas: her health too was seriously impaired. On Antonia's urgings she went to see Dr Carroll, who told her she was not crazy at all, 'thinks its change of life, not drink.'[25] She was extremely short of money, as always, and irritated by Peggy Guggenheim who floated about wearing a $60,000 pearl necklace while declaring she was too poor to help her friends. She proceeded to paint Peggy's portrait on a piece of mahogany, which not surprisingly Peggy loathed. 'Tony says she is going to wear a veil when she next comes to see me, shes so afraid of the horrid things I might do to her!! right too, I can just see what I would make of that great heifer like expanse of face, with its pretty golden curls!! A heifer loose among the Adams brothers, and the Wrens, and with spear grass in her teeth!!'[26]

Antonia and Ian had been steadily putting on weight during their relationship, and Antonia thought it had a psychological component; 'I suppose we are putting up some defence against each other for fear of being sucked dry.'[27] Antonia was now fatter than she had ever been, and her doctors, thinking there might be a physiological reason, were worried she might have diabetes. She went into a nursing home in Devonshire Terrace in Bayswater on 17 October to have her metabolism observed. 'After psycho-analysis comes glands' Phyllis wrily commented to Emily.[28] This observation involved measuring everything which went into her and everything which came out, 'including her breath' according to Phyllis, who had been summoned by Antonia in a panic.[29] Antonia was all right, only weak and intellectually confused from the spartan diet she was on. She emerged at the end of the month, her glands declared fit and healthy and her weight considerably reduced.

The following autumn she managed to write a play, *Three in a Room*, which was eventually produced at the Oldham Repertory Theatre in 1944 and occasional amateur companies in the years that followed. Antonia came to be ashamed of this attempt, 'it's a guilty secret . . . an efficient, manufactured little farce', which she wrote largely as an attempt to make some money.[30] She received £40 for all publishing rights and then fifty per cent of performing fees, which amounted to about £10 a year for at least fifteen years. She had always longed to write a good play but felt, as with novels, she lacked any real inventive power.

The long haul of analysis had only just ended when Antonia retreated into the womb-like routine of the nursing home. The end of analysis had marked a reluctant acceptance of her adult responsibilities. But she was to feel that they were responsibilities she accepted out of a sense of duty, not with love. In retrospect she believed that Dr Carroll had removed her 'chains of fear' but in the process she had further lost sight of her creativity. The analysis, however, had made 'sex relations possible' at last.[31] She wrote an unsent letter to Cyril Connolly a few years later, attempting to explain her return to the Church, where she mentioned her gratitude to Dr Carroll, and to Dr Freud himself who was still just alive, for 'removing the agonising obsessions and fears and making me capable of managing my life at least tolerably reasonably.'[32] Among the responsibilities she now felt prepared to shoulder were her two young daughters who, while increasingly interesting to her and companionable, were wounded, self-protective and understandably wary. In her diary, Antonia mused on her changed perspective:

> I do want (faintly) to do the best for them . . . and of course for myself too. I wish I knew what they needed most. I am distrustful of myself & a little frightened of them . . . find it hard to allow for their youth & their inevitable difference from me. I expected them to be . . . more interested in me. [After exhorting herself to learn how to manage her money better and not dissipate her energies in meaningless fantasies, she added,] I'm so afraid of losing myself I can't find myself.[33]

17
Peace and War

Irony if just as I am through with analysis, war breaks out. Impossible, of course, for the megalomaniac unconscious not to think the two connected.

11 September 1938, Diaries 1

At the end of September 1938, the English and French Prime Ministers, Neville Chamberlain and Edouard Daladier, flew to Munich to negotiate with Mussolini and Hitler the dismemberment of Czechoslovakia. Chamberlain returned to Britain with his notorious piece of paper and his claim 'I believe it is peace for our time!' The rapturous cheering which greeted him turned quickly to shame and unease. A far-away country had been sacrificed to a ruthless dictator; was there not a chance that each sacrifice would increase his people's appetite for blood? Chamberlain had made the fatal mistake of thinking that Hitler and Mussolini were reasonable, gentlemanly statesmen like himself, and he expected that everything would have been resolved within three months. Churchill, with war as his element and power his objective, was much closer in nature himself to these men and he warned that Hitler's annexing of the Sudetenland was just the beginning.

Despite temporary lapses, Antonia's mental state improved markedly as Britain prepared for war. She had always maintained that 'boredom, suspense and monotony are my "natural" bugbears', and that she felt more secure in times of violence when there was a good deal going on and varied and difficult demands were made of her.[1] She took driving lessons so as to be of greater use in the coming war effort. Her fashion writing for the *Sunday Pictorial* continued for a while; she was doing occasional work for *Picture Post*, where Tom was assistant editor and *Lilliput*, a small literary magazine whose founder, Phyllis Jones's friend

Stefan Lorant, occasionally used her skills in quirky frivolity like 'What a Woman does when she's Alone' – not much, it seemed, but fret and titivate.

Despite the distant thunder, she felt a new personal expansiveness and moved from Cecil Court into a maisonette in Cornwall Gardens. She also took on the lease of a cottage in the country near Rye in East Sussex, rented from a friend, Gerald Reitlinger, an artist and collector. She had one of her accesses of energy over furnishing this and the flat in town, spending recklessly and in advance, hoping that her earnings would somehow catch up. She recognised this manic energy as being similar to that which seized her when she first impressed her services on Saint-Denis and the London Theatre Studio. It made Antonia uneasy but, if she could contain it, it was preferable to the deadness and lethargy which lay at her other psychic pole. She thought she might try and make a home in the country for herself and her daughters and by the spring of 1939 felt financially secure enough to enrol them in a progressive girls' boarding school local to the cottage. Housed in an impressive half-timbered Elizabethan manor house in wonderful countryside near Northiam in East Sussex, the place was called, rather unpromisingly, Brickwall.

Both Susan and Lyndall recorded their memories of this school and its ill-favoured headmistress, Mrs Heath, whom Susan remembered as looking like 'a very old sheep.'[2] Horses were the main attraction for both girls, but the lack of any kind of discipline and academic expectation – even attendance at lessons was voluntary – gave an unsatisfactory formlessness to each day. Lyndall particularly was made uneasy at the enforced rule of nude bathing in the outdoor swimming pool. But increasingly fearful of Antonia's unpredictable temper, she never thought to confide to her mother her misery and loneliness. They only had to endure the summer term; a scandal when photographs of the nude bathers got into the press, and Antonia's realisation of her true financial situation, meant the girls were never to return. The alternative, however, the village school near their Hopkinson grandparents in Winster in Cumbria, was as unhappy an experience, with its harsh teacher, Miss Limb, and its low intellectual horizons. But with the outbreak of war officially declared in September, it seemed sensible for the children, who had spent the long summer holidays with their grandparents, to continue to live there and to go to school locally.

While the children were boarding at Brickwall, Antonia faced the shocking fact that she was pregnant again, this time with Ian's baby. She was forty and had already been a reluctant and unsatisfactory mother to her two daughters, although she was beginning to see the advantages –

just – of having children. She asked Dr Carroll's advice, and he felt that for her to go through with the pregnancy and have another child to care for would be too much strain on her newly regained equanimity. The imminence of war must have weighed in the balance also. He agreed that an abortion would be the safest option and suggested that she should have herself sterilised at the same time, to prevent the risk of any more unwelcome conceptions. Antonia went into hospital at the end of June, and offered her flat to Djuna, who was in London and in a thoroughly low state, with her health, her drinking and her hopeless love for Silas still haunting her. 'I have faded for him as a breath off a mirror. . . . He'll "love" a number of people and *hate me the least*' she wrote despondently to Emily.[3] Silas had been to see Antonia in hospital and Djuna reported to Emily how haggard she looked 'but then she's been through a terrible operation. . . . Tony longs for money and comfort, and with her tubes tied up, she may get it.'[4] Emily, on hearing about her friend's operation, wrote rather remotely from Arizona enquiring if she had any of her '*personal*' organs taken out. The whole business was a draining and uncomfortable experience. Antonia commiserated with Lyndall many years later who was facing an operation to remove an ovarian cyst: 'I had something of that kind when I had a rather nasty operation in 1939.'[5] Antonia was to regret this abortion, but not as profoundly as she had come to regret the first one: she never felt that she should have gone ahead with this pregnancy. She only told Ian after she had had the operation, which upset him at her lack of trust in him.

In retrospect, Antonia believed the declaration of war saved her sanity. She had become increasingly frenzied and frustrated in her attempts to write her next book. She had tried to construct a novel from an imagined situation but 'with relief, also with guilt, fell back on the old autobiographical subject.'[6] With some regret she acknowledged that she thought she was a reporter rather than an inventor, but then this factual approach threatened her with the implacable *idée fixe*: 'I feel . . . that he [father] would never forgive me if I wrote about him – that it is the unforgiveable sin to expose his nakedness to the world.'[7] She felt that until she could tackle his character, show 'the full force of my love and my hatred of him', she would never be free, either emotionally or in her imagination. And so, obsessively, Antonia was drawn back each time to try and write about him, the hero/villain of her life. And each time, 'it has the most awful effects. All my demons wake up, determined to shake me off it . . . and they do. Sometimes it is awful recurring dreams about my father & fearful depressions.'[8] Then if the response from those closest to her to what she had managed painfully to write was not enthusiastic enough, shame and anger inflamed her. She read one of the many versions of her first chapter to Ian, whose concentration slipped; 'I wrote to please him and he wasn't pleased.'[9] In fact he was just tired. But his inattention had been enough; Antonia promptly burnt the manuscript, hoping he would stop her, but he was too weary to try.

Having recently lost both a husband to divorce and remarriage, and a father figure, Dr Carroll, through natural progression, Antonia began to cast an increasingly longing eye at the certainty and security that faith can bring. 'A true belief in God would be the strongest spring of action and happiness', she wrote in her diary.[10] She had felt always that an extreme character like hers needed a cast-iron moral construct to contain it. But she was still resistant to the laws, the ideology and external trappings of an organised church. She was attracted to large and noble ideals, the soldier's morality, and could accept the proscriptions of such a life, but small-mindedness and arbitrary complications exasperated her. The Christian idea of meekness she considered unnatural, even repellent: organised charity, and always holding back, and making allowances, made for a bleak existence. She thought it was little wonder that lives spent trying to conform to arbitrary and unnatural patterns like these were often miserable and frustrated. Antonia was not ready yet to submit her own nature again to the template of Catholicism, but she was beginning to turn her face towards it, while protesting that she was not meant to be beautiful or good and that 'acquired virtues seem to me very much like rouge on a corpse.'[11]

She managed one last trip to Paris before the outbreak of war, travelling in August, but not seeing David Gascoyne this time, for he had come home to England in some despair. She may have seen Djuna Barnes who was staying at the Hotel Recamier, still ill and angry. She wrote to Emily that Antonia was a puzzle, so full of envy and meanness but with streaks of genuine goodness and generosity. Within ten months German troops would be marching down the Champs-Elysées, the symbol of France's humiliation. It would be seven years before Antonia left English shores again.

On Sunday 3 September 1939 at eleven o'clock in the morning, Britain was formally at war with Germany; by five o'clock that evening France had joined their allies. In Britain, after a summer of growing menace and political confusion, there was some relief in having the fateful decision made, although the future could only be a desperate struggle, a journey into the terrible unknown. In the first three days of September, Poland had been shattered by the *Wehrmacht*, and within eight days the Germans were at the gates of Warsaw, the *Luftwaffe* having destroyed the railway system and eradicated the Polish air force

Eirene Botting (Antonia White) at Convent of the Sacred Heart, Roehampton 1913, aged 14 (*front row, left*)

Cecil Botting, mid–1890s

Christine Botting and Antonia
in her hussar's hat, 1906

Binesfield, in Sussex, 1904, with Grandfather Botting and Antonia, aged 5

Antonia at 17, having cut her hair
and left school

Antonia and Reggie Green-Wilkinson
on their wedding day, 1921

Eliot Seabrooke

Robert Legg

Eric Earnshaw Smith

Antonia, 1924

Silas Glossop

Tom Hopkinson with Susan

Emily Holmes Coleman

Tom with Susan
and Lyndall, 1936

Antonia and Djuna Barnes at Hayford Hall, 1933, with Peggy Guggenheim
and John Holms inset

David Gascoyne,
drawing by Lucian Freud, 1943

Ian Henderson

Antonia, 1947

Antonia, South Bend, Indiana, 1959

Antonia with Susan and Lyndall, at Binesfield, 1939

Susan, *c.* 1951

Lyndall, 1952

Antonia, aged 65, with Minka

from their own skies. It was a terrifying experience to see the speed and devastation of a new kind of war, the *blitzkrieg*, or lightning war, set loose on an unprepared nation.

Antonia's journalism dried up virtually overnight. Similarly, the energy which had gone into writing her voluminous journals, the introspective telling herself about herself which had begun just before her first marriage in 1921 and was to accompany her throughout her life, was deflected elsewhere during the war years. She only managed a few pages and occasional jottings. No longer was she agonising over the failings of her own nature, her unresolved longings and the conundrums of faith. She was dealing with a threat from outside which was far greater than her self and the legacies of her past, and she rose to the challenge and thrived. 'Funnily enough I've never had such a peaceful life as I've had since Sept. 1st ... I feel very calm, only fretting at inaction' she wrote to Emily.[12] Her letters to Emily continued but their tone was different; there was a calmer philosophical sanity in her thoughts and a business-like productivity in her life.

Emily, far removed from the drama of war and never naturally empathic about the experiences of others, was living the life of a cowboy's wife on a ranch in Arizona, dispensing advice with her usual authority. She had fallen in love with Jake Scarborough, 'a cowboy, though he is – as you can imagine – a strange one', and gone to live with him in some heat and discomfort.[13] Djuna was sceptical at the thought that anyone could live with Emily. She thought she frightened every man to death, was too impulsive, too excessive; 'too bull-dog on the hem of heaven ... and men, well men dont like it. ... You see, a man wants a nicely ordered world on which he can put his feet and have it come up to him like Rover with his morning tea.'[14] In fact Jake bore up well and Emily seemed content at last with her ranch and the cattle and the distant Yosemites. She was reading avidly and thought that if she had been a man she would have been a second Blake, but being merely a woman she was just in trouble. Her idyll came to an end when she converted to Catholicism at the end of 1942, and was told that her divorce from her first husband was not valid. She could not therefore continue with her sexual relationship with Jake until she had had her first marriage annulled. Jake, being a real cowboy, did not take kindly to this sophistry, and told her if she was going to refuse to sleep with him then she could leave on the next train. Emily chose Catholicism over cowboy love and her phenomenal energies, which had needed the wide open spaces of Arizona to contain them, became channelled increasingly into religious fanaticism and the pursuit of personal beatification.

Antonia was living a very different life from her old friend out on the range. With her children being looked after by the Hopkinson grandparents in Cumbria, she felt she ought to accept the generous offer of a temporary home as a paying guest with Douglas McClean and Kathleen Hale. They lived near South Mimms in Hertfordshire in a house called Rabley Willow. Their two sons, Peregrine and Nicholas, were not much younger than Susan and Lyndall and Antonia got on well with them. Kathleen remembered, however, that on previous weekend visits when Antonia came with her children and one of her husbands or lovers, the girls hung around Kathleen, who was more practical and relaxed, and said how they wished that she was their mother. Antonia was initially happy at Rabley Willow, where she and Kathleen encouraged each other to work, meeting for coffee to compare progress. In the remaining time Antonia did some gardening, and talked to Kathleen's sons and read Spinoza at night. She told Emily that everything not directly connected with the war seemed shadowy and futile, and that although it was impossible to imagine a future, she did not feel as if she were ripe for death – but then perhaps no one ever did. Kathleen recalled in her autobiography that Antonia was almost comically impractical, and that even ordinary tasks such as sewing on buttons caused her trouble.

The war meant that Antonia's usual outlets for work had contracted. Theatres too were closing, and her play *Three in a Room* seemed unlikely to be produced in the foreseeable future. It had had an initially cool reception from an agent she had shown it to, and now Antonia was despondent, facing two alternative unpalatable truths – that she was not cut out to be a playwright, or that she had a good deal more work to do on this particular play. Money anxieties suddenly pressed hard on her. She wrote a 'bitter and resentful' letter to Tom about the difference in their financial situations, pointing out that he earned £1,500 and she earned nil. He was stung to reply, saying he earned £1,350 and had to support his household with Gerti, as well as contribute substantially to Antonia. He set down just what he had done financially for her and the children since he had moved out of the flat until their divorce, leaving just £5 a week for himself to live on; 'by last October, when this arrangement came to an end, I was £500 in debt, & everything I had was worn out.'[15] He proposed that for the coming years he pay Antonia £200 and an extra £100 support for Lyndall; Silas paid £60 towards Susan's maintenance; and Eric still gave Antonia an allowance, which had partially supported her analysis but could now go into the general pot. Tom estimated that as a minimum Antonia would have £450 a year (about £18,000 in current spending power), and felt that was a safe enough financial base for her, supplemented by whatever else she managed to earn. She felt cheated that he expected her to assume the insurance premiums that he had taken out for the girls. He pointed out that the children were costing her nothing while they continued to live with his parents, rent and board free.

The debate rumbled on, resentful on her side and conciliatory on his. Christmas was the next problem; both wanted to see Susan and Lyndall. Antonia probably had not seen them since the beginning of the summer holidays, as she found it difficult to visit the Hopkinsons after all the ill-disguised bad feeling between them. The McCleans were unable to house any more visitors, but Cecil and Margot King invited Antonia and her daughters to stay at Culham Court.

Then, on 17 December, Antonia's mother unexpectedly died at Binesfield. She was sixty-eight: Antonia was forty. She felt more natural grief, she said, at her mother's death than she had when her father had died ten years before. While she was alive her mother's vagueness, her lack of rigour and propensity to fantasy exasperated her daughter, but as Christine voyaged into old age with courage and generosity of spirit, Antonia began to appreciate the softer qualities for which, in her own youth, she had despised her. She was reminded again of her vanity and sense of humour, even beyond the grave. Christine had sought to prolong her fantasy of youth by pretending her middle-aged daughter was her step-daughter. Christine's priest met Antonia again while she was clearing up her mother's belongings at Binesfield; 'He said "I was so touched at the way you behaved at your *step*-mother's funeral." '[16] Rather too late for their relationship, Antonia recalled her mother's contribution to her own character and life. She thought that her ability to write had come from her: 'her imaginative, intuitive side, her interest in people – quite different from my father's', and that her mother's childlike simplicity about things would have served her better, she thought, than the intense, self-critical, demanding side which she shared with her father.[17] Antonia wrote of her:

> At the end of her life, when her religion became important to her, she never became intolerant towards my extraordinary goings on but always sympathetic and affectionate ... [she had a] real sweetness of disposition, an extraordinary capacity for forgiveness, a kind of independence in judging and, in the last months of her life, a really amazing courage and unselfishness. She made absolutely no demands on me, showed no self-pity but was quiet, humorous, patient and quite unafraid.[18]

With her mother's death, Antonia inherited – with certain strings attached – Binesfield, the magical cottage of her youth. Its air of ancient mystery and secret pleasures was inevitably diminished as she grew older, but her father's modernising and improvisations after his retirement were interpreted by Antonia as a kind of sacrilege; the suburbanisation of something wild and lovely, outside time and beyond convenience. However, now that it was her responsibility she wished herself to repair and redecorate it to make it more habitable. After the Christmas holidays, spent largely with her children at Margot and Cecil King's house, Antonia stayed that spring at Binesfield. By March 1940, the second draft of the play was finished and so was all the renovation work at the cottage. But rather than stay on there, when the Easter holidays came she took the children to a local farm as paying guests. Susan and Lyndall then went back to their grandparents and Antonia returned to lodging with the McCleans at Rabley Willow. She told Emily that she hoped to be able to move with her daughters into Binesfield in the autumn, but was anxious about the increasing dangers of air raids and invasion for those living in the south of England.

The thought of being together once more as a family in a house of their own may have been prompted by the news that Susan was exhibiting worrying signs of insecurity again by petty stealing. She had been caught spending a schoolfellow's money on sweets in the local village shop. Ever loyal to her sister, she had shared the swag with Lyndall. The two little girls were confronted with the deed and Susan confessed. Tom and Antonia were informed by the long-suffering Archdeacon Hopkinson and his wife, and Antonia asked Dr Carroll and Miss Searle's advice. (Miss Searle had subsequently given up being a psychoanalyst having found God, or so Silas told Djuna.) The experts' consensus of opinion was that the girls should return south to their parents, if the bombing permitted. Carroll thought they would benefit by being separated for a while. Lyndall was to go to Tom and Gerti, who were living in Summer Cottage, not far from Wyn Henderson's cottage in the Chiltern hills near Henley. Susan, he thought, should be housed with Antonia.

Antonia was still not about to set up home herself. At the beginning of May she had finally relinquished her flat in Cornwall Gardens, much as she had liked it. She packed up her furniture and prepared for an uncertain future, an uncertainty shared by everyone in some degree as Europe's own future become unremittingly dark during the desperate summer of 1940. In May Belgium and Holland were invaded; Queen Wilhelmina called on all the Dutch people to fight to the last. The heroic evacuation of more than 300,000 allied troops from the beaches of Dunkirk gripped the hearts and imagination of all those back home in the first week of June. The shock of the fall of Paris only ten days later made for a summer of grim foreboding. Britain was next in line, and the blitz bombing of London began in September. Antonia's state of mind was unusually calm, philosophical and outward looking; 'Italy came into the war last night. The Germans are 30 miles from Paris. . . . In a few weeks perhaps everything one has been accustomed to . . . care for may have been destroyed and one will be a prisoner in an invaded country waiting to be destroyed oneself.'[19] Her diary entry then described with curiosity and wonder the pellucid beauty of the natural world as she discovered it on an early morning walk.

By the beginning of June, Antonia had decided to leave Rabley Willow, as Kathleen Hale put it, 'to live with a more amusing group of people.'[20] These more amusing people were John Davenport and his wife Clement. He had been one of Cecil Botting's prize pupils and was now a distinguished critic and writer. A physically substantial and jovial man, he had a troubled marriage to the beautiful androgynous Clement, who was a painter. They lived in the elegant eighteenth-century Malting house on the High Street of Marshfield, a large Gloucestershire village between Chippenham and Bath.

In this house, one hundred miles from London, they held open house for artists during this difficult year. The composer Lennox Berkeley was already in residence, as was the musician and critic William Glock, with whom Clement was having an affair. Dylan and Caitlin Thomas and their baby Llewellyn were to join them, along with Antonia and her daughters. It was an easy cultured atmosphere, although the guests individually were far from easy. Music, ideas and alcohol were a unifying factor; 'The summer talked itself away' Dylan Thomas recalled.[21] Antonia entered into life at the Malting house with enthusiasm. 'To be able to talk freely, read, hear music . . . I had forgotten what it was like. I feel like one of the shades in Homer who had just had a good draught of blood.'[22] There was an atmosphere of creative mayhem, with Caitlin and Dylan Thomas drinking deeply and involved already in their bruising fights and noisy makings-up. But work too was in progress. There were two grand pianos at which Davenport and Glock would often play, and Thomas and Davenport were involved in writing a satiric novel called *The Death of the King's Canary* centred on a bohemian house party, much like the one currently running, with parodies of Augustus John, William Empson and Stephen Spender amongst the house guests. This interlude provided Antonia for a while with a sense of being part of an artistic and creative establishment, which helped to strengthen her faltering self-esteem and shadowy identity. But communal living was not easy for even the most placid and equable of temperaments. She was to consider it: 'four of the oddest months of my life . . . when I tell you I clung to them [Dylan and Caitlin] as rocks of sanity you will get an idea of what it was like!'[23] Antonia became aware that this could not be more than a short-term solution to her accommodation problems.

To begin with, her own daughters were part of the party. They muddled along with the motley group of adults and benignly neglected children, and went to the local rough school. Susan continued to play the elder sister role to the hilt, alternately organising and ignoring Lyndall but racing belligerently to her aid whenever anyone threatened to mistreat her. However, for some reason it was thought necessary for Antonia's children to be lodged elsewhere, and the Hicks sisters, who did most of the manual work around the house, suggested their father's farm, a mile distant, as a possible destination. Susan and Lyndall, who had just turned eleven and nine years old respectively, were put into the daily care of a farmer whose own mental state, as a result of shell shock from the previous war, meant he was subject to bouts of terrible ill-temper. It was a harsh but memorable few months, which encouraged their independence and physical resilience, and bonded the sisters even closer in the necessity to survive, where each was the only constant and secure presence in the other's uncertain life. Antonia once again appeared extraordinarily detached and unconcerned about the physical, emotional and intellectual well-being of both Susan and Lyndall. She treated her still pre-teenage daughters with the absence of parental guidance and responsibility usually accorded to university students as they approach adulthood.

Suddenly, Lyndall and Susan were in for another radical change. In the middle of October, Antonia was due to start a new job at the BBC working on their Canadian and American programmes. She had to settle the children and find somewhere to live herself. Susan was hurriedly inserted, mid-term, into boarding school life at the Godolphin School in Salisbury, a stolid, middle of the road Anglican establishment not ideally suited to a gifted, insecure and eccentric girl of eleven. Lyndall was sent off to Tom and Gerti at Turville Heath near Henley, rather a long distance from her sister. As she pointed out: 'after nine years of constant companionship with its squabbles and its moments of being very much united, Sue and I were separated and set off towards our different destinies.'[24] In passing responsibility for Lyndall back to Tom again, Antonia seemed to detach herself further from her second daughter, seeing her as an extension of Tom, and not needing much thought or consideration from her. She continued to prefer her elder daughter, endowing her with all the best qualities of herself, and more dangerously, the unfulfilled promise of her own youth. She now wrote to Emily, 'I miss [Susan] terribly. Lyndall is so much Tom's child that may be she'll want to live with him permanently but Susan is definitely mine & now that she is eleven, she is wonderful.'[25] Intellectually, what she said about her joy in her daughter's character and talents was true, but Antonia was not able to express this on an emotional level. Her children were seldom uppermost in her thoughts, and she could not empathise with their points of view and the suffering in their own lives. Neither daughter was ever to feel that she was loved, although when each was well into adulthood and Antonia herself had gained in insight and lost the worst of her sting, they could begin to understand intellectually that they did matter to her, that she was grateful for their loyalty and care, that she loved them in her own way, and was sorry.

Throughout Susan's time at school in Salisbury, Antonia visited her at half term and for the occasional Sunday exeat, making the long and uncomfortable journey in trains re-routed and lacking exact schedules due to the war. Susan admitted that she began to like her mother more at this time; Antonia was in a good mood on her visits and, although she may have looked comical in some of her fashionable outfits (turbans and capes were rather chic one year, but needed perhaps a taller, more elongated frame), Antonia managed to do the right things by her exacting daughter. She took her and a friend or two out for cream cakes and tea and then on to Beach's, the best second-hand bookshop in town. On good form, Antonia would make a most interesting companion, and Susan was at an age when she could begin to appreciate some of the merits in having an intellectual, professional mother with a talent for talk. Isabel Quigly, one of her friends, remembered the special thrill of Antonia's sophisticated and witty conversation, which marked her out from the more homely mothers.

Lyndall remained more remote. Now that her second daughter was ostensibly Tom's responsibility, Antonia did not feel it was necessary to be quite as conscientious as she was with Susan. Lyndall was lonely, living largely on her own with Gerti, as Tom worked up in town and only really returned home at weekends. She found it hard to be fully at ease with her step-mother, a young half-Jewish woman living in exile, having lost almost everything to the Nazis, and now a new wife responsible for an emotionally insecure young step-daughter, before she had even had children of her own. On the surface, however, it seemed to Susan, stuck away in a stuffy boarding school, that Lyndall was in a much more privileged position, with her own father, her own room and eventually a donkey of her own to groom and ride. But in effect Antonia had managed to do what she had expressed a wish to do more than three years earlier, when she was facing living on her own without a man in the picture; she had split the children up and taken responsibility only for her older and favourite daughter. She had written then, 'I wish I could have Susan and not Lyndall. I suppose it would be cruel to separate them?'[26]

At the end of September, the Germans had begun their blitz on London. Every night for three weeks the city was pounded with heavy bombing. Buckingham Palace was hit; some houses in Selwood Place, Eric's road, were also destroyed. The fires burned continuously and could be seen in the country for hundreds of miles around. In the skies of the southern counties of England the RAF had engaged the *Luftwaffe* in aerial dogfights: over everyone hung the imminent possibility of invasion and death. While many people were evacuated from London, even leaving the country for America, Antonia returned to the heart of the city, taking 'two nice white rooms' in the flat of one of her ex-lovers, Ian Black, in Linden Gardens, off Notting Hill Gate. Ian Black was now an expert on French economics, and a sensitive and introspective man. Like Antonia he had been married three times and had a fragile mental state which could slip rapidly into blackness and despair. They shared an Irish charwoman and only really met for meals. Antonia worked long and exhausting hours at Broadcasting House in the heart of the West End, learning the job as she went; 'It is more like the croquet game in Alice than anything I've ever struck & by the time I've got my flamingo tucked under my arm the hedgehog has unrolled and sauntered away.'[27]

Part of her brief at the BBC was to superintend parents sending messages to their children evacuated to Canada and America. Antonia was surprised at how moving it was to be confronted with such natural maternal passion. The first time she had to record a mother's messages to her child she burst into tears herself. On another occasion, rather than interrupt the woman's grief, she had continued to record a mother whose own tears started to flow in the middle of her message. Antonia then related to Emily just how admirable was this woman: carrying her baby in her arms, having just been bombed out of her home, she then insisted on re-recording a much cheerier message for her distant children.

Being in the thick of activity and danger was extraordinarily good for Antonia's state of mind. She had led a quiet and 'spectatorish' life in the country but on her return to a job and London she was engaged again in necessary action; 'the slight danger which certainly whets one's appetite for life made me begin to feel alive again.'[28] Suddenly she was looking outwards, appreciating the lives and unheralded courage of ordinary people. 'You can believe everything you read in the papers about how marvellous the people in the East End are,' she wrote to Emily. 'They are beyond all praise. . . . It is tragic to see them in the tubes every night, lining the platforms & sleeping on the stone stairs & it is obviously bad for the children, but they are extraordinarily gay and cheerful.'[29]

Emily was growing irritated with this new, un-neurotic, no longer circuitously introspective aspect to her old friend. She had sent Antonia one of her characteristic torrential fifty-page letters – and then had got very cross with Antonia for not receiving it. To Antonia's amusement, after the war it was discovered that the famous letter had gone down in a ship which had been torpedoed. Although it was beyond Emily to understand the everyday effects of this cataclysm that had overtaken Europe, Antonia persevered in trying to get her to share some of the momentous experiences that Londoners were going through. In a rare period of solidarity with the masses, she felt released from her own alienated and defensive self: for such a cerebral and fundamentally solitary individual, there was an exhilaration in being able to share a common humanity and make an emotional connection with people quite unlike herself. For Antonia, whose grief had been that her intimates were strangers to her, it was peculiarly moving to be able to make strangers fleetingly intimate: 'The war has even relaxed our great National Reserve. Everyone talks to everyone & no one even attempts to read in a railway carriage any more. You probably find yourself nursing a soldier's baby or sharing your sandwiches with a bombed-out family & everyone swaps bomb stories, cigarettes & opinions.'[30]

The two Henderson brothers, Nigel and Ian, were also transformed by the war. Nigel had immediately given up drinking once war was declared in order to be fit enough for the air force and Ian lost his wooliness and laziness with this new purpose in his life. Both qualified for commissions, Nigel in the RAF and Ian in the Gunners. The enormity of this external threat made personal irritations and incompatibilities shrink to flea-like proportions. Antonia saw Ian when she could, and they seemed to have moved on to a more mature footing. Ease and tolerance had replaced the edgy quadrille of demand and retreat.

Eric too, who was on highly secret Foreign Office business in Leighton Buzzard, saw her whenever he could, and in his letters dropped his cool, ironic style for a much more expressive affection, sending 'oceans of love' to his dear Poppet, his pussy-cat.[31] By then he was drinking full-time, starting the day at eleven o'clock with his first double whisky. He admitted he was an addict, but as yet there appeared to be no ill effects. Some time during this first year of the war, he proposed to Antonia again and, although she was always tempted by the comfort of the relationship he offered, she still had hopes at forty that she might yet manage to make an orthodox connubial relationship with a man. She turned him down, and lived to regret it.

For the first time Antonia, living unencumbered by children or men, working long hard hours at a job that was not particularly congenial to her temperament or talents, camping in someone else's flat, without a home, felt right in the heart of London. It was that great city's most desperate and yet heroic time and she seemed part of some fated momentum, a grand destiny: for once there was no individual choice, no moral dilemma, neither nostalgia nor regrets. The relief from her obsessional introspection and compulsive sense of inadequacy and failure released her into a landscape of clear vistas and calm philosophical certainty. She tried to explain how straightforward fear of physical injury and death freed her from the torture of the self:

> In the anxious hand-to-mouth life one leads at the moment, surprised & pleased every morning to wake up alive . . . one thinks without words. I find it harder than ever to be articulate, though some of one's faculites are sharpened by feeling death in the air every night. One will probably die without ever having *understood* anything and yet everything seems extraordinarily beautiful & inevitable. There is no time to speculate and yet one always has to be prepared. It is an impossible feeling to describe. You know how one feels just before they clap on the chlorophorm mask . . . that it is too late & yet it does not matter.[32]

Antonia herself was to come close to death. It was during a very bad air raid on the night of 16 April, 1941 when Piccadilly and Waterloo station were badly hit, Leicester Square station was demolished and Marylebone Goods Yard burnt out. The whole city appeared to be on fire again. She had been staying the night at Eric's and from 9.50 at night to 4.30 in the morning there was continual bombardment. A big bomb which brought down half the houses in Chelsea Square, only two hundred yards away, blew in the windows where Antonia had just got out of bed. The blast also tore a huge hole out of the wall above her bed. By bending down to find her slippers at the crucial time, she missed getting this blast full in the upper torso and head. She found Eric collapsed, but unhurt, in the corridor outside and they both sought shelter under the stairs, listening to the cacophony of bombs and sirens all around. 'However about half past four I cleared the debris off my bed and got into it again and SLEPT!'[33] In these early and most dangerous months of the war, Antonia had found at last the qualities in herself which she had so revered and longed for as a child; the simple courage and nobility of the soldier, the ability to get on uncomplainingly and ignore plain physical fear: to do what had to be done.

18

The Prodigal Uncertainly Returns

Oh! dream of joy! is this indeed
The light-house top I see?
Is this the hill? is this the kirk?
Is this mine own countree?

'The Rime of the Ancient Mariner' Samuel Taylor Coleridge

Antonia's return to the Catholic Church just before Christmas 1940 was sudden, unspectacular and profoundly ambivalent. It was not, however, unexpected. She had lapsed from belief as well as from practice in 1926 and for nearly fifteen years she existed outside the Church, yet remained obsessively connected to it in her own mind through a continuing dialogue of attraction and revolt. Extreme in everything, she would be drawn into a Catholic church on a wave of religious feeling, but this could as readily turn to loathing and recoil. She found much of contemporary Catholic writing and teaching both puerile and repellent but realised that it was not the Church so much as the apologists who roused her intellectual and moral distaste. At her most calm and equanimous she welcomed Catholicism as a richly poetical interpretation of the human and spiritual condition, a system of thought with its own pleasing internal logic but no necessarily divine authority. But she was never free of it: 'I still found myself furiously defending it to non-Catholics while with Catholics I furiously attacked it. . . . Sometimes I felt immense relief at having escaped from it all; sometimes I felt the whole core had gone out of my life.'[1]

In that spiritual lacuna, Antonia read constantly, searching for some kind of moral framework. She felt that one of her main defects was lack of the power to love, which sprang from her fear of exposure and vulnerability: within a strict moral framework she hoped she might learn the motions of love which would then lead her to love itself; 'I need so much to love so as to be able to use my aggressiveness creatively instead of destructively.'[2] In her search, Antonia wrote in her notebook telling and inspirational phrases culled from wide philosophical sources; Spinoza, Nietzsche, Lao Tze, Rilke, Blake, Buddhist teachings and Keats's letters. She considered fleetingly Quakerism, Communism and Bertrand Russell's Neutral Monism, his attempt to resolve the polarity of mind and matter. Struggle as she might to construct her own version of the truth, nothing supplied enough of the whole picture for Antonia to accept another religious or philosophical system. 'What a strange fish a "lapsed" Catholic is', she wrote to Emily, who became a Catholic herself at the end of 1942. 'The Catholic training persists & stamps one in spite of everything; one revolts & yet can be at home nowhere else – one really *is* a kind of monster.'[3] She was to feel all her life that Catholicism had tamed her and put its brand on her spirit; it was inescapable, ineradicable, it tugged her back time and again, and yet something in her could never fully submit.

Antonia felt that her analysis with Dr Carroll had released her from much of the burden of fear from her faith and from her father and this made it possible for her to contemplate a return to the Church. About a year after her analysis had finished, in the summer of 1939, she had the impulse to become a practising Catholic again and with some trepidation had sought out a priest, who happened to be an Oratorian and of an unsympathetic cast of mind. He told her harshly that her marriage to Tom in a Protestant church had automatically excommunicated her. Antonia had known that from a technical point of view her marriage was invalid, as far as the Catholic Church was concerned, that she had been living in sin, but to be told baldly that she was excommunicated and to be treated with neither understanding nor concern came as a shock. She found it 'almost insulting' to be asked if she expected to get an emotional kick out of religion, and for the priest to have recommended she read a fifth rate 'apologist' work with neither intellectual nor spiritual content.[4] He told Antonia that she could only be reconciled with her Church after a complex procedure involving the authorities at Westminster: she would have to sign a document accepting all the articles of faith and renouncing her errors. She left his presence humiliated and rejected, even more certain she would never return to Catholicism: it was obviously as rigid and life-denying as she had always feared.

But then a year later, having endured some of the worst bombing in London, Antonia slipped into the Carmelite church in Kensington Church Street where she had worshipped as a child. She had wanted to enquire about the time of the Midnight Mass on Christmas Eve which, because of the air raids and blackout conditions, was no longer held at midnight. She wished to attend it 'for purely sentimental reasons'; Christmas was a time which always carried enormous emotional significance for her, and hearing the first *Adeste fidelis* was an essential heralding of Christmas Day.[5] Antonia saw the queue for confession with no conscious intent at all to join it, yet, as she told Emily, something impelled her to. It felt almost as if she was being pushed by an invisible hand in her back. When her turn came she was quite unprepared, having spent most of the waiting time telling herself she would not stay. Suddenly she was in the confessional: her first words to the priest were 'I've no right to be here.'[6] This man was a simple Carmelite priest from a rural Irish community, whose own faith, Antonia came to recognise, worked through the heart. He obviously thought she had every right to be there, and in fact welcomed her as his own salvation from doubt. Father Hugh told Antonia later that he was weary and disheartened himself, and had been praying for a sign from God, hoping that perhaps through his offices a sinner might return. Antonia was that sinner, she was that sign, and the faltering priest could claim her as his 'Christmas present'.[7] Antonia blurted out her history, and to her surprise was told that because, due to the war, everyone was considered to be in danger of death, the conditions for reinstatement were not so stringent. Saying he would check this with the Vicar-General, the priest saw Antonia the following day, heard her confession and gave her absolution. He gave her permission to take communion on Christmas Day.

And so with little trumpeting or trauma Antonia slipped back into the Church – and almost immediately the debate was resurrected in her own mind between her faith and her reason. She did not deny the comfort in feeling that she had come home at last. And it was gratifying too to be of some spiritual help to someone else while seeking help herself; 'He is so frank and so human – and so humble', she wrote of Fr Hugh. 'He said: "I feel ten years younger since you came to me that day. I was beginning to feel tired and no longer friends with God and then that happened to me to show that there is a real point in being a priest".'[8] He had also admitted to her that he had never before come across anyone who suffered from such a complexity of religious doubt. However, that highly critical, intellectually scrupulous mind could not just accept and let things be. Antonia lacked hypocrisy and a desire for the quiet life. She was not confident in her faith, like many a cradle Catholic, nor was she pragmatic enough to take what she liked from Catholic dogma and ignore the rest: her extremeness of character, her love of truth, her black and white approach to everything meant that she had to accept the whole. Yet there were areas, such as the Church's attitude to sex and the power it vested in the Devil, from which she emotionally and intellectually recoiled. 'I still cannot conquer my strong repugnance to certain things in Catholicism. . . . I always have the feeling of being trapped and not released and I long to get into the fresh air again, however strong and uncomfortable it is and however secure and peaceful the Church seems.'[9]

Tom, who knew well the particular tortures of Antonia's mind, wrote with some perspicacity in his diary a year after Antonia's reconversion:

> The problem of Tony's [life] is the reconcilement of her reason & the readings of the Roman Catholic Church, so that her whole life seems & will always seem a slow-motion wrestling match between the Church & her, with each side many times gaining the upper hand but no side − by definition − ever winning − is the blending of opposites which will never mix.[10]

It was not easy to be both an intellectual and an English Catholic in the thirties and forties. Communism seemed to be a more natural spiritual home for thinkers and artists, while Catholicism appeared to smack of all things backward and degenerate, superstitious and against reason. The Catholic Church did not emerge well from the two world wars; too careful to protect its own interests, it had made pacts with the Fascists in Italy and with Nazi Germany and, although both popes Pius XI and XII had spoken out about the excesses of the Nazi regime, they did little to restrain it. In fact the papacy spoke out more often during the Spanish Civil War against the dangers of Communism. There was a tension between those within the Church who were sympathetic to the 'Modernist' movement, which advocated an evolutionary approach which respected historical and scientific developments, accepted a social responsibility and allowed a space for personal conscience, and the traditionalists who liked to exist within an immutable framework of hierarchy, proscription and papal infallibility. Modernism had been declared heretical in Pius X's 1907 encyclical, but this had not stifled liberal thinking and dissent, such as that of the excommunicated intellectual Father George Tyrrell. Intellectually Antonia belonged with this wing of the Church; 'Tyrrell is the only one who talks my language & they excommunicated him. . . . I understand Tyrrell so well when he felt the Church like a great octopus sitting on his chest.'[11] Emotionally, however, she seemed to need to believe in the authoritarian, fundamentalist Church, whose standards she could never attain and whose damnation she felt certain to merit.

This was the eternal dichotomy in her approach to Catholicism to which Tom referred, the conflict which could never be resolved. How much easier it would have been for her mental state and her daily happiness if, like many Catholics before and after her, she could have chosen either to accept or discard the tenets of her faith on the basis of personal condition and conscience. But it was not just her scrupulousness and honesty which made her so uncompromising; 'I have always respected the hard core in Catholicism. . . . In every art & every person I have ever cared for there has been this streak of harshness.'[12] It was as if she needed psychically to have a formidable rock of authority and executor of punishment against which she would fling herself repeatedly, only to bloody and bruise herself while the rock remained unmoved. 'I would rather worship a God who was indifferent to me and destroyed me (since my destruction is a manifestation of his law and power) than one who kept a petty personal account of my sins and virtues . . . and "suffered" if I did not love him.'[13]

Antonia had also feared her father more than she had loved him: only in her reconversion to her faith was she able to begin to understand her own father's anguish over her, and to feel for the first time the stirrings of an unclouded love for him. Her sense that rejoining the Church had released him from Purgatory shows how clearly Antonia saw her own frightening power; that her activities in life were responsible for the damning or redeeming of her father in death.[14] What supernatural power, what crushing responsibility, what exorbitant guilt. Although it can be explained as a manifestation of the inflated manic state of her disease, psychologically it revealed the apocalyptic way that Antonia had seen her father, and her relationship to him, ever since she was a tiny child.

Antonia's return to her Father Church was not an unalloyed homecoming. She was defensive about it in the company of her non-Catholic friends. To Cyril Connolly, who at that time was visceral in his dislike of Catholicism, she wrote a defensive explanation; 'though superficially civilised, I am a barbarian and a lunatic, I am naturally attuned to mysteries, hieroglyphs, symbols and what you call "beautiful muzziness". I am also a prig, but . . . one can be a prig anywhere.'[15] She was defensive also in her approach to telling Tom, who had seen her through so many crises, and was naturally concerned that the children should not be coerced in any way into following their mother into her faith, or unsettled themselves by Antonia's own restiveness. She felt that she ought to try and convince him, through a change in her own nature, that something fundamental had happened, that her reconversion was not merely 'a defence against the beast'. Tom had seen her at her most desperate and demonic, had stopped her killing herself in front of his eyes, had endured her tearing in to him full of spite and accusation, and then quietly despairing in his arms, begging him to kill her. Antonia determined she would become in contrast, 'calm, gentle and considerate . . . a change of nature as well as of conviction.'[16] That way he would believe her reconversion, and respect it.

Neither Antonia nor Tom had imposed any religion on Susan and Lyndall, and neither had been baptised into the Church of England or the Catholic Church. In a letter to Tom, Antonia confided her hopes for her children in this central matter of their spiritual being, and once more showed her fixed idea of how much Susan was like herself and how unalike, and therefore less considerable, was Lyndall. 'Lyndall, I feel, would be much the same sort of person, humanly speaking, whether she is a Catholic or anything else. But simply for happiness & proper functioning I think Susan is likely to be more successful in a religion with definite rules & a rich field for speculation & imagination. Only she must approach it by attraction & love & not by fear & coercion.'[17]

Antonia was even nervous of telling Eric, her intellectual mentor and the man who had introduced her to the philosophy of Santayana. She was afraid he would think it just a weak and lazy capitulation. But when she told him on New Year's Day he accepted the news with an unjudgmental serenity which gave her confidence in her decision. He offered a kind of paternal benediction: 'I'm not surprised and I think it a very good thing', he said, 'I've always thought that when you'd got free of all the terrifying associations it had for you, you'd be able to practise your religion again.'[18] He added that the very fact that she had been able to return was, to his mind, a proof that she was cured. For this he earned her heartfelt gratitude; 'if ever there was a Greek born out of his time and background, it is Eric.'[19] Ian Black welcomed her return to the Church, rather proud that it had happened under his roof, and he assured her that he had noticed a remarkable external change in her. This was something which Antonia found hard to believe, not least because Ian himself seemed to alternate between 'extreme depression and a kind of delirium.'[20] On the contrary Phyllis Jones, her stalwart friend, was shocked and upset. When Antonia told her over lunch that she had become a Catholic again, her whole face and manner changed: 'She said oddly, "But you of all people, Tony – *an intellectual*".'[21] Antonia thought Phyllis saw it as an escape, but also a betrayal of honesty and the search for truth. More personally, it interrupted their friendship: they were not to see each other for five years.

Antonia found it galling to her pride and threatening to her fugitive sense of self that by becoming a Catholic she seemed to be leaving 'nearly all the intelligent, the witty, the tolerant' on the other side of a wall to join a superficially much less attractive gang. 'It isn't hard, of course, to feel an "even-Christian" with whores and homosexuals, with the poor, the dirty, the ignorant and the stupid. But it is far harder to feel the same bond with the spiritual fascists, the sour old *dévotés*, the cocksure apologists, the hearty tankard-thumping Bellocians, the pilers-up of indulgences, the prurient defenders of "holy purity", the complacent and the snobbish.'[22] This blurring of identity and loss of solidarity with her friends was to worry Antonia considerably. To have a religion at all, amongst the circle of writers and artists she knew, was to be eccentric; she felt it created an abyss between herself and others. She could talk to David Gascoyne a little but his mental state was fragmenting rapidly, until in 1944 he was hearing persecuting voices and could not finish sentences without breaking off to listen to the clamour in his head. Other friends and acquaintances, she felt, looked at her with suspicion and contempt, and offered various hackneyed reasons for her reconversion: 'emotionally satisfying & comforting & "compensates" for having no sex-life, in making a mess of your life generally . . . too lazy to think or have a superstitious regard for authority. And of course, in my case, obviously I'm a Catholic because "they got hold" of me when I was a child & I've now reverted to childhood under the strain of the war!!'[23] The others, as Antonia continued in her protest to Emily, told her with a condescending sweetness what an excellent psychological adjustment she had made and how being within the Church was much the best place for a poor neurotic to be. Most galling of all for Antonia was the admission to herself that all these reasons were partially true.

Just over a month before her fateful appearance before Fr Hugh, Antonia had begun an intense correspondence with a man who had written to her out of the blue, enquiring about the spiritual whereabouts and well-being of Nanda, the heroine of *Frost in May*. His name was Joseph Thorp, although he liked to be known by his middle name of Peter. He was sixty-eight, almost the same age her father would have been had he lived. He had been born a Catholic and so devout was he as a young man that he had trained for ten years as a priest. He was judged to exhibit no true vocation and so spent the next thirty years out of the Church but, although he returned to his faith aged sixty-three, he remained troubled by much about the current teaching and practice of Catholicism. His letter prompted a lengthy reply from Antonia. Despite her long hours of work at the BBC (she sometimes did not get home until four in the morning) she realised that his interest in her spiritual development released a spring of religious debate and energy which she had been suppressing, for want of a congenial partner with whom to have a serious conversation about this central preoccupation of her life. She launched into a full account of her religious struggles and beliefs which, during a period of just over a year's correspondence with the receptive Peter, ran to over 80,000 words on her side alone.

Antonia was also lonely on a human level, and it was inevitable, perhaps, that this correspondence should turn into an epistolatory flirtation, then a love affair. As she herself explained it, 'I am selfish, impulsive and very ready to be caught up in a dream.'[24] It is a fascinating document of the ebb and flow of her faith, the endless workings of a mind worrying itself to a standstill over the conflict between belief and reason. Parallel to the intellectual and spiritual dialectic ran the story of the rapid inflation and violent demise of her romantic desire. In barely more than a month from that first formal letter, Antonia was writing to 'Dear, dearer, dearest Peter', and moving on to 'We have decided not to be "lovers" in the modern sense. But where does "love-making" begin and end? I can't help thinking of you as a man as well as a character and a spirit. . . . We know we are physically attracted to each other without ever having met.'[25] Peter was even keener on the personal, amorous nature of their relationship, on 'love in dreams'. However, when the unseen lovers finally did meet, the meshing of dream with reality was painfully inexact and both quickly came to their senses and retreated fast.

By then 'darling Peter' had become 'the poor old boy [who] half the time hadn't the least idea what I was talking about', as she reported briskly to Emily.[26] He was, nevertheless, the spur to Antonia's committing to paper her acute and interesting analysis of her shifting stance to her Church and the tides of her intellectual and spiritual responses. When the complete dialogue was eventually published in 1965 as *The Hound and the Falcon*, the Irish novelist Kate O'Brien, a lapsed Catholic herself, congratulated Antonia on the book: 'You sail out of that correspondence with all flags flying, tremendously justified under heads of intelligence, vision, modesty, tolerance and human warmth.' She then added what many of her other readers of the book must have felt, 'so you must forgive me if I say that your unheard correspondent *does not*.'[27] Antonia saw Peter Thorp and herself as the companion creatures of the 'heavenly huntsman'; he was the hound and she the falcon.[28] This book tracked her erratic and passionate flight, and the incidental landscape of work, the blitz, her children, over which she swooped.

Peter Thorp's first letter had started Antonia thinking, and she had dashed off a letter in reply, giving hints of her own troubled life and her continuing struggles with faith. He initially must have presumed too much, for quite quickly Antonia's tone became sharp and defensive; she did not care to be patronised or seen as a subject for conversion: 'don't try to "convert" me. Remember that, for many years, people of all kinds have been trying to do that. I suffered much from my father's coercion and also from the fact that I had to disappoint him bitterly by going my own way instead of his.' Antonia then unleashed her talons and gave him a forceful sideswipe; 'I find no difficulty in believing in God but I prefer Spinoza's conception of God to the Catholic conception of God and I find Spinoza's life considerably more edifying than most of the lives of the saints. Frankly, I detest most of the saints. I hate their morbid preoccupation with sin and guilt, I hate their smug intimacy with what they call God, and I hate their anxious, niggling concern with their own salvation.'[29] With that she gave notice that she was not a small confused parakeet but a raptor with a steel beak and a mind to match, a good deal more substantial and dangerous than he had supposed. In her next letter she was slightly more conciliatory, but still uncompromising about any kind of coercion; '[it] makes me feel like an animal in a trap and I'll bite my own paws off to get out.'[30]

Prior to her sudden reconversion, Antonia had maintained to Thorp the Santayanan position that Catholicism was poetically and psychologically true, that like any other great religion it was a fine and rich method for exploring the realm of the spirit, but that she found it hard to believe in its literal truth. Countering this rational position was her avowed need for worship, the religious side of her nature which craved a framework in which to practise an ancient and uplifting ritual, if not actually to believe in its transcendence. Then, in her letter to Thorp of 27 December, she broke the news of her return to the Church in a low-key and ambivalent manner, already expressing the concomitant grapeshot of doubts and divisions which would characterise her spiritual condition for the rest of her life. It was not until eight months later that she had a momentary insight into what 'faith' could mean, and recorded it in her diary as a reminder to herself when the inevitable doubts returned. 'All I know is that an eye seemed to open somewhere inside me, an eye very filmed and feeble, seeing nothing definite but yet knowing that there *was* something to see.'[31] She was to elaborate on this rare feeling of certainty in the unsent letter to Cyril Connolly: 'It was as if, with the eyes of the mind wide open, seeing all the loose ends, all the contradictions, all the gaps to be bridged, this inner eye perceived that the surface was not quite opaque and that an infinite perspective opened out beyond it. It was as if a two-dimensional creature realised for a moment the possibility of a third dimension.'[32]

But a more common experience was a continued intellectual

restlessness, a constant worrying over the truth or not of various dogmas, becoming too often distracted from the central substance of her beliefs by the arguments of various Catholic apologists whose style and manner still repelled her. Tyrrell she saw as an 'angel of light', and one of the few modern interpreters with whom she felt any sympathy. Her fear as a young woman that to be a Catholic was at direct odds with the necessities of being an artist, returned to unsettle her. She felt she had to find some way of living a spiritual life which was in accordance with her nature and her life's work to be a writer: 'To deny what I have laboriously found out as a human being, to present experiences only with an eye to their being edifying or at least "safe" seems to me a betrayal of one's function as an artist. And I don't feel strong enough to sacrifice that whole side which would be plucking out my eye.'

Antonia had always had problems with the lives and exemplars of the saints, their rejection, even necessary hatred, of the natural world and their repression of the senses. 'To what other end is deliberate *violation* of the senses as opposed to *restraint* directed? There is something so profoundly antipathetic to me in all this that I cannot help feeling many of these insistences are morbid, even pathological.'[33] And did one have to choose, she wondered, between being a saint and an artist? She was struck by Auden saying that 'a saint is an artist *manqué*', longing as she always had to be an artist but knowing that it was to sainthood that she ought to aspire.[34]

She felt very alone in her attempts to reconcile these disparate parts of her nature; the spiritual being and the creative artist, underlaid all the time with 'the nervous strains set up by the track of the beast in my mind'.[35] There was no one she knew or could turn to who had had to take into account these three particular tensions which strung up her life. By the end of her intense correspondence with Peter Thorp she had dismissed him as a kindly, well-meaning friend who could no longer offer her any real insights into the conundrum of faith. It mattered to him very much to be able to believe that he had been instrumental in her return to the Church. In fact he had been merely the catalyst who had reawakened the lifelong debate in her mind between reason and belief, and her personal need for some system of faith. He had been, too, a focus for her under-used intellectual energies and her lonely longing for love. Antonia had burned like a flame in her breathlessly fluent letters to him, and after nine months had snuffed it out without regret. She looked back with some surprise on the intensity of intellectual energy which she had produced after twelve-hour days or more at the BBC. And so in her solitariness Antonia determined to struggle on, living as if she did have faith, trying to conform to the Catholic map of the spiritual world which she felt was as true, perhaps, as any representation of the numinous could be. And she hoped that this conformity would not inhibit her destiny, as she saw it: to give form in writing to the experiences of her life.

19

War and Work

I've got to the point where I just feel I can't go on with this meaningless
office work much more.
When the war is over I want terribly to try & get 6 months freedom &
somehow finish my wretched book.
It's so hard to start one's life all over again at 45!

4 September 1944, letter to Emily Coleman

Antonia was apart from her children throughout the war. Susan was
still boarding at Godolphin in Salisbury and Lyndall was to become
a boarder at Headington School near Oxford in 1942, when she turned
eleven. She had been living full-time with Tom and Gerti, but had been
increasingly edged out with Gerti's pregnancy and the birth of her first
baby, Nicolette.

Tom had had a shed built at the bottom of the garden for Lyndall to
move into because they needed her room for the coming baby. Lyndall
did not feel particularly disadvantaged by this, although she was jealous
of Gerti, who was herself not very sensitive to the feelings of this needy
and lonely girl. For her part, Susan was beginning to shine academically
at school, but 'animals continued to be my consolation'.[1] Silas was seeing
more of his daughter, a situation which was to improve dramatically
when he remarried in the summer of 1944. Antonia was making the
occasional effortful journey to Salisbury to see Susan for days out from
school, but only visited Lyndall twice in the five years she was at
Headington. But at holiday time, she would try and take both girls off
with her somewhere. For the new year of 1941, the girls stayed in a
boarding house at Binesfield, the cottage having been let, and Antonia
could only get away from the BBC at weekends. There, Susan and
Lyndall had an afternoon's riding as part of their mother's Christmas
present to them. But for Antonia there were no thrills to balance the

physical discomforts of a 'horrid, cold, untidy, waterless, communal "guest house"' run not very well by a Mr and Mrs Perfect. She was so frozen one evening, dressed in a corduroy coat, 'a huge tweed cape' and fleece-lined boots, while she wrote one of her letters to Peter Thorp, that she wished she had 'a fur face' like a cat.[2]

While staying at this guest house, Antonia first took Susan and Lyndall to Mass. She was careful to explain the points and procedures of the service. Susan was serious and attentive; Lyndall less interested, and confused and bored by the endless Latin chanting. Antonia offered to buy both a statuette. Susan went for St Francis who, with his wolf, was the only one with any appeal. Lyndall thought the others were 'vile', and at Antonia's suggestion ended up with a Madonna, which her young daughter thought was 'one of the most revolting sentimental objects I had ever seen' and which she contrived to 'accidentally' break as soon as her mother had returned to London.[3]

Although she still seemed to be blind to their deepest feelings and needs, Antonia began to see that there were some advantages in having children. As the turmoil in her own mind was quieted a little, and as she faced with some equanimity the end of her sexual relationships with men, she valued more the enduring nature of blood ties; men loved and left but her children, for good or ill, remained. In the summer of 1941, she spent her last weeks with Ian who had returned for the summer to a training camp near London. Her struggle with her faith did not seem to inhibit their relationship; she was to recall the following year her 'very intense sexual life with Ian last summer'.[4] While she contemplated his departure for India, and faced the fact that she might never see him again, she was struck by melancholy at the things she no longer had; 'I have lost control of my life. This is on the surface due to money, as well as, of course, to the war. Although officially I have charge of the children, in practice I can do next to nothing about their lives. . . . I want my children back. I want a home. But do I want them back enough to make . . . any effort when the future is so uncertain.'[5]

Officially the BBC allowed Antonia only one and a half days off a week until 1942, but she managed to negotiate two weeks' leave in August 1941. This she spent with Susan and Lyndall in a small hotel in the picturesque fishing village and artists' retreat of St Ives on the rugged North Cornish coast. Lyndall remembered her mother being sweeter and more reasonable than ever before. Antonia, however, wrote to Peter Thorp about how St Ives did not really suit her, and that she was tired all the time. But the holiday was for the children, she reminded herself, and they were having a wonderful time. She was reading philosophical and religious teachings in her attempt to build her house 'on a rock and not on sand'.[6] She felt she must be ready with her intellectual arguments so as to be able to answer her interlocutors and critics, and not be caught out or made to look stupid.

Back in London, Antonia's work was unremitting and largely very tedious. The euphoria of the early part of the war was over; the sense of unity in the face of discomfort, fear and communal effort had faded. Drudgery, petty deprivations and difficulties began to wear the spirit down. And there were still threats of extreme danger and destruction, with sudden air strikes on modest houses and grand landmark buildings alike.

The BBC was first bombed in October 1940, wrecking the news library, the central switchboard and several thousand gramophone records. Six people were killed that night within the building alone. In December another bomb killed fewer people but wreaked an even greater havoc with the help of blast, fire and flood. Antonia was not there when it happened, but came into work the next morning to be confronted by shocking destruction. A colleague of hers on the Canadian unit described it thus: 'The unusual building, designed like a ship, stood with its "upper deck" on fire and its "keel" in pools of turgid water like some vessel at Trafalgar.'[7] Antonia rescued what she could of her papers and scripts from the mess of plaster dust, porridgy slime and broken glass, and shifted her secretary and office temporarily to Ian Black's flat in Linden Gardens. But nothing was allowed to halt the continuous transmission of programmes to the nation, the forces overseas and the listening world beyond. Even the catering staff were indomitable. Flooded out of their basement kitchens and with the electricity off, they managed to cook five hundred breakfasts amongst the wreckage of the building, using just two camping-size primus stoves. The spirit of make-do and mend, of enterprise and improvisation, of keeping the show on the road no matter what, prevailed triumphantly in such moments of crisis, and Antonia, for all her exhaustion and irritation with the tedium of the work, was exhilarated to be part of something bigger and more heroic than herself.

Antonia's office was re-established temporarily at Bedford College in Regent's Park. Her work there consisted of much administrative trivia and the production of various features and talks for the overseas service to North and South America and Australia, involving convoluted train trips to Bristol and Leeds and other provincial cities. 'BBC is a hair-shirt, such an exacting old job full of tiresome details and difficulties, some due to war, some not – you're on edge the whole time.'[8] Illness or the collapse of one piece of the organisation could undermine her hard-fought equilibrium. The range of what she was expected to do also wore her down; she was much better suited to pursuing one thing at a time in depth and to the satisfaction of her perfectionist self; 'I feel a cross between a kitchenmaid at Berchtesgaden [Hitler's Chequers] and a broken-down usher at Dotheboys Hall', she wrote to Peter Thorp.[9]

Having only just survived the bomb blast in the middle of April which rocked Eric's house, she had her office once more wrecked a month later by the destruction of two wings of Bedford College by incendiary and high-explosive bombs. Peter Thorp, who was of a less robust temperament, marvelled at how 'serenely' she wrote to him after suffering every kind of danger and disruption in one of the numerous bombing raids, but Antonia was clear that she preferred the physical danger of the blitz to the internal battles with depression and accidie. Having real practical exigencies absorbed the 'restless drive to action' which she recognised as one of her besetting sins, a compulsion which, combined with her impatience, brought misery. 'You don't give time for the corn to run into the mill and the result is that the wheels go on grinding in a vacuum which is one of the most horrible experiences you can have.'[10]

Despite the work, the discomfort, the lack of time, Antonia did manage to finish at last her short story about the terrible holiday she had taken with Tom in Brittany seven years earlier, which resulted in her attempted suicide. 'The Moment of Truth' was something of which she was proud, but most of all proud of finishing. She was rewarded with a rush of pleasure 'in having been able after all these dry years to have done some work again'.[11] Happening so soon after her reconversion to her old faith, Antonia felt gratitude to God and the hope that this was the beginning of a new fluency in the only work which mattered to her; 'if He'll let me use my faculty for writing again I feel I can bear anything'.[12] 'The Moment of Truth' is a story full of transfixing, menacing detail. It captures perfectly the shadow of madness and the fear of loss. The woman's disintegrating mind is terrifying to herself and her husband: his mixture of love and hatred, of complicity and detachment, are plausible and chilling. These are not warm, likeable human beings, but heartless and pitiable. Antonia's recreation of a sinister grotesque, the concierge Madame Berrichon, was a *pièce de résistance*, as memorable as Mrs Danvers in du Maurier's *Rebecca*. The story was published in the June edition of the literary magazine *Horizon*, which her friend Cyril Connolly had set up the previous year.

After being bombed out this second time, her BBC brief was changed in May 1941 to something more congenial, with more regular hours. Antonia was appointed the Corporation's chief publicist with responsibility for the foreign press. She was to move into a new interim office at the Langham Hotel, a grand Victorian building owned by the BBC, over the road from Broadcasting House – and another prime bombing target – just north of Oxford Circus. She shared her office with four others; two typewriters clattered all day and a colleague dictated his articles at the top of his voice. A chance of concentrated peaceful work there seemed remote.

As part of her new position in publicity, that December Antonia was asked to produce a booklet called 'The BBC at War'. She had three weeks in which to design, research, conduct interviews for and write it, all on 'a sudden whim of the Governors.'[13] This work exhausted her. To get it done within the deadline she worked constantly, without even a Sunday off. Her researches confirmed her jaundiced view of the 'deadheads', as she called them, at the top of the Corporation, who stifled the dedicated and enterprising people who worked away in the studios and engineering departments, producing and transmitting the programmes, and the thousands of other support staff who helped keep the voice of the nation heard throughout the worst hardships and dangers of the war.

At the end of June, Antonia visited the BBC studios at Bangor, first spending a long weekend with Peter Thorp and his long-suffering wife, Sylvia. It was their first meeting after nine months of intimate letter writing, and was not a success. Peter's extreme nervousness made him alternately overexcited, plying Antonia with questions and following her about, anxious to satisfy her every need, and paralysed with disappointment and apprehension. Antonia was increasingly irritated by his obtuse attentiveness, and 'often snappish.'[14] She much preferred his wife, although she was over-tired and ill. Antonia was to write that she felt fonder of Peter Thorp having seen him at last, but the visit seems to have had a traumatic effect on him. 'My coming to see you appears to have no pleasant results at all for you', Antonia wrote in answer to his unhappy letter. 'You find it an "ordeal"; you are miserable for twenty-four hours, and your belief in the devil is confirmed!'[15]

It says a great deal for her freedom from the blight of needing to be liked that this did not upset her more. Antonia made no attempt to mollify his hurt feelings or justify her own character and behaviour; 'over and over again I've warned you that I'm tough, harsh and impatient and it shouldn't be such a shock to find that I've told the truth', she scolded.[16] She then set into telling him what a pity he had had only a Catholic education for 'in these days it is rather thin soil', and moved on to an appreciation of the Devil, 'very useful . . . in the right place'.[17] This was fighting talk. The visit, and Antonia's uncompromising and unapologetic stand about the harsh streak in her nature, marked the final end of the intimacy between them. He had nothing more to offer her: she had always been the master.

At the bitter end of 1941, the bombing of Pearl Harbor by the Japanese brought the United States of America into the war, much to the Allies' relief. Even this did not bring home to Emily the convulsion of suffering and death that had extended over Europe and Asia during the last two years. She was happy with her horses and cattle in Arizona; cowboy Jake was in the army for only four months before being dismissed as 'an agriculturist over 38' and her son Johnny had been turned down, on psychiatric grounds, which had upset him but not surprised his mother.[18] Back in London, Antonia was house-hunting again. Ian Black's lease on his flat had come to an end and she returned temporarily to Eric's house in Selwood Place. He was away on war work for the Foreign Office, only returning for alternate week-ends, and it suited them both for Antonia to move back. She did not move out until spring 1942, and then only because Eric's housekeeper had had enough of her, or so Antonia reported to Peter Thorp.

Finding appropriate accommodation during the war was very difficult, and this time she decided to share with her sculptor friend Ronald Moody and his wife Hélène, whom he had married in Paris and escaped with only two days before the German occupation. She reported to Emily that having been 'so sick of living in the houses of unhappily married couples as I did for the first part of the war . . . it's a relief to be with a happily married one'.[19] After viewing thirty-three flats together, they found a home at last, a maisonette at 29 Thurloe Street, conveniently close to South Kensington underground station. The Moodys lived on the upper floor and Antonia the lower, and they shared a kitchen. Although she liked Ronald very much, he irritated her sometimes with his dogmatism, which clashed with her own; his being a follower of Gurdjieff also did not chime too easily with her Catholicism. Ronald told Antonia that he had noticed one side of her was dead. Perhaps it was her intellectual side, suppressed in her attempt to live at peace with her faith: 'I love the Church: it is almost a physical love. Sometimes it is compulsive. My intellect does not love it.'[20] Hélène, on the other hand, she found companionable and unchallenging: 'She's honest, amusing, intelligent and, above all, easy to live with.'[21]

Having a larger flat again made it easier to have the children to stay in the holidays. They split their time between Antonia and Tom and Gerti, with Susan going occasionally to Silas and Sheila. As a result of analysis, Antonia noticed that, as well as most of her morbid terrors and anxieties, she had lost the headaches which had plagued her since she was fifteen. At the same time, she noted, 'my relation with the children is enormously improved. But it's only a beginning.'[22] However, as Antonia's headaches disappeared, Lyndall began to suffer from crippling migraines, which were to strike without warning and wipe her out, sometimes for as much as three days at a time. Lyndall was still more uneasy and distant with her mother than was Susan, dreading her embarrassing visits to school in slightly too fashionable clothes or showy hats. Antonia became increasingly aware of her younger daughter's passion for Tom, and her emotional vulnerability. 'I am frightened for Lyndall with him for the child loves him like a *woman* & suffers very much. I do not think he *really* loves her though he is awfully kind to her. . . . The new baby is his real love'.[23] Meanwhile, Susan was feeling materially disadvantaged compared with her sister, and could not know that Tom was less satisfactory as a father now than he had been in their childhood. The emergence of her stepmother Sheila in 1944, bringing stability to Silas's life and benign interest to Susan's, offered her the potential of an alternative family just at the point that Lyndall was feeling her place with Tom and his new family under threat.

Despite her new role, Antonia's daily work continued to be a treadmill of long hours and administrative struggles. At the end of 1942 she became literary editor of the BBC's paper *London Calling*, which was aimed at listeners overseas. 'An exacting and not v. interesting job' was how she described it to Emily, who had by now left love on the range in Arizona for Catholicism and New York.[24] However, she found two diversions. Intermittently over the previous three years Antonia had been reading George Sand, fascinated by her letters to Flaubert and the relationship they revealed: Sand, the assertive, predatory, 'masculine' spirit; Flaubert, submissive, responsive and, in Antonia's terms, 'feminine'. Antonia found a resonance in the life and nature of this strong, demanding woman. While she was living with the McCleans in Hertfordshire at the beginning of the war, before she had begun work at the BBC, Antonia embarked on a free translation of the early part of George Sand's *Autobiography*, greatly cut and transposed. She was full of admiration for the grand sweep of it, with its portrayal of Sand's parents and grandfather against the background of the French Revolution; 'the *theme* is as good as *War & Peace*'.[25]

This was the first time that she had embarked on a lengthy work of translation and interpretation from the French language. Her French was fluent, thanks to her early training in Latin with her father, her natural aptitude for learning and languages, and the rigorous teaching of the nuns of the Sacred Heart at Roehampton. Sadly she did not continue with the work. The BBC, and the increased difficulties of daily life, absorbed all her energy and time. What little she had left had been expended on her extensive correspondence with Peter Thorp; 'I waste enormous mental energy on people who aren't really benefitted by it ... e.g. Thorp. It is much better for me to write for *people in general*.'[26] When Cyril Connolly made a chance remark to Antonia at the end of 1942 that she should write something for *Horizon* about her return to the Catholic Church, publishing extracts from her letters to Thorp seemed the truest way of charting the counterpoise of her faith and doubt, and the constant dialogue she was engaged in with herself at the time. It would also be a way to salvage something from all those words, that intellectual energy, which had poured into the letters rather than into her creative work. She felt she had doubly wasted time, for the recipient of all that energy had not even understood a half of it. Unfortunately, Connolly's own response was far worse than mere lack of understanding. Repelled and appalled, he refused to publish it. 'He said it was like watching a person making desperate attempts to retain their reason and finally lapsing into insanity.'[27] 'Escapism', 'betrayal of the intellect', 'a pathological case-history' were his descriptions of her religious struggles, a diagnosis shared by most of Antonia's old friends and fellow intellects.[28] She believed that Barker's absence from her life was due largely to recoil from her reconversion. 'The *prudery* of the intellectual-literary gang is amazing & disconcerting. I feel pretty lonely sometimes but it's good for my vanity.'[29]

Antonia had been back to a few of the reunion meetings for convent girls, the Children of Mary, and had met again one of the more sympathetic old nuns, Mother Clutton, with whom she kept up an epistolary conversation, 'but there is much one cannot say to nuns!!' as she protested to Emily. Eric was the only person who knew her in all her colours who did not disapprove, and calmly supported her when her doubts threatened to overwhelm her. But he was not often in London and available for consultation and consolation. Her loneliness made Antonia aware of lost opportunities: 'I would have been happy to have [a true love]. But I was too jealous, too self-centred, too demanding.'[30] Her real writing, the book about her father and herself, remained much agonised over but little progressed. Connolly's rejection of her went deep. She became more inward-looking, the religious doubts returning with a vengeance. With only herself to talk to, Antonia's mind began moving into a manic gear, the unproductive grind of obsessional anxieties causing dry panic and spiritual exhaustion.

Christmas that year took on an added significance and source of consolation. Susan and Lyndall, who were now thirteen and eleven respectively, were due to spend it at the flat with Antonia and the Moodys. 'Les Papas', Silas and Tom – and Gerti – were also due to come to lunch. Antonia planned it for weeks. There was a crib, with beautiful figures of Mary and Jesus carved by Ronald, and a stable, constructed and thatched by the girls. It was going to be a 'really good old-fashioned Christmas . . . a tree, crackers, stockings, quite a banquet on Christmas day with a duck, champagne, & a real pudding with blue flames!'[31] Susan and Lyndall sang carols, and Antonia felt she had managed at last to surround herself with the kind of family feeling she had longed for all her life, yet had managed to attain only in fleeting moments and memories.

Antonia's record of being sacked from every job she ever had was not about to be abandoned, even during the exigencies of wartime. She had become increasingly resentful of the daily grind at the BBC, all 'death & stagnation' as it seemed to her, and she was eventually asked to leave in the early summer of 1943.[32] Now depression joined the religious doubts, crippling her into a kind of torpid state which alternated with restless hypersensitivity. There was a lack of progress on every front: 'Careless & unorganised spending. Inability to feel. Irresponsibility, touchiness . . . eternal gnawing question, is Cath religion *true*? . . . reading mania . . . Try and swallow books whole. Sloth & impatience. . . . Everywhere conflicting creeds, opinions. Church offers security but do I really believe in the Church? still *odi et amo* as much as ever.'[33]

In August, Antonia began working in PID, the secret Political Intelligence Department of the Foreign Office in a section set up in Bush House. It operated under strict rules of secrecy: 'my real life is all underground.'[34] She was working largely with Americans, but concerned with propaganda operations in France. At the beginning of July the French Resistance leader, Jean Moulin, had died under torture from the Gestapo. There was a sense that the war was turning in the Allies' favour with Italy's unconditional surrender at the beginning of September. One of Antonia's jobs was to edit a monthly thirty-page illustrated booklet in French. Called *Accord*, this was a kind of compact *Picture Post* filled with rousing pictures of victorious allied soldiers and airmen. The limited text was upbeat and informative, and nearly half a million of each issue were dropped by the RAF over occupied France in the propaganda war. The December 1943 issue, probably the first one Antonia worked on, featured black and white photos of incredibly handsome French fighter pilots in Corsica, walking away from the doughty little Spitfire aeroplanes they had just landed. '*Avions anglais, pilotes français, equipment americain*' was the caption.[35] The only Germans you saw in these booklets were dishevelled and downcast, heading for one of the prisoner of war camps.

Antonia was working long hours every day, six days a week, 'very hard & harassing . . . but also very interesting.'[36] In the fourteen months she spent in this work, Antonia came increasingly to admire the French and form an even stronger attachment to France. The Free French movement had been set up in London with Charles de Gaulle at its head in June 1940, and this force in exile became the Fighting French in July 1942. They were a passionate and courageous group of men and women, and Antonia met some of them in her work. But the men and women of the Resistance were not predominantly devout Catholics, and Antonia found it difficult that she felt such affection and admiration for them and their cause, and yet came up against such antagonism in them to the religion she had placed at the centre of her life. 'It is very hard to do such work with people who are either rabidly anti-Catholic or lapsed Catholics' she explained to Emily.[37]

In early 1944, Antonia was involved in similar work but in a different section, headed by Graham Greene and based in Grosvenor Street, where a more literary booklet, without pictures, was produced to be dropped in the same operations over France. This was called *Choix* and ran to over a hundred pages of literary extracts of articles, such as an appreciation of Duke Ellington from the *New Yorker*, V.S. Pritchett writing on Anatole France in the *New Statesman* and Osbert Sitwell writing on London. *Choix* was a more subtle form of propaganda, as Graham Greene explained: 'propaganda of a cultural kind . . . making the French aware of what had been going on in literature whilst their country had been occupied by the Germans.'[38] The first issue was produced in April that year with a poem by Auden, 'Palais des Beaux Arts', among the serious prose pieces. There was a great deal of translating to be done, as the extracts were invaribaly from English language publications: it was likely that Antonia was responsible for most of it. Certainly it was in this work that Enid Starkie, an Oxford academic specialising in French literature, met Antonia and was impressed with her facility with French. This was to have a tremendous impact on Antonia's life when the war was over.

There was a certain companionship of like minds in this work. There was Graham Greene, himself a convert and novelist troubled by religious doubt, and the poet Kathleen Raine. The friendship between Antonia and Kathleen was for a while very important to them both, and although there were antipathies and fallings-out it lasted until Antonia's death. Both recognised the intellectual and spiritual quest of the other. Kathleen was nearly ten years younger than Antonia and in the midst of a passionate turmoil of love, spiritual necessity and ambition. She had been married twice and had two young children to whom, she admitted herself, she was a less than generous mother. She was attracted to

Antonia by her sense that behind the older woman's perfectly cultivated mask of control and civility was a highly-trained but fundamentally untamed creature. She recognised her 'soul of extreme sensibility', yet after hearing the story of her childhood, the convent, her madness, the lapse and reconversion, Kathleen was appalled and fascinated by Antonia's voluntary submission of her soul to the complex and arbitrary strictures of her Church.[39] Kathleen believed that 'the soul . . . has its innate form which must unfold according to its own mysterious inner laws; as in nature plant or animal forms. To interfere, by the imposition of external constraints, with this organic unfolding, was the great sin against life.'[40] The only discipline necessary was a scrupulous attendance to the voice of intuition, which would guide each soul towards its individual destiny. Yet to her own puzzlement Kathleen Raine, more naturally a neo-Platonist, was herself to convert to Catholicism soon after meeting Antonia. She discussed this at length in her own autobiography; in part it was wishing to make something positive of the suffering in her life, but it was an act of desperation too, a need for external restraints on her obsessional love for a man which she had not the will-power to resist alone. She compared herself to Ulysses having himself tied to the mast as his ship was rowed past the sirens.

Antonia was equally intrigued and alarmed by this 'charming, highly gifted, and ardent creature', whom she felt had rushed into Catholicism 'too subjectively'.[41] Although both women had respect for each other's intellect and the suffering in their lives, Antonia was rather taken aback to find in Kathleen a more extreme version of herself:

> She doesn't consider any woman alive her intellectual equal but she has a superstitious respect for men's judgement. . . . She really is a 'stone & flower' herself: stone uppermost at the moment. There is something curiously inhuman about her though she can be very kind, sweet & affectionate. She is passionate in the head only. She has a violent temper, is very rude & intolerant, though very sensitive herself. . . . She is very beautiful but her face goes hard & tight & cruel when anything annoys her . . . which is fairly often. She is small & slender, fair-haired, with wonderful blue eyes and very beautiful bones to her face. She has a lot of saint and a lot of fiend in her.[42]

She told Emily that she was the last person who could help Kathleen in her conflicts over her faith and her emotional life.

The two women attended a series of lectures on the Apocalypse by a brilliant young Dominican priest, Father Richard Kehoe, who had impressed them both, although Antonia longed to be able to talk to him informally as a confidante and friend. It was to the prior of the Carmelites in Kensington, however, Father Pius Dolin, that Kathleen Raine turned for instruction, believing him to be 'one of the most beautiful, most spiritually transfigured beings I have ever met'.[43] When Antonia first met him she at once blurted out her life story. He asked with some concern, 'Is there any single human being whom you trust?', and she replied yes, one, thinking of Eric; Father Pius said 'Thank God for that'.[44] It was like an angel speaking, Antonia thought, and suddenly it became clear to her what a problem she had with trusting anyone.

She was driven to asking his advice over what became an obsession with Kathleen and her own battle with Catholicism. Antonia objected to Kathleen's apparent contempt for her; 'she thinks I'm dreadfully earthbound & unperceptive & pedestrian'.[45] She also minded the way she had appropriated her religion: 'She goes on calling herself a Catholic but makes it clear that hers is a private, esoteric kind of Catholicism beyond the reach of ordinary people ... K is more like Djuna ... she loves beauty – "the wild beast, beauty" more than truth'.[46] Father Pius told her to look beyond such things and lift up her heart to God. Her obsession and dissatisfaction with Kathleen he put down largely to 'cattiness', with which Antonia willingly agreed – she longed to see her 'put in her place'.[47] In her later years Antonia was to come to love Kathleen, and to rely on her as the only person who could appreciate truly her struggle for meaning and truth. Kathleen too was on a painful journey of the soul, although it would lead her to a quite different place.

As the end of the war dragged on, Antonia became increasingly weary. Rationing of food, fuel, clothes, and even essential repairs of houses and machinery, was beginning to take its toll on the health and spirit of everyone. In a last flare of defiance, Germany had unleashed the 'Flying Bombs' – nicknamed the 'doodlebugs' – in the middle of June 1944, at the rate of 100 a day. They cruised in over the Channel, too low for the anti-aircraft guns, and then, running out of fuel, nose-dived to destruction over Kent, Sussex and London. At the beginning of August, Antonia took sick leave from the P.I.D. She had been suffering from the old symptoms of weeping, depression, inertia and 'maniacal reading'.[48] The news of the liberation of Paris on 25 August, however, for which she had been working for the last year, raised a small cheer in her heart. She longed to be able to go there herself; 'such hope, such radiance'.[49] Meanwhile, old London was 'so scarred and so shabby'. 'The war *has* affected us' she wrote to Emily, now back in Connecticut; 'yes – Five years of strain, uncertainty, break-up of our lives.'[50]

Antonia's only holiday was spent that year during the first two weeks of September, with Susan, Lyndall and Susan's friend Isabel Quigly, at an Assumption Convent evacuated to a beautiful seventeenth-century house in Shropshire. The girls helped with the harvest, which they loved, but Isabel remembered Antonia taking it very personally that they preferred to be out in the fields than with her, and would suddenly be overcome by a black rage. At other times she was as charming and funny as anyone could be.

Antonia hoped that here, on this grand but decaying country estate, her daughters might get some idea of what it meant to live a Catholic life – albeit of a rather rarefied kind. She went to communion every day in the family chapel, and she and Susan and Lyndall watched a lay sister make her final profession. This young Irish woman, crowned with a wreath of white roses, prayed for Susan and Lyndall on her profession day – no doubt in response to a request from Antonia who was always praying herself for the conversion of her daughters. Susan, who had been hesitating about committing herself to her mother's faith, decided the next day that she wanted to be instructed. This delighted Antonia; as she wrote to Emily with a striking lack of self-examination, 'I know nothing else will satisfy her. She is a strange child with a terribly clear critical mind and as she says herself a "shrivelled up heart".'[51]

Susan was baptised at the Brompton Oratory in August 1945. Some months later Antonia remarked with pride, '[She] is so quiet and firm in her faith. She is going to be brilliant scholastically and she is immensely attractive. I wouldn't be a bit surprised if she gave it all up one day & became a nun.'[52] With Susan's conversion, Antonia's over-identification with her elder daughter began in earnest. It was to lead to a similar kind of emotional oppressiveness, expectation and intrusion on her privacy to that imposed on her by her own father.

Lyndall's spirituality was never so clearly categorised by Antonia. She thought that her younger daughter's devotion to Tom made her nervous about showing any interest in Catholicism, which may have been partially true. But Lyndall had been given *Frost in May* to read by her mother and, having read her description of the nuns' behaviour, unbeknown to Antonia had vowed to have nothing to do with Catholicism. Lyndall was discovering also a needy passion for her motherly housemistress at school. This teacher had faith, but it was of the Protestant kind and, to ally herself with her and Tom's family, rather than her mother, Lyndall was baptised into the Church of England in the spring of 1945. Her Grandfather Hopkinson officiated.

Tom's growing unhappiness in his marriage was brought to a head when the family returned to London. In his own abstraction, he became increasingly distant from Lyndall. As Antonia pointed out, he behaved immaculately on the surface but emotionally was remote. Lyndall, whose nature was passionate and loyal and emotionally dependent, was made miserable by this abandonment. Antonia had her to stay for three days on her own at the end of March 1945 and for the first time really enjoyed and appreciated her company; Lyndall accompanied her without complaint to Mass. She also began to take the trouble to understand her daughter a little, and felt some real sympathy for her situation, although inevitably her sympathy had a reflexive quality: 'Poor pet, she has not an easy nature at all. She is like me – terribly jealous – and when she feels unloved she becomes unlovable. She broods on things till she gets in a fever of self-pity. She is a firm, radiant creature, very handsome, rather masculine, more like a son than a daughter; she is reserved and delicate like a boy. She is *upright*; she *endures*.'[53] At last, Antonia had found the upright, honest, courageous, son-like child she had always wanted.

As the war ended, Antonia became increasingly resentful of the office routine, knowing that it was inevitably to be run down. In fact, she was to continue there until the following March, when she was offered a permanent position at an excellent salary which would have meant a much more secure future financially. However, Antonia resigned in order to go back to her vocation of being a writer.

A further difficulty was the return of their landlord to the flat in Thurloe Street: Antonia and the Moodys had to be out by Christmas. The chore of flat hunting was made all the more difficult and depressing by the aftermath of the war. There was a great scarcity of anything decent, and what there was was run down and dirty. They visited forty-three flat agents and found one flat which was suitable, only to find that it had a colour bar. However weary she was, Antonia was not going to abandon the Moodys for something so shameful. The forty-fourth agent, however, produced a maisonette at 13 Ashburn Gardens, close to Gloucester Road underground station. It was filthy, undecorated and had lost all its windows from the blast of a nearby bomb, but they thought it had a friendly feel and it would do. Antonia now intended to award herself a few months in which to concentrate on her abandoned novel about herself and her father. She wrote to Emily that she had found the motto she wanted to use for it in the works of St Augustine. The book was to become *The Lost Traveller* and included St Augustine's words: 'In the sojourning of this carnal life each one carries his own heart and every heart is closed to every other heart.'[54] That bleak statement was a testament to her own lifelong isolation.

20

Dominating Women

Benedicta oddly prepared the way for the other two.
B dominated me through sex, religion mainly. . . .
D . . . [dominated through] writing, a fake form of religion, hope of
   release from neurosis, hints of success & money too. . . .
. . . this 'dominating women' period started in 1947.

18 February 1956 unpublished diaries

A ntonia first met Dorothy Kingsmill on 12 June 1945. Both women
had heard about each other through Kathleen Raine. Dorothy had
told Kathleen that she had had a dream about Antonia (something to do
with Antonia and the stage), and as dream analysis was her *métier* it was
fated that they should meet. Antonia was unlikely to resist such an
introduction, and accepted a lunch engagement with her, although
Kathleen had warned her: 'You may think her phony: Graham [Greene]
says she's sinister but I find her interesting. She walked out on her
analyst because he didn't believe in God.'[1] Dorothy was to be another
woman friend who veered, in the estimation of Antonia and others,
between saint and devil. These were all women with spiritual aspirations
and a well-developed will to power; qualities which Antonia shared.

   To begin with Dorothy's saintly side was more readily visible. She
was a pretty woman with soft fair hair and striking blue eyes which
retained their colour into very old age. For fifteen years she had been
married, not happily, to the stubbornly undomesticated writer Hugh
Kingsmill, who was much revered by his friends. In her powerlessness,
rooted in an unhappy childhood and nourished by an unsympathetic
marriage, Dorothy sought power for herself by directing the lives of
others. She chose to become a self-styled, untrained but intuitively
gifted, psychoanalyst. In this guise she was responsible, apparently, for
episodes of despicable manipulation of her clients and dangerous

indiscretions about their lives, as well as insights which seemed genuinely illuminating and helpful to their cases. Sometimes simultaneously, during a period of less than three years, she was 'analysing' Kathleen Raine, Antonia, Benedicta de Bezer, Susan, Lyndall, Tom, Gerti, and Tom's mistress Georgina Horley – and even the arch-rationalist Eric – and would use what she learned from each to fuel her own 'revelations' and interpretations to the others. It was a tangled web with damaging consequences.

During that first meeting Antonia initially had been distrustful of Dorothy's 'pretty little woman' side, and her over-earnest concern with the development of the soul, but had quickly warmed to her kindness and interest in her.[2] When, on their second meeting, Dorothy said she had read her short story 'The Saint' and had had a wonderful revelation about Antonia's writing problems, Antonia became interested in Dorothy. However, the demands of both of their lives kept them apart for nearly two years, although both heard of the other from Kathleen.

In the latter part of 1945, Antonia's determination to return to a writer's life was given encouragement by the unexpected windfall of a 'handsome advance' from Graham Greene who, as director of the publishers Eyre & Spottiswoode, had decided to bring out a new edition of *Frost in May*. (This was eventually published in 1948.) She began writing every day on her book – what would be her second novel, *The Lost Traveller* – as well as putting aside a few hours to read St Thomas Aquinas, 'properly, making notes as I go.'[3] By the beginning of March 1946, Antonia had written 105,000 words but, unused to 'this blessed release from the writing jam', she was afraid that anything that had flowed with some fluency would inevitably be poor; that only 20,000 of those words would be salvageable.[4] It was not as bad as she feared. By the beginning of May, having lost three weeks while she recovered from a serious bout of flu, she reported to Emily that she had finished Part I, Part II was in rough draft and she only had the last part to go. At this stage, she gave the manuscript to Eric to read. He responded positively; 'I think it is extremely good, and apart from anything else reads excellently as a mere narrative, which is what THE PUBLIC wants – and so do I, as a change from too much psychology, politics, symbolism etc. etc.'[5]

However, while work was going well, Antonia had made an uncomfortable discovery. She was losing her central position in Eric's life. Georgina Horley, a journalist aged twenty-seven, had been Tom's London mistress during the war, and had now turned her attentions to Eric, who was fifty-one. Antonia had been quite fond of 'Georgie', and helpful to her too. It hurt and unsettled her both to face this shift in her long relationship with Eric, and to have to reassess a woman who had become a friend. She wrote to Emily that this young person was a kind of Becky Sharp, '[who] would sit up all night with a sick friend & elope with her husband after first cooking her a nice breakfast.'[6] It surprised her too that Eric had capitulated so readily. However, this surprise was born out of a lack of perception; all the while good old Eric had been there for her, Antonia had not realised he was growing increasingly lonely and drinking heavily – and had been wanting a companion/ housekeeper/wife for some time. At one point he had proposed to Joan Souter-Robertson (who was by then divorced from the painter Frank Freeman). Joan, who had also caught Tom's eye and had a brief fling with him, recognised the domestic nature of Eric's offer and gently declined. Then along came this determined young woman, who wanted more than a resident housekeeper's role in his life. 'Eric was at first indifferent, then amused, then sympathetic, then apprehensive & finally, with a wave of the hand, succumbed & vanished' was how Antonia plaintively encapsulated it in a letter to Emily.[7]

It says something for Antonia's attraction, or abilities of persuasion, that, for the all-important festive lunch on Christmas Day 1945, she managed yet again to collect around herself every member of her 'irregular family' – Susan and Lyndall, Tom and Gerti, Silas and Sheila. Eric was only prevented from coming because Georgie's presence would have been understandably unwelcome to the wronged wife, Gerti. Silas appeared to be tremendously happy in his marriage to a woman whom Antonia recognised approvingly as being 'absolutely simple, direct, intuitive, sensible and loving', who was obviously very much in love with him.[8] Silas turned out to be the life and soul of the lunch, launching into an impression of Emily's old lover, Peter Hoare (who had become Silas's best friend) playing the same flute as a male friend who was three times his size. Difficult to imagine quite how this bizarre configuration was conveyed, but Antonia thought it marvellous.

Everyone was finding the increasing privations in daily life even harder to bear than during the war. Rationing continued; a weekly allowance consisted of 2 oz. of butter, 5 oz. of margarine, one egg if you were lucky, three rashers of bacon and enough meat for two meals. Fresh fruit was a very rare treat. 'We simply crave for *fresh* food & I find myself devouring raw cabbages with the utmost pleasure.'[9] Clothes, particularly nylon stockings, were hard to come by, and those you could get were expensive, thick, shapeless and so brittle that they laddered almost immediately. Antonia thought that Catholics ought to have a special allowance of nylons because kneeling was so ruinous to the things. In these daily deficiencies, Emily was able to help practically by sending parcels of cooking lard, sugar (rationed in the States, but she ate out all the time so did not use her allocation) and tinned Spam, wrapped in cast-off clothes from her own wardrobe and that of friends. One of the best things to come in such a parcel was an old coat of Peggy Guggenheim's which arrived in time for Christmas and which Antonia felt gave her that barely-remembered air of chic. She wore it for years afterwards. In contrast, she and Hélène Moody had between them, among their best clothes, a suit made out of a rug and a dress made from a dust-sheet, such were the forced ingenuities of post-war austerity.

Food parcels and second-hand clothes from the land of plenty could ease some of the material pressures of this time, but the emotional exhaustion and sickness of the spirit were more difficult to assuage. The full horrors of the concentration camps had only become apparent as allied troops liberated them at the end of the war; the atomic bombs dropped on Hiroshima and Nagasaki had shocked the world: suddenly here was a whole new level of human depravity and technological destruction. A natural force had been unleashed which was capable of destroying life on earth. Antonia was depressed and aware of a feeling of heaviness and despair which, for the first time, was more to do with what was outside her than what was within; 'The whole world is in such a state of horror & sickness; in some ways it is worse than the war – this oppressive sense of evil let loose.'[10]

Then, unexpectedly, Antonia was asked to go to Paris on 3 June for three weeks, to deliver a lecture on contemporary English fiction, in French, to a Dominican circle. She had made friends with three or four French Dominicans in London during the war. They had been variously incarcerated in concentration camps, beaten up and involved in the Resistance. Because of the extremity of their experiences, Antonia felt she could speak naturally to them about the struggles in her own life. There was a gritty reality which was lacking in so many of the Irish and English Catholic priests she came across, whose experiences were limited and whose minds were introspective. Her paper ended up as a discussion on salvation and liberation as expressed in Graham Greene's *The Power and the Glory* and Aldous Huxley's last novel, *Island*. Her talent as a teacher was once again revealed by the success of this lecture, delivered in her second language to an intellectually demanding audience. The three weeks extended to a month, and Antonia related to Emily how she was almost hysterical with excitement just to be abroad again, after so many years of hardship and narrowed horizons. It was striking how unspoilt and beautiful Paris still looked, compared to the battered and filthy London she had left behind, but if the buildings had been saved by the Occupation, the morality of its citizens, she felt, had become corrupted by greed, dishonesty and tension. Her disapproval of the Parisians' self-serving made her feel 'a bit priggish & British'.[11] Antonia, however, did note just how vital the Catholic Church was in France, and envy how much it was woven into the fabric of everyday life. She took part in a mass pilgrimage to Colombes (the huge Olympic stadium outside Paris built for the Olympic Games just before the war) where 150,000 people celebrated High Mass at midnight with the Cardinal and 200 parish priests; 'the *whole crowd* went to communion – the priests climbing up the tiers through the crowds. It was like the miracle of the loaves & fishes.'[12]

A much-longed-for but slightly anti-climactic highlight of her trip was meeting the novelist Julien Green at last. 'I've felt a most queer sympathy with this man for over 20 years.'[13] They were exactly the same age, were both Catholics, and had lapsed from their Church for about the same length of time. Her avid reading of his journal and novels had convinced Antonia that here was a sympathetic fellow artist, and a twin soul. When they did meet, she thought him extraordinarily like her in manner; 'like someone carrying a glass of water & terrified of spilling it.'[14] They both had on their social faces and were so 'completely conventional & embarrassingly polite' with each other that it took more than an hour's small talk before Antonia managed to move the conversation on to something more intimate, by mentioning she had been in an asylum.[15]

With the relaxation of both her work load and the everyday tension of the war, Antonia was in the possession of more free time than she had enjoyed for years. In this vacuum, she was struck again by the poignancy of her loneliness and the lack of a companion, especially now that Eric had remarried. A young man, who had been manoeuvring to meet her for two years having been impressed by *Frost in May*, suddenly declared himself in love and desiring to marry her, despite the existence of his own wife 'who has come to despise him'. Antonia, emotionally headlong and impetuous as ever, told Emily she 'had to hold on by the skin of my teeth not to yield', so violently did her emotions respond to his unexpected romantic interest. Ill-judged as it was, she could not help enjoying the long-lost pleasure of having someone profess to care about her. Phyllis Jones, who had been absent from Antonia's life since their lunch five years previously, visited Antonia in the middle of this abortive affair. Antonia had heard from Emily of Phyllis's hardship and had sent her £2, which touched her for she knew how short of money Antonia was too. Their renewed acquaintance did not become easily intimate again; 'Nor was the atmosphere improved by tonsillitis, the departure of an admirer who had been weeping for some reason or other, and the expected arrival of a Dominican priest. I felt completely out of place in this sandwich', was how Phyllis reported the meeting to Emily.[16]

Antonia's fundamental loneliness remained. After nearly five years of shared flats, she was once more on her own, the Moodys having moved on. Although she felt great relief at having a home of her own again, the lack of companionship loomed large. Since her reconversion, Antonia had also suffered an increased sense of spiritual isolation, with no one with whom she could share her intimate thoughts, doubts and struggles. Emily was now a devout convert herself, but she was both physically and emotionally distant, with no conception of the changes in Antonia's life since they had last seen each other in London, more than eight years before. Born with an assertive nature and bred on an emotionally explosive diet, alternating ecstasy and fear, Antonia always was made impatient and discomforted by equilibrium, calmness and the *status quo*. Now that the external threat of global oblivion had faded, she was ready to seek out some domestic trouble of her own.

She found it in the form of a mentally unstable, androgynous painter and musician called Benedicta de Bezer. This strange, compelling-looking woman, who was known as a lesbian and had led a wild life of fringe clubs and recreational drugs in Paris and London, had recently converted to Catholicism. Rejected from more than one convent in her quest to be a nun, Benedicta, assuming a simple black habit, had reinvented herself as a Dominican monk of slavish religious devotion. Antonia had first met her at the beginning of 1946 when she went to the Clothing of a mutual friend in the Carmelite nunnery in Notting Hill. She had liked Benedicta immediately, feeling an easy familiarity with her as if they had known each other before and were similar spirits. 'We both felt freaks & misfits in the Church in a way; we had such wild lives and spoke a language that seemed shocking & incomprehensible to most people.'[17] She continued to see her occasionally since, but it was not until a year later, in February 1947 when Benedicta fell ill and Antonia visited her every day, that she realised there was more to her than rebellion:

> *How* extraordinary she [is] . . . lives in absolute poverty, goes to Mass every morning, and is full of life, brilliance, gaiety, quick wit and the most intense Charity I've seen in a human being. She is extremely attractive, gifted so that it takes your breath away (she is a born musician and a magnificent pianist, a very good painter & sculptor – some of her religious pictures are almost like El Greco: very witty – in fact she seems to have every physical & mental gift there is).[18]

Antonia had fallen in love. Unfortunately she had chosen a woman who was close to the edge of insanity and whose mania expressed itself as religious delusions and a fervour for prayer. Antonia immediately entered into one of the most bizarre episodes of her life, when for a while she believed herself to be in mortal danger. The diary she kept that charted the short blazing trajectory of mutual obsession was unlike any other in her journals. It was small and the entries were written not only in a small cramped hand, but were themselves uncharacteristically cryptic and abbreviated. This abbreviation was particularly marked in the early entries, from the middle of February to the middle of March, when it seems likely she was recapping on events, having burnt the original diary on the urging of Benedicta. She returned to her lucid, expansive style in her later diary entries and dream diary, which discussed the Benedicta phenomenon with the benefit of some hindsight.

In one of her later ruminations, Antonia explained that Benedicta's attraction for her was a generalised sexual attraction, for a woman this time who seemed entirely present in her own body, a kind of ' "spiritual-physical" body . . . both tangible & intangible'. However, this generalised physical attraction became focused on physical desire: it was this change of focus which Antonia felt spelt doom for the relationship, much as it had when her feelings for Tom changed from general attraction to a more specifically carnal desire; '. . . the Benedicta feeling got localised: sheer sexual hunger. Then it went all wrong.'[19] This suggested that there might have been some attempt at sexual expression of their feelings, immediately abandoned in some panic on Antonia's side. Benedicta was in her early forties, a few years younger than Antonia, with a bony, sallow-skinned beauty. Susan, who was also attracted to her when they met, described her memorably; 'her short dark hair seemed to stand on end like a flame, which gave her the appearance of having recently landed.'[20]

Antonia and Benedicta then began passionate pilgrimages together to various churches and Westminster Cathedral, praying, saying the Office, attending religious lectures, and paying reverent attention to every ritual and symbol both in each other's flats and in the more public spaces of church and chapel. They exchanged religious pictures and holy medals. Benedicta's mania for prayer resulted more than once in her getting locked in at St Mary of the Angels in Bayswater, one of their favoured churches. Antonia decided that as part of her devotion she should offer her services as a cleaner at the church. Benedicta was already a Dominican Tertiary, a lay member of the Order in the world: influenced by her admiration for her, Antonia became a postulant in the

Dominican Order, having pestered the Prior at the Dominican Priory in Haverstock Hill in Hampstead.

All this was enacted within an increasingly hysterical relationship between the two women. Both Antonia and Benedicta appeared to inflame in each other the mental instability they shared. Their relationship became symbiotic, their moods swinging violently between ecstatic euphoria and religious certitude, and fearful depression and doubt; first Benedicta would have 'a terrible day', then Antonia recorded, 'I have a terrible day She [Benedicta] takes it over the phone for $3\frac{3}{4}$ hours and I am cured.'[21] Antonia would have a menacing dream about Benedicta which, when she related it to her, plunged Benedicta into 'a terrible state', and was then impelled to turn up with a samurai sword which she gave to Antonia.[22] Two days later Antonia noted in her diary that having said the rosary and litanies together and made the Stations of the Cross, they waited to see the Prior but he did not come. Then she returned to Benedicta's flat 'in a fearful mood'. She then added the oddly cryptic phrase, 'Sex and the fingernail. I think I have wrecked everything.'[23] The following day Antonia suffered her own crisis and was found by Benedicta weeping by the crucifix in the Dominican Priory. Benedicta was so insistent that the Prior come and see them that when he eventually turned up, just as they were ready to leave, he received Antonia's confession and accepted her as a postulant. Immediately the mood had swung from panic and despair to the opposite extreme, where both were 'deliriously happy'.[24]

The Feast of St Benedict (Antonia had taken to heading her diary entries by the feast days of the saints) marked another crisis. It started well with Benedicta bringing a bunch of daffodils and a bottle of Pommard '37, but ended with Antonia urged by Benedicta to burn her two earliest notebooks, the first one started just before she married Reggie Green-Wilkinson in 1921. Possibly she also burnt the notebook chronicling her most recent thoughts and activities with Benedicta. Antonia's diaries were much more important to her than mere records of events and passing thoughts; intimately bound up in her own mind with her identity, they helped to reconfirm her existence when she began to feel shadowy and transparent. 'Somehow more truth and less distortion gets into these notebooks than anything else . . . they are like a photograph of myself to which I refer.'[25] The destruction of these two diaries was a violent erasing of part of her past and her emerging self. It was inevitable that there was some reaction. After the conflagration, Antonia wrote in her new diary that something had gone wrong. She felt lost and bewildered again: she and Benedicta said part of the Office for the Dead together.

This religious manic-depressive axis became more extreme as Holy Week approached. Susan came home for the Easter holidays and was immediately subsumed into their mania. At first she was a willing participant; she too found Benedicta an attractive and compelling individual. In her own memoir, Susan recalled that she felt spellbound by her and experienced something akin to the excitement of falling in love. However, although Antonia was to come to regret that she had not protected Susan from what she later recognised as an evil influence, she make no attempt at the time to keep this unbalanced religious behaviour between herself and Benedicta, and to shield her vulnerable adolescent daughter from the worst of their excesses. In fact, it was Susan who was the first to sense that there was something unwholesome in the emotionality and extreme behaviour of these two women. She had joined them on Maundy Thursday for High Mass at Westminster Cathedral and had been profoundly moved by the sight of Benedicta praying. All three women then had returned to Benedicta's gloomy studio where her looming religious paintings dominated the room. That evening they had walked through the rain to the Dominican Priory on Haverstock Hill for *Tenebrae*, one of the offices of Holy Week. Praying beside Benedicta and her mother, as each candle was extinguished to symbolise the approaching death of Christ, Susan was overcome with a fearful emotion. 'I had a sensation of terrible evil. I knew there would be no Resurrection. The creature who knelt beside me, whose tilted nose I could just see in the gloom, was damned for eternity. Ashes seemed to fall perpetually. My sorrow for Benedicta was enhanced by sorrow for the Crucifixion, and I shed tears for both.'[26]

Susan's unhappiness continued, but Antonia's pricking of unease was deflected again by the 'happy "family" feeling' of Easter Sunday, when both her daughters and Dorothy Kingsmill and her daughter Edmée all sang round the piano, while Benedicta played.[27] Lyndall was staying with Tom and Gerti, but had come over for Easter Sunday and there met Benedicta for the first time. She had been completely excluded from the religious fervour leading up to the weekend because she was not a Catholic, and could not participate with her mother and Susan in the worship. However, she too found Benedicta extremely attractive, with her handsome manly looks, her theatrical mannerisms, and expansive character.

Shortly afterwards, Susan was confirmed at Westminster Cathedral. The tea party afterwards at Ashburn Gardens would have appeared, to an outsider, a bizarre event, with Benedicta dominating proceedings in 'sponge-bag check trousers with a crucifix larger than anything the Bishop had about him'.[28] It was during this religiously fervid time that

Silas and Sheila began to feel seriously alarmed by Antonia's influence on her elder daughter. In fact Susan's religious crisis was deepening. Finally, a week after her first intimations of evil, she collapsed. She felt she had lost 'Our Lady': she could neither pray nor even hold her rosary. She could not bear to be in the same room as Benedicta, so powerful was her sense of evil present. Antonia gave her her own crucifix to hold instead. Father Victor White was due for dinner and when he entered the flat all three women asked for his blessing. Antonia requested that he also exorcise the flat: Susan was most insistent that he particularly bless the bathroom. Dorothy Kingsmill also arrived to add her interpretation to the situation. She spoke extremely well and impressed Father White, but irritated Antonia ('she seemed a little boastful').[29] The following night Susan heard a voice calling her. Certain it was Antonia she went to her mother's room only to find her sound asleep. But at her feet Susan noticed an enormous black beetle squeeze out from under her mother's door. When she told Antonia the next day they both decided that it was the voice of Our Lady who had called and Antonia declared that this required that another priest, this time Father Pius, should be consulted. Father Pius's last words to Antonia were 'Do not be dominated.'[30]

This marked the end of Antonia's extreme infatuation with Benedicta. She told her that she intended to be received as a Tertiary, not at the Dominican Priory in Haverstock Hill where Benedicta had been received, but in Paris. Benedicta was deeply hurt and took this as a cruel snub. She accused Antonia of not having loved her enough, of shabby treatment and lack of gratitude. Antonia was mortified and grief-stricken. She did not accuse Benedicta of being a person possessed of evil; instead she saw a pathetic, frightened and lonely woman. Antonia was always ready to take the blame for the breakdown in her relationships. But then, when Benedicta attempted to dismiss with a laugh the whole highly charged last weeks, implying that Antonia was far too serious and self-important and had misunderstood the whole thing, Antonia countered this by categorising such levity as just another face of the Devil. She prayed fervently to find God's will in all this. She felt she had to purify her own heart: 'A dream showed me there was more flesh in my love than I knew.'[31] Somehow, she made a kind of peace with Benedicta: 'She is a noble soul . . . I pray, if it is God's will, that we two should be a pair.'[32] Antonia took the scapular that Benedicta had sewed for her, and with Susan set off for France. There in Paris on 24 April, the Dominican feast of the Crown of Thorns, Antonia was received as a Dominican Tertiary in a far more elaborate ceremony than she would have had at Haverstock Hill. Although she felt it was rather presumptuous, she took the name of Sœur Thomas d'Aquin because

Thomas Aquinas had brought her much consolation through the years, not least with his belief that faith falls between opinion and scientific knowledge; an intellectual act of will becomes necessary in order to believe. If she could not have a brother in the world she could at least have a spiritual brother in faith. She and Susan sent Benedicta a postcard with a picture of the Crown of Thorns on it.

Antonia then accompanied Susan on to Alsace, where she had been recommended to a good Catholic family, the Gruneliuses, who lived with their six children in a grand eighteenth-century pink and white chateau at Kolbsheim. Susan was to stay with them for five months, having that summer won an exhibition to Somerville College, Oxford. The month of mutual fascination with Benedicta, followed by the violent recoil and a feeling of shared loss and grief, had drawn Susan closer to her mother than ever before: 'In loving Benedicta, I came to like, or at any rate understand, my mother. For a time our thoughts ran parallel and were often identical.'[33] However, this psychological interconnection would have its destructive aspects, when both mother and daughter began to find her psychological disintegration mirrored in the other.

On Antonia's return to London, almost immediately she fell into the arms of Dorothy Kingsmill, the second and perhaps more influential of her dominating women. She also acquired a small black and white female kitten and called her Domina, and dominatrix she turned out to be. Antonia identified closely with this cat's difficult and demanding nature, and described herself perfectly in describing her: 'She is very witty and has no sense of humour and is terribly touchy. But though exceedingly intelligent (and rather a prig) she has moments of endearing pure idiocy. She can look sillier than any cat I've ever seen but it is not wise to remind her of this in her Roman Empress mood.'[34]

Tom had greeted his ex-wife's return with the news that he thought Lyndall should go and see an analyst. Antonia suggested that a talk with Dorothy first might be a good idea. She arranged to see Dorothy herself to give her own gloss on the situation between Lyndall and Tom, but almost immediately started talking about Benedicta. Dorothy was equally keen to talk about this unaccountable woman. She mentioned that she had found Benedicta in a café looking very unhappy: she had explained her discomposure as due to the fact that a woman she knew had dreamt of her 'as a devil'.[35] When Dorothy realised that this woman was Antonia she promised that she could help both her and Benedicta. More importantly for Antonia, however, she said she would also be able to release her writing block. Lyndall was almost forgotten in this exchange. When Antonia, however, did describe her daughter's problem as she saw it, she told Dorothy not to mention a letter that Lyndall had written to Tom. The first thing Dorothy brought into the discussion, when she did get to talk to Lyndall, was the letter to Tom. However, this failed to alert Antonia to the levels of indiscretion and manipulation to which Dorothy frequently stooped.

Dorothy did confide to Antonia that she was untrained and that there was a risk involved for both of them in embarking on this 'analysis', given the seriousness of Antonia's previous breakdown. For a few weeks both she and Benedicta were seeing Dorothy independently, without conflict. Then Benedicta rang Antonia out of the blue, and in a terrible state. Sounding paranoic, she warned Antonia that it was dangerous to go on seeing Dorothy because she was a Buddhist. Antonia was phlegmatic; she knew about Dorothy's spiritual interests, she said, and was not concerned. Benedicta, however, broke off all relations with Dorothy, on the grounds of her indiscretion as well as her heretical beliefs, hurting Dorothy's feelings very much in the process.

Dorothy Kingsmill was not a Buddhist but was a prominent follower of an Indian mystic called Meher Baba. He believed that all things which are real are given and received in silence, and so he maintained silence for most of his life, communicating through gesture alone. Meher Baba considered himself to be the avatar for that age, ranking among such universal religious figures as Rana, Krishna, Buddha, Jesus and Muhammed: he believed that all major religions were but revelations of 'the One Reality which is God'. Unwilling to have an institution of devotees set up around him, and bound by his own commitment to serve the poor and dispossessed, he nevertheless attracted many followers. Dorothy Kingsmill was one of his most committed followers in England: she was involved also with the Theosophists, members of the Arcane Society and followers of Gurdjieff. Antonia believed that one of the lessons her extraordinary time with Benedicta had taught her was 'how the supernatural is *here* all the time in our everyday life.'[36] Dorothy's more inclusive beliefs did not worry her at this stage, and she launched into an analysis with her that May. Antonia was not expected to pay for her sessions because, as Dorothy explained, she considered this to be her vocation. However, her insistence on it being a favour and a gift, rather than a business transaction, was to prove another powerful way of controlling her through the unexpressed sense of obligation: Antonia was to come to rue the day that she did not clarify the terms of their relationship.

On Dorothy's urgings she began to keep extensive dream diaries in which she wrote every dream fragment which she could salvage from her waking mind. Antonia went three mornings a week to Dorothy's house, often not leaving until 1.30 in the afternoon, and by the time she returned to her own flat she was too tired to do anything but lie down and recover.

In August and September 1947, Antonia suffered a psychological crisis; 'it alternates between extreme nervous tension & jitters & complete lethargy.'[37] Unfortunately this state coincided (or was exacerbated) by a visit to London from Emily Coleman. Emily was in a bad way herself, and thought that the lack of an effusive welcome from Antonia was due to the fact she did not love her any more. In truth, these old friends were never easy companions in the flesh; so manic was Emily, Antonia so thin-skinned and easily irritated. Antonia explained that her friend's violent and shifting preoccupations made it difficult for her to react sympathetically; all she could register was 'a painful feeling of bewilderment and impotence.'[38] When their relationship was conducted by letter, Antonia was able to overlook Emily's conviction of her own saintliness and possessiveness of Christ as her personal lover. Face to face, her violently-held opinions and absolute self-righteousness were more difficult to ignore. But the underlying affection and admiration still remained. In their different ways they both had survived madness, and had struggled on with the burden of their extreme and volatile natures. They shared too a quest for religious truth and meaningful experience. At the time Dorothy, too, was little help to Antonia, having suffered some kind of nervous breakdown herself, caused by 'the psychic strain of dealing with [Antonia's] "shadow side"', as Dorothy saw it.[39] Her husband, Hugh Kingsmill, thought otherwise: he accused his old friend William Gerhardie of having gone too far in an argument about reincarnation in which he had laughed at something Dorothy had said, sending her into hysterics.

By November, both Antonia and Dorothy were restored to equilibrium, and Emily had returned to Connecticut. Antonia wrote her an apologetic letter; the timing of Emily's visit had been unlucky. Now Antonia was also struggling with a sense that God, having increased her capacity to love by bringing Benedicta into her life, had dealt with her rather cruelly by suddenly removing that object of love. Antonia tried to think of this piously as a useful cross for her to bear, but her sense of abandonment was strong, particularly given Eric's forthcoming marriage. To add to her frightening feelings of loss, her financial affairs were on a knife-edge again. Enid Starkie, whom she had met during her time in the Political Intelligence Department during the war, suggested Antonia try translating to supplement her income. She put her name forward to her own publishers, Hamish Hamilton. Antonia did a sample chapter and was taken on at thirty-one shillings and sixpence per thousand words translated.[40] Her first full-length novel was Guy de Maupassant's *Une Vie*, which became in translation *A Woman's Life*. Published in New York and London in 1949, it was this book which won for her the respected Clairoun prize for translation. Here began her lengthy, prolific and distinguished career as a translator from the French.

Her own writing, having progressed so well for a while, now languished as she concentrated on recovering from her analytic sessions and the resultant exhaustion and depressions. However, in the autumn of 1948, Joan Souter-Robertson, a kindly and eminently practical woman, had agreed to stand over her and make sure she finally finish the novel which was to be called *The Lost Traveller*. She rang or saw her every day and demanded updates on her progress. In a copy she gave her when the book was eventually published, Antonia wrote 'For Joan, without whose gentle inflexibility this book would never have been finished.'[41]

Antonia's analysis, and her association with Dorothy, continued to disturb her. At the beginning of 1948, Antonia had survived a sudden and catastrophic mental collapse under the auspices of Dorothy's analysis which had frightened them both very much, but from which Antonia emerged, apparently cured. That January, Dorothy and Hugh Kingsmill had moved into Antonia's cottage, Binesfield, as tenants. While she was living there Dorothy said she was certain it was haunted by someone with a peculiar sigh. When she reproduced it, Tom had leapt out of his chair: he immediately recognised it as the exact sound characteristically made by Christine, Antonia's mother. On one of Antonia's early visits to Dorothy, in this ancient house with so many associations, the analysis uncovered something very unsettling which propelled Antonia into a state of near insanity, 'babbling in a kind of trance'.[42] Dorothy sat up with her until three in the morning, terrified that she would go out of her mind again. She said that on that night she had handed Antonia over to Baba's safekeeping. Antonia told Emily that it felt like going down into the underworld. She emerged intact, but weeks of deepest depression followed – and then unexpectedly something fundamental about her self in relation to the world was revealed: 'It happened during one night, very quietly. You could call it a kind of revelation . . . for the first time in my life I can make a free choice. I've no excuses any more. . . . Anyway, I chose to be a Catholic, freely, for the first time, without any fear or compulsion.'[43] Antonia was nearly fifty. She considered herself cured at last. 'It rather stuns one when something that has been wrong with one for over forty years suddenly comes right.'[44] She wrote to Benedicta to tell her the wonderful news: Benedicta sent one line in response, a warning that there was more to come; 'she turned out to be right.'[45]

Antonia continued to feel very well in the early part of the summer. But then she began to have a sense that she was somehow in contact with Baba. She thought she could discern his 'telling' her to do things, like give up smoking for a day. Anxiety and a feeling of menace began to build in her. Dorothy was coming up to London from Sussex three days a week and staying with Antonia at Ashburn Gardens. Initially Dorothy's company and her practical skills in decorating and home-making gave Antonia the rare pleasure of being looked after, but soon their relationship became complicated by hidden tensions and posses-siveness. Then her beloved cat Domina, with whom she closely identified, had an unexplained and terrible fall from the roof, through four floors to a stone area below. She was found by Antonia under her bed, having dragged herself back into the flat, with her mouth full of blood and apparently dying. The little cat had split her palate with the impact on landing, and had damaged her legs. For four days Antonia fed her with a spoon.

Antonia also had a series of dreams which Dorothy interpreted as warnings of trouble brewing with Susan. Indeed, after a carefree first term at Oxford, Susan was growing increasingly depressed and returned to Ashburn Gardens in the middle of her second term with an incipient nervous breakdown. Antonia's diary for 1948 was almost entirely taken up with analyses of the character of Susan, endlessly working over where she had gone wrong as a 'rotten mother' and how this had contributed to Susan having become, despite her wonderful qualities of intelligence and beauty, 'like a creature poisoned at the source'.[46] Despite declaring herself cured and transformed, in these entries Antonia is so obsessional in her negative and critical dissection of her daughter, so paranoid about Susan's desire to hurt her and the possibility of her seeing Benedicta and forming a hostile alliance, that she seems to be far from the well person she professed to be.

By the summer, Antonia was in a crisis again, and at risk, both she and Dorothy felt, of a violent accident much as Domina had suffered. Dorothy even saw fit to warn the caretaker at Ashburn Gardens. In a semi-cataleptic state, worrying about the divinity or otherwise of Baba, the saintliness or not of Dorothy, Antonia began a downward spiral. In retrospect she realised that her sanity was saved by Lyndall's return to the flat in need of nursing herself. Lyndall had come home, unwell, and found her mother in a strange state, lying on her bed and staring at the ceiling. She explained that she was in a sort of trance, debating in her own mind whether she should comply with Baba's latest edict –

communicated to her through thought – that she should demonstrate her obedience to him by eating a turd from the cat's litter tray in the corridor outside her bedroom door. Was he the avatar of God or a disciple of the devil? For once Lyndall's needs were greater than Antonia's own desire to settle this spiritual point. She took her daughter's temperature, put her to bed and called a doctor.

That autumn, in a final grinding push, *The Lost Traveller* was at last finished and handed in to her publishers; 'I feel most queer without it, this old man of the sea of 14 years!'[47] With the completion of the book, Dorothy felt that her analysis with Antonia was over, and told her so in December. She considered that her work had been directly responsible for this great freeing of Antonia's ability to write, a conclusion which Antonia herself accepted. Dorothy had helped her sort out the relationship she had with her mother. She also supported her through the ordeal of confronting both her mother and her father in her novel. Most exhilarating of all for Antonia, however, was the sense of breakthrough: '[I] really believe I've lost my horror of writing.'[48] But nothing for Antonia was ever that simple. Dorothy the saviour became Dorothy the evil controller; 'there has been a struggle between me, trying to carry out D's instructions which I am sure were right: viz to stand on my own feet & D's efforts to get me back in her power & order every detail of my life.'[49] Meanwhile Benedicta's role changed from prince of darkness to bringer of light, by revealing how it suited Dorothy to play on Antonia's deep-seated feelings of guilt and unworthiness, keeping her susceptible to manipulation. 'To be "NOT GUILTY" in Benedicta's sense doesn't mean I have a beautiful nature or am not liable at any moment to behave disgracefully. It simply means that I am not responsible for the Fall of Man.'[50]

Antonia's personal life was also in flux. She was going through the menopause, which seemed connected to her sense of 'some radical change in the organism . . . almost as if the body itself were changing & new centres beginning to come alive.'[51] There were also more difficult symptoms; 'one's nerves are raw & on edge' which made it more difficult to deal with the stresses in her children's lives.[52] Now the daughter with whom she so closely identified became the focus of her negative feeling; her other unregarded daughter attracted her belated favour; ex-husbands who had always been reliable supports slipped from her immediate circle. But, in her fiftieth year, Antonia decided that God had set her a piece of 'homework' which would last her for the rest of her life: 'that is to give up the enormous luxury of being unhappy.'[53] The following night she joined a mass pilgrimage of 10,000 people to Walsingham where she had to kneel in a wet field in Suffolk, suppressing her distaste for the priests who had jumped on the people's bandwagon, for the 'cheery' old girls from Roehampton, and the young convert who called herself 'God's Cactus'.[54] Her work had begun.

21

Mother Love

How much unthinking love, care and the money which symbolises these things have gone to people who were not my first natural care and my children have only had the pickings and leavings.

6 June 1949, *Diaries*

The two 'dominating women' who demanded so much of Antonia's attention and time both had uneasy relationships with their own mothers. Benedicta identified Antonia with hers, a woman who had let her down by succumbing to melancholia, and whose illness consequently demanded close nursing from her daughter. Antonia felt that both Susan and Benedicta wanted her to be 'a strong & loving mother' and both were rivals with each other over this.[1] Of course the only one who had a right to expect this of Antonia was Susan – and Lyndall too, but she was not part of this equation in Antonia's mind at the time. Despite the very explicit needs of Susan and the implicit need of Lyndall, it was Benedicta who received most of Antonia's thoughts and energy during those febrile months. Antonia thought that she herself had 'suffered from too much father and [Susan] suffers from too little'. This had enabled her to be quite a good 'father' to her daughter but meant she was much less capable of being a 'mother', which in her psychological lexicon meant being sympathetic, supportive, nourishing, and able to sublimate one's selfish desires to the needs of the child.

Antonia believed that although both she and Susan had fallen in love with Benedicta, it was not with her as a woman but as 'the romantic prince on the white horse ... the prince without a penis'.[2] Sexually attractive, she was also safe. To Antonia she seemed the perfect husband figure who would support her and help her parent Susan, while Susan desired her as the father figure of which she had been largely deprived.

Each longed for the deficiencies in their lives to be filled by the idealised version of the other.

Dorothy Kingsmill too, had had too little love from her mother, and was compelled to shore up the shipwreck of her self-esteem by exercising her power over others. This, combined with her manipulativeness and her occasionally brilliant intuitions into the significance of dreams, could be very dangerous indeed. Her relationship with her daughter Edmée, who was a near contemporary of Susan's and Lyndall's, was also one of resentment and guilt. Antonia suspected that Dorothy, working out some of her own unresolved wounds in the process of analysing others, unconsciously fuelled Antonia's painful ambivalencies towards her own daughter.

When Susan came home from Oxford in the spring term of 1948, pale and ill and on the verge of a nervous breakdown, Antonia recognised this was a chance for her to try and fulfil, belatedly, some of her maternal duties of care, support and encouragement. Here was the calling to account of the neglect and lack of love from her in the past; here was the opportunity to do better the second time round:

> I have just *got* to love her & stand by her now, even if she is hostile, cold and ungrateful. All her very sharp critical faculties, conscious and unconscious are focussed on me & I've got to stand up to it . . . and smile! After all, why *should* she trust me? How many times, consciously and unconsciously I have let her down, exploited her, hurt her.[3]

Antonia was never slow to realise intellectually just how much she had failed as a mother, and to identify the qualities she needed in order to help her daughters move on confidently into adult life. Through her analysis with Dr Carroll she had come to accept that she had responsibilities to her children, but she realised it was *'responsibility without love'*.[4] This meant that nothing Antonia offered them could be unconditional and without cost; she resented what she had to do for her children, and was inevitably in search of gratitude and recognition when she had done it. The terrible pressure of expectation from her own father had been the parental model she had absorbed rather than her mother's more tolerant acceptance.

The emotional connection in the mother-child relationship was not automatically engaged in Antonia, although as Susan and Lyndall had grown older she realised, with some surprise, that she did love them; however, her bleak opinion of her own lovableness meant that she could not conceive of being loved in return. Instead she desperately wanted them to respect her, in particular for her work, and to show a certain sense of filial duty. One of Antonia's greatest weaknesses in intimate relationships was her lack of emotional empathy. She was aware of this but found it hard to rectify: 'For years and years and *years* though I could be terribly fond of people & even very much "in love", I just could not *imagine* how the other party *felt*! I knew what I *wanted* them to feel . . . which is not quite the same thing!'[5]

Knowing something intellectually, however, was a quite different matter from putting all those good intentions into practice in the face of problematic, self-absorbed, individually-minded adolescents, whose own insecurities were more marked as a direct result of the neglect they had suffered as children. By biting her tongue and constantly reminding herself of Dr Carroll's advice, 'to be as even and natural as possible . . . treat her in a light and friendly way', Antonia managed for a while to accommodate Susan's predictably demanding behaviour.[6] She wrote in her dream diary lucid, rational exhortations to herself. '[Sue] has been clever to have this illness which puts her back to babyhood. It is a great chance for me instead of the burden I have seen it. It is NOT blackmail, merely asking for deferred rights. Only she can't stay in that stage. She must be fed, then weaned, then made to learn to stand and walk.'[7]

Antonia was hardest of all on herself, self-critical, and full of self-disgust. When faced by a daughter who exhibited so many of her own qualities she was sometimes overwhelmed with fear and aggression towards the person who reflected her worst self back, at twice its natural size. Susan's irresponsibility with money made Antonia wildly resentful; her untidiness outraged her; her self-centredness and 'apparent total unawareness of what she has done and does' frightened her.[8] Conversely, those parts of her daughters' natures which were unlike her own she found hard to appreciate or understand. They had a blistering row when Antonia realised that Susan intended to visit Lyndall in Cambridge, where she had been staying since leaving school. Was this jealousy and fear of the girls having fun without her, strengthening their own alliance? Dr Carroll was consulted once again and he suggested it might ease the situation if Susan lived away from home while she sorted out her feelings about returning, or not, to Oxford. The Waleys, her schoolfriend Isabel's family, took her in. But Susan and Antonia were still intimately connected, with the kind of desperate, obsessional bond which damaged relationships breed. Sue was back at Ashburn Gardens again for Easter – she was ill and her friend had gone away for the holiday. She told her mother she had decided to return to Oxford, but was obviously still in a broken mental state.

The obsessive and highly critical analysis of Susan's character and behaviour which dominates Antonia's diary at this time shows very little empathy, tolerance or compassion. There was such a degree of harshness and coldness in her judgements, it was as if she was talking about herself. Susan, only nineteen, and, in the middle of her own mental collapse had symptoms of panic, depression and despair which Antonia herself knew intimately. At this point in her life, Antonia believed herself to be cured, and therefore with more energy for the concerns of others. Yet she could write; '[Susan] said to me the other day "I haven't lived since I was five years old". That is not true. She was alive last year all right. She forgets her past.'[9] This 'aliveness' was the ecstasy followed by fear and loathing which Susan had experienced in the dubious religious triad of herself, Benedicta and her mother. This was more a sign of unhappiness and emotional imbalance than 'aliveness' in any normal sense; however, to Antonia such swings of emotion were a vital sign of life. Her diary entry continues in the same chilly, uncompromising tone:

> Life absolutely terrifies her. You can watch her trying hard to escape into illness. I know she is suffering terribly. She is always trying to score off me, make me look a fool. She doesn't want to be with me yet she is always coming round here or ringing up on some pretext or other. I suppose I ought to be able to deal with the 25% of her that is like me. But I'm quite at sea with the rest.[10]

Envy was also a factor in the uneasiness between Antonia and her daughters. From a purely physical point of view, Antonia had never liked her looks or her body. Inheriting her father's short, square build rather than her mother's finer proportions, she had longed to be taller and more elegantly made. There was also a snobbishness in this, absorbed from her mother's attitudes towards her husband's family. Christine Botting's only weapon against the opinionated, self-righteous Cecil and his over-influential parents was a barely suppressed contempt for their humble origins; their peasant build and execrable taste were part of that deplorable inheritance. When friends commented on how '*distinguished*' Susan looked, Antonia could only see this as a negative reflection on herself; 'I feel the implication is "And *you* look so common".'[11] Instead of rejoicing in her daughters' elegance and beauty, Antonia felt diminished. Once again she considered her children not as enrichers of her life but as robbers of something intrinsically important:

> I think it is rather difficult for a short mother to have a very tall daughter. They are always bending down their swan like necks to you or putting things on shelves you can't reach and taking such

long strides you can't keep up with them. I think it is almost
impossible not to develop an inferiority complex and to become a
bit of a tyrant by way of compensation. You can neither effectively
cuddle or scold a creature a head taller than yourself who seems to
be almost out of earshot. I feel like a hen who's hatched a crane.[12]

It was not just the physical beauty of her daughters which caused
Antonia trouble. Both Susan and Lyndall felt that any happiness they
found with other people was seen in some way as a betrayal, another
source of envy. They felt their mother was happier herself when they
were unhappy. But in effect this was rooted in Antonia's pathological
need for power. If her children were unhappy then she had the potential
to do something for them; if they were happy independently of her then
that power resided in themselves or the people with whom they were
happy, and she was left unable to affect their lives, except for the worse.
As with all her maternal emotions, both positive and negative, the full
force was focused on Susan, who consequently carried the brunt of
Antonia's jealousy and envy. 'Part of *me* fears *her* as a rival, that if she
developed properly she would be such a wonderful, beautiful creature
that she would eclipse me entirely. . . . Of course there are times when I
do play the identification trick but I can't keep it up. So another part of
me sees every appreciation of Sue as a *de*preciation of myself.'[13] Writing
a postcard to a friend, Antonia found herself about to sign her own name
as 'Susan', evidence she realised of both her obsession with that daughter
and also that fatal identification.[14]

  Deficient she may have been in imaginative feeling, and cruelly
cutting when angry, but in rational discussion Antonia was at her best –
subtle, honest and unflinching. In her dream diaries she detailed a couple
of the conversations she had with Susan at this time, in one of which she
decided to tell her the full circumstances of her birth, taking full
responsibility for the wrongs she had done her when a baby. This
seemed to draw mother and daughter closer. But then, in the same
unflinching fashion, Antonia described going with Susan to the first
night of a French play for which she had been sent complimentary
tickets. They went out for dinner first and both were in the best of
spirits, enjoying each other's company and the treat of an interesting
night out. During the interval, while they enjoyed surveying the critics
and celebrity-filled crowd, Susan said, 'I can't think why on earth they
sent *you* tickets. *You* can't do them any good.' The combination of her
daughter's dismissive tone of voice and the implication of her words,
unleashed a temper tantrum in Antonia which shocked even herself.
Susan had hit the raw nerve of her fear of insignificance, powerlessness

and non-existence. She described vividly the terror of her own extreme reactions: 'I felt my temper rising madly: in fact I was shaking all over . . . I broke down completely & behaved shockingly . . . I was nearly in tears [this was a woman who found it impossible to cry even when her father died, a husband betrayed her or lovers left]. I just managed not to rush out of the theatre . . . But I was in despair.'[15] She then lambasted herself for her childishness, vanity and lack of control, and felt that she had destroyed the fragile goodwill and trust rebuilt between them.

Susan returned to Oxford and decided to spend as much of the long summer vacation away from home as possible, pursuing art and freedom in Italy. Lyndall, therefore, became belatedly the focus of Antonia's maternal concern, and for a while this shift in emphasis healed and comforted them both. Lyndall had gained a place at the Old Vic Theatre School, where Antonia's old collaborator Michel Saint-Denis had become general director. She was due to start in September. In August, she returned to live with her mother at Ashburn Gardens. She was ill and unhappy. Tom had finally made it clear that she was no longer welcome under his roof, a roof she had considered home since she went to live with him and Gerti eight years before. Tom was a faithless husband and Gerti had grown increasingly depressed; they had moved into a smart but unwelcoming house in Cheyne Row and Gerti, who was expecting her second baby, was unwilling to continue accommo-dating Lyndall.

Lyndall appeared on Antonia's doorstep in need of help and support at a point when Antonia was becoming increasingly preoccupied by the divinity or otherwise of Baba: 'My own unsolved mystery is Baba. Because that doesn't seem to me all delusion. . . . Many of his words affect me deeply. I feel something awfully authentic. . . . I've never met him. Yet in dreams and other contacts, he inspires love and respect.'[16] She was confused too as to how he fitted in with the tenets of the Catholic Church. She told Father Richard Kehoe and Father Victor White about her 'contacts' with the one Dorothy called sometimes '*the great Master*', at other times just 'loving soul' or 'fellow mystic', and these progressive priests seemed to be unconcerned. But this was not enough to stop Antonia's endless quest for the Truth; worrying, dissecting, comparing, praying, interpreting and reinterpreting and then starting all over again. What she returned to constantly was whether there was something more universal than the Church, and whether a spiritual individual like Baba was not more intimately connected to this universal truth than organised religions could ever be.

Her daughter's arrival, to find Antonia contemplating Baba's instruc-tion about the litter tray, and her prompt collapse with tonsillitis, put the manic theorising out of Antonia's mind. Lyndall felt this saved their relationship, or at least moved it into a space where fear of her mother was not the dominant factor. During a convalescence in Aldeburgh, where she had to share a hotel room with Antonia, a prospect she had rather dreaded, Lyndall was pleased and surprised at what good company her mother could be, especially as she did not lose her temper once during the week. Instead they walked, talked a good deal and browsed in bookshops before heading for one of the numerous little teashops for tea. Most surprising of all was Lyndall's realisation that Antonia was as tentative at following up an introduction to Benjamin Britten as she was herself. To discover that this overpowering, forceful and at times terrifying woman actually could be as socially unsure as she was, an unconfident girl of seventeen, was a revelation: 'I was amazed that my mother also suffered from shyness, and began to realise this person I had always feared as a monster was also a human being.'[17]

But despite having gained this greater understandng of each other, living with Antonia was fraught with problems. The internal chaos of her mind and emotions were only contained, and then barely, by a carefully maintained external ordering of her life. Spontaneity and improvisation threatened her fragile control. Her weapons against disintegration were lists, rigidity and a martinet insistence on routine. Just as her father had imposed order on his household, meals for Antonia were at set times; she had to know if Lyndall would be back for dinner and woe betide her if something came up at college which meant she had to ring in and say she would be late or miss it altogether. The dinner which awaited her was too often an unwelcome penance because it cost Antonia so much in nervous tension to produce, a tension and resentment which nothing but lavish gratitude and praise could assuage. Antonia's own loneliness, and lack of daily encouragement from others for her writing, meant she leant very heavily on her daughters when they were present. For Lyndall, living by day in an atmosphere of impulse, freedom and extemporisation, the heavy expectations at home were an oppressive burden. She began to dissemble in order to evade disappointing and angering her mother. There were occasional moments of real connection and mutual support; one night Antonia came to Lyndall's rescue with help with a poem, which she was writing to be set to music for the end of term revue. 'The most startling rhyme, however, is her own: hippopotami & "what am I?" I felt I couldn't improve on *that!*' she reported in a letter to Emily.[18] However, the familial relationship which Lyndall most relied on was the sisterly bond she had with Susan, and she longed for the vacations when she would return from Oxford.

Susan, however, was not able to conform her life and suppress her true nature in order to fit better with her mother's dictates and expectations. Consequently, harmony at Ashburn Gardens was always short-lived when she was home. The triangular relationship did not work well either. Susan and Lyndall got on well and then Antonia felt excluded and was jealous. However, there were also areas of resentment between the girls. Susan had the bigger bedroom and more spending money; she was wildly untidy and Lyndall ended up doing more than her fair share of domestic chores. However, Lyndall, through subterfuge and evasion, managed to live a double life, displaying an obedient and conformist face to their mother while gaining confidence with a socially more sophisticated set. And all the while Antonia, less admiring, supportive mother than insecure, neglected only child, was jealous of both her daughters for their freedom, for their sibling relationship, and for the material help extended to them by their fathers.

> Of course I'm horribly jealous too. I'm jealous that les Papas will produce money, holidays, clothes etc. for S. and L. but never dream of practical help for me. That is what makes me feel sore sometimes: that there is no one who concerns themselves about my welfare. I feel sometimes that I could die here and no one would ever know.[19]

As always, it was not the money so much as the care and love that the money symbolised which she felt she was denied. Antonia longed to be first with everyone but felt she was not even special to one. She wrote that this feeling of inconsequentiality was like drowning in sight of land – so near to human contact and certainty, and yet left floundering, invisible, her distress unnoticed, her self beyond rescue. Her feeling of insignificance was underlined by the increasing importance of Silas – and particularly Silas's wife Sheila – in both Susan and Lyndall's lives. She was a much more naturally maternal and capable woman, presiding over a more easy-going and welcoming alternative home, who extended her love of Silas to embrace both of Antonia's daughters.

Increasingly, Lyndall filled the uneasy role of the 'worldly but good' daughter while Susan was cast in a variation of her long-term and burdensome role of favourite; she had become 'brilliant but bad'. They were limiting caricatures and were not pleasant parts for either to play. After completing her stage production course at the Old Vic School, Lyndall fled the oppressive associations of her mother's flat to return to Cambridge to do a secretarial course. However, in the summer of 1950 she returned to London and the flat to look for a job.

That summer Susan turned twenty-one. She suggested to Antonia, rather boldly Lyndall thought, that she would like a birthday party. Celebration of her own birthday mattered to Antonia immensely: the contrast between Susan's party and the fact that she had not had one of her own for her fiftieth birthday the previous year would have exacerbated her sense of rivalry and deprivation. 'I am awfully childish about my birthday: still think people ought to make it a little feast for me & of course they don't: there's no one to make it. It is silly to be so "lonely" or to mind it but oh, I do, I do.'[20] The party was held at Binesfield, the tenants having a lease which required that they leave the house free for Antonia's use during the month of August. Friends from university, Silas and Sheila, Antonia and Lyndall were all there, as was Thomas Chitty, a fellow undergraduate with whom Susan had fallen in love when they had met the previous spring on a university drama tour of France. The party was a great success, although Antonia recorded a small incident the following morning which symbolised for her her sense of being peripheral to the lives of others. 'Sue and the young things all dashed out into the garden in their pyjamas. I was in the kitchen washing up while Thomas was posing everybody for a picture. Just as he'd snapped the group, Sue suddenly said, "Gosh, Mother wasn't in it." But it was his last film so nothing could be done.'[21]

That year Antonia took the brakes off her spending, in the hopes of more money from royalties yet to be earned on *The Lost Traveller*, published in April that year. She threw her energies into decorating the flat and bought a new stair carpet, the whole lot costing £110 which she confidently expected would be covered by money to come. But in the short-term it left her physically tired, rather lethargic and even more financially constrained. Both daughters were home, Lyndall as a paying lodger, Susan for her summer vacation, and her irritations and obsessions with Susan and her character returned. Antonia had long realised that she had always to have someone who was the focus of her compulsive thoughts; after husbands and lovers had swung out of orbit and no longer preoccupied her, she turned to women: first Benedicta, then Dorothy and now Susan. 'My present nagging preoccupation is Susan', she wrote at the beginning of September, 'who for some time has been the person with the most power to make me unhappy'. She then proceeded to catalogue the ways in which her daughter's erratic and self-centred behaviour threatened the necessary routine of her everyday life.[22] To be the focus of all that piercing intelligence, that hyper-critical energy, was uncomfortable, even damaging. David Gascoyne loved and admired Antonia as 'one of the most wonderful people I have ever known, or am likely to know', but even he feared the negative power of her gaze:

> On the whole, I think her influence on the people she comes in contact with is bad . . . she gradually undermines everyone's self-confidence. There are very few who can stand the dazzling (but how depressing!) light of moral Truth she radiates. Exposed to their selves, her intimates begin to wilt . . . and with what ruthlessness she tears their illusions to shreds! – very often, I believe, out of revenge for (imagined?) neglects or slights.
>
> One can hardly be surprised that, after a time, people begin to avoid her. . . . So she is left alone – with her terrors.[23]

Into this difficult triangle Antonia inserted a third young woman, a daughter in God, Elaine Lingham. Elaine was the daughter of a friend who had left the Catholic Church, married an Anglican man and brought her children up without formal religion. She had died young. Elaine, one of her daughters, had converted to Catholicism when she was twenty and when, four years later, she first contacted Antonia, in May 1950, she was about to enter the Carmelite order on the way to becoming a nun. Antonia had impulsively taken straight to her heart this 'enchanting, golden creature . . . attractive, intelligent & absolutely full of life and love and real, strong spirituality': inevitably she compared her with her own daughters, to their detriment.[24] In the meantime, Antonia had to deal with her real daughters. Lyndall was not much trouble to her, contorting her own life to impact as little as possible on her mother's. On her return to London she became part of an entertaining set of young people who included Simon Raven, who was to write the ten-volume series of novels *Arms to Oblivion*, Hugo Philipps, son of the novelist Rosamond Lehmann, and Mark Boxer, who was to become influential as a social cartoonist and magazine editor. Lyndall suffered still from the shyness and lack of confidence which had dogged her through childhood. She fell in love with one of this new set of friends, Richard Temple Muir, known as Dicky Muir to his friends, an urbane, charming man more than ten years her senior, who was involved in setting up a magazine publishing venture. Lyndall could confide neither in her sister, whom depression had made more inaccessible, nor in her mother.

Susan continued to loom larger in Antonia's mind. She was in her last year at Oxford and was acting in an increasingly inflated way; Antonia believed that her natural profligacy was exacerbated by the £400 she had received from the maturation of an insurance policy started by Tom and contributed to by him, Silas and Antonia. Antonia complained that her elder daughter had become more arrogant in her attitude to others, particularly to her own mother, and was rapidly spinning out of control. 'Whenever I write about Sue, I am frightened. How much of her there is in me . . . I don't see how I can love what is bad in her any more than I can love it in myself.'[25]

In Easter 1951, after attending all the Holy Week ceremonies with Antonia, Susan suddenly gave up her religion with apparently little heartsearching or regret. As Finals approached she became increasingly depressed. 'At last I pushed 100 compound codeine tablets down my throat. It was a dull job and I read *Of Mice and Men* most of the night to pass the time.' When Thomas Chitty came round to her digs the next morning to pick her up he found her semi-conscious and rushed her to the Radcliffe Infirmary. This act of desperation effected a fleeting vision of what it might have been like to have a conventional loving family: 'When I came round I thought I was in heaven. I saw Mother and Silas side by side at the foot of the bed, looking like a normal mother and father.'[26] Susan was discharged from hospital and returned to Ashburn Gardens still in a deeply depressed state. When Lyndall found her in her bedroom, unresponsive to her presence, with the cable to her electric fire severed with a pair of scissors, it was obvious she was still in danger. Antonia rang Dr Carroll who insisted Susan go to the Maudsley Hospital immediately. For three weeks, Antonia managed to behave 'with unnatural calm and efficiency', visiting her virtually every day.[27] But she became aware how closely she and her elder daughter were psychically connected 'when I developed a state as bad as Sue's', and the doctors treating Susan suggested that she did not visit for a while.

There were two other shocks that spring which, with the guilt and anxiety of Susan's collapse always on her mind, destabilised the other major props of Antonia's life. She learnt that Tom and Dorothy Kingsmill were lovers. This was a terrific blow, for she had never really relinquished Tom in her mind as support and literary mentor. This now forced her to acknowledge that she had truly lost him, and to a formidable rival. The second blow was a tough, 'almost blackmailing', demand from Eric for £50 of the £250 which she owed him. She realised that he needed the money and was in a bad way, but she had to hand over her rent money to satisfy him and, even worse, his uncharacteristically uncaring manner meant she had to relinquish her fond and long-held conception of Eric as 'the intelligent, understanding "good" father'.[28] In her already shaky state of mind, the final recognition of the emotional loss of the two most important men in her adult life left her weakened and bereft.

In her anxiety about Susan, Antonia asked Silas if they could have a meeting to discuss their daughter, without Sheila. She felt that Sheila did not acknowledge the importance of the spiritual life, and so could be too pragmatic, Antonia believed, in her advice. Her fierce protectiveness towards Silas also meant that any intimation of neglect or guilt on his part was forbidden, and so shared assumptions of responsibility for Susan's unhappiness were difficult. Antonia was very ready to admit that she was jealous too of Sheila's place in Susan's affections, but her first concern was to ensure that she and Silas were thinking along the same lines over the best way of caring for Susan. Doctors at the Maudsley Hospital were so concerned at the continuing severity of Susan's depression that they suggested electric shock treatment, but Antonia and Thomas Chitty in a concerted effort argued to get such extreme treatment deferred. She was home by mid-June, having spent three months in hospital. Still depressed, she was 'gentle, melancholy, gradually becoming apathetic, lacking all confidence'.[29] Antonia too had been struggling with a recurrence of her own depression. She had a feeling of constant pressure inside her head and had burst into tears and cried 'uncontrollably' in the street.[30] The direness of her current financial situation also overwhelmed her. 'I have nothing for rent or the quarterly bills', she wrote in familiar desperation.[31]

Susan's unhappiness and depression were hard enough for Antonia to bear, but when her daughter's behaviour began to spin to the opposite pole of inflation and extravagance, Antonia was disgusted and afraid. The parallels were too close and threatening: 'The swing from acute depression & total lack of confidence to wild optimism & extreme self-confidence seems suspicious. Her life in some ways is horribly like mine.'[32] Antonia's obsession with her increased; her diary one more revealed the compulsive revisiting of every slight and disappointment. She saw moral failure and turpitude where there was mental fragility and despair. Years later Antonia was moved by something W.H. Auden had written which she thought painfully applicable to her relationship with Susan at this time: 'To be well-bred means to have respect for the solitude of others, whether they be mere acquaintances or, and this is much more difficult, persons we love.'[33] Antonia's own illness made this kind of detachment and support impossible. All she could register was a rising panic and anger as she confronted the external chaos created by her daughter, which threatened to undermine her precarious control on her own internal demons:

> . . . a crescendo of insolence, extravagance, endless demands, crazy disorder until I said if she could not behave reasonably she had better go off on her own . . . endless trouble for me and Lyn.

Incredible vanity and conceit: out to exploit everyone. . . . She has worn me down till I am tired and trembling and can't settle down or concentrate but this time I am not going to give in to her . . . There are times when it is extremely difficult to believe that the whole suicide and Maudsley episodes were not quite consciously and coldly planned and executed.[34]

When Susan began to feel better she started work as an assistant at the children's zoo attached to Battersea Fun Fair. It was the year of the Festival of Britain, and the fun fair was part of the celebrations. Thomas Chitty was one of the drivers at the fair and both of them were earning about £4 a week for relatively congenial outdoor summer work and Susan still had Silas's allowance of £2. Then, at the height of Antonia's outrage over Susan's behaviour, she asked her to leave and live independently in a bedsit. For Susan this was a much more traumatic event than Antonia appeared to understand. She wrote in her own memoir that it was her statement that her furniture from Oxford was going to be delivered to Ashburn Gardens later in the week which set Antonia off on a furious rant, which ended with a forcible ejection: 'On the first Saturday in August 1951 Mother threw me out of the flat . . . She stood up and said, This is *my* house and *I* decide when furniture shall be delivered. You will leave this place within twenty-four hours. I will burn anything you leave behind. Except books.'[35] Once Susan had moved out she made a few trips back to the flat to pick up her things, including some objects which Antonia considered belonged to the general household rather than personally to her daughter. In one of her disastrous impulsive outbursts of ill-temper, Antonia then changed the locks to keep Susan out. She wrote a chilly letter justifying her actions as being necessary to satisfy her insurers.[36]

Antonia had been given a second chance to show that she could be a true mother to Susan, and had categorically failed. The effects of this second rejection of her daughter were to reverberate right through the remaining years of her life. Antonia's obsession with her daughter, like her obsession with Catholicism, was to remain a continual power struggle, an unrequitable love which aroused in her alternating feelings of frustration, anger and supplication. Susan's own hurt and anger burn still in the pages of her memoir, written thirty-four years later.

Within three weeks, Susan had secretly married Thomas Chitty in a civil ceremony with only Lyndall, Sheila and Silas Glossop in attendance. Susan and Thomas each sent Antonia a letter to tell her of what they had done, posted so that they arrived when they were safely on honeymoon. Susan's attempt to cast off her mother and her mother's religion, was a desperate reflection of Antonia's own attempt to escape from her father's overweening influence. In her valedictory letter there was one phrase which puzzled Antonia but gave her some hope of reconciliation; 'we both want our Mother back again'.[37] Antonia replied individually to both. She admitted her shock and distress at not being trusted enough to be told. To both she was unequivocal that she never doubted their feelings for each other, thought them 'right for each other', and wished them every happiness. But to Susan she made her renouncement of her religion seem to be one of her main concerns. 'If you had decided to try and be married in a Catholic church, I should have been in the horrible position of having to intervene in order to prevent what, from the Church's point of view, would have been sacrilege.' Assuring her of her love always, Antonia brought up the old fear that Susan had always thought her 'the great grim ogre of your life' and now could be rid of her.[38]

This was the beginning of the wilderness years for Antonia when Susan withdrew from her completely for nearly six years. She was supported and encouraged in this by Thomas, who recognised what a potentially destructive effect Antonia could have on Susan's vulnerable state of mind. Silas and Sheila too supported this iron curtain approach to Antonia's influence; they had never been happy about the more extreme expressions of Catholicism with which she had involved her daughter during the Benedicta fiasco, and had been deeply concerned by Susan's breakdown and attempt at suicide. Her newfound equilibrium, with a devoted husband who had stood by her in the extremity of her illness, seemed to be a far healthier environment in which to begin anew.

Antonia alternated between bitterness, acceptance and bleak misery. She missed her daughter terribly, and was hurt and genuinely uncomprehending as to why such a turn of events should have come about. She seems to have been blind to the effects of her past behaviour, and the young couple, in refusing any concrete explanation of their silence, were unaware of the confusion and fear this engendered in her. 'All I got [in reply to two letters] was a brief note from her husband, signed by them both, saying politely but firmly that they thought it better not to see me', she explained to Emily.[39] In her rational moments, Antonia would accept that Thomas was a person who could bring Susan security and happiness, and that the marriage might be successful; 'In many ways I think this marriage may be very good for her & may be a real beginning of something when all the dust has died down.'[40] Her occasional letters to them alternated between chilly accusations, which she signed 'E.A. Hopkinson', and desperate abjection: 'although when you didn't answer my letter of 6 months ago, I said I wouldn't write again, I am weakly doing so. . . . I am always thinking about you. I can't help it. And praying for you. However much one might wish to put a daughter out of one's mind, one just can't.'[41] Antonia was particularly concerned that the spiritual nature which she had always identified in Susan would be starved amongst the heathen with whom she chose now to live. She was further wounded and dismayed by the fact that her friends and ex-husbands continued to see the newly-married couple and yet, she believed, made no effort to intercede with Susan on her behalf. The marriage seemed to have opened a permanent breach between Silas and Sheila and herself. They resisted all attempts at communication. This denial of her filled Antonia with painful emotion; her hand was shaking as she wrote to Silas at his office, 'it was only common courtesy to let me know *why* I was being treated as non-existent.'[42]

Antonia turned increasingly to Lyndall and found in her a sympathetic and affectionate spirit she had barely managed to notice before. But even in celebrating her good qualities she could not resist using them in damaging comparison with her sister: 'I *like* Lyn more and more. I don't suppose she can ever cause me as much agony or as much exquisite delight as Sue. But she is immensely lovable and attractive and there is something terribly sweet in her dogged little way of paying her way . . . Lyn is the more generous of the two and immensely sensitive to any feeling she understands. Sue, like Eric, understands the impossible but has no middle register.'[43] Although being appreciated by her mother was a novel and welcome experience, Lyndall too had to protect her most vulnerable self from the full glare of Antonia's gaze. Through love for her sister and unwillingness to expose her mother to further hurt, and through fear of both, she was forced into a Janus role of keeping Susan's secrets and passing on unwelcome and edited versions of Antonia's messages.

Susan's implacable withdrawal from her mother's life had the effect of visiting upon Antonia the over-riding experience of her daughter's own childhood. The abandoning mother was now abandoned by her child, and suffering something of the same emotions. Desperate obsessional longing followed by resignation was then interspersed with recurrent stabbings of loss: 'I am too weak not to complain about the hurt and long for Sue to be friends with me again. It is horrifying to realise that one must often have hurt other people as much as they are hurting me now.'[44] By refusing to participate in her mother's struggle, Susan had gained a new power: 'Sue perhaps is the last of my dominating women.'[45]

22

Moving the Mountain

This suggestion – so universal – that with every book I was fast
  declining. . . .
I felt I ought to stop any further attempt at serious writing. . . .
Eric said 'You can't stop even if you want to.
You are bound to a fiery wheel'

9 August 1952, Diaries I

Dorothy Kingsmill, with all her dubious methods and ulterior
motives, had had at least one positive effect on Antonia's life. *The
Lost Traveller*, her first novel in the seventeen frustrating and arid years
since *Frost in May*, was written almost entirely during her 'analysis' with
Dorothy. In fact so grateful was she for the illumination offered into the
psychic tangles of her life, that Antonia had originally dedicated her
book to 'The Master', a reference to Meher Baba, only to change it at
the last moment to Hugh Kingsmill's name as a compromise. By the
time she was editing the novel in proof Antonia had fallen out with
Dorothy, and she decided that the last two sections were too influenced
by her 'occultism'. She feverishly rewrote them in the August of 1949,
delaying publication for six months.

The breakdown in Antonia's relationship with Dorothy had happened shortly after Hugh Kingsmill died of bleeding from an
undiagnosed duodenal ulcer in May 1949. Dorothy had brought
Antonia's analysis to an end the previous autumn but was still in close
and, Antonia felt, increasingly controlling contact with her, putting
pressure on her to cut all ties with London, her friends and family, to
move permanently into Binesfield, and there to see only Dorothy.
Things came to a head when Antonia refused to concur with her plans.
She had also upset Dorothy by requesting that the tenancy Dorothy had
on the cottage should come to an end. The flashpoint came when

Antonia decided to tell Dorothy that she felt that she was in touch with dangerous occult influences. 'She turned on me & wrote me the most violent, abusive, really crazy letters I have ever had in my life. She threatened me that dreadful things would happen to me if I broke away. . . . Bit by bit I am piecing out the incredible tangle of untruths she told me: I truly think she *is* insane in some ways', Antonia explained in a highly confidential letter to Emily ('*I must implore you, dear Emily, to keep what I have written about D. to yourself*').[1] The venom in Dorothy's letters shocked Antonia profoundly. They attacked her where she felt most vulnerable; 'Something all wrong with me. . . . I am "depraved", and she must withdraw from me and my situation.'[2] Dorothy called up Antonia's immanent sense of her own monstrousness, her fear that she was unlovable and fundamentally irredeemable, that she contaminated everything she touched.

Emily's interpretation of the related events was straightforward and uncompromising – Dorothy had always struck her as 'terribly "Lesbian" ', and she was obviously in love with Antonia. The abusive letters were clearly of the 'hell hath no fury' kind.[3] As Emily believed at this point that homosexuality was Satan's stronghold, this could explain why evil was able to work through Dorothy in her intimate analytical dealings with her clients. Antonia replied that this theory had been put forward by other friends and could account for a number of puzzling things, but if it was true of Dorothy's feelings for her she was sure it was only on an unconscious level. Both agreed, even as they accused her of being a conduit for evil forces, that Dorothy was also capable of great goodness, despite her hatred of the Catholic Church.

Antonia had not seen Dorothy for almost a year by the time the book to which she had been midwife finally saw the light of day. Significantly, it seemed to Antonia, *The Lost Traveller* was published on 3 April, three days after her fifty-first birthday, '36 years after that fatal birthday that gave me such awful guilt about writing novels'.[4] She had wanted this to be a 'proper novel' in that she wished to widen the perspective to encompass the viewpoints of the heroine's parents too. In an attempt to separate the two novels, Nanda Grey's name had been changed to Clara Batchelor, but her character and the influences of her life were a continuation in every sense from the more intensely focused *Frost in May*.

In *The Lost Traveller*, Antonia powerfully evoked the conflicts in the adolescent Clara; the seduction of the spiritual life she had experienced in her years in the Convent and a love of the world '[which] meant her father, Paget's Fold [the cottage based on Binesfield], the country, freedom to read and say and eat and wear what she liked, freedom to choose her friends and even, as a faint possibility, marriage.'[5] Her longing to express herself as an artist also seems difficult, if not impossible, to reconcile with the expectation that as a Catholic everything she did should be to the edification of God. This emerging self is buffeted by the demands of perfection from her father and the Church, and the tender stirrings of individual expression and desire. In this Clara has the support of her mother, who carries lightly the proscriptions of husband and Church, but so great is her daughter's contempt for this instinctive, loving and unrigorous side of her mother that she cannot accept the compassion and understanding which she offers. Indeed, so closely does Clara identify with her father, that the only quality of her mother's which she wholeheartedly admires is her beauty:

> 'Why Mother,' she said. 'You're a really beautiful woman. But *isn't* she, Daddy? Seriously. Quite as beautiful as any of the heroines in her old novels.'
>
> 'My dear,' said her father, beaming, 'have you never noticed it before? Unobservant as I am, it struck me the very first time I set eyes on her. Four . . . five . . . twenty five years ago.'[6]

Antonia allowed the mother her beauty but denied her wisdom, respect or influence. She also allied Clara firmly with her father in every situation, keeping her mother on the other side of a psychological divide. Only at the very end of the novel is there a moment of rare sympathy between mother and daughter, but by then the pattern of Clara's life has been set – devotion and fearful recoil from the authoritarian father/Church; suspicion of the feminine; headstrong action combined with passivity and indecisiveness; an overwhelming sense of unworthiness. On the verge of womanhood she is, as the title poignantly suggested, lost in an alien landscape, uncertain of herself and lacking either signpost or direction.

Antonia, in trying consciously to make *The Lost Traveller* into a 'proper novel' not only broadened her viewpoints but also departed in places from the strictly autobiographical, something she was not to experiment with again in her full-length fiction. Her major invention was the accidental death of the boy in her care, Charles Cresset, but she came to regret this, believing that it skewed the novel and threw the following one off course. In this, as in all her novels, Antonia was striving after subjective truth: she needed to explain herself to herself, to make sense of this isolated, unknown being. Confessional in tone, cool and precise in her use of language; her self-knowledge and absolution came in the telling, the silent reader the equivalent of the listening priest. Her fiction writing was always a means to another end, seldom driven by its own momentum and lacking in internal impetus. 'I certainly feel NOTHING that could be called "inspiration".'[7] Her occasional poems, on the other hand, came from a different place, and were freighted with an emotional force lacking in the novels. 'All I am interested in at the time is to *express* something which moves me deeply.'[8]

But something had been eased in Antonia's psyche. Even before publication of *The Lost Traveller*, she had managed to begin work on the next novel in her autobiographical sequence. Having set aside an attempt to write about Eric and Tom, both because she felt it would not be fair on her daughters, and because the two main protagonists and their new wives were too present in her life, she turned to the idea of a direct continuation from *The Lost Traveller*. This was to deal with her brief time as an actress in a touring company and her eccentric marriage to Reggie Green-Wilkinson, incarcerated in the bijou house in Chelsea, the eponymous Sugar House. Antonia set up a regime, which she hoped to maintain, of writing '3 pages a day, with Sunday off if I like'.[9] At about the same time, she was proposed for a grant from the Royal Literary Fund. She went through a series of 'alarming' interviews and a means test, and was awarded a sum which paid off all her pressing debts. Much more valuably, however, it gave her a sense of being offically recognised as a writer whose work was worth supporting. Antonia subsequently noticed an 'extraordinary change' in her attitude to this work; 'it must have symbolised a pardon of some kind: an official permission from Society to go on writing.'[10]

Perhaps Dorothy's insistence on the importance of dreams, and the opportunity they gave one to resolve conflicts in relationships long gone, had helped to lance some of Antonia's anger and fear of her father, releasing the creative and intellectual energies needed for her peculiarly autobiographical works. There was a sense of reconciliation that spring. She had begun reading and translating Latin and Greek again and had found it 'a *huge* joy'.[11] In order to earn money she was also reviewing new fiction for the *New Statesman* from January through to July (and intermittently thereafter throughout the fifties), and for the Jesuit publication the *Month*.

When the editor of the *Month*, Father Philip Caraman SJ, asked Antonia if she had any ideas for an article, she recalled the edited version of her letters to Peter Thorp which she had put together for Cyril Connolly eight years before. Unlike Connolly, Caraman did not refuse to publish it. He took it without any changes, and included it in his

August 1950 edition under the title 'Smoking Flax: The Story of a Reconversion'. This article was to impress many, not least the writer Neville Braybrooke, whose lasting memory of it was to be the impetus for the publication, fifteen years later, of the whole collection of Antonia's letters to Thorp, entitled *The Hound and the Falcon*.

The reviews for *The Lost Traveller* were 'madly contradictory', but Antonia accepted them philosophically. 'I am pleased that I have stood up quite well to many very "misunderstanding" and even insulting notices of the book.'[12] The *Times Literary Supplement* thought Miss White carried on the tradition of Charlotte Brontë 'in [the book's] unfolding of a young girl's experiences in coming to grips with the world', although it also attempted to rap her knuckles for making what seemed like a Public Relations pitch for the advantages of belonging to the Catholic Church.[13] The *Guardian* found the novel rich in texture and in the diversity of its scenes, and again mentioned the Catholic viewpoint but with greater sympathy. Emily wrote that she thought it a 'humdinger', although the sudden death of the boy in Clara's charge marred it: 'he could have died more quietly'.[14]

Antonia felt that the fact that she had managed to produce a second novel which had been taken seriously had 'established' her.[15] Another positive step, she believed, was the regular reviewing work she had maintained for the *New Statesman*; for the first time in her life this was a job she had continued to do well, and choosing herself when to quit was a great improvement on her record of being sacked from most of her previous jobs. There was some pleasure in hearing that Janet Adam Smith, the impressive literary editor at the *New Statesman*, had said Antonia was 'irreplaceable' after she resigned at the end of June.

Douglas Jerrold, Antonia's editor at Eyre & Spottiswoode, was keen to follow up *The Lost Traveller* with another novel, and commissioned her to produce the next by the end of June 1951. Writing without constant encouragement was always very difficult for Antonia. She had a revelation about this: 'something so obvious that it is amazing I never spotted it before: the need of an audience. . . . I want the direct impact . . . the actor's vanity . . . whereas the writer must put up with an invisible audience.'[16] *Frost in May* was written solely because Tom had listened; and Dorothy, and latterly Joan Souter-Robertson, had supported her through the production of *The Lost Traveller*. For *The Sugar House*, not only did Antonia lack a friend who could respond with unflagging interest, but she actually had to deal with the emotional demands of someone else in greater need. The writing of her third novel coincided with Susan's nervous breakdown, her incarceration in the Maudsley Hospital and her subsequent painful exit from Ashburn

Gardens. Antonia could be selfless for a short while, and respond with real care and concern when she felt that her actions were beneficial and appreciated, but her natural impatience and her hunger for attention and recognition of her needs were too insistent to ignore for long. As explained to Emily, 'I get so much the feeling of working in a vacuum: no one among my immediate "circle" really cares or is interested & as I always have had great difficulty in believing I could write at all I often feel like a kind of a ghost.'[17]

That summer Antonia took a few weeks' holiday at Binesfield, intending to make real progress on the book, but instead spent time, energy and money on modernising and decorating the cottage. All this expenditure, however, could not alter its basic character which did not suit her, except as a dream, a nostalgic accompaniment to her life since childhood. Practically, it was quite different; 'so dark, decidedly damp and the small rooms and low ceilings are oppressive.'[18] Then, on her return to London in the second week of September, Elaine Lingham, her 'daughter in God', came to see her, having left the Convent before taking her final vows. Antonia's obsessive hurt over Susan's withdrawal from her life was a constant ache 'like an open wound'.[19] Elaine's sudden 'almost miraculous' reappearance in her life meant she could replace the defective favourite daughter with a simulacrum of the ideal and perfect one.[20] Antonia was grateful too for Lyndall's benign presence in the flat. 'Lyndall is very sweet to me & growing up to be quite delightful', but they now lived more independently of each other, which suited both, and Antonia accepted with some residual resentment that Lyndall was absorbed in her own life, and naturally rather keen to keep her mother out of it.[21] With Elaine's help three days a week as her secretary, typing and encouraging, Antonia worked steadily on and by November had finished *The Sugar House* without further anxiety. Jerrold liked the book, although he explained he did not intend to publish it until the following summer.

Antonia thought this third novel more successful than the last. It rambled less, and made use of an acute psychological understanding, learned through her own sufferings and the painful explication of part of their source through psychoanalysis. It revealed an increasingly terrifying vision of the disintegration of a young woman's self, and in the portrait of her marriage we see the touching but doomed relationship between two unhappy, frightened, inadequate people. Subtle and courageous in its candour about sexual fear and madness, *The Sugar House* was a highly personal book and one which Antonia really hoped would be appreciated and understood. She had all along intended to dedicate it to Susan, but by the time she had finished writing they were no longer in communication with each other. Antonia asked Lyndall to find out if her sister still wanted the book to be dedicated to her and was inevitably disappointed and hurt by the casual response; 'Lyn said she just laughed & said "If she wants to, I don't mind."'[22] In a sense Antonia had vested in her daughter the same power over her which her father had once exercised to such ill effect; of approval or disapproval, of acceptance or veto, of love or indifference, of happiness or despair. It was a poisoned chalice to offer in any relationship. By the time *The Sugar House* was published Antonia had become much more sensitive to criticism; Susan was witholding the recognition and approval she craved from those close to her, and she thought that even her friends were more sympathetic to Susan's point of view than to her own. Antonia felt isolated and uncertain again of her own identity; open to others' ridicule and *schadenfreude*.

The literary landscape also was in a process of change. It was the beginning of the ascendancy of the Angry Young Men, epitomised by, among others, William Cooper's *Scenes from Provincial Life*, which was to be followed by Kingsley Amis's *Lucky Jim* and John Osborne's plays, among them *Look Back in Anger*, first performed in 1956. Alongside the swagger of these anarchic, ambitious men, the tentative struggles of an over-sensitive suburban girl, shy of sex and concerned with virtue, seemed irrelevant, even outdated. Antonia also felt that current opinion was peculiarly out of sympathy with Catholicism. Often she felt she was like a social leper, and this and her loneliness made her over-sensitive to the fact that her daughters wanted to get on with their own lives independently of her. She broached with Lyndall her conviction that both her daughters despised her, were unimpressed by her writing and did not wish to introduce her to their friends. Lyndall explained that her main difficulty was with her mother's religion. 'She likes my short stories – especially "The Moment of Truth" – if there is no Catholic reference.' This made Antonia feel better and take Lyndall's lack of enthusiasm less personally, especially as her daughter had said she felt the same embarrassment when she read Graham Greene. However, it gave her pause for thought; 'It certainly is strange, that in modern "intellectual" ... society, no one is in the least disconcerted by homosexuality, but to be a Catholic or to be at all seriously religious is definitely a social handicap!'[23] As for the charge that her daughters lacked affection and respect for her, Lyndall's bleak answer was 'I'm not proud of Tom either'. 'She was rather sweet & trying to be both honest and tactful'; Antonia recognised belatedly how difficult such a question was to answer and was grateful that, at least, she was not alone in her inadequacy as a parent.[24]

The reviews of her novel, Antonia felt, were 'the coldest and most hostile I have ever had'.[25] She was in fact reviewed widely, something which reflected how seriously her work was received, and any publicity department could have put together a glowing collection of cleverly edited quotes. Most reviews were curate's eggs; John Betjeman in the *Telegraph* found that 'as a study in frustration it is subtle and kind'.[26] The *Spectator* thought it 'light, slight and slangily shrewd in its feminine way, Miss Antonia White's new novel is engaging reading. It is, however, only a pale replica of *Frost in May*.'[27] It was Robert Kee's review in the *Observer*, however, which cut deepest of all. It struck Antonia as 'really cruel and spiteful'. In fact it was a review more concerned with the reviewer's own cleverness than with any animus against the book. Holding up certain of her descriptions to ridicule, he ended his piece with, 'As one might expect from a Catholic writer on an off day it is Paradise that suffers; Hell remains fairly convincing.'[28] The hurt for Antonia lay more in the fact that Kee was a friend of her son-in-law, Thomas Chitty, who had himself just published his first novel to great acclaim (*Mr Nicholas*, as Thomas Hinde). Antonia's resultant fear was that, just as she had been shown publicly to be redundant in her daughter's life so was she revealed, by this dismissive reception of her hard-wrought writing, as equally inconsequential to the world of literature. With no word from Susan, it was easy to think that Kee's opinion was also hers and Thomas's. She feared that Susan 'was sniggering over [the review]', but Lyndall assured her mother that Susan had told her she liked the book and preferred it to *The Lost Traveller*. However, it was hard for Antonia not to feel she was considered by everyone who mattered to have had her day, and even that was a short-lived and rather cheerless one. With Thomas's singular critical success with his first novel, and Susan's recent winning of the *Vogue* Talent Contest, which guaranteed a job with Condé Nast, it seemed that the next generation were swiftly sailing away to new adventures on sunlit seas while she, old and no longer seaworthy, was anchored in port and far from home.

This highlighted all the more for Antonia the importance of Elaine Lingham's presence in her life; the help she offered with typing and the all-important encouragement to write continued to great effect. 'I do 3 times as much work having her here.'[29] At the beginning of the year, Antonia had taken on four long translations, *A Pathway to Heaven* by Henri Bordeaux, *Reflections on Life* by Alexis Carrel, *The Cat*, her first Colette translation and Marguerite Duras's novel *A Sea of Troubles*, which she really admired. Antonia had been so inspired by having Elaine to work alongside that she had finished one in two months and finished all four in ten. Paid between £150 and £200 for each translation, she now found herself for the first time in many years in a relatively healthy financial situation; she had managed to pay off most of her debts and felt optimistic about continuing to earn enough from her writing and translating to live. She had also let Susan's old bedroom to a lodger, Daphne Borrett, a friend of Lyndall's, and this added a valuable £8 a month to her income.

The writing of the next novel was slow to start. Before she could really tackle it, however, she was involved with another dramatic flight from home; this time it was by her second daughter, and not, ostensibly, from her mother. Lyndall's affair with Dicky Muir had been gathering apace, accelerated more by his desire than hers. Too unconfident to assert her own wishes and having grown wary, through long training, of emotional scenes, Lyndall had allowed herself to be rushed along on a tide of others' expectations. Suddenly she found herself engaged, a society wedding in the offing, and the world closing in round her before she was even twenty-one. Other supports of her life were falling away. She lost her job, and Susan and Thomas seemed to be moving into a different, increasingly glamorous circle of their own. Perhaps, most unsettling was a strangely critical and almost valedictory letter that Tom gave her on her twenty-first birthday. How much of this was written under Dorothy's influence cannot be known, but he launched into a lecture exhorting Lyndall 'to resist the temptation to blame other people, bad luck, circumstances – or whatever it may be' for the unhappiness she had suffered in her life.[30] With more in this vein, shifting blame for emotional negligence and irresponsibility from the parents on to their children, Tom then turned to the subject of money. He mentioned he had added a present of £50 to the £387 that her matured insurance policy produced, blew her a kiss and wished her well. This was the last time he offered her any financial support. Closed in on by Dicky and marriage, Lyndall fell into the arms of another attractive young man in her social set before running away, with the help of her birthday money, to Italy. Antonia was only told part of the story and through a series of mistimings ended up having to break the news herself to the distraught fiancé and his mother. Only then did she learn that her daughter had got herself into a terrible tangle, telling half-truths to everyone in her desire to avoid causing and enduring more unhappiness.

Lyndall's flight, however traumatic for everyone involved, saw the beginning of a more honest and affectionate mother-daughter relationship between Lyndall and Antonia. Conducted at a distance within the safety of letters, there was a candour and generous-heartedness, with a few hiccups on Antonia's side, which had been difficult to achieve when they were absorbed in the tension of daily life under the same roof. Instead there developed sympathy and mutual support, while Antonia struggled to contain her egotism and envy and her obsessional paranoia about everyone double-crossing her over Susan. Antonia's first letter to Lyndall, once she had fielded the jilted lover and discovered the extent of her daughter's perfidy, was insightful and understanding. Having admonished her for her dishonesty, she set out to reassure her of her support: 'But, my pet, if I don't trust you just at the moment, I *do* love you and you will just have to sneer at that because I shall continue to do so [Dicky had told her Lyndall was "always bitchy"' about her]. . . . But I *do* trust you to this extent . . . that you will let me know if there is anything of any kind I can do for you. Because, my rather naughty Pussy, your idiot Mother does love you and *always* will.'[31] Lyndall, profoundly lonely and shocked by what she had done, however, only took to heart the passages where her mother chided her for her dishonesty and untrustworthiness.

By October 1952, after a hard push to finish the translations, Antonia slipped into a depression which lasted for six months, during which time she was unable to keep up the renewed flow of her own writing. She managed just nine pages of a first draft and 'LONGED to die . . . just so as not to have to go on', as she admitted to Emily. She had eventually gone to her doctor who gave her the 'usual dope', tranquillisers which made her brain feel even more befuddled, and banned her from intellectual work for a fortnight.[32] She cleaned the flat instead, but at the back of her mind was the fear of having a stroke and being unable to work. A sudden stroke had killed her father, and when the pressure in her head became acute Antonia worried that this might be the precursor of something more serious. Her sense of humour did not desert her entirely, however, for she received a late review of *The Sugar House* from one of the provincial papers with a big banner headline: 'COLOURLESS CLARA FADES OUT'. She related in a letter to Lyndall just how apt this seemed to be at the time; 'As that was exactly what Colourless Clara felt as if she were doing at that particular moment, I had to laugh!'[33]

In the midst of her depression the hurt she felt over Susan's silence and Sheila and Silas's cold-shouldering was intensified. When Antonia heard that Sheila had had her baby, she had written a few lines of congratulation and received no acknowledgement; she felt bewildered and erased. 'When people remain deliberately unaware of me, I cease to exist, can make no decisions, do no work . . . a form of mental suicide. . . .'[34] Her loneliness increased with the absence of Elaine from her life; she could no longer afford to employ her, so she had been forced to take on other work and was due to leave for Germany after Christmas. Friends seemed to have fallen away from her. It was distressing to receive a desperate, begging letter from Eric, for so long the stalwart of her life. Alcoholic, poverty-stricken, suicidal, he seemed to be inhabiting an even worse hell than her own and she could offer him little practical or spiritual support, so impoverished were her own resources. Christmas was always of utmost emotional and symbolic importance to Antonia and as she faced this one, with Susan more estranged from her than ever and Lyndall absent and depressed herself in a foreign city, despair overwhelmed her. She wrote a frightening, half-crazed letter to Lyndall, which she knew should not have been sent; the sight of her disintegrated and broken handwriting as terrible as the message it conveyed:

> I don't know how to stand this depression & isolation any more. I can put on an act when I see people or speak on the phone but that is all. . . . Forgive me darling. Take no notice. Sue's cruelty is quite simply destroying me. She wishes I were dead. She cannot wish it more than I do. Do not worry. I am not allowed to kill myself. If I were not a Catholic I would. . . . Nothing I have ever done or could do would make you or Sue unashamed of me. . . . Believe me I do understand. But believe too that I tried to do what I could. I don't know how one lives when all one's springs are broken & one is not allowed to die. . . .[35]

The writing trailed off as if she was slipping over into oblivion. Luckily Lyndall noticed that the envelope had been addressed in the usual firm handwriting and hoped this meant that Antonia had managed to overcome the terror herself. Two days later another letter arrived, apologising for sending the last, but still at the lowest ebb of misery, slipping the knife in again by blaming implicitly both Lyndall and Sue's contempt for her work for her continuing fear of writing. However, in more rational moments Antonia was clear-sighted about the part her own neurosis played. 'This morbid fear of "disapproval" & this awful guilt about writing goes back to the episode at the end of *Frost in May*. Now that my father isn't there to disapprove, I've transferred the terror on to my children as the arch-disapprovers!'[36]

Having not written a poem for years, Antonia suddenly found her dread of a lonely Christmas and pity for herself translated into a heartfelt cry:

In dulci jubilo.
Once in the candleglow
Two faces seraph-bright
Opened round mouths to sing
'*Ubi sunt gaudia*
If that they be not there?'

Wild solstice: all the caked snow of the year
Iron to summer, melted to that sound.
The winter heart awoke; the curtained eye
Couched of its cataract let in the light.

Christmas returns and other children cry
Alpha et O! pursing as sweet mouths round:
Shuttered and dark beneath the clotted snow
No star, no angel penetrates my night. . . .

She called it 'Ubi Sunt Gaudia?' and it was printed in the New Year edition of the *New Statesman*. Tentatively she sent it to Lyndall to read and was delighted that she liked it.

Antonia's demands for approval from her daughters could only bring guilt and recoil on their side, and humiliation and pain on hers. Her relationship with Elaine, on the other hand, was free of these retrogressive associations. She told Lyndall that when she could afford to change her will she intended to make Elaine her literary executor. But this was, like so many things, dependent on her emotional state at the time, and changed after Elaine was absent from her life for a while. When Antonia turned away from her own snagged feelings to discuss Lyndall's life, her affectionate, encouraging self re-emerged and in almost every letter she reiterated her admiration for this daughter's independence and courage. To Emily, Antonia explained something of this growing respect: '[Lyndall] is so sweet but headstrong and inflexible. I have some of her confidence and I think some affection. I feel less worried about her because she has such strong feelings. She's a wild young woman and crazy for pleasure and excitement but she's not afraid of suffering.'[37] For too long Lyndall had existed in the shadow of her mother's obsession with Susan, and now Antonia seemed at last to embrace her with something approaching mother love. It was a love which was lacking in the identification, neuroticism and intrusiveness of her feelings for Susan, something much closer to an unconditional love, and a growing recognition of her individual self. As Susan disappeared into unreality in her mind, Antonia began to appreciate the depths of Lyndall's feelings and nature: 'If I write to you, even if I am shy & conscious of being in uncharted territory, at least I know I am writing to a real person.'[38] It seemed that Antonia felt easier with her daughters opposed in her mind; she did not like to think of them as having a relationship separate from her, but was uneasy also with the idea of all three of them together, with an equal share in a united family. She still could not bear the idea of sharing love, and continually longed to be the only one, the important one, in the lives of her lovers and children.

Meanwhile, Susan was working hard at *Vogue*. She had been profoundly shocked by her breakdown and the depths to which her depression had taken her. Antonia's lack of understanding and sympathy with her mood swings following her discharge from the Maudsley Hospital had reinforced her sense of rejection; both were insulated from appreciating the seriousness of each other's illness and despair. 'My sanity, even my life, were matters that did not concern my mother' was Susan's bleak interpretation of this blindness to her needs.[39] Having made her painful progress back to a new life, Susan was afraid that any contact with her own mother might destroy this hard-won stability. She told Bridget Speaight, a friend of Antonia's, '[Mother] was a destructive influence & must not be allowed to cross the threshold of their "little citadel".'[40] Of course, Susan and her mother were also engaged in a covert power struggle; having been at the mercy all her life of Antonia's wilfulness and critical attention, there was some satisfaction in holding the whip hand in the relationship at last. The sense of anxiety such powerlessness caused Antonia reached such a pitch that she was afraid to go to a film or a play in case Susan should be there, almost as if she had been a jilted by a lover.

Antonia's obsessional nature and desperate need to punish herself did not help. Emily had such confidence in her own righteousness that she was capable of being brutally frank – and sometimes strikingly true in her observations. She gave her unsolicited analysis of the situation in a letter to Antonia: 'You think of yourself . . . as a poor abused little loving mother! You can't see yourself as a jaw that threatens to swallow them.'[41]

However, as the depression lifted, Antonia's mind could turn to more productive things. The book, ever waiting in the wings, needed to be addressed. One of the positive results of her suffering over Susan's withdrawal was her greater understanding of and sympathy for her own parents. She was particularly moved by the thought of what they endured during her incarceration in Bethlem Hospital, when they were having to come to terms with the possibility that they would never see their beloved only child again. 'One comes to love and understand them in an *entirely* new way. Also one rediscovers them in oneself which is awfully queer and disconcerting . . . and yet rather wonderful too.'[42] She used to think lovers suffered most, she wrote in her diary, but now she knew it was parents who really suffered. It was parents also who were the most loyal to their children, as Antonia was to write in her next novel, *Beyond the Glass*. 'Mothers are more faithful than lovers'; however, when the fictional mother said that, with tears in her eyes, she was thinking of the suffering of her daughter, rather than of herself.[43]

Antonia wanted to explore in this next book her parents' experiences, dealing with their characters with more insight and compassion. 'I'm very moved by the father. At the time it all happened I was too absorbed in my own predicament even to *think* of what *he* must have felt.'[44] She drew a poignant, well-rounded portrait of them both, keeping faith with her all the while, and suffering, while she retreated into her own much more vivid reality. There was a fond drawing of Eric too, in the incarnation of the wise and whimsical pedant, Clive Heron. In a sense it was a memorial to him also for, although still alive, in a sense he was lost to her, the harshness and disappointments of life having robbed him of the unruffled, philosophical intellect which had been the calm eye for her in many storms. But *Beyond the Glass* was fundamentally about madness, about disorientation, disconnection, free-wheeling in a different dimension where ordinary laws, expectations and the external constraints of the self, and that self's relation with others, no longer held sway. 'I *wanted* to get the irony that when she feels most "real", she is, actually, most false', she explained to Emily.[45] Antonia conjured brilliantly in this book the thrill of extreme experience, the ecstasy and terror of a mind cut loose to race with the the wind and the tides, never certain how, or when, or whether, it could return. Like the Ancient Mariner, with whom she closely identified, Antonia was on a journey over which she had no direct control: her nightmare visions described in prose of poetic power. Like the Ancient Mariner, she believed her suffering was punishment for some terrible sin she had committed inadvertently, echoing the terror from her convent days that she might fall from a state of grace, risking eternal damnation – yet never know.

The beginning of the book was hard labour, and only by June 1953 was Antonia really under way, having scrapped her previous attempts. When she got to the part where her altered consciousness began the ascent to madness, the euphoric, telepathic love story with Robert, her writing started to flow; 'something "took over" and I'm not sure if it's good or bad.'[46] Recreating the period when she was out of control and freed from inhibitions and constraints seemed to have a similar liberating effect on her writing; 'I also feel almost as if someone else had written it . . . especially the asylum part where I worked with a speed and intensity that I've never known before so that it was almost like being possessed.'[47] By April 1954 she was finished, amazed that she had managed to produce another novel and proud of it, 'rather "in love" with it' in fact, certain that there was more power in it than anything she had done before. The critics generally responded well; no longer was *Frost in May* the ghost at the feast. Antonia was satisfied that this book had brought her the recognition she craved.

The novel ended with Clara reluctant to go forward into life, with the asylum, a broken marriage and a lost lover all behind her, a featureless horizon ahead. Rather ominously, perhaps, the extremity of experience in the grip of 'the beast' still seem to Clara more seductive and real than any of the vaunted advantages of a life in the palm of sanity. Antonia was fifty-five and almost until the day she died, twenty-six years later, she tried desperately to write the next stage of Clara's journey. So compulsive were her attempts, so pathological the reasons for her failure, that the effort at times almost drove her to madness. Clara was never to leave that limbo, but Antonia nearly killed herself with the contradictory impulses which urged her on to pursue her story and the public explication of her life, and yet drove her back cramped by fear of exposure, her impossible drive for perfection, and her obsession with the past.

Antonia felt she had been a terrible failure as a woman; with sadness she could accept this and still go on, but her true identity could only be confirmed by her writing. If she was not a writer then she was nothing. If all the sacrifices had been in vain, then she was just a destructive force who had laid waste to her life. So the struggle to touch others, and in the process to save herself from nonentity, had to go on, even though it became painfully self-defeating in the end. A passage Antonia had found in Dickens's *Little Dorrit*, which she had opened at random, was resonant with her own nature and she copied it into her diary: ' "She was inspired to be something which was not what the rest were and to be that something, different and laborious, for the sake of the rest". That's what I forget: [she added] it is, in the end, *for the sake of the rest*.'[48]

23

More Troublesome Women

No one was ever less self-sufficient than I. . . .
Or more helplessly undecided and at the mercy of impulse. . . .
I need *incessant* encouragement.

8 June 1955, unpublished diaries

Loneliness, fear of poverty, and vanity now made Antonia prey to another of her mad, mystical women: it took her months to recognise the fact and more than six years to extricate herself from her clutches, the trap having been honeyed with extravagant praise and offers of money. In January 1953 Antonia was at a low and lonely point in her life, recovering from a bout of flu, her daughters flown from her, Elaine about to leave for Germany, Tom and Eric distanced and estranged. Suddenly a woman called Virginia Johnes 'exploded' into her life.[1] She was the deranged Catholic wife of a Kensington antiques dealer, Raymond Johnes, and she bombarded Antonia with letters – sometimes up to three in one day – phone calls and visits. Obsessed with Antonia's work, she claimed it as a joint effort and eventually as her own – 'The Catholic Novel', as she called the Nanda/Clara quartet collectively.

Antonia described her in a letter to Lyndall as 'a kind of Catholic Kingsmill without the Kingsmill liveliness and good looks. . . . She's bossy . . . morbid and fearfully & unnecessarily unattractive'.[2] Rather late in the day, Antonia realised that like Dorothy, Virginia Johnes set out to make her feel guilty. Father Bartlett, a Catholic priest who knew the woman well, had advised Antonia to be brutal '[he] says she is mad and "has her breakdowns on other people".'[3] But Antonia was not to be warned. In part she felt sorry for someone who was in a crisis '& feel I'm the last person to slam the door in a neurotic's face'.[4] Perhaps Antonia saw in this one the possibility of an encouraging friendship, someone who admired her work and would give her the sort of reassurance she needed now that she felt so isolated and alone. Certainly, the intimations of financial help were always a hook on which she would impetuously impale herself. Virginia Johnes had recently come into an £8,000 inheritance and her offers of gifts or loans against royalties were hard for Antonia to ignore: 'receiving money does give me a particular thrill – a sense of warmth, security & exhilaration.'[5]

Johnes's next strategy for gaining a measure of control over Antonia was more insidious; she started to deposit, anonymously, sums of money in Antonia's account. The first miraculous materialisation of £50 appeared in July 1953 and, naturally, was welcomed as if it was an answer to a prayer. By February 1956, when Antonia discovered for sure exactly who was the 'Anonymous Donor', she had already accepted a loan of £500 which Johnes had put pressure on her to take as an advance on royalties. In this way, Antonia was caught in the trap of obligation and gratitude. But she also liked Virginia Johnes who, in her lucid moments, was intelligent, generous-hearted and affectionate. She was liable, however, to terrible reversals in character and behaviour and, during the bad spells, frightened and exhausted Antonia. Like Emily, she had 'enormous energy' and was 'unsnubbable' but lacked Emily's grandeur of character and lovableness.[6]

Until she could pay off the loan, and now the anonymous donations too, which Virginia Johnes then claimed she needed back to stave off her own financial collapse, Antonia could not ignore the woman and extricate herself easily from her life. After a particularly distressed letter from Mrs Johnes, threatening suicide as the only honourable alternative to banckruptcy, Antonia sought help and advice from the Prioress at the Carmelite priory and from Father Victor White. Within a day she received a cheque for £300 from the Carmelites with which to pay off Mrs Johnes, so that the money then was owing to them. The Prioress suggested Antonia forget about the anonymous donations, for she had known about them and would be a witness that they were gifts. This 'pure, exquisite, heroic charity' was compounded by the Prioress telling Antonia that she had 'genius' and must continue to write novels because 'the world needs them'.[7]

What had begun as a flattering mystery had turned into a time-consuming irritant and eventually a persecution which distressed Antonia and distracted her from the real necessities of her own life and the demands of her work. But while the donations continued to arrive anonymously (and she had hoped for a while that they were from a genuine admirer, probably male) they had increased her feelings of security and the sense of being appreciated. The book was written, the flat decorated and clothes bought. Some good came out of an unpromising brew of derangement, duplicity, domination and personal distress.

Before she could enjoy this treat, however, Antonia had to deal with various legal disputes and problems, the first of which was the unhappy custody battle between Gerti and Tom Hopkinson following their divorce, and Tom's immediate remarriage to Dorothy Kingsmill in March 1953. Tom and Dorothy had requested that his daughters, Nicolette who was now eleven and Amanda, aged four, should spend most of the holidays with them, but Gerti and Nicolette felt unable to countenance such an agreement, largely due to their antipathy towards Dorothy. Most people who knew Tom had been struck by how much of his will and personality seemed to have been subsumed in Dorothy's. Never the most definite of men, he had seemed to have become even fonder and more foolish under Dorothy's Circean spell. Dorothy was widely held to have 'occult' powers of some kind which she used to influence susceptible people. In fact 'the Witch' was one of the descriptions given to her by Antonia and others, like Graham Greene, who recognised some power in her for good or ill. Even Tom's generous-hearted and sensible sister Esther, an Anglican nun, was dismayed at the change in her brother; 'he seems unrecognisable as the person she knew.'[8]

Antonia felt partly responsible for the whole unhappy business; she had been the one to introduce Dorothy to Tom, thinking she might help Gerti through her debilitating depression and save the marriage. In fact the absolute opposite had happened, with more than a little help, it was suspected, from Dorothy who was newly-widowed, unhappy, impoverished and fearful for her own future. Nevertheless, it was with some reluctance that Antonia acceded to Gerti's request that she write an affidavit supporting her case that the children should not be required to spend so much time with their father and step-mother. So difficult was this delicate task that she took a whole week to write it and emerged from the ordeal wrung out like a rag. Part of her case was a statement that 'although I had been willing for [Lyndall] to go & live with Tom & Gerti, if his wife had been Dorothy, I should have objected strongly'.[9] Both Gerti and Antonia felt that Dorothy would attempt to estrange the children from Gerti. Antonia also enclosed the threatening letters she had received from her after their friendship had broken down, as evidence of Dorothy's unpredictable nature. With this help from Antonia, when the case was eventually heard the following year, Gerti was successful, in so far as the judge modified Tom's custody rights to eight days each holiday. But despite Antonia's care in her wording of her statement, her support of Tom's second wife against him was to widen the rift between her and him, a matter of sadness for Antonia who liked to keep an emotional connection with all her ex-husbands and lovers.

Possibly in punishment for this alliance against him and Dorothy, Antonia received a solicitor's letter, less than two months later, informing her that at Tom's request they were applying to have her maintenance order annulled. This pushed all the panic buttons; her fear of penury, her sense of powerlessness and her loss of a loved one. Not only was she frightened as to how she was to manage without the £20 a month which represented her only regular income, 'my basic life-line', but she also felt it was dismissive and uncaring of Tom not to have spoken or written to her himself, but to put it into the cold, and expensive, hands of solicitors.[10] She could not believe that this was behaviour which 'the old Tom' ever would have contemplated, and could only blame the change on Dorothy's influence.

Fortunately, her solicitor felt she had a good case, and in an out-of-court settlement Antonia was to get the legal minimum, a sum she would have been happy to accept in the first place; £12 a month net of tax. But it distressed her deeply to think what a complicated web of deceits, hurts, estrangements, partisan camps and double-dealing had enmeshed her closest family relations. She and Susan were adamantly estranged; Susan was very close to Silas and Sheila who had cut off all communication with Antonia; Susan was growing closer to Tom and Dorothy with whom Antonia had very little contact because of Dorothy; Susan's husband Thomas had been appointed to a job at Shell after some initial introductions from Tom. Lyndall was in largely affectionate communication with Antonia and with Susan, but was increasingly estranged from Tom over Dorothy; Gerti did not trust Lyndall because she tried to maintain her relationship with Tom; but Lyndall was also very fond of her half-sisters, Nicolette and Amanda and wished to go on seeing them. Antonia became jealous and suspicious when Lyndall continued on friendly terms too with Silas and Sheila; she also felt fundamentally betrayed by everyone who was friends with both herself and Susan, and yet had not intervened on her behalf. The atmosphere was rancid with accusations, suspicions and duplicity. The person who needed to travel most freely between these factions was Lyndall and only when reminded of this did Antonia become aware of how impossible it was for her younger daughter to be the go-between in such poisonous circumstances, and not get blamed by everyone.

According to Lyndall and Joan Souter-Robertson, Susan was in fact more ready to mend the breach between herself and her mother, particularly after she became a mother herself. But those who were close to her, most notably Sheila and Silas, for their own reasons, as well as a genuine love for her and concern for her state of mind, counselled maintenance of the *status quo*. Silas came to believe at some point after his disastrous love affair and engagement to Antonia that she was possessed of something evil. This may have come from his own observations and knowledge of her character and deeds; it may have been an expression of his dislike of the more lurid forms of Catholicism in which he had witnessed her involvement during the Benedicta experience; or it may have been as a result of conversations with Djuna, who never really liked Antonia and who had accused her, during their Bacchantic holidays, of being a wicked little Borgia in her treatment of her men, especially Silas.

A small incident heightened Antonia's feelings of being a complete pariah, an outcast in her own country, convicted of crimes to which no one had put a name. While shopping in Harrods one day, she suddenly found herself alone in a lift with Sheila Glossop. She had not seen or spoken to her for nearly two years. Sheila greeted her stiffly with a 'Good Morning' which Antonia returned, but so shaken was she that she said nothing else. However, finding Sheila next to her as they both went to return library books, she thought perhaps the time had come to try and make contact again – after all she had always liked Sheila, and hated this continuing cold war. Following her out of the department she caught up with her and said, ' "I'd so much like to have a word with you, Sheila, but it's entirely up to you." She turned & stared at me stonily for a full minute and then said icily "I can't imagine anything I could possibly say to you, Tony." '[11]

This confrontation came the day after the letter had arrived from Tom's solicitor, and the two blows together cracked the fragile peace of mind Antonia had constructed for herself, which had allowed her to work steadily for the past few months. Once more she felt paralysed, worthless and alone. But earning money was as imperative as ever and when she was offered a last minute job reviewing *The Taming of the Shrew* at Stratford for the *Spectator* she took it, even though it would earn her no more than a couple of guineas. After six hours of travelling there and back, she ended up finishing her piece in the Ladies' lavatory at Paddington having returned on the 8.30 train the following day. Her copy was delivered to the office by noon, 'Pheugh!', as she exclaimed in a letter to Lyndall.[12]

For some time Antonia had been trying to get out more and do as much as she could in an effort to stop herself from brooding about the unhappy familial situation. Three months previously she had accepted an invitation to give a lecture to the Newman Society dinner in

Birmingham. In her usual perfectionist way she spent a long week working on it, twenty pages of notes, a frantic eight hours' polishing and rewriting at the last minute, only to deliver it to sixteen people who would have preferred an impromptu talk – and told her so. The last time she had been in Birmingham was for her stolen weekends with Silas twenty-four years before, and now amongst the priests, respectable Catholics of the old school and earnest undergraduates, she felt as out of place 'as a cat at a dog-show.'[13]

Then, without warning on April Fool's Day, Antonia learnt of another difficult female intent on affecting her life, claiming she had been injured intentionally by something Antonia had written. A little-known actress called June Sylvaine objected to the fact that Antonia had called a dim actress who had a walk-on part in *The Sugar House* by the same name as hers. She claimed to look like the fictional character whom Antonia had described as 'a voluptuous redhead ... who was only twenty and had an extremely pretty face [and] had hoped to play the leading ingenue but, being decidedly fat, had been cast as the comic elderly cook.'[14] Sylvaine's solicitors were trying to make out that Antonia was a rival actress trying to ruin their client's career. Antonia pointed out that as this novel was set in the early 1920s it was before the real June Sylvaine was born and could not possibly be referring to this young woman. Her publishers, Eyre and Spottiswoode, however, thought they had better take the threat seriously, and all copies of the book were recalled; they refused even to sell one to Antonia to give to Emily. The case, delayed by Miss Sylvaine's solicitors, took three and a half years to come to court and grew in self-importance on the way. The bit part, who had sixteen lines in the original story, became, through the prosecuting solicitors' distorting lens, the 'principal character' of the novel.[15] Antonia had her suspicions that it was all a publicity stunt worked up by the real Miss Sylvaine's press agent. When it finally came to court, with the now famous libel expert Peter Carter-Ruck acting for Antonia, it was a historic case, the first to be tried since the new Defamation Act was passed, an act meant to prevent these actions about a pure coincidence of name. Although Antonia had persuaded influential writers like Sir Compton Mackenzie and Graham Greene to be witnesses for her, she had no one to support her personally. Lyndall had sent a much appreciated telegram of encouragement but no word had come from Susan, although Antonia had hoped, rather wanly, that this case might have breached the wall of silence. However, Eric Siepmann, with his wife Mary, was back in Antonia's life again. When Mary Siepmann realised Antonia was to endure this court appearance alone she volunteered to accompany her, and sat beside her for the two days, stifling giggles when accusations got too preposterous (it was all a Catholic plot, it was suggested by Miss Sylvaine's counsel, to discredit the young actress because her father was a lapsed Catholic). A gruelling cross-examination by a 'really *nasty*' opposing counsel, in front of an unsympathetic judge, was relieved of its full sting by this friend's presence; 'she was an angel . . . just the right mixture of sympathy & fun.'[16] The defence was a shambles, Antonia thought the whole trial a cross between Kafka and *Alice in Wonderland*. She lost the case, or rather her publishers lost, and had awarded against them costs of £1,000 and compensation of £200 for the damage to Miss Sylvaine's reputation. When Antonia's publisher heard the verdict he declared 'This is the end of publishing'.[17]

Just after the news of June Sylvaine's projected libel case against her, Antonia received one of Emily's characteristically headlong letters; in intimate contact as always with the Holy Family she now had them acting as unofficial travel agents. 'I'm going to give you a shock! If I can get my passport in time, I am sailing for England *May* 6, on the *Queen Mary*. Can you beat it? It was all arranged by our Lady.'[18] In her lonely fastness, struggling with a book which was proving to be as intractable as the rest, Antonia was overjoyed at the thought of Emily back in her life. She said she would meet the boat train and offered to put her up for as long as she needed. Her impetuous overblown expectations could never be fulfilled in real life, and the last time Emily had come to England in 1947 had not been a success. But this time Emily and Antonia in the flesh were not such a disappointment to each other. 'She was here two nights . . . in splendid form & *very* sweet', Antonia reported to Lyndall.[19]

Emily informed her she was here for the rest of her life but, to Antonia's puzzlement, her entire luggage consisted of a small weekend case containing one pair of shoes, nylon pants, blouse, dressing-gown and nightdress, and two carrier bags – one filled with books, the other with tinned food and cigarettes for friends. The only thing being sent on by her daughter-in-law was the sheepskin lining for her coat when the weather got cold. As it turned out, Emily was to live in Rye in Sussex for many years before moving into a retreat guesthouse at Stanbrook Abbey, an enclosed Benedictine convent at Callow End near Worcester. She was only to return to America fifteen years later in 1968 to stay at a Catholic Worker's farm, where she eventually died in 1974. Hers was the great lasting friendship of Antonia's life; she was the one person who could weather Antonia's emotional storms without harm, for they paled in comparison with the force of Emily's own tempestuous nature. ' "The Kingdom of Heaven suffereth violence and the violent take it by force" – I always used to think that applied to Emily', Antonia wrote in memory of her, adding, 'She was more than life size, with enough vitality for at least half-a-dozen people.'[20] People were attracted to her for this all her life: generous-hearted and optimistic, she included Antonia with herself in the category of genius, and cheered her friend on when she too appeared to be striving for the saintly. 'No, darling, I am most emphatically NOT a saint,' Antonia was moved once to remark, 'only trying desperately to behave dimly like a Catholic!'[21] Both in their different ways strove to be artists and good Catholics, both bemoaned the mess they had made of their lives as women, in the guise of wives, lovers and mothers. 'You & I have genius', Emily had once explained to Antonia. 'This is a Force, & must go its own way. It is not the way of others. When such people have children, a terrible current & counter-current is set up, that almost kills the children.'[22] She was thinking of Antonia's anguish over Susan's defection when she wrote that, and also the psychiatric problems of her only son Johnny.

The two women also shared a love of cats. Domina, Antonia's beloved and demanding black and white cat, died in September, at the end of Lyndall's first visit to London since her escape to Rome the previous year. She and Antonia had had a very happy couple of weeks in each other's company and it was a relief for Antonia to have a sympathetic presence with her at Domina's end. When Lyndall went round that evening to see Susan and Thomas she told her sister about Domina's death. She reported back to her mother; 'Sue was very sweet: she even asked Lyn if she thought I would like one of her next litter of Siamese kittens.'[23] Thomas then apparently came into the room and forbade such a gift, but Antonia told Emily that she was deeply touched by this sign of her daughter's humanity towards her.

Emily immediately wrote offering Antonia a kitten from her own cat's litter which had yet to be born. Antonia's reservations about not being able to bear the pain of loving another pet who would one day die were quickly overcome, and a little marmalade Tom was selected for her. He was to be named Coeur de Lion or Curdy, and Antonia was due to pick him up from Rye at the end of November. But before she could keep her date with Curdy, the head of the Children of Mary, the old convent girls' organisation, rang her up to ask her to take a four-month-old female Siamese who was in urgent need of a good home. Antonia had always secretly longed for a Siamese cat, and despite demurring at replacing Domina with even one cat she now decided on a 'crazy conclusion to have Both Pussies'.[24] This is how the famous Minka arrived in her life. Antonia's series of letters to Emily charting the introduction of these two to each other, her discovery of their natures and how she adapted her life to fit, have all the delightful detail, affection, charm and insights which she put into the two *jeu d'esprits* named after them, the novellas *Minka and Curdy* and *Living with Minka and Curdy*.

> Dearest Emily,
> Hasty first report from the battlefront! NO signs of truce yet. Minka is practically having a nervous breakdown from rage & jealousy. . . . As soon as I got home (Curdy slept peacefully all the way in the train: was let out of basket in taxi & promptly stood up and admired the lights of London, purring with excitement) I handed basket with Curdy for Denise [lodger] to unpack behind closed door. Minka flew into my arms, purring madly, so delighted to have me home. But oh, oh, when I tried a tactful introduction! She not only swore at kitten but when I took her out to comfort her, swore and chattered at me in a nervous frenzy of emotion.
> I took her into the kitchen to give her some food to calm her. She wouldn't touch it. At that moment Curdy escaped from Denise, trotted into the kitchen & seeing some nice rabbit, ate it under Minka's nose which did not improve their relations. I took Curdy up to show him his tray: he examined it & decided he preferred Minka's & used *that*! . . .
> Thank goodness for Curdy's wonderful temperament. He is rather frightened but stands up to her. She has not attacked him but growls & threatens him all the time. I *daren't* fuss him in front of her which is agony because he is *adorable*. I'm afraid of making her more jealous. She is so deeply hurt in her feelings that even when playing on her own she suddenly remembers her grievance and starts growling at her ping-pong ball. . . .
> At the moment they are in my room & mercifully asleep. Curdy has been trying to type & also to eat a page of my manuscript. . . . Minka, sulking even in sleep, is in her basket. There is no immediate prospect of peace but I have hopes of time healing etc. etc. . . . [25]

Showing far greater empathy, patience and psychological insights than she ever managed with her own young children, Antonia gave up work for a week while she concentrated on learning about these two disparate characters, and encouraged and reassured them into a real friendship. Minka and Curdy continued to provide Antonia with endless diversion and much appreciated affection for the rest of their lives: a few days later, she wrote a postscript on the back of the envelope of another letter to her friend: 'Five minutes ago, C de L came up & planted himself in the chair where M was sleeping. She looked cross, said nothing. I held my breath, did not push him away. I praise her for her forbearance and she purred. As I write this, they have settled down to sleep with C de L's head propped against M's flank! VICTORY!'[26]

Joan Souter-Robertson recalled how to watch Antonia with her cats was to see her transformed by love. Nothing was too much trouble for her. Despite her efforts to maintain a strict control on her external life – exactly the right cups for tea, a particular order for performing of household tasks – in the shape of two independent-minded felines Antonia welcomed into her working and living space an energy she could neither order nor control. Minka and Curdy, like her cats before them, slept with her, waking her up at unsociable hours if they needed entertainment, letting out or just wanted more space in the bed. They squeezed behind her on her desk chair, forcing her to write perched on the end. They sat on her manuscript and played with her pens. When kittens, they crapped on her bed, swung from the curtains and tipped over the milk. One of her fashionable turbans was appropriated by Curdy as a daybed. In order to distract them from distracting her when she was working, Antonia made the dining room into a 'Cats' Gymnasium' with branches suspended from the ceiling and ping-pong balls from the chairs. Her cats dictated their terms to Antonia and she seemed happy to comply. It was a relationship which, in its simplicity, was quite unlike any human relationship for her. Her love and care for her animals was rewarded with unquestioning devotion, quiet accept-ance and their companionship for life. They were the living versions of the toy dog Mr Dash, the passionately-loved companion of her solitary childhood; her cats were the confidantes and faithful partners in her solitary personal life.

Just as Antonia was taking delivery of the two new kittens who were going to share her life for nearly eighteen years, so her daughter Susan's life was changing with the birth of her first child, Antonia's first grandchild, Andrew Chitty. When Lyndall had last seen Susan in September and told her about Domina's death she had been sworn to secrecy about the imminent baby. On the verge of returning to Rome, having had such a close and easy time with Antonia, she was unhappy at having to keep such a huge secret from the mother who was now much more a friend than the enemy. 'I couldn't bear you to find out by chance . . . and know that I'd known for months', Lyndall explained to her mother, and went on to say that Susan was not to know that she had broken her confidence.[27] Antonia's first reaction was one of hurt and shock that once more she was deliberately to be left in the dark about something so important. But this gave way to a more philosophical calm. 'I feel more concerned about *her* now, knowing about the baby, and less about my own hurt feelings. A good thing, too! I can't do anything but pray for her more than ever & that's mercifully something no Sheila or Thomas can stop me from doing!'[28] However, she was put into a difficult position by a letter from Tom's father writing in early November, taking for granted that she knew about the expected baby and saying how concerned she must be about its apparent tardiness in coming into the world. On the spur of the moment and in the middle of writing a letter to Lyndall, Antonia rang up her elder daughter. Susan answered the phone; this was the first time Antonia had heard her voice in twenty-two months. There followed an affable conversation, as she reported in breathless style to Lyndall:

> I said I had to answer Grandfather's letter somehow & that now I knew & was awfully pleased she was having a baby I naturally wanted to know how she was said she probably had her own reasons for not telling me & for the whole thing & she said she had & I could probably guess what they were. I said I couldn't & I'd constantly written asking her to tell me. And she actually said, quite nicely, that she wd. write to me & explain. I told her not to do anything that wd. upset her. She said she was feeling fine & expecting the baby any moment & had meant to tell me when it arrived.[29]

The explanatory letter was not forthcoming, and Antonia continued to comb the Announcements column of *The Times* in order to know when the baby was born. Andrew Chitty finally came into the world on 20 November, and Antonia sent a telegram of congratulation. Two weeks after his birth, when she had still heard nothing, the bitterness of her exclusion struck again. It was particularly galling to think that Tom and Dorothy, for instance, would see her grandson before she would be allowed to. She swore to Lyndall that she had at last reached the limits of her ability to endure and she was giving up hopes of any kind of reconciliation; exhausted by two years of speculation, anxiety, hurt, anger, remorse, and hopes raised only to be dashed again. This callous treatment of her had destroyed her affection for Susan, she declared.

None of this in the end was true, and by the following summer she was tiptoeing up to a pram parked outside the Chittys' flat in the Little Boltons, hoping to catch a glimpse of her grandson, only to find it empty. When she heard from Lyndall that the baby had red hair, she wrote back 'I've always longed for a red-haired grandson!'[30] But for a while the snippet of news relieved Antonia of the gnawing obsession with the situation, which had driven her thought processes into ever-decreasing circles of accusation, abjection and self-pity.

The end of 1953 saw Antonia more philosophical about all the areas of her life. Consoled always by the structure of lists, she summed up the year in the customary end of term report in her diary:

> I think the *nicest* thing in 1953 was having Lyn at home for a fortnight. The most painful Sue's not telling me about the baby. The most upsetting that meeting with Sheila in Harrods. The most alarming, Tom's solicitors threat. The luckiest, the [anonymous] donor. Most comforting, Emily's return.
>
> Spiritually, what can I say? I think nothing but an *enormous* need for gratitude. . . . Our Lady has showered me with kindness all the year . . . even to the two kittens. . . .[31]

24

Loss, Love and Loss

'Our family situation – one could almost call it our family curse – goes on & on.'

17 September 1955, *Diaries I*

The Anonymous Donor had sent Antonia a return air ticket to Rome for her fifty-fifth birthday in March: after a prolonged period of solid work her last novel, *Beyond the Glass*, was finished by mid-April, and suddenly she was on her way. She was to spend most of May in Italy. Lyndall was working at the Food and Agriculture Organisation at the United Nations and for the first two weeks of Antonia's stay the routine consisted of Antonia visiting the sights in the morning while Lyndall worked, meeting for lunch in the FAO canteen and then catching the bus back to the villa Lyndall shared with two friends, to rest and study her Italian. For the last ten days, Lyndall joined her on holiday. They set off together on a tour up to Tuscany and Umbria. The weather was disappointing but the holiday was a great success for them both, despite having to share a room and Antonia being an irrepressible snorer. Even to a sensation-seeker like Antonia, Rome was almost too intense an experience; the richness and contrasts of its visual character and the insistent and polyphonic noise were too much for her to capture in her diary, instead she needed to reflect and savour the memories; 'I just want to chew the cud peacefully.'[1] Ancient ruins lay around like pieces from a grand stage set while people and traffic vied for right of way down the narrowest of alleys. Antonia had always been wary of crossing even sedate London streets; here in the maelstrom of Vespas, Lambrettas, lurching buses and anarchic speedsters she gave up and remained on her bus, sometimes until it was on its return journey if it meant being deposited on the right side of the road for the museum or gallery she wanted to visit. The beauty of the countryside Lyndall drove her through was easier to evoke in words: 'The pleated mountains outside Siena: the castle-crowned hills: the cream oxen with long horns. . . . The altar boy tucking his little brother under his arm. The great moths outside the window at Assisi. . . .'[2] It was much more than a holiday; it was an experience which was to nourish her for months. The film *Three Coins in a Fountain* she saw solely to be able to revisit Rome in memory.

Lyndall had shown her a recent photograph of Susan with Andrew, who was then almost seven months old. Antonia was struck by the well-shaped head and charm of the baby and how Susan's face, inclined, had a likeness to her own. Momentarily, the old serpent raised its head; the suspicion that Lyndall – and everyone else she knew – had some secret knowledge about why Susan, and the Glossops specifically, were treating her in this way. But this was fleeting. Antonia was sensitive to Lyndall's generosity in organising such a wonderful tour and giving unstintingly of her time and energy. She wrote on her return to London full of thanks and a real admiration for her ability to manage the artistic and practical in life with such aplomb; 'I felt so proud of my beautiful daughter and I was absolutely dazzled by your prowess as driver & interior decorator & your general savoir-faire and savoir-vivre.'[3] The greatest pleasure of all, she said, was being able to see so much of her.

The return to London brought further complications with her will. Antonia had finally got round to making a new will just before she left for Italy, leaving her possessions and royalties to Lyndall, whose financial precariousness she was concerned about, taking for granted that her father's will leaving the cottage and his royalties to Susan was valid. She had also made Lyndall her literary executor. However, when her solicitor Eichholz was dealing with this he mentioned something that had been worrying him for more than a year. He had discovered that, due to a technicality, Susan was not the beneficiary of her grandfather's will. He had used the words 'eldest grand-daughter' (he died before Lyndall was conceived) and had not named Susan specifically. Her illegitimacy meant that legally she would be passed over in favour of Lyndall, who was legitimate. This then meant that Antonia had to 'turn my own will completely upside down' and leave everything she had to Susan, now that it seemed that Lyndall would inherit the cottage and whatever royalties still emerged from her grandfather's share in the Hillard and Botting textbooks. (The will was to go through a few more metamorphoses before she died and the seemingly so scrupulous Eichholz, after his death a few years later, would be unmasked as a prodigious embezzler of his clients' money: nearly half a million pounds, it was suspected.) Antonia had mixed emotions about this unexpected complication. She genuinely felt sorry for Susan, who had always thought, as they all did, that the cottage would be hers one day, and was guilty too that it was Susan's illegitimacy, which Antonia accepted as her fault, that was to deny her elder daughter her rightful inheritance.

However, Antonia could not repress a slight thrill at the sense of power regained, of retribution delivered, as she contemplated the possible impact of this news on Susan's fortress stance against her: 'I wonder if this *real* blow and grievance might not even have a good effect. . . . She was such a grabber in the old days, even to shamelessly grabbing things of mine on the pretext that they would automatically be hers one day.' Antonia wondered if in fact only Susan's conceit would suffer, but then she reminded herself that that too could be laid at her own door; 'of course that pathological conceit may be her defence against insecurity. And security, though I tried really hard to give it to her from the Tom divorce time, I never could make her feel. How could I when I not only felt, but was, so desperately insecure myself? . . . I sometimes wonder if there was ever such a tangle as ours.'[4] In fact, Susan took the news very well, when it was unemotionally explained by the diplomatic family solicitor. After Eichholz's death, the solicitor who replaced him, on Antonia's urging, looked into the terms of her father's trust again and discovered that Lyndall could make 'a deed of gift' renouncing her interest in Binesfield in favour of Susan. This Lyndall gladly did, and everyone felt the spirit of the will was finally honoured.

Lyndall's view, which she periodically expressed, was that her sister was not violently opposed to seeing Antonia again but was unduly influenced by Sheila and Silas's concern for her welfare which, in their interpretation of the situation, meant continuing the embargo. Thomas too, was not about to encourage his wife's renewal of relations; he was an atheist who was naturally suspicious of the toils of Antonia's religion. He also had not had much opportunity to get to know Antonia before the frightening rollercoaster of Susan's mental breakdown, attempted suicide and incarceration had overtaken events. Thomas and Antonia had joined forces effectively to prevent electric shock treatment being administered to Susan, but the subsequent falling out between mother and daughter followed close behind, and events overtook the individual relationships involved. Thomas felt then that Susan's relationship with her mother was directly responsible for her breakdown, and Antonia could only agree that, subconsciously at least, that could well have been true. It never occurred to her that her manic-depressive mental illness and Susan's had a genetic component which had little to do with will. Antonia carried such an inflated view of her own sinfulness and guilt that she had truly believed that her lapse from the Church had doomed her father to purgatory, and her return had sent him to Heaven: how certain then she must have been that she alone, in her neglect of Susan, had caused her daughter's illness.

During the long years of exile from their lives, Antonia realised that although she did not like Thomas, and feared his influence over her daughter, particularly in matters of the soul, she respected his honesty and courage. Perhaps these feelings were mutual. Certainly Thomas only really came to appreciate, and even to like, his mother-in-law when he finally read her diaries after her death.

While Antonia waited for the publication of, and critical responses to, two books that year – *Strangers*, her collection of short stories published in the summer, and the last of her quartet, *Beyond the Glass*, published in the autumn – she was struck by how much she missed the company of others interested in her writing. There was always Emily, who was a stalwart and enthusiastic supporter, but she was so prolific herself and unboundedly confident in the quality of her own work that the agonies of uncertainty, unproductiveness and writer's block were quite alien to her. Elaine was a most valuable collaborator, but at this time Antonia was not in regular enough contact with her. Good friends like the Catholic writer Robert Speaight and his artist wife Bridget, and the art historian Anthony Bertram and his wife Barbara, made a great difference to Antonia emotionally. But always the men would begin talking about their writing, going on self-importantly for hours, even pronouncing 'with such superiority that they never read any novels except masterpieces etc.' while the women listened: not once did they turn to Antonia to enquire about her work.[5] At moments like these, she could not help but feel invisible in the one area which really mattered to her. Friends like Viola Garvin and the Irish writer and academic Dr Enid Starkie, who both lived in Oxford, were also good friends to her but not the kind of writers with whom she could mull over ideas and seek encouragement. Antonia told Emily she missed having a neighbourhood pub, like The Union in Rye, to which Emily and Phyllis had taken with such pleasure. Here they were welcomed by a group of bizarre and interesting regulars and had met, amongst others, the poet Patric Dickinson and Sheila, 'his high-brow young gay nice thin wife'.[6] Antonia, longing sometimes for congenial company at the end of a solitary and frustratingly unproductive day, would think of Emily and Phyllis in the warmth and chatter of their pub and wish she were there too.

Despite her own lack of writerly support, Antonia was tireless in her efforts on the behalf of others struggling to write or to place their work. Emily's son John had finished a vast novel, 'The Grasshoppers', which Antonia read and on which she offered help and advice: sympathetic to his plunges of despair, she urged him not to give up. Just as time-consuming were her attempts on John's behalf to get the book taken on by an agent, publishing scout or publishers' editor. Emily's great explosion of a book, 'The Tygon' was still doing the rounds, and to her too Antonia offered contacts and suggestions. She also undertook to teach her cousin Helen White how to write stories for women's magazines in order to try and supplement her inadequate pension. Needful of recognition, Antonia was modest nevertheless about her talents; she had once described her measure: 'I am the ordinary bourgeois Catholic with the luck to be a little odd and a little mad.'[7] And she could be generous too, never seeking to treat her profession as an esoteric art kept only for herself. More than once she was moved to remark to Lyndall, having received a particularly eloquent or moving letter from her, that she too had potential; 'you happen to have this rare gift of "attention" which is why I think you may turn out to be a writer in the end.'[8] This was a sweet accolade from a mother who considered writing on a level with her faith: the two most important areas of her life.

Strangers was published to the widely mixed reviews which her work always inspired. There seemed to be an increasing sensitivity to the Catholic content of her fiction, which was often treated with suspicion. Although Antonia felt that the critics were generally favourable, nearly everyone harked back to *Frost in May*, usually to mark her decline since then. The book of her precocious youth had become, she felt, like a withered wreath about her neck. In the *Daily Telegraph* the reviewer departed from his colleagues to heap such baroque abuse on the book that Antonia was moved to copy out the best bits for Emily to read: 'Miss White's suicidal wives, with their dreary psycho-neurotic dreams, her cold Catholics and scrubbed nuns, querulous & dogmatic by turns, leave a taste in the mouth as nasty as it is unsubstantial. Wistful children, the longeurs of mental and sexual imbalance – these have become almost conventional short stories sufficient in themselves. . . .'[9] And then the *New Statesman* review, impressed deeply by 'The House of Clouds', ended with an exhortation which puzzled Antonia; if she could be persuaded to 'go into training, [she would] write all the other professional sensitives off the map'.[10] The Catholic paper the *Tablet*, however, took an opposing line to most of the other critics; its reviewer loved all the stories except 'The House of Clouds', which it found unattractive and precious.

Tom was once more very much on Antonia's mind. He had begun a regular slot as a commentator on *The Critics*, an intellectual weekly arts review programme on the Third Programme on BBC radio. Antonia listened avidly, still trying to fathom out what had happened to the man she used to know. On the whole she thought he was rather good except when he got on to the subject of love, which he did quite often, when he went off into a mystical fog suggesting love was a frightening thing when 'you *exchanged* your self for another person's', all of which Antonia found psychologically significant.[11] She was left offering succour to his second family after the break up of the marriage. Nicolette was twelve years old and suffering particularly from the bad feeling between her father and deeply depressed mother. She had a strong antipathy to Dorothy, possibly through loyalty to her mother who was hurt and very bitter, but probably just as much because Dorothy seemed to be insensitive to the children's own feelings and need for privacy. She tried to beam the intrusive analytical eye on to them too, asking Nicolette to tell her her dreams. Both Nicolette and Amanda were to grow very fond of Antonia at different times of their lives: at this point Nicolette wanted to come and talk seriously to Antonia about the situation between her mother and father, and aspects of the relationship which puzzled her. Antonia's clarity and intellectual honesty was a refreshing thing for this confused child. Having been heavily encouraged by Tom to read the book he had written with Dorothy, *Love's Apprentice*, on relations between men and women, she had given up in despair. She asked Antonia pathetically 'Aunt Tony, what is the sex war?'[12]

Then, at the beginning of November, Antonia was faced with a desperate Gerti with nowhere to stay. She offered her a room at her flat for a few weeks until she found the right house to rent. Antonia was struggling herself with an enormous amount of translating work to try and finish before Lyndall arrived for the Christmas holidays. She had almost finished a novel by Paul André Lesort, with a heavy-footed style and the tongue-twisting English title *The Wind Bloweth where it Listeth*, which ran to well over 100,000 words. She had to immediately start on another. Under this kind of pressure of work, she found Gerti's presence extremely disrupting, much as she was pleased to help her. Harassed, she told Emily the situation was probably good for her; 'Nothing to ordinary people. Hair-shirts to selfish old neurotics like me!'[13] But nevertheless, to be force-fed even more of the selfish and bizarre doings of Tom and Dorothy gave her indigestion. There were some unwelcome discoveries too. Tom had apparently told Gerti that he had only married Antonia because his father had forced him to. This shocked Antonia, whose fond picture of Tom was as a basically honest but naïve man – until he got into the clutches of Dorothy.

The critical reaction to *Beyond the Glass* was everything Antonia had hoped for. This was the book that she felt herself had more power than all the rest: it was certainly bought by an interested public, having sold more than 5,000 copies by the end of the year. If she had to come to it fresh, however, Antonia thought she would find it almost too unbearable to read. More important than the professional reviews were the reactions of her friends and family. Lyndall wrote to say she really liked it; this carried a great deal of weight, assuaging Antonia's fear that everything she wrote was embarrassing or contemptible to her children. Georgie Earnshaw Smith, who for months had been railing angrily against her, sent her 'a most remarkable letter' to say she loved the book; 'Best of all, she said it had made her appreciate Eric!!!'[14] Emily's verdict was the most eagerly awaited. She had loved it too she said, particularly the section dealing with Antonia's madness, although she had not been convinced about the ecstatic love affair with Richard.

Just at the point when Antonia had begun to feel that she had established something of a literary reputation at last, not based solely on the memory of that one brief shooting star more than two decades before, her translating work took off. Her intelligence, wide cultural references, precise feel for language and sensitivity to nuances of meaning made Antonia a talented translator, in increasing demand from a wide range of literary publishers. Her translation of Colette's Claudine series of novels was her greatest triumph. Although she was never to meet her, Colette had always been a heroine of Antonia's and there already existed a strong sympathetic similarity in their work. Colette's sensuous use of language and sharp psychological insights were well-served by a writer with an equal feel for her own language, and a sensibility which could empathise with the world Colette inhabited. During the mid-fifties to the mid-sixties, Antonia's translating work was at its peak. She was working at a terrific pace; within the twelve months from September 1954 to September 1955 she had translated four full-length novels, amongst them Colette's *Claudine at School* and Christine Arnothy's *I am Fifteen and I Do Not Want to Die*. Always short of money and anxious about her financial situation, this was a tempting way of earning a living while she attempted to continue with her own fiction. But such a pace did not allow very much concentrated time for Antonia's more demanding work, 'the much more bloodcurdling task of my own new novel.'[15]

In preparing for this novel, in which she intended to cover the Eric and Silas years, Antonia began to reread Silas's letters to her when she was pregnant with Susan. She was struck for the first time just how much he had suffered, away from home, in grim Canadian and Mexican mining towns, worried about her and money, homesick, very much alone. A terrible feeling of guilt overcame her. Antonia wrote at length to Lyndall about that muddled, unhappy time; her love for Silas, her fear that his inexpressiveness meant he did not love her, the effect of Tom's contrasting fluency. 'Oh dear . . . if *you* ever feel guilty, darling, believe me you've never caused a fraction of the unhappiness that I have.'[16] She expressed her remorse and sadness too, for the effects on her children of the choices she had made.

In a letter she wrote to Emily later in the year, while still attempting, unsuccessfully, to get her book under way, Antonia revealed one of the possible reasons for her inability to write about this period of her life: 'My book is a penance . . . I have to look inwards & face some HORRID facts . . . which may well prove Sue has every (natural) right to treat me as she does. Believe me, I lived for my own will all right in those days!'[17] In a later letter, still pondering how to write about this period of her life, Antonia admitted to her friend; 'What I am paying for is years & years ago, when she was a baby when for a year, because it was "difficult" I didn't have her with me. I put myself before her – and it all seemed "reasonable" at the time – but it was a wicked thing to do & no love & care . . . which I *did* give afterwards – can make up for it.'[18] How difficult it was to reveal what she saw as her own deeply-flawed nature, and the damaging actions of her selfish youth, to readers, like Silas and Sheila, whose good opinion she craved and yet, she feared, were already implacably judgemental and hostile towards her. This was enough to strike her mute. In her diary, she again returned to the anxieties of dealing with such a fraught and unheroic time: 'To *me*, of course, the Dougal episode is something I would like to rule right out since it is so trivial . . . as well as being so shaming. Also, one feels, for the book, it will destroy any sympathy the reader might feel for Clara.'[19] The foundations for the tragic deadlock were in place; Antonia had learnt painfully that invention in fiction was dangerous for her, only by sticking close to the facts of her life could she continue her literary career. But by revealing the facts truthfully she exposed herself, and those she loved, and risked their contempt and rejection. This book, honestly written, could only hand over more ammunition to damage her further.

Then Antonia was suddenly distracted from her struggle against the stasis of writer's block by a letter from Lyndall containing astounding news. She had fallen in love, quite suddenly, instantaneously, with a man she had known on and off since she was a girl. Lionel Birch, known as Bobby, was a charming journalist friend of Tom Hopkinson's who had become editor of *Picture Post*. Married and divorced four times he had proposed to Lyndall on the spur of the moment on a visit to Rome.

She had accepted, and then both embarked on a whirlwind love-affair. Unbenownst to Lyndall he had then proposed to his previous wife, the photographer Inge Morath. At forty-six Bobby was exactly twice as old as Lyndall, and only four years younger than her father. There was another more worrying connection; his charm, his labile emotions and even his kind of looks were rather too familiar for comfort. Now that she was increasingly estranged from her much-loved father, those who cared about her wondered if this *coup de foudre* was more to do with reclaiming Tom. In an immediate response to Lyndall's news and request for advice, Antonia wrote an exemplary letter of maternal affection and concern, asking the right questions and assuring her of her continuing support and love whatever she decided:

> My darling Lyndall,
> . . . I *do* understand and I am terribly happy that you have fallen in love but you *will* understand, pet, won't you, that I can't help being worried that it is Bobby Birch? . . . how *can* I help being apprehensive? . . .
> No, I'm NOT going to say 'for heavens sake don't do it, darling!' The very most I would dare say is . . . wait a little, if you can bear to. You can see what disturbs me most . . . there *seems* a fatal similarity of temperament between Tom & Bobby. . . . Darling, you *know* how I wish I could give you my wholehearted blessing with *no* misgivings. And you know that *whatever* you do, nothing will make any difference to my love for you. . . .
> I can't 'advise', darling, only say the obvious things. It isn't the past but the fear of the future repeating the past that worries me. On the other hand, it may be so important for you to love someone so wholeheartedly that it may be right for you to take such an enormous risk. And I don't hold all that much to 'playing for safety' as you know. . . .[20]

Within a week, Bobby Birch had taken Antonia round to his flat in London and cooked her a chop: they had talked for more than six hours, and he dealt with all her anxieties so candidly that she was charmed. Her reservations, however, were not entirely erased. When Bobby had broken the news to his old friend and past boss, Lyndall's father, Tom was initially disconcerted and upset. Perhaps he was envious too. Lyndall and Bobby were married in May a month after their fateful reunion in Rome. Antonia, however, felt a certain confidence return when she saw her daughter on her arrival in London, where she was once more to make her home; 'she is radiantly happy' she reported to Emily; 'I've never seen her *happy* before . . . only *excited* . . . it is touching.'[21] But Antonia also reported to Emily the familiar emotion of envy, which she explored in greater detail in her diary: envy of Bobby who, with such a catalogue of emotional disasters behind him and middle-age beckoning, could still start again with a beautiful young woman; and envy too of any woman like Lyndall, 'with an adoring husband'; 'will nothing *ever* take away those old longings of mine for a fresh beginning, a man to love me, all the rest?'[22] Whenever Antonia wrote of her need for love, it was always someone to love her for which she longed, not someone for her to love.

Too soon, Lyndall awoke from her midsummer night's dream to see poor Bobby for what he was, rather sad and growing old; a pale reflection of the man she had thought she loved. A temporarily grief-stricken Bobby told Antonia that the marriage had lasted eight days. Lyndall, anguished and guilty, agreed to go to an analyst to try and reverse this sudden antipathy which had replaced her fleeting passion. The most miserable year of her life had begun.

By the beginning of August Antonia was already uneasy at Lyndall's apparent restiveness. She had also been jolted with another reminder of her estrangement from Susan. A second baby, her daughter Cordelia, had been born in July and once more Antonia had been reduced to watching the Birth columns of *The Times*. When the news came, she sent her congratulations telegram, and could not help hoping for a response. When no answer was forthcoming, Antonia was cast down again, certain that Silas and Sheila had completely ousted her in her daughter's and grandchildren's lives.

Antonia had just finished translating Colette's novel, *Claudine at School* and this, combined with her family worries meant she was exhausted by the time she set off on a ten-day holiday at the end of August. She was accompanying an American doctor friend, Katharine Gurley who, in professional guise, had sprung to Antonia's (and Clara's) defence against a weasley review of *The Sugar House*, in which scorn was poured on the naïvety of a heroine who could neither recognise, nor use her wiles to overcome, her husband's impotence. She admired and encouraged Antonia's writing and was rewarded with a dedication in *Beyond the Glass*, thanking her for her support. This sensible, good-hearted doctor from New Jersey had only met Antonia once before, but had invited her along on a tour of the west coast of Ireland, in the car of Jim Twomey, an undertaker and part-time taxi-driver, whom Katharine Gurley had met four years before. As Antonia wrote to Emily, 'So with a doctor & an undertaker for company I shall be well set . . . & – at the moment – feel I might need *both* services!'[23]

Their journey lasted nine days and covered 1,500 miles. Mr Twomey was endlessly good-natured; a fund of information, he entertained them with superstitious stories, jokes and anecdotes, often breaking into song as he drove, smoking all the while. Only once did he take a wrong turning, and then only because he was studying a hearse with professional interest. He explained to the two women the traditions of his undertaking trade, and the different colour shrouds for different status corpses. He told a story, which Antonia copied into her diary, of two corpses, one a Catholic and one a Jew. The Jewish corpse had a coin put into his hand to pay the ferryman over the river Jordan. The undertaker pocketed the coin, saying, 'if Paddy has to swim for it, that fellow can too & we'll drink Paddy's health.'[24] In the middle of the tour, Antonia and Dr Gurley went to have dinner with the Anglo-Irish writer Elizabeth Bowen at Bowen's Court, her crumbling mansion in County Cork. She was an exact contemporary of Antonia's and had written the now famous preface for *Frost in May* which appeared in the 1948 Eyre & Spottiswoode edition, and every subsequent edition of the work.

Antonia was to return to Ireland the next year when Dr Gurley, who had Addison's disease and was not expecting to live much longer, asked her to join her for her farewell visit to Ireland, all expenses paid. She had reluctantly agreed, although she was desperate to finish another overdue translation: the trip was not a success. Katharine was cantankerous and difficult with everyone, even her much-loved Mr Twomey, and Antonia was relieved to get home, despite the tens of thousands of words which awaited her for translation.

But back in London, that summer of 1955, the full unhappiness of Lyndall's and Bobby's situation was brought home to her. Over what was meant to be a celebratory meal in their new house, both of them told Antonia the extent of their woes. Lyndall out of love and miserable, Bobby desperate to win her back, both of them in financial straits; it turned into a grim evening where nobody could offer much consolation. 'Lyndall is the discontented one. . . . Bobby acutely unhappy. Her old trouble – not wanting what she has got – being unable to *accept* love. . . . I am terrified of interfering. . . . I *hope* they will stay together and get things right.'[25]

Antonia had also returned to the grind of trying to write her next novel. She had been thinking about attempting a contrast, even experimenting with inventing part of the plot; 'something short, light & ironical because so STALE & I'm so *sick* of Clara!!', she wrote to Emily.[26] What she came up with was a melodramatic and sentimental novelette she called *Happy Release*. It started with the death from a broken heart of a loving mother who had been separated from her only daughter by the connivance and interference of the daughter's platitudinous stepmother. Antonia wrote it in an intensive eleven-week dash, enjoying writing for the first time since she was a child. She could express all her pent up hurt and self-righteousness, and reward herself with a delicious, if fictional, posthumous retribution when the daughter, filled with bitter remorse, cast her stepmother out of her life. It had all the psychologically satisfying elements of that childhood expression of powerlessness and hurt pride – I'll die and then you'll be sorry! Antonia wrote 'this rum hybrid' in a 'sort of *fever*'. This excitement continued in the aftermath, as she had high hopes of placing it in America (where the main protagonists would be unlikely to read it) and making some badly-needed cash. She had got into an obsessive post-watching state, desperate to hear something positive back from her American agent. Then Emily, always so reliable in her literary criticism, knocked her hopes well and truly on the head. Apart from its intrinsic interest to anyone who knew the people involved, *Happy Release* was dire, she declared. And with that uncompromising verdict, Antonia's fever subsided and she accepted its fate; 'I *meant* to do something light & "competent". . . . and it turned into a sort of psychological monster.'[27] Once more, it had been made clear to her that she could not be inventive in her fiction, and that any enjoyment in her writing was highly suspect; 'I never get that when I'm trying to write all-out seriously. That is *always* nausea, impotence & drudgery.'[28]

About this time Antonia began to mention occasionally in her diaries another young daughter substitute; 'I have, in an odd way, my "good" daughters – Elaine and Gudrun.'[29] She added that Lyndall, of course, was a good daughter, but the 'good daughter' appellation she gave to these unconnected young women was more to do with their status as young protégées, people who were primarily interested in and encouraging of her work. They were intellectual 'daughters' rather than real daughters, with all the practical, emotional and historical baggage that that implied, and therefore much easier for Antonia to deal with. Other than her name, there are few other clues in Antonia's diaries as to who this other young woman might be. In a letter to Emily at the end of 1955 Antonia described a new young acquaintance whom she embraced with characteristic hyperbole and impetuous enthusiasm: 'A new Female charged into my life via Sacred Heart nuns. German, about 30, &, I fear a genius . . . or a lunatic . . . or both. She is in Ireland [?] at the moment which gives me time to breathe . . . She *writes*, dear! Alternate slices of marvellous and *less* than good. Tremendously intelligent. May or may not be a liar.'[30] This woman shares a good deal of the qualities Antonia noted in Gudrun in her few diary entries.

Interest in Antonia's writing, intelligence but intrusiveness, seemed to be a common thread: 'Some people just have to be pushed out of my mind *while* I'm writing . . . Gudrun is [one] – immensely intelligent as she is. Geniuses who haven't quite found themselves are dangerous to have around during the actual process.'[31] In a diary entry in early February 1956, Antonia displayed a certain anxiety that Gudrun was becoming another of her demanding neurotics. Then in early March she described to Emily the unnamed German turning up uninvited at the flat one day, just when she was settling down to work, with the excuse that she had lost Antonia's telephone number. 'She stayed 2 hours & wrecked my day. Not that I didn't quite enjoy seeing her. But work is going so BADLY. . . .'[32]

In the meantime, Antonia had begun to lose confidence in her relationship with her real daughter. When she and Lyndall had lived in different countries and supported each other with affectionate letters she had felt she had discovered a treasure she had not known she had. But with Lyndall's return to London Antonia found it hard to deal with the fact that Lyndall was conducting her own life, not closely involved with her mother's, and seeing more of Susan and her family again. Her anxieties about Lyndall's loyalty to her resurfaced. She experienced the old sad rivalry over who was most loved, a contest she felt she could only lose. '[Lyndall's] obviously avoiding being alone with me. I feel Sue has somehow re-established her old domination . . . she is obviously desperately anxious again for Sue's approval . . . &, in a crisis, would give me up rather than Sue, I think . . . in a way, unconsciously probably, I don't think she *wants* me to be reconciled with Sue.'[33]

25
Grandmother's Footsteps

Of course it is beyond anything I could have hoped.
And I see that now I *had* at last given up hope. The restoration of it is
almost more painful than what I had grown used to.

20 March 1957, Diaries I

In the five years since she had last seen Susan, there were periods when
Antonia could resign herself to having lost her for good. At other
times the anger, bewilderment and pain of loss flared up to ambush her.
She had been reading Susan's articles in *Punch*, 'Diary of a Fashion
Model', and had found them 'uproariously funny . . . full of *life*'.[1] Her
powerlessness to effect any response in her daughter still rankled, as did
her frustration in being prevented from even expressing pleasure in her
work. Antonia wrote a stocktaking letter to Susan in the middle of
January, alternating between veiled anger and pathetic supplication, the
conflicting emotions of victim and bully:

> How often have I asked you to tell me why you cut me off so
> completely. You don't even deign to answer. Surely you must feel
> that I have done something unforgivable. But wouldn't it, at least,
> be common courtesy to tell me what it is? . . . I keep humbling my
> pride by, at intervals, writing to you. You are my daughter & I
> love you. If you don't answer this, there will be no more signs
> from me. If that's what you honestly and wholeheartedly want,
> you shall have it.[2]

Two months later, Antonia received a letter from Susan. At first she did
not recognise the writing, then she did not dare open it for an hour 'in
case it wasn't, in case it *was*. . . .'[3] She was invited to tea and dinner in a
month's time at the Chittys' house in Sussex, on the proviso that she did
not bring up the past 'as our two versions of what happened will never
agree'.[4] Antonia's first reaction was one of shock and numbness. There

was fear too; having become deadened to hope, it was painful to have those feelings re-awakened. She likened it to the pain that is felt as circulation is restored in a body that had nearly frozen to death. She had had a series of dreams over the intervening years in which she was reconciled with Susan, sometimes with both daughters and all three of them happy together, but the dreams were often clouded with delays and misunderstandings, making for a certain unease. It was as if her psyche had rehearsed this momentous and longed-for reunion so many times that when the call finally came she was almost too incredulous or fatigued to respond with ready delight.

Her reply was very careful, her stance submissive; 'can you just tell me who I'm supposed to be as regards Andrew and Cordelia? Am I your mother and their grandmother or just some vague party? I don't want to drop any bricks! I'll accept any part you choose to assign me!' She was told that she was the children's other grandmother, which delighted her; Sheila Glossop had not usurped that role, as she had feared. From now on, the emotional side of life would always be uneasy between the two women: Antonia ever fearful she might put a foot wrong, and Susan afraid of becoming enmeshed again. Antonia felt much more confident dealing with her daughter on an intellectual level. The only spontaneous part of her letter was to do with work; at last she could tell her, 'I have been laughing like anything over your Punch articles: I think they are brilliantly funny.'[5]

Before she could go down to see the Chitty family Antonia had to take part in a four day symposium on Christian art at Downside Abbey, where she was to give a paper on the problems of the Catholic novelist. She stayed with Lance and Emmi Sheppard, who were subsequently to become friends, and was given a lift every day to the Abbey, four miles distant, in a sidecar. Antonia had been dreading it all but told Emily that in fact the whole experience did her good, calming her down and making her more philosophical about the reunion with Susan the following Saturday.

Although Antonia did not write about this day in her diary she wrote in detail to Lyndall and Emily. Everything passed off so well, and Susan and Thomas and their children appeared to be so perfect in their relationships with each other and in their hospitality to her, that the dreamlike feeling continued. Antonia feared she would awake and find that none of it was true. '*Either* I was dreaming last Saturday *or* I have been dreaming for five years.' She found her daughter even more radiant and attractive than ever, exhibiting great sweetness to her children – and a measure of domestic competence which amazed and delighted her mother. She was afraid to accept that this friendly and charming young woman actually was her daughter and that things could continue so harmoniously. Thomas she liked better than ever before, 'that dour, official Angry Young Man, is a heavenly father. . . . Well THEY [Andrew and Cordelia] can never complain like Sue & Thomas of having cruel, domineering, repressive, insensitive parents!' she reported to Emily.[6] The special moment of Antonia's day occurred on an expedition to see the new Exmoor pony Susan had bought for the family. She was pushing Cordelia in her cart when Andrew ran up and slipped his hand under her arm; suddenly she felt a confirmation of her existence. 'There I was . . . JUST LIKE A REAL GRANDMO-THER.'[7] Although she feared that she would return to London and not see or hear from Susan again – for another five years perhaps – this was the beginning of a renewed relationship, with both parties respectful and affectionate in their dealings with each other, but never risking the over-close emotional connection of Susan's youth. It seemed to be important for Susan to maintain control of the situation, to keep the upper hand so that she need never again feel vulnerable and in thrall to her mother's power. Antonia recognised this and accepted it as part of the pact now between them. She reported to Lyndall: 'Her manner to me? Gay, a trifle mischievous, rather charmingly patronising . . . *very* much in command of the situation!'[8]

On the very day that Antonia was mending bridges with Susan, Lyndall was taken to hospital in Rome for an emergency operation to remove her appendix. She was in the middle of a desperate love affair with a spoilt and ambivalent playboy, 'in that fatal way I have, when I want to build a situation up I can do it with hardly any bricks to help; and when I want to destroy something I can do it with practically no ammunition', she explained later to her mother.[9] Earlier in the year she had been struck down by a serious bout of hepatitis and had been hospitalised: her physical and emotional health were in a fragile state. Antonia was quick to commiserate on both occasions with a 'Darling Lyndall' letter, which was largely what she called her younger daughter now – along with 'pet', 'my beloved pussy' and 'sweetie'. Antonia was able to be as affectionate as she liked in her letters to Lyndall, maternal in her concern and exhortations to take care of herself, to think better of herself. She was insistent with her praise of her qualities and encouragement of her self-esteem. With Susan, however, her letters from now on were genuinely affectionate, friendly and admiring, but always watchful. She felt she was on approval and that approval could be withdrawn. The old fear lurked from her convent days of inadvertently sinning and falling from grace.

Antonia had always been afraid of her children – of their disapproval, of their pointing up her failure, of the power they seemed to drain from her, of the attention they attracted. In feeling at last that she was cared for by Lyndall more than she was judged by her, Antonia lost her fear and gained the chance of a more normal mother-daughter relationship with her; 'I love Lyndall dearly, I love her as my child and I long to see her and worry over her.'[10] Her feelings for Susan remained much more complicated and less healthy; Antonia's fear of her increased as her admiration grew. Her deference was exacerbated by the emotional distance between them: 'when I think of those five years of alienation and the incredible joy of having her back in my life on any terms, however seldom I see her . . . the person who means most to me in the whole world.'[11]

During 1956 there were further reversals in Antonia's life. She overcame her suspicions about Lyndall's dealings with Susan, which consolidated her relationship with her younger daughter. She described it as 'the one great positive joy that has emerged for me in the last five years or so'.[12] She worried about Lyndall's increasingly difficult relationship with Tom; '[he] is being not merely horrid but plumb crazy in his dealings with her'.[13] However, Antonia could not suppress a little satisfaction in the fact that Lyndall and Tom now had nothing to say to each other, and sat on the edges of their chairs, making polite conversation – much as she and Lyndall had done before establishing their own solidarity. By the middle of August Lyndall, now single again, had returned to an uncertain future in Rome. Antonia was almost in tears as she listened to *Mrs Dale's Diary* on the radio a few days later and heard Mrs Dale's daughter tell her mother she was leaving to live in Wales. Her letters to her own daughter were full of encouragement, especially of a novel Lyndall was writing: 'I'm *sure* there's something very good there if you can force yourself through the horrors.'[14] She emphasised how proud she was of her, not just of her beauty but the competent and courageous way that she managed her life. Lyndall may lie to others, she declared, but she was always honest with herself, and that quality of clear-sightedness she admired.

Lyndall's absence in Antonia's life was soon partially, if temporarily, filled by the large personality of Eric Siepmann, who came to stay for ten eventful, conversation-filled days. He and his wife Mary had met up with Antonia again through the auspices of Emily. They had become good friends with Emily and Phyllis Jones, and had converted to Catholicism in late summer – with Antonia acting as godmother. Phyllis, friend and stalwart to everyone and Emily's companion in Rye, had also converted to Catholicism earlier that year. For so long Antonia had felt that her faith had made her an odd exile; now she was less alone as others whom she admired joined the fold. It meant a great deal to her that even hardened cases like Basil Nicholson, the reprobate ex-lover of herself and Phyllis all those years ago, had converted on his deathbed. Eric Siepmann was due to start a new job before he and Mary could move into their new flat, and so became Antonia's lodger in early September. Much as Antonia disliked cooking, finding it a source of anxiety and a major distraction in her working day, she had offered to give Siepmann an evening meal as well. He was a great talker, a great drinker and a man of intellectual power who, when he was in the mood, was the most stimulating of company. His time with Antonia was almost too energising for her, despite her professed craving for excitement, even violence, to counteract the dread monotony of life.

One of the most memorable points of his stay was a sudden conflagration which almost destroyed the flat. In the middle of a supper party the company were suddenly disturbed by a commotion and a voice crying 'Fire!' A passer-by had seen flames leaping up at the window of what turned out to be Antonia's work-room, and had rushed across the road to warn them. Then he and Antonia used the cats' pails and jugs to try and damp down the flames which had started in a waste-paper basket and spread to her father's old oak desk, the curtains, half the kelim and the window frame. Three fire engines were there in five minutes and, after extinguishing the fire, the firemen told Antonia just how close she had been to the whole building going up in flames. The laborously produced few pages of her novel were safe but some chapters of a Colette translation and her letter file, with letters waiting to be answered, along with her fountain pens, had all been reduced to ashes.

Antonia, often completely thrown by trivial disruptions of routine, was heroic in emergencies. She had dealt with the fire, made sure the cats were safe, charmed the firemen, and kept the atmosphere so calm that everyone was able to return to their dinner, albeit now cold, to stay talking until two in the morning. The next day she was feeling shaky, she reported to Lyndall, but was dealing with the mess, salvaging what she could and sorting out the insurance claims. Apparently someone had tossed a live cigarette butt into the wastepaper basket as they all went upstairs to eat. Antonia had some suspicions it was Siepmann, but he had assured his wife that he had not even been smoking. She bore no resentment about it all, even though it made it difficult to work and meant she had to relinquish her father's old desk and get another one. In fact, Antonia, who had what she considered to be a mania for redecorating, for new beginnings, was able to look forward to making 'a fresh start in a tidy remodelled study'.[15] It seemed significant to her that now she would have her own desk at last, a reconditioned Georgian one. Her work-room was obviously highly combustible, for there was a second fire within only three months of the first. Minka and Curdy had pushed a piece of paper from a parcel through the bars of an electric fire. The hearth rug was already in flames when Antonia came into the room, alerted by the smell.

Within a month of the Great Fire, Antonia faced the Sylvaine libel case which had come to court at last. Again she was cool under enemy attack but crumbled afterwards. However, she was feeling better about her novel, perhaps, she admitted, only because she had shelved it for the time being, under pressure to finish a *New Statesman* review on 'Nuns with a Difference', and to start again on the Colette translation. Elaine, however, had read what she had written for the first chapter of her own work and had liked it: this was always a spur to her confidence and energy.

Antonia's ability to empathise with the sufferings of her friends, and her persistence in her friendships, were called on during the long and painful terminal illness of Alick Schepeler. Antonia had known Alick for nearly thirty years. She had had an impoverished and disappointed life, the last act of which was a bleak diagnosis of cancer. Antonia saw a great deal of Alick during the last eighteen months of her life, visiting her every day during the long decline. She was moved by her courage and nobility, despite her implacable denial of religion, and particularly of Catholicism. Alick had accused her friend Edith Sitwell, when she became a Catholic, of committing 'intellectual suicide'.[16] Despite this antipathy, after Alick's death in February 1957 Antonia intended to have a Mass said for her; 'I feel God *will* be good to her and she will find now *what* was the perfection (for nothing human was *ever* good enough in her eyes) she was looking for all her life', she told Emily with a modified sense of Emily's own self-righteousness.[17] To Lyndall she wrote how touched she was, and guilty too, that Alick, who had so little, had left her in her will her only valuable possession, a diamond ring, together with a gold watch and a fine gilt mirror, gifts which had stirred up some envy in friends who had known her for longer.

This sensitivity to the suffering of others was also extended in another very different direction. Leslie Earnshaw Smith, who was known universally as Lel, was Eric's sad and lonely younger brother. He had already tried to commit suicide twice, was estranged from his brother and in despair when Antonia stepped hesitantly into the breach. Homeless, penniless, in deepest depression, Leslie seemed to have nothing to live for and Antonia felt she was the only person in a position to offer him some company and a temporary home. In December 1956, he moved into her spare room in Ashburn Gardens, barely able to pay even for his keep. He was to remain there for two years. Antonia liked Lel, finding him sweet-natured and touchingly grateful for any kindness shown him. There were times too when his presence made her own loneliness less burdensome. She thought he even helped her to economise – by depressing her so that her manic spending sprees were less frequent. He squashed her conceitedness by liking her but being unimpressed by her work; '[he] has a very low opinion of my writing.'[18] Being manoeuvred into living with him, she thought, could be interpreted as an expression of God's sense of humour towards her. The importance to Antonia of a certain routine, however, and her increasingly desperate attempts to write, meant the lack of privacy and the loss of a spare room, which she had always been able to offer to friends, seemed at times a heavy price to pay.

Just as Lel joined her, Antonia was threatened with a doubling of the rent she paid for her flat. This sort of sudden extra stress set her off in the kind of mental frenzy she knew too well. Immediately her brain was working in obsessional circles of anxiety and speculation; should she live at Binesfield in Sussex and give up London or sell the cottage and use the interest from the capital to top up her income? Should she try and get an increase in rent from the cottage and, staying in the flat, charge her two lodgers, Shirley and Lel, slightly more rent? All too easily Antonia could lose herself in this kind of reflexive worry, alternating with elaborate daydreams about new flats, different houses, redecorating rooms, the purchasing possibilities of an imaginative inheritance of £50,000, new beginnings, freedom from care. Meanwhile, while she was translating virtually full-time with two Colette volumes in the pipeline, and had dashed off *Minka and Curdy*, her first book about the cats, in sixteen happy days, she was no nearer producing anything in the Clara series, after thousands of hours of work and hundreds of pages written and destroyed.

During the last year or so, Antonia's social life had opened out again. Having not given a big party herself for years she had more than seventy-five friends and acquaintances for summer drinks at her flat in May 1956. There were all sorts of collisions and near confrontations which were too complicated for her to relate in a letter to Emily, but the excitement and attention did Antonia good. Just before her libel case she went off rather jauntily to Antonia Packenham's grand wedding to Hugh Fraser. The bride was an acquaintance of Antonia's, and a long-term admirer of *Frost in May*. Antonia was wearing her new 'rose-net flower-pot. Not as awful as it sounds'. In fact, she felt she was terrifically up to the minute as flower-pots were being worn by all the female guests who were not under a 'fluffy meringue'.[19] Then in June, she went to another even grander wedding – that of the younger daughter of Alan Walker, the friend of Eric Earnshaw Smith to whom she was briefly engaged in the heady months after her escape from the asylum. She told Lyndall that she almost collapsed into giggles in the church when she first saw him escorting his daughter up the aisle. He had grown a most extraordinary moustache of Squadron Leader proportions and now had 'about 6 ins of fleecy grey whiskers that looked indescribably funny'.[20]

Elizabeth Bowen invited her to Bowen's Court for a week in June 1957, for a working holiday, where they would both write by day and only socialise at night. Antonia's house fantasies and delusions of grandeur could be given full rein in this romantic, slightly dilapidated Georgian mansion, surrounded by 250 acres of parkland and the beautiful landscape of County Cork. She toyed for a while with the idea of giving up everything to buy a nine room derelict house on the shores of an estuary there for £100. In the big house, Antonia had a whole suite of rooms to herself, was brought breakfast in bed and then driven to other large Georgian houses dotted round the countryside for dinner with various other Anglo-Irish friends. After twenty-five years of casual acquaintanceship, Antonia felt she had begun to know Elizabeth Bowen better at last, and found her fascinating – if contradictory; 'Extraordinary mixture of shy & sophisticated, chatelaine and down-to-earth good fun; scholarly, masculine, feminine, frivolous, serious, neurotic, warm-hearted and GOOD.'[21]

The composer Malcolm Williamson, who had come into her life via Emily, also extended his hospitality to Antonia. She went to stay for 'two wild week-ends' with him and Sylvio, a charming and feckless Brazilian youth whom Emily and Phyllis had taken under their wing, and tried to pass on to Antonia (which had not worked) and other surrogate mother hens.[22] He was then living with Williamson in bohemian rapture. The weekend was chaotic with neither linen nor cutlery but Antonia enjoyed the lively company of 'the "boys".'[23] George Barker, another presence from her past, was invited for lunch on one of these weekends. Having driven twenty miles, he immediately excused himself saying he had to go and settle 'an urgent domestic problem' and would be back in half an hour. He disappeared and never returned.

Williamson suggested to Antonia a plan which touched her with his interest but filled her with dread. He wanted her help in making a ballet out of *The Sugar House*. She was to condense the action and he to write the music, but after a gruelling two days' work on it and then a five-hour session together the following February, which left them both exhausted, Antonia felt that the ambitious project was beyond her. She admitted to Emily, 'I *don't* understand M's music but, like you, believe in him.'[24]

The Christmas after her reconciliation with Susan was also a much happier and more sociable time than any of her recent ones. Although the rent increase was still looming over her, her chronic financial worries were eased by generous presents of money from Daisy Green-Wilkinson, her first mother-in-law, and from Emily and Phyllis, even though Phyllis was always even worse off than Antonia and struggling to nurse her demented mother. Then a few days before Christmas, Antonia received a letter from Susan asking her to join them on Christmas Day. She cancelled her arrangement with some friends and set off for Sussex. Once more she was touched by the 'adorable' children and by how charming both Susan and Thomas were; when she gave Thomas his present of a pullover he immediately took off the one he was wearing and wore Antonia's gift the whole day, much to her delight. Thomas's job with Shell meant that the family were off to Nairobi for two years the following June, but this seemed no time at all, she confided to Lyndall, given the 'blank *five*' she had survived already.[25]

Antonia's translating commitments were unremitting. She was always harried, working against deadlines, driving herself on, at times even resorting to barbiturates to get the final chapters finished when she thought she had exhausted every resource of mental and physical energy. Her eyes would give up on her, and her hand become cramped with the writing. She had bought herself a typewriter and was trying to become proficient at using it, but the hundreds of thousands of words she wrote every year were written in pen and ink in her clear rounded handwriting. In 1958 alone six works translated by her were published, including Colette's short stories and *Claudine in Paris*. Her frantic activity in 1957 rewarded her with three precious months at the beginning of the following year for her own work, the novel with the working title 'Clara IV'. However, Antonia remained blocked, mentally exhausted as much by this creative aridity as by the previous year on the translating treadmill. Instead she turned to her other mania, decorating the flat. With the help of her cleaner Mrs Linturn and her husband she spent three weeks washing, cleaning and painting everything in sight. Suddenly the three months were up and the next 84,000 words of Colette loomed: Antonia feared she was once more merely a translation factory.

Her daughters too in their different ways, were entering new and challenging stages in their lives. Susan left that summer for Kenya with Thomas and the children, their writing careers having begun to take off with great promise. They were to find Joan Souter-Robertson and her husband Jacques Cochemé, who were also out in Kenya, good company and fellow adventurers. Meanwhile Lyndall was living, by her own admission, a Cinderella-like life in Rome. Returning to her modest room in a 'slum house' after nights out in night clubs 'in the company of young, carefree princelings who spend as much in an evening as I earn in a week.'[26] She was still lonely and unhappy, although her circle of friends and acquaintances was large and superficially extremely glamorous. She had the thrill too of a small speaking part as a pale nun in Zinnemann's film *The Nun's Story*. A friend from her old London social life passed through Rome in March. Edward Montagu had inherited at three the vast house and estates of Beaulieu in Hampshire, had started the vintage car collection, had been imprisoned for homosexual offences, and was now in need of a wife. Lord Montagu had fallen in love with Lyndall: she was uncertain of her feelings for him. She was also reluctant to give up Italy for England, which seemed to have a profoundly depressing effect on her. She was understandably anxious about how much of her life would have to be sacrificed to providing the heir and maintaining the inheritance – cars, paying visitors and all. She havered; he agonised; they both consulted Antonia, who wisely said she could not give anyone advice, but could only pray for the right decision. In the middle of all this Lyndall found that her abdominal pain was not appendicitis after all but a cyst on her ovary, and she flew to London for the operation. Montagu's family were very keen on the marriage; Lyndall was unwell, unhappy and evasive; Antonia was once more dodging a potential mother-in-law who wanted to talk wedding details for the proposed November nuptials. 'I am also madly avoiding a new potential son-in-law who does not know the sword of Damocles is suspended over his handsome head and is already practically furnishing the nursery in his ancestral home!!' she reported to Emily.[27]

All summer, Antonia frantically worked on clearing her translation backlog, with three more due to be finished before the end of the year. By October the Press were on to the engagement story and Lyndall, caught by surprise in Rome, had to extemporise her story, which did not tally with Montagu's version. She felt vulnerable, humiliated and abandoned as Montagu publicly denied her importance in his life. He had been to see Antonia and she decided she liked him a great deal (he was her type): 'I adore courage & honesty & my goodness, he's got them!'[28] Antonia always responded to people, not prejudice, and took little account of race, sex or class. Unlike her Church, Montagu's homosexuality did not trouble her except in her human concern as to whether he would be able to be a good husband to Lyndall. After all,

Eric had been the man with whom she had been most happy: to a woman who found sexual love a difficult and disappointing area of human relationships, the possible lack of a sexual life in marriage did not loom as too great a disadvantage. She was careful, however, not to try and influence Lyndall either way. She genuinely wanted to see her settled and happy, without the loneliness and struggles of her own life, but she did not diminish the risks involved for her daughter in such a match. Lyndall remained haunted by the unease she had felt while convalescing at Beaulieu that summer: she needed more time. He was business-like and pressing; he wanted to be married and his honeymoon over by the time his new motor museum was due to open.

By January the following year Lord Montagu announced his engagement to another more accommodating woman. Antonia was quick to back Lyndall, pointing out that she would discover there would be little to regret, particularly as he had so quickly became engaged to someone else; perhaps the marriage rather than the person was the important thing. Friends and acquaintances offered Lyndall their advice; Sonia Orwell, who had become a Pitt-Rivers and knew from experience the potential heartbreak of such a marriage, sent Antonia a message for Lyndall: 'Be Careful'; she did not believe that Edward would ever 'give up the boys'.[29]

Antonia felt more appreciative than ever of her daughters, but was incapable of offering much except support for what they chose to do. She was no longer critical and exasperated by the way they chose to live their lives, as she had been when they were under her roof, when the smallest inconvenience or extra demand unsettled her fragile equilibrium and called out the demons of her disease. However, so harassed was she by deadlines that the lengthy letters she wrote to an unhappy daughter, a demanding Emily and other friends in need of succour or news took large chunks out of her allotted working day. During these years she was continually stealing time and looking over her shoulder. But emotionally she had reached a certain stability which she hoped she could maintain. 'It is extraordinary how, at my age, one's children are so important that it is impossible to recapture the state of mind when one's "love life" seemed so desperately important – as, of course, it does to them at their age. I definitely am older than my father was now. And my life will probably not be very different from what it is now until I die. Three more books to translate by the end of the year. My own book? Goodness knows when.'[30]

26
High-Heeled Sneakers

Miss White donned sturdy boots and a heavy leather coat which she
purchased in South Bend to withstand the winds and rains of the huge
Notre Dame stadium. She didn't miss a game.

She roared, clapped, groaned, sighed, jumped and faithfully shouted the
Saint Mary's cheers, including the famous 'handkerchief cheer' where
all the Saint Mary's students wave white hankies to the boys in the
Notre Dame stands.

13 December 1959, *Our Sunday Visitor*, Fort Wayne, Indiana

Just when she thought that life for her was never again going to be
unpredictable, as she was deep in yet another translation – the only
means, it seemed, now left to her by which she could earn a living –
Antonia received an unexpected invitation. In the middle of a
sweltering August in 1958, she opened a letter from Sister Madeleva, the
principal of St Mary's, a Catholic girls' college in South Bend, Indiana
affiliated to the male college of Notre Dame, suggesting that she join
their faculty and teach 'creative writing'. 'No mention for how long
(seemed to be for life but I don't understand American) no mention of
how much . . . and they expected me there on *September 16th!!*'[1] After
various letters back and forth, advised by her friend Bobby Speaight,
who had been a guest lecturer there himself, she agreed to teach for a
term, from September 1959, for the fee of $2,500 all found, which at
about three and a half dollars to the pound would reward her marginally
better than three translations. Sister Madeleva was the charismatic and
self-promoting President-nun who had a weakness for grand tours, on
which she picked up celebrities. Antonia described her to Susan as a self-
styled 'poet, saint and scholar'. Her energy was prodigious; it exhausted
Antonia, who was more than a decade younger, just to think of her still
climbing mountains in her old age, having written an autobiography
entitled *My First Seventy Years*. Despite the content of her poetry, which
Antonia described as '*awful* sexy religious stuff',[2] Sister Madeleva seemed
to have little patience with the real thing; 'Well, I suppose [sex] has to

be there. Maybe I'm lucky – I've never been tempted to waste *my* time & energy on it' she said within Antonia's hearing.[3]

The months prior to this adventure were spent frantically working to finish translations due, organising who would look after her cats and the flat, and dealing with the on-going friendships and dramatic interruptions. Virginia Johnes, the 'Anonymous Donor', anonymous no longer and spasmodically persecuting and disrupting, was still rearing up to shatter her concentration and calm. Denyse Sawyer and her husband Geoffrey had become friends when Denyse, a Belgian, had asked Antonia to translate her novel from the French. This she did, with all sorts of interference from the author and her husband, and it was eventually published by Collins as *Till the Shadow Passes*, under the nom de plume of Julie Storm. Their interest in and affection for Antonia, however, backfired badly when they told her bossily to abandon the 'Clara' saga and write a 'rattling good yarn', the banal plot of which they had kindly provided.[4] For Antonia, who was brought to a frenzy by her compulsive struggle to write the book she felt she had to write, this kind of insensitivity added a match to already combustible feelings of desperation and impotence. She felt the inchoate musings on the Dougal book were stopped in their tracks, she was '*castrated*', misunderstood, devalued; 'The obvious thing is to ignore it but they've planted this poisonous dart in my consciousness.'[5]

Antonia was cheered up by hearing that she had won $300 as second prize for an article she had written, 'Problems of a Christian Novelist', which had been reprinted in America. It gave her an excuse for a small spending spree. She took Nicolette Hopkinson to see *The Nun's Story* and they were delighted with it, their enjoyment given extra frisson by being able to spot Lyndall, and her hands, at key moments in the film; 'You were quite identifiable and *very* good . . . I felt so proud and thrilled. . . . You were excellent . . . so dignified . . . & you moved beautifully!'[6]

Antonia was beginning to long for the trip to America, as much as an escape from the hectic routine of translating, the block on the book and the demands of all her friends, as because she wanted to experience something new. To get in the mood she waited in the Cromwell Road to see President Eisenhower when his motorcade passed on his official visit to London at the end of August. She cheered and surged forward with the crowd towards his car, shouting out 'Ike' and feeling quite patriotic. On 5 September Antonia was aboard the *Liberté* and sailing for New York. She was fascinated by her cabin-mates and felt that she could write a short story about them; '3 of us ill-assorted females crammed into embarrassing intimacy'. Both were Jewish, one elegant and embittered from Vienna and the other, called Queenie, who was an enormous, voluble, back-slapping manageress of a laundry in Clapham. Both decided they liked Antonia and stuck close to her, leaving her little privacy or peace: 'I was like Alice between the Red Queen & the White Queen'[7]. It was a French ship and the food was better than anything Antonia had tasted in any restaurant in London; also the staff were not very proficient in English and so her French came in useful. She was the centre of admiring attention.

The letter she dashed off to Emily on her arrival at the college was so vivid and expressive and funny that it brings home what a loss it is that Antonia never managed to write the 'American novel' she was to struggle over – or even the American short story. Here is a taste of what was missed:

> . . . dripping with sweat in my basement apartment with the students playing jazz overhead, I will. . . . If not interrupted . . . try & roll a frenzied eye and wave a distraught hand at you across the Atlantic . . . .
>
> Your country has just *exploded* on me & I am reeling . . . and fascinated! . . . Well, after waiting 2 1/2 hours cooped up with the other aliens, a long-legged angel . . . rescued me as if from purgatory & I left the boat escorted by her & an enormous Irish cop, revolver on hip. She'd got round him to let her on board (I think I'd still be there otherwise) & he smuggled us out a back way (Ann, (the angel) saying 'You lovely man, Inspector O'Casey' & the benevolent cop holding my arm & saying 'Scram, ladies, or you'll be in trouble.' Somehow I was in a vast red & yellow taxi driven by an obvious gangster smoking a cigar & talking JUST like the movies and bawling to another driver 'Red, you git de hell out of here, you do dat ting, will you?' and I've got my head upside down trying to look at sky-scrapers through the taxi window & Ann was babbling about West Side & East Side & Fifth Avenue & I was entranced by seeing Chinese names over laundries & Beefburgers & BASKET burgers written up over cafes. And then I was in a luxury flat looking over East River & little gardens & feeling dead (I'd got up at 5) & being shown into my hostess's new bedroom suite crammed with every kind of Dresden, bric-a-brac, Italian primitives . . . statues, satin cushions in unimaginable profusion. And a pink bathroom crammed with *more* Dresden (not room to put down even a lipstick) & *piles* of rich pink monogrammed towels in at least 5 sizes & a waste-paper basket with a china rose attached to it & a lavatory seat painted with roses

and when you lifted it there were more roses and the inscription 'Gentlemen Only'. And then I was having lunch with my hostess & Sr Madeleva & another nun who were also staying there & it seemed to begin with coffee before the soup & there was a salad of melon balls & greenery & cream & mayonnaise & cheese & a lot of other things. My hostess was a darling Catholic lady, madly rich & devout, & a Grand Dame of the Holy Sepulchre and they'd got some glorious medieval ivory statues and lots of complete trash & all the walls were hung with certificates of good works & Papal blessings & awards for selling bonds (her late husband's) and holy pictures (bad) & Italian primitives (good) and mottoes like 'Don't worry it may never happen' & photos of the lady taken at six different angles so that she seemed to be having herself to a multiple lunch party . . . which is just about how I feel at the moment. . . .

. . . Of course the train was a revelation to me! I dined with the nuns in what was like a real restaurant & they gave us each . . . an ORCHID!! My 'roomette' was fascinating . . . it had a miniature wash-basin & loo but when they pulled the bed down for you to sleep in it filled the whole space & you couldn't use the loo so I had to keep wandering out in my nightdress & coat & dodging business men and Train Hostesses & coloured Stewards (sweeties)

. . .. We passed Peekskill & I thought of you . . . & wide river (Hudson?) as big as an English lake. When we finally got to St Mary's (V. handsome buildings . . . about 10 . . . haven't learnt half yet . . . lawns . . . lake . . . masses of English-looking trees but crickets singing in them . . . Mediterranean sound like cicadas. Girls in white were singing on porch to greet us & blackboard was chalked WELCOME SR MADELEVA & ANTONIA WHITE.

. . . I'm too exhausted to write another word. Dripping with sweat. They've fixed a sweet little room for me but it's in the basement & gives me claustrophobia. At high noon I have to have the electric light on & it's STIFLING.

. . . I am killed with kindness but can't catch breath. Mixture of being a film star & going back to school. I'm always getting lost in these vast bldngs & being in wrong place at wrong time. Meals with the other schoolmarms are at unnatural times . . . breakfast 7.45 sharp, lunch 12, dinner 6 & 5.30 on Sundays. . . . The place abounds with FASCINATING characters. . . . I'm *besieged* with life-histories, unpublished novels, the Lord knows what. Everyone adores my 'English accent'. I am v. popular with everyone but the Dean & the Head of the English Dept. who had written a vol on

Shakespeare entirely from the point of view of the number of
rhetorical devices he employs. She has dug up 274 of these such as
entrepismus, restrictio, erotema and amphibology. Did you know
these words? I didn't. The result is beyond belief & she doesn't
know the first THING about writing or poetry or any*thing*. 'My
real joys are 1) The American girl ... who is pretty, intelligent,
deliciously well-mannered, gay & full of life. I'm crazy about my
students and HOW they respond to a breath of life & interest in
their work. Yes, I LOVE the American enthusiasm and warmth!
    2) American kindness. It's *heavenly*. The way everyone here,
Adam the carpenter, Minnie the maid, the coloured girls, the Irish
nightwatchman, smiles at me, calls me 'Honey', fall over
themselves to help me in my innumerable troubles in this foreign
land where EVERYTHING is different down to the way keys &
switches & taps turn on.
    3) Going in ALONE to explore South Bend – a REAL
midwestern town – & shopping in drugstores and five & ten cent
stores & supermarkets & having lunch in something called
KUPNSORCR [KUPNSAWCR, Emily corrected her]. I now
know that TONITE is not a strange Latin expression & have learnt
to watch the traffic LITES. I got a piece of bubble gum stuck to
my shoe & felt acclimatised. . . . Best love . . . shattered . . . Tony.

Antonia's classes were attended by a select twenty young women who
showed interest and promise in writing and appreciation of literature.
She was immensely impressive to the girls who had never been taught in
such an intelligent and open-minded way. And she loved and admired
them in return, 'each of whom I cherish as if she were a potential
Djuna.'[8] She was amazed at how much she enjoyed working with these
young enthusiastic minds, watching them expand in the fresh air of
intellectual freedom and encouragement which she offered: Antonia
recognised for the first time the possibility of a true reciprocal creativity
in the best teaching relationships; 'I get as much as I give', she told
Emily.[9] The thought that she had run too hard from teaching because it
was what her father had most wanted her to do occurred to her again.
To Lyndall she admitted, 'it really seems as if my destiny had caught up
with me. What I really *was* intended to be a schoolmarm! I really seem
to be good at it! I adore my students, find the work thrilling & absorbing
& am getting results already beyond my wildest hopes.'[10]
    One of her pupils was to become a friend and helpmeet for the rest of
her life, another 'good daughter' figure, Lyn Cosgriff (later Isbell). Lyn
bounded into Antonia's life and quickly became 'my pet'. Antonia

described her to Emily as 'a girl from the West . . . a real wild colt, generous, extravagant, mad for life.'[11] She was the daughter of a much-loved father and a beautiful and neurotic mother whom she felt did not approve of her intellectual and gawky self. Antonia was a much more appreciative mentor and they both recognised what they needed in each other. Lyn was responsible for the new and unlikely enthusiasm for American football which Antonia genuinely shared with her girls – and the Notre Dame boys. She went to the prematch rally and learnt her chants with 5,000 students from both the men's and women's colleges and then the next day she sat for three hours in the massive stadium and got drenched to the skin, obediently bawling ' "Go I-RISH" . . . and "Get that ball and FIGHT" and "Hit 'em again and HARRRD" etc. etc. . . . I'm *madly* trying to discover the rules – the only one I can deduce is that you knock everyone down at sight, even if he's on your side. But I'm fascinated.' The mass experience, the communal excitement and collective will, Antonia found refreshing and oddly soothing. To be part of something larger than yourself, when you were often uneasy with that self, brought a freedom and relief that was exhilarating. 'I haven't enjoyed anything so much for years as this ritual sport or tribal dance, complete with magic incantations.'[12] Along with the thousands of fellow beings, she ate a hot dog out of a paper bag, her feet frozen and her clothes clammy with the wet and cold. Her interest in the game earned her respect from the janitors and workmen who would stop her for a discussion and to impart the latest news.

As an Englishwoman and a published writer she was a rarity in this rural community and the local press came to interview her. In an article which romped through her life story, making comments like, 'It is far afield to assume that Miss White's eminence has made her either stuffy or visionary', Antonia saw fit to kill Tom Hopkinson off rather than to admit that she was divorced once, let alone three times. She had also tidily married first before having children and then, as a poor widow without masculine company of any kind, and two daughters to bring up, had struggled to make her way in the world. It is possible, however, that the young journalist had got carried away – already she had turned Antonia's masterpiece into *Frosted May* and her literary daughter and son-in-law had become Lady Crotty and Sir Thomas Crotty. But then 'The term is all too quickly galloping toward a parting with this exhilarating mentor'.[13] Antonia was also interviewed on television, and had not been warned about the commercial breaks; 'my interviewer kept saying things like "Just a moment, Miss White – I think I smell something good cooking, don't you?" & I would have to sniff enthusiastically & ask what it was so that they could interpolate a boost for O-so-tasty Instant Cheeseburgers or what have you.'[14] It was a holiday of the spirit that was long overdue. The appreciation of so many people, from the girls she taught to the service staff around the college and the shopkeepers in town, made her feel for a time that she was a valued and rare addition to the community. It was an intellectual holiday too, giving her the freedom just to think and to discuss literature, a subject in which she was both knowledgeable and inspiring, and could talk with mesmerising fluency. 'My life here is the *absolute* reverse of my English one in every way. . . . I'm just *immersing* myself, love it, get bewildered, don't mind, can hardly remember England & bless the Lord for this marvellous complete upsetting of my old routine.'[15] She escaped from the 'pioneer-battle-axe type', who presided uncompromisingly over the faculty dining table, in order to eat a steak and go bowling with a welder and his wife, a waitress at the College whom she had befriended. She also showed a remarkably sympathetic understanding of the unloved Classics mistress, drawing a portrait of her and the tragic lineaments of her life with such economy and tenderness it gave her a kind of immortality:

> I admire this strange character. . . . I believe she's as good at her game as my father was . . . & here she is . . . with only 8 students out of 1000 taking her subject & that is *English* [translation] . . . she's only allowed to teach *Greek* every other year . . . to about 2!! It's a martyrdom. . . . I *know* she's a first class classicist . . . ought to be a don at Oxford or Cambridge & has been isolated here 22 years. Everyone is afraid of her . . . she repels friendships & has a sharp tongue. But she's softened to me because of Classics and Cats & I feel honoured.[16]

Just when she was beginning to get homesick and miss her friends, Lyn Cosgriff and her father came to Antonia's aid with an expedition to Chicago to celebrate Thanksgiving. Mr Cosgriff was the owner of an empire of banks across the West, with the seat of power in Salt Lake City. He was intelligent, good-looking and shy – and he knew how to give an impoverished Englishwoman a good time; limitless champagne, a deluxe hotel, fine meals, lots of laughter and a glitzy show, Antonia was half in love. 'Positively the ONLY unspoiled rich man I have *ever* met . . . looks rather like Si – but thin. In fact, if you can imagine Si plus a strong character and minus all the neuroses, you have the man!', she reported to Lyndall.[17]

As the end of November approached, Antonia began to find the rigid routine of institutional life rankled more. She was never very sure about nuns and too much exposure to them made her increasingly critical. Sister Madeleva's charm had also worn thin. She had had enough, Antonia told Emily, of 'sham and big talk and general INFLATION.'[18] There was an undercurrent of something amongst the nuns which made Antonia uneasy. She thought the trouble partly lay with Sister Madeleva and the legend that had built up around her. Rereading her poems a year later she told Emily: 'They are unspeakably bad & embarrassing, and . . . at times . . . well, I think *indecent!* If I were the Pope, I'd forbid nuns to wear wedding dresses when they enter. It gives them ideas!'[19] She was carrying also the weight of the knowledge that Lyn Cosgriff wanted to become a nun and had yet to tell her mother. Antonia's joy at the news was not unconfined. Furthermore, she missed her cats; there were none to adopt around the place and she had only caught sight of one in the far distance, but had grown quite fond of the cockroaches, except when they climbed into bed with her. But it was the rich layering of European culture, and all the references that she usually took for granted which she now began to miss most of all: 'one longs now & then for . . . what is it? . . . older *minds*? I'm not thinking of the students but the nuns & the faculty.'[20] As she approached the end of her semester, Antonia was begged to return for another term. But she felt she had to get back to her own life and surroundings. Many people were in tears as she left, from the old battle-axe who ruled the faculty table with a dictator's fist, through 'my "lambs" – my darling students', to the maids who cleaned her room.[21]

For the two weeks before Christmas Antonia went to New York and met her American publisher and, by lucky coincidence, Elizabeth Bowen, on her way to be a writer-in-residence at Vassar. Although she had had more than enough of nuns and convents she went on up into Connecticut to stay with Mother Benedict, whom she had known from her convent days, who had begged her to come. Christmas she spent with friends of Dr Gurley, and went to Charleston, which she loved. She found Julien Green's birthplace in Savannah, the city he had written of as extraordinary and enchanting, but thought his family house gothic-ugly, with the pokiest staircase possible 'twisting up in an almost furtive way from the main hall'.[22] This explained to her Green's obsession with staircases. Julien Green's first cousin, Julian Hartridge, came to Christmas dinner. Hartridge's father had spent thousands of dollars, he said, putting the ungrateful wretch through the University of Virginia, and his books were hardly worth the bother; 'like a wet Sunday afternoon in Bonaventure' – the great graveyard in Savannah.[23]

By February Antonia was home in Ashburn Gardens, forgiven by her cats, and thankful that the money she had earned at St Mary's would buy her time until September to work on her book. However, this prospect, instead of being greeted with relief, was profoundly frightening. For seven years Antonia had been struggling with the Clara sequel, in various guises, with the growing dread that she had lost whatever ability she had to write fiction. She tried to distract herself from the task with small spending sprees on unnecessary clothes and things for the flat. She bought another hat, 'MOST unsuitable' for a sixty-one year old she thought, but a beautiful object which she liked looking at; 'It is all Renoir-like roses with a whiff of veil'.[24]

She decided to go to Paris for a week in April, to stay with Christine Arnothy, a young Hungarian novelist writing in French for whom Antonia had already translated four books. She would also see Julien Green. And in between, Antonia sat at her desk, writing, revising, crossing and recrossing out, throwing away, and beginning again, in the most painful and pathological expression of creative impotence. She felt that as she consistently destroyed each piece of writing so effortfully produced, she was a protesting Penelope unravelling her day's weaving every night in a life and death struggle with her fate. All this she recorded in agonising and repetitive detail in her diaries and letters to her closest friends. The book had been due at her publishers, Eyre and Spottiswoode, in August. They had been patient beyond reason, but in September 1960 she was still on the first few pages.

She catalogued an average day's work: 'I sat down at 11.... I thought I wd. just "tidy up" a sentence or two ... perfectly easy ones. When I looked up it was 4.30. I had spent 5 1/2 hours – absolutely unproductively.... I didn't even make a "final version" of those 2 sentences ... I find this rather frightening ... it has happened ... over & over again these past weeks – this extraordinary flight of time ... my mind really has almost ceased to function.'[25]

In addition to her old fears, Antonia was paralysed by her concern that she might upset the fragile truce with her daughters by bringing up the more recent past. She also felt guilty about having received an advance for the book and therefore being indebted to her publisher until she could produce something for him to sell. Antonia was troubled too about the possible interpretation of her fiction as 'unedifying'; 'all my old guilt about there being something corrupt (even without my knowing it) in my novels as my father read corruption into the one I wrote at school'.[26] This explained some of the 'terror and guilt and nausea' Antonia felt when trying to write novels. It was not helped by the violent reactions she provoked in some establishment figures in her Church. Virginia Johnes had told her that a priest she knew (and Antonia had met once) had said that she ought to give up writing and

concentrate on translating 'as a penance for her immoral life'. This shook
Antonia and, try as she might, she could not dismiss it from her mind.
She decided to check if it was true and found that the priest, an eminent
and devout man, had only ever read her short story, 'The Moment of
Truth', and as a result had returned *Strangers*, in which it appeared, to
Mr and Mrs Johnes saying 'he refused to read any more of such
disgusting stuff.'[27] Another priest had asked Antonia in public if she had
written any more dirty books lately. He too was well-regarded within
the Catholic hierarchy – and to make matters worse was an ardent
admirer of Colette. This sort of disparagement of her work from the
father-figures in her Church had a terrorising effect on her.

But the nuns too, who seemed to be fond of her and admire her
work, could shock Antonia with how little they understood, how naïve
and irrelevant their views were on lives which were complex and
outside their experience. Antonia had written to the Carmelite Prioress
to thank her for coming to her aid so generously over Virginia Johnes
and the Anonymous Donor business, and had mentioned in passing that
she thought her next book (the Dougal and abortion one) would shock
her. This unwitting woman replied along the lines of: we all know that
there are wicked people in the world and that Antonia had to write
about them so that the good would shine out all the brighter. Antonia
expostulated to Emily, 'Never seems to have occurred to her that we're
all wicked & *all* good!'[28] Intellectually she could dismiss these individual
opinions as irrelevant, but emotionally and spiritually such comments
stuck in the flesh of her shell-less self like poison darts. As her concerted
efforts to produce the next book seemed more and more futile, the
terrible doubts arose. Did God not intend her to write? Was the whole
purpose and struggle of her life built on false ambition and base vanity?
Were the shameful failures of her life not suitable material for her work?
Was she fundamentally worthless and corrupt? Antonia was not helped
by her fixation on telling her own story, chronologically and accurately.
She had got so bored with 'Clara'; the life she was recalling was now too
long ago, the mood of flippant elation when she had escaped from the
asylum, too difficult to recreate. Yet she could not lose the fixation. 'I
seem to be able to do *nothing* except out of my experience – years &
years after it happened . . . I have absolutely NO inventive power, I
think & it is an appalling handicap', she wrote in reply to a much
appreciated letter from Susan urging her not to give up.[29]

Emily, despite her own creative logorrhoea, was also a ready ear for
Antonia's problems. Six months after the book was due to be delivered
she still had not managed really to begin; 'I continue to have HELL over
the book (honestly, Emily, I don't know why I don't just CHUCK it

... every page I write is LOUSY ... I have 4 lousy versions of the next 10 lousy pages ... my brain is so tired and stale I don't think I'll *ever* be able to write decently again. O[ur] F[ather] is providing a nice penitential Lent for me.'[30] She was oppressed with the thought that her faith would have her believe that this was God's will, that she should suffer this barrenness in a compulsive routine of striving and failing, only to strive and fail again. It exhausted and distressed her yet she seemed involuntarily bound in this fruitless ritual, like an obsessive washing her hands until they bled.

This ongoing state of despair and aridity, accompanied by panic, characterised Antonia's creative life virtually until her death. She had small recessions when she managed to produce something, most notably her autobiography which she started with some pleasure in 1965, but then struggled with as surely. She was never to escape the feeling that, fundamentally alone, she was forced to write in a vacuum, 'absolutely stuck inside a bell-jar & unable to communicate at all.'[31] She mourned that she could never again recreate the mentor/protégée intimacy she had with Tom which had brought forth *Frost in May*. And so, her creative spring sealed off from herself and others, Antonia continued to torture herself at her desk even when she was old, in pain and half-blind.

During her last analysis of 1966–67, Dr Ployé, her psychoanalyst, had been particularly concerned about her writing block. She told him of a dream which he felt was highly significant. At that time there was no hot water in the flat because a ball-cock in the tank on the roof had jammed and the tank drained dry, cracking the cylinder of the boiler as a result. In her dream she was descending an iron ladder into a swimming pool to get to a model submarine lying on the bottom. About to put her foot on a lever, she wondered what would happen: would it turn something off? Someone made a suggestion that it might cut off the air supply to the people in the submarine. Dr Ployé had long thought that much of Antonia's problems went back to a pre-natal experience: in this dream he saw an indication of the kind of trauma she might have suffered. Perhaps something had happened when she was in the womb which had cut off her oxygen supply, he suggested. Antonia agreed that she always described her writing problems in terms of blockage or jamming, and yes, the accompanying anxiety was always acute. On her way home she tried to think further about the associations; 'what could represent the "ball-cock" that had got jammed. The first word that came into my head was religion.'[32]

Her years of unproductivity had made Antonia despair of ever being accorded a place in even the second division of Catholic writers, let alone the pantheon of English writers. She often felt she was invisible to the literary establishment. However, at a Society of Authors party in the autumn of 1960 she realised she was not so much invisible as in disguise. Someone came up to her and said how much they loved her books – it transpired that they thought her the well-known children's author Noel Streatfield. Then the real Noel Streatfield came up to her (they had been at drama school together) and said how much she adored her books: Antonia stopped purring when she added 'Especially the way you read them on the wireless'. She had mistaken Antonia for Antonia Ridge, who read her novels on *Woman's Hour*. Then Rebecca West's husband came up and was charming; 'You know I have *never* forgotten that delightful book of yours about the Three Rivers of France.' Rebecca herself, whom Antonia had not seen for ages, did recognise her as herself and said '"My dear, you must meet a friend of mine from S. Africa who is DYING to meet you". So I was duly introduced to a lady who was indeed dying to meet me, not because she'd read so much as one word I'd written, but because she'd been staying with Tom & Dorothy & was *dying* of *curiosity* to know what Tom's first wife had been like.'[33] She could only smile and watch the tide rush on.

27

Drowning in Sight of Land

And yet I am, and live with shadows tost
Into the nothingness of scorn and noise,
Into the living sea of waking dreams,
Where there is neither sense of life nor joys,
But the vast shipwreck of my life's esteems;
And e'en the dearest – that I loved the best –
Are strange – nay, rather stranger than the rest.

'I am', John Clare

Antonia had read this poem of despair to David Gascoyne when she was thirty-eight, and attempting to piece her life together again after a breakdown and four and a half years of Freudian analysis. Although there had been many alarms since, she had been free of her Beast for more than twenty-five years. Now it began slowly to gain on her again.

Dr Carroll, her Freudian analyst, had warned her that she could experience another crisis between fifty and sixty, but a gruelling regime of translating work, Antonia believed, delayed her recognition of her state. It was during her sixties that the writing block became petrified into stone. Her compulsive battering of fists and brain against this monumental psychological edifice was the underlying stress of her life. When other people with sensible professions and modest pensions were retiring, Antonia was frantically trying to work still, sick with anxiety over paying the rent and bills, then breaking out on spending benders which would increase the fear of penury. Having faced the anxiety of the rent rises on her flat at Ashburn Gardens and the threatened extra costs of renewing the lease, Antonia heard at the end of February 1961 that the owner of the building had died and the heirs wanted to sell as soon as possible. She might only have three months' notice to quit. This new threat loomed over everything and dominated her thoughts for the next four months. She decided she had to try and find somewhere else to live which would give her more security, but the price of everything half-decent alarmed her. After the usual desperate financial calculations, rising panic, worrying that kept her awake at night, she decided, with the agreement of the trustees to her father's estate, that the only way to finance the move would be to sell Binesfield, her family cottage in Sussex. Her father's will gave Antonia the use of the place or the capital, should it be sold before reaching Susan.

However, it was with great trepidation that Antonia wrote to Susan to tell her that this seemed to be the only route open to her; the lease on the new flat would of course go to her on her mother's death. She feared that this would be the trigger for another withdrawal, but after a few days' anxious wait she received a note from her daughter saying that although it was sad it was much more important that Antonia have a home '& peace from the eternal menace of eviction'.[1] So anxious had she made herself, Antonia felt pole-axed with gratitude. Her idea of Susan, for good or ill, was often much more extreme than the reality; again, as with her father, she somehow needed to be in awe, afraid and yet admiring. It was hard for her to think of either as being merely human.

For weeks Antonia had not been able to sleep very well and was habitually waking up at five in the morning, and starting to worry, write letters and think about work. She was very keen to sell Binesfield to her current tenants, who loved the house and knew it well, but she had to battle with one of the trustees who wanted her to try and get more money out of them, or wait for a better offer from someone else. Suddenly in early April she saw the place she wanted. Just round the corner from Ashburn Gardens, it was a third floor flat in 42 Courtfield Gardens, which was still big enough to allow her a work room and a room for a lodger. She had been in Ashburn Gardens for eighteen years and this new flat would be her last home. The price of the lease and the costs of moving would be more than she was getting for Binesfield and she immediately started to sell anything she could, her only bits of good furniture, her piano, the jewellery left to her by Alick Schepeler, even in a frantic moment Tom's aquamarine engagement ring which she had actually given to Lyndall, who had left it behind in the flat. Full of remorse at what she had done on the panicked spur of the moment, she wrote apologetically to Lyndall. She had only been given £5 for it. She offered to pass the money on to her when she could. 'WILL YOU FORGIVE ME? I FEEL AWFUL. . . . I wouldn't have done it if I weren't up against the crisis of all time & the *desperate* need to have a home.'[2]

Antonia was in an obsessive drive to get this flat at all costs; it was perfect for her, she believed, no other would ever do so well. She asked her praying friends to pray for it. Phyllis, who was worse off even than she, sent a donation of £100 and Emily, who was increasingly generous to her old friend, continued to send the odd £30 – £50 to help her out. (The equivalent today would be a multiple of about ten.) Lyndall, rather than asking for the £5 back, sent £25 for Antonia's birthday, which delighted her. Emily and Lyndall were to continue to send what money they could to Antonia to temporarily ease the chronic anxiety she had when expenditure threatened to exceed income, a situation which became increasingly common as she grew older and the translations became harder to come by and took longer to do. As her contribution over the following years, Phyllis offered to type even the roughest drafts for her, hoping to extricate the pages before Antonia could get too locked into the revision/destruction mania. Occasionally it worked.

Antonia said herself that during these four months of flat-moving unheaval, she was so obsessed and exhausted she felt barely human. She drove herself not only to clear up the old flat but to repaint parts of it and the furniture in it, so that it was nice for the incoming tenants. But her mental and physical exhaustion was not just a result of her current efforts and anxieties. The selling of Binesfield also had deeper significance and caused inevitable psychic disturbance. In the Clare poem she had read so affectingly to David Gascoyne, the final lines recalled her own feelings for the place. 'There to abide with my Creator, God,/And sleep as I in childhood sweetly slept:/Untroubling and untroubled where I lie,/The grass below – above the vaulted sky.' Although she had never wished to live there permanently, it represented a prelapsarian innocence and rural delight which she was able to revisit for spiritual nourishment in barren times. It was a place through which she remained connected to her forebears: her father's parents; his dear old aunts who loved her unconditionally; her father himself, who in his brief retirement was happier there than anywhere; her mother, living on in vague and pleasurable widowhood. By relinquishing the house, Antonia was cutting this material link with her past. She was making also another move towards emotional independence; 'an assertion (*not* a rebellion!) against my father'.[3] But she recognised the guilt this assertion still gave her. She wondered whether this disconnection from the past should not be mirrored in her writing about a part of her life more allied to the present, the American book, for instance, which in embryo she called *The Polished Apple* and then *The Golden Apple*. All these surface anxieties and subterranean stresses took their toll.

Antonia still had two Colette books to translate by the end of the

year, one of them the last in the Claudine series, *Claudine and Annie*, and
a lengthy review for the *Month*. After a solid stretch of working so
intimately with the writer she felt overborne by the weight of her ego;
'I really don't think ANY woman was as much in love with herself as
Colette. . . . She is so overwhelming! I am worn out having to live in
her personality, translating her! I love her . . . but I need a rest from
her!'[4] And even when she was finally and happily settled into her new
home, money continued to trouble Antonia and keep her awake at
night. She had spent more than she meant to on new things for the flat,
and was always feeling she had to run to try and catch up with herself.
Sudden siren thoughts that there might be a better place for her gripped
her imagination again and she began to look at flat particulars in the
paper, and daydream. Lodgers continued to be a necessary source of
regular income but she was tentative with them, and her loneliness and
quick affections made her indulgent and exploitable.

By now Antonia had spent most of her life alone, but still felt she
would have been happier sharing it intimately with someone else,
although she admitted that she could not imagine a man to whom she
could have been 'a real wife'.[5] Lodgers were the half-satisfactory
alternative. Giorgio was a charming Venetian lad, a protégé of Alec
Guinness's, but he had never been away from a doting Mamma and
Antonia had to show him how to wash his clothes and cook, and ended
up doing most of these chores for him herself. Then in Courtfield
Gardens, after a young woman called Griselda and a neurotic young
South African, she took in a charming and wildly camp Mr Chapman, a
Catholic convert who had had to return to England from Madrid for a
year for 'tax reasons'. He was a part-time actor and very keen cook who
made his hair cream in Antonia's food mixer. He would dance into her
work room when she was sweating over her desk to tell her funny
stories, and would bring her on a tray a plate of his dinner party food
while all his guests cavorted noisily in the next room. She felt it was
probably good for her to live with such an out-and-out extrovert, with
the sweetest nature, she thought, of anyone she knew. Unfortunately he
turned out to be an immensely plausible Walter Mitty character who
cheated her of more than three months' rent with promises that he
would return to clear his room and debts. Antonia continued to believe
him when anyone else had long given up and the nervous strain on her
was considerable. She had never been able to deal with suspense and
uncertainty and was periodically obsessed about him for over a year –
would he ring as he said? would he pay her back as he promised? –
staying at home specially, hanging by the phone. 'This war of nerves
after all the misery of suspense . . . is nearly killing me'.[6] She was

outraged when Emily and Phyllis suggested that she had hoped of his return (and believed in his honesty) for so long because she was in love with him, yet her obsessional nature and her desperate need for the money owed made her unable to cut her losses. In the end she took possession of his belongings, largely a treasure trove of fashionable clothes, a dubious passport and photographs of handsome young men in swimming trunks, as hostage against the rent. Her next lodger was a young Catholic woman, and much less trouble.

Antonia was always susceptible to hard luck stories, and headlong and enthusiastic in her embrace of a wide variety of people. In July 1962 Mr Mumford, the local 'Squire' and prison visitor, asked Antonia to write regularly to George, a prisoner in Pentonville for burglary, who had no one to write to him. There began an unlikely relationship, with Antonia writing every week a letter which could take her well over two hours to compose. George's interests were pop music, boxing and motor-racing and he had hoped for a young and pretty pen-pal, but was an optimistic opportunist who seemed grateful enough for this mother-in-law figure, sticking her photographs and those of her daughters up in his cell. Antonia was heroic in her efforts on his behalf. She got Susan and Lyndall, Emily and Mary Siepmann, even Dame Marcella, a devout nun at Stanbrook Abbey where Emily was a guest, and numerous other friends, to send cards at Christmas and even write letters and visit. She herself visited him a number of times in Pentonville, before he was moved to Dartmoor, spending two and a half hours travelling and hanging around the waiting room, just for the allotted twenty minutes' chat over a formica-covered table. Her letters about George and these visits were funny and vivid; it was clear she expended a great deal of emotional and practical energy on him, even though she realised he was a recidivist who had no desire to be either converted or cured.

Antonia was drawn to his cheeky exuberant character, 'as quick-witted as they come & *bursting* with life'.[7] In the first flush of her enthusiasm for George, she left his company feeling energised by his animal spirits and the glimpse he gave her of an alternative system that was completely alien to her way of life – and rather exciting. He was quite honest about what a crook he was, told her about his bank jobs with pride, shared his burgling lore and gave her the insider's tricks on cracking the combination code on any safe, 'but I have promised not to reveal it. I can't use it myself on account of my deafness' she solemnly told Emily.[8] Antonia thought him an endearing rogue, a born fiddler with no more moral sense than a magpie, but she recognised something of the robber mentality in herself – the need to get something for nothing.

Antonia's need for money made her easy prey for another kind of conman. Jacob Schwarz was an American manuscript dealer who had bought in 1962 various manuscripts from her for £50. Antonia was not then in the habit of keeping her manuscripts, once the book was published, and when he learnt that she no longer had *Frost in May* he suggested she copy the whole thing out in longhand and he would pay her £35. Her own writing was going badly, she was ever short of money, and so she complied, but said she needed £60. It was humiliating to be reduced to this, and also to be reminded of the success of this first book, this albatross around her neck. Three years later at a party she learnt from Olivia Manning just how conned she had been; Olivia had sold a manuscript to the same man for £25 who had sold it on to one of the rich American university archives for £1,500.

However, there were happier moments. The event she had been praying for every day for nearly eleven years happened in the early summer of 1962. Susan told her that she had returned to her religion and had had her marriage regularised by the Catholic Church. Antonia wrote to Emily saying she was so dumbfounded that she could barely take it in. All she did was hug her daughter and try not to cry. Her own months of misery and religious deadness suddenly seemed to have had a point and a reward. For a while Antonia felt an unfamiliar contentment; 'as if the most important task in my life had somehow got done & what happens to me now doesn't matter much'.[9] She continued to go down to Sussex to see the Chitty family for high days and holidays and they were always harmonious, uncontroversial occasions, with both sides careful not to tread on sensitive ground. Only a couple of years later, when Susan was visiting her mother in Courtfield Gardens, did she feel confident enough to explain for the first time the impetus behind her withdrawal:

> She said she had to get away, to be herself. What surprised me was that she said she felt 'inferior' because of having such a 'clever' mother. This seems extraordinary to me, because *I* always felt Sue to be as intelligent as myself if not more so, as well as having many gifts I have not, including beauty.[10]

This openness had made Antonia feel again the special bond between them; the sense that each understood the meaning beyond the words; 'I have something in common with her that I have with no one else'.[11] Although Antonia was wary about mentioning Catholicism in front of Thomas, his kindness to her and his tolerance of his wife and children's own religious choices increased her liking and respect for him. She prayed for the conversion of 'that tough subject, Thomas!' and her own younger daughter, whom she felt needed something firm at the centre of her life.[12]

Lyndall was still unsettled and at times suicidally depressed. She spent a miserable nine months in America, working on the Festival of Two Worlds, but longed to return to Italy. On her journey back from New York she stopped off in London to see Antonia and then set off for a week's holiday alone with Susan. She left the manuscript of a novel she had written for her mother to read, the person whose opinion mattered most. Antonia found this novel extraordinary and moving, and 'hair-raising' too. 'Some of the book is really marvellous' she reported to Emily, 'But my goodness, what it tells me about Lyndall & her state of mind! It is God's miracle she hasn't been murdered, killed herself, gone mad or been utterly corrupted.'[13] To Lyndall she sent a long appreciative, encouraging letter, pointing out the 'marvellous' things and those which did not work so well. 'Whatever you say, you CAN write – & write unusually well & it would be the greatest pity if you didn't go on writing' was her mother's verdict.[14] Lyndall did not make much effort to get her book published; she had heard what she needed to hear from the person for whom it had been written.

One of the advantages of Antonia's detachment as a mother was that she could take devastating criticism on the chin, as long as it was taken in through her intellect. In Lyndall's novel there was a highly unflattering picture of the heroine's mother and Antonia was able to accept this without pique as being true of how Lyndall saw her, at least when she was a teenager and still living at home: 'An embittered frustrated woman, devoured with jealousy of her daughter, always frustrating the daughter, angry if she is happy, only sympathetic when she is in trouble. I have few friends, having driven them away by my sour temper, am "an intellectual with no normal intelligence" "unable to face life" always complaining about lack of money (true enough!) . . . cynical, neurotic and possessive . . .' was how she characterised in her diary her fictional character.[15] In the postscript on her letter to her daughter, Antonia wrote penitentially; 'Your portrait of me in your book makes me realise what a dreary old grouser I was (& often am!) & I must STOP it. But I truly *did* want you to be happy – it's awful that I made you think I didn't!'[16]

Spiritually, she may have always felt a much closer bond to Susan, but in her emotional life Antonia could recognise too well Lyndall's febrile search for purpose and identity. This made her book 'haunting' and 'terrifying' to a mother who had travelled that way herself; 'her lack of any centre, her desperate isolation, her sense of not existing unless involved in some violent emotion. . . . I understand better than she thinks'.[17] Rather remarkably perhaps, there is no evidence that Antonia felt jealous of her own territory being invaded by her daughters' novel-writing, even though she was barely able in these last years to occupy the landscape she hoped was hers. Although initially shocked by Thomas's novels and unsettled by how out of touch as a writer they made her feel, she had grown reconciled to him and no longer bristled at his enviable creative fertility and critical acclaim. Susan's second novel, *White Huntress*, was published in 1963 and Antonia found it 'brilliantly funny . . . more than a touch of the young Evelyn Waugh'.[18] To Lyndall she wrote that, witty as it was, she wished Sue would tackle a more serious book closer to her own nature.

Lyn Cosgriff, her favourite student at St Mary's and another of her adopted 'God daughters' was an extra bright light in her life at this time. When she was passing through London in September 1961 she helped Antonia with notes for the American book she hoped she would write, refreshing her memory, soothing her despair and urging her on to tackle in fiction her time at St Mary's. They had so many laughs that Antonia had to remind herself that, if she managed to do such a book, she had to avoid being too funny – or too unkind to Sister Madeleva. A month later Antonia heard from a nun at the college that Lyn's much-loved father had been killed in a car crash. Lyn was only twenty-one and as Antonia perceptively pointed out, 'She isn't nearly as tough physically as she looks.'[19]

Antonia had opened an intellectual door for Lyn Cosgriff which had changed her life: she had also offered her an unconditional love and admiration which her own mother had not been able to give. Lyn was heartsore at the state of anxiety into which Antonia's fear of penury drove her: she felt that freedom from the worst worries might help release the writing jam which dominated her life. She was young and had recently come into part of her inheritance; it seemed a natural and right thing for her to give a little of her own wealth to someone to whom it might make all the difference. Lyn was concerned, however, that it could damage their friendship. At the beginning of April 1963, on her return to America from teaching in Japan, Lyn spent two days with Antonia in London. They had been corresponding and Lyn knew the pressure Antonia was working under, her fears of not having enough money even for bills. For months she had been getting up at five in the morning, sometimes even at four, in order to translate to an implacable deadline a secret book on de Gaulle. Banned in France, *The Trial of Charles de Gaulle*, an indictment of the General by Alfred Fabré Luce, was rushed through for publication in England and America. Antonia had to pass sections on to experts and then incorporate their changes and additions, rewriting parts herself. When she visited, Lyn saw an elderly woman whom she loved and admired, almost old enough to be her grandmother, driving herself still through a gruelling schedule of work, her mental health declining, with no easy retirement, pension or financial protection ahead. With tears in her eyes, she offered Antonia a gift of £1,000 to help buy her peace of mind for a year, with time to work, or just to stand and stare. It did just that. But also a few more interior decorations and new clothes, all of which temporarily cheered Antonia but then as quickly filled her with guilt. She was still trying to persuade herself that this flat was home. During this build-up to her third breakdown, she embarked on re-painting sprees nearly every year.

Antonia recognised that this compulsion to spring-clean and remodel the flat was becoming pathological; quite obviously a distraction from the terror of her writing block, it was also an attempt to keep the external carapace of her life pristine and controlled while inside she fell apart. She remained fastidious about her own appearance, her hair always coiffed, make-up perfect, neat and tidy in her dress. While she was unable to make a fresh start in her life, to throw off the rotting albatross, blow away the staleness and begin again, she could at least make that fresh start on the more manageable features of the flat, with paper and paint, new bits of furniture and spruced up fabrics. But it never did the trick for long.

Lyn's gift, however, also meant Antonia could pay off debts which weighed on her conscience, like the £80 she had borrowed thirty years before from Charlotte Denman (née d'Erlanger, her convent friend Léonie in *Frost in May*). Within a year the gift was gone, except for £100 left in premium bonds. Charlotte, in fact, refused to accept the cheque and insisted it had been a gift, but Antonia's contacting her again renewed their friendship. They continued to correspond and see each other intermittently until Antonia died. Charlotte had always been a heroine to Antonia, elegant, distinguished, and a cradle Catholic who could wear her faith lightly and with humour. The fact that she had lapsed and felt no need to return was always a source of fascination to Antonia – and some admiration, for it seemed that she had slipped from the silken net and truly managed to break free. Ever since her own return to the Church, Antonia's faith had been a cerebral and soul-less thing, where she faithfully went through the motions and prayed for heat and light. In the lead up to her mental collapse, the aridity of her faith weighed her down; 'I wish I felt devout, I don't, not a bit. I don't feel *any* conscious love of God. I just say to myself "I *know* I believe this" but it all *feels* quite unreal ... I really feel at a very low ebb spiritually as well as every other way.'[20]

A part answer to her dustiness of spirit was provided by Kathleen Raine, who introduced Antonia to the works of the philosopher-theologian Frithjof Schuon. He was a Swiss, living in America and a convert to Islam, who belonged to a group called the Traditionalist Movement which believed in the transcendent unity of religions. He approached all religions, but particularly Catholicism, in the tradition of sacred knowledge. 'The scriptures are *inspired* – that is what matters', Antonia wrote in her diary and this thought freed her for a time from the irresolvable debate in her own mind about biblical literalness, historical truth and how many angels can dance on the head of a pin.[21] A great deal of controversy had been stirred up by the Second Vatican Council convened by Pope John XXIII, who intended to modernise both the organisation and the teaching of the Church. Through Schuon's insistence that one's personal religious tradition was God's revelation to oneself, that truth had no conditions, she could see how immaterial were the arguments about traditional versus modern when the fundamental revelation was 'ever ancient, ever new'.[22]

As the Pope lay dying in the summer of 1963, Antonia and Emily exchanged anxious letters, concerned for him as a person and worried about the political and spiritual ramifications of the choice of his successor. In fact Pope Paul VI continued with the reform Pope John had begun. But concurrent with the old Pope's deathbed vigil there was a terrible row between Emily and Phyllis which further heightened the emotional temperature at home. Antonia, in the middle of her own crisis of translating the de Gaulle book, was dragged into the fray. Phyllis, who was a recent convert, had expressed religious doubts to Emily, a woman who had no doubt. Furthermore, Phyllis, who had a prodigiously generous heart and capacity to endure, had finally had enough of being Emily's 'slave friend' and decided to move away from the cottage at Callow End, near where Emily was living.[23] The shock of her rejection of this demanding relationship appeared temporarily to tip Emily into madness. Once before she had been psychotic, after the birth of her son John, as she had described in her poetic novel *The Shutter of Snow*. Now in her sixties, Emily wrote furious, hurt, accusatory, torrential letters to all her friends, incapable of seeing Phyllis's point of view in the situation. Antonia admitted to Emily that she was terrified of her violent side and was incapable of confronting her for this reason, but she did attempt a tortuously diplomatic letter suggesting that Emily might be just slightly insensitive to the everyday struggles that assailed others less exalted than herself; such things as religious doubt, exhaustion, demands of work and failures of will. This letter was returned annotated by Emily with angry and emphatic denials, and for a while she remained furious with Antonia too. As it turned out, just over a year later she was operated on for a brain tumour and its effects on her mind may have been already evident.

This torrent of bitterness from one of her oldest friends, against a woman whom she considered heroic in her generosity of spirit, preyed on Antonia's mind. She was already regularly rising at four in order to finish her enormous de Gaulle translation by May. Now she began to force herself out of bed ever earlier, in order to write calm, reasonable, sympathetic letters to Emily before she started work. She was still managing her letters to George too, to other friends and to Lyndall. Briefly, Antonia returned to the battle with her own book, 'Clara IV'; 'one sentence a day which is scrapped the next. It is really a nightmare.'[24]

Then, by the early summer of 1964, she began a translating task which Emily and the French Catholic philosopher Jacques Maritain had been urging on her for months, the translation of Raissa Maritain's journal. Raissa had recently died: Jacques had lived with her in an exclusive hothouse of mutual devotion and spiritual certainty and was devasted with grief. Antonia's work was emotionally complicated by the power of the personality she was having to interpret and by the grieving husband's interference with the translation. The former, who had been considered saintly by all who knew her, made Antonia feel her own spiritual life was meagre in comparison; she could only hope that this work would be good for her soul – 'a mean, cowardly little soul, as different as possible from R.'s great generous courageous one'.[25] In an already diminished state, Antonia was intimidated by the intensity of Raissa's vision. Her elevated thoughts brought back the old fear that her own writing belonged in 'the devil's world'.[26] It therefore relieved Antonia immensely to hear from Emily that the saintly mystic had dyed her hair and varnished her nails.

In recent years Antonia had made firm friends again with Georgie Earnshaw Smith, despite the virulence of her attacks in the early days of her marriage. Since reading *Beyond the Glass*, Georgie turned to Antonia both for help with her own writing, and for support in the stormy inadequacies of her marriage to Eric. Antonia had deep sympathy for her and the frustrations of her life, and a great continuing affection for Eric, whom she saw as a tragic figure ossified by alcohol, disappointment and fear of change. The old intellectual connection still remained and a nostalgia for that kind of easy sodality that they shared. Each turned to her when they became distraught about the other. After one such occasion, with Eric on the phone to her for more than an hour, Antonia returned to her Clara book with renewed vigour: 'I suddenly realised to the *full* how much Eric meant to me & what I feel (& I think he does too, but I won't let him say it) about our not being able to do what we'd always meant to do – spend our old age together.'[27]

Another of her ex-husbands and his wife made an uninvited foray into her life in 1965. After years of silence, Dorothy Hopkinson suddenly wrote to Antonia suggesting she might like to send a birthday cable for Tom's sixtieth birthday. Antonia, determined as ever to maintain good relations, sent one off. When Tom replied in a sweet and friendly way, saying he would like to see her again when he came to London at the end of May, Antonia was perfectly happy to comply. However, it transpired that it would be Tom and Dorothy with whom she would be dining, and that Tom, first of all, wanted to clear up with Antonia 'the bitter injustice of my affidavit about Dorothy in Gerti's case over the children'.[28] This was the first occasion Antonia had to explain her actions and she did so at length in a measured but unflinching tone, mentioning Dorothy's 'ferocious' letter with the half-crazed threats to set Baba's curses upon her. Not unsurprisingly the meeting was called off with a very chilly note from Tom, implicitly believing Dorothy's version of events over Antonia's. She would have liked to see Tom again and found it hard to accept that he thought her a liar, but was more than a little relieved that she did not have to make polite conversation to them both; she had long ago realised that the Tom she had thought she knew had somehow absented himself, leaving an affable simulacrum to go through the motions.

Meanwhile, however, Antonia's closeness to her daughters was increasing. Susan and Thomas's elder daughter Cordelia had decided to become a Catholic like her mother and grandmother, and at her confirmation in December 1964, Antonia had been touched by the poignancy of the occasion. She experienced fleetingly that rare feeling which she had wanted ever since she was a child, but never really known how to achieve – that of being part of a warm united family. She only wished that Lyndall could have been there too, although she had sent her niece 'the sweetest, most touching letter.'[29]

Antonia for her part went home and wrote a long, affectionate letter to Lyndall. She was increasingly touched by her daughter's affection and generosity to her. After one of her gifts of money, Antonia wrote: 'you have given me marvellous *moral* support, as well as material! And I'm very touched & *very* grateful. But *don't* worry about me. I'm fine.'[30] She remained troubled by how unsettled and fragmented was her daughter's life, despite its outward glamour. Lyndall's picaresque romantic experiences had finally taught her mother that beauty did not automatically bring in its train happiness, security or lasting love. In fact, Antonia thought there was a sense in which Lyndall's 'fatal beauty' and the attention she had always attracted from men had distracted her from her true self and the pursuit of her own goals. She was an Atalanta figure, beautiful, fleet of foot, losing the race only because she had been deflected by the golden apples, tossed down by a tricky suitor, and had paused to pick them up along the way. Antonia thought Wolfgang Reinhardt, her daughter's boss and lover, the nicest of Lyndall's men she had met so far, but was concerned at how selfish and blind he could be to her needs; 'I am not sure that he realizes that he is, in his gentle way, eating her up.'[31]

Susan and her family were off to Champaign-Urbana, Illinois in the late summer of 1965, where Thomas was to take up an academic position at the University of Illinois. They were to be gone for two years, with Susan suffering from depression herself the first months after arrival as they entered a bitter winter. Deep in the mid-west, they were 130 miles south of Chicago, rather isolated from big city culture and with extremes of weather to endure. Antonia missed her daughter very much and missed too the occasional but precious conversations about writing or faith. She was concerned also for Susan's health, particularly when, in her late thirties, she became pregnant with her third child while she was away.

Antonia continued to plod on with her faith, no longer expecting much, going to Mass, praying for herself and others. To her amazement, however, her honest religious struggle, unselfconsciously recorded, was to prove an unexpected success. In August 1964, at dinner with her old friends, the writers Neville and June Braybrooke, Neville had started talking about how good he thought the extracts from her diary which had appeared fourteen years ago in the *Month*. Antonia realised he was talking about her extracted war-time letters to Peter Thorp. John Guest, an editor at Longman who was also at dinner, expressed interest in seeing the article she had written for Cyril Connolly, and then wanted to read the whole correspondence. Phyllis had typed out all her letters (she had sent Thorp's back to him, as requested). Antonia was embarrassed by her impetuosity of feeling, and struck by how her struggles with the problems of faith had not changed in these twenty-four years. She was also amazed by the sheer volume of writing, written in one year at the height of the blitz, while working full-time at the BBC. 'Did I really write those letters? Is it *me* they're excited about?', she asked herself.[32] In the middle of her implacable writer's block, such unselfconscious facility gave her pause for thought.

Longman were delighted with the letters, and published *The Hound and the Falcon* in the autumn of 1965. The book was well-received, particularly among her friends and the public at large who responded to her candour and the depth of her feeling, her passionate engagement with the truth. She was inundated with letters: intimate, moving ones from strangers outlining their own problems of faith, and enthusiastic admiring ones from old friends and almost forgotten acquaintances. A mysterious telegram from Benedicta said merely 'Wonderful. Love. Bezer.'[33] This was the last communication she had from her. Cyril Connolly, ironically, recommended the book to Sonia Orwell. Antonia was exhilarated that she had written something that might actually help people and she exhausted herself answering these letters, sometimes at length. Father Hugh, the Carmelite priest whose acceptance of her at confession had brought her back into the Church, had written too. He had been given *The Hound and the Falcon* to read by his bishop and had not known her as the author but had recognised her as he read. He sent her 'a wonderful letter' about how much happiness the book had brought him; 'it had encouraged him in his own bad times to see how God had looked after both of us.'[34]

Just before the publication of *The Hound and the Falcon*, Antonia went to her GP with swellings round her eyes. She had been extremely tired for months, and now a bad cold and the sore eyes meant that she was unable to work. She did not see her usual doctor and was taken aback to be asked by the unfamiliar Dr Galway how she was generally, in herself. His kindness and interest in her suddenly opened the floodgates. She told him about Bethlem, her further breakdowns, her worries about work, the load on her conscience about money given to her by friends and in public grants, and nothing to show for it. She even wept. There was such relief in being able to talk to a sympathetic professional, so aware was she that in a busy general practice doctors did not have time for counselling sad old ladies. Rather than treat her as if she was wasting his time, this doctor thought her complaints were more serious than she had allowed, and suggested she see a psychiatrist. Although she had prided herself on being sane at last, she was relieved to know that there was something more to this nervous exhaustion and mental stagnation than just weakness of will, depravity of character, laziness or old age. 'It is a great relief to me not to have to keep *forcing* myself.'[35] When she returned to Dr Galway the following week, he said he would like to try her on anti-depressant pills initially. This was the first time in Antonia's life that her mental problems were treated by anti-depressant drugs. In the past she had had the occasional blanket tranquillisers which suppressed the personality, rather than just freeing it of some of its compulsions and anxiety. To begin with they made her feel pleasantly peaceful: 'How odd that a drug should give one peace of mind', and then for a while worked well in releasing her from the most debilitating aspects of her depression and crippling perfectionism.[36]

Dr Galway attempted to allow a set time each week during surgery for Antonia to see him. He told her he thought she had split off a whole part of herself which she considered to be bad and terrifying and that this schism had happened in babyhood. Antonia, remembering Dr Carroll's warning, realised that this third breakdown had been building for many years. It finally came to a head just after an intensive ten-year grind of translating had come to an end. That work had distracted her from misery at her own inability to write: now with money from friends and the Royal Literary Fund grant of £400 which arrived at the end of 1964, she was awarded time to write at last and was hit with overwhelming guilt that she could not do so. In her own mind, she was as much a robber as George: in her subsequent analysis she caught herself substituting her own name for his when she was relating his story to the doctor. Antonia also thought it significant that, just after receiving the longed-for grant, she had a series of accidents and ailments which made it difficult for her to get down to the dreaded work; a fall in the street which damaged her knee, a cracked rib, a prolonged attack of excruciating lumbago, a mysterious eczema-like rash and then the cold and swollen eyes.

Dr Galway's therapy, chemical help from the pills, together with the excitement of having a book published again gave Antonia a few moments' clarity and peace; 'Fresh air?' *That* is how all this feels.'[37] She also found her writing block temporarily relax as she continued with some ease on the beginning of her autobiography, a project suggested by Malcolm Muggeridge. By the end of 1965 she had sent a hundred pages to Phyllis to type. Antonia was trying a new tack. The written pages went off immediately to Phyllis before she had time to read them, start correcting, and then destroy. She did not even consider this a serious attempt at writing a book, more 'a kind of serial to amuse Phyllis'.[38] *Frost in May* had been written with the same intention – as a weekly serial to amuse Tom. But in a few months the symptoms of depression and despair were as bad as ever. This was not helped by her being touched by the tragic deterioration in the mental and physical state of Elizabeth Coutts, a widow in the basement flat in her building, whom Antonia had known for five years and for whom she did small neighbourly kindnesses. She had been found wandering and incoherent in her nightdress: her flat in a chaotic and filthy state.

The depredations of age and infirmity were brought even closer to home; Curdy was chronically ill. Antonia was going to have to make the painful decision to put him down; it was that weighing up of when was the right time to have a beloved animal killed which caused so much grief. He had gravel in his bladder and she knew his time had come. 'All this reflects for me my own mental trouble – the old cat under sentence of death, the old woman mouldering away in her flat as I feel myself mouldering away inside.'[39] She did not want to upset Emily unduly with the news of Curdy's sentence; Emily was battling with her own depression having been through the traumatic operation for a brain tumour and subsequent radiotherapy. But when the fateful decision was made Antonia wrote to her old friend, the person who had given her Curdy as a kitten when she thought she would never have the heart to have another cat again. Having almost stopped purring as he got more ill, Curdy began to purr continuously after the vet had given him the fatal injection with Antonia sitting stroking him, '& went on purring the whole time, even after he was unconscious, right up to his last breath. It was as if he were reassuring me that he knew I was doing the kindest thing for him & he was grateful'.[40] She told Emily she felt his gentle presence still in the flat: she was sure that everyone would have their beloved animals in heaven with them when they died. 'Bless you for having given him to me.'

Antonia's own depression, despite the pills, would not lift. Dr Galway thought she needed more intensive help, and wrote to the Cassel Hospital in Richmond to ask for her to be taken on as an out-patient. She felt every day was an ordeal she had to drag herself through. Death and degeneration and the sufferings of old age overwhelmed her; '[Dr Galway] says that I see myself as the old, incurable cat. But not even to be put away by merciful euthanasia – to be subjected to cruel torture.'[41]

28

An Old Soldier

Fr Broderick SJ: 'Antonia's *Hound and Falcon* interested me *intensely*.
I read and re-read it *three times*. She is a heroic soul.'
That is an *extraordinary* idea for anyone to have of me!
'Heroic' – of all things!

13 October 1966, *Diaries II*

At the end of February 1966, Antonia went to the Cassel Hospital to
meet Dr Philip Ployé to see if he would take her on as a patient on
the National Health. At first Antonia took exception to him, he was
small and dark, 'he looked most sinister & is a hunchback', but very
quickly he had impressed her with his intelligence and her confidence in
him grew.[1] He agreed to see her every two weeks, at the hospital, a
commitment which involved Antonia in a long journey by public
transport. The analysis continued for three years and was only broken
off, rather abruptly, because Dr Ployé's in-patient list was too
demanding for him to find enough time for his out-patients. He was
worried and distressed at having to abandon Antonia prematurely;
'when I said "It is like an unfinished story" he agreed.'[2] Antonia hoped
that this analysis with Dr Ployé would free her to write again. This did
not happen. Her depression and anxiety, however, diminished and the
compulsion to return repeatedly to things, expressed in her constant
revisiting of the past and the endless revision of each word in her
writing, was reduced to more manageable proportions.

Early on in the analysis, as the sense of oppression and depression
began to lift a little, Antonia received two extensive 'schoolmistressy'
letters from Lady MacAlister, the former pupil of her father's who had
been instrumental in his conversion. They had not seen each other for
more than forty years, and Antonia had never really liked her. These
letters accused her of betraying her father by writing about him; 'that it

was wicked of me to write about him at all unless I had simply composed a pious memoir', as she explained in a letter to Susan.[3] She and Tom promptly ordered some wine to be delivered to Antonia's flat as a 'gloom-chaser'. With Dr PloYé's help, her understanding of her mother's qualities, and her father's forbidding perfectionism, was deepened. 'I am my mother's child as well as his. I think he often forgot that.'[4] The inhibition of Antonia's imaginative and creative self was connected perhaps with the eclipse of the archetypal mother in the subtle workings of her soul.

With this increased emotional connection to her mother, Antonia gained confidence in her own maternal relationship with her daughters. They had become the most important people in her life and she was able, belatedly, to offer them the love which she had been too self-absorbed, fearful and blind to be able to give them when young. In her experience, the mother of a daughter was of little importance and not a focus for that daughter's love: with her own young daughters she had sensed a hostility and fearfulness in them towards her, which she was neither mature enough nor confident enough to overcome; 'I didn't dare to be demonstrative: I got well & truly snubbed if I did!'[5] But in her old age, Antonia settled happily into motherly pride and supportive affection, interested in their projects and unintrusive in their lives. Antonia loved to talk to Susan about her writing or the eternal questions of her faith; 'she still thank goodness has this peculiar quality that she had when she was a girl – what I used to call the "streak of platinum" – and which I can't define. It is a kind of severity or integrity – something which makes me value her judgement.'[6] Having made Lyndall her literary executor (with Elaine Lingham's help) during the wilderness years when Susan was lost to her, Antonia in 1967 decided that Susan should now be her executor after all. Susan argued against the inclusion of Elaine. Rather than have a joint-executorship, Lyndall thought it less complicated if she withdraw in favour of her sister; she had always been reticent about claiming her full rights and inheritance.

Antonia was included in the whirl of Chitty family life for birthdays and Christmas and Easter, and occasional weekends and treats in between. As she watched Susan and Thomas dealing in a permissive and loving way with their young children, the contrast with her own childhood, and her behaviour when her children were young and being cared for largely by Nurse, was almost too vast to contemplate. 'I can't imagine any better parents than Sue and Thomas. These young modern parents who share coping with the baby and the domestic chores are really splendid. . . . Sue and Thomas put me to shame when I think of my own selfishness and cowardice.'[7] The major difference, she noted, was that her young grandchildren had a voice in the family; they could ask for things and expect to be listened to, their needs respected. As a small girl, she had no voice, no rights and little respect. At times she thought that they were allowed too much of a voice but, even when her hearing aid screeched in her ear in protest, she never wished for a return to the silence and repressions of her childhood. Antonia even found she could admire her son-in-law for more than just his creative energy and the abundance of his literary output. She was reading an advance copy of Thomas's novel about America, *High*, due to be published at the end of 1968 and reported to Emily how much she enjoyed it; 'Had to swallow last ounce of my prudery. It's very dirty, hilariously funny & has got an extra *something* as well. . . .'[8] Although she had initially blamed him for her breach with Susan, over the years Antonia had come to admire what she recognised as his integrity and his qualities as a father: she was particularly grateful for his kindness towards her.

Lyndall's relationship with her mother was more emotional and intimate. It was a bond which flourished in the medium of letters. She and Antonia confided in each other over the trials and tribulations of their lives and celebrated the victories which came their way. They went to great lengths to offer support to each other, and some philosophical framework for the suffering in their own lives and the lives of others. Lyndall's financial contributions to her mother, even when she was herself a struggling working woman, eased some of the worst anxieties of Antonia's life.

In 1967 Lyndall met Count Lorenzo Passerini whom she married in 1972. After the initial euphoria, Antonia was aware that life with Lorenzo would not be easy. He was capricious and demanding with no real motivation and little pleasure in his life; 'Lorenzo, charming as he is, is really a life-work in himself!' she consoled her daughter.[9] Lyndall also suffered from intermittent black depressions and an immanent sense of aloneness, which Antonia recognised as something she too had felt all her life. Now that she was older, however, she told Lyndall she found being alone and an outsider did not matter so much; '[I] even find certain advantages in it.'[10]

Being alone, however, had serious drawbacks when accidents or failing health assailed her. In August 1966, Antonia tripped over a paving stone at seven in the morning on her way to Mass. She fell flat on her face, bashing her nose, splitting her lip and breaking all four fingers of her right hand. Antonia staggered to her feet, blood pouring from her nose, which she thought she had broken. Nobody came to her aid except one woman who merely pointed out in passing that her handbag had sprung open in the fall. Although she was shaky and bleeding she walked the three-quarters of a mile to the nearest hospital alone, where the staff were surprised that she was still upright, given the shock and the hairline fracture of her skull they discovered on X-raying her. Her fingers took a long time to mend and for a while Antonia was going to hospital three times a week for painful physiotherapy to restore them to use. Antonia thought it 'fishy' that, just as she felt she was managing to write a little, she had crippled her writing hand. Kate O'Brien, her 'lapsed' friend, thought the fishiness was more to do with the fact that she fell on her way to Mass, while suffering one of her crises of faith. Her old friend Margot King took her to see a practitioner of alternative medicine, Mary Austin, who used 'radionics' and acupuncture on Antonia over an extended course of treatments, all paid for by Margot.

Illness and decrepitude surrounded her. Elizabeth Coutts, the woman in the basement flat, was an exhausting burden for Antonia for much of 1966. She was rapidly going out of her mind, her deterioration accelerated by drink. Antonia was naturally sympathetic to people struggling with mental troubles and she became the main focus for Mrs Coutts's frightening and disruptive behaviour. Raved at and wept over, Antonia took the responsibility for her which her own relatives seemed to evade. But it wore her down and frightened her, for this poor mad lonely woman seemed to mirror her own condition; 'I feel, myself, empty, half-crazed, deadly tired, unable to concentrate on anything. I'm nearly as crazy as poor Mrs C. but put on a better show.'[11] She saw Mrs Coutts shuffling about in her dressing-gown, or merely just a vest, her hair unkempt, her flat in chaos, and Antonia knew that her own carefully maintained exterior, her visits to the hairdresser, her manicure, her immaculate clothes, the redecorated flat, all kept from sight this mad beast inside. It was this meticulous mask which Kathleen Raine had recognised when she met her during the war; 'All she did was carefully self-conscious to a degree that seemed at times almost perilous, like some delicate feat performed by a juggler.'[12] The energy required to maintain this feat, to keep all those balls in perfect synchrony, was exhausting: to let go was to risk catastrophe, the same exposure of internal disintegration which faced her every time she saw her neighbour.

Antonia had a key to Elizabeth Coutts's flat, and it was she who let the police in to find her dead, slumped over the kitchen sink in her husband's dressing-gown, looking more like a bundle of old clothes than a person. The old woman had been determined that she would not go to a mental hospital or other institution and had at least managed to die at home. But Antonia was the only person available to be responsible for sorting out the remnants of her life, and it was a sad and salutary job; 'It's a frightening thing, watching the disintegration of a human being.'[13] Inevitably it made her think of her own approaching infirmity and death. Neither of her parents were long-lived and Antonia was half-expecting death from her sixties onwards.

Antonia's eyes had been troublesome for some years. She had incipient cataracts in them both which would need two operations, ordeals she was happy to put off for as long as possible. However, by the summer of 1968, when she was trying frantically to finish *Living With Minka and Curdy*, her eyes had deteriorated so much that she knew something radical had to be done. Her oculist suggested that Antonia have the worst eye done first, and privately if she could, so that she could be operated on quickly and have her own specialist supervise her post-operative care. BUPA medical insurance did not cover the full costs of the operation and nursing home, and Lyndall offered to pay the shortfall, an offer which took the worst of the worry off Antonia's shoulders. She was always made most miserable by anticipation and uncertainty. 'I'm *so* touched & grateful to you darling for all you're doing for me. I'll let you know how it all goes & I'm sure it will go splendidly.'[14] But she was not so sure it would all go well. She was afraid of blindness and in that fear her aloneness seemed more frightening. She lay awake one night a few weeks before the operation 'feeling very isolated. Not exactly depressed but very much alone, glad of the living presence of Minka, purring when she woke and making curious little grunting noises in her sleep'.[15] She could not be alone in the immediate aftermath of the operation, as she could not see well, was not allowed to bend her head down, and needed to have eye drops administered regularly through the day and night. Phyllis, who was living in Devon now Emily had gone back to America, offered to come and look after Antonia.

The first operation was performed at the Nuffield Nursing Home in Woking in the middle of October 1968 and Phyllis, 'angel friend if ever there was one!', escorted her home and cared for her for over two weeks.[16] They shared a taste for crosswords and good whisky and had almost a lifetime of mutual friends and memories to chuckle over. When they were younger there was no natural understanding between these two very different natures, although Phyllis had come to Antonia's aid even then, during her breakdown in the mid-thirties. Phyllis was practical, earthy, sexually adventurous, with a liveliness of spirit and generosity of heart which made Antonia think of her, in her later years, as truly saintly. There had been many men she had loved but she never married or had children. She had an extraordinary capacity for caring for others which she expressed unstintingly with her friends. For years she

nursed her mother in the terrible slow decline of dementia. For the
eleven years Emily Coleman was in England, Phyllis had dealt with all
the practicalities of their lives, often in very difficult circumstances,
accused and raved against by Emily in her illness and despair. Phyllis
then became a rock of comfort and support to Antonia when she was ill,
or most afraid and alone.

However, once Phyllis had returned to her own life, Antonia had to
get used to her newly incapacitated self. She could not see to write even
after three weeks, and was beginning to worry about how she was to
earn a living. After a dearth of nearly two years on the translating front,
Antonia had suddenly been offered two at the end of the previous
summer and had accepted both, even though it meant working without
a break for five months with her sight failing. Both were 'lousy', she told
Emily; one an early Colette, *The Innocent Libertine*, which was
'*unbelievably* bad – it was like a cruel parody of her and has almost
disillusioned me about her other books'.[17] The other was Thérèse Saint
Phalle's *The Candle*. After another fallow time while she recovered from
the operation and then finished her second cat book at last, Lyndall
introduced Antonia to Anthony Blond, an attractive young publisher
whose star was ascendant. He immediately gave her not only *The
Memoirs of Chevalier d'Eon* to translate but also wangled a translator's
grant for her from the Arts Council, which gave her a little more time to
try and produce something of her own again. Unfortunately Antonia
had to turn down his next translation because, although she considered
it better written than *Lolita*, she felt that its theme of complicit child
abuse was pornographically depicted and 'as a Catholic, I feel I shouldn't
do it.'[18]

Increasingly Antonia's mind returned to her doubts about her faith.
Inspired by *The Hound and the Falcon*, letters continued to come to her
from distant friends and strangers, often reporting how she had helped
the reader renew his or her faith. She had more than seventy in all and
answered each one carefully, some at great length. But her own faith
was as troublesome to her as ever. After a happy day out with Susan and
her family at their house in Sussex, she had turned to Virginia Woolf,
the inspiration of her youth. Rereading *The Years* she was struck again
by the bleak truth that we do not know ourselves and cannot know
others. This sent her worrying again at the intractable bone of religion,
her 'eternal, eternal, more and more insoluble problem and conflict. It is
awful to say it, but so much in Catholicism is positively *repellent* to me.
More and more so. It is most of all this insistence on sin, Christ's
atonement, the angry Father who will condemn to hell those who are
not "saved".'[19] Antonia also believed, however, in the 'Real Presence'

which she experienced for a few moments when she went to Communion. But then she beat herself with the impossibility of knowing that anything so personal is true: 'All we can say, this has happened to me, I have reacted in such and such a way.'[20]

Despite Antonia's instinctive recoil from her Church's insistence on sin and retribution, she felt no more at ease in the modern psychological wing of Catholicism, when a sympathetic priest who heard her confession admitted to having as many doubts as she did. The sixties was a decade of upheaval in the Catholic Church as elsewhere. There were daily reports of priests leaving the priesthood in order to marry. Latin Mass was abandoned and services were conducted in the vernacular. Trendiness was in danger of breaking out in manner and belief. Nuns were stripped of their traditional wimples and habits and got up to look like district nurses, Antonia complained, with short skirts, an excuse for a veil, and their hair showing. All very hard on the fatter ones, she noted. At St Mary's College in Indiana the modernisation had swung even further; 'The nuns wear ordinary dress and even make-up and go in for slimming. They are also allowed to drink.'[21]

Father Broderick, who on reading *The Hound and the Falcon* had thought Antonia a heroic soul, admitted to being 'constantly riddled with doubts himself' and consoled her with his lack of concern about whether the Garden of Eden, for instance, was myth, although he admitted it conveyed a profound religious truth. However, his breeziness did not release her for long from her obsessional mental wrangling with what was actually true. She wanted an authority to tell her what were the fundamentals which she had to believe in order to be free of hypocrisy in practising her religion. Yet that authority itself was antipathic to her nature. She found problematic the fact that the whole doctrinal structure of the Catholic Church was based on 'the literal Adam and Eve, the fall, original sin, the atonement to an offended God, salvation only through baptism, the divinely guided Church, the inerrancy of scripture, the possibility of eternal damnation and all the rest.'[22] When she put the same question about whether Adam and Eve was literally true or poetically true to Father Anselm, who came to see her when she was convalescing after her cataract operation, he said he would have to consult and think it out and then write to her. But he went on to say 'Adam *did* live a long time (900 years)' and once again she was sprung back into the old mental turmoil.[23]

Both Fr Broderick and Fr Anselm suggested that her problems with belief were more emotional that doctrinal, which was close to the mark, but Antonia could not agree. She did not want the attaining of grace to be easy; her view of The Father was not of a benign God of Love. She needed to believe in an uncompromising, unforgiving, implacable God against whom she could beat her brains and rail. This was an expression of her comfortless view of life and her professed need for the platinum streak, as she called it, the pitiless line that would brook no compromise. Yet her human, feeling side longed for the very qualities which she could not find in such a faith; understanding, tolerance, acceptance, love. She found the changes in society, as mirrored by the Church, equally confusing. 'The key words of praise now seem [to be] "erotic" "revolutionary". The dirty words "bourgeois" "Victorian morality" (i.e. Christian morality) "unaware of social issues". "Society" has now become a kind of abstract god or devil.'[24] An interview with John Braine in the *Guardian* horrified her; here was an apparently ardent Catholic who could boast about his 'pretty revolting' latest novel, *Stay With Me till Morning*, full of immoral goings-on.[25] On another occasion the marital irregularities of a friend who had married an ex-priest left her wondering; 'One just doesn't know where one is with Catholics these days'.[26]

Although Antonia was not convinced by aspects of the newly modernised Church, neither was she a convinced traditionalist; she was personally too open-minded for that. Some years later, at a Requiem Mass for the translator and writer Bernard Wall, Antonia was ill-at-ease; 'I did not realise how used I'd become to the vernacular Mass. Much as I miss the Latin and think much of the English translation abominable, there seemed something in the Tridentine Mass that one missed – the sense of participation'.[27] She had always liked best the inclusivity of Catholicism, and had no time for the mannered elitism of certain sections of the Catholic fold. She fought down aesthetic fastidiousness at the religious artefacts sold at Lourdes, and one part of her wished she could have the unquestioning faith of an unsophisticated Irish woman she had met who truly believed, for instance, that a Carmelite who died on a feast of Our Lady would go straight to heaven 'or "if not, on the following Saturday"'.[28]

Antonia was reading Santayana again; she was still moved by him and 'haunted by the idea that Christianity is a myth' but she was afraid that any lapse again on her part might have repercussions on the belief of people who mattered greatly to her: Susan and her other Catholic friends.[29] The publication of *The Hound and the Falcon* had made her faith public. She identified with the heretical priest Fr Tyrrell and read his autobiography again with horrified recognition. Antonia felt that both of them shared this state of permanent inner conflict, that both had buried their doubts alive. Of course, hers came back to haunt her. Catholicism was something she longed to relinquish but feared to lose.

But these very doubts, formalised in the published letters to Peter Thorp, were also responsible for bringing a great deal of warmth and friendship into her life. Among the people who became new friends was an actor who had studied at the Academy of Dramatic Art when Antonia was a student there, Denys Blakelock. He was a bachelor who lived with his sister Renée and her husband. Brother and sister became like the brother and sister Antonia had never had, she explained in a letter to Lyndall. Denys was a devout Catholic who suffered from debilitating depressions, but when he was well he was an amusing companion and sometimes escorted Antonia to social events. He looked after her in the aftermath of the accident which broke her fingers, giving her a bottle of Lourdes water to sprinkle on her hand – although she found a compress of witch hazel more effective. He was also of practical help, doing shopping for her when she had her cataract operations and was not seeing well enough to feel confident walking in the street. Denys was aware of her lack of money, and gave her a gift of £100 and other smaller presents and loans. He died, in the depth of one of his depressions, just after Antonia's second cataract operation in 1970. His sister Renée was as affectionate a friend as her brother, and when she died, three-and-a-half years later, she left her a legacy of £1,000 in her will. The neglected Irish writer, Kate O'Brien, a friend of Denys's and like him homosexual, re-entered Antonia's life also as a result of those shared religious doubts. She and Antonia had first met in 1934, after the success of *Frost in May*, and she wrote to Antonia again, having read *The Hound and the Falcon* with admiration and affection. She too was making no headway against a writer's block that had turned to stone. Impoverished and living in Kent, Kate invited Antonia down to stay, but the accident to her hand and the death of Mrs Coutts intervened. When the Arts Council awarded Antonia, at the end of November, the unexpectedly large grant of £1,200, 'The biggest sum I have ever received in my life', she immediately sent a cheque to Kate O'Brien, knowing herself how difficult it was to make any sort of living as a writer when one was old and ailing and faced with the terror of the blank page.[30] Kate was overwhelmed; 'How mad can you be? I am so much touched by your quixotic generosity, your absurdity. . . . Simply I don't know how to say "thank you" for your marvellous & absurd X-mas present – you lunatic!'[31]

As she grew older, Antonia was an attractive mentor figure to young women. A marvellous talker herself, she extended to young friends an unshockable and open-minded concern for them and their lives. She was particularly helpful and sympathetic in matters of spiritual quest and doubt. Amanda Hopkinson, the younger daughter of Tom and Gerti, converted to Catholicism at the end of 1966 when she was just eighteen. Up to this point Antonia had had more to do with Nicolette, her older sister, but Amanda entered her life with a request that she stand in for her absent godmother at her confirmation. There began a relationship in which there was a good deal of mutual admiration and affection, although some of Amanda's subsequent wildness and adventurousness with life had her honorary Aunt wide-eyed with amazement: 'such a mixture of childishness & maturity, so much tremendous energy – and nervous frailty – such terrific obstinacy & such incessant changes of direction – well it's an explosive mixture, isn't it?'[32] Every conversion to her faith boosted Antonia's flagging belief momentarily; she saw it as a message of encouragement from God. However, at Amanda's confirmation, there was also an apparition from the past. Tom was invited, without Dorothy, and Antonia, who had not seen him for seventeen years, studied the familiar demeanour of the man she used to know; 'Tom was very affable & utterly remote. . . . He was *most* courteous to his two ex-wives. He struck me as a little sad, outwardly the same Tom, grown a little flabbier, but somehow *hollow* inside.'[33]

31 March 1969 was Antonia's seventieth birthday and she was once again surrounded by all her family. There was a party in Sussex with Susan, Thomas and their children. Amanda Hopkinson and Isabel Quigly were also there. Lyndall had arrived from Italy with a huge bottle of Rochas perfume and a gift of £20 a month for the year to come. Antonia felt guilty at accepting more money from her daughter when she already had given her so much the previous year towards her cataract operation, but now, with her powers failing, she was grateful for anything her family and friends could offer her. As a treat she was taken to the theatre but would have happily stayed at home just to be able to talk more to Susan and Lyndall: 'it was wonderful having them both together which is such a rare treat and for me now the peak of happiness.'[34]

Her old cat Minka was now over sixteen years old and ailing, with kidney failure and arthritis. Antonia's keen young vet suggested a strict diet of meat or fish with added grated carrot. Minka did not care for fish and more times than not Antonia ended up eating the carefully prepared (and expensive) meal herself. The cat had to endure an operation to remove some of her decaying teeth, the anaesthetic was risky at her age, but she survived to Antonia's great relief, although 'She was very miz & cross for 2 days after – and squinted outwards instead of inwards!'[35]

The sense of inexorable decline was halted temporarily by the appearance of an American academic, Professor Samuel Hynes, who was writing an appreciation of Antonia's writing for the *Times Literary*

Supplement. He took her to lunch and impressed her with his knowledge and enthusiasm for her work. When his article appeared in the first week of July 1969, it made Antonia believe in herself for a while; 'It made me feel like a Real Writer!!!'[36] Hynes wrote: 'Failures and rejections are the substance of her novels, and seem to define the human condition as Miss White sees it. . . . If *Frost in May* is cool, the Clara Batchelor novels are icily objective: if *Frost in May* is deficient in kindness, the trilogy is heartless. "Heartless" may seem an odd term of critical approbation, but . . . the quality that I am trying to identify is that aloofness that prevails when honesty and art converge upon the artist's self.'[37] Antonia was rather disappointed that he should find her writing so chilly, but what mattered was that she had been treated seriously in a serious paper. It was fourteen years since she had published *Beyond the Glass* and this recognition of her work seemed a reflection from the literary world which confirmed her fugitive identity as writer, and reassured her she was real. Unfortunately, all her books were out of print so the article could not have any immediate effect on her sales.

Driving herself on with the *Chevalier d'Eon* translation, Antonia managed to finish the 138,000 words by the end of October, having taken just over five months. She was by now very deaf without her hearing aid, and her sight, even with a variety of glasses with special lenses, was not good for walking purposes. The lens distorted her surroundings and made the floor appear to come up and hit her. Shopping was increasingly an ordeal and carrying bags of provisions up the sixty-nine steps to her flat was exhausting. In her letters and diary entries, however, there was very little complaint and no self-pity. A sudden and threatening attack of double pneumonia following flu put Antonia back into hospital in December 1969. One night her breathing had become very laboured, but Antonia was afraid of calling out her bad-tempered doctor: it was her lodger Diane who eventually decided this was too serious to leave any longer. Antonia was whisked off to Princess Beatrice Hospital and spent three weeks over Christmas in the general ward. Although she was in pain, and never at ease with communal living, she made the best of her time there and found Christmas Day 'a riot. . . . Fr Xmas, complete with sledge, attended by 7 prettiest nurses in tinsel & spangles as THE PLANETS'.[38] The deputy Mayor and Mayoress of Chelsea also joined in the jollities, 'shaking hands with the Inmates'.[39] She wrote a memorably funny letter to Lyn Isbell, describing how Father Christmas had given each of the old ladies in her ward a face flannel and cake of soap, after which Sister then put them all to bed early 'because she couldn't run the risk of any of us getting over-excited.'[40]

Susan was in Boston with her family, Thomas having accepted an academic job there until the following June. Lyndall was in Italy struggling with illness herself. So Phyllis once again came to Antonia's aid, visiting her and caring for Minka while Antonia was in hospital. 'Poor Tony. She battles on with extraordinary courage', she reported to Emily after Antonia had been in hospital for more than two weeks. 'She can hardly see . . . is practically deaf – a mass of terrors and frustrations. I wish I could really love her.'[41] Phyllis then stayed for a week once she was home, anxious that Antonia get her strength back so that she could cope on her own. She was concerned about Antonia managing without her and wished that she would take up Charlotte Denman (d'Erlanger)'s offer to go and stay with her in Chelsea. But Phyllis feared Antonia was too much in awe of Charlotte to accept, and anyway would not countenance any suggestion which disturbed Minka. Antonia's plan was to have Gladys, her cleaning lady, do her shopping, even though she only came twice a week, and rely on Diane, her lodger, to keep an eye on her when she was back from work.

All her friends rallied round and both daughters telephoned offering to fly over. Antonia was particularly surprised and grateful for evidence of Susan's thoughtfulness towards her.

Even old husbands and lovers, alerted by Susan, were anxious; Tom wrote to Phyllis suggesting he might visit Antonia in hospital, but she was home by then, and Silas rang; 'I actually SPOKE to him – first time I've heard his voice for nearly 19 years!'[42] She was touched by all this care and concern for her; 'I've been VERY spoilt.'[43] From this time onwards as her health declined, it was very clear that Antonia did not want to burden her daughters with her suffering. Her letters made light of what she was going through, often reiterating that she was fine: she never issued an SOS by letter or phone. It was Phyllis, and latterly Carmen Callil, who she turned to first in her gravest states of physical or mental distress.

Phyllis returned to Devon in a hurry to help Mary Siepmann in the terrible aftermath of her husband Eric's death. Antonia had tried in vain to get her to accept reimbursement for her train fare and other expenses, but was grateful that Lyndall independently had sent Phyllis a cheque which she hoped she would cash. Lyndall offered her mother a holiday with her and Lorenzo in Cortona as a birthday present and period of convalescence. Antonia had become increasingly afraid of making long journeys, but decided it was a good idea to find the energy and courage and go. Delighted to see her daughter and soothed by the beauty of Lorenzo's ancient villa and the surrounding landscape, she nevertheless longed to be home. She felt decrepit and tottery walking on the ancient uneven floors. She was also worried by Lyndall's health and lack of happiness; she seemed to be overwhelmed with work and responsibilities: Lorenzo himself was more of a burden than a support. There was not much opportunity for mother and daughter to be together and talk, as there had been on Antonia's first and happiest visit, when she stayed with Lyndall in Rome in 1954.

On her return home, the outside world intruded unpleasantly on her cosy little flat. There was another letter waiting for her from the censorious Lady MacAlister implying that all her books, with the exception of a few passages in *The Hound and the Falcon*, should have been burnt in manuscript. This left Antonia unable to sleep, brooding over the old problem of reconciling truth-telling in her writing with making her subject matter suitably edifying. Then George, the burglar she had gone to great lengths to befriend, turned up late and uninvited on the evening of the day she had flown in from Italy, and stole the money her lodger, Diane, had left on the mantelpiece. She decided that he probably needed it more than she did, but it was the end of their friendship. The world was getting bleaker and more difficult to understand. A couple of months later Antonia answered the phone to an obscene caller from a callbox, 'The poor maniac must have spent 6 d . . . to mumble "I've got my hand on it and it's six inches".'[44] She was also worried about a call from a journalist at the *Sunday Express* who had rung up to interview her about her translation of the *Memoirs of the Chevalier d'Eon*, and had asked impertinent questions. Extremely hard of hearing on the phone, and naturally helpful and polite to strangers, she feared she panicked and said too much.

Antonia's sight was now so poor that the second cataract operation was unavoidable. Phyllis reported to Emily that she found Antonia much aged and weakened by the pneumonia and really dreading the next operation, booked for the beginning of October. Kathleen Raine wrote her 'a most beautiful letter, hoping the operation might restore my inner vision and creativity. If only it would!'[45] Again Phyllis had promised to care for her and friends and family offered the necessary financial help; Denys Blakelock lent her the money, another friend, Clare Nicholl, gave her a share of a legacy she did not need, and Lyndall promised her another £100. This time the ordeal was worse than anticipated. Antonia contracted an eye infection, which caused her greater pain and prolonged her stay in hospital. Phyllis was concerned that she was becoming mentally overwrought again; 'She is in a bad mental state, as you can imagine – Giving the nurses hell', she wrote to Emily in America.[46] Eventually Antonia was discharged from hospital; Susan, who was back from their year in the States, came with champagne and they had a little party at the flat. Three kinds of drops, three times a day, bandages on her eye at night; Minka also had to have three lots of pills – Phyllis felt she had her time cut out nursing them both, but she cared about Antonia and admired her fortitude.

The death of old friends further depressed her spirits. Lel Earnshaw Smith, Eric's unhappy brother who had been her lodger and with whom she shared a birthday outing every year, had died at the very end of 1967. Robert Demenge, a devout Catholic friend whom she had known for twenty years, also died in 1967, as did Douglas McClean, the doctor who had certified to her sanity when she was about to marry Tom Hopkinson. Eric Siepmann and Denys Blakelock both died in 1970. At Denys's funeral, Antonia gazed in some horror at the large square coffin which encased him, a small man but with a pathological claustrophobia, and she recalled how he had asked that his heart be pierced before he was buried, so terrified was he by the thought of being conscious of his entombment. She also lost her two Oxford-based friends and stalwart allies, Enid Starkie and Hilda Graef. Clare Nichols died unexpectedly of lung cancer when she and all her friends had thought she was recovering merely from pleurisy. This might have given Antonia pause for thought; she had herself been a heavy smoker all her life, and had already suffered from a pleuro-pneumonia. And, closer to home, in April 1971 Antonia lost the constant companion of her bed, desk, lap and board from her early fifties until now, at seventy-two, 'Dear Minka. . . . My last cat.'[47] The tumour the vet found was too big to be safely removed, and she was not brought round from the anaesthetic. Antonia wrote to Lyndall, 'I was lucky to have had her with me so long – nearly 18 years – just on a quarter of my own lifetime & I think she had a happy life.'[48]

Several weeks before, a messenger had arrived on her doorstep from Downing Street, bearing a huge envelope marked importantly 'Prime Minister' and inside the happy news that Antonia had been awarded a Civil List Pension 'for services to literature'.[49] All of £250 a year; Antonia grasped it with gratitude. In January the following year, after an interview, she received notice that the Royal Literary Fund had seen fit to award her £400 per annum for five years. It had been her devout and attentive friend Fred Marnau who had proposed her as a worthy recipient of such recognition and help. Her translation work was now very infrequent and these small yet reliable sources of income helped ease her anxieties about the rapidly rising prices accompanying increasing inflation.

However, on the same day as Antonia heard about the Royal Literary Fund, she was telephoned by Georgie Earnshaw Smith to tell her that

Eric had had an operation for a very severe duodenal ulcer. Antonia visited him in hospital a few days later, and was shocked by how old and frail he looked; at first she did not recognise him. She managed to have him to herself for a while before Georgie arrived, and they talked in the old way, even though Eric's voice was nothing but a whisper. She was never to see him again. A few days later he had a sudden haemorrhage and died. It took Antonia more than a week before she could write about his death, even in her diary. It was more than a week before she could cry. She had lost someone who had been much more than a husband or lover. For a woman like Antonia, to have a companion of the mind, as Eric was to her, was a more precious and rare relationship than anything based on the stirrings of the heart. He had been her master, her mentor, her guide; 'the most important person in my life – and unique. All those other people, Si and Tom, with whom I was in love, of course, meant much but my extraordinary relationship with Eric – it lasted over 50 years – was something quite different and entirely on its own.'[50] The day after Eric's death, Antonia went with Georgie to the hospital when the staff gave Georgie his effects. She was about to get rid of them when Antonia plucked up the courage to ask for Eric's watch. Georgie was happy to give it to her; 'it's for some reason very comforting. I wear it all the time, except when I'm with Georgie.'[51]

29
Virago Vindex

Inevitably I think much about death. I am 79 & so many of my
contemporaries, including younger ones, are already dead.
Funny to have press interviews in prospect [for *Frost in May*'s publication
by Virago] – like being exhumed. I'd accepted the fact of being quite
forgotten as a writer.

7 April 1978, Diaries II

Eric had been a backbone of authority and omniscience in Antonia's
life, taking over the godhead role from her father. 'I defied my
father only when I had Eric to back me up – who had as much influence
on me as my father & was "God" to me too. But no *guilt* in my relation
with Eric. *That* was the blessed difference.'[1] Unlike her father, however,
Eric's influence had lain in his expanding of Antonia's mind; his was not
a proscriptive nature, but one which sought the possibilities in life,
although he may have lacked the drive himself to explore them. Unlike
any of the other men in her life, Eric had never recoiled from her worst
nature, and had therefore reassured her of her lovableness and the
possibility of redemption. At his death Antonia was truly orphaned. She
was comforted especially by the large physical presences of men like
Fred Marnau and Ronald Moody.

Ronald's tears for Eric, and his warmth, consoled her. 'When they
[he and Fred Marnau] envelop me in a big affectionate hug I feel happy
and cherished and not so isolated from human contact.'[2] She and
Georgie were united in their very different griefs, Antonia feeling she
needed to make herself available for the younger woman, who
alternated between brusque plans for the future and explosive bursts of
crying. She promised to ring her up every day and saw her often, yet
remained puzzled by her nature, admiring and wary. Kathleen Raine,
grief-stricken herself at the death of a love, had written to Antonia a

couple of years earlier to commend her generosity to her friends; 'I have seen how you, over the years, have kept faith with the people in your life – all of them. *Being* long suffering, kind, not envying, not resenting.'[3] It was this quality which Antonia offered to Georgie, which was only spasmodically appreciated.

As Antonia's own life necessarily became more circumscribed and predictable, her dream life took on the hyper-realism of her memories of madness. In intense detail, she dreamt of another world where landscapes, clothes and meals were charged with a vivid reality. Perhaps this creative dreaming was the only easy access she could have to that part of her mind disconnected from her normal waking life, her working life, by her writer's block. These wonderfully detailed dreams also compensated for the increasing failure of her sight and hearing. She often dreamt of Eric, and two years after his death she was amused by a dream in which she had been hoping to live with him again: he greatly disappointed her by saying he had rooms in the most rarefied of Oxford colleges, All Souls. 'It was quite a while after I woke up that I realised that "All Souls" was a very significant name for what he was going to be!'[4]

The summer after Eric's death brought two cheering events. A change in the Italian divorce laws had allowed Lyndall at last to marry Lorenzo Passerini, which made Antonia hope for happier and more secure times for her. She had come to rue her unsubtle generalisation of her children's potentials when young, when she had confidently predicted that Lyndall would have an uncomplicated life as a 'charming and devoted wife and mother', surrounded by a brood of happy children.[5] The regularising of their relationship brought Lorenzo officially into Antonia's fold, and reinforced her own sense of family; 'I feel quite a matriarch with two daughters, two sons-in-law & four grandchildren!'[6] Her later diaries are full of quick asides about how lucky she feels to have her two lovely daughters and kind friends.

Her honorary daughter, Lyn Isbell, was touring in England that summer with her husband and three children. They stopped by to spend some time with Antonia. They took her out one day on a sightseeing trip round London in an open landau, and Antonia's anecdotes about the areas they passed through enlivened the guide's own narrative. Lyn was struck by how physically valiant and strong she seemed still, although her sight was so bad, and her fear of crossing roads consequently exacerbated, that she walked the long way round the square to their hotel rather than cross the road without a zebra crossing. Susan joined them for what Antonia described as a 'hilarious evening here. . . . I enjoyed it enormously & they said they did too'.[7]

Even in her mid-seventies, Antonia was attracting new friends still. Elizabeth Sprigge, an actress and writer who had been a contemporary at St Paul's Girls', now became a friend with whom she liked to share occasional meals and do the crossword puzzle, in the absence of Phyllis. Gavin Young also, only twenty-one and yet to make his name as a writer, was an admiring young friend for a while. Staff and students she had met during her semester at St Mary's College in Indiana continued to seek her out. Shirley Hooker, one of her brightest girls, came to visit; she had become a Holy Cross nun after college and was in the middle of her PhD thesis on Shakespeare and Spenser. Antonia was impressed by a realism and confidence she saw in this young woman, and interested to hear of the new generation of nuns; 'Very much "in the world" yet "not of it".'[8]

Having feared she would not earn again, Antonia was pleased to be offered more translations, but like London buses, after a long gap these travelled in threes. In the summer of 1972, Hamish Hamilton, the publishers who had set her off on her long and distinguished translating career, asked her to translate a Georges Simenon novel for them, *The Glass Cage*. This was only 40,000 words and she finished it in two months. Then in the spring of the following year, Longman offered her a large, scholarly book, *The Novels of Tobias Smollett*, which would need continual correspondence and collaboration with the author. Luckily Paul-Gabriel Boucé, a professor at the Sorbonne, was charming, an amusing and intelligent man whom Antonia liked; 'he livens me up with all his warmth and gaiety.'[9] The work was a great labour, however, repetitious and pedantic, and she ended up thinking even less of Smollett than when she had started. But Boucé became a friend; only thirty-eight and 'looking like a cross between Henry VIII and Billy Bunter', they continued to see each other occasionally after their collaboration was over.[10] Just as she had accepted this vast commission, the Folio Society asked her to translate Voltaire's *The History of Charles XII, King of Sweden*, written while he was in exile in England, and which she would have preferred as a task. Although she had to turn it down on account of time, Folio waited and her translation was eventually published in 1976. Apart from the ever-necessary injection of money, these translation jobs brought the 'huge relief of. . . . being let off the rack of working fruitlessly daily on the autobi'.[11]

Antonia treated her writing much as a religious devotion, a ritual which she had to observe every day in order to affirm her vocation. She was still susceptible to the convent's teaching in her youth of the correct sequence of duties and devotions. Without completing one, she was somehow prevented from progressing to the next and so her continuing failure to finish the page, the paragraph, the sentence, in her own literary creation, kept her obsessively trying – only to end each day exhausted and frustrated, with no sense of wholeness or rest. The epic fruitlessness of Antonia's labours had echoes in her much-loved myths. Like Sisyphus she painfully pushed her boulder up the hill every day only to find it roll back to where she had started, forced to toil upwards again the following day. Her desk was littered sometimes with fifteen versions of a first paragraph, so crossed through and reworked it had become an entanglement of barbed wire. And she saw in herself a reflection of Penelope whose weaving was unravelled every night, in Antonia's case through a prohibitive search for perfection. Antonia remained caught between the drive for perfection, and her longing for wholeness, the path to which lay through imagination and feeling.

As Antonia made herself observe daily the comfortless task of writing, the practice of her religion became more mechanical and less frequent. For a long time after her return to her faith Antonia had gone daily to Mass, or at least three times a week. Now in her old age she only went on Sundays and Holidays of Obligation and the three days of Holy Week. Her prayers were sketchy and mainly for people she knew who needed help. She found the rosary '*impossible*' and any other form of prayer difficult: 'Yet I am perpetually preoccupied with religion.'[12]

Kathleen Raine's friendship continued to comfort and stimulate her. Antonia felt that she could talk to her about anything, particularly her religious doubts and her search for meaning. Kathleen's natural acceptance of the mysteries of humankind and the world was refreshing to a nature like hers, which was too rigidly schooled to trust the intuitive, the inexplicable and mysterious. After an evening with Kathleen in September 1973, Antonia was touched by her heroic efforts to care for her aged parents. She was grateful for the freedom of their own conversation, their friendship having endured for nearly thirty years; 'I have become very, very fond of her; she is a rare, a unique person. I know no one else of quite that quality.'[13]

Perhaps Kathleen's own courage and individuality in her approach to religion soothed for a while Antonia's ceaseless worrying over belief, historical truth and literalness; a month later she seemed much more philosophical and pragmatic. 'I *do* believe in a spiritual realm and that, in some mysterious way, it both transcends and interpenetrates the physical. And that perhaps only Catholicism is the truest religion because it most fully expresses this. It *is* a faith one can live by.'[14] But this was a short respite. She had set herself the task for much of the seventies to read her way through the Bible, starting with Genesis. Having been taught by the nuns that everything in the Bible was literally true and divinely inspired, Antonia still seemed to have trouble in overlooking some of the grosser manifestations of a God made by man in his image: 'More of Deuteronomy this morning. The laws laid down by Yahweh are incredible. Savage destruction of the enemies (all non-Israelites), a virgin raped in the city to be stoned to death along with her seducer because she did not cry out. . . . As for "racialism" the Jews are as bad as the Nazis. A "bastard" i.e. a man of mixed race "shall not enter into the congregation of the Lord even to his tenth generation".'[15] This all gave Antonia cause for increasing worry and speculation. She had been educated as a fundamentalist; this made her constitutionally unable to follow her own intelligence and intuition, to believe what seemed to her to be spiritually coherent, and disregard the rest.

Antonia's seventy-fifth birthday was celebrated by going to Binesfield with Susan, to revisit the old house that had been so much a part of her sense of family connections and the rural past. The previous day, Susan had come to interview her for an article in *Harper's & Queen* to be published in the June 1974 edition of the magazine. Mother and daughter talked for two hours of her life, her loves, her work and her faith; and the article was entitled 'An Un-classic Case of Success'. When Antonia read an advance copy she thought the racier elements of her life had been rather cleverly disguised, 'though I felt rather as if I were reading a witty obituary of myself!'[16] Susan's own biography of Charles Kingsley was due out in January the following year, dedicated to Antonia, who was 'so proud of being the author's mother & publicly declared to be such!'[17]

This article, together with the Samuel Hynes piece in the *Times Literary Supplement*, five years earlier, helped to prompt interest in a writer whose last novel had been published two decades before. Although she tried daily to write the sequel to *Beyond the Glass*, and progress her autobiography, Antonia feared she had ceased to exist as a writer to all but her friends and acquaintances. But she was not forgotten. The literary biographer Michael Holroyd had, many years before, come across *Frost in May* when he was researching his biography of Hugh Kingsmill. He remembered it as a wonderful oddity which was top of his list of works in need of resurrection. When the opportunity to recommmend this to the right person arrived, a train of events were set in motion which would charge Antonia's literary reputation with new life, and in the process start a significant new publishing venture.

In May Antonia went to Italy to spend three weeks with Lyndall. Feeling very decrepit, and afraid that she was an extra burden on Lyndall's already over-strained shoulders, she longed to see her daughter happier and free of nervous tension, with fewer responsibilities and more enjoyment in her life. 'Living with you for these three weeks has given me a very clear picture of your life and I have thought of you constantly since', she wrote to her after being back in London a week.[18] She was grateful to Lorenzo for his kindness but she thought him an impossible man to live with. She felt increasing admiration for both her daughters' ability to endure in their marriages, and make them last, when she herself had been so unsuccessful in her attempts to live the married life. She did not envy them either husband.

Antonia was also pleased to renew her acquaintance with Count Umberto Mora, the head of the Italian Institute in London, and to meet for the first time Iris Origo, a well-known writer, Anglo-American by birth, who spent most of her life in Tuscany writing about Italy's history and its people. Antonia was amazed that the Marchesa Origo had read every one of her novels, and she longed to talk to her about her life, her own books, and Santayana, whom Origo had known as an old man at the Blue Nuns convent in Rome. Her father had been his pupil at Harvard and she had heard all sorts of details about his character and quirks. Antonia met at the same time Joan Martini, a friend of Lyndall's who would become a great practical help to her later, as her health further declined. She met too 'the rather-dreaded Germaine Greer who turned out to be so charming'.[19]

A possible repercussion of Susan's interview with Antonia in *Harper's & Queen* was an invitation to a Royal Garden Party at Buckingham Palace. It was an exhausting waste of an afternoon. She longed to have someone to giggle with, could not face the queues for the tea and walked miles trying to find her way out. Although she was nearly mowed down by Prince Philip as she strayed on to unauthorised ground, the only Royal she saw properly was the Queen Mother. She was much the same age as Antonia, who was gratified to find her 'fatter than I am', looking just like she did in the photographs, 'arrayed in flowered georgette & a herbaceous toque'.[20] Another repercussion was an enthusiastic nostalgic letter from Geoffrey Grigson to Susan. Antonia copied a paragraph into her diary: 'I was moved remembering those Chelsea Sunday parties. I owed a lot to your mother, though I don't suppose she realizes it. . . . Your mama, plump, pink, laughing, & wonderfully attractive. . . . Your mother was very kind to such gauche young men as myself.'[21]

Antonia was worried about both her daughters. She signed off a letter to Lyndall with 'Lots & lots of love, darling, & a bear-hug. . . . Bear up, braveheart!'[22] Susan was looking terribly tired, having nursed Andrew through hepatitis picked up while he was in India. She had also had a great deal of publicity for her Kingsley biography which had excited her but taken its toll. Thomas had set his heart on making an epic journey with the family; Susan had steered him away from a sea voyage but had given in to the suggestion that they walk from Santiago de Compostela in Spain to Salonika in Greece with their two youngest, Miranda and Jessica, who would be barely four, riding on donkeys. Antonia was alarmed by how physically demanding 'this crazy expedition' would be for Susan and the children, but relieved that Andrew, who was then twenty-two, would be going with them.[23] The little party set off at the end of April 1975, expecting to be gone for eighteen months in all: Antonia was not sure she would live to see them return.

Each year now was marked by the deaths of further friends, and 1974 saw the end of a few who had meant a great deal to her. Emily had been living a communal life at a Catholic Worker farm in New York State where she had turned her prodigious energies almost exclusively to painting primitive and largely religious paintings. She had recognised finally that her extreme polarities of being were symptoms of a manic-depressive temperament, and Phyllis told Antonia that during these last years she had been less emphatic about her saintliness and genius. However, her portraits of Christ all had an Emily look about the face. Whenever she had heard of anyone's death, Emily's first emotion had always been one of envy. She had very little patience with human grief, particularly in the devout. Ever since she had become a Catholic, Emily had been preparing for her own death with an unflagging confidence about the status which awaited her: when it came she was peaceful and free of doubt and pain. Antonia did not grieve for her so much as feel for Phyllis, for whom Emily had been such an important focus for her thoughts and care: 'it's no good trying to console her for Emily's loss, it's one of those huge private griefs people have to bear alone, and no friend, however affectionate, can do more than stand by and sympathise'.[24] Antonia had known Emily for more than forty years and remembered her fondly and in awe as a human phenomenon; 'She was a unique person with *incredible* vitality – fierce, passionate, generous, violent, wildly unreasonable in some ways, fascinating and often exasperating'.[25] Although Emily could never understand Antonia's spiritual doubts, nor the practical problems associated with having to earn a living and run a household, there were occasions when she had 'the most dazzling spiritual & imaginative insights', which made her infuriating dogmatism worth bearing.[26] She was often extremely funny – sometimes intentionally – as when she called herself a sensitive hippopotamus, a description which had endeared her to Antonia immediately. The valiant Kate O'Brien had also died in 1974, as had Antonia's more recent friend, Elizabeth Sprigge. And although Cyril

Connolly was not an intimate friend, his passing was like losing one of the cultural landmarks of her life.

The translating of Voltaire's *The History of Charles XII, King of Sweden* had turned out to be as difficult in its own way as the Smollett. The elliptical style and complicated syntax were not in sympathy with Antonia's own unembellished style, and she spent much time struggling to decipher his exact meaning, then expressing it clearly without losing the essential Voltairean spirit. She finished the task eventually at the end of March, feeling 'dispericraniated' by the effort, and knowing that she now had no excuse for not returning to the daily punishment of trying to continue her own writing.[27]

Antonia began to read some of her old diaries, hoping for information and inspiration, and became involved again in aspects of her life she had forgotten. She was dismayed to find how little the old obsessions had changed; her writing block, her religious doubts, her worries over money. Inflation in the seventies was giving real reason for concern for those people, like Antonia, on fixed incomes who had never before experienced such a relentless rise in prices. For most of the decade and the beginning of the eighties, inflation was in excess of fifteen per cent, and 1973–4 saw it peak at around twenty-five per cent. This was frightening for older people who could only watch the hike in prices, incapable of earning the matchingly inflated salaries to pay for them. Antonia noted that £300 dresses in Harrods were no longer a rarity; the post seemed to go up every few months; and Binesfield, which she had sold fourteen years ago for £5,000, was being resold for £30,000. Her leasehold flat was now worth four times what she had paid for it, but even at that price she would be unable to get another nice flat in the area, for everything else seemed to have increased in value even more.

Lyndall was over in England twice in 1975, house-hunting for a London base for herself and Lorenzo. She was very keen to try and get Antonia to move into the ground floor flat in her building, rather than have her increasingly struggle with the five flights of stairs. Antonia could not face another move, however practical, and was thrown into a panic merely by the thought of it. Phyllis was up in London during Lyndall's visit in May; Lyndall remembered the sight of the two old friends, sitting, their heads together, hunched over *The Times* crossword.

In the autumn, Susan returned from Italy with Miranda, who had fallen off her donkey and broken her arm. They had rented out their house in Sussex, and so she went to stay with the Glossops in Cornwall while Miranda's arm healed and she herself recovered her strength. Susan flew back in November to rejoin the expedition only to find that in her absence Jessica had done exactly the same thing and was also nursing a broken arm. Thomas went back with her to England while Susan and her diminished party of children and the donkeys stayed in Italy with Lyndall. Antonia was surprised to hear this latest turn of events from Lyndall, having heard nothing from Thomas or Susan. However, she seemed to be no longer afraid that Silas and Sheila Glossop were usurping her maternal and grandmotherly roles in Susan and her family's lives.

Meanwhile Antonia's mind and daily life were becoming ever more besieged by her cousin Helen White who, unbeknownst to Antonia, was suffering from a premature senile dementia. On Helen's retirement, Antonia had given her a great deal of patient help with the short stories she was trying to write. She had been sympathetic and had liked her; family members were a rare treat for Antonia. Unfortunately, Helen's mental state deteriorated in such a way that she was a perfectly reasonable and personable woman one day and a screaming, incoherently distressed and uninhibited banshee the next. Antonia tried to treat her as a rational person who was behaving badly, but quickly became the focus of much of Helen's obsessional behaviour and uncomprehending misery. This in turn exacerbated Antonia's own nervous anxieties and drew her into a mutual obsession; 'This trouble with Helen has really dominated my life ever since September [1976]. She doesn't realise, poor thing, that I am almost as neurotic as she is, and has no idea what a burden she has become to me'.[28] Helen bombarded Antonia with raving phone calls, once as many as seventeen in a day: Antonia had never thought that she would ever get to a point when she would be grateful to answer the phone to a wrong number. However, although she was driven to distraction by this, when Helen did not ring her, she would start wondering what was wrong and ring Helen herself, starting up the whole obsessional pattern again. Antonia thought of her all the time, feared her intrusions and yet was uneasy with her silences: 'I've spent the day, very stupidly, ringing H's number. I can't get her out of my mind. . . .'.[29] When Helen was in her persecuting and persecuted mode, ringing almost continually, never once did Antonia put the phone off the hook to gain herself some respite.

Helen physically intimidated her too. One Saturday in January 1977 Antonia invited her to lunch at Courtfield Gardens only to have her screaming and banging on the street door, causing such a commotion that Antonia's neighbour in the ground floor flat had to come to her aid. After Helen had been persuaded by her brother to go quietly, the neighbour, Mrs Given-Wilson, took Antonia into her own flat to feed her coffee and brandy to stop her shaking. On other occasions, Helen would become distressed and abusive in restaurants or the street and

Antonia had not the physical or emotional resources to cope with her. Once she had to escape on a passing bus, but usually her own physical handicaps made speedy evasive action impossible. Antonia always recognised in the madness of others something of herself, and she was both fascinated and repelled by her implication. She was faced with the unpredictable beast which she knew well and had long both feared and valued. Here was Helen, a calm and respectable woman, out of which leapt without warning a snarling, screaming harpy, making animal faces, grunting and tearing up paper. Although Antonia feared this elemental force, a part of her longed for the freedom and expressiveness of that energy.

In Antonia's life at the time, the madwoman alternated with the sane. Phyllis Jones, representing the impeturbably sane, was increasingly important as the encourager of her writing, the listening teacher who read her work and urged her onwards with kind words. She was also Antonia's protector, writing almost daily to her to bolster her after the traumatic confrontation with Helen at Courtfield Gardens. Phyllis too had taken to sending Antonia unsolicited cheques for small sums of money from her own meagre account. Antonia, grateful and guilty, accepted them: 'I feel mean to take it for she is worse off than I am but this reckless generosity is part of her nature'.[30]

Antonia's concern and anxiety over her cousin continued virtually until Helen's death at the beginning of 1979. She wrote so many words in her diary on this obsessive and long-running saga of misdiagnosis, madness, sudden lucidity and despair, it became almost a gripping, claustrophobic novella in itself. However, Antonia's inability to make any headway in what she considered her real writing had become so petrifed there seemed no chance of release: the barrenness even extended to her reviewing. She beat herself into a frenzy for three weeks trying to write a review for the *Tablet* but was incapable of even making a start. When Susan returned from her Great Trek she told her mother to send the book back with apologies, and in fact wrote herself to Bobby Speaight to explain the situation. The relief for Antonia in being let off the hook was enormous.

But there were happier things to distract her from decay, stagnation and death. Antonia was relieved and delighted to have Susan back in England again; she would drop in for tea when she was up in London, although her exhaustion was an increasing worry. In March, Antonia saw Silas again, for the first time in more than twenty-five years. They had both lent pictures to an exhibition of John Tunnard's work held at the Royal Academy. Knowing that Silas and Sheila would probably come up from Cornwall for the private view, Antonia had asked Susan if she would accompany her to give her courage. The meeting was better than she had hoped and she was grateful that they were able to talk a little in the old way, and moved to discover that the poet in him still existed. Sheila arrived later and was perfectly friendly: Antonia felt that a gulf had been bridged at last. She was so excited by meeting Silas again she did not sleep well and got up twice during the night to think, smoke and revisit old memories, reading the memoir in the catalogue which Silas had written for his friend.

Accepting the loss of her creative impulse, and expecting nothing more disconcerting now than death, Antonia was surprised instead by a miraculous renaissance in her literary works and reputation. Michael Holroyd had recognised in a young Australian publisher, Carmen Callil, the spirit who would respond to *Frost in May*. She was running the feminist publishing house, Virago, and always ready for new publishing ideas. He suggested she read Antonia's book, it reminded him of Carmen's own experiences as a young Catholic girl. Carmen read it in one sitting, electrified by the truth of what Antonia described. If Catholicism was a nationality, overarching race, class and generation, then this book charted precisely the conformations which bound an individual to that inescapable destiny. With this book, Carmen's idea for the Virago Modern Classics was born. *Frost in May* was to be the first and carried its number as a proud badge on the inside front page. In the middle of September 1977, she wrote to Antonia to ask if Virago could buy the rights.

At the end of October 1977, Carmen Callil herself entered Antonia's life; 'Dark, goodlooking, 39 but looking much younger. I took an instant liking to her and we talked for 2 hours. . . . I've a feeling that C.C. will be "in my life". She interests me extremely'.[31] She was the reviving angel of Antonia's life's work, breathing vitality into her out-of-print novels, providing introductions where none existed and clothing them in the distinctive evergreen jackets, decorated with little-known paintings of charming girls, which was to become the distinctive trademark of the Virago Modern Classics series. Whole new generations of readers, to whom Antonia White had meant nothing, were introduced to Nanda and Clara and the fine-drawn, coolly-observed catastrophes of her life. It was an almost miraculous vindication of her lifelong struggle to be true to her life and her art.

Carmen was even more important personally to Antonia. Hers was the last great friendship Antonia was to make. Carmen visited her, calmed her frenzies, and did practical chores for her, shopping on her way back from work, helping organise home and nursing help when arrangements broke down. 'Carmen Callil could not be kinder about my work – or kinder to *me!*'[32] She and Antonia had recognised each other immediately as wild survivors of a Catholic girlhood. Carmen had endured thirteen years of a convent schooling and had been unable to forgive the nuns for the spiritual terrorism she suffered. She and Antonia would talk for hours about religion, relationships, life, with much more laughter than regrets. Antonia had an open-mindedness and unshockability which meant Carmen could tell her anything. In the evolving of this friendship Carmen recognised too the extreme sensitivity of Antonia's skinless self; she gained an insight into the way she struggled daily to cope with her manic-depressive illness: 'the endless lists, the obsessive analyses, the tortured anxieties and the fractured temper: all of this was behaviour she had little control over'.[33] One of the most valuable things Carmen did for Antonia was to understand the nature of this illness and embrace even the most extreme expressions of it in her character. Carmen, like Eric, did not recoil from Antonia's occasional outbursts of anger or irritation. This reassured Antonia that she was not the monster she feared; that she could be loved for whom she really was, naked and unconstrained. And Carmen did grow to love her. And Antonia's letters to her just before she died showed how much she had valued that love and turned to her in the extremis of her despair.

Frost in May was reissued in the summer of 1978 to great interest and acclaim. There were interviews and a flurry of letters from people who had been drawn to read the book by the recent publicity. Antonia seemed rather detached from all the interest and praise which was suddenly focused on her and her work. She had become something of a phenomenon, but she had moved on herself beyond the clamour of fame, fashion and the lure of literary celebrity. Recognition as a writer was something that had mattered to Antonia all her life, but now it was almost too late. She was seventy-nine and felt her life fast ebbing; deaf without her hearing aids, nearly blind without her thick glasses, and increasingly unsteady on her legs, she had advanced osteoporosis and an as yet undiagnosed cancer of the bowel. The concerns of the world seemed to recede in the face of the practical necessities of daily life.

It mattered to Antonia that the old rifts in her intimate relationships were bridged as well as they could be in the tidying of her life in readiness for death. Unexpectedly, Dorothy Hopkinson had suggested a meeting with herself, Tom and Antonia and Lyndall, and they had all had tea at Courtfield Gardens at the end of November 1977. Antonia was relieved how easily everyone was able to talk, despite her not having seen Tom for ten years and Dorothy for much longer. Georgie had suggested that the timing of this reunion had everything to do with the New Year Honours which were published in the paper just five weeks later; Tom had been knighted for his services to journalism, and Dorothy was now Lady Hopkinson. But Antonia did not subscribe to such a cynical view of men's – or women's – motives.

Within days of this news, Antonia was told that Susan's depression had become so severe she had had to go into a mental nursing home in Hellingly near Eastbourne. Antonia believed that she had never really recovered from the stress and exhaustion of the great donkey walk, although the book that she and Thomas had jointly written had been a great success, which had partially revived her. However, Susan had been commissioned to write a biography of Gwen John and had difficulties over access to papers held by a rival biographer: this seemed to have been the tripwire which had tipped her into despair. The news of her daughter's mental breakdown was a shock to Antonia; 'All yesterday I was in a kind of daze. . . . I was so weak and shaky that I could not walk down Gloucester Road'; instead she stayed in the flat, reading a Le Carré novel and waiting for Thomas to ring with news.[34] Susan endured two particularly severe bouts of depression in 1978 and another in early 1979 which necessitated hospitalisation and drug treatment, and talk of electro-convulsive therapy. Susan was not submitted to this, but Lyndall thought it surprising that Antonia this time appeared so philosophical about the possibility.

Since the total withdrawal by Susan soon after her first breakdown, Antonia was never again to be so possessive of her elder daughter nor to identify with her so closely. She had learnt to tread carefully, to allow Susan privacy and keep her own distance: she had even relinquished a little the long-cherished idea of Susan as the genius daughter. Antonia had finally realised that she had imposed the same impossible and intrusive expectations on this daughter as those with which her father had oppressed her: just as she had had to wrench herself away from his weighty hand, so Susan had had to free herself violently from her.

Antonia was smoking too much again, managing to write nothing yet driving herself always to try, and feeling '"désoeuvrée". . . . in every sense of the word'.[35] Ill again with a bronchial infection, a constant pain in her back sent her to her doctor who asked for an X-ray which showed the middle vertebrae of her spine were fused. Her hairdresser was doing shopping for her and Lyndall, who was able to come to London more frequently, arranged for her friend Joan Martini to stay in her flat for a month, when she herself had to return to Italy, so that there was someone to drop in daily on Antonia with shopping and other necessities. Joan and Antonia got on very well and for a birthday treat Joan took her by taxi to the Tate Gallery to see the Blake exhibition. Lyndall had also insisted on buying her mother her first television set which she began to watch rather guiltily, for it was time spent when she felt she ought to have been doing work or other duties. So important and rigid, however, was Antonia's need for external order that even the minor rearrangement of her sitting room, to accommodate the television, disturbed her for days with uneasiness and anxiety. The chaos she recognised in her cousin Helen's life was only just contained in her own. Even when ill and nursed by 'saintly' Phyllis, the wrong cups for tea on the wrong tray could throw her into a frenzy of anxiety and ill-temper.

Just as she was expecting the republication of *Frost in May* and all the attendant emotional disturbances of reviews and interviews, Antonia's back pain became so severe that she had to spend nearly ten days in a nursing-home. When she managed to escape on 1 May, Phyllis came to London for two weeks to care for her in her flat. Then her home help, the redoubtable Joan Harris, took over where Phyllis had left off. She was to be so much help to Antonia that with her money from the Virago reissues she was able to employ her privately. Despite her physical decrepitude, Antonia managed a sparkling interview with Maureen Cleave for the *Observer* in which she admitted her life was 'in such *bad taste*. . . . so messy and complicated. I'm a natural conformist. I so wanted to be like everybody else.'[36] An interview she did as the introduction to a radio play had even the technicians coming over afterwards to tell her how fascinated they were by her story; 'It really is all *most* peculiar – this sudden interest in me. . . .'[37]

Although unexpected events in her life, or uninvited changes to her routine, could induce in Antonia anxiety attacks, she rose like a trooper to challenges such as being interviewed on camera about intimate and traumatic upheavals in her life. The soldier and the actress in her nature united to acquit her with honour. Mavis Nicolson interviewed her for a television programme to be broadcast in the autumn; 'Mavis was a marvellous interviewer; couldn't have made things easier for me. I think I was truthful in all I said. . . . Pretty probing questions but couldn't have been put more tactfully.'[38] She had not only managed to be truthful but touching too: on the day it went out Mavis rang up to tell Antonia 'she had been "moved" by our television piece'.[39]

Antonia had also had to get used to a new lodger, Pippa, who was very kind to her but disconcertingly neurotic herself, 'Yet I think she was really the nicest and most amusing of all my lodgers'.[40] At the beginning of the following month, July, Antonia went to bed with a terrible headache one night only to wake up the next morning having lost the power of speech and the ability to read. She had had a mild stroke. Pippa proved her niceness by doing all the ringing of doctors and cancelling appointments for Antonia. Gradually over the next few days her memory returned along with her ability to talk; her reading took longer, and at first she found it easier to read French than English. Her hearing and aural understanding seemed to remain in a deteriorated state for much longer.

In none of her struggles with ill-health, pain or despair did Antonia communicate any need for her daughters to be anxious about her, or to do more than they already did. Her letters to them, apart from the half-crazed one she wrote to Lyndall in Italy, when Antonia was facing her third breakdown, were often more concerned with cheering them up and on, tending to gloss over her own problems. In fact, worried by Susan's and Lyndall's own health and mental states at various times in the late seventies, she could write in her diary that her current lot in life was easier than theirs.[41] By her middle and old age, Antonia had realised how much she had neglected them as children, how they had had to bear the nerve-wracking effects of her own illness and inability to cope. Although there were still the occasional outbursts of irritability and temper, over which she had managed to gain a little more control and for which she was filled always with remorse, Antonia had decided not to burden her daughters again with her suffering. To Susan, who was recovering from acute depression, she wrote in the autumn of 1978; 'It is *so* sweet of you to worry about me when *you* are having such a miserable time! So let me assure you that everything is going *wonderfully* well for me. . . . Getting a letter from you today has "made my day".'[42]

She was not fully aware, however, of the lasting wounds which her unpredictable and tempestuous behaviour had induced in both Susan and Lyndall; a wariness in Lyndall's relationship with her mother extended almost to her death, while Susan, whose five-year withdrawal had altered the balance of power between them, was less affected by Antonia now and more distanced.

Just as Helen's behaviour had obsessed her, now Antonia got caught up in an anxious, obsessional way with Lyndall's arrangements for buying and letting a house in Knowsley Road. Antonia worked herself into a state over the problems which Lyndall was having with the practical details of the transaction. Due to Antonia's interference Phyllis was involved as a possible tenant, and misunderstandings abounded, feelings were hurt and stress levels escalated.

Meanwhile, the success of *Frost in May* continued apace. Carmen was also Antonia's agent and had sold the television and radio rights, and foreign rights were being negotiated. Television rights alone were due to bring Antonia more than £2,000, twice what she had ever managed to earn previously in one year. Carmen had also decided to reissue the

Clara trilogy simultaneously as Virago Modern Classics, in the summer of 1979. The only problem for Antonia was the need for an Introduction, detailing something of her life and how closely it was followed in the fiction. In an attempt to trick the writing block, Antonia decided to try and write it as a letter to Carmen, but too soon she was in a frenzy of anxiety, unable even to begin. Carmen agreed to come and interview her, as if they were just having one of their many easy talks, but even that became an agonising ordeal for Antonia. Carmen was amazed and horrified to see this woman, who would naturally talk with great fluency and wit about any aspect of her life, disintegrate into a panic-struck child, squirming in her chair, as if she was being forced to find the right answer to questions she did not understand: 'I sat opposite her . . . and I watched pain so great overcome her it twisted her body. I was dumbstruck. She was a living ball of pain'.[43] With much reassurance and changing of tack, the interview was completed eventually: Carmen wrote the Introduction and the next three novels were readied for publication. The Dial Press in America ended up taking all four. Antonia was richer than she had ever been in her life.

Less than two weeks after that excruciating interview, Antonia was in St Stephen's hospital for a biopsy on a tumour in her lower bowel. In the first week of January 1979 she was confirmed as having cancer. Before the end of the month a course of radiotherapy at the Marsden Hospital, the world-famous specialist hospital for cancer, was organised for her; five days a week for five weeks. Lyndall was not due to return to London but had caught the coach from Italy with her invalid husband and turned up at Antonia's bedside. Susan also came to the hospital; friends wrote, telephoned and offered help. Antonia, once again, was surprised by how much others seemed to care for her; 'People's kindness to me is *incredible*'.[44]

30

Struggling Free

Another world,
Its walls are thin,
But, oh, I cannot
Enter in.

I feel its touch,
I breathe its air,
How long before
I enter there?

The key hangs close,
My grasp is weak;
Oh, you who know,
Take pity: speak.

'The Key', Antonia White

With the diagnosis of cancer and the commencement of intensive radiotherapy treatment, Antonia entered a hermetic kind of life, centred around the daily wait for an ambulance to turn up to take her for treatment. Lyndall was with her daily and accompanied her on her first visit to the radiotherapy clinic at the Royal Marsden: 'As we sat waiting, holding hands, I felt like a mother taking a frightened child to the dentist, and a wave of tenderness suffused me as a nurse led away the hunched little figure.'[1] Antonia's life was suspended; reading was the only easy activity open to her. She and Lyndall went to a bookshop and bought seventeen books to get her through. Antonia was delighted to reread Henry Handel Richardson's first novel, *Maurice Guest*. This was her favourite, and she had recommended it enthusiastically to Carmen who reissued it in Virago. Both thought Richardson a genius: Antonia then launched into the epic Australian trilogy, *The Fortunes of Richard Mahoney*; she ended it breathless with admiration, 'surely the greatest woman novelist ever. I think she is an even greater novelist than Tolstoy'.[2]

Susan's depression had deepened and she had returned to hospital again; Antonia wrote that she 'told Lyndall the last thing she wanted was to go back to Hellingly. And now she has had to. . . . I feel utterly helpless'.[3] Lyndall was staying on in London and seeing or ringing her mother daily. She had been researching another, private, hospital which might make better headway with Susan's depression; it cost £125 a week which Lyndall and Antonia thought they could manage between them, if it proved to be a better alternative to Hellingly. Susan, however, was improving a little and managed to help organise Antonia's eightieth birthday on 31 March, when she and Thomas brought up to Courtfield Gardens food they had cooked at home. Phyllis also came to London from Devon to celebrate, and stayed on a few days. She was delighted to meet Carmen who had turned up with a contract for Emily Coleman's one published novel, *The Shutter of Snow*, which was set to join Antonia's novels in the growing list of Virago Modern Classics.

From the spring of 1979, after her radiotherapy treatment, Antonia's physical state deteriorated rapidly. In pain from her osteoporosis, she grew increasingly immobile. Even shuffling down the passage in her flat to the bathroom seemed at times to take a superhuman effort. During waking moments in the night, she contemplated her future. If only her leg would work, she felt, she could continue to live in her flat, with friends or her home help, Mrs Harris, shopping for her. Her mind also turned to the more pressing problem of her faith and her readiness for death; 'I am more and more conscious of my own sinfulness. How selfish, how cowardly, how self-indulgent, how *un*loving I have always been. I look back with shame on my selfishness – Susan, Aunt Agnes, all the people I've shamelessly neglected.'[4] Antonia's religion had taught her that all her life was a preparation for this definitive event, the reckoning with her God. She had never been able to believe that she was worthy of anyone's love, particularly of a Divine love when a tolerant, loving kind of Father had never been part of her spiritual landscape. 'One sees a superb Intelligence at work in the natural order . . . but it is *very* hard to see a supreme Love – in any sense that "love" means to a human being. It is much easier to believe that the world was under the dominion of Satan. . . . I really have no difficulty in believing in the devil!'[5] Too ingrained in her being was the conflation of the Divine Father with the most uncompromising qualities of her own human one; perfectionist, implacable, unreasonable, deaf to explanation, blind to pity. She knew that she would fail this last great test; that she could only be found wanting. It had become just a matter of time.

Antonia found the periods she had to stay in hospital very difficult and disorienting, and was most miserable in St Mary Abbots, where she thought the nurses particularly unsympathetic. She loathed being treated like a geriatric and made to join in with communal physiotherapy sessions. During one of these stays in early June, Lyndall was over from Italy and mentioned to her mother that she felt that she did not need to be a beneficiary, along with Susan, of Antonia's will. She had no children and was well enough provided for, whereas Susan had four children and was in greater need of whatever financial benefits might be forthcoming from Antonia's estate.

Antonia was momentarily hurt that she did not want anything from her, and fretted about the administrative problems in changing the will. Lyndall said she would arrange for the solicitor to come with the revised will. The most recent will Antonia had made had Susan once more as her literary executor, with her bank as the second executor. Lyndall met Carmen by chance at the hospital and they began to talk of Antonia's future, now that her days staying in the flat seemed to be numbered. As Lyndall recalled later, both of them admitted they were 'worried and perplexed that a *bank manager* should be Lit. Exec. with Sue. I told Carmen then that I felt as Antonia's "resurrector", publisher and agent she definitely ought to be one. I think *she* then said she would agree if I would be one too'.[6] This was put to Antonia who agreed and Mrs Harris, the solicitor, was given the new terms to draw up. No one mentioned to Lyndall that by renouncing her financial interest in Antonia's estate, her influence over the literary estate was correspondingly reduced.* Antonia had asked Lyndall to choose one thing to remember her by and 'suggested a John Tunnard oil painting which she thought had become rather valuable', but Lyndall preferred a little still-life oil of a half-peeled lemon, a green glass and a shell, 'which I had always loved'.[7]

Antonia's bones were weakened by the osteoporosis, and while she was in St Mary Abbots her hip was broken as a result of getting out of bed unaided. Lyndall had to return to her sick husband and Susan had only just had a major abdominal operation and was at the beginning of a long convalescence. Antonia was rushed to St Stephen's hospital to have the hip repaired. She was in great pain and 'Darling Phyllis' came up from Devon to be with her.[8] She, and the mother of Harriet Spicer, a Director of Virago, witnessed the new will. However, Antonia's hip did

---

* Susan Chitty points out that she was not informed at the time of the new will. If she had known of the problems that having three literary executors would bring she would have been opposed to this change.

not mend quickly, and she was in a good deal of pain when she returned to St Mary Abbots, 'trying not to be too depressed'.[9] She counted her blessings religiously, but the more immediate sufferings were very hard to bear.

During these last couple of years, Lyndall had developed a kind of telepathic bond with her mother which made her suddenly aware that she was needed in London: she would set off to find each time that Antonia had reached a crisis point. On the most traumatic occasion, at the end of July, Lyndall's sense of urgency sent her straight to St Mary Abbots from the airport, to be told that her mother had insisted on being sent home a few hours before. When Lyndall let herself into Courtfield Gardens she heard moaning. She found Antonia propped at her desk, in the same place she had been left by the ambulance men, unable to move even to get the telephone to phone Carmen, her doctor or home help. 'When she saw me she wept from shame as much as relief, for she had wetted herself several times.'[10] Lyndall washed her, put her to bed and organised a night nurse. It was Friday, Susan was on a recuperative holiday abroad, Phyllis was in Devon, her new lodger was away for the weekend and no one else knew that Antonia had discharged herself. The district nurse was only due to call the following Monday. This state of affairs frightened Lyndall; when Susan returned the two sisters decided that they had to suggest to Antonia that she leave her much-loved flat and go into a nursing home.

Phyllis had written to Susan the previous year, when the state of Antonia's health and lack of mobility were beginning to worry them all. She had told her to put out of her mind any idea of taking Antonia to live with her and her family. 'She wouldn't want it I know. One thing about most of us oldies is that we hate the idea of being dependent on friends or relatives. . . . Oh dear – OLD AGE!'[11] But, as she pointed out, it was so difficult to gauge the extent of Antonia's suffering, both mental and physical; 'she is so brave and uncomplaining that it is hard to know.'[12]

In the meantime Antonia managed to stay on at her flat with the almost constant attention of a day and night nurse from a private agency, paid for by the newly-earned royalties from her books. Crippled, in pain and uncertain of the future, she still managed to offer support to others. Lyn Isbell was another of the younger women who had grown to love her and had written, alarmed by the news of her cancer. Exhausted by her radiotherapy treatment, Antonia nevertheless managed to write four pages filled with interest in Lyn's life and support and encouragement in her struggles. Lyn's own relationship with her mother was a hurt and troubled one and Antonia not only offered her an encouraging and affectionate friendship but also some insights into her mother's complexities. Antonia recognised these as being very like her own in her relationship with her daughters: 'Interesting that Harry [Lyn's husband] thinks that [your mother] is very jealous of your feeling for me. That may well be true. I also suspect that she is jealous of my feeling for you. I think she has a desperate desire to be loved – to come indisputably first in someone else's affections. But along with this goes a certain kind of power-mania – the need to dominate other people – sometimes by "buying" them, sometimes by doing her best to destroy their self-confidence. I realise how painfully insecure she must feel herself.'[13]

Lyn could not bear to think she would never see Antonia again and so flew over from Salt Lake City to spend a week in London in September, visiting Antonia every afternoon during the three hours she most dreaded, when the day nurse had finished duty before the night nurse arrived. She had not seen her for seven years and in that time age and illness had taken their toll. Antonia's face, when she turned to greet Lyn, 'bore the expression of a child who has fallen and knocked the wind out of herself, that combination of pain and surprise.'[14] Her voice and conversation, however, were as full of life and wit as ever. Lyn was shocked how painful and difficult any movement was for her but, cigarette between her fingers, drink by her hand, Antonia behaved as if the disaster that had overtaken her body was something unrelated to the real Antonia, just another burden to accommodate along the way. It surprised Lyn to see her slightly cringing attitude to her nurses, even to Monica Hayes whom she really liked and trusted and who too grew to love and admire her. Antonia explained that she had never felt more powerless in her life and was probably a bit afraid – it was like being back in the Convent again, when the nuns had all the power and she had none. On one of the occasions when Lyn had let herself into the flat, she had found Antonia asleep at her desk, leaning forward with her head cradled in her arms, just like a schoolchild. When she awoke it was instantaneous: she greeted Lyn, sat up a little straighter and poured the drinks, lit a cigarette and the conversation started up again.

A Catholic nursing home run by nuns, in Danehill in Sussex, close to Susan and Thomas's home, was recommended by Isabel Quigly. When a place eventually became vacant there at the end of October, Antonia reluctantly agreed to her daughters' plea that she consider moving there. They would keep the flat on and not sell it. Antonia knew that she had to go, that her newfound capital would not support for very long the cost of two full-time nurses that allowed her to remain at home. She did not want to be a burden to anyone, but dreaded the move. When she heard that her room at St Raphael's would be only eight feet wide she panicked and began to clear up her possessions, throwing out and redistributing. She neatly sorted out the letters and papers she was keeping, and, in a surprising move, labelled Silas's letters to her for Carmen to look after.

At some point during this process, Antonia also threw away the bulk of both her daughters' letters to her, from their schooldays on through the dramas and vicissitudes of their lives. Short of space, she could have easily given them back to Susan and Lyndall; she could have put them with the other letters she had kept from much less central people in her life, neatly filed and in good order. The destruction of these important, emotionally affecting and informative letters was a puzzle. Symbolically it was a violent act against her daughters, and greatly wounding to them both. Susan wrote in her memoir: 'Antonia revenged herself on Lyndall and me.'[15] But cold-blooded revenge was not in Antonia's nature whereas hot temper and impulsive bloody rages were. She had told Lyn Isbell on her last visit, with some remorse and shame, how she had lost her temper with a temporary night nurse who had inadvertently hurt her when moving her in bed. She had kicked her feet like a child, feeble as she was, and she had sworn at her, aware of how ridiculous and unfair she was being, but unable to stop. Her hyper-sensitivity and irritableness could only take so much stress; beyond that point she was suddenly in a frenzy and out of control. Perhaps she had had a similar and equally temporary frenzy of rage against her daughters; they inadvertently represented the forces of power when she herself felt so frightened and weak. Antonia did not want to leave her flat and go into a nursing home, and yet she knew that there was no other way; old age and illness had overtaken her at last.

Lyndall flew over once again from Italy to stay the last night with her mother at Courtfield Gardens and then to accompany her down to Sussex and, with Susan's help, instal her in her last home. Twice in the night, she was woken by her mother's screams. As Lyndall tried to calm her she asked her what had she been dreaming. Never before in Lyndall's memory had Antonia refused to answer a question put to her, but this time she just said; 'It's too obscene to tell you. . . . It was about my father'.[16] She clung on to Lyndall's hand in the ambulance all the way down to Sussex, but could still joke with her that she had begun her life delivered by her father into the hands of nuns and now was ending it in the same way, but this time delivered by her daughters. There may have been deeper feelings beneath the joke. This time she entered the care of the nuns, not as Eirene Botting, at nine years old, but as Mrs Hopkinson, aged almost eighty-one, and still afraid.

Initially Antonia tried to make the best of it. The room had a big window with a view of the beautiful garden. She had asked specifically if Thomas could set up her small desk so that she could continue to prop herself up to write. She told Lyndall she was happy there and left her free to return to Italy, relieved that at last her mother was going to be securely cared for. The shock of the move affected all Antonia's senses. For a while, she could barely read, write or hear properly. She lost track of time. She may have suffered another stroke, because in one of her letters to Carmen she wrote that she had had to teach herself the alphabet again. Or perhaps it was just the severe shock of the disruption of her essential routines. Susan and Thomas visited her on Fridays, but Susan was in the thick of her Gwen John research and more often than not it was Thomas who came alone to deal with the practical needs of his mother-in-law. The position of the desk and chair became a distressing obsession, so desperate was she to maintain something of her old life and order, and Thomas 'nobly' dealt with the experimental combinations she thought might give her comfort.[17] Isabel Quigly tried to visit whenever she was in Sussex most weekends, and the old friends, the Marnaus, Mary Siepmann and Phyllis, came when they could, talking, listening to reminiscences of the past and attempting to console. Kathleen Raine wrote with news of David Gascoyne's surprising marriage, and sent her blessings: 'Life is one unending story, running now, like the Tale of Genji, into the third and fourth generations for you and me. How I wish one could see the whole story – perhaps we will, but not here. Please God all the knots will then be unravelled and all the wounds healed. Dear Antonia, I send you all my love in this ordeal you are having. Bless you dear friend who have given me so much.'[18] Her night nurse at Courtfield Gardens, Monica Hayes, wrote to send Antonia her love and tell her how much she missed her and how greatly she admired her courage.

But it was her daughters whom Antonia longed most to see. She did not write to either of them to tell them of her fears and utter despair. The letters which she sent to Phyllis, to whom she wrote daily at first, and to Carmen, were harrowing. She was seeing double and finding it hard to write, and her spidery words spelt out her misery: 'It's like being amputated of all one's former life. Nothing has ever been so complex & frightening', she wrote to Carmen soon after she had moved in.[19] Letters of increasing incoherence and misery continued to arrive in London and Devon. Antonia worried over the chair and in an internal frenzy tried to work out alternatives. She felt the nuns were very busy and brusque, with little time to reassure her or help with small things like putting her clock right: to a naturally impatient person, trapped by physical disability and afraid of her powerlessness, their slowness to answer the bell requesting help or a painkiller seemed unbearable. Despite her unhappiness, Antonia's letters to Carmen continued to show her concern for her, her 'superb cats' and 'the other Viragos' and express the affection and gratitude she felt for her friendship. 'This is only to thank you for all the miracles you've done & to send you fervent love & thanks'.[20]

So reluctant was Antonia to burden her daughters that she had destroyed a 'wildly unhappy letter' written to Susan in the depth of misery.[21] Despite accepting intellectually the reasons for their absence – Lyndall back home in Italy with a sick husband, Susan trying to beat a rival Gwen John biographer and under stress with her research – emotionally Antonia felt abandoned by them both. In February of 1980, some extra sense told Lyndall Antonia might be dying and she packed Lorenzo, who was himself now chronically ill, into their camper van and drove back across Europe. A few days before they arrived, Phyllis had gone to see Antonia and was shocked at what she found. She was now completely bed-ridden and incapable of reading or doing anything else for herself at all. Although she could barely talk above a mumble, she had managed a few weak laughs with her old friend, her sense of humour still struggling to the surface. But what had most shocked Phyllis was the fact that Antonia seemed to be 'in constant fear'.[22] She wrote to Carmen that she did not know how to ease this mental suffering: she was afraid of mentioning such distressing concerns to Susan who was not yet properly recovered from her breakdown and was clinging on to her Gwen John research.

Two years earlier, on Holy Thursday, Antonia had had a powerful dream which she had felt embodied a fundamental truth about her fears of death. She had been ill in bed in a building opposite the Brompton Oratory, the famous Catholic church in Knightsbridge. She knew she was probably dying and had asked a priest to give her the Last Sacraments. While she was waiting she saw through the window opposite an 'extraordinary cloud formation – most vivid and clear life-size representation of Christ on the cross'. She was deeply moved, actually to tears, and full of sorrow for her sins. The priest then suggested that she was 'perhaps not so much afraid of death as what might happen to me after'.[23] In her dream she agreed that this was indeed so and woke with the feeling that this had been a kind of revelation.

All her life Antonia had been a fighter: she was fighting still to hold on to the little life that was left to her. Resignation, philosophical acceptance and quiet hope were never part of her nature. At nine years old, in the Convent of the Sacred Heart, she had begun to learn to distrust herself and to fear her God. At her father's knee, she had known she could not be loved for what she was, only for an elaborately constructed mask of what she ought to be; the good daughter, who should have been a son, the good scholar, the good wife and mother, the good Catholic, the good writer. And she had failed in them all. All she had ever wanted was to be good, without realising that that kind of comformable goodness could be the enemy of the great. How could she offer a pitiless God her real self, this divided being, this impulsive burning spirit, an intellectual woman in lifelong quest for the numinous; selfish, irascible, madder than most, yet with more compassion and sanity than many?

Antonia had once consoled a friend with the words of one of her favourite mystics, Julian of Norwich, to whom it was revealed; 'yet all shall be well and all shall be well and all manner of thing shall be well', who, when she asked to be shown hell, 'saw no shewing'.[24] Yet Antonia was unable to draw on such intuitive consolation for herself.

Lyndall and Susan arrived together at her bedside not long after Phyllis's visit. They were just as shocked to see the deterioration in their mother. Lyndall was horrified by Antonia's obsessive fears that she was being punished, and the images of horror which she described, the screaming of demons, the rising of wraiths from their graves. On her second visit, Antonia seemed to drag Lyndall's name out of the recesses of her memory and then proceeded to ask her about a wounded cat she had rescued in Cortona. When Lyndall explained that he had happily survived an amputation, Antonia murmured 'I wish I were brave like him'.[25] Lyndall felt that all she could do was to spend as much time with Antonia as she could. Over the Easter holiday, she and Lorenzo travelled down to Sussex, deciding to sleep in the back of the van, so that Lyndall could be there most of the time, sometimes not recognised by Antonia, sometimes mistaken for Susan. Unable to soothe her fears, overwhelmed with pity, even love, for the mother she now no longer feared, Lyndall now made her peace.

One day, as she sat by Antonia's bed, Lyndall heard her mother whisper 'Which one?' For a moment she thought she ought to lie and say Susan, because she felt she was the daughter whom her mother would most want to be there with her at the end. But this was not a time for lies. Instead she said her own name, and was glad that she had. Antonia gently squeezed her hand and then with agonising slowness brought her other hand to meet it and lift it, with enormous effort, to her lips. This one effortful kiss was filled with significance for Lyndall, the daughter she felt her mother had never really wanted. 'With one gesture, which seemed to convey affection, remorse, gratitude and apology, she had placated the past by acknowledging me finally as her own'.[26]

The day was approaching when she would have to return to London with Lorenzo for an appointment he could not miss. Lyndall prayed for Antonia to be released from suffering, to be allowed to die. She wanted to be there with her at the end, but still her mother struggled on. The day after Lyndall left, due to return the following day, Isabel Quigly dropped in to see Antonia. She had sat with Antonia for a couple of hours most Sundays, and as she explained in a letter to Susan in early March, she would hold her hand and listened to her talk 'often vividly, it was almost like hearing odd lines of poetry. . . . At one point she suddenly smiled and turned right round & said: "I'm so glad you've got such a nice son." (This was quite unprompted! . . . It was strange, sad and in a way fascinating to hear her "rambling" talk – it was almost like listening in on a stream-of-consciousness thing, because it showed what her mind was dwelling on – her parents, you (very lovingly), *some* dread & guilt ("am I doing right?"), worry about pain and being "such a coward", and a few things of course it was hard to follow'.[27]

On this visit, Thursday 10 April 1980, Isabel found Antonia peaceful and apparently asleep. As she began to leave, Antonia suddenly opened her eyes wide; she still had occasional moments of extreme responsiveness. Isabel returned to her bedside to speak a few more words and stroke her hair and cheek. She then said goodbye. That evening, the nun sitting sewing by Antonia's bedside heard a little sob. The masks slipped away with the years. Mrs Hopkinson, Mrs Earnshaw Smith, Mrs Green-Wilkinson, Antonia White, Eirene Adeline Botting: Eirene, the child named after peace, need struggle no more.

Antonia's last written communication was left with the nuns for her daughters, in an envelope addressed to Lady Hopkinson and Contessa Passerini, even at the last conflating Susan with herself. Written on Boxing Day 1979, it was barely legible, words missing or mixed up, the sentences radiating outwards and fragmented – but the heartfelt meaning was clear:

> My darling Sue & Lyndall,
>   Forgive this muddled kind of note but I am absurdly muddled in my head.
>   Can't see very well which doesn't help!!
>   It's only to say how much I love you both & always will and do hope you'll have lots of happiness in spite of all the inevitable worries & miseries.
>   Love to Renzo & Thomas too of course.

This is only to ask you to forgive me for my incredible selfishness and thoughtlessness about you [when you] were little. . . . There is nothing to say really but how fonder & prouder [of] you [I] got with my old age & [hope] that there'll be nice things as well as one's horrid to remember.

Antonia then signed off with what appeared to be a plea:

Pray for both of me,
Mamma[28]

Afterword

After her death, Antonia White's literary reputation was riding higher than it had been since she first burst on the publishing scene with *Frost in May* in 1933, almost half a century before. All her novels were in print again, as was her collection of short stories, *Strangers*, and *The Hound and the Falcon*, and a collection of previously unpublished writings under the title *As Once in May* was being prepared by Susan for publication. All were published by Virago, who had introduced Antonia White to a completely new readership, and generated a good deal of interest and excitement in the process. Carmen Callil, in her role as agent, had also re-energised the American market and persuaded Dial Press in New York to republish an American edition of the novels. The BBC broadcast a dramatisation of Antonia's novels in a four-part serial in the summer of 1982, to universal acclaim. Nanda/Clara's painful progress from childhood to an unenticing future was etched into the collective consciousness of millions of television viewers. Antonia White had a wider range and greater number of fans than ever before.

But her personal legacy remained a complicated one. To begin with her three executors got on well. Aware of the problems of triangular relationships, perhaps, they agreed that any decisions should be unanimous. This worked harmoniously in the discussions about which of the unpublished works should go into *As Once in May*. Susan also had embarked on a personal memoir of her mother. Then the PEN Club, a society for writers, organised an evening in memory of Antonia White which was held in June 1982. Susan was asked to talk, as was Carmen Callil, Kathleen Raine, Neville Braybrooke and Tom Hopkinson. At the last minute Tom Hopkinson was unable to attend and Lyndall offered to speak instead. She spoke last and her talk, written at the last moment, electrified the gathering. She spoke passionately of how frightening Antonia had been as a mother, of the fear which had dogged her childhood, but also of how she had realised in her adulthood the reasons for Antonia's tempers and terrible unpredictability. When she had finished, Carmen and others urged her to write a book about her mother too.

The inevitable competition engendered by having both sisters writing about this difficult and complex woman and their differently unhappy relationships with her (coupled with the objection of Susan's publishers to a second book on the same subject) was the beginning of conflict between them. When Susan's book was published in 1985, *Now to My Mother: A Very Personal Memoir of Antonia White*, it was reviewed widely and sympathetically. Lyndall wrote to a couple of newspapers to point out inaccuracies in some quotes from Antonia's diaries, and also to deny the statement that she too, when young, had hated their mother and wanted to kill her. With this, and Susan's response, the family spat became a public row, fuelled by a keen press.

Others publicly entered the fray. At a televised Folio Society debate on biography in 1986, Germaine Greer, one of the main speakers for the motion 'Literary biographers are a disease of English literature', attacked Susan's book and was answered from the floor by the pale author in a trembling voice. The press again relished the fight. Lyndall's book, *Nothing to Forgive: A Daughter's Life of Antonia White*, was finally published in 1988, and also received by the critics with interest and sympathy. But by now, the relationship between the sisters had further broken down, and they were unable to agree on who should edit the last remaining work of Antonia's. Susan thought she should be the one to edit the diaries; Lyndall and Carmen were as emphatic that she should not, that no daughter who had had such a troubled relationship with her mother could be expected to do an unbiased job on such intimate, and at times hurtful, material. Susan argued that she was a biographer and anyway could not afford to pay an outsider to do a task she felt perfectly well qualified to do herself. Impasse was reached.

Susan then took legal action: as a result, the other executors had to accept that they had no case and that Susan, as sole beneficiary under Antonia's will, was also entitled to the sole inheritance of her copyrights. The diaries were duly edited by her, and two volumes appeared in print in 1991 and 1992. The breach appeared to be final. Antonia's strengths and failings live on in this story of her daughters' estrangement; independence, sensitivity, rivalry and hurt. And despite the efforts of Virago, the sales of Antonia White's works have dwindled again. At least she is still in print and young women, particularly, are still reading *Frost in May*, wondering at the horror of its content, admiring its truthfulness, directness and control.

Select Bibliography

Published works by Antonia White:

Frost in May (London, D. Harmsworth 1933; Eyre & Spottiswoode 1948, 1957; Virago 1978; New York, Dial Press 1980)
The Lost Traveller (London, Eyre & Spottiswoode 1950, 1953; Virago 1979; New York, Dial Press 1980)
The Sugar House (London, Eyre & Spottiswoode 1952; Virago 1979; New York, Dial Press 1981)
Beyond the Glass (London, Eyre & Spottiswoode 1954; Virago 1979; New York, Dial Press 1981)
Strangers (London, Harvill Press 1954; Virago 1981)
The Hound and the Falcon: The Story of a Reconversion to the Catholic Faith (London, Longmans 1985; Collins 1969, Fontana 1969; Virago 1980)
Minka and Curdy (London, Harvill 1957; Virago 1992)
Living with Minka and Curdy (London, Harvill 1970; Virago 1992)
Three in a Room: A Comedy in Three Acts (London, French's Acting Edition 1947)
BBC at War (Wembley Middlesex, BBC 1942)
As Once in May: the early autobiography of Antonia White and other writings, ed. Susan Chitty (London, Virago 1983)
Diaries 1926–1957, Volume One, ed. Susan Chitty (London, Constable 1991)
Diaries 1958–1979, Volume Two, ed. Susan Chitty (London, Constable 1992)

Translations by Antonia White:

Maupassant, Guy de, *A Woman's Life* (London, Hamish Hamilton 1949)
Bordeaux, Henri, *A Pathway to Heaven* (London, Gollancz 1952)

Carrel, Alexis, *Reflections on Life* (London, Hamish Hamilton 1952)

Colette, Sidonie Gabrielle, *Gigi* tr. R. Senhouse and *The Cat* tr. A. White (London, Secker & Warburg 1953; Harmondsworth, Penguin 1957)

Duras, Marguerite, *A Sea of Troubles* (London, Methuen 1953; Harmondsworth, Penguin 1969)

Groussard, Serge, *A German Officer* (London, Hamish Hamilton 1955)

Lesort, Paul André, *The Wind Bloweth Where It Listeth* (London, Collins 1955)

Arnothy, Christine, *I am Fifteen and I Do Not Want to Die* (London, Collins 1955)

Colette, Sidonie Gabrielle, *Claudine at School* (London, Secker & Warburg 1956)

Arnothy, Christine, *Those Who Wait* (London, Collins 1957)

Colette, Sidonie Gabrielle, *Claudine in Paris* (London, Secker & Warburg 1958; Harmondsworth, Penguin Books 1963)

Colette, Sidonie Gabrielle, *The Stories of Colette* (London, Secker & Warburg 1958); as *The Stories* (London, Heinemann 1962); as *The Rainy Moon and Other Stories* (Harmondsworth, Penguin 1975)

Lesort, Paul André, *The Branding Iron* (London, Collins, 1958)

Langlois-Berthelot, Jean Marc, *Thou Shalt Love* (London, Methuen 1958)

Arnothy, Christine, *It Is Not So Easy to Live* (London, Collins 1958)

Rouget, Fanny, *The Swing* (London, Bodley Head 1958)

Arnothy, Christine, *The Charlatan* (London, Collins 1959)

France, Clair, *Children in Love* (London, Eyre & Spottiswoode 1959)

Mahyère, Éveline, *I Will Not Serve* (London, F. Muller 1959)

Masson, Löys, *The Tortoises* (London, Chatto & Windus 1959)

Colette, Sidonie Gabrielle, *Claudine Married* (London, Secker & Warburg 1960; Harmondsworth, Penguin 1963)

Storm, Julie, *Till the Shadow Passes* (London, Collins 1960)

Arnothy, Christine, *The Serpent's Bite* (London, Collins 1961)

Colette, Sidonie Gabrielle, *Claudine and Annie* (London, Secker & Warburg 1962; Harmondsworth, Penguin 1963)

Fabre-Luce, Alfred, *The Trial of Charles de Gaulle* (London, Methuen 1963)

Masson, Löys, *The Whale's Tooth* (London, Chatto & Windus 1963)

Arnothy, Christine, *The Captive Cardinal* (London, Collins 1964)

Colette, Sidonie Gabrielle, *The Shackle* (London, Secker & Warburg 1964; Harmondsworth, Penguin 1963)

Leulliette, Pierre, *St Michael and the Dragon: A Paratrooper in the Algerian War* (London, Heinemann 1964 [tr. by Tony White])

Colette, Sidonie Gabrielle, *The Innocent Libertine* (London, Secker & Warburg 1968; Harmondsworth, Penguin 1972)

Saint Phalle, Thérèse de, *The Candle* (London, Toronto, Harrap 1968)

Gaillardet, Frédéric, *The Memoirs of Chevalier d'Éon* (London, Blond 1970; London, Corgi 1972)

Simenon, Georges, *The Glass Cage* (London, Hamish Hamilton 1973)

Boucé, Paul Gabriel, *Novels of Tobias Smollett* (London, Longman 1976)

Colette, Sidonie Gabrielle, *The Complete Claudine* (New York, Farrar Strauss & Giroux 1976)
Voltaire, François Marie Arouet de, *The History of Charles XII: King of Sweden* (London, The Folio Society 1976)

Related works:

Djuna Barnes, *Nightwood* (London, Faber 1936)
Penny Brown, *The Poison at the Source: The Female Novel of Self-Development in the Early Twentieth Century* (London, Macmillan 1992)
Hugh and Mirabel Cecil, *Clever Hearts: Desmond and Molly MacCarthy – a biography* (London, Gollancz 1990)
Susan Chitty, *Now to my Mother: A very personal memoir of Antonia White* (London, Weidenfeld 1985)
Emily Holmes Coleman, *The Shutter of Snow* (London, Virago 1981)
Stanley Coren, *Left Hander* (London, Murray 1993)
Dido Davies, *William Gerhardie: A biography* (Oxford, OUP 1990)
Paul Ferris, *Dylan Thomas* (Harmondsworth, Penguin 1977)
Andrew Field, *The Formidable Miss Barnes: A Biography of Djuna Barnes* (London, Secker & Warburg 1983)
David Gascoyne, *Collected Journals 1936–42* (London, Skoob Publishing 1991)
Goodman & Gilman, *Pharmacological Basis of Therapeutics* (London, Macmillan 7th ed. 1985)
Frederick K. Goodwin and Kay Redfield Jamison, *Manic-Depressive Illness* (Oxford, OUP 1990)
Geoffrey Grigson, *Recollections* (London, Chatto & Windus 1984)
Peggy Guggenheim, *Out of this Century* (London, André Deutsch 1979)
Kathleen Hale, *A Slender Reputation: An Autobiography* (London, Warne 1994)
Michael Holroyd, *Hugh Kingsmill: A Critical Biography* (London, The Unicorn Press 1964)
Lyndall Passerini Hopkinson, *Nothing to Forgive: A daughter's life of Antonia White* (London, Chatto & Windus 1988)
Tom Hopkinson, *Of This Our Time, A Journalist's Story 1905–50* (London, Hutchinson 1982)
Tom Hopkinson, *Under the Tropic* (London, Hutchinson 1984)
Compton Mackenzie, *My Life and Times: Octave Two, 1891–1900* (London, Chatto & Windus 1963)
Kathleen Raine, *Autobiographies* (London, Skoob Books 1991)
Norman Sherry, *The Life of Graham Greene: Volume II 1939–1955* (Harmondsworth, Penguin 1996)
Julian Symonds, *The Thirties: A Dream Revolved* (London, Faber & Faber, 1975)

Notes

Antonia White's diaries are published in two volumes: *Diaries 1926–1957, Volume One,* edited by Susan Chitty (London, Constable 1991) and *Diaries 1958–1979, Volume Two,* edited by Susan Chitty (London, Constable 1992). These are referred to in the Notes as *Diaries I* and *Diaries II.*

The bulk of her diaries remain unpublished, and where this material is quoted, the Notes refer to it as 'unpublished diaries'. When a quotation is from an entry which is only partly published, the reference will be, for instance, '*Diaries I* and unpublished diaries'.

Parallel to the main diaries were other diaries, written by Antonia for a specific reason, and often simultaneously to the main diaries. The 'analysis diary' was kept when she first started her Freudian analysis in 1935. In the Notes, extracts from this diary are referred to either as 'unpublished analysis diary' or as part of the published '*Diaries I*'. The 'Basil Nicholson diary' was written during her affair with him in 1937. This too is referred to by name in the Notes, either as 'unpublished' or part of '*Diaries I*'. There are also the 'dream diaries' which were written as part of her 'analysis' with Dorothy Kingsmill during 1948–49. These are unpublished, and so in the Notes are just referred to as 'unpublished dream diaries'.

Any references to letters written to or from Antonia abbreviate her name to her initials, AW.

Foreword

1. Sir Tom Hopkinson, review of *Nothing to Forgive, Sunday Telegraph* August, 1988
2. 23 June 1980, Kathleen Raine to Susan Chitty
3. Virgil, *The Georgics* IV, trs. James Rhoades (London, Kegan Paul 1881)
4. 6 July 1935 AW to Tom Hopkinson

One: Born in Captivity

1. Kathleen Raine, *Autobiographies* p. 239 (London, Skoob Books, 1991)
2. 28, 29 January 1937 Dylan Thomas to Emily Coleman
3. 4 August 1949, unpublished diaries
4. *The Hound and the Falcon* p. 16
5. AW to Cyril Connolly, *The Hound and the Falcon* p. 157
6. *The Hound and the Falcon* p. 87
7. *The Hound and the Falcon* p. 56
8. *The Hound and the Falcon* p. 107
9. AW to Susan Chitty, 21 September 1958
10. 'Autobiography', *As Once in May* p. 257
11. *The Hound and the Falcon* p. 72
12. 6 October 1935, unpublished diaries
13. 6 October 1935, *Diaries I*
14. *As Once in May* p. 258
15. 26 January 1933, unpublished diaries
16. 26 January 1933, unpublished diaries
17. Cecil Botting to Nevinson de Courcy, *As Once in May* p. 209
18. 6 September 1968, *Diaries II*
19. ibid
20. *As Once in May*, pp. 214–15
21. *As Once in May*, p. 218

Two: Consciousness

1. 3 March 1966, unpublished diaries
2. 28 December 1948, unpublished dream diaries
3. ibid.
4. 3 April 1948, unpublished dream diary
5. 15 September 1937, *Diaries I*
6. 15 June 1938, unpublished diaries
7. 3 April 1948, unpublished dream diaries
8. 'Autobiography', *As Once in May* p. 260
9. 15 June 1938, unpublished diaries
10. 31 October 1947, unpublished dream diaries
11. ibid.
12. 13 November 1947, unpublished dream diaries
13. ibid.
14. 31 October 1947, unpublished dream diaries
15. 29 October 1935, *Diaries I*
16. *As Once in May*, p. 191
17. 'Autobiography', *As Once in May* p. 267
18. 1 June 1935, *Diaries I*
19. 'Autobiography', *As Once in May* p. 234

20. 'Autobiography', *As Once in May* p. 226
21. 31 October 1947, unpublished dream diaries
22. 6 February 1956, unpublished diaries
23. 'Autobiography', *As Once in May* p. 245
24. 28 December 1948, unpublished dream diaries
25. 'Autobiography', *As Once in May* p. 270
26. 17 July 1936, AW to Emily Coleman
27. 7 July [1937], AW to Emily Coleman
28. 'Autobiography', *As Once in May*, p. 273
29. 'Autobiography', *As Once in May*, p. 275.
30. 15 June 1938, *Diaries I*
31. 1 March 1939, *Diaries I*
32. 'Autobiography', *As Once in May*, p. 289
33. undated letter [probably 1915–17] AW to Rhoda Dawson
34. 'Autobiography', *As Once in May* p. 303
35. 16 August 1954, *Diaries I*
36. 19 March 1949, unpublished dream diaries
37. 'Autobiography', *As Once in May* p. 320
38. 'Autobiography', *As Once in May* p. 321
39. 1 January 1948, unpublished dream diaries
40. ibid.
41. 28 June 1932, *Diaries I*
42. Kathleen Hale, *A Slender Reputation* (London, Frederick Warne 1994) p. 232

Three: The Garden of Good and Evil

1. 28 December 1948, unpublished dream diaries
2. AW to Cyril Connolly. *The Hound and the Falcon* p. 160
3. 23 April 1966 q. in unpublished diaries
4. *The Lost Traveller* p. 23
5. Lyndall Hopkinson, *Nothing to Forgive* (London, Chatto & Windus 1988) p. 27
6. From an interview with Maggie Pringle
7. 28 December 1948, unpublished dream diaries
8. 23 January 1948, unpublished dream diaries
9. 'A Child of the Five Wounds', *As Once in May* pp. 151–2
10. *Frost in May* pp. 15
11. 4 April 1939, *Diaries I*
12. August 1955, AW to Emily Coleman
13. 11 May 1951, unpublished diaries
14. 28 December 1948, unpublished dream diaries
15. 1948, unpublished dream diaries (p. 84)
16. *Frost in May* p. 112
17. 12 October 1948, unpublished dream diaries

18. From an interview with Maggie Pringle
19. *The Hound and the Falcon* p. 35
20. *Frost in May* pp. 144–5
21. From an interview with Maggie Pringle
22. *Frost in May* p. 137
23. *The Hound and the Falcon* p. 14
24. *Frost in May* p. 169
25. From an interview with Maggie Pringle
26. 21 November 1961, *Diaries II*, unpublished diaries
27. 29 June 1935, *Diaries I*
28. Interview by Neville Braybrooke, published in the *Critic*, June/July 1959 Vol. XVIII no. 6
29. 'A Child of the Five Wounds', *As Once in May* p. 161
30. From an interview with Maggie Pringle
31. ibid.
32. *Frost in May* p. 216
33. 25 June 1938, *Diaries I*
34. 10 June 1955, unpublished diaries

Four: Outside the Railings

1. Roehampton School Register, Provincial Archives, Society of the Sacred Heart p. 172
2. 22 February 1953, first sentence *Diaries I*, second sentence unpublished diaries
3. 22 July 1939, unpublished diaries
4. From an interview by Maggie Pringle
5. 7 July 1938, unpublished diaries
6. AW to Cyril Connolly, *The Hound and the Falcon* p. 155
7. 12 July 1950, *Diaries I*
8. From an interview by Maggie Pringle
9. 4 August 1949, unpublished diaries
10. 4 August 1949, *Diaries I*
11. 'A Child of the Five Wounds', *As Once in May* p. 162
12. 4 April 1939, *Diaries I*
13. 24 November 1948, unpublished dream diaries.
14. 'Memoir of Antonia White', Rhoda Dawson, courtesy of St Paul's Girls' School
15. *The Lost Traveller* p. 178
16. 26 May 1948, unpublished dream diaries
17. *The Lost Traveller* p. 37
18. *The Hound and the Falcon* p. 10
19. 12 July 1938, *Diaries I*
20. *The Hound and the Falcon* p. 66
21. 7 October 1968, AW to Nevinson de Courcy Jr

22. Undated letter [probably 1915–17], AW to Rhoda Dawson
23. *The Lost Traveller* p. 170
24. 9 August 1937, *Diaries I* and unpublished diaries
25. *The Lost Traveller* p. 225
26. 29 February 1936, Emily Coleman's diaries
27. 'Memoir of Antonia White', Rhoda Dawson, courtesy of St Paul's Girls' School
28. 6 March 1946, AW to Emily Coleman
29. From an interview with Maggie Pringle
30. 12 July 1950, *Diaries I*
31. 26 May 1948, unpublished dream diaries
32. 'The First Time I Went on Tour', *As Once in May* p. 163
33. From an interview with Maggie Pringle
34. 25 June 1938, unpublished diaries
35. From an interview with Carmen Callil
36. ibid.
37. 'The First Time I Went on Tour', *As Once in May* p. 173
38. 21 June 1954, *Diaries I*
39. *The Sugar House* p. 217
40. From an interview with Carmen Callil
41. *The Sugar House* p. 129
42. 16 March 1934, *Diaries I*
43. 27 August 1938 *Diaries I*
44. ibid.
45. *Nothing to Forgive* p. 39
46. *The Sugar House* p. 129
47. *Nothing to Forgive* p. 40
48. *The Lost Traveller* p. 242

Five: The Land of Lost Content

1. 15 March 1936, unpublished diaries
2. 12 July 1950, *Diaries I*
3. *The Sugar House* p. 209
4. 5 January 1966, unpublished diaries
5. 27 August 1951, *Diaries I*
6. 13 December 1960, unpublished diaries
7. *The Sugar House* pp. 153–4
8. *The Sugar House* p. 212
9. 12 December 1936, Emily Coleman's diaries
10. 11 December 1936, Emily Coleman's diaries
11. *The Hound and the Falcon* p. 27
12. q. in Susan Chitty, *Now To My Mother: A Very Personal Memoir of Antonia White* (London, Weidenfeld 1985) p. 16
13. *The Hound and the Falcon* p. 67

14. 27 August 1951, *Diaries I*
15. *The Sugar House* pp. 239–41
16. AW to Cyril Connolly, *The Hound and the Falcon* p. 155
17. ibid.
18. 12 July 1950, *Diaries I*
19. *Beyond the Glass* p. 65
20. *The Hound and the Falcon* p. 24
21. *The Hound and the Falcon* p. 40
22. From an interview with Carmen Callil
23. 3 October 1960, *Diaries I*
24. 27 August 1938, unpublished diaries
25. 5 March 1951, unpublished diaries
26. 23 April 1954, AW to Emily Coleman
27. *Beyond the Glass* p. 144
28. 23 August 1954, AW to Emily Coleman
29. *Beyond the Glass* p. 154
30. 12 September 1951, unpublished diaries
31. *Beyond the Glass* p. 181
32. 24 November 1962, AW to Emily Coleman
33. Bethlem Royal Hospital Archive
34. 27 November 1922, Cecil Botting to Senior Assistant Physician, Bethlem Royal Hospital
35. 28 July 1954, unpublished diaries
36. 1 July 1937, *Diaries I*

Six: Breaking the Glass

1. 17 November 1922, Dr R. W. Merrick, Bethlem Royal Hospital
2. 27 November 1922, Cecil Botting to Senior Assistant Physician, Bethlem Royal Hospital
3. *The Hound and the Falcon* p. 16
4. ibid.
5. 1948 unpublished dream diaries. (p. 87a)
6. 'The House of Clouds', *Strangers* p. 46
7. *Beyond the Glass* p. 213
8. *Beyond the Glass* p. 213
9. *Beyond the Glass* p. 214
10. *Beyond the Glass* pp. 218–19
11. *Beyond the Glass* p. 211
12. 9 January 1956, unpublished diaries
13. *Beyond the Glass* p. 232
14. 4 June 1978, *Observer*
15. *Beyond the Glass*, p. 216
16. *Beyond the Glass* p. 218
17. *Beyond the Glass* p. 245

18. *Beyond the Glass* p. 262
19. *Manic-Depressive Illness*, Frederick K. Goodwin and Kay Redfield Jamison (Oxford, OUP 1990) p. 597
20. *Pharmacological Basis of Therapeutics*, Goodman & Gilman (London, Macmillan 1985) pp. 361–2
21. *Beyond the Glass* p. 271
22. 4 June 1978, *Observer*
23. *The Hound and the Falcon* p. 15
24. AW to Cyril Connolly, *The Hound and the Falcon* p. 157
25. 26 May 1948, unpublished dream diaries
26. 17 June 1954, *Diaries I* and unpublished diaries
27. 24 November 1962, AW to Emily Coleman
28. 23 August 1954, AW to Emily Coleman
29. 28 July 1945, Emily Coleman's diaries
30. March 1936, Emily Coleman's diaries
31. 24 January 1956, *Diaries I*
32. 30 November 1937, unpublished diaries
33. 17 September 1955, *Diaries I*
34. 2 May 1937, unpublished diaries
35. 26 May 1948, unpublished dream diaries
36. 23 June 1955, *Diaries I*
37. From an interview with Maggie Pringle
38. 26 January 1952, *Diaries I*
39. 23 February 1951, unpublished diaries
40. 25 June 1938, unpublished diaries
41. 15 March 1949, unpublished diaries
42. From an interview with Maggie Pringle
43. 12 May 1941, *Diaries I*
44. 6 January 1935, *Diaries I*
45. 23 February 1951, unpublished diaries
46. 6 February 1956, *Diaries I*
47. 21 August 1954, *Diaries I*
48. 21 August 1954, unpublished diaries

Seven: The Rational Construct

1. 22 February 1969, *Diaries II*
2. Unpublished dream diaries, p. 37
3. Kathleen Hale, *A Slender Reputation* (London, Frederick Warne 1994) p. 191
4. 9 February 1959, *Diaries I*
5. 12 September 1960, unpublished diaries
6. 18 October 1958, *Diaries II*
7. 8 September 1974, *Diaries I* and unpublished diaries
8. 27 September 1953, AW to Emily Coleman

9. 16 July 1928, Eric Earnshaw Smith to AW
10. 29 December 1971, AW to Lyndall Hopkinson
11. Susan Chitty, 'An Un-classic Case of Success', *Harper's & Queen* June 1974
12. *There is a Tide*, G.H. Saxon Mills (London, Heinemann 1954) p. 50
13. 25 June 1938, unpublished diaries
14. 4 December 1937, *Diaries I*
15. 24 October [1931] AW to Virginia Woolf
16. 'Julian Tye', *As Once in May* pp. 91–2
17. 1948, unpublished dream diaries (p. 37)
18. 'Julian Tye', *As Once in May* p. 108
19. 1 May 1933, Emily Coleman's diaries
20. Conversation with Joan Souter-Robertson
21. 11 August 1974, *Diaries II*
22. AW to Cyril Connolly, *The Hound and the Falcon* p. 156
23. *The Hound and the Falcon* p. 45
24. AW to Cyril Connolly, *The Hound and the Falcon* p. 157
25. 22 February 1969, *Diaries II*
26. *The Hound and the Falcon* p. 36
27. AW to Cyril Connolly, *The Hound and the Falcon* p. 157
28. AW to Cyril Connolly, *The Hound and the Falcon* p. 158
29. 'Julian Tye', *As Once in May* p. 92
30. 8 September 1974, *Diaries II*
31. 'Mon Pays c'est la Martinique', *As Once in May* p. 130
32. 'Mon Pays c'est la Martinique', *As Once in May* p. 133
33. 10 October 1966, *Diaries II*
34. 17 June 1954, *Diaries I*
35. *The Hound and the Falcon* p. 88
36. 18 August 1961, *Diaries II*
37. 'Julian Tye', *As Once in May* p. 92
38. 22 January 1926, Bertrand Russell to AW
39. 29 April 1926, Bertrand Russell to AW
40. 2 September 1926, Bertrand Russell to AW
41. [early 1928], Bertrand Russell to AW
42. Lyndall P. Hopkinson, *Nothing to Forgive* (London, Chatto & Windus 1988) p. 56
43. 4 July 1974, AW to Kenneth Blackwell
44. 'Clara IV', *As Once in May* p. 60
45. 'Clara IV', *As Once in May* p. 64
46. 'Clara IV', *As Once in May* p. 65

Eight: Striking Out from the Shore

1. *The Hound and the Falcon* p. 56
2. q. in *Clever Hearts*, Hugh and Mirabel Cecil (London, Gollancz 1990) p. 229

3. *Virginia Woolf*, Quentin Bell (New York, Harcourt Brace Jovanovich 1972) vol. 1 p. 103
4. *The Hound and the Falcon* p. 26
5. 24 August 1937, *Diaries I*
6. ibid.
7. 4 January 1935, AW to Emily Coleman
8. 13 May 1937, *Diaries I*
9. 15 May 1937, *Diaries I*
10. 10 September 1937, Djuna Barnes to Emily Coleman
11. 9 August 1937, unpublished 'Basil Nicholson diary'
12. 22 September 1928, Silas Glossop to AW
13. 14 March 1935, *Diaries I*
14. *The Hound and the Falcon* p. 30
15. 15 May 1937, *Diaries I*
16. 2 May 1937, unpublished diaries
17. 9 January 1935, *Diaries I*
18. 9 March 1961, AW to Susan Chitty
19. 14 March 1935, unpublished diaries
20. 25 May 1937, *Diaries I*
21. 17 February 1929, Silas Glossop to AW
22. 17 May 1929, Silas Glossop to AW
23. 14 June 1929, Silas Glossop to AW
24. 4 July 1929, AW to Silas Glossop
25. ibid.
26. 2 May 1948, unpublished dream diaries
27. 20 December 1963, *Diaries II*
28. 25 June 1938, *Diaries I*
29. 20 August 1929, Silas Glossop to AW
30. 18 August 1929, Eric Earnshaw Smith to AW
31. 3 April 1948, unpublished dream diaries
32. 2 September 1929, Bertrand Russell to AW
33. 3 April 1948, unpublished dream diaries
34. 21 February 1948, *Diaries I*
35. ibid.
36. 1948, unpublished dream diaries (p. 73)
37. 12 April 1967, *Diaries II*

Nine: We Have Shot the Lovely Albatross

1. 17 June 1954, unpublished diaries
2. 18 February 1952, AW to Lyndall Hopkinson
3. 18 February 1955, AW to Lyndall Hopkinson
4. 14 February 1972, *Diaries II*
5. 3 October 1960, *Diaries II*

6. 2 December 1952, *Diaries I* and unpublished diaries
7. ibid.
8. *The Hound and the Falcon* p. 8
9. November? 1947, unpublished dream diaries (p. 76)
10. 'Julian Tye', *As Once in May* p. 82
11. 25 January 1935, unpublished diaries
12. 17 June 1954, *Diaries I* and unpublished diaries
13. 17 June 1954, unpublished diaries
14. 19 March 1949, unpublished dream diaries
15. 17 June 1954, unpublished diaries
16. 17 December 1948, unpublished dream diaries
17. Tom Hopkinson's autobiography, q. in *Nothing to Forgive*, Lyndall P. Hopkinson (London, Chatto & Windus 1988) p. 81
18. 4 January 1935, Tom Hopkinson's diaries
19. 17 June 1954, unpublished diaries
20. 18 February 1955, AW to Lyndall Hopkinson
21. 20 December 1948, unpublished dream diaries
22. ibid.
23. ibid.
24. [Spring] 1930, Tom Hopkinson to AW
25. 18 February 1955, AW to Lyndall Hopkinson
26. From an interview with Carmen Callil
27. *The Hound and the Falcon* p. 37
28. ibid.
29. 23 October 1951, AW to Emily Coleman
30. 24 October 1953, AW to Virginia Woolf
31. 12 November 1935, Tom Hopkinson's diaries
32. [Summer 1930], AW to Tom Hopkinson
33. 28 February 1930, Silas Glossop to AW
34. 18 February 1955, AW to Lyndall Hopkinson
35. 7 May 1930, Silas Glossop to AW
36. [12 May 1930], Silas Glossop to AW
37. [15 September 1930], Tom Hopkinson to AW
38. 12 November 1935, Tom Hopkinson's diaries
39. ibid.
40. Silas Glossop's memoirs
41. 25 November 1952, unpublished diaries
42. 26 September 1930, Tom Hopkinson to AW
43. 11 August 1937, *Diaries I* and unpublished diaries
44. 13 February 1939, *Diaries I*
45. 13 February 1939, unpublished diaries
46. Susan Chitty, *Now to my Mother* (London, Weidenfeld 1985) p. 40
47. 24 August 1937, *Diaries I*
48. 14 March 1935, *Diaries I*

49. November? 1947, unpublished dream diaries (p. 76)
50. 3 August 1938, unpublished diaries

Ten: The Writer . . .

1. 31 December 1942, Tom Hopkinson's diaries
2. 22 October 1947, unpublished dream diaries
3. 30 April 1931, AW to Tom Hopkinson
4. [2 May 1931], Tom Hopkinson to AW
5. *Recollections*, Geoffrey Grigson (London, Chatto & Windus 1984), p. 6
6. *Recollections*, p. 5
7. [21 July 1931], Tom Hopkinson to AW
8. 15 September 1937, *Diaries I* and unpublished diaries
9. Susan Chitty, *Now to My Mother* (London, Weidenfeld 1985) p. 41
10. [19 November 1931], Tom Hopkinson to AW
11. [13? November 1931], Tom Hopkinson to AW
12. 12 November 1931, Logan Pearsall Smith to AW
13. [13 November 1931], Tom Hopkinson to AW
14. *Frost in May* p. 216
15. 19 April 1950, *Diaries I*
16. From an interview with Maggie Pringle
17. ibid.
18. *The Authors', Playwrights' and Composers' Handbook* (London, A & C Black 1935)
19. 23 January 1933, *Diaries I*
20. ibid.
21. 20 July 1933, *Times Literary Supplement*
22. 7 July 1933, *Spectator*
23. [summer 1933], Tom Hopkinson to AW
24. [December 1933], Tom Hopkinson to AW
25. 16 July 1933, Eric Earnshaw-Smith to AW
26. 26 May 1948, unpublished dream diaries
27. *Of This Our Time*, Tom Hopkinson (London, Hutchinson 1982) p. 140
28. From an interview with Maggie Pringle
29. 19 April 1950, unpublished diaries

Eleven: . . . and the Wild and Weeping Woman

1. *The Hound and the Falcon* p. 37
2. 13 June 1938, *Diaries I*
3. 7 June 1933,*Diaries I*
4. 16 July 1941, Tom Hopkinson's diaries
5. *The Hound and the Falcon* p. 26
6. *The Hound and the Falcon*, p. 15

7. 14 March 1935, unpublished diaries
8. 9 February 1933, *Diaries I*
9. 22 March 1933, Emily Coleman's diaries
10. *Out of This Century*, Peggy Guggenheim (London, André Deutsch 1979) p. 78
11. 22 September 1937, Emily Coleman's diaries
12. *The Formidable Miss Barnes*, Andrew Field (London, Secker & Warburg 1983), p. 199
13. *The Story and the Fable*, Edwin Muir, quoted in *Out of this Century* pp. 101–2
14. 12 July 1934, Emily Coleman's diaries
15. 16 August 1934, Emily Coleman's diaries
16. 26 November 1935, Tom Hopkinson's diaries
17. 10 September 1936, unpublished diaries
18. 21 July 1933, Emily Coleman's diaries
19. 24 February 1936, Emily Coleman's diaries
20. *The Formidable Miss Barnes* p. 198
21. 21 July 1933, Emily Coleman's diaries
22. ibid.
23. 5 August 1934, Emily Coleman's diaries
24. 24 July 1933, Emily Coleman's diaries
25. 10 September 1933, *Diaries I*
26. 14 September 1933, *Diaries I*
27. 23 January 1934, *Diaries I*
28. *Everything to Lose*, Frances Partridge (London, Gollancz 1985) p. 105
29. 10 August 1934, *Diaries I*
30. 7 July 1934, Emily Coleman's diaries
31. 13 July 1934, Emily Coleman's diaries
32. 14 July 1934, Emily Coleman's diaries
33. 15? July 1934, Emily Coleman's diaries
34. q. in *Nothing to Forgive*, Lyndall P. Hopkinson (London, Chatto & Windus 1988) p. 103
35. 25 May 1937, *Diaries I*
36. 15? July 1934, Emily Coleman's diaries
37. 15, 16, 17 July 1934, Emily Coleman's diaries
38. ibid.
39. 'The Moment of Truth', *Strangers* p. 29
40. 'The Moment of Truth', *Strangers* p. 28
41. 'The Moment of Truth', *Strangers* p. 41
42. 5 August [1934], AW to Emily Coleman
43. 23 March 1935/36, Tom Hopkinson to AW
44. 12 August 1954, AW to Emily Coleman
45. 16 August 1934, Emily Coleman's diaries
46. [1934], Tom Hopkinson to AW

47. 22 October 1947, unpublished dream diaries

Twelve: Dicing With Death and Life-in-Death

1. *Minka & Curdy* p. 13
2. 12 December [1935], AW to Tom Hopkinson
3. 10 August 1934, *Diaries I*
4. 17 August 1934, *Diaries I*
5. 30 August 1934, Emily Coleman's diaries
6. 18 August 1934, Emily Coleman's diaries
7. [1934], Tom Hopkinson to AW
8. *Of This Our Time*, Tom Hopkinson (London, Hutchinson 1982) p. 151
9. 12 March 1935, Tom Hopkinson's diaries
10. 22 March 1936, AW to Tom Hopkinson
11. [1934], Tom Hopkinson to AW
12. 15 November 1934, Tom Hopkinson's diaries
13. [4 December 1934], Tom Hopkinson to AW
14. 9 January 1935, *Diaries I*
15. 25 February 1935, Tom Hopkinson's diaries
16. 11 September 1938, *Diaries I*
17. *The Hound and the Falcon* p. 37
18. 11 September 1938, *Diaries I*
19. 24 February 1936, Emily Coleman's diaries
20. 3 September 1938, *Diaries I*
21. [? March 1935], Tom Hopkinson to AW
22. 5 August [1934], AW to Emily Coleman
23. 28 May 1935, *Diaries I*
24. *Out of this Century*, Peggy Guggenheim (London, André Deutsch 1979) p. 143
25. 11 February 1935, Phyllis Jones to Emily Coleman
26. 9 March 1935, *Diaries I*
27. 14 May 1935, AW to Emily Coleman
28. 11 September 1938, *Diaries I*
29. 6 July 1935, *Diaries I*
30. 9 March 1935, analysis diary in *Diaries I*
31. 13 March 1935, analysis diary in *Diaries I* and unpublished diaries
32. 14 May 1935, AW to Emily Coleman
33. 12 March 1935, Tom Hopkinson's diaries
34. 14 March 1935, *Diaries I*
35. 17 August 1934, unpublished diaries
36. 14 March 1935, *Diaries I*
37. *Of This Our Time* p. 154
38. 20 March 1935, unpublished diaries
39. 22 March 1935, Tom Hopkinson's diaries

Thirteen: Living With the Stranger

1. 26 May 1935, *Diaries I*
2. ibid.
3. 28 May 1935, *Diaries I*
4. 7 October 1935, unpublished revised diary
5. undated, Christine Botting to AW
6. 1 June 1935, unpublished revised diary
7. 6 October 1935, unpublished revised diary
8. 3 April 1935, Phyllis Jones to Emily Coleman
9. 4 June 1935, unpublished diaries
10. 4 June 1935, *Diaries I*
11. 14 June 1935, *Diaries I*
12. 4 January 1936, unpublished diaries
13. 6 July 1935, analysis diary in *Diaries I*
14. 28 January 1936, *Diaries I* and unpublished diaries
15. 10 August 1935, analysis diary in *Diaries I*
16. 18 August 1935, *Diaries I*
17. [Summer 1935], AW to Phyllis Jones
18. *The Thirties*, Julian Symonds (London, Faber & Faber 1975) p. 78
19. 13 January 1936, Tom Hopkinson's diaries
20. *Cyril Connolly*, Jeremy Lewis (London, Jonathan Cape 1997) p. 274
21. *The Thirties* p. 79
22. 7 August 1935, *Diaries I*
23. 28 August 1935, *Diaries I*
24. 19 September 1935, *Diaries I*
25. [September 1935], Tom Hopkinson's diaries
26. 3 July 1935, Tom Hopkinson's diaries
27. 29 December 1935, Tom Hopkinson's diaries
28. 5 December 1935, Tom Hopkinson's diaries
29. ibid.
30. ibid.
31. 7 January 1936, analysis diary in *Diaries I*
32. 1 June 1936, Tom Hopkinson's diaries
33. 12 October 1935, unpublished revised diary
34. 21 November 1935, *Diaries I*
35. 20 November 1935, unpublished diaries
36. 15 March 1936, *Diaries I*
37. 8 April 1936, Tom Hopkinson to AW
38. 7 January 1936, analysis diary in *Diaries I*
39. 29 December 1935, Tom Hopkinson's diaries
40. 14 January 1936, Tom Hopkinson's diaries
41. 20 February 1935, Emily Coleman's diaries
42. 15 March 1936, *Diaries I*
43. 22 October 1936, *Diaries I*

44. 16 January 1938, AW to Emily Coleman
45. *The Hound and the Falcon* p. 21
46. *As Once in May* p. 340

Fourteen: Young Poets' Society

1. 28 January 1936, *Diaries I*
2. 3 February 1936, Tom Hopkinson's diaries
3. 12 May 1936, *Diaries I*
4. 17 January 1936, Emily Coleman's diaries
5. 5 April 1936, Emily Coleman's diaries
6. 11 March 1936, Emily Coleman's diaries
7. 16 April 1936, Emily Coleman's diaries
8. 28 September 1936, *Diaries I* and unpublished diaries
9. 1 March [1936], Eric Siepmann to AW
10. 27 April 1936, Emily Coleman's diaries
11. 12 May 1936, *Diaries I*
12. [25] June 1936, Emily Coleman's diaries
13. 9 July 1936, *Diaries I*
14. 2 June 1936, Emily Coleman's diaries
15. 28 September 1936, *Diaries I*
16. 2 August 1936, George Barker to Emily Coleman
17. 17 July 1936, George Barker to Emily Coleman
18. 8 July 1936, AW to Emily Coleman
19. [17 July 1936] letter from AW to Emily Coleman
20. ibid.
21. ibid.
22. 1 June 1936, unpublished analysis diary
23. 22 October 1936, *Diaries I*
24. 20 [July] 1936, AW to Emily Coleman
25. *Nothing to Forgive*, Lyndall P. Hopkinson (London, Chatto & Windus 1988) p. 144
26. 20 [July–September] 1936, AW to Emily Coleman
27. 21 July [1936], AW to Emily Coleman
28. 5 September 1936, Emily Coleman to AW
29. 9 September [1936], AW to Emily Coleman
30. Kathleen Raine, *Autobiographies* (London, Skoob Books 1991) p. 226
31. 18 September 1936, *Diaries I*
32. 25 September 1936, *Collected Journals*, David Gascoyne (London, Gollancz 1985)
33. 9 October 1936, *Collected Journals*
34. ibid.
35. 22 October 1936, *Collected Journals*
36. 16 November 1936, *Diaries I*
37. ibid.

38. 4 December 1936, *Diaries I* and unpublished diaries
39. 4 December, unpublished diaries
40. *Collected Journals*, David Gascoyne pp. 368–9
41. 8 January 1937, unpublished diaries
42. [December] 1936, Tom Hopkinson's diaries
43. 22 February 1937, Tom Hopkinson's diaries
44. 18 December 1936, Emily Coleman's diaries
45. 30 December 1936, Tom Hopkinson's diaries
46. 24 April 1948, unpublished dream diaries
47. 30 December 1936, Tom Hopkinson's diaries
48. *Dylan Thomas*, Paul Ferris (Harmondsworth, Penguin 1978), p. 147
49. 27? December 1936, Emily Coleman's diaries
50. 28 & 29 January 1937, Dylan Thomas to Emily Coleman
51. ibid.

Fifteen: The Lithopaedion

1. 4 January 1934, *Diaries I*
2. 6 January 1935, *Diaries I*
3. ibid.
4. 9 March 1935, analysis diary in *Diaries I*
5. [12 December 1935] AW to Tom Hopkinson
6. 2 August 1948, unpublished dream diaries
7. From an interview with Carmen Callil
8. *The Lost Traveller* pp. 113, 115
9. From an interview with Carmen Callil
10. [12 December 1935], AW to Tom Hopkinson
11. 3 April 1948, unpublished diaries
12. 17 September 1955, unpublished diaries
13. 28 June 1938, *Diaries I*
14. ibid.
15. 6 November 1948, unpublished dream diaries
16. 4 November 1952, *Diaries I*
17. 7 July [1937], AW to Emily Coleman
18. 27 July 1969, AW to John Broom
19. 13 March 1945, AW to Emily Coleman
20. 7 July 1937, AW to Emily Coleman
21. 6 April 1937, *Collected Journals*, David Gascoyne (London, Gollancz 1985)
22. 9 September 1937, *Diaries I*
23. 4 April 1937, David Gascoyne to AW
24. 15 May 1937, *Diaries I*
25. 21 May 1948, unpublished dream diaries
26. 24 June 1937, unpublished 'Basil Nicholson diary'
27. 10 July 1937, Phyllis Jones to Emily Coleman
28. 20 June 1937, *Diaries I*

29. 21 May 1948, unpublished dream diaries
30. 1 June 1937, unpublished diaries
31. 26 June 1937, *Diaries I*
32. 2 September 1937, *Diaries I*
33. 31 July 1937, Tom Hopkinson to AW
34. 15 August 1937, *Diaries I*
35. 27 September 1937, *Diaries I*
36. 24 July 1937, Djuna Barnes to Emily Coleman
37. 22 September 1937, Emily Coleman's diaries
38. 27 September 1937, 'Basil Nicholson diary' in *Diaries I*
39. 27 September 1937, unpublished 'Basil Nicholson diary'
40. ibid.
41. ibid.

Sixteen: Sexual Swansong

1. 15 August 1937, *Diaries I*
2. 28 December 1948, unpublished dream diaries
3. 25 June 1938, unpublished diaries
4. 30 November 1937, 'Basil Nicholson diary'
5. 31 January 1938, *Diaries I*
6. ibid.
7. 7 July 1938, *Diaries I*
8. ibid.
9. 20 October 1937, Djuna Barnes to Emily Coleman
10. 29 October 1937, Phyllis Jones to Emily Coleman
11. Susan Chitty, *Now to my Mother* (London, Weidenfeld 1985) p. 90
12. *Nothing to Forgive*, Lyndell P. Hopkinson (London, Chatto & Windus 1988) p. 156
13. 2 July 1938, Djuna Barnes to Emily Coleman
14. *Nothing to Forgive*, p. 174
15. q. in PhD thesis *The Booster/Delta Nexus, Henry Miller and his Friends in the Literary World of Paris and London on the Eve of the Second World War*, Von Richthofen, (PhD. thesis, Durham 1987), p. 146
16. 10 February 1938, *Collected Journals*, David Gascoyne (London, Gollancz 1985)
17. 18 June 1938, *Diaries I*
18. 18 June 1938, unpublished diaries
19. 29 May 1938, unpublished diaries
20. 3 August 1938, *Diaries I*
21. 10 October *Diaries II*
22. 28 June 1938, *Diaries I*
23. 13 March 1939, AW to Emily Coleman
24. 28 June–20 September 1938, Emily Coleman to AW
25. 7–8 August 1938, Djuna Barnes to Emily Coleman

26. 2 September 1938, Djuna Barnes to Emily Coleman
27. 29 August 1938, unpublished diaries
28. 17 October 1938, Phyllis Jones to Emily Coleman
29. 28 October 1938, Phyllis Jones to Emily Coleman
30. 'England to America', Neville Braybrooke in the *Critic* June/July 1959
31. 3 April 1948, unpublished dream diaries
32. q. *The Hound and the Falcon*, p. 159
33. 11 September 1938, *Diaries I* and unpublished diaries

Seventeen: Peace and War

1. 18 February 1956, *Diaries I*
2. Susan Chitty, *Now to My Mother* (London, Weidenfeld 1985) p. 117
3. 5 January 1939, Djuna Barnes to Emily Coleman
4. 25 June 1939, Djuna Barnes to Emily Coleman
5. 20 April 1957, AW to Lyndall Hopkinson
6. 13 February 1939, *Diaries I*
7. 1 March 1939, *Diaries I*
8. 13 March 1939, AW to Emily Coleman
9. 1 March 1939, *Diaries I*
10. 13 February 1939, *Diaries I*
11. 22 July 1939, unpublished diaries
12. 28 May 1940, AW to Emily Coleman
13. 22 January 1939, Emily Coleman to AW
14. 20 March 1939, Djuna Barnes to Emily Coleman
15. [November 1939], Tom Hopkinson to AW
16. Interview with AW, *Observer* 4 June 1978
17. 10 October 1966, *Diaries I*
18. 12 May 1941, *Diaries I*
19. 12 June 1940, *Diaries I*
20. *A Slender Reputation*, Kathleen Hale (London, Frederick Warne 1994) p. 232
21. *Dylan Thomas*, Paul Ferris (Harmondsworth, Penguin 1978) p. 181
22. 8 June 1940, *Diaries I*
23. 6 November 1940, AW to Emily Coleman
24. *Nothing to Forgive*, Lyndall P. Hopkinson (London, Chatto & Windus 1988) p. 203
25. 6 November 1940, AW to Emily Coleman
26. 24 August 1937, *Diaries I*
27. 6 November 1940, AW to Emily Coleman
28. *The Hound and the Falcon* p. 19
29. 6 November 1940, AW to Emily Coleman
30. ibid.
31. 25 September 1940, Eric Earnshaw Smith to AW
32. 6 November 1940, AW to Emily Coleman

33. *The Hound and the Falcon* p. 113

Eighteen: The Prodigal Uncertainly Returns

1. AW to Cyril Connolly, *The Hound and the Falcon* p. 158
2. *The Hound and the Falcon* p. 35
3. 11 December 1944, letter from AW to Emily Coleman
4. *The Hound and the Falcon* p. 66
5. 30 December 1942, letter from AW to Emily Coleman
6. ibid.
7. ibid.
8. *The Hound and the Falcon* p. 56
9. *The Hound and the Falcon* p. 41
10. 27 December 1942, Tom Hopkinson's diaries
11. 9 April 1942, letter from AW to Peter Thorp
12. *The Hound and the Falcon* p. 54
13. *The Hound and the Falcon* p. 8
14. 13 March 1945, letter from AW to Emily Coleman
15. AW to Cyril Connolly, *The Hound and the Falcon* p. 157
16. *The Hound and the Falcon* p. 60
17. 19 January 1941, letter from AW to Tom Hopkinson
18. *The Hound and the Falcon* p. 44
19. *The Hound and the Falcon* p. 45
20. *The Hound and the Falcon* p. 102
21. 12 January 1943, letter from AW to Emily Coleman
22. April 1942? AW to Cyril Connolly, *The Hound and the Falcon* p. 162
23. 11 December 1944, letter from AW to Emily Coleman
24. *The Hound and the Falcon* p. 18
25. *The Hound and the Falcon* p. 52
26. 12 January 1943, AW to Emily Coleman
27. 19 July 1966, Kate O'Brien to AW
28. *The Hound and the Falcon* p. 87
29. *The Hound and the Falcon* p. 8
30. *The Hound and the Falcon* p. 10
31. 18 August 1941, *Diaries I*
32. April 1942?, AW to Cyril Connolly, *The Hound and the Falcon* p. 164
33. *The Hound and the Falcon* p. 95
34. 13 March 1945, AW to Emily Coleman
35. ibid.

Nineteen: War and Work

1. Susan Chitty, *Now to My Mother* (London, Weidenfeld 1985) p. 136
2. *The Hound and the Falcon* p. 51
3. *Nothing to Forgive*, Lyndall P. Hopkinson (Chatto & Windus 1988) p. 206

4. 22 February 1942, analysis diary in *Diaries I*
5. 13 July 1941, *Diaries I*
6. *The Hound and the Falcon* p. 42
7. *The BBC at War*, Antonia White p. 10
8. *The Hound and the Falcon* p. 82
9. *The Hound and the Falcon* p. 103.
10. *The Hound and the Falcon* p. 133
11. *The Hound and the Falcon* p. 127
12. ibid.
13. 7 January 1942, letter from AW to Peter Thorp
14. *The Hound and the Falcon* p. 132
15. *The Hound and the Falcon* p. 134
16. ibid.
17. ibid.
18. 21 August 1942, Emily Coleman to AW
19. 12 January 1943, AW to Emily Coleman
20. September, analysis diary in *Diaries I*
21. 12 January 1943, AW to Emily Coleman
22. 22 February 1942, analysis diary in *Diaries I*
23. 19 March 1944, AW to Emily Coleman
24. 12 January 1943, AW to Emily Coleman
25. 6 November 1940, AW to Emily Coleman
26. 22 February 1942, analysis diary in *Diaries I*
27. *The Hound and the Falcon*, p. xix
28. 12 January 1943, AW to Emily Coleman
29. ibid.
30. ibid.
31. 12 January 1943, AW to Emily Coleman
32. 19 March 1944, AW to Emily Coleman
33. 4 June 1943, *Diaries I* and unpublished diaries
34. 19 March 1944, AW to Emily Coleman
35. Public Records Office *Accord*, December 1943 (*FO 898/521*)
36. ibid.
37. 13 August 1944, AW to Emily Coleman
38. *The Life of Graham Greene*, Norman Sherry (Harmondsworth, Penguin 1996) vol. II p. 187
39. *Autobiographies*, Kathleen Raine (London, Skoob Books 1991) p. 239
40. *Autobiographies*, p. 240
41. 13 August 1944, AW to Emily Coleman
42. 15 November 1944, AW to Emily Coleman
43. *Autobiographies* p. 246
44. 13 March 1945, AW to Emily Coleman
45. 12 June 1945, AW to Emily Coleman
46. 28 July 1945, AW to Emily Coleman
47. 5 August 1945, *Diaries I*

48. 5 August 1944, *Diaries I*
49. 10 October 1944, AW to Emily Coleman
50. ibid.
51. 4 September 1944, AW to Emily Coleman
52. 6 March 1946, AW to Emily Coleman
53. 12 June 1945, AW to Emily Coleman
54. 3 December 1945, AW to Emily Coleman

Twenty: Dominating Women

1. 7 July 1949, *Diaries I*
2. 12 June 1945, AW to Emily Coleman
3. 6 November 1945, AW to Emily Coleman
4. 6 March 1946, AW to Emily Coleman
5. 22 June 1946, Eric Earnshaw Smith to AW
6. 27 January 1946, AW to Emily Coleman
7. ibid.
8. 1 January 1948, unpublished dream diaries
9. 6 March 1946, AW to Emily Coleman
10. 4 April 1946, AW to Emily Coleman
11. 8 July 1946, AW to Emily Coleman
12. ibid.
13. 30 May 1946, AW to Emily Coleman
14. 8 October 1946, AW to Emily Coleman
15. 8 July 1946, AW to Emily Coleman
16. 6 October 1946, Phyllis Jones to Emily Coleman
17. 20 February 1947, AW to Emily Coleman
18. ibid.
19. 22 October 1947, unpublished dream diaries
20. Susan Chitty, *Now to My Mother* (London, Weidenfeld 1985) p. 144
21. 2 March 1947, *Diaries I*
22. 12 March 1947, *Diaries I*
23. 14 March 1947, *Diaries I*
24. 15 March 1947, *Diaries I*
25. 27 August 1938 *Diaries I*
26. *Now to My Mother* p. 145
27. 6 April 1947, *Diaries I*
28. *Now to My Mother*, p. 146
29. 7 July 1949, unpublished diaries
30. 13 April 1947, *Diaries I*
31. 16 April 1947, *Diaries I*
32. 1 May 1947, unpublished diaries
33. *Now to My Mother* p. 148
34. 14 July 1948, AW to Emily Coleman
35. 7 July 1949, *Diaries I*

36. 3 May 1947, AW to Emily Coleman
37. [September 1947], AW to Emily Coleman
38. 23 February 1948, AW to Emily Coleman
39. 7 July 1949, unpublished diaries
40. From an interview with Carmen Callil
41. In the author's possession
42. 7 July 1949, *Diaries I*
43. 23 February 1948, AW to Emily Coleman
44. ibid.
45. 7 July 1949, unpublished diaries
46. 21 March 1948, *Diaries I*
47. 25 January 1949, AW to Emily Coleman
48. ibid.
49. 7 July 1949, unpublished diaries
50. 4 August 1949, *Diaries I*
51. 7 February 1948, unpublished dream diaries
52. 2 September 1976, AW to Lyndall Hopkinson
53. 14 July 1948, AW to Emily Coleman
54. 18 July 1948, AW to Emily Coleman

Twenty-One: Mother Love

1. 3 April 1948, dream diaries
2. 23 March 1948, dream diaries
3. ibid.
4. 3 April 1948, dream diaries
5. 17 December 1960, AW to Emily Coleman
6. 27 March 1948, dream diaries
7. 3 April 1948, dream diaries
8. 21 March 1948, *Diaries I*
9. ibid.
10. 21 March 1948, *Diaries I* and unpublished diaries
11. 28 March 1949, dream diaries
12. 19 February 1948, *Diaries I*
13. 23 March 1948, dream diaries
14. 18 August 1948, dream diaries
15. 7 April 1948, dream diaries
16. 4 July 1949, *Diaries I* and unpublished diaries
17. *Nothing to Forgive*, Lyndall P. Hopkinson (London, Chatto & Windus 1988) p. 242
18. 25 January 1949, AW to Emily Coleman
19. 4 August 1949, *Diaries I*
20. 25 March 1949, dream diaries
21. Susan Chitty, *Now to My Mother* (London, Weidenfeld 1985) p. 161
22. 9 September 1950 *Diaries I* and unpublished diaries

23. *Collected Journals*, David Gascoyne (London, Skoob Books 1991) p. 70
24. 16 May 1950 AW to Emily Coleman
25. 3 August 1951, *Diaries I* and unpublished diaries
26. *Now to My Mother* p. 161
27. 10 May 1951, *Diaries I*
28. ibid.
29. 3 August 1951 *Diaries I*
30. 5 June 1951, *Diaries I*
31. ibid.
32. 20 August 1951, unpublished diaries
33. 23 July 1963, *Diaries II*
34. 3 August 1951, *Diaries I*
35. *Now to My Mother* p. 162
36. 11 August 1951, letter from AW to Susan Chitty
37. 31 August 1951, *Diaries I*
38. 30 August 1951, AW to Susan Chitty
39. 23 October 1951, AW to Susan Chitty
40. 31 August 1951, unpublished diaries
41. 25 October 1953, AW to Susan Chitty
42. 12 March 1952, *Diaries I*
43. 31 August 1951, *Diaries I* and unpublished diaries
44. 18 May 1952, *Diaries I* and unpublished diaries
45. 20 August 1951, *Diaries I*

Twenty-Two: Moving the Mountain

1. 4 February 1950, AW to Emily Coleman
2. 4 August 1949, *Diaries I*
3. 21 February 1950, Emily Coleman to AW
4. 3 April 1950, AW to Emily Coleman
5. *The Lost Traveller* p. 141
6. *The Lost Traveller* p. 146
7. 23 July 1960, unpublished diaries
8. ibid.
9. 12 February 1950, AW to Emily Coleman
10. 26 February 1950, *Diaries I*
11. 12 February 1950, AW to Emily Coleman
12. 12 July 1950, *Diaries I*
13. 31 March 1950, *Times Literary Supplement*
14. 6 July 1950, Emily Coleman to AW
15. 19 April 1950, *Diaries I*
16. 8 July 1949, *Diaries I* and unpublished diaries
17. 23 October 1951, AW to Emily Coleman
18. 12 September 1951, *Diaries I*
19. 5 December 1951, *Diaries I*

20. 16 November 1951, *Diaries I*

21. 3 December 1951, AW to Emily Coleman

22. ibid.

23. 23 January 1952, *Diaries I* and unpublished diaries

24. 23 January 1952, unpublished diaries

25. 9 August 1952, *Diaries I*

26. 25 July 1952, *Daily Telegraph*

27. 8 August 1952, *Spectator*

28. 27 July 1952, *Observer*

29. 6 February 1952, AW to Emily Coleman

30. [August] 1952, Tom Hopkinson to Lyndall Hopkinson

31. 17 September 1952, AW to Lyndall Hopkinson

32. 31 October 1952, AW to Lyndall Hopkinson

33. 13 November 1952, AW to Lyndall Hopkinson

34. 25 November 1952, unpublished diaries

35. 20 December 1952, AW to Lyndall Hopkinson

36. 12 January 1953, AW to Lyndall Hopkinson

37. 23 August 1953, AW to Emily Coleman

38. 12 January 1953, letter from AW to Lyndall Hopkinson

39. Susan Chitty, *Now to My Mother* (London, Weidenfeld 1985) p. 165

40. 1 January 1953, AW to Lyndall Hopkinson

41. 25 September 1953, Emily Coleman to AW

42. 6 February 1952, AW to Emily Coleman

43. *Beyond the Glass* p. 251

44. 17 June 1954, unpublished diaries

45. 23 August 1954, AW to Emily Coleman

46. 17 June 1954, unpublished diaries

47. 17 June 1954, *Diaries I*

48. 2 January 1953, *Diaries I* and unpublished diaries

Twenty-Three: More Troublesome Women

1. 31 January 1953, *Diaries I*

2. 1 April 1953, AW to Lyndall Hopkinson

3. ibid.

4. 1 February 1953, AW to Lyndall Hopkinson

5. 4 February 1956, unpublished diaries

6. 3 February 1956, unpublished diaries

7. 15 February 1956, unpublished diaries

8. 3 May 1953, AW to Lyndall Hopkinson

9. 23 May 1965, AW to Lyndall Hopkinson

10. 27 May 1953, AW to Lyndall Hopkinson

11. 10 June 1953, AW to Lyndall Hopkinson

12. 10 June 1953, AW to Lyndall Hopkinson

13. 22 February 1953, AW to Lyndall Hopkinson
14. *The Sugar House*, p. 14, Eyre & Spottiswoode edition, 1952
15. 14 October 1956, *Diaries I*
16. 18 October 1956, AW to Lyndall Hopkinson
17. ibid.
18. 23 April 1953, Emily Coleman to AW
19. 20 May 1953, AW to Lyndall Hopkinson
20. 15 June 1974, *Diaries I*
21. 5 September 1953, AW to Emily Coleman
22. 25 September 1953, Emily Coleman to AW
23. 24 September 1953, AW to Emily Coleman
24. 7 November 1953, AW to Emily Coleman
25. [30 November 1953], AW to Emily Coleman
26. 4 December 1953, AW to Emily Coleman
27. 24 September 1953, AW to Emily Coleman
28. 21 September 1953, AW to Lyndall Hopkinson
29. 15 November 1953, AW to Lyndall Hopkinson
30. 31 January 1954, AW to Lyndall Hopkinson
31. 31 December 1953, *Diaries I*

Twenty-Four: Loss, Love and Loss

1. 8 June 1954, AW to Lyndall Hopkinson
2. 13 June 1954, *Diaries I*
3. 8 June 1954, AW to Lyndall Hopkinson
4. 15 June 1954, *Diaries I* and unpublished diaries
5. 21 June 1954, *Diaries I*
6. 27 October 1953, Emily Coleman to AW
7. 31 October 1953, AW to Emily Coleman
8. 25 January 1953, AW to Lyndall Hopkinson
9. 23 August 1954, AW to Emily Coleman
10. 19 July 1954, AW to Lyndall Hopkinson
11. 29 August 1954, AW to Lyndall Hopkinson
12. 17 October 1954, AW to Lyndall Hopkinson
13. 10 November 1954, AW to Emily Coleman
14. 21 October 1954, AW to Emily Coleman
15. 12 February 1955, AW to Emily Coleman
16. 18 February 1955, AW to Lyndall Hopkinson
17. 20 June 1955, AW to Emily Coleman
18. 3 August 1955, AW to Emily Coleman
19. 23 June 1955, *Diaries I* and unpublished diaries
20. 19 April 1955, AW to Lyndall Hopkinson
21. 30 May 1955, AW to Emily Coleman
22. 8 June 1955, unpublished diaries

23. 3 August 1955, AW to Emily Coleman
24. 20 August 1955, unpublished diaries
25. 17 September 1955 *Diaries I* and unpublished diaries
26. 29 September 1955, AW to Emily Coleman
27. 3 March 1956, AW to Emily Coleman
28. ibid.
29. 1 January 1956, *Diaries I*
30. 22 December 1955, AW to Emily Coleman
31. 24 June 1956, *Diaries I*
32. 3 March 1956, AW to Emily Coleman
33. 9 January 1956, *Diaries I* and unpublished diaries

Twenty-Five: Grandmother's Footsteps

1. 24 February 1957, AW to Emily Coleman
2. 16 January 1957, AW to Susan Chitty
3. 24 March 1957, AW to Emily Coleman
4. 20 March 1957, *Diaries I*
5. 12 March 1957, AW to Susan Chitty
6. 'Good Friday' [19 April] 1957, AW to Emily Coleman
7. ibid.
8. 20 April 1957, AW to Lyndall Hopkinson
9. 30 May 1957, Lyndall Hopkinson to AW
10. 13 November 1961, *Diaries I*
11. 13 November 1961, unpublished diaries
12. 11 August 1956, unpublished diaries
13. 1 July 1956, AW to Emily Coleman
14. 9 September 1956, AW to Lyndall Hopkinson
15. 1 October 1956, *Diaries I*
16. 24 February 1957, AW to Emily Coleman
17. ibid.
18. 25 September 1957, unpublished diaries
19. 7 October 1956, AW to Lyndall Hopkinson
20. 4 June 1957, AW to Lyndall Hopkinson
21. 14 July 1957, AW to Emily Coleman
22. 28 December 1957, AW to Emily Coleman
23. ibid.
24. ibid.
25. 13 January 1958, AW to Lyndall Hopkinson
26. March 1958, Lyndall Hopkinson to AW
27. 1 August 1958, AW to Emily Coleman
28. 22 October 1958, AW to Emily Coleman
29. 3 December 1958, AW to Emily Coleman
30. 26 July 1958, *Diaries II*

Twenty-Six: High-Heeled Sneakers

1. 21 September 1958, AW to Susan Chitty
2. *Diaries II* p. 331
3. 'All Saints' [1 November] 1959, AW to Emily Coleman
4. 28 May 1959, *Diaries II*
5. ibid.
6. 3 August 1959, AW to Lyndall Hopkinson
7. 8 October 1959, AW to Lyndall Hopkinson
8. 4 October 1959, AW to Emily Coleman
9. ibid.
10. 8 October 1959, AW to Lyndall Hopkinson
11. 4 October 1959, AW to Emily Coleman
12. 7 October 1959, AW to Emily Coleman
13. 13 December 1959, *South Bend Tribune*
14. 2 January 1972, AW to John Broom
15. 4 October 1959, AW to Emily Coleman
16. 7 October 1959, AW to Emily Coleman
17. 29 November 1959, AW to Lyndall Hopkinson
18. 10 January 1960, AW to Emily Coleman
19. 18 September 1961, AW to Emily Coleman
20. 'All Saints' [1 November] 1959, AW to Emily Coleman
21. 19 March 1960, AW to Lyndall Hopkinson
22. 22 December 1959, *Diaries II*
23. 30 December 1959, *Diaries II*
24. 10 April 1960, AW to Lyndall Hopkinson
25. 26 September 1960, *Diaries II* and unpublished diaries
26. 8 February 1959, AW to Emily Coleman
27. 8 February 1959, AW to Emily Coleman
28. 28 December 1957, AW to Emily Coleman
29. 6 October 1960, AW to Susan Chitty
30. 26 February 1961, AW to Emily Coleman
31. 6 October 1960, AW to Susan Chitty
32. 1 September 1967, *Diaries II*
33. 3 October 1960, AW to Emily Coleman

Twenty-Seven: Drowning in Sight of Land

1. 9 March 1961, AW to Emily Coleman
2. 11 March 1961, AW to Lyndall Hopkinson
3. 6 August 1961, AW to Emily Coleman
4. 3 December 1961, AW to Emily Coleman
5. 20 December 1960, *Diaries II*
6. 4 November 1962, *Diaries II*
7. 9 August 1962, AW to Emily Coleman

8. 28 August 1962, AW to Emily Coleman
9. 1 May 1952, AW to Emily Coleman
10. 28 October 1964, *Diaries II*
11. ibid.
12. 1 May 1962, AW to Emily Coleman
13. 13 May 1962, AW to Emily Coleman
14. 1 May 1962, AW to Lyndall Hopkinson
15. 12 May 1962, *Diaries II*
16. 1 June 1982, AW to Lyndall Hopkinson
17. 12 May 1962, *Diaries II*
18. 1 October 1963, AW to Susan Chitty
19. 4 October [1961], AW to Sister Franzita
20. 'Good Friday' 1962, AW to Emily Coleman
21. 2 April 1964, *Diaries II*
22. ibid.
23. 1 June 1963, *Diaries II*
24. 7 March 1964, AW to Lyndall Hopkinson
25. 14 June 1964, *Diaries II*
26. 29 July 1964, *Diaries II*
27. 11 November 1962, AW to Emily Coleman
28. 22 May 1965, *Diaries II*
29. 20 December 1964, *Diaries II*
30. 14 October 1965, AW to Lyndall Hopkinson
31. 2 April 1964, *Diaries II*
32. 25 November 1965, *Diaries II*
33. 9 December 1965, AW to Susan Chitty
34. 12 June 1966, AW to John Broom
35. 3 October 1965, AW to Susan Chitty
36. 3 October 1965, *Diaries II*
37. 15 December 1965, *Diaries II*
38. 11 December 1965, AW to Lyndall Hopkinson
39. 9 February 1966, *Diaries II*
40. 15 February 1966, AW to Emily Coleman
41. 16 February 1966, *Diaries II*

Twenty-Eight: An Old Soldier

1. 3 March 1966, AW to Susan Chitty
2. 25 February 1969, *Diaries II*
3. 19 March 1966, AW to Susan Chitty
4. 26 April 1966, *Diaries II*
5. 4 April 1971, AW to Lyndall Hopkinson
6. 19 [20?] May 1967, *Diaries II*
7. 18 December 1967, *Diaries II*

8. 28 October 1968, AW to Emily Coleman
9. 3 May 1970, AW to Lyndall Hopkinson
10. 14 January 1971, AW to Lyndall Hopkinson
11. 6 July 1966, *Diaries II*
12. *Autobiographies*, Kathleen Raine (London, Skoob Books 1991) p. 239
13. 6 October 1966, *Diaries II*
14. 27 September 1968, AW to Lyndall Hopkinson
15. 30 August 1968, *Diaries II*
16. 27 September 1968, AW to Lyndall Hopkinson
17. 18 February 1968, AW to Emily Coleman
18. 28 October 1969, AW to Lyndall Hopkinson
19. 23 September 1968, *Diaries II*
20. ibid.
21. 8 September 1969, *Diaries II*
22. 22 December 1968, *Diaries II*
23. 20 November 1968, *Diaries II*
24. 22 December 1968, *Diaries II*
25. 6 September 1968, *Diaries II*
26. 7 May 1970, *Diaries II*
27. 15 June 1974, *Diaries II*
28. 13 November 1968, *Diaries II*
29. 7 April 1966, *Diaries II*
30. 30 November 1966, *Diaries II*
31. 13 December 1966, Kate O'Brien to AW
32. 27 September 1968, AW to Lyndall Hopkinson
33. 28 December 1966, AW to Emily Coleman
34. 4 April 1969, *Diaries II*
35. 20 July 1969, AW to Lyndall Hopkinson
36. ibid.
37. 'Reputations', *Times Literary Supplement*, 3 July 1969
38. 14 January 1970, AW to Kathleen McClean
39. 11 January 1970, AW to Susan Chitty
40. Recalled in conversation with Lyn Isbell
41. 1 January 1970, Phyllis Jones to Emily Coleman
42. 20 January 1970, *Diaries II*
43. 10 January 1970, letter from AW to Lyndall Hopkinson
44. 26 August 1970, *Diaries II*
45. 4 October 1970, *Diaries II*
46. 19 October 1970, Phyllis Jones to Emily Coleman
47. 15 April 1971, *Diaries II*
48. 22 April 1971, AW to Lyndall Hopkinson
49. 31 March 1971, AW to Lyndall Hopkinson
50. 25 January 1972, *Diaries II*
51. 26 January 1972, AW to Lyndall Hopkinson

Twenty-Nine: Virago Vindex

1. 29 April 1973, unpublished diaries
2. 12 February 1972, *Diaries II*
3. 14 October 1969, Kathleen Raine to AW
4. 8 September 1974, *Diaries II*
5. *The Hound and the Falcon* p. 62
6. [June? 1972], AW to Lyndall Hopkinson
7. ibid.
8. 5 January 1973, *Diaries II*
9. 8 September 1974, *Diaries II*
10. 22 October 1973, AW to Nevinson and Nora de Courcy
11. 29 April 1973, *Diaries II*
12. ibid.
13. 9 September 1973, unpublished diaries
14. 14 October 1973, unpublished diaries
15. 18 December 1976, *Diaries II* and unpublished diaries
16. 27 May 1974, AW to Lyndall Hopkinson
17. 8 December 1974, AW to Susan Chitty
18. 27 May 1974, AW to Lyndall Hopkinson
19. ibid.
20. 13 October 1974, AW to Lyndall Hopkinson
21. 9 June 1974, unpublished diaries
22. 13 October 1974, AW to Lyndall Hopkinson
23. 11 May 1975, *Diaries II*
24. 15 June 1974, unpublished diaries
25. 15 June 1974, *Diaries II* and unpublished diaries
26. 15 June 1974, unpublished diaries
27. 5 April 1975, *Diaries II*
28. 16 December 1976, *Diaries II* and unpublished diaries
29. 12 June 1977, *Diaries II*
30. 1 February 1977, *Diaries II*
31. 26 October 1977, *Diaries II*
32. 7 April 1978, unpublished diaries
33. From a paper given by Carmen Callil to the Kate O'Brien Society, 'Blood Sisters', 1996
34. 6 January 1978, *Diaries II*
35. 6 January 1978, unpublished diaries
36. From an interview with Maureen Cleave, *Observer* 4 June 1978
37. 25 November 1978, *Diaries II*
38. 23 November 1978, *Diaries II*
39. ibid.
40. 1 September 1978, *Diaries II*
41. 3 August 1978, *Diaries II*
42. 5 October 1978, AW to Susan Chitty

43. From a paper given by Carmen Callil to the Kate O'Brien Society, 'Blood Sisters', 1996
44. 20 January 1979, *Diaries II*

Thirty: Struggling Free

1. *Nothing to Forgive*, Lyndall P. Hopkinson (London, Chatto & Windus 1991) p. 353
2. 29 January 1979, *Diaries II*
3. ibid.
4. 22 April 1979, *Diaries II*
5. 7 April 1974, unpublished diaries
6. 11 March 1998, Lyndall Hopkinson to the author
7. ibid.
8. 18 June 1979, *Diaries II*
9. 24 August 1979, *Diaries II*
10. *Nothing to Forgive* p. 353
11. 11 March 1978, Phyllis Jones to Susan Chitty
12. ibid.
13. 12 March 1979, AW to Lyn Isbell
14. Quoted from an unpublished story by Lyn Isbell about this last visit, 'A Bit Afraid'
15. Susan Chitty, *Now to My Mother* (London, Weidenfield 1985) p. 184
16. *Nothing to Forgive* p. 254
17. December 1979, AW to Carmen Callil
18. 6 February 1979, Kathleen Raine to AW
19. [November 1979] AW to Carmen Callil
20. December? 1979, AW to Carmen Callil
21. [November] 1979, AW to Carmen Callil
22. 3 March 1980, Phyllis Jones to Carmen Callil
23. 23 March 1978, *Diaries II*
24. 12 June 1966, AW to John Broom
25. *Nothing to Forgive* p. 3
26. *Nothing to Forgive* p. 7
27. 4 March 1980, Isabel Quigly to Susan Chitty
28. 26 December 1979, AW to Susan Chitty and Lyndall Hopkinson

Index